THE FOLK MUSIC SOURCEBOOK

THE FOLK MUSIC SOURCEBOOK

New, updated edition

LARRY SANDBERG AND DICK WEISSMAN

A DA CAPO PAPERBACK

Library of Congress Cataloging in Publication Data

Sandberg, Larry.
  The folk music sourcebook.

  Rev. ed. of: The folk music source book.
1st ed. 1976.
  Includes bibliographical references.
    1. Folk music—North America—Directories.
  2. Folk music—North America—Bibliography.
  3. Folk music—North America—Discography.
  I. Weissman, Dick. II. Sandberg, Larry.
  Folk music source book. III. Title.
  ML12.S26 1989   016.78162'00973   89-23389
  ISBN 0-306-80360-7

All new information representing 1989 updates is
presented in sans-serif type.

This Da Capo Press paperback edition of the *Folk Music Sourcebook*
is an updated and expanded edition of the book published in New York
in 1976. It is reprinted by arrangement with the authors.

Published by Da Capo Press, Inc.
A Subsidiary of Plenum Publishing Corporation
233 Spring Street, New York, New York 10013

CONTENTS

II
LEARNING

FOREWORD

In the *Foreword* to the first edition of this book in 1976, Dick Weissman wrote: "This book deals with the folk and folk-based music of North America in the English language, with additional materials covering American Indian, Cajun, Spanish music of the Southwest, and French-Canadian music. Further, selective attention is given to Caribbean, British, and Irish music....The purpose of this book is to provide the reader with information about all the aspects of North American folk and folk-based music." The goals of this new updated edition are the same.

This book originated in the 1966 Denver Folklore Center mail-order catalog compiled by Harry Tuft and Phyllis Wagner. Almost all the resources of the folk music community—books, records, instruments, accessories, and a good deal of almanac-style background lore—could then be encompassed in an eighty-page octavo paperback.

The possibility of a commercially-published folk music catalog arose in the mid-seventies. Harry Tuft obtained a contract with the publishing firm of Alfred A. Knopf, and turned the job over to Dick Weissman and myself. We got more than we bargained for. The field had grown. Building on Phyllis Wagner's preparatory work, we turned what had been a slender almanac into a hefty, highly organized encyclopedia.

The magnitude of what we had done surprised us. We were equally surprised when a committee of musicians, scholars, and writers voted us an ASCAP Deems Taylor Award for Excellence in Writing About Music, and when we received accolades from critics outside the folk music community as diverse as those of *Rolling Stone* and *Library Journal*. Less surprising were some of the key words that appeared again and again in newspaper and magazine reviews: "feisty," "opinionated," "lively." We already knew we were feisty and opinionated, and we were trying our best to be lively.

But I wouldn't now defend everything I wrote then. Some of my opinions have changed, and I'm sure that's true of Dick's as well. (Nor do we necessarily share all the opinions each of us expresses.) I'm certainly embarrassed that, in the *Listening* section on England, Scotland, and Ireland, there appeared a misinformed pronunciation for *ceili*, the Gaelic word for a get-together that we all now know is pronounced "kay-lee." And I'm sorry that beneath some rug on Seventeenth Avenue in Denver must still be the index card for the Incredible String Band. (I remember setting it aside to try to find some way of expressing how equally delightful and erratic their so highly original meanderings could be. It's still a relevant challenge, now that they're reissued on the Carthage label.)

The present edition differs from the original in the following ways:

All new information representing 1989 updates is presented in sans-serif type. This distinguishes 1989 information from 1976 information, which is presented in the original serif typeface of the first edition.

The Listening section has been given a new introduction which highlights recorded folk music since 1976. The record company directory is updated and expanded. Fol-lowing this, the original (1976) *Listening* section is reprinted. As in the first edition, this is Larry Sandberg's section.

The *Learning* section has also been given a new introduction, including reviews of significant new books and instructional materials published since the first edition. The directory of book publishers has been brought up to date. As in the first edition, this is Dick Weissman's section.

Subsequent directory sections of the *Sourcebook*—film, video, organizations, folk music centers, and so on—have been updated and reorganized as necessary. As in the first edition, sections by Larry Sandberg or Dick Weissman are signed with their initials.

The new edition, then, is something more than a reprint and less than a completely revised edition. Some of the materials discussed in 1976 have now gone out of print, but are still available in libraries, collections, and specialty shops. Some terminology (e.g. "American Indian" rather than the now-preferable "Native American", "Spanish-American" rather than the preferable and more accurate "Hispanic-American," "Chicano," etc.) has for the sake of consistency in places been retained from 1976. The author's tastes and opinions remain as they were intended: no more than starting points for the cultivation of your own. We mean this edition to be both an historical document of the seventies and a useful resource for the nineties.

FOLK MUSIC INTO THE NINETIES

The good news is that the market has found itself and achieved economic stability. Not many people in the folk music industry—which is finally admitting to itself that that's what it is—are getting very rich. Enough have found it possible to achieve an acceptable level of comfort. More than enough survive at least.

The bad news is that we're all getting older. The advertising demographics of a leading folk music magazine show a bell-shaped curve peaking near what, a few years ago, I would have called middle age. The market tends to serve, and is served by, the sixties generation. There hasn't been a continued influx of teenagers during the eighties, which is probably how it should be. (But there's probably due to be one soon, which is also as it should be.)

This market is now ably served by organizations and mail-order businesses, which sets *The Folk Music Sourcebook* free to become a true sourcebook. Wherever possible, we refer you to original resources outside the *Sourcebook*.

The years since 1976 have also seen the growth of an institutional folklife establishment. I don't think the word "folklife" appeared in the 1976 *Sourcebook*. It's since gained currency as a useful term to describe the study of all aspects, social as well as cultural, of folk and ethnic communities. (At the same time, it serves to emphasize a weakness in the academic study of folk music: the conceptual inability to track that which is purely musical across boundaries of social class. Much of the folk music canon is now played primarily by educated middle and professional classes.)

With the growth of folklife activities has also come a healthier appreciation of ethnic cultures in America. The great romantic folksinger's odysseys of the forties and fifties—Pete Seeger's, Jack Elliott's, Alan Lomax's—all led Down South, or Out West, or perhaps Down East. But not into the South End, or The Stockyards, or any place where communities of ethnic Americans made their homes. As a child in the fifties I was taught that our nation's background was English and Northern European (except for Negroes, who had been made separate and noble by oppression), and that shorter, swarthier immigrants would in time be made more blond, and concomitantly more wealthy, by a mysterious process called "the melting pot."

But since then we've learned that the melting pot never really worked that way. With an understanding of the folklife of ethnic groups has come a deeper appreciation of their musics. Norwegian fiddle tunes from Wisconsin, Italian music from the east coast cities, Balkan and Slavic music from the industrial midwest have all been recently documented. "Klezmer"—Yiddish entertainment music—has made an astounding comeback. The influence of Southeastern Asian music is beginning to be felt. As Celtic music became a vital force on the folk scene during the seventies, we discovered that cultural societies and private academies in our big cities had been quietly keeping Irish dance and music traditions alive, with old master fiddlers like Martin Mulvihill and newcomers like Liz Carroll both equaling the best of the old country. Cajun and Hispanic-American musics are not only widely appreciated in their original forms, but have been incorporated into contemporary popular and country music.

As the children of the sixties became professional musicians and record producers and music directors, the sounds of American traditional music were assimilated into every aspect of our musical experience. The ring of the five-string banjo and the bluesy twang of the slide guitar, known thirty years ago only to remote rural populations and a bohemian underground, are now commonplace in radio commercials and TV and movie scores. It seems that soon the reedy pulse of the button accordion will join them there. They're accepted by listeners who have never heard or thought of folk music. They're likely as not scored and played by musicians to whom the term "folk music" is an irrelevancy. They have entered the cultural mainstream.

OTHER RESOURCES

The American Folklife Center's *Folklife Sourcebook* (1986) is a valuable directory of institutional resources in this country and Canada. Like all published directories, its usefulness is qualified by the volatility of addresses of small companies and volunteer organizations. (The Center, however, maintains internal update files and publishes update sheets from time to time.) We have relied heavily on this directory, and on unpublished update information from the Center and other sources, in compiling our own directories. However, we have omitted many folklife resources not primarily concerned with music. (Another useful sourcebook, though also outdated, and now out-of-print, is *The Grass Roots International Folk Resource Directory*. Nonetheless, a copy, if one can be found, belongs in the library of every folk professional.)

The Center also publishes an annual *Selected List* of American folk music and folklore recordings. Each booklet describes in detail about thirty recordings recommended primarily on the basis of fidelity to unadulterated tradition and quality of annotation, as well as availability and esthetic value. Address: American Folklife Center, Library of Congress, Washington DC 20540.

Sing Out! magazine, a not-for-profit organization, has at this writing been funded to set up a resource center which will network the folk music community. Plans are to keep information online and furnish printouts as a way of dealing with the update problem. Address: *Sing Out!* Resource Center, Box 5253, Bethlehem PA 18015.

The Folk Music Sourcebook is not formally affiliated with *Sing Out!* or The American Folklife Center. However, we urge those wishing to update or correct the directory information contained in this book to provide them with new information on a continuing basis.

The authors wish to extend their joint thanks to the many individuals who provided the support, inspiration, and information that made this book possible. Of special help to the entire project has been the continuing work Joe Hickerson, Gerry Parsons, Sebastian LoCurto, and the rest of the staff at the American Folklife Center. At Da Capo Press, the book has been seen into print through the considerable and much-appreciated efforts of Bea Friedland, Ruth Jensen, Els Olesk and Adam Segal. Numerous others have helped as well, including our friends of the first edition, and we regret the omission of many names that undoubtedly should appear here.

From Larry Sandberg: I'd like to thank the following individuals for their help with my part of the work: Mary Armstrong (WXPN-FM), Leslie Berman and Heather Wood (*Grass Roots International Folk Resource Directory*), Jennifer Cutting (American Folklife Center), Roberta Goren (WXPN-FM), Ginny Musico, Mary Newman (NAIRD), Charles Sawtelle, Lynn Sengstack (Birch Tree Group), and the many record companies which offered generous assistance.

From Dick Weissman: Special thanks to Oak Publications, Mel Bay Publications, Alfred Music, Happy Traum (Homespun Tapes), Don Johnson (*Musical Merchandise Review*), and most especially to Glenda Herro at Hal Leonard Publications. I am particularly grateful to Dick Burns and Lillian Krelove at Legacy Books. Although they are not responsible for any errors of fact or interpretation, special thanks go to Hal Cannon, Elizabeth Dear, "Sawyer Tom" Hayden, John Nielsen, and Sarah Sweetwater for introducing me to the world of cowboy poetry. Meg Glaser at the National Council for the Traditional Arts, and the travelling portion of the Fife Cowboy Poetry and Song Collection that came to the 1989 Cowboy Gathering, provided helpful research materials.

—LARRY SANDBERG, February, 1989

I
LISTENING

We live in a world filled with the noise of machinery. Our environment teaches us not to listen; the sharp ears of the hunter are a disadvantage in modern urban society. Our apartments truly keep us apart; they are filled with expensive phonographs and tape recorders, and we use them to create walls of sound to shut out the noise of the machinery and of our neighbors as they build their own walls of sound. We build more and more walls in more and more ways, and grow ever more lonely within them.

Our traditional music is a rural music that exists at peace with a quieter and more spacious environment. In Burl Hammons' fiddle playing you can hear the sounds he has heard: birds, a creek, the mountain wind coming down across a stand of timber. All you have to do is listen.

(—L.S.)

INTRODUCTION

LISTENING is the discography section. The section begins with a list of recommended records issued since the first edition of the *Sourcebook*. It's a highly select and eclectic list intended only to suggest a few potent starting points and points of reference, especially for readers new to the music. Since it's an update, it leaves out many names which already appear in the 1976 discography.

You'll also notice that I cite some artists by record title and number, but also drop a lot of undocumented names. These are intended to point you in other interesting directions. Please track down these artists through your local folk record source, or in the catalogs available from the mail-order houses and record companies listed in the directories following the record recommendations. Though LPs are cited, many items are also available on cassette or CD.

The record company directory has been updated completely for the 1989 Da Capo edition. More information about recommended records can be found in the directory section.

Following the directory, the discography from the original 1976 edition is reprinted without change. It's meant to be more than an index of individual records, for the observations made in many of the captions add up to an analysis of folk music style.

(—L.S.)

THE AGE OF SYNTHESIS

The most exciting development since the first edition of *The Folk Music Sourcebook* has been the coming-of-age of a generation of cosmopolitan, sophisticated performers capable of high professional standards, and able to move freely through an eclectic field of different musical traditions. The urban revivalists who started from square one in the mid-fifties have now been learning and performing for over thirty years. The younger players who started later didn't have to start from square one. And all have had the benefit of exposure to a world full of music.

For most performers, it's enough to do one thing well. But some do many things well—even mastering more than one idiom; even developing personal styles in more than one idiom.

We're living in a highly creative post-traditional period. Songwriting may never have been more widely practiced. Recording studios abound. Traditional styles are being mixed and redefined, and in ways beyond the scope of folklorists, for the music is no longer being performed on a folkloric level. (Perhaps in the future it will even be seen as "art music," or as a late-twentieth-century analog of that music of past times which we now call "courtly.") In the selections that follow, I've tried to give special emphasis to records which epitomize the new synthesis of old traditions.

BLUEGRASS

There are still bluegrass performers who sing with great heart, like Dave Evans and Larry Sparks, and young musicians like Alison Krause who are very much traditionalists without sounding imitative or old-fashoned. And there is no lack of good music-making by solid performers like John Starling, the now-disbanded Johnson Mountain Boys, Dry Branch Fire Squad, or the Bluegrass Cardinals.

But bluegrass has also shot off in new and different directions. It's not just a simple case of fine bluegrass musicians crossing over to country music, as Ricky Skaggs and Keith Whitley have done. Musicians like mandolinist Dave Grisman and guitarist Tony Rice have come out of bluegrass, looked at such influences as Django Reinhardt, cowboy jazz, and western swing, and created a new acoustic music (*see* Grisman and Rice, next section). Peter Rowan, a fine songwriter and lead singer whose latest incarnation is in the Nashville Bluegrass Band, has worked in a variety of musical contexts during his career, and greater fame has mysteriously eluded him in each. Banjoists like Bela Fleck, working on the foundations laid by Bill Keith, Bobby Thompson, and later voyagers like Tony Trishka and Marty Cutler, have brought new styles to their seemingly intractable instrument as well. Jerry Douglas has revolutionized dobro playing. Sam Bush (New Grass Revival) and Tony Trishka (Skyline) lead bands that are essentially pop or rock bands with bluegrass instrumentation. And then the music moves full circle again, and an older player like Eddie Adcock so casually adapts modernisms to his basically traditional banjo style that they slip by almost unnoticed.

DAVE EVANS *Goin' Round This World*. Rebel 1602. Dave Evans is a beautiful, expressive "high lonesome" singer. His sound is conservative; his songwriting and choice of others' songs isn't. His banjo tone is gorgeous. He does traditional bluegrass proud.

HOT RIZE *Untold Stories*. Sugar Hill 3756. The most dynamic bluegrass band now working, they preserve a traditional feeling while really being thoroughly modern. And if that's not enough, they also switch clothing, instruments, and personalities to double as a western swing take-off band called Red Knuckles and the Trailblazers. (You'll enjoy Red's records too.)

Hot Rize (Pete Wernick, Nick Forster, Tim O' Brien, and Charles Sawtelle): New ways to respect the old ways of bluegrass)

Richard Thompson: Acoustic, electric, and eclectic

CONTEMPORARY INSTRUMENTAL MUSIC

THE DAVE GRISMAN QUINTET. Kaleidoscope F-5.

THE TONY RICE UNIT. Kaleidoscope F-10. Guitarist Rice and mandolinist Grisman have done more recent work than this, and cohorts like violinist Darol Anger have gone off to make their own music, but these were among the seminal albums that defined new acoustic music.

TINY MOORE AND JETHRO BURNS *Back to Back*. Kaleidoscope F-9. Tiny Moore played mandolin with Bob Wills in the forties. Jethro Burns was the mandolin-playing half of the country comedy act Homer and Jethro. They're both virtuoso players. In a selection of tunes by Duke Ellington, Dizzy Gillespie, Django Reinhardt, and other jazz composers, they take to a high point the sociologically distinct interpretation of swing and bebop created by white musicians of the south and west who came out of country and western music. It's a style that many Nashville session musicians sharpen their axes on, and much of the new acoustic music has its spiritual and conceptual roots in it. It's jazz, but not exactly: call it "cowboy jazz." It's string-rooted rather than horn-rooted; it stayed hot after jazz got cool; and every so often a couple of two-step dancers cast their shadow across the bandstand.

PETER OSTROUSHKO *Sluz Duz Music*. Rounder 0204.

BERTRAM LEVY AND PETER OSTROUSHKO *First Generation*. Flying Fish 392. Well known from his "Prairie Home Companion" appearances, fiddler/mandolinist Ostroushko stands with the very different eclectic Ry Cooder as a quintessential musician for our time. He's not the only one to have synthesized elements of American and Irish fiddle tunes, Western swing, old-time novelty tunes, forties pop, and other twentieth-century American vernaculars—that's a common enough patch to hoe—but he's certainly one of the best, and to this mix he's added a unique brand of spice from his Ukrainian

heritage. The Rounder album is the more dynamic and varied; if you value subtlety, you'll also enjoy the very graceful Flying Fish album with concertina player Bertram Levy.

BONNY PHIPPS *Autoharpin'*. Kicking Mule 228. An engaging singer, good ensemble arranger, and surely the most interesting autoharp player around. The "idiot zither" is actually an instrument as challenging as you care to make it. Phipps sets new limits by working with original mechanical configurations and tunings.

BILL SPENCE *The Hammered Dulcimer*. Front Hall 01. Others play this music too, but it was this album that probably did most to establish the sound of the hammered-dulcimer/fiddle band. Spence is a traditionalist. More recently the sound has moved in other directions: listen to Metamora's latter-day work (Windham Hill 1068) to hear how easily the textures of this instrumentation slip into a commercially acceptable new age sound, and to No Strings Attached (Turquoise 5060) for a younger band, still growing, that's unafraid to explore extended sounds and repertoire.

RICHARD THOMPSON *Strict Tempo*. Carthage 4409. Englishman Richard Thompson is well versed in British and American tradition, a veteran of major British folk-rock bands, and a cult figure as rock singer-songwriter-guitarist. Here he takes acoustic and electric guitars and an arsenal of other instruments on a quick and very polished tour of fiddle tunes, swing, polkas, and exotic melodies. Like all his work, it's never quite like anyone else's.

ARTIE TRAUM *Cayenne*. Rounder 3084. This album has been perceived as rock, jazz, and new age. Listen to the acoustic guitar work embedded in textures of other instruments and of the modern studio itself: you'll hear echoes of country blues, bluegrass, the English folk guitarists of the sixties, bossa nova, and contemporary pop sounds. A good example of contemporary synthesis from a musician who grew up with traditional music and kept his ears open as he changed over the years.

GUY VAN DUSER *Stride Guitar*. Rounder 3059. Many finger-style guitarists try their hand at a piano-rag style; too many get overcomplicated and lose the beat and the music. In Van Duser's playing, it all hangs together with a good swing and just the right notes.

SONGSTERS AND SONGWRITERS

There's no way to do justice here to the many songwriters and singers of contemporary songs who are associated with the folk music community. In recent years only a few contemporary artists have moved, like The Roches, Suzanne Vega, Tracy Chapman, and Nanci Griffith, from the folk community to major-label contracts. Many talented performers have stayed behind, making good music, probably wishing for a break on the majors, and meanwhile managing to make a career with an independent-record-label contract. It's a living.

Here are a few singers and songwriters of various styles and attitudes; see how many of them you like. I wish I had room for more, but these will start you on your way to hearing intelligent contemporary writing. I've deliberately promoted a few obscure names. For your convenience in searching them out, I'll cite them by record label:

The Dinner Ladies (Mick Jackson, Julia Palmer, Ben Davis, and Lorraine Bowen): Acoustic music moves into the eighties.

Bare: Mary Flower. *Carthage/Hannibal:* Kevin Brown, The Dinner Ladies, Kate and Anna McGarrigle. *Cypress:* Cheryl Wheeler. *Dragonwing:* Eileen McGann. *Flying Fish:* Eric Bogle, Bright Morning Star, Anne Hills, Si Kahn, Sally Rogers, Claudia Schmidt. *Front Hall:* Cindy Mangsen. *Kaleidoscope:* The Bobs. *Neworld:* David Mallet. *Rampur:* Tricia Alexander (cassette). *Raw Deal:* Judy Roderick (cassette). *Red House:* John Gorka. *Redwood:* Holly Near. *Rounder:* Rory Block, John Mc-Cutcheon. *Philo:* Nanci Griffith, Christine Lavin. *Sugar Hill:* Guy Clark, Jesse Winchester. *Unrecorded* (at this writing): Shawn Colvin.

Si Kahn; Continuing the topical song tradition.

OLD-TIME MUSIC

Like the bluesmen, the great old singers and musicians of the Appalachians are passing on. County Records' albums of the great fiddler and banjo player Tommy Jarrell are a fitting epitaph for an age.

Younger players coming out of the sixties folk music revival are left to carry on the traditions in their own ways. Listen to fiddler Brad Leftwich's polished Jarrell, or Bob Carlin's deft touch on the banjo, or Jody Stecher's soulful singing, or the drive and unabashed modernisms of the Red Clay Ramblers, or the way contemporary performers like Cathy Fink, Mike Cross, Blue Rose, and John McCutcheon bring an intimate knowledge of tradition into contemporary professional usage.

Visit the Brandywine Old Time Music Festival or the Augusta Heritage Festival and you'll see fields full of fiddlers, acres of banjoists, keeping alive what twenty-five years ago appeared to be an endangered species of music.

TIM AND MOLLIE O'BRIEN *Take Me Back.* Sugar Hill 3766.

RICKY SKAGGS AND TONY RICE *Skaggs and Rice.* Sugar Hill SH 3711. Tim O'Brien, here joined by equally clear-voiced sister Molly, performs with the bluegrass band Hot Rize and writes country hit songs. Ricky Skaggs started in bluegrass and became a country music star. Tony Rice started in bluegrass and became a prime shaper of new acoustic music. On these separate but equal albums, they all return to the roots of the classic old-time duet style with old-time and gospel songs (a few modern ones from Tim and Mollie), elegant picking, beautiful harmony singing, and an obvious love for the music. You won't hear better duet singing than this.

MIKE SEEGER (AND OTHERS) *Fresh Oldtime String Band Music.* Rounder 0262. Moving into the role of elder statesman of the old-time revival, singer/multi-instrumentalist Mike Seeger has, more than any other urban musician, become one with the music—yet he remains sadly under-recorded. Here he is joined from piece to piece by various musicians, mostly younger, and all devoted to extending the limits of the tradition while remaining faithful to it. A band called The Horseflies are among the guests on this album; their own Rounder albums offer an even

Tim and Mollie O'Brien; Old time harmony

wilder vision of how far you can bend tradition without breaking its spirit.

BLUES AND GOSPEL

The blues go on. The form hasn't changed, but faces have changed: old masters have passed away, and significant talents have come into prominence or achieved overdue recognition. Reissues of country blues have slowed down since the sixties, and the age of the rediscovery of old blues singers is effectively over. Many important electric blues records are now being reissued, including worthy but little-known midwestern blues-men on the Nighthawk label, and the massive MCA reissue of the great fifties and sixties Chess classics including Muddy Waters.

In addition to the artists listed below, you'll also enjoy electric bluesmen Son Seals and Robert Cray, and Koko Taylor, perhaps the last of the women blues shouters. Taj Mahal remains pre-eminent among the few black performers of the urban country blues revival. He's turned his fine voice and great talent to modern pop styles as well, with mixed success.

ALBERT COLLINS *Cold Snap*. Alligator 4752. The most dynamic showman on the electric blues scene today; a strong singer/guitarist.

WILLIE DIXON *Hidden Charms*. Bug/Capitol CI-50595. A major writer of Chicago blues, bassist/singer Dixon expands the structure and content of the idiom at an age when others retire.

PROFESSOR LONGHAIR *Crawfish Fiesta*. Alligator 4718. Everything that's special about New Orleans r & b is epitomized in the work of this singer/pianist. New Orleans musicians have a unique way of playing around the beat, a lightness of spirit, and sometimes a heart of darkness beneath the surface gaiety.

KATIE WEBSTER *The Swamp Boogie Queen*. Alligator 4766. A hard-driving Texas pianist-singer out of fifties r & b, but with deeper roots.

DOROTHY LOVE COATES *A City Built Four Square*. Savoy 14500. Little known outside gospel music circles, Coates has one of the very greatest voices ever recorded, a powerful rhythmic drive, and a clear sense of her texts—many of them written by herself. Look also for her reissues on the Specialty label.

SWEET HONEY IN THE ROCK *Live at Carnegie Hall*. Flying Fish 106. This women's a cappella group uses the black gospel tradition to address contemporary political and feminist topics, as well as to preserve the original idiom. They sing beautifully.

VARIOUS ARTISTS *Georgia Sea Island Songs*. New World 278. The great Bessie Jones and others, carrying on the traditions of Afro-American choral singing that survived on the isolated coastal islands.

CAJUN/ZYDECO AND CHICANO MUSIC

(The Cajun/Zydeco and Chicano notes and selections are by Mary Armstrong of WXPN-FM, Philadelphia.)

Cajun/zydeco and live recording are an unbeatable combination. If it's a choice between a studio session and a concert recording, you'll get more excitement if you go with the show. Rounder Records has several *Live at Richard's* albums that capture the energy between musicians and dancers that can't be duplicated in the studio. Many of the recordings below are live.

CLIFTON CHENIER *Live at the San Francisco Blues Festival*. Arhoolie 1093.

Willie Dixon: Past master of the blues.

Sweet Honey in the Rock: contemporary content for the gospel sound.

(ANTHOLOGY) *Festival de Musique Acadienne '81 Live.* Swallow 6032.

(ANTHOLOGY) *Louisiana Cajun and Creole Music 1934.* Swallow 8003/2. John Lomax field recordings: the real roots of the music.

(ANTHOLOGY) *Music of French America.* Rounder 6010. Presents the Balfa Brothers in the context of music of other Francophone regions: Missouri, Maine, and Quebec.

Among recordings by younger musicians, you can trust any with accordionist Marc Savoy; likewise fiddler Michael Doucet with his band Beausoleil as they range from Creole blues to contemporary hybrids. Bruce Daigrepont, Queen Ida, and Zachary Richard are the names to search out for rocking music. Country music has been important to Cajuns too. The under-celebrated Vin Bruce is an exquisite baritone and wonderful songwriter; Belton Richard blends traditional Cajun with country, and D.L. Menard brings Nashville and Louisiana comfortably close.

FLACO JIMENEZ *El Sonido de San Antonio.* Arhoolie 3014. Jimenez has emerged as the best-known Tejano musician for his ability to bring his authentic accordion sound to the work of country and contemporary singers like Ry Cooder, Peter Rowan, and Dwight Yoakum, but this is my personal favorite among his many records.

LOS LOBOS *La Pistola y el Corazón.* Slash/Warner 25790-1. Much of the current popularity of Mexican-American music is due to the success of this rock-oriented band. Here, to the surprise of their rock fans, they blend a number of regional styles in original songs played entirely on traditional instruments, exhibiting an eclectic knowledge of the Hispanic musics of this hemisphere.

For classic Tejano and Mexican music, listen to the many artists on Arhoolie records, including anthologies of various styles (string bands, etc.) and the great singer Lydia Mendoza. Trust Rounder Records ¡Conjunto! series for the best of South Texas bands leased from regional labels.

CELTIC MUSIC

A Celtic music revival took hold in the seventies and exploded into the eighties, when performers of Irish music found an enthusiastic market in the States. In a style derived from the English school of Davy Graham and John Renbourn, Irish players followed the lead of Frenchman Pierre Bensusan in devising new techniques to express Celtic dance tunes. Bands were formed and re-formed (De Danaan, Planxty, The Bothy Band, and The Boys of the Lough being the big names), and the Irish musician became an organization person.

The new generation includes players of high character and great skill, like fiddler Kevin Burke, piper Paddy Keenan, and accordion player Jackie Daly, conscientious musicians all, who love and respect their tradition and take it brilliantly into a new world of professional possibilities.

But the essence of the old music was in the subtle and individualistic reshaping, the twists and turns of ornamentation, that the masters applied to a canonic repertoire of dance tunes and airs, occasionally adding a new tune of their own. It's not an approach that lends itself to slick ensemble playing: sometimes it sounds crude to the uncultivated ear, and it can be hard to follow as it reaches back to distant times and places.

In the modern bands, regional characteristics and individual eccentricities disappear as musicians instead work toward an international style and think in terms of ensemble unity, professional polish, album structure, and studio techniques. And in so thriving a market, there's a more than fair share of bad music from bad musicians, though from the best of the younger ones, we haven't heard the end of beautiful music. But I think we won't hear the likes of Willie Clancy's pipering, or the fiddling of Tommie Potts, or the voice of Joe Heaney, ever again.

MARY BERGIN *Feadoga Stain.* Shanachie 79006. The title is Irish for "little flute," which actually signifies tin whistle. You'll be moved by Bergin's fluency and expression on it.

Alistair Anderson, virtuoso of the concertina and Northumbrian pipes.

KEVIN BURKE AND JACKIE DALY *Eavesdropper*. Green Linnet SIF 3002. Playing, from delicate to intense, by polished younger players on fiddle and accordion. Elegant; no pounding guitars.

MAIRE NI CHATHASAIGH *The New Strung Harp*. Temple 019. Ni Chathasaigh, who also sings in Gaelic, has extended the courtly repertoire of the Irish harp to encompass the dance music tradition as well.

JOE HEANEY AND GABE O'SULLIVAN *Joe and the Gabe*. Green Linnet 1018. Tracks of flutist/whistle player O'Sullivan pleasingly alternate with the magnificent, sometimes chilling songs of Joe Heaney, a profound singer in the ancient, ornamented style. Most songs are in English, a few in Gaelic.

KORNOG *Premiere: Music from Brittany*. Green Linnet SIF 1055. The Breton contingent adds continental traditions and instruments like the reedy bombarde to the Celtic mix.

CHRISTINE PRIMROSE *Aite Mo Ghaoil*. Temple 006. Sweet Scots Gallic singing by a Hebridean native living in Glasgow.

PADDY TUNNY *The Stone Fiddle*. Green Linnet 1037. Ballads and airs sung gracefully in the old style; yet a more easily approachable singer than Joe Heaney (above).

(ANTHOLOGY) *Flight of the Green Linnet*. Green Linnet 103 (cassette, CD) A sampler of music on the Green Linnet label; a good way to hear many contemporary bands in one place.

ENGLAND

Much strong singing has come out of England. Martin Carthy has established his excellence as loremaster as well as singer and original guitarist, while American audiences have become aware of such other fine traditional performers as Frankie Armstrong, Vin Garbutt, Bernard Wrigley, Mick Hanley, and

Dick Gaughan. Stateside-resident Britishers Lou Killen, John Roberts, and Tony Barrand perform here frequently.

England has also seen a revival of the spicy Northumbrian smallpipes, a particularly agile member of the bagpipes family, as well as a concertina revival and the further development of a proud guitar tradition in the hands of Martin Simpson, Richard Thompson (*see* CONTEMPORARY INSTRUMENTAL MUSIC, above), and others.

Note also that many of the important English folk-rock bands of the seventies, and their spin-offs, are now reissued by Shanachie and Carthage/Hannibal.

ALISTAIR ANDERSON *Dookin' for Apples*. Front Hall 020. Dance tunes by a virtuoso of the concertina and Northumbrian smallpipes.

JOHN RENBOURN *Ship of Fools*. The eclectic guitarist's new group includes voices and instruments old and modern in a selection of traditional, medieval, and contemporary material. Within the styles that have always interested him, Renbourn doesn't stop growing.

JUNE TABOR *Airs and Graces*. Shanachie 79055. Ballads ancient and of today, beautifully and movingly sung.

MUSIC FOR CHILDREN

The children of the sixties have grown up and have children of their own, so now there's a new generation of children's music as well. In addition to the music below, also look into tales told by David Holt, the Folktellers, and Robin Williamson, and the products of A Gentle Wind. (In addition to their individual cassettes of tales and music, A Gentle Wind also publishes a good sampler series.)

JONATHAN EDWARDS *Little Hands*. American Melody 102.

CATHY FINK *Grandma Slid Down the Mountain*. Rounder 8010. *When the Rain Comes Down*. Rounder 8013.

TAJ MAHAL *Shake Sugaree*. Music for Little People 272 (cassette).

MARCY MARXER *Jump Children*. Rounder 8012.

PHIL ROSENTHAL *The Paw Paw Patch*. American Melody 104.

VARIOUS ARTISTS *Grandma's Patchwork Quilt*. American Melody 103. (Jonathan Edwards, Cathy Fink, John McCutcheon, Larry Penn, Phil and Naomi Rosenthal.)

MAIL ORDER RECORD HOUSES

Each of the mail-order houses listed here has a different stock list, price structure, and personality. Most of those I've chosen stock a good cross-section of the musical styles described in this book. There are others, some of which specialize more deeply. You can find out more about them by reading the advertising in the magazines listed in our PERIODICALS section. Note also that many of the individual record companies listed in the next section also sell directly by mail.

ALCAZAR Box 429, Waterbury VT 05676. 120-page annual catalog covering all idioms. (Also wholesales as SILO.)

ANDY'S FRONT HALL Box 307, Wormer Rd., Voorheesville NY 12186. 80-page catalog of records, books, instruments, etc.

JIM BOND, INDIAN TRADER, 34030 Totem Pole Road, Lebanon OR 97355. Native American recordings, craft supplies, etc.

CANADIAN RIVER MUSIC 4106 Tyler St., Amarillo TX 79110.

Informative newsletters; strong in small labels hard to find elsewhere.

COUNTY SALES Box 191, Floyd VA 24091. Strong in old-time and bluegrass; good newsletter in this area.

DOWN HOME MUSIC 10341 San Pablo Ave., El Cerrito CA 94530. Catalog and good bimonthly 40-page newsletter. All areas of traditional and ethnic music, rock, jazz, etc.

ELDERLY INSTRUMENTS Box 14210, Lansing MI 48901. Comprehensive 72-page catalog of all idioms; also books, instruments, etc.

FESTIVAL RECORDS 3271 Main St., Vancouver BC V5V 3M6. 72-page catalog includes Canadian/foreign labels hard to find in U.S.

FLOYD'S RECORD SHOP Drawer 10, Ville Platte LA 70586. Regional Cajun and zydeco artists and labels, plus country, etc.

LONGHORN RECORDS Box 93457, Hollywood CA 90093. Country cutout specialists, but the catalogs contain all sorts of Cajun, rockabilly, and bluegrass surprises. A must for discophiles.

ROUNDUP RECORDS Box 154, N. Cambridge MA 02140. 116-page catalog of all idioms plus bimonthly bulletin with excellent reviews by Bob Coltman and others. Also books, videos, etc.

SHANACHIE RECORDS 37 E. Clinton St., Newton NJ 07860. Issues general and special-area bulletins. Strong in Celtic, historical blues, guitar, reggae, African, and "world beat" music.

TALKING TACO RECORDS 5402 Timber Trail, San Antonio TX 78228. Hispanic, Native American, and modern southwestern music.

RECORD COMPANIES

This section provides a descriptive list of specialist folk music record companies. (For major labels, consult the *Billboard Buyer's Guide* or your local record source.) Our list contains only recently authenticated addresses. Consult the American Folklife Center's *Folklife Sourcebook* for a supplementary, though possibly outdated, address list. For updates after the publication of this book, consult the *Sing Out!* Resource Center (*see Foreword.*)

Many of the companies listed below sell directly to the public. I've noted those that publish particularly useful mail order catalogs, but most have some sort of catalog available.

The industry trade association is the National Association of Independent Record Distributors and Manufacturers (Box 568, Maple Shade NJ 08052).

ACORN 323 Marine St., No. 5, Santa Monica CA 90405. Well-known dance tunes executed literally on hammered dulcimer by Tony Elman.

ADELPHI Box 7688, Silver Spring MD 20907. Varied contemporary.

ADVENT Box 772, El Cerrito CA 94530. Blues, British, and Irish.

AFS *see* LIBRARY OF CONGRESS.

AIRBORNE 10 Music Circle South, Nashville TN 37203. Singer-songwriters (Mickey Newbury, etc.); also pop, country.

ALABAMA TRADITIONS Brierfield Ironworks Park, Route 1, Box 147, Brierfield AL 35035. LP documenting Alabama fiddling.

ALASKA HIT SINGLES Box 707, Juneau AK 99801. LP of songs, many good, about Alaskan life by contemporary Alaskan singer-songwriters.

ALCAZAM! *see* ALCAZAR.

ALCAZAR Box 429, Waterbury VT 05487. Varied contemporary folk.

ALL-EARS REVIEW *see* ROM.

ALLIANCE Box 1176 Station Q, Toronto ONT M4T 2P4. Dist. in U.S. by FRONT HALL. Children's album by Michael Cooney.

ALLIGATOR Box 60234, Chicago IL 60660. The pre-eminent catalog of contemporary electric blues. Also rockabilly, reggae, etc. *The Genuine Houserockin' Music* anthologies and *Living Chicago Blues* series are a good introduction to the label.

AMERICAN COWBOY SONGS Rt. 7, Box 220, Mount Juliet TN 37122. Country-style cowboy songs by Chris LeDoux and others.

AMERICAN HERITAGE 1208 Everett St, Caldwell ID 83605. Western competition-style fiddling.

AMERICAN MELODY Box 270, Guilford CT 06437. Traditional songs for children by performers with established adult-music careers.

ANTONE'S 2928 Guadaloupe St., San Antonio TX 78705. Live recordings of contemporary blues from the Antone's nightclub.

ARCHIVE *see* EVEREST.

ARCHIVE OF FOLK CULTURE and ARCHIVE OF FOLK MUSIC *see* LIBRARY OF CONGRESS.

ARHOOLIE 10341 San Pablo Ave., El Cerrito CA 94530. Extensive, important catalog of blues, Cajun, country, old time, Chicano, and other ethnic and regional music. Large mail order catalog.

ASCH *see* FOLKWAYS.

ATOMIC THEORY *see* FLYING FISH. Small mixed bag of acoustic, rock, unusual contemporary, and Willie Murphy's blues piano.

AUGUST *see* ROUNDER. LP of the popular novelty-rag singer-guitarist Leon Redbone.

AUGUSTA HERITAGE Davis & Elkins College, Elkins WV 26241. Albums documenting West Virginia traditional musicians. *See also* SCS.

AURAL TRADITION Vancouver Folk Music Festival, 3271 Main St., Vancouver BC V5V 3M6. Varied world, U.S., and Canadian.

AVOCET Box 6769, Portland OR 97228.

BALKAN ARTS Ethnic Folk Arts Center, 325 Spring St., New York NY 10013. LPs of Balkan music; also distributor and mail order.

BANJAR Box 32164, Minneapolis MN 55432. Midwestern Scandinavian.

BARE c/o Zither Shop, 525 E. Ohio, Denver CO 80209. Singer-songwriter Mary Flower. Good songs well done; good musicians.

BAY 1741 Alcatraz Ave., Berkeley CA 94703. Specializes in Bay-area musicians: varied folk and acoustic, Jody Stecher, etc.

BEREA COLLEGE RECREATION EXTENSION CPO 287, Berea KY 40404. String band instrumental settings for Appalachian folk dances.

BIG ROUND *see* ALCAZAR. LP of children's music by group Peggosus.

KAREN BILLINGS Box 277, Bloomington IN 47402. Cassettes of lullabies: a trained voice and folk instruments.

BISHOP MUSEUM PRESS, Box 1900-A, Honolulu HI 96819. Hawaiian and Polynesian cassettes and correlated books. The real stuff.

BIOGRAPH 16 River Street, Chatham NY 12037. Historical jazz and blues; some sixties revival performers.

BLACK TOP see ROUNDER. Contemporary electric and New Orleans blues.

BLIND PIG see FLYING FISH. Contemporary bluespersons.

BLUES CLASSICS see ARHOOLIE. Early country and piano blues reissues.

BLUE GOOSE see SHANACHIE. Seventies blues revival.

BOULDER FOLK 2888 Bluff St., No. 402, Boulder CO 80301. Singer-songwriter Jon Sirkis.

BRI (Blue Ridge Institute), Ferrum College, Ferrum VA 24088. *Virginia Traditions* series documenting Virginia traditional music, and *Folk Music of Virginia* radio airplay series.

BUTLER 1086 Meandering Creek, Uniontown OH 44685. Bluegrass from the Hotfoot Quartet; other groups.

CABBAGE 1015 Mariposa Ave., Berkeley CA 94707. Scottish dance music.

CANADIAN FOLK MUSIC SOCIETY Box 4232 Sta. C, Calgary Alberta T2T 5N1.

CANADIAN RIVER 4106 Tyler St, Amarillo TX 79110. Cassette by singer-songwriter David Rea. *See also* under MAIL-ORDER above.

CANYON RECORDS 4143 N. 16 St., Phoenix AZ, 85016. Music and other Native American arts, also distributor.

CARTHAGE Box 667, Rocky Hill NJ 08553. Varied small but tasty catalog ranging from important seventies reissues (McGarrigle Sisters, Phil Ochs, Steeleye Span, Fairport Convention, Sandy Denny, etc.) to African, world, and contemporary music.

CASSANDRA c/o Schroder Music Co., 2027 Parker St., Berkeley CA 94704. Music of topical singer-songwriter Malvina Reynolds.

CATALYTIC Box 120316, Nashville TN 37212. Unusual arrangements of pop and traditional tunes on dulcimer by David Schnaufer.

CENTER 885 Clayton St., San Francisco CA 94117. Topical songs sung by Fath Petric.

CENTIPEDE Box 121832, Nashville TN 37212. Singer-songwriter Nyle Frank.

CHAMELEON 3355 El Segundo Blvd., Hawthorne CA 90250. Marketing group for MOUNTAIN RAILROAD, SIERRA, and VEE-JAY.

CIMIRRON/RAINBIRD 607 Piney Point Rd., Yorktown VA 23692. Bluegrass and country.

CLEAN CUTS see ROUNDER. Varied contemporary.

CMH (Country Music History), Box 39439, Los Angeles CA 90039. Good modern recordings of important first-generation performers in bluegrass, country, and western swing: Merle Travis, Osborne Brothers, Johnny Gimble, many other valuable LPs and CDs.

COLE HARBOUR see ALCAZAR. LP by Stan Rogers. *See also* FOGARTY'S COVE.

COLLECTOR'S CLASSICS see ZIM.

COLLEGIUM see MINSTREL.

COLORADO COUNCIL ON THE ARTS AND HUMANITIES 770 Pennsylvania St., Denver CO 80203. *Do Not Pass Me By* cassette of folklife profiles narrated by Harry Tuft, primarily for airplay.

COPPER CREEK 2623 Cedarhurst Ave., Roanoke VA 24012. Small selection for bluegrass collectors: Stanley Brothers live shows, etc.

CORNBELT Box 3452, Madison WI 53704. LPs by Peter and Lou Berryman. Homespun vocals, funny and entertaining songs.

COUNTRY HERITAGE Rural Route 1, Box 130, Madill OK 73446. Pretty, old-style dobro: Brother Oswald, Bev King, instruction, etc.

COUNTRY MUSIC FOUNDATION 4 Music Square East, Nashville, TN 37203. Classic country reissues; historically important items.

COUNTY Box 191, Floyd VA 24091. Large, important catalog of reissues and contemporary recordings. String band, fiddle, banjo, bluegrass, and early country music, including Doyle Lawson, Kenny Baker, Tommy Jarrell, many more major performers.

COWLICK see ALCAZAR.

CRANFORD PUBLICATIONS Box 42, Englishtown NS B0C 1H0. Cape Breton fiddler Jerry Holland's cassette of careful, exemplary solo selections from an interesting, separately published tunebook.

CRYSTAL SONG Box 91-A, HCO 1, West Shokan NY 12494. Cassette of Amy Fradon and Leslie Ritter. Good soulful vocal duets imported into contemporary style; contemporary and some original songs.

CYPRESS 1523 Crossroads of the World, Los Angeles CA 90028.

LES DANCERIES DE QUEBEC Box 516, Haute-Ville QUE G1R 4R8. Traditional music of Quebec.

DANDELION see Silver Stream.

DARING see ROUNDER. Varied contemporary.

DAVY LEE Box 4024, Portsmouth NH 03801. Cassette of David Levine's original songs developed for high school peer leadership programs.

DELMARK 4243 N. Lincoln, Chicago IL 60618. Major figures in country, Chicago, and piano blues: Sleepy John Estes, Roosevelt Sykes, Otis Rush. Also traditional, mainstream, and modern jazz.

LOTUS DICKEY MUSIC 8920 South Shore Dr., Unionville, IN 47468. Cassettes of an Indiana old-time fiddler and songwriter.

DRAGONWING 67 St. Dunstan Dr., Scarborough ONT M1L 2V4. Music of the highly regarded Canadian singer-songwriter Eileen McGann.

DUNKELD see ALCAZAR. Contemporary Scottish.

EARWIG 1818 W. Pratt Blvd., Chicago IL 60626.

ELDERBERRY West Virginia Dept. of Culture and History, Cultural Center, Capitol Complex, Charleston WV 25305. LPs documenting West Virginia fiddlers and other traditional musicians.

ETHNIC FOLKWAYS LIBRARY *see* FOLKWAYS.

EV. ARCH. *see* EVEREST.

EVEREST 2020 Ave. of the Stars, Century City CA 90067. Markets ARCHIVE, LEGACY, OLYMPIC, TRADITION.

F & W *see* ALCAZAR. New England contradance music.

FALCON 783-A Queen St. West, Toronto ONT M6J 1G1. Scholarly albums documenting old-time fiddling in Western Manitoba.

FAST FOLK Box 938 Village Station, New York NY 10014. Subscription series featuring rising singer-songwriters; strongest on New York scene; special topical and regional issues as well.

FIDDLESTICKS Box 7 Margaree Harbour, Inverness Co., NS B02 2B0. Nice Cape Breton fiddling cassette from Jerry Holland.

FINE CATCH *see* FLYING FISH. Varied contemporary.

FIRE ON THE MOUNTAIN *see* KALEIDOSCOPE.

FLORIDA FOLKLIFE PROGRAM Box 265, White Springs FL 32096. LPs documenting black Florida musicians and the Florida Folk Festival programs of the past quarter-century.

FLYING FISH 1304 W. Schubert, Chicago IL 60614. Extensive, important catalog of eminent contemporary performers in all areas. Good descriptive mail-order catalog available.

FLYING HEART 4026 NE 12th Ave., Portland OR 97212.

FLYRIGHT *see* ZIM.

FOGARTY'S COVE *see* ALCAZAR. Recordings by the late singer-songwriter Stan Rogers, whose strong, clear voice and original songs about the sea made him a favorite performer.

FOLK ERA 6 S. 230 Cohasset Rd., Napierville IL 60540. Reissues of sixties commercial folk groups: Kingston Trio, etc.

FOLKRAFT Box 404, Florham Park NJ 07932. 45s and LPs for folk dance and movement activities.

FOLK LEGACY Sharon Mountain Rd., Sharon CT 06069. A varied catalog favoring low-key, unaffected traditional and revival singers.

FOLKLYRIC *see* ARHOOLIE. Tex-Mex, Hawaiian, regional/ethnic, historical jazz.

FOLKWAYS *Curatorial:* Office of Folklife Programs, Smithsonian Institution, 955 L'Enfant Plaza, Suite 2600, Washington DC 20560. *Sales distribution: see* ROUNDER. After the death of founder Moses Asch, the massive, confusingly rich Folkways catalog, with all its treasures and aberrations, passed into the care of the Smithsonian. The original materials now form a core archive known as "The Frances and Moses Asch Collection."

FOUR DOTS Box 233, Denton TX 76202. Pre-Rounder Brave Combo albums, smooth cowboy singer Randy Erwin, and off-beat Texans.

FRETLESS *see* ALCAZAR and ROUNDER. Varied contemporary and revival.

FRONT HALL Box 307, Wormer Road, Voorheesville NY 12186. Contemporary revival performers, emphasizing Anglo-American and British song and instrumental traditions.

GCS, Box 41062, Memphis TN 38174. Soul, blues, gospel.

A GENTLE WIND Box 3103, Albany NY 12203. Songs and stories for children, attractively performed and presented on cassette. Sampler series available. Attention: children's librarians.

GLOBAL VILLAGE Box 2051 Cathedral Station, New York NY 10025. Varied, interesting catalog of traditional and ethnic music; some contemporary idioms. Revival performers, older traditional performers, archival reissues, oddball surprises, etc. Not since Folkways has a catalog so strongly reflected the eclectic personality of its manager. Yiddish, black gospel, and Italian areas are the strongest among many others.

GOLDBAND Box 1485, Lake Charles, LA 70602. Cajun, zydeco, and swamp rock; regional performers.

GREENHAYS *see* FLYING FISH. Jean Richie and varied contemporary revival performers including Happy Traum.

GREEN LINNET 70 Turner Hill Rd., New Canaan CT 06840. A strong catalog which represents and defines the new generation of Celtic revival and new acoustic performers. Many eminent soloists and groups; also more conservative performers, some U.S. folk and contemporary figures, etc.

GREEN MOUNTAIN *see* ALCAZAR. Vermont contemporary and traditional.

GUITAR ARTISTRY *see* SHANACHIE. A Shanachie imprint featuring contemporary folk and blues guitarists (John Renbourn, Stefan Grossman, Happy Traum, etc.) with printed tablatures.

GUSTO *see* IMG.

HAN *see* ALCAZAR. Varied contemporary.

HANNIBAL *see* CARTHAGE.

HDS *see* FLYING FISH. LP of hot Nashville acoustic jam.

HEPATICA Box 569, Lemont PA 16851. Carrie Crompton (hammered dulcimer) and the Baroque Folk: pleasant arrangements of British Isles and renaissance through classical-period music.

HERITAGE Route 3, Box 278, Galax VA 24333. Bluegrass and old time.

HERWIN *see* SHANACHIE. Historical blues, jazz, ragtime, and gospel.

HIGH WATER Dept. of Music, Memphis State Univ., Memphis TN 38152. Under the leadership of David Evans, Memphis State University's departments of Commercial Music and Ethnomusicology/Regional Studies join in professional-level recording of contemporary Memphis blues and gospel performers.

HIGH WINDY Box 28, Fairview NC 28730. Tales with music for children by proficient revival singer/multi-instrumentalist David Holt.

HOGEYE *see* FLYING FISH. Contemporary singer-songwriters including Cindy Mangsen, Anne Hills, and Tom Paxton.

HOMESPUN *see* LEARNING section.

HULA *see* BISHOP MUSEUM PRESS.

HUMMING BIRD 1921 Walnut St., No. 1, Berkeley CA 94704. Exploratory contemporary music based on world and American traditions.

HURRICANE Route 2, Box 130, Hurricane WV 25526. Old-time songs and banjo music of Elmer Bird.

ICEBERGG 207 E. Buffalo St., Milwaukee WI 53202. Women's/feminist.

IMG 1900 Elm Hill Pike, Nashville TN 37210. At this writing reported new owner of GUSTO, KING, and STARDAY.

INDIAN HOUSE Box 472, Taos NM 87571. Native American.

INDIAN RECORDS Box 47, Fay OK 73646. Native American.

INSTITUTE OF ALASKAN NATIVE ARTS Box 80583, Fairbanks AL 99708. Documentary cassette of Athabaskan old time fiddling.

IONA see ALCAZAR. Contemporary Scottish.

IROQRAFTS RR 2, Ohseken ONT N0A 1MO. Iroquois social dances.

JEMF (John Edwards Memorial Foundation) see ARHOOLIE. Blues, country, and traditional reissues.

JIN see SWALLOW.

JUNE APPAL Appalshop, Box 743, Whitesburg KY 41858. Traditional and revival Appalachian-area musicians.

KALEIDOSCOPE, Box O, El Cerrito CA 94530. Mixed bag of good-quality contemporary folk, seminal new acoustic music, and cowboy jazz antecedents: Dave Grisman, Tiny Moore and Jethro Burns, important Bob Wills reissues, Kate Wolf, The Bobs, etc.

KICKING MULE Box 158, Alderpoint CA 95411. Virtuoso instrumental stylists, especially on guitar, dulcimer, and banjo, in traditional and modern styles; most with tablature transcriptions. Large mail order catalog.

KID'S RECORDS 68 Broadview Ave., Suite 303, Toronto, ONT M4M 2E6. U.S. distributor: ALCAZAR. Includes Bonnie Phipps cassettes.

KING see IMG.

KOPN-FM attn: S. Newstead, 915 E. Broadway, Columbia MO 65201. Missouri Legacy series of taped profiles, including folk musicians, for airplay.

LA LOUISIANNE 711 Stevenson St., Lafayette LA 70501. Cajun, etc.

LADYSLIPPER Box 3130, Durham NC 27705. Music by women performers.

LANOR Box 233, Church Point LA 70525. Cajun, country, zydeco, and swamp rock; regional performers.

LEGACY INTERNATIONAL see EVEREST.

LIBRARY OF CONGRESS Motion Picture, Broadcasting, and Recorded Sound Division, Washington DC 20540. Recordings from the Archive of Folk Culture (formerly AFS, the Archive of Folk Song).

LINCOLN HOUSE see ALCAZAR. LP of singer-songwriter Wendy Grossman.

LIVING FOLK see ALCAZAR. New England revival performers.

LUCRATIVE Box 90363, Nashville TN 37209. Homey, enjoyable cassette of country hit songwriter Fred Koller's wacky side.

LYRICHORD 141 Perry St., New York, NY 10014. Varied international.

MAGPIE see ZIM.

MALACO Box 9827, Jackson MS 39206. Contemporary blues and r & b.

MARIMAC Box 5, Little Ferry NJ 07643. Cassettes of traditional music.

DAVID MASSENGILL 179 E. Third St., No. 20, New York, NY 10009. Cassettes of talented post-Dylan singer/songwriter

many of whose songs are well known through the recordings of others.

MEADOWLARK see SHANACHIE. Traditional Irish, ethnic, and reggae.

MEGSHEILIAN 19231 E. Nassau Dr., Aurora CO 80013. Country-folk singer-songwriter Alan Kelly, who likes to write evocatively in the character of the romantic drifter.

MELODEON see BIOGRAPH. Historical blues, bluegrass, and jazz.

METAMORA 8920 South Shore Drive, Unionville, IN 47468. Cassettes by Grey Larson, Malcolm Dalglish, and Pete Sutherland; polished traditional instrumentals, hammered dulcimer, etc.

MINERAL RIVER see ALCAZAR. LP of singer-songwriter Bill Staines.

MINSTREL 35-41 72nd St., Jackson Heights NY 11372. Small catalog of sixties-style revival performers (especially Bob Coltman); also Arkansas traditional singer Almeda Riddle, etc.

MISSISSIPPI DEPT. OF ARCHIVES AND HISTORY (dist. by SOUTHERN CULTURE). LP of 1939 Mississippi fiddling field recordings.

MORNING STAR see SHANACHIE. Early traditional and ethnic reissues.

MOUNTAIN RAILROAD see CHAMELEON. Sixties and seventies revivalists.

MUSIC EDUCATORS NATIONAL CONFERENCE 1902 Association Dr., Reston VA 22091. Sounds of the World cassette series profiling music of immigrant and ethnic communities in the U.S., with teacher's guides for elementary through college use.

MUSIC FOR LITTLE PEOPLE Box 1460, Redway CA 95560. Varied catalog including folk songs and tales; good Taj Mahal cassette.

MUSIC OF THE WORLD Box 258, Brooklyn NY 11209. Cassetes/CDs of folk, ethnic and contemporary music. Many interesting items including the Frantz Casseus Haitian Suite for guitar.

MUSKADINE see ADVENT.

NAP (National Assoc. for the Preservation and Perpetuation of Storytelling), Box 309, Jonesborough TN 37659. Folktellers et al.

NATIONAL COUNCIL FOR THE TRADITIONAL ARTS 806 15th St. NW, Washington DC 20005. Southwestern Hispanic music and cowboy poetry.

NEWORLD see ALCAZAR. Music of singer-songwriter David Mallett.

NEW WORLD 701 Seventh Ave., New York NY 10036. American music of all idioms, including valuable ethnic, bluegrass, blues, etc.

NIGHTHAWK Box 15856, St. Louis MO 63114. Contemporary blues and reggae; forties and fifties blues and r & b reissues.

NOUMENON Box 287, West Province Rd., Mt. Sunapee NH 03772. Albums of singer-songwriter Tom Pirozzoli. Formerly OASIS.

OGHAM see SHANACHIE.

OH BOY see ALCAZAR. Music of singer-songwriter John Prine.

OHIO ARTS COUNCIL 727 E. Main St., Columbus OH 43205. Interesting, unusual LP of Balkan Slavic music from the midwest.

OJL (Origin Jazz Library), 330 California, No. 302, Santa Monica CA 90403. Country blues (mostly early reissues) and early jazz.

OLD HOMESTEAD RECORDS Box 100, Brighton MI 48116. Bluegrass.

OLD TIMEY *see* ARHOOLIE. Early string band, Cajun, country reissues.

OLDIE BLUES *see* ZIM.

OLYMPIC *see* EVEREST.

OLD DOMINION Box 1385, Gallatin TN 37066. Bluegrass albums by Jim and Jesse McReynolds.

OLIVIA/SECOND WAVE 4400 Market St., Oakland CA 94608. The pre-eminent feminist label, including acoustic stylists Nancy Vogl and Lucie Blue Tremblay.

ONE SKY *see* ICEBERGG. Judy Gorman-Jacobs: topical contemporary folk.

ORIGIN JAZZ LIBRARY *see* OJL.

ORIGINAL BALKAN JAM Box 712 E, Victoria BC V8V 1P9. Contemporary interpretations of Balkan music.

OUTER GREEN *see* ALCAZAR. Sea songs by Schooner Fare, and others.

OUT OF TIME Box 4498, Silver Spring MD 20904. Piano rags, etc., arranged by accomplished finger-style guitarist Steve Hancoff.

PAMLICO SOUND *see* SUGAR HILL.

PARADISE Box 594, Middleton WI 53562. Electric bluesman Paul Black.

PASQUINADE *see* CANADIAN RIVER. Singer-songwriter Lu Mitchell.

PEDLAR PRESS 53 Whittemore Rd., Sturbridge MA 01566. Albums of New England traditional and historical topical music and tales performed by Jim Douglas. Songbooks separately available.

PEARL *see* DELMARK. Traditional jazz; fifties blues.

PEOPLE'S RECORDS 8929 Apache Dr., Beulah CO 81023. Country/folk cassettes of children's and peace songs by the Van Manens.

PHILO *see* ROUNDER. Contemporary performers and singer-songwriters, including Patty Larkin, Nanci Griffith, and Christine Lavin.

PIEDMONT *see* OJL.

PIGEON INLET Site 13, Box 26, RR 1, Torbay, Newfoundland ADA 3ZO. Albums of traditional music and stories from Newfoundland.

POTATO SATELLITE Box 472, Martindale TX 78655. Texas songwriters.

PRAIRIE DRUID 219 11th St. East, Saskatoon, SASK S7N OE5. LP of traditional and contemporary songs sung by Paddy Tutty.

PRAIRIE SMOKE 250 W. 99th St., No. 8C, New York NY 10025. Album of colonial songs sung by National Park Service balladeer Linda Russell, with polished arrangements by the band Prairie Smoke.

PROPINQUITY Box 9036, Denver CO 80209. Pleasing albums by the versatile singer/multi-instrumentalist Carla Sciaky: tradi-

tional, international, and children's music. Also cassette of The Mother Folkers, informal group of fine Denver-area women musicians whose annual concerts are a cult event.

PULSAR 1880 Bogey Hills Plaza No. 1880, Suite 11, St. Charles MO 63302. Contemporary blues.

PUNCHDRUNK Box 27125, Washington DC 20038. Wanamaker Lewis and the Lewis Brothers: bluegrass band and finger-style guitar albums.

RAG BABY *see* ARHOOLIE. LPs of Country Joe MacDonald.

RAINBIRD *see* CIMIRRON.

RAINBOW SNAKE Box 922, Greenfield MA 01302. The group Bright Morning Star: good, well-performed contemporary satirical and topical songs in styles from folk, pop, and cabaret traditions.

RAMBLER *see* ARHOOLIE. Early western swing and white jazz reissues.

RAMPUR 2018 Delaware St., Berkeley CA 94709. Songwriter Dev Singh and others, including a nice jazzy cassette from Tricia Alexander also available from 1744 W. Devon, Chicago IL 60660.

RAW DEAL c/o Oprea, Benton Rd., Sardinia NY 14134. Judy Roderick with electric band. Country and blues material includes some good original songs from a fine, gutsy singer.

RBF *see* FOLKWAYS.

REBEL Box 3057, Roanoke VA 24015. Contemporary bluegrass; many important performers including Ralph Stanley, Larry Sparks, Bill Harrell, Dave Evans, etc.

RED BEANS 2240 N. Magnolia, Chicago IL 60614. Blues (mostly acoustic Chicago musicians) and contemporary.

RED HOUSE Box 4044, St. Paul MN 55104. Small mixed bag of high-quality traditionalists, pickers, and songwriters: John Gorka, Peter Ostroushko, virtuoso guitarist Pat Donohue, etc.

RED PYJAMAS *see* ALCAZAR. Music of the late Steve Goodman.

REDWOOD 6400 Hollis St., Emeryville CA 94608. Contemporary high-quality artists, mostly with a social message: Holly Near, Ronnie Gilbert, Ferron, feminist music, Victor Jara and other Latin-American topical music (nueva cancion).

RELIX Box 92, Brooklyn NY 11229. Acoustic and folk-rock spin-offs by Grateful Dead and Jefferson Airplane members and associates.

REX REINHARDT 240 S. 39th St., Boulder CO 80303. Cassette of modern banjo pieces and songs by *Folk Music Sourcebook* co-author Dick Weissman.

RIVIERA Box 1848, Orange CA 92668. Contemporary blues.

ROAR *see* ALCAZAR. Children's music by Rory Zuckerman.

ROM Box 491212, Los Angeles CA 90049 (dist. by WELK RECORD GROUP.) CDs of Sandy Bull, contemporary eclectic bands, etc., plus ALL-EARS REVIEW, CD subscription anthology of recent contemporary releases on various labels.

ROOSTER Box 315, Pomfret VT 05053. Varied traditionalist performers.

ROOSTER BLUES *see* FLYING FISH. Contemporary electric blues.

ROSE QUARTZ *see* FLYING FISH. Album of revival singer Odetta.

ROSETTA 155 W. 16th St., New York NY 10011. *Women's*

Heritage Series of women performers of blues, jazz, and gospel. Some little-known artists worth hearing.

ROUND 6470 Eighth Ave., Grandville MI 49418. Albums of Jay Round on hammered dulcimer, with string band.

ROUNDER One Camp St., Cambridge MA 02140. Extensive, important catalog includes eminent performers in all areas. Useful sampler anthologies published in various categories.

RUBY SLIPPERS 6 Franklin Ct., Northampton MA 01060. LPs of Judy Polan; contemporary acoustic.

RURAL RHYTHM Box A, Arcadia CA 91006. Old-time, country, bluegrass.

SAMPLER Box 19270, Rochester NY 14619. Albums of traditional dance tunes, etc., by Mitzie Collins (hammered dulcimer) and others.

SANTROFI 2322 NW Kearney St., Portland OR 97210. Good cassette of Ghanian drummer/singer Obo Addy, now active in the U.S.

SAWMILL Box 447, Evergreen CO 80439. Cassette of contemporary and traditional songs about cowboys and the West engagingly performed by "Sawyer Tom" Hayden; some good songs here.

SCS SOUND 1332 West Eddy, Chicago IL 60657. Cassette tapes of selected Augusta Heritage Festival concerts.

SECOND WAVE *see* OLIVIA.

SEQUATCHIE Star Rt., Box 73, Dunlap TN 37327. Bluegrass bands centered on songwriter/banjoist Edward Brown. Album *Coke Oven Slave* has some good original mining songs.

SHANACHIE 37 E. Clinton St., Newton, NJ 07860. Extensive, important catalog of African, Irish, ethnic, blues, historical jazz, finger-style guitar, and reggae music. Leading purveyor of self-styled "world beat" and "ethno-pop."

SIERRA Box 5853, Pasadena CA 91107 (dist. by CHAMELEON). Varied contemporary: Gram Parsons, country rock, bluegrass, etc.

SILVER STREAM 20 Wills Ave., Stanhope NJ 07874. Contemporary and original songs nicely sung by Elaine Silver.

SKY *see* ALCAZAR. LP of virtuoso finger-style guitarist Preston Reed.

SLEEPY MORNING Box 393, Scarsdale NY 10583. LP of Joe Heukerott, whose sweetly sung and un-preachy topical songs can suddenly hit you in the gut when you're not watching.

SMITHSONIAN FOLKWAYS *see* FOLKWAYS.

SONG BANK Box 933 Peck Slip Station, New York NY 10272. Cassettes of multi-ethnic lullabies.

SOURCE UNLTD. 331 E. 9th St., New York NY 10003. Post-Dylan singer-songwriter Santo; songs often about New York City street life.

SOUTHERN CULTURE Center for the Study of Southern Culture, University MS 38677. Late-sixties Mississippi blues, etc.

SOUTHERN FOLKLORE Center for Southern Folklore, 1216 Peabody Ave., Box 4010, Memphis TN 38104.

SOUTHLAND Box 1547, Arlington TX 76010. Albums of Texas swing pioneer Leon Rausch.

SPINDRIFT *see* ALCAZAR. English folk-rock.

SPIRIT FEEL *see* SHANACHIE. Black gospel music.

STARDAY *see* IMG.

STASH 611 Broadway, New York NY 10012. Primarily jazz; some blues.

STINSON Box 3415, Granada Hills CA 91344.

SUGAR HILL Box 4040 Duke Station, Durham NC 27706. Large, aggressively growing list includes important performers currently active in modern bluegrass, new country, and new acoustic music: Hot Rize, Peter Rowan, Mike Cross, Red Clay Ramblers, Ricky Skaggs, John Starling, New Grass Revival, etc.

SWALLOW Flat Town Music, Drawer 10, Ville Platte LA 70586. Cajun, country, zydeco; regional and national performers.

TAKOMA Allegiance Records, 620 Hampshire, Westlake Village CA 91362. Mostly sixties and seventies recordings; some important artists.

TARA dist. in U.S. by SHANACHIE. Irish traditional and contemporary.

TEMPLE dist. in U.S. by FLYING FISH. Contemporary Irish and Scottish.

TENNESSEE FOLKLORE SOCIETY Box 201, Middle Tennessee State Univ., Murfreesboro TN 37132. Tennessee archival/field recordings.

TESTAMENT *see* OJL. Contemporary country and Chicago blues.

THINKING DOG Box 591, Montclair NJ 07042. Songwriter Dennis Dougherty.

TOAD *see* ALCAZAR. Children's music by Willie Sterba.

TOPSOIL 22283 Cass Ave., Woodland Hills CA 91364. Small selection includes Hawaiian slack-key guitar, Hawaiian field recordings, and contemporary singer Ross Altman.

TRADITION *see* EVEREST.

TURQUOISE Box 947, Highway 931, Whitesburg KY 41858. Rising young bluegrass and new acoustic music performers: New Coon Creek Girls, fiddler Glen Duncan, other good musicians.

VANGUARD *see* WELK RECORD GROUP. Many distinguished recordings of earlier decades are now being reissued or repackaged on LP/CD.

VARRICK *see* ROUNDER. Contemporary blues, folk-rock, and varied performers; repackages from earlier or foreign releases.

VEE-JAY *see* CHAMELEON. Blues and r & b.

VOYAGER 424 35th Ave., Seattle WA 98122. Varied small catalog. Emphasis on good fiddling including Vivian Williams and such distinctive Canadian-style players as Louis Boudreault, Frank Ferrell, Gerry Robichaud, and Graham Townsend.

WEBCO 10005 Banner Country Ct., Gaithersburg MD 20879. The small listing of good contemporary bluegrassers includes such tasty performers as Bill Emerson and Larry Stephenson.

WELK RECORD GROUP 1299 Ocean Ave., Santa Monica CA 90401. Marketing group for ROM, VANGUARD, and other labels.

WEST VIRGINIA UNIVERSITY LIBRARY (West Virginia and Regional History Collection) Colson Hall, Morgantown WV 26506. Documentary album from West Virginia fiddling archives.

WESTERN *see* ARHOOLIE. Reissues of early western swing.

WINDHAM HILL Box 9388, Stanford CA 94305. New age and new acoustic.

WISCONSIN FOLKLIFE CENTER, 100 S. 2nd St., Mount Horeb, WI 53572. Albums of the music of Norwegian and other ethnic groups in Wisconsin and correlated print materials.

WORLD Bowmanville ONT L1C 3Z3. Includes CBC satirist Nancy White.

WORLD MUSIC INSTITUTE 109 W. 27th St., New York NY 10001. Traditional and ethnic music; also mail-order distributor.

WORLDWIDE COMMUNICATIONS 320 Stewart St., Reno NV 89502. Cassettes of performances from the annual Cowboy Gathering.

WYOMING ARTS FOUNDATION Box 2015, Laramie WY 82070. Double-cassette album documenting Wyoming fiddle traditions.

YAZOO *see* SHANACHIE. Extensive, important catalog of reissues of country blues and related areas: string ragtime, etc.

YELLOW MOON PRESS Box 1316, Cambridge MA 02238. Tapes and books of storytelling, music, poetry, and spoken word.

ZIM Box 158, Jericho NY 11753. Importer and selling agent of many hard-to-find foreign and domestic labels including jazz, blues, some traditional music.

BLACK AMERICAN MUSIC
THE BLUES

Blues refers to several musical-poetic forms, one of which is very common, while the others are relatively rare. The common one is the "twelve-bar" blues. In twelve-bar blues the verse form is three lines long; one line repeated, and then another, in AAB form:

Why does the rooster crow at the break of day
Why does the rooster crow at the break of day
To let the playboy know the working man's on his way.
(—traditional)

Each of the three lines potentially takes up four measures of musical time; hence the term "twelve-bar." Actually, most lines end three to seven beats before the end of the fourth measure, leaving space for a fill by the accompanying instrument(s). This relationship between the vocal and accompaniment phrasing is an important structural feature of folk blues, and it influences blues phrasing into the jazz period. Measure for measure, the typical chord structure of the twelve-bar blues is:

a) I IV or I I I
   IV IV I I
   V IV I I

b) I IV^7 I I^7
   IV IV^7 I I^7
   V^7 IV^7 I/IV I/V^7

Example b shows one of numerous possible variations involving chord extensions and a half cadence (turnaround). This variation, like others, clearly relates to the basic model

of example a. In folk blues, the added seventh is more common than the simple chord.

Occasionally, sixteen-bar forms occur, with a verse structure AAAB. In this case the chord structure of the second line is repeated. There are also quite a few variations on an eight-bar musical structure, having the verse form AB. Here is a common traditional verse in eight-bar blues, and one of the several chord patterns with which it is sometimes sung:

I'm goin' away, babe, I won't be back 'til fall.
If I find me a new gal, I won't be back at all.
(—traditional)

I V I IV
I/VI^7 II^7/V^7 I I

The older folk blues just use the tonic, subdominant, and dominant chords; some primitive forms that antedate the formal twelve-bar pattern even omit the dominant. The cycle of fifths progression in the last line of the above example represents a ragtime influence. Enough bluesmen use ragtime-influenced rhythms and chord structures for it to make sense to speak of a whole category of songs called ragtime blues, in addition to the twelve- and eight-bar forms.

The twelve-bar form is open to any number of additional variations, such as displaced chord changes, phrases in which the time is cut or doubled, and extended or abbreviated measures. It is a favorite device of bluesmen (along with some fiddlers, ballad singers, and other performers of harmonically unsophisticated music) to vary their music by altering the metrical structure. This is an easily accessible area for variation, since harmonic devices for variation, such as modulation and sophisticated chord extension or substitution, do not occur in these traditions. Listeners who are knowledgeable in the ways of European, jazz, or pop music, but not in the ways of folk blues, frequently regard such alterations as mistakes. They are not. Further study will reveal that they are the deliberate result of a difficult art, the art of knowing a structure well enough to transcend it.

For all the research that has been done on blues, no one knows the origin of the form or even of the name. Historians relate the blues to two earlier forms. One is the field holler, an unaccompanied monody of irregular length and structure. The other is the choral work song, which preserves the "call-and-response" pattern of some African choral singing. In this form, similar to southern white church singing, a leader "lines out" a phrase which is then echoed, varied, or completed by the chorus. The pattern is not strictly antiphonal; often the parts of the leader and chorus overlap polyphonally. In the blues format, the call is represented by the vocal line, the response by the instrumental fill. This style continues as a basic structure in jazz ensemble writing until the present day.

Whatever the origins of the blues form, it had achieved such great currency by the beginning of the recorded era that far fewer examples of other traditions of Black-American song have been recorded.

The great bluesmen possess an imposing array of talents: those of song collector, composer, or improvisor, as well as those of poet, arranger, vocalist, instrumental virtuoso, and sometimes showman and social analyst. Few musical cultures have demanded so much of the individual artist. European culture, for example, sets up a division of labor between composer and performer, composer and librettist, vocalist and accompanist, and so on, just as it sets up divisions of labor in the economic sphere. A single bluesman must incorporate all the varied skills that are parceled out among several persons in the European tradition. Of course, a given individual bluesman may be stronger or weaker in some areas than in others.

Folklorists like to make a distinction between a bluesman and a songster. A bluesman, in ideal terms, is a composer or improvisor, a unique contributor to his musical culture. A songster, on the other hand, is a transmitter of that culture, a performing collector of the traditional material current in his musical environment. But in fact these categories often overlap. I use the word "songster" more loosely, to refer to anyone who sings songs that are not formally defined blues. It even makes a certain amount of sense to use the word "blues" in a very loose way, to encompass all sorts of material that have a blueslike feeling or are accompanied by a blueslike instrumental part.

Not only are most blues structurally similar, but they also draw from a fairly limited common pool of possible melody lines. Each singer makes his own choices about how he will draw from that pool and vary the lines; in addition, it's possible to speak of regional and chronological characteristics. But the most important way for a country bluesman to establish his musical identity is in his guitar parts. The great bluesmen are unique instrumental stylists, and sometimes virtuoso technicians as well.

Country blues records are divided into regional categories largely as a convenience, in order to avoid having them all listed in one large and possibly cumbersome section.

Sleepy John Estes

But it is certainly possible to distinguish between regional guitar styles, just as long as you bear in mind that I'm making rampant generalities that have many exceptions.

Mississippi, central, and Louisiana bluesmen tend to favor the keys of E and A, in addition to the open tunings. These keys are "deep" for blues guitarists. (Flamenco guitarists would conceive of them in the same way for similar reasons.) In terms of the way the notes tend to lie under the fingers, "deep" keys permit the easiest changeover between the major and minor modes, the easiest fingering accessibility of the altered tones of the blues scale within the voicings of open chords, and likewise the easiest accessibility of suspended fourths. These are all characteristic of tonalities that suit the kind of vocal lines favored in that region. In addition, these are the keys in which drone notes on the bass strings are most accessible—another characteristic of the regional style.

The east coast, or "Piedmont," style, on the other hand, favors a different sort of finger-picking technique. In this style, the thumb of the picking hand produces repeated arpeggiated bass figures, or even moving bass lines, while the fingers work out melody or fills on the treble strings. In addition, the style favors ragtimey cycle-of-fifths chord progressions and cadences. All these aspects of style are best realized on the guitar in the keys of C, G, and D.

It's impossible to generalize about a southwest guitar style. The greatest older stylist was Blind Lemon Jefferson. He occasionally strummed or used a drone bass figure, but not characteristically enough to define his style. The most important aspect of his playing was the use of single-line or double-stopped treble figures in counterpoint to his vocal line.

Later blues styles come farther on in the listings. Most could be called urban, which is primarily a stylistic and only secondarily a sociological term. The most obvious characteristic of urban blues is that they are played by ensembles rather than by self-accompanied soloists. This leads to further differences. Guitar styles—for that matter, the styles of harmonica, piano, and all other instruments, too—must be modified to fit into the ensemble context. Then the tonality changes: the notes of the country blues scale, analyzed in terms of vibrations per second, do not correspond exactly to the notes of the European well-tempered scale. (*See* Glossary.) But the presence or influence of that very European instrument the piano tends to pull the voice of the urban singer closer to the well-tempered scale.

Later on, in the introduction to the section on white southern songs and singers, I'll be saying that it's the *guitar* that pulls the voices of white singers away from *their* non-European scales. You will be entitled to wonder why the guitar does this for white but not for black singers. It is partly because the black and white scales are not identical, and partly because of the approach to different choices of chord voicings in the different instrumental traditions. But mostly it is because black guitarists have developed a tradition of certain techniques of "bending" the guitar strings in order to make the pitch conform more closely to the pitches of the blues scale. This is a persistent tradition in black musical style. For example, jazz tenor-saxophonist Stanley Turrentine, an excellent blues player, is particularly adept at using lip work and breath dynamics to adjust the intonation of his instrument far more closely than mere fingering would allow. The piano, of course, cannot produce such microtonal variations in pitch, though a good pianist can suggest them by slurred fingerings, adept chord voicings, carefully controlled minor second intervals, etc.

To return to urban blues, another characteristic is that the twelve-bar structure becomes more precisely standardized in order to provide a consistent structural common denominator for all members of the ensemble. And then there are influences from jazz—the use of jazz and swing rhythms not found in country blues and of a melodic line that has greater freedom from the beat and the bar line. Finally, the subject matter of the blues, which is open to the whole range of the singer's experience and emotions in country idioms, tends to narrow down to themes of love and sexual relationships in the urban blues.

COUNTRY BLUES

MISSISSIPPI AND CENTRAL

BARBEE, JOHN HENRY
———. Storyville SLP 171. Sixties recordings of an older Memphis bluesman who first recorded in 1938.

BRACEY, ISHMAN. *See* Tommy Johnson, page 10.

BROONZY, BIG BILL (William Lee Conley, 1898?–1958) Like Sonny Terry and Josh White, Broonzy was a bluesman of rural origins who spent the latter part of his life entertaining white urban audiences. He alternated between rhythm-and-blues work on Chicago's South Side and folkish associations in New York with Sonny Terry, Brownie McGhee, Pete Seeger, and Woody Guthrie. His early recordings reveal a raggy, good-time performer with a guitar style after the manner of Blind Blake. As he grew older, Broonzy seemed to lose interest in the guitar, and turned his attention to a maturing and deepening voice. He concentrated over the years on the difficult art of ornamented singing at slow tempos, and his voice became one of the strongest and most expressive in this tradition.
The Young . . . (1928–35). Yazoo 1011.
Do That Guitar Rag (1928–35). Yazoo 1035. These two albums represent his earlier ragtimey work.
1930's Blues. Biograph BLP C15. His Chicago period, with rhythm-and-blues bands.
His Story (1957). Folkways 3586. Songs and reminiscences with interviewer Studs Terkel.
Folk Music Blues on WMFT (1956). Folkways 3864. Broonzy and Pete Seeger swap songs and interesting dialogue on Studs Terkel's radio show.
The Blues (1957). Folkways 3817. A Studs Terkel radio interview, with performances by Broonzy, Brownie McGhee, and Sonny Terry.
Sings Folk Songs. Folkways 2328. Satisfactory performances of some of his less interesting songs.
Sings Country Blues. Folkways 31005. Good performances and songs; recorded shortly before his death, when he was not in his best voice, but a good introduction to his work.
———. Ev. Arch. FS-213.
Whoopin' and Hollerin'. Melodisc 12-115.
Big Bill's Blues. Columbia WL 111 (OP). His finest vocal work.

———. Storyville 143.
An Evening With. . . . Storyville 114.
Feeling Low Down. GNP Crescendo 10004.
Blues, Folk Songs, and Ballads. Joker 3608.
Hollerin' and Cryin' the Blues. Vogue 30198.
———. Trip 7500 (2-rec. set).

CALLICOTT, MISSISSIPPI JOE
Blues Masters, vol. 6. Blue Horizon BM 4606.

CARTER, BO (d. 1961)
Greatest Hits. Yazoo 1014. Blues, rags, and hokum songs with interesting guitar work by a popular entertainer of the thirties.
Twist It Babe. Yazoo 1034.

CAT-IRON
Sings Blues and Hymns. Folkways 2389. Fifties recordings of a typical older Mississippi bluesman; some good songs.

CHATMON, SAM
The Mississippi Sheik. Blue Goose 2006. A recent album by an older bluesman originally associated with the Bo Carter and Mississippi Sheiks string band circle.

COLLINS, CRYING SAM
And His Gitfiddle. OJL 10. A most interesting bluesman of the late twenties, in the Charlie Patton vein. Sound quality of original recordings very poor. Also includes four pieces by King Solomon Hill.

CRUDUP, BIG BOY (Arthur) A fine rhythm-and-bluesy Mississippi bluesman—he typically recorded with rhythm section or at least bass—who was acknowledged as an influence by Presley and who contributed to the early rock-and-roll repertory.
The Father of Rock and Roll. RCA LPV-573. Good 1941–54 recordings of his best songs.
Mean Old Frisco. Blue Horizon 763855.
Look on Yonder's Wall. Delmark 614.
Crudup's Mood. Delmark 621.
Mean Ol' Frisco. Trip 7501.

DOUGLAS, K. C.
The Country Boy. Arhoolie 1073.

ESTES, SLEEPY JOHN An excellent Memphis-area bluesman.
———. (1929–40). RBF 8. Recordings from his prime, solo and with band.
The Blues of . . ., vols. 1 (1934–37) and 2 (1938–40). Swaggie 1219, 1220. Classic sessions, some with harmonica and exciting interplay with mandolin or second guitar.
———. (1935–37). Collector's Classics 24.
The Legend of . . . Delmark 603. His first rediscovery recordings, mid-sixties.
Broke and Hungry (1964). Delmark 608. Yank Rachell's blues mandolin is especially prominent.
In Europe. Delmark 611.
Brownsville Blues. Delmark 613.
Electric Sleep. Delmark 613. With Chicago blues band.
———. Storyville 172.

Delta Blues: Fred McDowell

GIBSON, CLIFFORD
Beat You Doing It (1929). Yazoo 1027. A St. Louis bluesman whose guitar parts are exceptionally clear, with a beautiful right-hand technique.

GRIFFETH, SHIRLEY
Mississippi Blues. Blue Goose 2011.

HAWKINS, BUDDY BOY
And His Buddies. Yazoo 1010. 1927–29 recordings by an excellent blues and ragtime player; cuts also by Will Day, Texas Alexander, and others.

HOLTS, ROOSEVELT
Presenting Country Blues (1966). Blue Horizon 7704.

HOUSE, SON (Eddie James House, b. 1902) A seminal figure in the development of the Mississippi Delta blues style, and a strong vocal performer.
———. Folk-Lyric 9002 (= Roots RSE-1 = Saydisc RSE-1). Excellent performances recorded for the Library of Congress in 1941–42.
Vocal Intensity of. . . . Roots SL-504.
Father of Folk Blues. Columbia CL 2417. Performances from the sixties, still intense in spite of the passage of years.
The Real Delta Blues. Blue Goose 2016.
See also J. D. Short, this section, page 11, and Blind Lemon Jefferson, in the section on Louisiana, the Southwest, and the West, page 16.

HOWELL, PEG LEG
The Legendary (sixties). Testament 2204.

HURT, MISSISSIPPI JOHN (1892–1966) Hurt played blues and songs mostly of his own composition, accompanying himself with a finger-picking style more characteristic of the eastern seaboard, and comparable to Elizabeth Cotten's for its well-conceived sense of arrangement. His songs reflect the gentleness and wry humor that made those who knew him love him. As an old man, his voice was unpolished but tender and expressive. Most recordings date from the early sixties until his death a few years ago.
His First Recordings (1928). Biograph BLP C-4. The recordings that assured his reputation even before his re-emergence as an entertainer in the sixties.
Folk Songs and Blues. Piedmont 13157.
Worried Blues. Piedmont 13161.
The Best of . . ., 2 vols. Vanguard VSD-19/20. Live concert recordings; good but not his best.
The Immortal. . . . Vanguard 79128. Excellent performances, though they don't include several important standards of his repertory recorded elsewhere.
Last Sessions. Vanguard 79327.

JACKSON, PAPA CHARLIE
Fat Mouth. Yazoo 1029. Blues, rags, and novelty songs with guitar and (mainly) six-string banjo. Poor sound quality on the original 78's. Jackson, in the early twenties, was the first popular self-accompanied blues recording artist.
——— (1925–28). Biograph BLP 12042.
———. Collector's Classics 6. Other side has Blind Blake.

JAMES, SKIP (Nehemiah, 1902–69) A unique stylist, usually singing blues, folk songs, and spirituals in an eerie falsetto accompanied by a sparse, personal guitar or piano style. James was an especially subtle composer.
Early Recordings (1931). Biograph BLP 12029.
A Tribute (1964). Biograph BLP 12016.
Greatest of the Delta Blues Singers. Melodion MLP 7231.
Devil Got My Woman. Vanguard 79273.
Today. Vanguard 79219.

JOHNSON, LONNIE. *See* Sophisticated Blues section, page 18.

JOHNSON, ROBERT (d. 1937)
King of the Delta Blues Singers, vols. 1–2 (1936–37). Columbia CL 1654, C 30034. For the intensity of his performances, the originality of his compositions and arrangements, and the intricacy of his guitar work, Johnson was the greatest of the Mississippi bluesmen of his generation. As this book goes to press, Columbia Records is planning to issue a three-volume series of Johnson's complete recordings, edited by Steve LaVere. Further information is not available at this date.

JOHNSON, TOMMY (1896?–1956)
The Famous 1928 Tommy Johnson/Ishman Bracey Session. Roots 330. Johnson was a great and original bluesman, whose songs and arrangements are still played today.

KOKOMO ARNOLD
——— (1934–37). Blues Classics 4. A good singer and bottleneck guitarist; other side has Peetie Wheatstraw.
———. Collector's Classics 25.

LEWIS, FURRY A good Tennessee bluesman, whose work is inconsistent.
Shake 'em on Down (sixties). Fantasy 24703. Good performances of his best songs; much bottleneck work.
_____ (1959). Folkways 3823. More good performances, though occasional problems keeping his guitar in tune—a characteristic of Lewis'.
Back on My Feet Again. Prestige 7810.
. . . and Fred McDowell. Biograph BLP-12017.
Blues Masters, vol. 5 (1968). Blue Horizon 4605.
In Memphis. Saydisc SDR-190.

MACON, SHORTSTUFF (d. 1973)
Miss. Delta Blues. Spivey 1005.

McCOY, GEORGE AND ESTHER
Early in the Morning (sixties). Adelphi 1004. Blues duets with archaic and very funky harmonies.

McDOWELL, FRED (1904–72) A strong singer with excellent songs and a driving bottleneck guitar style, McDowell recorded prolifically from 1963 until his death. He was a popular performer on the college and festival circuit, and his "You Got to Move" was made popular by the Rolling Stones.
Miss. Delta Blues. Arhoolie 1021. His first record; it remains his best.
_____, vol 2. Arhoolie 1027.
. . . and His Blues Boys. Arhoolie 1046. (With rhythm section.)
Keep Your Lamp Trimmed and Burning. Arhoolie 1068.
My Home Is in the Delta. Testament 2208. Includes vocal harmonies on several spirituals with his wife, Annie Mae McDowell. Has an unusually restrained feeling.
Amazing Grace. Testament 2219. Spirituals, with sanctified gospel choir.
Live in New York. Oblivion OD-1. McDowell sings in a less strict vocal style than in his studio recordings. Includes several songs unrecorded elsewhere.
_____ *1904–1972.* Just Sunshine JSS-4.
I Do Not Play No Rock and Roll. Capitol ST 409. With inhibiting and distracting bass and drums.
_____. Ev. Arch. FS-253.
Long Way from Home. Milestone 93003.
See also Furry Lewis, above.

MEMPHIS MINNIE (Minnie Douglas)
_____, vols. 1–2. Blues Classics 1, 13. One of the few women to record in the country blues idiom, a good singer and guitarist. Often with husband, Joe McCoy, as second guitar.
_____, vols. 1 (1934–41) and 2 (1941–49). Flyright 108, 109.

NIGHTHAWK, ROBERT, AND HOUSTON STACKHOUSE
_____. Testament 2215. Older Mississippi bluesmen recently recorded; both excellent slide guitarists.

OWENS, JACK, AND BUD SPIRES
It Must Have Been the Devil. Testament 2222. 1970 Mississippi field recordings.

PATTON, CHARLIE (1887?–1934) Patton was the key figure in the development of the Mississippi Delta style. He played not only blues, but a wide variety of songs, rags, and spirituals as well. His recordings reveal a repertory of country blues rhythmic figures that still survive today, though not all in the work of any one player. Unfortunately, the poor sound quality of the surviving 78's makes his work inaccessible to all but devoted listeners. Of the two almost identical sets below, the Yazoo sound is somewhat clearer.
Founder of the Delta Blues. Yazoo 1020 (2-rec. set).
The Immortal . . . , vols. 1–2. OJL 1, 2.

RACHELL, YANK A blues mandolinist and sometimes guitarist and singer, best known as Sleepy John Estes' favored accompanist, but a strong soloist in his own right.
_____ (1973). Blue Goose 2010.
Mandolin Blues. Delmark 606.

RHODES, EUGENE
Talkin' 'bout My Time. Folk-Legacy FSA 12. Blues and spirituals, with spoken introductions, recorded in the Indiana State Prison in the sixties.

SHORT, J. D.
_____ (1962). Sonet SNTF 648. A strong singer in the old Delta style, Short also made a few recordings in the thirties.
Blues from the Mississippi Delta. Folkways 2467. Other side has Son House.

SMITH, FUNNY PAPA
The Original Howlin' Wolf. Yazoo 1031.

SMOKEY BABE (Robert Brown)
Hot Blues (1960). Arhoolie 2019 (formerly Folk-Lyric 118). A good older Mississippi–Louisiana singer with twelve-string guitar and sometimes friends on harmonica and second vocal.

STACKHOUSE, HOUSTON An older Mississippi bluesman with a fine though not greatly varied bottleneck touch. *See also* Robert Nighthawk, this section, above.
_____. Adelphi 1024.

WHITE, BUKKA (Booker, b. 1909) A native of Mississippi, White began his recording career in 1930, but disappeared from sight from 1940 until his rediscovery by Ed Denson and John Fahey in 1960. He plays guitar in a rhythmic strumming style, preferring fast tempos, and excels at extemporized or only tentatively aforethought composition—though he has produced excellent composed lyrics, too.
Parchman Farm. Columbia C 30036. The 1940 session that produced his well-known "Fixin' to Die" and "Jitterbug Swing," along with two pieces from a 1937 session. The songs here are structured and arranged, reflecting the influence of Robert Johnson.
Mississippi Blues (1960). Takoma B1001 (= Sonet SNTF 609). His first rediscovery album, joyful and enthusiastic.
Sky Songs, vols. 1–2. Arhoolie 1019, 1020. The emphasis is on his extemporized lyrics; he calls them sky songs because "I just reach up and pull them out of the sky."
Big Daddy (1973). Biograph BLP 12049. Good performances, not well-recorded.
_____. Blues Beacon 3.
_____. Blue Horizon 4604.

WILLIAMS, BIG JOE (b. 1903) A strong and sometimes dramatic singer, who has been recording since 1935, Williams accompanies himself with a rough and forceful guitar style characterized by strumming alternating with rapid fills. He usually extemporizes his lyrics. As a result, the quality of his recorded work varies from session to session or even from song to song, depending on whether or not he is "on." He usually plays an eight-, nine-, or ten-string guitar (like a twelve-string, but with a few strings missing).

Tough Times. Arhoolie 1002. A good example of his work, from the sixties.

Thinking of What They Did to Me (1969). Arhoolie 1053.

Back to the Country. Testament 2205. With fiddle and harmonica backup.

_____ (1972). Sonet SNTF 635.

Blues from the Miss. Delta. Blues on Blues 10003. With electric backup band.

Classic Delta Blues. Milestone 3001.

_____. Folkways 3820.

Piney Woods Blues. Delmark 602. Another good session, accompanied by J. D. Short.

Ramblin' and Wanderin'. Storyville 163.

Malvina My Sweet Woman. Oldie Blues 2804.

WILLIAMS, ROBERT PETE (b. 1914) A Louisiana bluesman, who has been included in this section on stylistic grounds, Robert Pete Williams is the extemporizer *par excellence.* Like Big Joe Williams, he uses a strumming guitar style with bursts of energetic fills—carefully made arrangements are inhibiting to bluesmen who like to improvise their lyrics. Williams uses a number of different tunings, producing somewhat more varied guitar accompaniments than others in his style.

Those Prison Blues. Arhoolie 2015 (formerly Folk-Lyric 109). 1959–60 field recordings from the Angola State Penitentiary.

Louisiana Blues. Takoma B1011. A spontaneous, almost instinctive blues session; his strongest recorded performance.

Rural Blues. Fantasy F 2416. Double-record set shared with Snooks Eaglin.

_____. Sonet SNTF 649. Recordings from the early seventies, reflecting the more settled and orderly life Williams has recently led.

Sugar Farm. Blues Beacon 1.

ANTHOLOGIES AND COLLECTIONS

Beale Street Mess Around. Rounder 2006. Sixties field trip recordings by George Mitchell, of Furry Lewis, Will Shade, Charlie Burse and other Memphis bluesmen of the older generation.

Blues from the Delta. Saydisc 226. Recent field recordings by William Ferris, to complement his book of the same name.

Blues in the Mississippi Night. United Artists UAL 4027 (OP). Performances, commentaries, and conversations with collector Alan Lomax. Should be reissued, this time with name credits for the performers.

Blues Roots—Mississippi. RBF 14. Classic recordings by the greatest bluesmen of the twenties, thirties, and forties, well chosen by Sam Charters. Includes Tommy Johnson, Bo Carter, Robert Johnson, and others.

Fort Valley Blues. Saydisc SDM 250. Library of Congress field recordings, 1941–43.

Frank Stokes' Dream. Yazoo 1008. Memphis blues 1927–31: Tom Dickson, Frank Stokes, Memphis Minnie, Cannon's Jug Stompers, the original Furry Lewis recording of "Turn Your Money Green," and others.

I Have to Paint My Face. Arhoolie 1005. Blues, songs, and other music from the Mississippi Delta; 1960 field recordings.

Jackson Blues (1928–38). Yazoo 1007. Good recordings by Tommy Johnson and others from this creative center of Mississippi blues activity.

The Legacy of Tommy Johnson. Saydisc SDM 224. Recent Mississippi field recordings—not of Johnson—made by David Evans to complement his book on Johnson.

Lonesome Road Blues (1926–41). Yazoo 1038. Sam Collins, Skip James, Robert Lockwood, and other lesser known figures.

Low-Down Memphis Barrelhouse Blues. Mamlish 3803. Will Shade, Jack Kelly, and others of the twenties and thirties.

The Memphis Blues Again, 2 vols. Adelphi AD 1009s, 1010s. Older Memphis bluesmen, pianists, and jug band players still active in the sixties, including Furry Lewis, Nathan Beauregard, and Sleepy John Estes.

Memphis Blues Favorites (1928–39). Magnolia (no number).

Memphis Jamboree (1927–36). Yazoo 1021. Jim Jackson, Memphis Minnie, Furry Lewis, and others.

Miss. Blues, vols. 1 (1927–42), 2 (1927–40), and 3 (1928–42). Roots RL 302, 303, 304.

Miss. Blues, vols. 1–3. OJL 5, 11, 17.

Miss. Blues, Yazoo 1001. Excellent 1927–41 performances by Skip James, Charlie Patton, Son House, Robert Johnson, and others.

Mississippi Bottom Blues. Mamlish 3802.

Mississippi Delta Blues, vols. 1–2. Arhoolie 1041, 1042. Sixties field trip recordings by George Mitchell issued in conjunction with his book *Blow My Blues Away.* Vol. 1: Como Fife and Drum Band, Fred McDowell, Houston Stackhouse, and others. Vol. 2: R. L. Burnside, Rosa Lee Hill, and Joe Callicott.

Mississippi Moaners (1927–42). Yazoo 1009. Excellent recordings by Charlie Patton, Son House, and many lesser known figures.

Mississippi River Blues. Saydisc SDM 230. 1940 Library of Congress field recordings: Lucius Curtis, Willie Ford, and George Boldwin.

On the Road Again (1969). Adelphi 1007s. Furry Lewis, Bukka White, and Gus Cannon.

Really the Country Blues. OJL 2. An excellent anthology of 1927–33 recordings by major Mississippi bluesmen and others. Includes Son House, Ishman Bracey, Bullet Williams, and Tommy Johnson.

Saint Louis Blues (1929–35). Yazoo 1030. Henry Townsend, Charlie Jordan, and others.

Saint Louis Town (1929–33). Yazoo 1003. Jim Jackson, Charlie Jordan, and others.

The Sound of the Delta. Testament 2209. Sixties field recordings by Pete Welding of obscure Mississippi singers recommended by Big Joe Williams.

South Mississippi Blues. Rounder 2009. Older Mississippi bluesmen and string band players, recently recorded by

David Evans. These recordings demonstrate that the older musicians still adhere to the conventions and themes established by Patton, Tommy Johnson, and the other innovators and synthesizers of blues style in the twenties and thirties.

Ten Years in Memphis (1927–37). Yazoo 1002. Robert Wilkins, Frank Stokes, Furry Lewis, and others.

Things Have Changed. Adelphi 1012s. Older St. Louis bluesmen still active in 1969, such as Henry Townsend, Henry Brown, and George and Ethel McCoy.

Up and Down the Mississippi. Roots RL 319.

THE EAST AND SOUTHEAST

ANDERSON, PINK

————, vols. 1–3. Prestige/Bluesville 1038, 1051, 1071 (all OP). Anderson was a medicine show entertainer and one of the most important sources of songs, routines, and ragtime blues from the strong Carolinas tradition. *See also* under Rev. Gary Davis, this section, page 14.

BARBECUE BOB (Robert Hicks)

————. Collector's Classics 36.

BLIND BLAKE (Arthur Blake, d. circa 1940) Blake was the most fluent of the great ragtime blues guitarists of the southeast, and he probably had the best right-hand touch and coordination of all finger-picking guitarists. In addition to his own recordings, he often worked as an accompanist to others in the Chicago studios. His influence on Gary Davis and Blind Boy Fuller was great, and through them as well as through these recordings, his influence is still felt today. (This Blind Blake should not be confused with Blind Blake Higgs, a calypso singer and banjoist.)

Bootleg Rum Dum Blues (1926–30). Biograph BLP 12003.

Search Warrant Blues (1926–32). Biograph BLP 12023.

No Dough Blues (1926–29). Biograph BLP 12031.

Rope Stretchin' Blues (1926–31). Biograph BLP 12037.

COTTEN, ELIZABETH (b. 1893) A songster who hardly plays blues at all, Cotten has cultivated the most graceful and dignified of all finger-picking styles. She plays a regularly strung guitar left-handed, making her style even more unusual. Her repertory includes a variety of songs, dance tunes, picking tunes, and a few banjo pieces. One among her many original songs, "Freight Train," has become a standard.

Folksongs and Instrumentals for Guitar. Folkways 3526.

Shake Sugaree. Folkways 31003.

"Freight Train": Elizabeth Cotten

DAVIS, REV. GARY (Blind Gary, 1896–1972) Originally a ragtime bluesman in the Carolina tradition, Davis later joined the church and took up spiritual singing. The last years of his life were spent as a street singer and then as a preacher in Harlem and Brooklyn, as well as in entertaining white audiences. His right-hand touch was hard and heavy, as that of street singers tends to be, but his left-hand technique was the most highly developed of all traditional guitarists and expressed unusually advanced harmonic and contrapuntal concepts. So much attention has been paid to his virtuosity as guitarist and arranger that his being a great singer as well is often overlooked.

_____ (1935–49). Yazoo 1023. Davis' guitar work was somewhat cleaner here than in most of his later recordings, his voice not as deep, his tempos somewhat faster. His style was clearly consolidated by 1935, and though it developed, it did not change much with time.
Children of Zion. Kicking Mule 101 (= Transatlantic 249). A 1962 concert appearance, including the show-off guitar piece "Soldier's Drill" and several little-known spirituals.
Ragtime Guitar. Kicking Mule 106. Unusual guitar instrumentals recorded in Davis' later years, especially chosen to demonstrate his unique concepts of melody-chord playing and moving bass lines.
Guitar and Banjo. Prestige 7725. A good representation of the different aspects of his instrumental virtuosity, including banjo and harmonica pieces.
The Singing Reverend. Stinson SLP 56. With Sonny Terry, harmonica. This recording sounds as if it were made inside a large boiler, and his guitar work is almost totally obscured. But it may be his best vocal performance on record; worth listening to in spite of the bad sound.
New Blues and Gospel (1971). Biograph 12030.
Lord, I Wish I Could See (1971). Biograph 12034. An unforgivable lack of care was taken in recording these sessions. Recording quality is simply unworthy of the man, and it would have been considerate to both Davis and his audience to have helped him, advanced as he was in years, to keep the twelve-string guitar used in tune.
When I Die I'll Live Again. Fantasy 24704 (2-rec. set). Spirituals culled from earlier releases on the Prestige label.
O, Glory (1969). Adelphi 1008. Recordings of Davis in unusual contexts: in addition to guitar he plays harmonica, banjo, and piano; on three songs he is accompanied by a chorus in white hymn style, on one by his wife in sanctified style. Larry Johnson's harmonica mars the other cuts, dragging severely.
The Boy Was Kissing the Girl . . . (1968). Kicking Mule 110. Live concert performance, featuring unusual and rarely heard pieces from his blues and ragtime repertory.
Lo, I Be with You Always. Kicking Mule 111. 1959–62 recordings from his secular and spiritual repertory, in a variety of settings from his living room to concert performances.
. . . and Pink Anderson: American Street Songs. Riverside 12–611 (OP). One side of each artist. Most unfortunately out of print, since it represents some of the very best recorded work of both men.

EDWARDS, FRANK
Done Some Travelin' (1972). Trix 3303. A good Atlanta singer.

FULLER, BLIND BOY (Fulton Allen, 1903–40)
_____ (1935–40). Blues Classics 11. Blues and rags by an excellent and influential Carolina performer, with washboard. Sonny Terry, harmonica. Fuller was an early associate of Blind Blake, Reverend Davis, and Brownie McGhee. *On Down.* Flyright 110.

GUITAR SHORTY
Alone in His Field (seventies). Trix 3306. A rough North Carolina bluesman with a personal sound.

GUITAR SLIM AND JELLY BELLY (Alex Seward and Louis Hayes)
_____. Arhoolie 2005. Disciples of the Fuller–Brownie McGhee school, late forties.

JACKSON, BILL
Long Steel Rail. Testament 2201. A Maryland bluesman and songster.

JACKSON, JOHN
Blues and Country Dance Tunes from Virginia, vols. 1–2. Arhoolie 1025, 1035. Mostly standard tunes in the eastern finger-picking style.
In Europe. Arhoolie 1047.

JOHNSON, HENRY
The Union County Flash (1973). Trix 3304. Blues, songs, and spirituals by an older exponent of the multifaceted South Carolina tradition.

JONES, EDDIE LEE
Yonder Go That Old Black Dog. Testament 2224. A Georgia bluesman and singer.

KIRKLAND, EDDIE (b. 1928) A resident of Macon, Georgia, Kirkland was active in Detroit during the fifties as a recording artist and as John Lee Hooker's accompanist. A strong singer, although without Hooker's depth, he shares with his former employer a lack of structural sense. He also lacks the sense of phrasing that Hooker does have, and he accompanies himself with a rather stiff and erratic guitar style.
Front and Center (1970–72). Trix 3301.
The Devil and Other Blues Demons. Trix 3308.

LEWIS, JOHNNY
Alabama Slide Guitar. Arhoolie 1055. An older bluesman with a typical bottleneck guitar style.

McGHEE, BROWNIE (b. 1914) A bluesman of the Carolina school. His partnership with Sonny Terry has become a popular act on the college and folk club circuit.
Blues. Folkways 2030 (10 inch).
Traditional Blues, vols. 1–2. Folkways 2421, 2422.
Sings the Blues. Folkways 3557. See also Sonny Terry, page 15.

McTELL, BLIND WILLIE An Atlanta twelve-string ragtime bluesman with many good songs who recorded prolifically, often repeating himself though in differing versions. I recommend the Atlantic and Melodeon albums for starters.

The Early Years (1927–33). Yazoo 1005.
Death Cell Blues (1929–33). Biograph C-14.
_____. Melodeon 7323. 1940 field recordings for the Library of Congress.
Trying to Get Home (1949). Biograph 12008.
Atlanta 12-String (1949). Atlantic SD 7224.
Last Session (1956). Prestige 7809. Includes some new original songs.

Moss, Buddy
Rediscovery (1966). Biograph 12019. A Georgia bluesman, who recorded with Josh White in the thirties.

Peg Leg Sam
A good harmonica player and medicine show entertainer in the vanishing eastern seaboard tradition.
Medicine Show Man. Trix 3302. Blues, ragtime, and twenties pop tunes, as well as rhythmic monologues and other medicine show routines. Recorded about 1970, with singer-guitarists Herman Johnson and Baby Tate. A valuable document, as well as good music.
The Last Medicine Show. Flyright 507/8 (2-rec. set).

Seward, Alex
Late One Saturday Evening (1966). Blue Labor 103. Recordings with Brownie McGhee and Sonny Terry. Seward is a Carolina bluesman who has frequently worked with McGhee, and who recorded in the forties with Leadbelly, Woody Guthrie, and others in that circle. Occasionally his name appears misspelled as Alec Stewart, etc.; he also recorded as Guitar Slim.

Tampa Red.
See Sophisticated Blues section, page 19.

Terry, Sonny
(Sanders Terrell, b. 1911) An excellent harmonica player in the southeast tradition, which is considerably different from the Mississippi–Chicago tradition that has been a great influence in contemporary blues and rock. Alternating so quickly between singing and accompanying himself that his voice and instrument seem at times to overlap, Terry can still pull more notes out of his instrument than just about anyone.
Harmonica and Vocal Solos. Folkways 2035 (10 inch).
. . . and His Washboard Band. Folkways 2006 (10 inch).
On the Road. Folkways 2369. With J. C. Burris and Sticks McGhee; the seeds of what later came to be called rhythm-and-blues.
_____. Ev. Arch. FS-206.
New Sound. Folkways 3821. With jew's-harp as well as harmonica.

Terry, Sonny, and Brownie McGhee
A popular performing act, Terry and McGhee have recorded to the point of repetition. Consult the Schwann catalogue for all available recordings. For starters, the following is recommended.
Brownie McGhee and Sonny Terry Sing. Folkways 2327.

Trice, Willie
Blue and Rag'd. Trix 3305. Early seventies recordings of a North Carolina songster with an interesting repertory.

White, Josh
(1908–69) An excellent southeastern guitarist with a unique touch, White achieved great popularity as an entertainer among left-wing urban white audiences during the forties. He found it convenient to become a "folk singer" and developed a rather mannered style, which he uses on most of his available recordings. (See Schwann catalogue.) The following records demonstrate his overlooked prowess as a superb and unique guitarist.
_____, vols. 1–2. Stinson SLP 14, 15.

Williams, Bill
Low and Lonesome. Blue Goose 2004.
The Late Bill Williams. Blue Goose 2013. These are early seventies recordings, when Williams was himself in his early seventies. He was not a clean player or a proficient singer, but his picking style and his songs were nonetheless interesting. Although his roots are in the classic eastern seaboard picking style, his playing incorporates a wide range of sounds and influences, including blues, rags, ballads, and instrumental pieces of both black and white origin.

Williams, Blind Connie
_____. Testament 2225. A Philadelphia street singer of blues, songs, and spirituals.

Willis, Ralph
Carolina Blues. Blues Classics 22. 1946–52 recordings, some with Brownie McGhee and Sonny Terry.

ANTHOLOGIES AND COLLECTIONS
Alabama Blues (1927–31). Yazoo 1006.
The Atlanta Blues (1927–33). RBF 15. Barbecue Bob, Lonnie Coleman, Tampa Red, Buddy Moss, and others.
Blues in Georgia (1924–31). Magnolia (no number). Mary Willis, Ed Andrews, Irene Scruggs, and others.
East Coast Blues (1926–35). Yazoo 1013. Excellent recordings emphasizing the guitar virtuosity of William Moore, Bayless Rose, Blind Blake, and others.
East Coast Country Blues. Muskadine 104.
Georgia Blues (1927–33). Yazoo 1012. Barbecue Bob, Blind Blake, Gitfiddle Jim, and others.
Georgia Blues. Rounder 2008. Recent field trip recordings.
Guitar Wizards (1926–35). Yazoo 1016. Excellent performances, with the emphasis on instrumental work, by the great southeast guitar stylists: Carl Martin, Blind Blake, Billy Bird, Sam Butler, and others.

LOUISIANA, THE SOUTHWEST, AND THE WEST

Black Ace
_____. Arhoolie 1003. A Texas bluesman, with slide guitar.

Bonner, Juke Boy
(Weldon Bonner, b. 1932) Bonner, who accompanies himself on electric guitar and harmonica, is a good performer and writer. He has not achieved the recognition gained by other writers of his stature, possibly because he likes to use irregular metrical structures which make it impossible for him to get together the band he would need for greater commercial success.
_____. Sonet SNTF 634.
I'm Going Back to the Country (1968). Arhoolie 1036.
The Struggle. Arhoolie 1045.
Things Ain't Right. Liberty (British) 83319.

"Things Ain't Right": Juke Boy Bonner

DUNBAR, SCOTT
From Lake Mary. Ahura Mazda SDS 1.

EAGLIN, SNOOKS A fine singer, with a soft and melancholy personal voice seemingly influenced by Ray Charles and Lightnin' Hopkins. His guitar style is unique and proficient, as both a solo and an accompaniment style.
New Orleans Street Singer. Folkways 2476. A fine and influential album, representing Eaglin's work of the late fifties. At this point in the development of his style, he was not particularly interested in the songs themselves, and at times he sang lyrics without much continuity, although they were still given meaning by the quality of his voice. This album offers his best and most interesting guitar work, ranging from blues to amazing adaptations of Dixieland band pieces.
Rural Blues. Fantasy 24716. A double-album set shared with Robert Pete Williams. Solid performances and good singing; mainly blues.
_____ (1971). Sonet SNTF. At the time of these recordings, the emphasis in Eaglin's guitar work is on strumming: evenness and accentuation. This enables him to concentrate more on vocal delivery and the qualities that go into making up a polished performance. At this point Eaglin is no longer a street singer but is working rooms like the New Orleans Playboy Club. This record presents him as a unique figure: a pop-soul singer accompanying himself on a folk-style acoustic guitar.
Possum Up a Simmon Tree. Arhoolie 2014. Originally issued as *New Orleans Washboard Blues* on Folk-Lyric 107.

Eaglin does not play a dominant role in this washboard band with Percy Randolph and Lucius Bridges.

HAZELTON, EDWARD. *See* Eddie "One String" Jones, page 17.

HOPKINS, LIGHTNIN' (Sam Hopkins, b. 1912) At his best, Hopkins is superb as both performer and blues writer. His large recorded output is inconsistent, and I have not listed all his available albums. *See also* the Schwann catalogue and *Phonolog;* the few recordings here listed are all recommended. Hopkins has a highly expressive blues voice, full of nuances and melancholy with an underlying hardness. His vocal style, like his guitar style, is only superficially a simple one. His best playing, writing, and overall performances, although not recorded with the best studio techniques and equipment, can be found on his early recordings from the forties. Since the early sixties, Hopkins has been a favorite performer on the folk circuit. He can still be great, but like other entertainers he has been subject to the ravages of the road and its distractions. The first three albums focus on his work from the late forties.
Early Recordings, vols. 1–2. Arhoolie 2007, 2010.
Low Down Dirty Blues. Mainstream 405.
The Blues Giant. Olympic 7110. Especially good vocals; irrelevant trombone on some selections.
Double Blues. Fantasy 24702 (2-rec. set).
. . . *in Berkeley.* Arhoolie 1063.
Texas Blues Man. Arhoolie 1034.
Roots of. . . . Folkways 31011.

JACKSON, LI'L SON
_____ (1960). Arhoolie 1004. An older Texas singer; good songs.

JEFFERSON, BLIND LEMON (d. 1930) A strong singer, who relied on a limited repertory of basic melodies to which he set episodic lyrics, Jefferson was an excellent guitarist with wonderful time and a highly developed sense of altered blues structure. His guitar lines typically had the effect of a second voice rather than mere fills, and he achieved the greatest independence of simultaneous guitar and vocal line of any singer-guitarist in any idiom. His recordings, made in the late twenties, vary considerably in sound quality, ranging from almost inaudible to acceptable at best.
_____ (1926–29) Biograph 12000. Relatively poor sound quality, but a more varied selection of material than most other recordings.
Master of the Blues. Biograph 12015.
. . . *and Son House.* Biograph 12040. One side of each performer.
_____. Collector's Classics 22.
. . . *and Ramblin' Thomas.* Collector's Classics 5. One side of each performer.
Black Snake Moan. Milestone 2013.
The Immortal, vols. 1–2. Milestone 2004, 2007.
_____. Milestone 47022. The Milestone recordings have cleaner sound, but not one of them offers the variety of the first Biograph.
_____, vols. 1–3. Roots 301, 306, 331.
Early Blues (1926–29). Olympic 7134. Edited and engineered for good sound quality. Jefferson developed a small number of guitar accompaniment parts, which he used

over and over for various songs; this record does not present a good variety.
Classic Performances. Joker 3103.

JOHNSON, HERMAN E.
Louisiana Country Blues (1961). Arhoolie 1060. A primitive, dynamic, older bluesman with a personal style of writing and playing.

JONES, EDDIE "ONE STRING"
One String Blues (1960). Takoma B1023. Jones, a California street musician, accompanies himself on a homemade single-string instrument played with a glass-bottle slide. It would be a mistake to dismiss this record as a curiosity. These are first-rate primitive blues performances. Also includes several cuts by harmonica player Edward Hazelton.

LEADBELLY (Huddie Ledbetter, 1888–1949) An outstanding figure in American music, Leadbelly was a walking archive of southern and southwestern black musical tradition. He had an immense repertory of blues, hollers, work songs, ballads, and dance tunes as well as songs of his own composition. He had a high, strong voice, superb pitch, and a unique, driving twelve-string guitar style. Of the numerous recordings below, the Columbia, RCA, and Folkways *Last Sessions* sets are recommended for starters.
———— (1935). Columbia C 30035. Emphasizes his blues repertory, with some unusual six-string bottleneck guitar work.
Midnight Special. RCA LPV 505.

"Trouble in Mind": Mance Lipscomb

Leadbelly's Legacy, vols. 1–4. Folkways 2004, 2014, 2024, 2034 (10 inch).
Last Session, vols. 1–2. Folkways 2941/2 (2 rec. per vol.).
Sings Folk Songs. Folkways 31006. With Woody Guthrie, Cisco Houston, Sonny Terry, and Brownie McGhee.
Take This Hammer. Folkways 31019.
Negro Folk Songs for Young People. Folkways 7533.
The Library of Congress Recordings (1933–42). Elektra EKL 301/2 (3-rec. set, OP).
Early Leadbelly (1935–40). Biograph 12013.
The Legendary. . . . Olympic 7103.
The Legend of. . . . Tradition 2093.
Shout On. Folkways 31030. Air shots of 1948 radio broadcasts.
Memorial, vols. 1–4. Stinson SLP 17, 19, 48, 51.
Play-Party Songs. Stinson SLPX 39.
. . . Sings and Plays. Stinson S 91.
———— (1948). Playboy PB 119. Live concert recordings, made the year before his death.
————. Fantasy 24715 (2-rec. set).
————. Collector's Classics 23.
————. Ev. Arch. FS 202.
————. Storyville 124, 139.

LIPSCOMB, MANCE A fine rural Texas songster and excellent guitarist. His repertory was varied and unusual, encompassing all sorts of songs, with well-conceived guitar accompaniments. He was a popular performer on the folk festival circuit during the sixties.
————, vols. 1–6. Arhoolie 1001, 1023, 1026, 1033, 1049, 1069.
Trouble in Mind. Reprise RS 6404.

SHAW, THOMAS
Born in Texas. Advent 2801.
Blind Lemon's Buddy. Blue Goose 2008.

STOVALL, BABE
———— (1964). Verve VPM-1. A New Orleans songster.

THOMAS, HENRY
Texas Blues. OJL 3. A distinctive, somewhat erratic songster; good songs.

RAMBLIN' THOMAS (Willard Thomas) Thomas had a particularly clear bottleneck style; good songs.
———— (1928). Biograph 12004.
. . . and Blind Lemon Jefferson. Collector's Classics 5. One side of each performer.

WILLIAMS, ROBERT PETE. *See* Mississippi and Central section, page 12.

ANTHOLOGIES AND COLLECTIONS
Blues from the Western States (1927–49). Yazoo 1032. King Solomon Hill, Texas Alexander, and others.
California Country Blues. Muskadine 103.
Country Negro Jam Sessions (1959). Arhoolie 2018. Field recordings from the Louisiana countryside. Many good, rough performances.
Southern Prison Blues (1959). Tradition 2066 = Storyville 125. Field recordings from the Louisiana State Penitentiary at Angola. Some good performances.

Tex-Arkana-Louisiana Country. Yazoo 1004. 1927–32 performances of the best southwest bluesmen, including Henry Thomas, King Solomon Hill, and Blind Lemon Jefferson.

Texas Blues, vol. 1 (1948–51). Arhoolie 2006. Lightnin' Hopkins, Li'l Son Jackson, and others.

Texas Blues, vol. 2. Arhoolie 1017. More recent recordings by Mance Lipscomb, Mercy Dee, Alex Moore, Lightnin' Hopkins, and others in the Arhoolie catalogue.

COUNTRY BLUES ANTHOLOGIES AND COLLECTIONS

The anthologies listed in this section combine musicians from two or more of the previous regional categories, or center around characteristics other than regional.

The Blues. Asch A-101. Music from the film of the same name by Sam Charters, performed by J. D. Short, Furry Lewis, and others.

Blues 'n' Trouble, vols. 1–2. Arhoolie 1006, 1012. A good introduction to the various country blues artists represented in the Arhoolie catalogue.

Blues Rediscoveries. RBF 11. Twenties and thirties recordings by bluesmen who reemerged in the sixties: Henry Townsend, Bukka White, Peg Leg Howell, and others.

The Blues Tradition. Milestone 2016. Excellent early recordings by Bill Broonzy, King Solomon Hill, Willie Brown, Buddy Boy Hawkins, and others.

Bottleneck Blues. Testament 2216. Contemporary exponents of the style: Muddy Waters, Johnny Shines, Robert Nighthawk, and others.

Bottleneck Blues Guitar Classics. Yazoo 1026. 1926–37 recordings of varying quality; includes a superb Hawaiian-style version of "St. Louis Blues."

The Country Blues, vols. 1–2. RBF 1, 9. Excellent anthologies, well chosen by Sam Charters, representing classic performances of the twenties and thirties. Recommended as a starting point for building a blues record library; almost all of the most important artists of the time are included.

Country Blues Encores. OJL 8.

Country Blues Obscurities. Roots RL-334. William and Versey Smith, George Owens, and others.

The Country Girls. OJL 6. 1927–35 recordings by women country blues artists of the period. Few women played country blues.

Down South (1927–41). Roots RL-313.

Fillin' in Blues. Herwin 205. Rare 1928–30 recordings not elsewhere reissued: Furry Lewis, Cannon's Jug Stompers, and others. (Other side has blues pianists.)

Going Away Blues (1926–35). Yazoo 1018.

Going Up the Country (1966). Decca (British) LK 4931. Mississippi and Louisiana field recordings by David Evans.

The Great Harmonica Players, vols. 1–2. Roots 320, 321.

I'm Wild About My Loving (1928–30). Historical HLP 39. Memphis Minnie, Joe McCoy, Ishman Bracey, Jim Jackson, and others.

Kings of the 12-String. Piedmont 13159. Mostly thirties recordings by Willie McTell, Seth Richard, Barbecue Bob, George Carter, Charlie Lincoln.

The Male Blues Singers. Collector's Classics 3. Twenties and thirties recordings by Casey Bill, Skip James, Jim Jackson, Mississippi Sheiks, and others.

Mama Let Me Lay It on You (1926–36). Yazoo 1040. Recordings of southeasterners predominate.

Masters of the Blues (1928–40). Historical HLP 31. Robert Johnson, Curley Weaver, Texas Alexander with Lonnie Johnson and Eddie Lang, and others.

The Party Blues. Melodeon 7324. Twenties to forties good-time and bawdy blues and rags.

Please Warm My Weiner. Yazoo 1043. Hokum and bawdy blues, rags, and novelty tunes.

Ramblin' on My Mind. Milestone 3002. Train and travel blues, mostly from the sixties, by Johnny Young, Big Joe Williams, Honeyboy Edwards, and others. Mostly good writing.

The Rural Blues: A Study of the Vocal and Instrumental Resources. RBF 202 (2-rec. set). Compiled by Sam Charters: mostly selected from the early thirties. Selections have been made in order to exemplify certain categories of style and technique which Charters has constructed.

San Diego Blues Jam. Advent 2804. Older rural bluesmen of mostly central and southwest origin who were discovered in the San Diego area during the late sixties: Sam Chatmon, Tom Shaw, and others.

Sic 'em Dogs on Me (1927–39). Herwin 201. Obscure artists and recordings.

Sugar Mama Blues (1949). Biograph 12009. David Wylie, Frank Edwards, Dennis McMillian, and others.

They Sang the Blues, vol. 1 (1927–29). Historical HLP 17. John Hurt, Bobby Baker, KiKi Johnson, and others.

They Sang the Blues, vol. 2 (1927–34), Historical HLP 22. Recordings by Jelly Roll Anderson, Robert Wilkins, Josh White, and others, including Skip James with piano and a blues reed flute solo by Big Boy Cleveland. An interesting collection.

CLASSIC, URBAN, AND ELECTRIC BLUES
SOPHISTICATED BLUES

I have devised this category to include the work of several early bluesmen whose roots were in the country style but who developed a more advanced style due to professional contact with early jazz players and the more sophisticated blues pianists. Their music is sometimes described as "rhythm-and-blues," but it is distinctly different from the better-known schools of rhythm-and-blues that developed in urban centers after World War II.

BLACKWELL, SCRAPPER (d. 1962)
The Virtuoso Guitar of . . . (1928–32). Yazoo 1019. Solo recordings of an excellent guitarist best known as an accompanist to others, along with other recordings of him in that role. *See also* Leroy Carr, Piano Blues section, page 25.

BROONZY, BIG BILL. *See* Mississippi and Central section, page 9.

JOHNSON, LONNIE Johnson was one of the most versatile guitarists of the twenties and thirties, a strong solo performer who also worked in the bands of such jazz figures as Louis Armstrong, Jimmy Noone, and Johnny Dodds. Later in his career, he made many rhythm-and-blues rec-

"Losing Game": Lonnie Johnson

ords, lapsed into obscurity for a while, and made a comeback as a soloist in the late sixties, performing frequently in the years before his death.
The Blues of . . . (1937–38). Swaggie 1225. Classic sides from his prime.
————. Collector's Classics 30.
Losing Game. Prestige 7724. Representing his work of the sixties.
————. Storyville 162.

JOHNSON, LONNIE, AND EDDIE LANG Lang was the leading white jazz guitarist of the twenties. With Johnson he formed the first integrated recording duo. They complemented each other beautifully, and their work still stands as a classic example of the guitar duet idiom.
————, vols. 1–2 (1927–29). Parlophone PMC 7019, 7106.
————, vols. 1–2 (1927–29). Swaggie 1229, 1276.

LANG, EDDIE, AND JOE VENUTI
Venuti–Lang (1927–28). Swaggie 1266. White and integrated jazz groups, featuring Lang's fine guitar work. Venuti was an early jazz violinist.

TAMPA RED
The Guitar Wizard (1935–53). Blues Classics 25. Recordings spanning Red's later career. There are only glimpses of his guitar work, despite the album title; the dominant instrument is the piano, played by Big Maceo, John Davis, and others. By placing a rural blues guitar sound, a classic blues vocal line, and a commercially composed blues and novelty repertory in the context of an urban piano, bass, and drums sound, Red pioneered the early Chicago rhythm-and-blues idiom in which he, as well as Bill Broonzy, Lonnie Johnson, and Washboard Sam, achieved commercial success during the thirties.
Bottleneck Guitar (1928–37). Yazoo 1039. His earlier ca-

reer, under his own name or as accompanist to others, including Ma Rainey. Presents more of his guitar work than the Blues Classics album.
Guitar Wizard. RCA AXM2-5501 (2-rec. set).

WASHBOARD SAM (Robert Brown, d. 1966)
———— (1941–42). RCA LPV 577. With Bill Broonzy, guitar; Memphis Slim, piano.
———— (1935–41). Blues Classics 10.

CLASSIC BLUES

The term "classic blues" is used to describe the work of those professional blues entertainers of the twenties, usually women, who were accompanied by pianists or small jazz ensembles.

ARMSTRONG, LOUIS The following recordings present Armstrong, in the very early stages of his career, as an accompanist to various blues singers.
Rare Recordings of the 20's, vols. 1–4. Columbia J 23, 25, 26, 28 (OP).
Louis Armstrong/Blues Singers. Collector's Classics 32.
Mr. Armstrong Plays the Blues (1925–27). Biograph C-6.
The Sideman (1924–27). Decca DL7-9233.

COX, IDA
The Blues Ain't Nothin' Else But. . . . Milestone 2015.
————. BYG 529.073.
————. Fountain 301. With Tommy Ladnier.

The Great Blues Singers. Joker 3098. A wide-ranging selection of female blues singers of the twenties: Trixie Smith, Mary Johnson, Chippie Hill, Odetta Gorden, Ma Rainey, Ida Cox, Sara Martin; and Bessie Smith's soundtrack recording of the title tune from the movie *St. Louis Blues.*

GREEN, LIL
Romance in the Dark. RCA LPV-574. A forties singer of blues, pop, and novelty tunes. Good catchy songs, especially interesting as nostalgia items, though lightweight. Bill Broonzy is among her accompanists.

HALL, JUANITA
. . . Sings the Blues. Storyville 113.

HILL, CHIPPIE (Bertha)
_____ (1925–27). Raretone 24009. With Louis Armstrong.

OLIVER, JOE "KING," LOUIS ARMSTRONG, AND BESSIE SMITH
The Blues Heritage. Olympic 7104. Six pieces by Oliver's classic but poorly recorded 1923 band, one piece by his 1926 band, one by Smith, and three by early Armstrong groups. A useful introduction to the New Orleans-in-Chicago sound that was the classic blues matrix. Includes Armstrong's "I'm Not Rough," a blues with a fine Lonnie Johnson guitar solo.

RAINEY, MA (Gertrude)
Blues the World Forgot. Biograph 12001.
Oh My Babe Blues. Biograph 12011.
Queen of the Blues. Biograph 12032.
_____. Milestone 47021.
Down in the Basement. Milestone 2017.
Blame It on the Blues. Milestone 2008.
The Immortal. Milestone 2001.
_____. BYG 529.078.

SMITH, BESSIE Bessie Smith is regarded as the greatest of the classic blues singers. Her accompaniments were provided by some of the best blues players among the jazzmen of the twenties and thirties.
_____, vols. 1–3. Swaggie 1255, 1263, 1264.
The Bessie Smith Story, 4 vols. Columbia CL 855–858. This set is being superseded by the following series, which will ultimately comprise eight sets of two records each, covering her entire career.
Any Woman's Blues. Columbia G 30126.
The Empress. Columbia G 30818.
Empty Bed Blues. Columbia G 30450.
Nobody's Blues But Mine. Columbia G 31093.
The World's Greatest Blues Singer. Columbia GP 33.

SMITH, TRIXIE
_____. Collector's Classics 29.

SPIVEY, VICTORIA
Recorded Legacy (1927–37). Spivey 2001. With Louis Armstrong, Tampa Red, and others. The following are post-1961 recordings in the contemporary Chicago blues style.
. . . And Her Blues. Spivey 1002.
Three Kings and the Queen. Spivey 1004. With Roosevelt Sykes, Big Joe Williams, Lonnie Johnson.
The Queen and Her Knights. Spivey 1006. With Lonnie Johnson, Memphis Slim, Little Brother Montgomery, and others.

WALLACE, SIPPIE
_____. Storyville. SLP 198.

Women of the Blues (1926–39). RCA LPV-534. Alberta Hunter, Margaret Johnson, Lizzie Miles, Monette Moore, Mamie Smith, Victoria Spivey, Sippie Wallace.

POSTWAR COUNTRY AND URBAN RHYTHM-AND-BLUES, DETROIT BLUES, AND OTHER ELECTRIC BLUES

This catchall section encompasses stylistically similar material from several regions, along with their stylistically less similar offshoots. A few major figures whose recordings are well publicized are not listed comprehensively. Other excellent singers, such as Bobby Bland, Little Milton, and Johnny Taylor, not to mention Ray Charles, are not listed because their work is pretty far removed from traditional style, especially in regard to choice of accompaniment.

BROWN, CLARENCE "GATEMOUTH"
The Blues Ain't Nothin'. Black and Blue 33.033.

FULSON, LOWELL (b. 1921)
In a Heavy Bag. Jewel 5003.
Soul. Kent 516.
_____. Arhoolie 2003.
Hung Down Head. Chess 408.

HARMONICA FRANK (Frank Floyd)
The Great Original Recordings (1951–58). Puritan 3003. Recordings of a white master of the white rockabilly and black rural rhythm-and-blues styles.
_____. Adelphi 1023.

HOGAN, SILAS
Trouble. Excello 8019. Electric Louisiana blues; a good writer.

HOOKER, EARL (d. 1970)
First and Last Recordings. Arhoolie 1066.
Hooker 'n' Steve. Arhoolie 1051. With Steve Miller, keyboards.
Don't Have to Worry. ABC Bluesway 6032. With Chicago sidemen.
See Schwann catalogue for other listings.

HOOKER, JOHN LEE (b. 1915) An inconsistent Detroit bluesman, primitive in style. When he is at his best, his performances can be emotionally shattering experiences, and many of his songs, often extemporized, are excellent. From among his many recordings of varying quality, I recommend the following:
Detroit Special (1953, 1961, 1972). Atlantic SD 7228.
Original Folk Blues. Kent 525.
Goin' Down Highway 51 (1948–51). Specialty 2127.
Alone. Specialty 2125.
_____. Ev. Arch. FS 222.
Mad Man Blues. Chess 2CH 60011 (2-rec. set).
It Serves You Right to Suffer. Impulse S-9103.
Detroit (1948–52). United Artists UAS-127 (3-rec. set).

HOUSTON, BEE
_____ (1968–70). Arhoolie 1050. An electric bluesman from San Antonio, with band.

A Family Group

KING, ALBERT
Born Under a Bad Sign. Stax 723. *See* Schwann catalogue for other listings.

KING, B. B. (Riley King, b. 1925)
From the Beginning. Kent 533 (2-rec. set).
———— (1949–51). Kent 9011.
Best of . . . (late sixties). ABC X767.
Live at the Regal. ABC ABCS-724.
See Schwann catalogue for other listings.

KING, FREDDIE (b. 1934)
His Early Years. Polydor (British) 2343.047. *See* Schwann catalogue for other listings.

LAZY LESTER
True Blues. Excello 8006.

LIGHTNIN' SLIM
Rooster Blues. Excello 8000.
Rhythm & Blues Songs. Excello 8004.
High and Low Down. Excello 8018.
London Gumbo. Excello 8023.

ROBINSON, L. C.
Ups and Downs. Arhoolie 1062. An Oakland bluesman and fiddler, accompanied by the Muddy Waters band.
————. ABC Bluesway 6082.

SLIM HARPO (b. 1924)
Rainin' in My Heart. Excello 8003.
Baby Scratch My Back. Excello 8005.
Tip On in. Excello 8008.
Best of. . . . Excello 8010.
Knew the Blues. Excello 8013.

THORNTON, BIG MAMA (Willa Mae)
She's Back. Backbeat 68.
In Europe (1965). Arhoolie 1028. Well-recorded sessions by the greatest contemporary woman singer, with good sidemen including Buddy Guy and Walter Horton. Includes two duets with Fred McDowell.
————, vol. 2. Arhoolie 1032. More strong performances, backed by Muddy Waters' band.

WALKER, T-BONE (d. 1975) Originally a country bluesman from Texas, Walker went on to develop a modern jazzy rhythm-and-blues style. He records in contexts ranging from small Chicago-style ensembles to big bands.
I Want a Little Girl. Delmark DS 633.
Stormy Monday. ABC Bluesville 6008.
Funky Town. ABC Bluesville 6014.
Dirty Mistreater. ABC Bluesville 6058.

ANTHOLOGIES AND COLLECTIONS
Blues Live in Baton Rouge. Excello 8021. Live concert recordings by Louisiana bluesmen Silas Hogan, Guitar Kelly, Whispering Smith, and Clarence Edwards.
Blues Sounds of the Hastings St. Era. Fortune 3012. Detroit blues of the Fifties: Big Maceo, Eddie Kirkland, Gracie Brim, John Lee Hooker, and others.
Detroit Blues. Blues Classics 12. Good fifties recordings by Baby Boy Warren, Dr. Ross, One-String Sam, John Lee Hooker, and others.
The Excello Story. Excello DBL 28025 (2-rec. set). A good sampling of mainly fifties and sixties Texas and Louisiana rhythm-and-blues, including Lightnin' Slim, Lazy Lester, Slim Harpo.
Juke Joint Blues (1948–59). Blues Classics 23. Urban and rural rhythm-and-blues.
Louisiana Blues (1970). Arhoolie 1054. Recordings by Baton Rouge bands led by Silas Hogan, Henry Gray, Whispering Smith, and others.
Memphis and the Delta—The 1950's. Blues Classics 15. Elmore James, Sunnyland Slim, Roosevelt Sykes, and others.
Oakland Blues (1948–54). Arhoolie 2008. K. C. Douglas, Mercy Dee, L. C. Robinson, Jimmy McCracklin, and others.
Packin' Up My Blues (1950–61). Muskadine 102. Rural southern rhythm-and-blues bands.
Roots: Rhythm-and-Blues. RBF 20.
Roots: The Rock-and-Roll Sound of Louisiana and Mississippi. Folkways 2865.
Swamp Blues. Excello 8015/16 (2-rec. set). Seventies recordings by Silas Hogan, Whispering Smith, and other Baton Rouge bluesmen.

CHICAGO BLUES

Chicago blues is an intense, high-energy blues style, usually played in ensembles consisting of electric guitars and bass, harmonica, piano, bass, drums, and perhaps a saxophone. Essentially an offshoot of the Mississippi style, it developed after the movement of many rural blacks to Chicago during World War II. The earlier recordings of many of the older artists listed here were actually made in the south. The younger Chicago bluesmen tend to have more of what could superficially be called a soul or rock sound than their elders do, and occasionally bands and musicians depart radically from tradition in their use of highly arranged horn sections. Although there are some differences in approach, the music in general uses a common and fairly limited set of conventions. Standards of excellence do not involve musical originality so much as good lyric writing and intensity of performance.

ALLISON, LUTHER One of the strong younger performers.
Love Me Mama. Delmark 625.
Luther's Blues. Gordy G967 VT.
Bad News Is Coming. Gordy G946 VT.

BELL, CAREY
Blues Harp. Delmark 623.
Last Night. ABC Bluesway 6079.
See also Big Walter Horton, below.

BIG WALTER. *See* Big Walter Horton, below.

The Bluesmen of the Muddy Waters' Chicago Blues Band, vols. 1–2. Spivey 1008, 1010. Waters' band minus the leader.

CHICAGO BLUES ALL-STARS
Loaded with Blues. BASF MPS 20707. An excellent band led by bassist Willie Dixon, with Sunnyland Slim, piano; Walter Horton, harmonica; Johnny Shines, guitar; and others. They favor a light jazzy shuffle sound, staying generally away from the usual heavier Chicago beats.

COTTON, JAMES (b. 1935)
Blues Band. Verve 3023.
Cut You Loose. Vanguard 79283.
100% Cotton. Buddah 5620.

DAWKINS, JIMMY "FAST FINGERS" A younger player, currently achieving recognition as a powerful writer.
———. Delmark 623.
———. Excello 8024.
Tribute to Orange. Black and Blue 33.038.

DIXON, WILLIE (b. 1915)
I Am the Blues. Yambo 777–15. Bassist Dixon, one of the great writers of contemporary blues ("Spoonful," among others), here sings songs written for him by others. Good backup band includes Big Walter.

GUY, BUDDY (b. 1936) An intense, sometimes over-dramatic singer-guitarist, who often favors arranged horn sections in his recorded work.
Hold That Plane. Vanguard VSD 79323.
Left My Blues in San Francisco. Chess 1527.
I Was Walking Through the Woods. Chess 409.
. . . and Junior Wells Play the Blues. Atco 33–364.
Buddy and the Juniors. Blue Thumb BTS 20. A good and very unusual record. Guy plays acoustic guitar with Junior Wells, harmonica, and Junior Mance, piano; no rhythm section.

HOMESICK JAMES (James Williamson, b. 1914) A good writer, with a bottleneck guitar style derived from Elmore James.
Blues on the Southside. Prestige 7388.
Ain't Sick No More. ABC Bluesway 6071.

"Luther's Blues": Luther Allison

HORTON, BIG WALTER (b. 1918)
Southern Comfort. Sire SES 97011.
. . . with Carey Bell (1972). Alligator 4702. Fine, highly electric playing by the foremost older and younger harmonica players.

HOWLIN' WOLF (Chester Burnett, b. 1910)
Live and Cookin'. Chess 50015.
Back Door Wolf. Chess 50045.
AKA Chester Burnett. Chess 60016 (2-rec. set).
Original Folk Blues. Kent 526.

HUTTO, J. B. (b. 1929) An Elmore James-style bottleneck player.
Hawk Squat. Delmark 617.
Master of Modern Blues. Testament 2213.

JACOBS, LITTLE WALTER
Boss Blues Harmonica. Chess 2 CH 60014. Jacobs was an important figure in the development of the Chicago harmonica style.
Confessin' the Blues. Chess 416. With Robert Jr. Lockwood, Otis Spann, Willie Dixon.

JAMES, ELMORE (1918–63) James' bottleneck guitar style, essentially a simplified but more energetic adaptation of the Mississippi style to the electric guitar, influenced many subsequent players.
Original Folk Blues. Kent 522.
The Legend of. . . . Kent 9001.
The Resurrection of. . . . Kent 9010.
Blues Masters, vol. 1 (1963). Blue Horizon 4601. His last recording session, including retakes, false starts, and studio conversation.
. . . and Walter Horton. Polydor (British) 2383.200.

JOHNSON, LONNIE. *See* Sophisticated Blues section, page 18.

JOHNSON, LUTHER
Born in Georgia. Black and Blue 33.503.

JONES, FLOYD, AND EDDIE TAYLOR
————. Testament 2214. One side of each, with Walter Horton and Otis Spann.

LENOIR, J. B. (1929–67)
Natural Man. Chess 410.

LITTLE WALTER. *See* Little Walter Jacobs, page 22.

LOCKWOOD, ROBERT JR.
Steady Rolling Man. Delmark 630.
Contrasts (1973). Trix 3307. A loose and untogether session unworthy of Lockwood's reputation.

MAGIC SAM (Sam Maghett, 1937–69) One of the most promising of the younger bluesmen until his recent death.
West Side Soul. Delmark 615.
Sweet Home Chicago. Delmark 618.
Black Magic. Delmark 620.
Blues Masters, vol. 3. Blue Horizon 4603.

ODOM, ANDREW
Farther On Down the Road. ABC Bluesway 6055.

REED, JIMMY (b. 1926)
Roots of the Blues. Kent 537 (2-rec. set).
Wailin' the Blues. Tradition 2069.
The Ultimate. ABC Bluesway 6067.
See Schwann catalogue for other listings.

ROBINSON, FENTON (b. 1935)
Somebody Loan Me a Dime (1974). Alligator 4705. A good singer and writer, with polished arrangements including a horn section.

ROGERS, JIMMY
Chicago Bound. Chess 407. With Muddy Waters and Little Walter.

SEALS, SON
The Son Seals Blues Band (1973). Alligator 4703. An intense younger player, who favors a highly electric sound; a good album especially accessible to listeners who are coming into Chicago blues through an earlier interest in hard rock.

SHAKEY JAKE
The Devil's Harmonica. Polydor PD 5014.

SHINES, JOHNNY (b. 1915) A bluesman of Mississippi origins, who frequently performs in country blues style on the folk circuit, in addition to his Chicago-style work.
Standing at the Crossroads. Testament 2221. Solo performances in country blues style.
Master of Modern Blues. Testament 2211. Chicago ensemble session.
. . . and Big Walter Horton. Testament 2217. Chicago ensemble session.
Blues Masters, vol. 7. Blue Horizon 4607. Chicago ensemble session.
————. Advent 2803. A cross section of his work, acoustic-solo and electric-ensemble.
Sitting on Top of the World. Biograph 12044. Solo perfor-

mances, with acoustic guitar, of original blues and country blues standards.
. . . and Company (1974). Biograph 12048. In addition to solos with acoustic guitar, Shines also performs with a Dixieland-style band and with commercial soul-style backup singers in ensembles led and arranged by David Bromberg. The arrangements—highly unorthodox for a bluesman of Shines' tradition—are quite successful. Some of Shines' best writing, including an unusual story song, is on this album.
Chicago Blues Festival. Black and Blue (French) 33.502.

SPANN, OTIS. *See* Piano Blues section, page 26.

TAYLOR, EDDIE
I Feel So Bad. Advent 2802. *See also* Floyd Jones, above.

TAYLOR, HOUND DOG (b. 1916), **AND HIS HOUSEROCKERS.** Nothing new musically or in the way of writing, but the band name is apt. Rocking, hard-driving dance music, infectious and well-recorded.
————. Alligator 4701.
Natural Boogie. Alligator 4704.

TAYLOR, KOKO
I Got What It Takes. Alligator 4706.

WALKER, JOHNNY "BIG MOOSE"
Ramblin' Woman. ABC Bluesway 6036.

WATERS, MUDDY (McKinley Morganfield, b. 1915) The south side Chicago blues tradition derives mainly from the influences of Elmore James, Sonny Boy Williamson, and Waters. Of the three, it was Waters, singer and slide guitarist, who as bandleader perfected the most personal ensemble sounds of the tradition. His influence has been immense, especially on white blues revival players (such as the Rolling Stones), and many of his songs and arrange-

Buddy Guy and Junior Wells Play the Blues

ments have become classics. In recent years, he has perhaps recorded too frequently, often repeating himself without enthusiasm, but his best recordings set a standard for the idiom.

Down on Stovall's Plantation. Testament 2210. 1941–42 Library of Congress field recordings, made while Waters was still in Mississippi. They reveal a younger musician emerging from the influence of Robert Johnson and Son House, an excellent country blues player showing signs of becoming his own man.

McKinley Morganfield AKA Muddy Waters. Chess 2CH 60006 (2-rec. set). Includes the classic recordings by his great band of the fifties.

The London Sessions. Chess CH 60013. More recent recordings with younger British bluesmen.

Brass and the Blues. Chess 1507. With irrelevant horn section parts, apparently overdubbed; the parts are hardly organic and are often out of tune with the tracks.

Folk Singer (1963). Chess 1483. Nonelectric sessions, with Buddy Guy, second guitar. Apparently, an attempt to recapture the spirit of the Library of Congress recordings, but not a successful one.

Fathers and Sons. Chess 127. Waters and pianist Otis Spann are joined by younger white associates Paul Butterfield and Mike Bloomfield in well-organized sessions from the sixties.

See Schwann catalogue for other listings.

WELLS, JUNIOR (b. 1932) A strong singer and harmonica player, who often works with Buddy Guy.
Hoodoo Man Blues. Delmark 612.
South Side Blues Jam. Delmark 628.
Comin' at You. Vanguard 79261.
It's My Life Baby. Vanguard 79231.

WILLIAMSON, SONNY BOY NO. 1 (John Lee Willamson, d. 1948) A singer and influential harmonica player, who did much to popularize the harmonica-led ensemble-with-piano sound that is characteristic of the Chicago style.
Bluebird Blues (1938). RCA Victor (British) 731.014.
Sonny Boy and His Pals (early forties). Saydisc SDR 169.
_____, vols. 1–3. Blues Classics 3, 20, 24.

WILLIAMSON, SONNY BOY NO. 2 (Rice Miller)
_____. Arhoolie 2012 = Blues Classics 9.
_____ (1963). Vogue CLVLX 410. Live concert recordings made in Paris, with Memphis Slim, piano. Not a good session; they need a larger ensemble to carry it.
My Story. Chess 50027.
_____. Storyville 158, 170.

YOUNG, JOHNNY (b. 1917) One of the few blues mandolin players.
Blues Masters, vol. 9. Blue Horizon 4609.
. . . and His Chicago Blues Band. Arhoolie 1029.
. . . and Big Walter: Chicago Blues (1967). Arhoolie 1037. Young plays guitar here.

YOUNG, MIGHTY JOE
_____ (1972). Sonet SNTF 633. Good recordings by a younger singer. Trumpet and tenor saxophone are used in the ensemble, along with guitar and rhythm section.
Chickenheads. Ovation 1437.

ANTHOLOGIES AND COLLECTIONS

The Best of the Chicago Blues. Vanguard VSD 1/2 (2-rec. set). James Cotton, Junior Wells, Buddy Guy, Otis Spann, Walter Horton, Johnny Young, J. B. Hutto, Homesick James. Replaces the three-volume set *Chicago: The Blues Today,* from which it is culled.

Blues Jam at Chess (1969). Blue Horizon 7-66227 (2-rec. set). An informal session with eminent British and Chicago players: Walter Horton, Otis Spann, Willie Dixon, John McVie, Mick Fleetwood.

Chicago Blues. Spivey 1003. Rough, exciting performances, not very well recorded, by Sunnyland Slim, Jimmy Oden, Homesick James, Koko Taylor and others, in various combinations.

Chicago Blues Anthology (forties and fifties). Chess 2CH 60012. A good cross section of the idiom; performances by Bill Broonzy, Robert Nighthawk, Johnny Shines, Elmore James, J. B. Lenoir, and others.

Chicago Blues: The Beginning (1946). Testament 2207. Muddy Waters, Johnny Shines, Homer Harris, James Clark.

Chicago Boogie (1947). Barrelhouse 04. Jimmy Rogers and Little Walter, Othum Brown, Johnny Young, Sleepy John Estes, and others.

Chicago: The Blues Today, vols. 1–3. Vanguard 79216, 79217, 79218. Vol. 1, Junior Wells, J. B. Hutto, Otis Spann. Vol. 2, Otis Rush, James Cotton, Homesick James. Vol. 3, Johnny Shines, Johnny Young, Walter Horton. An excellent anthology from the sixties; the best introduction to the music of the post-classic period.

Drop Down Mama. Chess 411. Fifties recordings by Johnny Shines, Robert Nighthawk, and others.

Electric Blues Chicago Style. Buddah 7511. Reissues from the defunct VeeJay label: Junior Wells, Earl Hooker, and others.

Encore for the Chicago Blues. Spivey 1009. Memphis Slim, Koko Taylor, Homesick James, and others.

Heavy Heads. Chess 1522. Selections from earlier albums, many of the fifties, by Muddy Waters, Sonny Boy Williamson, Howlin' Wolf, Little Milton, Bo Diddley, Washboard Sam, and others.

Modern Chicago Blues. Testament 2203. Robert Nighthawk, John Lee Granderson, Walter Horton, and others.

On the Road Again (1947–54). Muskadine 100. Floyd Jones, Delta Joe, Little Walter, John Brim, and others.

Really Chicago's Blues (1969). Adelphi 1005 (2-rec. set). Rather disorganized ensembles, including Johnny Shines, Sunnyland Slim, Walter Horton, and Big Joe Williams.

Sweet Home Chicago (late sixties). Delmark 618. Good performances by high-intensity singers and guitarists, including Luther Allison, Big Mojo, and Louis Myers.

PIANO BLUES

This section is devoted to rural and urban piano soloists and to singers who accompany themselves on the piano, in all styles and periods. Excluded are blues pianists, such as Ray Bryant and Mose Allison, who clearly locate themselves in a contemporary jazz tradition. The Classic Ragtime section, page 29, should also be consulted for listings of a few borderline players, and for anthologies.

AMMONS, ALBERT (1907–49)
_____ (1936–49). Boogie Woogie 1001.

BARRELHOUSE BUCK
———. Folkways 3554.

BLYTHE, JIMMY A solid, raggy barrelhouse pianist active in Chicago.
——— (1927–31). Swaggie 1324. Solos and with jazz groups.

BOGAN, LUCILLE, AND WALTER ROLAND
———. (1927–35). Yazoo 1017.

BYRD, ROY OR ROLAND. *See* Professor Longhair, page 26.

CARR, LEROY (1905–35) The leading Indianapolis pianist and a popular early rhythm-and-blues composer and recording artist.
Blues Before Sunrise. Columbia C 30596. 1932–34 sessions with guitarists Scrapper Blackwell and Josh White.
Singin' the Blues (1934). Biograph C-9.
———, vols. 1–2. Collector's Classics 38, CC 50.
Naptown Blues. Yazoo 1036. 1929–34 sessions with Scrapper Blackwell, models of the guitar-piano duet idiom.

DAVIS, BLIND JOHN
The Incomparable. . . . Oldie Blues 2803. Recent European recordings by the pianist who worked on many recording sessions of the thirties and forties with Bill Broonzy, Tampa Red, Lonnie Johnson, and Sonny Boy Williamson.

DAVIS, WALTER An interesting singer-pianist. Appears at first to be erratic, going out of key and disregarding structure, but on further listening, a unique method emerges; he uses tonal and metrical alterations as a systematic aspect of style.
Think You Need a Shot (1932–35). RCA Victor (British) INT 1025.
. . . and Cripple Clarence Lofton. Yazoo 1025.

DEE, MERCY (Mercy Dee Walton)
——— (sixties). Arhoolie 1007. A good blues writer, with guitar and rhythm section.

DUPREE, CHAMPION JACK A good pianist in the modern barrelhouse style, also a fine singer, now popular as an entertainer in Europe. A native of New Orleans, he records in a variety of styles, ranging from a clear solo sound in the Yancey tradition to Chicago-style ensembles to highly arranged rhythm-and-blues bands.
———. Sonet SNTF 614. Solo sessions from the early sixties.
———. Sonet SNTF 626. With a Chicago-style ensemble composed of younger English musicians, who play well and leave him plenty of room.
. . . and His Blues Band. Sire SES 97010. With large soul band.
———(1970). Atlantic 8255. With saxophone and rhythm section; a Kansas City jump jazz feel.
When You Feel the Feeling. Blue Horizon 7702.
Happy to Be Free. GNP Crescendo 10005.
———. Storyville 107, 145, 151, 161, 193, 194, 216.

FOWLER, LEM
———. VJM 18. Solos and with washboard band.

GEORGIA TOM (Thomas A. Dorsey) Gospel songwriter Dorsey used the pseudonym Georgia Tom for his secular work: good-time bawdy blues and ragtime blues. *See also,* Professional Gospel Music section, page 36.
——— (1928–31). Riverside (Europe) 8803. With Big Bill Broonzy, Tampa Red, and others.
Come On Mama, Do That Dance (1928–32). Yazoo 1041.

HELFER, IRWIN, AND JIMMY WALKER
Piano Duets and Solos. Flying Fish 001.

JOHNSON, PETE
Master of Blues and Boogie. Oldie Blues 2801.

JONES, CURTIS
Lonesome Bedroom Blues. Delmark 605. Delicate, subdued singing with piano; some fine songs.
Now Resident in Europe. Blue Horizon 763.206.
Super Black Blues. Goody 10.007.

LEWIS, MEADE LUX (d. 1964) A well-known performer in the popular boogie-woogie style of the thirties.
Barrelhouse Piano. Ev. Arch. FS 268.
Barrelhouse Piano. Storyville 208.
———. BoogieWoogie 1002.

LOFTON, CRIPPLE CLARENCE (1886–1957), **AND MONTANA TAYLOR**
Low Down Blues. BYG 529.065. One side of each pianist, recorded in 1939 and 1946, respectively. Lofton has achieved an historical reputation as a hard-driving pianist of the early Chicago school, but Taylor's more simple, subtle work and unpolished, melancholy voice have been underrated. Poor remastering, but this is the only available recording of Taylor, except for anthologized single performances.

LOFTON, CRIPPLE CLARENCE, AND WALTER DAVIS
———. Yazoo 1025. Selections from each, recorded in the thirties.

LOFTON, CRIPPLE CLARENCE, AND JIMMY YANCEY
Pitchin' Boogie (1939 and 1950, respectively). Swaggie 1235.

LUCAS, LAZY BILL
———. Philo 1007. A singer-pianist now resident in Minneapolis after years of work in Chicago. Most of the selections are without additional accompaniment, giving his individual character a chance to be heard clearly.

MEMPHIS SLIM (Peter Chatman) Slim's recording career includes work on dozens of 78 rpm record dates, beginning in Chicago in 1940. First associated with Big Bill Broonzy, he later went into rhythm-and-blues work; he is equally comfortable as an old-style singer-piano soloist and as a member of Chicago or jump blues ensembles. In recent years, he has worked mostly in Europe. The first three albums are oriented toward his solo piano work.
The Real Boogie Woogie. Folkways 3524.
The Real Honky Tonk. Folkways 3535.
Chicago Boogie Woogie. Folkways 3536.
Songs. Folkways 2385. With Willie Dixon.

. . . and Willie Dixon at the Village Gate. Folkways 2386.
Favorite Blues Singers. Folkways 2387. Songs composed or recorded by Bessie Smith, Bill Broonzy, and others.
Mother Earth. Buddah 7505. Reissues of earlier rhythm-and-blues material with band, probably from the fifties. Cliché arrangements of the period; not a good session.
Raining the Blues. Fantasy 24705.
_____ (1973). Sonet SNTF 647. A well-arranged session with guitar (Billy Butler), tenor saxophone, bass, and drums. Slim is the vocalist; his piano work is ensemble-oriented and does not predominate. Relaxed and enjoyable; some of the best rhythm-and-blues studio men in New York are on the recording session.
The Blues Is Everywhere. GNP Crescendo 10002. With a jump jazz feeling; tenorist Benny Waters is the prominent instrumentalist.
. . . and Buddy Guy: South Side Reunion. Warner BS 2646. A Chicago blues band session.
Blue Memphis. Warner WS 1899. An autobiography in song, with British horn and rhythm men.
Bad Luck and Trouble. Barnaby ZG 31291. With harmonica by Jazz Gillum and guitar by Arbee Stidham. Guitar is played badly and out of tune.
_____. Storyville 118, 138.
_____. Trip 8025 (2-rec. set).
See Schwann catalogue and *Phonolog* for other listings.

MERRIWETHER, MACEO (Big Maceo)
Big Maceo (1941–47). RCA Victor (French) 730.577. Vocal and piano recordings by the Texas-Detroit musician best known for his work with Sonny Boy Williamson. With bass, drums, and guitar (Tampa Red).

MONTGOMERY, LITTLE BROTHER (Eurreal, b. 1906) A good singer, writer, and pianist, who often repeats himself on his many recordings. His two best pieces on record, really excellent versions of songs he has often recorded, are available on *After Hours Blues,* listed in Anthologies and Collections, page 27.
_____. Saydisc SDR 213.
Home Again (1972). Saydisc SDM 223.
_____. Blues Beacon 3.
Urban Blues. Fantasy 24717 (2-rec. set). Set shared with Roosevelt Sykes.
Tasty Blues. Prestige 7807.
_____ (1969). Adelphi 1003. With Jeanne Carroll, vocals, and Backwards Sam Firk, guitar. Montgomery, usually a fluid player with a fine sense of doubling or dividing his time, sounds stiff and confined here. The piano and the guitar are out of tune, and Carroll's vocal style is not appropriate to the idiom. However, the record includes a valuable seven-minute interview on style, with musical examples by Montgomery.
_____. Folkways 3527.
Farro Street Jive. Folkways 31014.
_____ (1935–36). Collector's Classics 35.

MOORE, ALEX These are sixties recordings by a fine old Texas singer-pianist with a good command of rhythmic devices reminiscent of Little Brother Montgomery and the New Orleans pianists.
_____. Arhoolie 1008.
In Europe. Arhoolie 1018.

PIANO RED
Dr. Feelgood Alone with His Piano. Arhoolie 1064.
Rockin' with Red. Camden ACL1-0547.

PRICE, SAMMY
Blues and Boogie. Black and Blue 33.040.
_____. Joker 3075.

PROFESSOR LONGHAIR (Roy Byrd)
New Orleans Piano. Atlantic 7225E. 1949 and 1953 sessions, with horns and rhythm section, of the most exciting New Orleans pianist-singer-composer. New Orleans musicians, open to Caribbean and Latin influences, have always been ingenious in dividing the time and developing cross rhythms; the interplay between the drummer and Byrd's vocal and piano lines is some of the funkiest and best from that city's rhythm-and-blues tradition.

ST. LOUIS JIMMY (James Oden)
Going Down Slow. Prestige Bluesville 1028 (OP).

SHAW, ROBERT
Texas Barrelhouse Piano (1963). Arhoolie 1010. Shaw plays in a ragtimey, irregular style with a hint of "stride" bass figures, as well as with the more customary arpeggiated bass.

SPANN, OTIS (d. 1970) A Chicago pianist best known for his work with the classic Muddy Waters band. Spann sang on his own records. His piano style was sometimes frilly and ornamental, coming close to what jazzmen dismiss as "noodling," but he relied on good time and touch to make an impact.
The Blues Never Die. Prestige 7719.
Chicago Blues. Testament 2211. Solos and with blues band.
Walking the Blues. Barnaby KZ 31290. With Robert Jr. Lockwood, guitar, and St. Louis Jimmy Oden, additional vocals.
The Blues Is Where It's At. ABC Bluesville 6003.
Bottom of the Blues. ABC Bluesville 6013.
Heart Loaded with Trouble. ABC Bluesville 6063.
Blues of . . . (1964). Decca (British) LK 4615. With Muddy Waters.
Good Morning Blues. Storyville 157.
Sweet Giant of the Blues. RCA BT29006.

SPECKLED RED
Barrelhouse Blues. Folkways 3555.
The Dirty Dozens. Delmark 601. Late fifties recordings in a raggy blues style.
The Dirty Dozens. Storyville 117.

SUNNYLAND SLIM (Albert Luandrew, b. 1907) Another good singer-pianist who has recorded more frequently as a sideman in others' bands, mainly Chicago blues ensembles.
Sad and Lonesome. Jewel 5010.
Slim's Shout. Prestige 7723.
Ragtime Blues. ABC Bluesville 6068.
_____. Storyville 169.

SYKES, ROOSEVELT A singer, writer, and pianist who had several hits in the thirties and whose career has perse-

"New Orleans Piano": Professor Longhair

vered. Most of the recordings below are from the fifties and sixties. His influence on the blues piano tradition was great, especially in the work of Memphis Slim and Little Brother Montgomery.

_____ (1929–32). Yazoo 1033.
In Europe. Delmark 616.
I Feel Like Blowing My Horn. Delmark 632.
Blues. Folkways 3827.
Urban Blues. Fantasy 24717 (2-rec. set). With Little Brother Montgomery.
The Honeydripper. Prestige 7722.
Dirty Double Mother. ABC Bluesville 6077.
_____. Storyville 189.
Hard Driving Blues. Delmark 607. With Homesick James.

TAYLOR, MONTANA. *See* Cripple Clarence Lofton, page 25.

WALKER, JIMMY. *See* Irwin Helfer, page 25.

WHEATSTRAW, PEETIE (d. 1941)
_____ (1930–38). Blues Classics 4.

YANCEY, JIMMY (1894–1951) Yancey was the most graceful, elegant, and profound of the early Chicago pianists, despite an apparent simplicity in his playing.
Chicago Piano. Atlantic 7229. A good recording made shortly before his death, reflecting a slight but noticeable diminution of his powers. Usually a soloist, he is aided here by a bassist. Includes four vocals by his wife.

Pitchin' Boogie. Swaggie 1235. One side of 1950 recordings, one side of Clarence Lofton, 1939.
Piano Solos (1939). Joker 3101. An excellent session.
The Immortal. Oldie Blues 2802. Most selections are from a 1943 session in which Yancey played rather stiffly. Includes several vocals by Mama Yancey and one by himself, two selections on electric organ, and two 1940 home recordings.

ANTHOLOGIES AND COLLECTIONS

After Hours Blues. Biograph 12010. St. Louis Jimmy Oden, Sunnyland Slim, and Little Brother Montgomery (1949), and two fine Montgomery pieces from 1930.
Barrelhouse, Blues, and Boogie Woogie, vols. 1–3. Storyville 155, 183, 213. Jack Dupree, Memphis Slim, Jimmy Yancey, Roosevelt Sykes, Henry Brown, and others.
Barrelhouse Blues and Stomps, 2 vols. Euphonic 1204, 1205. Speckled Red, Henry Brown, Dink Johnson, and others.
Barrelhouse Piano (1927–36). Yazoo 1028. Will Ezell, Cow Cow Davenport, Montana Taylor, and others.
Blues Piano Chicago Plus. Atlantic 7227. Early fifties recordings, some with band or rhythm section, by Floyd Jones, Little Brother Montgomery, Frank Williams, and Meade Lux Lewis.
Blues Piano Orgy. Delmark 626. Previously unissued cuts by singer-pianists in the Delmark catalogue: Speckled Red, Curtis Jones, Sunnyland Slim, Little Brother Montgomery, Roosevelt Sykes, and Otis Spann.
Boogie Woogie. RCA (French) 730.561. Albert Ammons, Pete Johnson, and Jimmy Yancey.
Boogie Woogie. Jazz Piano JP 5003. 1938 Library of Congress Archives recordings by Meade Lux Lewis, Albert Ammons, and Pete Johnson.
Boogie Woogie Piano Greats (1938–41). Columbia KC 32708. Meade Lux Lewis, Pete Johnson, and Albert Ammons.
Boogie Woogie Rarities (1927–32). Milestone 2009. A good collection of early pieces by Wesley Wallace, Leroy Garnett, Will Ezell, Charlie Spand, Jabbo Williams, Cow Cow Davenport, Henry Brown, Charles Avery, and the original version of Meade Lux Lewis' "Honky Tonk Train Blues."
Boogie Woogie's Greatest Hits. BoogieWoogie 1000. Pinetop Smith, Clarence Lofton, Joe Sullivan, Meade Lux Lewis, Art Hodes, Red Nelson, and others.
Classic Jazz Piano. RCA LPV-543. Albert Ammons, Pete Johnson, Fats Waller, Earl Hines, Jelly Roll Morton, and Jimmy Yancey.
Favorite Country Blues Piano-Guitar Duets. Yazoo 1015. 1929–37 recordings by Leroy Carr, Blind Blake, Willie Harris, and others.
Fillin' In Blues (1928–30). Herwin 205. Rare recordings not reissued elsewhere; one side of pianists, one of country bluesmen.
Great Jazz Piano (1926–40). Joker 3121. Fats Waller, Cow Cow Davenport, Jelly Roll Morton, and Montana Taylor.
Piano Blues. RBF 12. Good to excellent performances by important pianists of the twenties and thirties: Walter Roland, Walter Davis, Romeo Nelson, Louise Johnson, and others.
Piano Blues, vols. 1–2. Storyville 168, 187. Otis Spann, Speckled Red, Memphis Slim, Henry Brown, and others.

Pitchin' Boogie. Milestone 2018. Classic 1924–30 sides by Meade Lux Lewis, Clarence Lofton, Jimmy Blythe, Roosevelt Sykes, Will Ezell, and Bob Call. A good sampling of the Chicago school.

Ragged Piano Classics (1923–43). OJL 16. Recordings by Jimmy Blythe, Alonzo Yancey, Will Ezell, Leroy Garnett, Frank Melrose, and others.

Ragged Piano Classics (1927–39). OJL 15. Recordings by Cow Cow Davenport, Romeo Nelson, Henry Brown, Skip James, Clarence Lofton, and others.

Uptown Blues (1927–37). Yazoo 1042. Guitar-piano duets by Bill Broonzy, Leroy Carr, Bo Carter, Clarence Lofton, and others.

GENERAL BLUES ANTHOLOGIES

This section lists anthologies that draw from the work of artists who come from one or more of the previous categories. Some additional relevant listings can be found in the Other Black American Traditions and General Anthologies of Black American Music section, page 38.

All-Star Blues World. Spivey 1011. Willie Dixon, Smokey Hogg, and Roosevelt Sykes.

American Folk Blues Festival (1962). Excello 8029. Munich studio recordings by Memphis Slim, T-Bone Walker, John Lee Hooker, Brownie McGee and Sonny Terry, and Shakey Jake.

Anthology of the Blues. Kent KST 9001–9012. A twelve-volume anthology of fifties blues and rhythm-and-blues.

Ball and Chain. Arhoolie 1039. Sixties recordings by Big Mama Thornton, Larry Williams, and Lightnin' Hopkins.

Berkeley Blues Festival. Arhoolie 1030. Mance Lipscomb, Clifton Chenier, and Lightnin' Hopkins.

Bluebird Blues. RCA LPV 518. Reissues of recordings originally made for Bluebird, RCA's budget 78 rpm label, between 1932 and 1942. Includes Willie McTell, Tommy McClennan, Sonny Boy Williamson, Sleepy John Estes, Lonnie Johnson, and others.

Blues at Newport. Vanguard 79145. 1963 Newport Folk Festival recordings by Brownie McGhee and Sonny Terry, John Hammond, Jr., Gary Davis, John Hurt, John Lee Hooker, and Dave van Ronk.

Blues for Mr. Crump. Polydor (British) 2383.257. Howlin' Wolf, Bobby Bland, Junior Parker, and Sonny Blair.

Blues Roots. Poppy 60,003 (2-rec. set). Selections from albums originally issued on the Arhoolie label. Serves as a good introduction to the vast range of artists available on Arhoolie. Includes Clifton Chenier, Mance Lipscomb, Fred McDowell, and Lightnin' Hopkins among many others.

Can't Keep from Cryin'. Testament S-01. Topical blues on the death of President Kennedy.

Dark Muddy Bottom Blues. Specialty 2149. Early recordings by John Lee Hooker, Lightnin' Hopkins, Mercy Dee, and others who are more obscure.

The Great Bluesmen. Vanguard VSD 25/6 (2-rec. set).

Memphis Swamp Jam. Blue Thumb 6000. Not a jam session, but a two-record anthology of 1969 recordings by Bukka White, Piano Red, and others, including some very pleasant guitar duets by the little-known R. L. Watson and Josiah Jones.

Montreux Blues Festival (1972). Excello 28026. Doctor Ross, Lightnin' Slim, Whisperin' Smith, Bessie Griffin, and Jimmy Dawkins.

Rare Blues of the 20's. Historical HLP 1, 2, 4, 5. A four-volume anthology (available separately) of rare country and, especially, classic blues sides.

Recording the Blues. Columbia (British) S2797. Musical examples chosen to accompany the book of the same name by Robert Dixon and John Goodrich. Includes Lucille Bogan, Bertha Hill, Blind Lemon Jefferson, Blind Willie Johnson, and others.

Spivey's Blues Parade. Spivey 1012. Sippie Wallace, Lonnie Johnson, Walter Horton, and others.

Stars of the Apollo. Columbia KG 30788. A two-volume anthology of recordings from 1933 to 1964, especially strong in the thirties and forties, that ranges from early blues through raggy novelty acts and Harlem swing on up to Aretha Franklin.

Texas Guitar from Dallas to L.A. Atlantic 7226. Country, urban, and rhythm-and-blues stylists: T-Bone Walker, Guitar Slim, Lawyer Houston, Al King, Ray Agee, and R. S. Rankin.

JUG BANDS, STRING BANDS, AND RAGTIME

JUG BANDS, STRING BANDS, COUNTRY RAGTIME, AND ONE-MAN BANDS

American Skiffle Bands. Folkways 2610.

CAMPBELL, JAMES
_____ (1962). Arhoolie 1015. An exuberant, most unpolished Nashville street band. Campbell, vocals and guitar, with fiddle, trumpet, tuba, and percussion.

Cannon's Jug Stompers. Herwin 208 (2-rec. set).

The Chicago String Band. Testament 2220. Urban bluesmen Carl Martin, Johnny Young, John Wrencher, and John Lee Granderson attempt to re-create the rural string band sound of their youth.

EAGLIN, SNOOKS. *See* Louisiana, the Southwest, and the West section, page 15.

FULLER, JESSE (1896–1976) A spectacular one-man band on 12-string guitar, harmonica, kazoo, and an assortment of odd foot-percussion instruments of his own devising. Fuller, originally from Georgia, had a large and entertaining repertory of blues, rags, and novelty tunes; the popular "San Francisco Bay Blues" is one of his compositions.

Greatest of the Negro Minstrels. Folk-Lyric 126 (OP).

The Lone Cat. Good Time Jazz 12039.

Jazz, Folk Songs, Spirituals, and Blues. Good Time Jazz 12031.

San Francisco Bay Blues. Good Time Jazz 12051.

Brother Lowdown. Fantasy 24707 (2-rec. set).

Move on Down the Line. Topic 12T134.

The Great Jug Bands (1926–34). Historical HLP 36.

The Great Jug Bands (1927–33). OJL 33.

The Jug Bands. RBF 6. Recordings by the best bands of the twenties and thirties, including the Old Southern Jug Band, Cannon's Jug Stompers, the Memphis Jug Band, and the Dixieland Jug Blowers with Johnny Dodds.

Jug, Jook, and Washboard Bands. Blues Classics 2. Memphis Jug Band, Walter Taylor, Ed Kelly, Birmingham Jug Band, and other groups of the thirties.

Jugs, Washboards, and Kazoos. RCA LPV-540. White vodeodo music of the twenties.

LOUIS, JOE HILL
The One Man Band (1949–52). Muskadine 101. Recordings by a Memphis street entertainer with guitar, harmonica, and foot-cymbals. Although most such musicians are in the country tradition, Louis' roots are in rhythm-and-blues.

MARTIN, BOGAN AND ARMSTRONG Older black string band musicians who have formed a band, which is popular at folk festivals. They play a wide selection of blues, rags, and jazzy songs. It is interesting to observe how black string band musicians got many of their ideas from white string band and early jazz players, who of course got many of *their* ideas from still earlier black players.
Barnyard Dance. Rounder 2003.
Let's Give a Party. Flying Fish 003.

"The Lone Cat": Jesse Fuller

Memphis Jug Band. Collector's Classics 2. The most popular of the early jug bands.
———— (1929–34). Joker 3104.

THE MISSISSIPPI SHEIKS A popular black string band of the twenties.
————. Mamlish 3804.
The Mississippi and Beale Street Sheiks. Biograph 12041. The Beale Street Sheiks were Memphis bluesmen Frank Stokes and Dane Sane. The Mississippi Sheiks usually included Bo Carter, but these selections are duets by the two other members, Walter Vincent and Lonnie Chatmon.
The New Mississippi Sheiks. Rounder 2004. A recent reunion, with additional friends.

Ragtime: The Country. RBF 18. Black and white string ragtime music of the twenties and thirties.

Skoodle Um Skoo. Saydisc SDR 199. Ragtime blues, hokum songs, and raggy folk songs recorded between 1924 and 1932 by Sam Jones, Winston Holmes, and others. Includes some rare Gus Cannon–Blind Blake duets.

String Ragtime. Yazoo 1045. Black and white bands of the twenties and thirties, including Jim and Bob, John Dilleshaw, Lonnie Johnson, and Dave Apollon.

Terry, Sonny, and His Washboard Band. Folkways 2006 (10 inch).

Tub, Jug, and Washboard Bands. Riverside (Europe) 8802.

Washboard Rhythm (1926–32). Ace of Hearts 55. Recordings of raggy novelty tunes, somewhere between jug band music and early jazz, by Jimmy Bertrand, Beale Street Washboard Band, Alabama Washboard Stompers, Clarence Williams, and others. Jazz musicians Johnny Dodds, Louis Armstrong, Buster Bailey, and Herb Morand appear in several ensembles.

CLASSIC RAGTIME

A piano and occasionally an ensemble or orchestral style, classic ragtime is a schooled music. It is included here because (1) it derives from traditional folk forms, (2) many of the people who listen to the other styles of music dealt with in this book also listen to classic ragtime, and (3) a comprehensive survey of recorded ragtime is needed.

I have included several figures whose styles differ from classic ragtime but who are commonly thought of along with the classic ragtime pianists and composers, such as James P. Johnson and other great pianists of the Harlem school, whose octave-jumping "stride" bass figures, and other characteristics, were radically different from those of the classic ragtime school. The great Jelly Roll Morton played in a style close to ragtime, but took great pains to insist that he was a jazzman, and once spent a whole afternoon at the Library of Congress recording examples showing how his playing differed from that of Turpin, Joplin and other midwest ragtimers. His piano records are listed here, but his jazz ensemble work is not. Nor is that of another pianist, Fats Waller.

I have also listed select recordings by contemporary revivalist players, including classically oriented players. There is considerable debate about just how ragtime should be played on the piano. Serious exponents agree that the music is meant to be taken at a stately tempo—brass band marching music was a factor in the genesis of ragtime. Less serious exponents favor a rinky-dink rapid tempo manner. In general, however, it is not the question of tempo that is debated, but rather the question of touch and feel—whether the accentuation should tend toward a marchlike two or a jazzier four, and whether the touch should be flat-fingered, as in jazz, or with the wrist and fingers more arched, as in classical piano technique.

There are still many player pianos in existence. Piano rolls of the great ragtime pianists, and lesser figures as well, are available from QRS Piano Rolls, 1026 Niagara Street, Buffalo, N.Y. 14213. Player piano parts, accessories, and rebuilding materials are available from Player Piano Co., 620 E. Douglas Street, Wichita, Kan. 67202.

BLAKE, EUBIE A native of Baltimore, Blake was active as a pianist and composer before the turn of the century. In the years after World War I, he achieved success as the earliest black composer of Broadway musicals. He has been interested in pop and show tunes as well as in ragtime; this is reflected in a style somewhat less swinging and rhythmically aggressive than, say, that of his colleague James P. Johnson. Most of the recordings listed have been made since the late sixties; rarely do they indicate Blake's advanced years.
Blues and Ragtime Piano Rolls, vols. 1 (1917–21) and 2 (1917). Biograph 1011Q, 1012Q.
The Eighty-Six Years of. . . . Columbia C2S 847 (2-rec. set).
. . . Featuring Ivan Harold Browning. EBM 1. One side of piano solos, one side accompanying Browning, a polished interpreter of spirituals and show tunes.

The Ragtime of Eubie Blake

Rags to Classics. EBM 2. Ragtime pieces and original light classical studies.
. . . with Edith Wilson and Ivan Harold Browning. EBM 3. Wilson was a popular entertainer on the black vaudeville circuit during the twenties.
Sissle and Blake (1920–27). EBM 4. Blake and Noble Sissle, later a bandleader, were a major black vaudeville, Broadway, and songwriting act of the twenties.
Live Concert. EBM 5. With interesting reminiscences and biographical and stylistic comments.
Introducing Jim Hession. EBM 6. One side of Blake and one of Hession, a young protégé who plays older and contemporary material in a Walleresque style.

HUG, ARMAND
Rags and Blues. Golden Crest 3064. A pleasant pianist in the white Dixieland school.

JOHNSON, JAMES P. Like Blake, Johnson was also active in the world of Broadway musicals; he also recorded with blues singer Bessie Smith and with numerous jazz figures. He was the leader of the early Harlem piano school and foremost exponent of stride piano style. His recordings reveal a good tradition-based composer's sense, a clear and articulate technique and sense of arrangement, and an immensely powerful sense of swing, within the limits of the rhythmic concepts of his time.
Rare Piano Rolls, vols. 1 (1917–21) and 2 (1917). Biograph 1002Q, 1009Q.
Father of the Stride Piano. Columbia CL 1780.
W. C. Handy Blues. Folkways 3540. Katherine Handy Lewis sings her father's songs accompanied by Johnson, who also plays several of his own pieces.
The Original. . . . Folkways 2850.
Piano Solos. Swaggie 1211.
Piano Solos. Joker 3108.
Father of the Stride Piano. Sounds 1204.
_____ (1921–26). Olympic 7132. Superb piano-roll performances; playback tempos for the rolls are judiciously set and they hardly sound mechanical at all.

JOPLIN, SCOTT The preeminent composer of ragtime music, Joplin was active in St. Louis in the early part of the century.
Scott Joplin (1916). Biograph 1006Q. One side of piano rolls cut by Joplin, the other side of piano rolls cut by other composer-pianists. In 1916 Joplin was suffering from what his death certificate, a year later, diagnosed as dementia paralytica, and the quality of the performance is not up to quality of the writing. The rolls reveal occasional fingering errors and a consistent inability to maintain steady tempo. Stylistically, the rolls reveal a rather heavy touch, a somewhat more legato phrasing than that favored by classical pianists playing ragtime, and accents tending toward one and three rather than two and four.
Piano Rolls, vols. 1–5. Biograph 1006Q, 1008Q, 1010Q, 1013Q, 1014Q. The first number is reviewed above; the others reflect his work of other years.
Ragtime, vols. 1–3. Nonesuch 71248, 71264, 71305. Played by Joshua Rifkin, a good player with a sympathetic classical touch who, by the way, happens to be the arranger of *The Baroque Beatles Book* and of several Judy Collins records.
A Joplin Bouquet. Sonet SNTF 631. Played by Ann Charters, with a graceful, somewhat classical touch.

Scott Joplin with a Back-beat: New Orleans Rag-time Orchestra

The following records are of Joplin's arrangements of his compositions for chamber wind and string ensemble, with percussion. They make for extremely pleasant listening.
The Red Back Book. Angel 36060. New England Conservatory Ragtime Ensemble, conducted by Gunther Schuller.
Palm Leaf Rag. Angel 36074. New England Conservatory Ragtime Ensemble.
More Scott Joplin Rags. Golden Crest CRS-31031.
The Sting. MCA 2040. Music from the film score, "adapted" by Marvin Hamlisch.

LAMB, JOSEPH Lamb is considered second to Joplin as a composer.
A Study in Classic Ragtime. Folkways 3562. A 1959 interview with Sam Charters, recorded at Lamb's home. The few examples of his piano playing here recorded reflect his advanced age.
Piano Rags. Golden Crest 4127. Played by Milton Kaye.

MORTON, JELLY ROLL (Ferdinand, 1885–1941) A great, dynamic pianist from New Orleans, Morton has asserted that he was the inventor of jazz. He just may come closer to deserving the title than anyone. Consult the Schwann catalogue for additional listings, particularly of his work as jazz ensemble leader.
Piano Solos (1923–24). Joker 3091.
Piano Rolls (1924). Ev. Arch. FS-267.
Piano Roll Solos. Collector's Classics CC 7.
Piano Roll Solos (1924–26). Collector's Classics 7.
Rare Piano Rolls (1924–26). Biograph 1004Q.
Piano Roll Solos. Swaggie 1214.

————. Milestone 47018 (2-rec. set). Solos and early bands.
The Immortal. . . . Milestone 2003. Solos and early bands.
Blues and Stomps (1924–26). Biograph 1004Q.
The Library of Congress Recordings, vols. 1–8 (1938). Swaggie 1–8. Songs, piano solos, stories, comments, and reminiscences from one of the most colorful and brilliant figures, and probably the greatest egotist, in American music. These recordings provided the material for Alan Lomax' biography, *Mr. Jelly Roll.* Morton's career took him from New Orleans to Chicago, Texas, California, St. Louis, Harlem, and every place in between, and he has a story or song for each city and town.
The Library of Congress Recordings, vols. 1–12. Riverside 9001–9012 (OP). *Note:* At time of compilation of this book, the Library of Congress series is being issued on the Swedish CJM label, in addition to the Swaggie series. A multivolume series of Morton's complete RCA recordings is also being issued by French RCA.

NEW ORLEANS RAGTIME ORCHESTRA
————. (1971). Arhoolie 1058. Recordings of orchestrations for small chamber ensemble, taken from Joplin's *Red Back Book* as well as from other composers' orchestrations—most from the Robichaux archive at Tulane University. This band plays with more of a backbeat, and a much raggier feeling in general, than the New England Conservatory Ragtime Ensemble, listed under Scott Joplin, does.
————. Delmark 214.

ROBERTS, LUCKEY. *See* under Willie "the Lion" Smith, this section, page 32.

SMITH, WILLIE "THE LION"
The Lion. GNP Crescendo 9011.
Live at Blues Alley. Chiaroscuro 104.
_____. Jazz King 1207.
The Lion. Vogue 9860.
Memorial. Vogue 20.
The Lion and the Tiger, vols. 1–2. Jazz Odyssey 006, 009.
. . . and Luckey Roberts: Harlem Piano. Good Time Jazz 10035.

SMITH, WILLIE "THE LION," AND DON EWELL
Grand Piano Duets (1967). Swaggie 1228 (= Sackville 2004). Smith belongs to the older Harlem school, and Ewell is a good white pianist who works in many styles.

SULLIVAN, JOE
_____ (1944–46). Folkways 2851. An excellent pianist and composer in ragtime and related styles, Sullivan is associated with the "Austin High" group of white jazzmen who came out of Chicago in the early thirties. Folk devotees do not usually know that the bluegrass banjo showpiece "Little Rock Getaway" (also played on guitar by Les Paul) was originally a Sullivan piano composition. (The piece is not included on this album; see *Piano Ragtime of the Teens, 20's and 30's* listed in Anthologies and Collections, below.)

WALLER, FATS (Thomas)
Rare Piano Rolls, vols. 1 (1923–24) and 2 (1924–31). Biograph 1002Q, 1005Q.
   See Schwann catalogue for other listings, particularly for his jazz ensemble work. Very much his own man in his later work, his early recordings clearly show he was James P. Johnson's protégé.
   A multivolume series of Waller's complete RCA recordings has been issued by French RCA.

ANTHOLOGIES AND COLLECTIONS

Black and White Piano Ragtime. Biograph 12047. Early recordings by James P. Johnson, Eubie Blake, Fletcher Henderson, Zez Confrey, and others.

BOLCOM, WILLIAM
Pastimes and Piano Rags. Nonesuch 71299. Rags by Artie Matthews and James Scott.
Heliotrope Bouquet. Nonesuch 71257. Rags by Tom Turpin, James Scott, Joseph Lamb, Scott Joplin, and others less well known.

CHARTERS, ANN
Essay in Ragtime. Folkways 3563.

Classic Jazz Piano. RCA LPV-543. Albert Ammons, Pete Johnson, Fats Waller, Earl Hines, Jelly Roll Morton, and Jimmy Yancey.

Great Jazz Piano (1926–40). Joker 3121. Fats Waller, Cow Cow Davenport, Jelly Roll Morton, and Montana Taylor.

Harlem Stride Pianists. RCA (French) 741.118–119 (2-rec. set). James P. Johnson, Eubie Blake, Pat Flowers, Donald Lambert, and Cliff Jackson.

Hot Pianos (1926–40). Historical HLP 29. Jelly Roll Morton, Montana Taylor, Fats Waller, Cow Cow Davenport; some blues, some ragtime-jazz stylists.

KAY, MILTON
Ragtime at the Rosebud. Golden Crest CRS 31032. A two-record anthology of the compositions of Scott Joplin, Arthur Marshall, Tom Turpin, Artie Matthews, and other classic composers, played with a classical touch. Good for setting Joplin in perspective, since there is a tendency otherwise to identify the classic ragtime school with his name alone.

Parlor Piano (1917–27). Biograph 1001Q. Piano rolls by Fats Waller, James P. Johnson, Luckey Roberts, and others; mainly rags, some blues.

Piano Ragtime of the Teens, 20's, and 30's. Herwin 402. Jelly Roll Morton, James P. Johnson, Joe Sullivan, and other black and white players.

Piano Roll, The. RBF 7. Early original piano roll music.

Piano Roll Hall of Fame. Sounds 1202. Steve Lewis, Fats Waller, Richard M. Jones, Jimmy Blythe, and other blues and ragtime pianists.

Piano Roll Ragtime. Sounds 1201. Tom Turpin, Scott Joplin, James Scott, and others.

Ragtime, a Recorded Documentary. Piedmont 13158. Rare 1899–1929 cylinder and disc recordings.

Ragtime, the City: Banjos, Brass Bands, and Nickel Pianos. RBF 18.

Ragtime Entertainment. RBF 22. 1911–22 cylinder and disc recordings of popular white ragtime sounds.

Ragtime Piano Interpretations. RBF 24.

Ragtime Piano Originals. RBF 23. Early recordings by Zez Confrey and other performers, mainly white.

Ragtime Piano Roll Classics. BYG 529.063. Early piano rolls originally cut by the composers: James Scott, Tom Turpin, Scott Joplin, and Joseph Lamb. Good performances; also of great documentary value.

Ragtime Piano Rolls. Jazz Piano JP 5001.

Red Onion Rag (1917–39). Herwin 402. Piano rolls by Abe Oleman, Willie "The Lion" Smith, Jelly Roll Morton, James P. Johnson, and Cow Cow Davenport.

They All Played the Maple Leaf Rag. Herwin 401. Various noted musicians all play banjo, piano, or band versions of the great Joplin standard.

Toe-Tappin' Ragtime. RBF 25. Orchestrated ragtime and early jazz performances of the twenties and thirties. Compositions of Joplin, Lamb, Bennie Moten, James P. Johnson, and others, played mostly by white ensembles.

In conclusion, I would recommend that the ragtime devotee try to extend his knowledge to other pianists usually considered jazzmen rather than ragtimers. Much satisfaction can be gained from the works of players such as Earl Hines, Cliff Jackson, Art Hodes, Don Ewell, and many others whose names are not often mentioned in a ragtime context.

RELIGIOUS MUSIC

SACRED BLUES, COUNTRY SPIRITUALS, AND SANCTIFIED SINGING

Note: For other relevant listings, consult Other Black American Traditions section, page 38.

BROWN, REV. PEARLY
_____. Arhoolie 2017.

DAVIS, REV. GARY. *See* the East and Southeast section, page 13.

JOHNSON, BESSIE
_____ (1928–29). Herwin 202. Sanctified hymns and spirituals, with some instrumental accompaniment. See also *Country Sanctified Series*, Anthologies and Collections, below.

JOHNSON, BLIND WILLIE A great Texas singer with a gravelly, expressive voice; the best slide guitarist in any blues tradition. His repertory was largely traditional, but he seems to have composed a number of songs as well. While he occasionally recorded slow songs with a delicate and haunting quality, most of his material was energetic and hard-driving, as befits the repertory of a street singer. He often recorded with a female harmony vocalist, yet his guitar parts always played the role of a second voice, sometimes in unison or harmony, sometimes contrapuntally distinct. The quality and depth of his performances are unmatched in the tradition.
_____ (1927–30). RBF 10.
His Story. Folkways 3585. Also has selections by Blind Lemon Jefferson, Blind Boy Fuller, and others. Side 2 is an interview with Johnson's widow.

REED, DOCK, AND VERA WARD HALL
Spirituals. Folkways 2038 (10 inch). Early fifties recordings, unaccompanied solos and duets, by two fine, clear-voiced Alabama singers also present on the *Negro Folk Music of Alabama series. (See* Other Black American Traditions section, page 38.)

SMITH, DAN
God Is Not Dead. Biograph 12036.

WILKINS, REV. ROBERT
_____. Piedmont 13162. Sixties recordings of traditional and interesting original spirituals by a rediscovered singer-guitarist who, before he took up religion, recorded numerous blues during the thirties.

ANTHOLOGIES AND COLLECTIONS

Christ Was Born on Christmas Morning (1927–36). Historical HLP 34. Gospels, spirituals, and holy blues by Willie McTell, Blind Willie Johnson, Rev. Clayborn, and others.

Country Sanctified Series
   Vol. 1, *Bessie Johnson* (1928–29). Herwin 202. Johnson, Phipps Holiness Quartet, Memphis and Chicago Sanctified Singers, McIntorsh and Edwards.
   Vol. 2, *God Give Me Light* (1927–31). Herwin 203. Holy Ghost Sanctified Singers, Elder Curry, Elder Bryant, and others.
   Vol. 3, *Whole World in His Hands* (1927–36). Herwin 207. Roosevelt Graves, McIntorsh and Edwards, many others.

Country Spirituals. Storyville 135. Snooks Eaglin, Rev. Pearly Brown, Cage and Thomas, and others.

In the Spirit, vols. 1–2. OJL 12, 13. Spiritual blues and sanctified singing and preaching recordings of the twenties and thirties: Bukka White, Charlie Patton, Skip James, Willie Davis, Joe Taggart, and others.

Negro Religious Songs and Services. AFS L10. 1934–42 Library of Congress field recordings in the south.

The Rural Blues: Sacred Tradition (1927–30). Herwin 206. Recordings by Mother McCollum, Rev. Clayborn, Eddie Head and family.

Sanctified Singers, vols. 1–2. Blues Classics 17, 18. A well-chosen selection, mainly featuring solo singers of the twenties and thirties accompanying themselves on guitar, with occasional harmony vocals: Joe Taggart, Willie Johnson, Lil McClintock, Rev. Edward Clayborn, and others. The selections amply demonstrate that then, as now, the black talent devoted to religious music was no less great than that devoted to secular music.

Singing Preachers and Their Congregations. Blues Classics 19.

Sorrow Come Pass Me Around. Advent 2805. Religious music from rural communities.

Southern Sanctified Music. Roots 328.

TAGGART, BLIND JOE
Guitar Evangelist (1926–31). Herwin 204.

Ten Years of Black Country Religion (1926–36). Yazoo 1022. Recordings of sacred blues by bluesmen whose repertory and attitudes were primarily secular: Charlie Patton, Blind Willie Davis, Bo Weevil Jackson, Blind Lemon Jefferson, and others.

This Old World's in a Hell of a Fix. Biograph 12027. Good selections from sacred blues and gospel recorded between 1927 and 1969: Robert Wilkins, Fred McDowell, Skip James, and others.

Urban Holiness Service. Folkways 8901.

NOTHING HAS CHANGED BUT THE TEMPO

by Wesley Westbrooks

On the west bank of the Ouachita River is the city of Arkadelphia, Arkansas, which has often been called a city of talent. During World War I there were some influential colleges in the area, including Ouachita Baptist College and what is now known as Henderson State Teachers College. And on the west end of town there were two important schools, the Presbyterian Academy and the Baptist Academy for blacks.

Arkadelphia was a city of talent for two primary reasons: Doodley Williams and Christine Hunter.

Doodley Williams was an unusually talented man. Though he had no formal education or musical training, he could learn to play any instrument in a matter of hours. Not only *learn to play*—he mastered the instrument, worked the standard melodic lines, and then improvised, whether he was handling strings or brass. In addition, Williams was an expert singer. Students at various colleges invited him to perform during the twenties and thirties, and usually ended up giving him money. He knew more songs than he ever had time to sing; what really baffled his audiences was where he'd learned them all.

Christine Hunter was an accomplished pianist as well as a singer. When she and Doodley got together at the Arkadelphia Methodist Church on Sunday nights, the place was always packed. As a combo, they were truly miraculous. After hearing a song on the radio once, they could play and sing it, how I don't know. This is what we call playing by ear.

Most Arkadelphia concerts, especially church programs, were held in the west end of town. There were three black churches, all of which still exist today, that dominated the religious life of the area. The Sanctified church always had a pianist present. They'd sing a song and testify, and each time it would be in a different key. The songs were always up-tempo songs. The Baptist church was a "middle-of-the-road" church. But the Methodists swung their gospel songs, especially when Christine and Doodley appeared.

In those days invitations to a revival were sent out "by the winds," without any formal announcement to people in other churches. People would come all the way from Hot Springs, a much larger town some twenty-nine miles distant, and the word would be passed around. When the gospel revival began, the singing could be heard throughout the west end of Arkadelphia. In fact, many radio stations today are playing songs from those years. The rhythm's different, however, although the words may be the same. People in the west end sang "Oh Happy Day" thirty-five years before it became a nationwide hit in America.

By 1935 a lot of younger people had left Arkansas and gone to Chicago and St. Louis. When they returned home, they brought the latest word on what was happening to gospel music in the big cities. Wednesday night was prayer meeting night, and all the youngsters listened to the service. To this day, I've never seen music printed that matches the way they sang their songs. One person would walk into the church and start singing, "This time another year I may be dead and gone." If the church was empty, the singer would just pick up the theme and repeat it until someone came in and took it over from him. The chord pattern used was usually I, IV, V, V^7, then back to I. But I've never seen it captured exactly as it sounded, even by gospel music writers who come from this same background. The singers sang from a special feeling, and minutes later the church would be filled. The youngsters were still outside during the prayer service, and the prayers were sung. The young people could say the prayers because they were usually the same from week to week. They knew who was testifying or singing these songs. This type of prayer service still exists today.

So many people eventually went to Chicago that one couldn't walk two blocks on the south side without seeing somebody from Arkadelphia. And all the little towns on the outskirts of Arkadelphia—Manchester, Gum Springs, Curtis, Gurdon, Shadygrove, and Amity—were producing gospel sounds as each generation grew up.

Things started moving faster in the years from 1936 to 1938. People traveled more. In Kansas City they used a jazzier beat, but in Chicago one could find all styles because so many people came from different places. During World War II some of the people who sang gospel music traveled all over the world, and they brought back new songs and styles. Thomas Dorsey, the composer of "Precious Lord Take My Hand," and the Roberta Martin Singers became popular. Some ministers didn't like the new styles of gospel music. Roberta Martin wrote a song, "God Is Still on the Throne," which became accepted everywhere. I remember one city in Italy where a group sang many of the Roberta Martin Singers' songs, and sang them very well.

Although jazz gradually became more influential at the end of the war, many of the churches in cities like Chicago, Los Angeles, Washington, D.C., and Baltimore held onto the traditional gospel music. The Staple Singers came out of Mississippi to Chicago and sang there at Roebuck Staples' brother's church. They did one tune in particular, "Uncloudy Day," which launched them on a successful singing career.

Quartet singing originated during the early thirties. It is a combination of hymnal, jazz, and rock music with guitars and drums as accompaniments. Many black ministers sang in quartets while attending college; they would perform in school auditoriums because they were not allowed to sing in the Baptist or Methodist churches. Even today, in many of the larger churches with black ministers who have had formal college training, the ministers still resent this type of singing.

After the war, the doors swung open to gospel music.

*Doodley Williams (with guitar)
and the Band*

With people leaving the south and moving north and west, the field of gospel music was more widely spread. Because so many men had been in the army, women began to dominate the recording of gospel music. Some of the first women to achieve popularity were the St. Paul Choir of Los Angeles, Bessie Griffin, the Davis Sisters, and the Famous Caravans. Mahalia Jackson was a Baptist minister's daughter, and she knew how to get the churches to support her singing.

As gospel music achieved prominence, the Staples Singers became the number one group in popularity. They are now a "gospel-rock" group, and with this slight change they have become known throughout the world with such tunes as "Respect Yourself," "I'll Take You There," and "Be What You Are." Some other gospel artists that have made the top one hundred record chart are the Art Reynolds Singers with "Glory, Glory" and the Edwin Hawkins singers with "Oh Happy Day." The Mighty Clouds of Joy have recently joined the list with their hit single "Time." I can't say enough about the singers that are listed in this chapter of the record guide.

As you can see, gospel music has various styles and with its increase in versatility, it is becoming more and more accepted throughout the world. It's moving along with the times.

The following records are vocal-oriented, with instrumental accompaniments of various kinds. Any instrumental solo record is indicated by the abbreviation "instl."

AMMONS, GENE
Preachin (instl.). Prestige 7270.

ANDREWS, INEZ
Close to Thee. Song Bird 213.

ART REYNOLDS SINGERS, THE
Tellin' It Like It Is. Capitol T2534.

BEVERLY GLENN CONCERT CHORALE
Coming Again So Soon. Cross 333.

BOLDEN, ALFRED
We Shall Overcome. Atlantic R019.

BRADFORD, REV. ALEX
Keep on Praying. Checker 10041.

CAESAR, REV. SHIRLEY
Thompson Community Choir and Caesar Singers. Hob 21-32.

CAESAR, REV. SHIRLEY, AND THE CAESAR SINGERS
Strangers on the Road. Hob 299.

DAVIS SISTERS, THE
He That Believeth. Savoy MG 14014.

DIXIE HUMMINGBIRDS, THE, AND THE ANGELIC GOSPEL SINGERS
Move on Up a Little Higher. Hob 296.

EDWIN HAWKINS SINGERS
More Happy Days. Buddah 5064.

FAMOUS CARAVANS, THE
————. Gospel MG 3049.

FRANKLIN, ARETHA
The Gospel Soul of Aretha Franklin. Checker 10009.

FRANKLIN, ARETHA, WITH JAMES CLEVELAND AND THE SOUTHERN CALIFORNIA COMMUNITY CHOIR
Amazing Grace. Atlantic SD2-906.

FRANKLIN, REV. C. L., AND ARETHA FRANKLIN
Never Grow Old. Checker 10083.

FRANKLIN, ERNEST
Dynamic. Jewel 0094.

GREEN, GRANT
Feelin' the Spirit (instl.). Blue Note 84132.

GRIFFIN, BESSIE
Gospel Soul. Sunset SUM 1195.

HARMONIZING FOUR, THE
Golden Bells. Vee-Jay 5025.

HAROLD SMITH MAJESTIC CHOIR FEATURING JAMES CLEVELAND
Lord, Help Me to Hold Out. Savoy 14319.

JACKSON, MAHALIA
Make a Joyful Noise unto the Lord. Columbia 1936.

KING, B. B.
Doing My Thing, Lord. Kent 563 X.

LAWS, HUBERT
Morning Star (instl.). CTI 6022.

MIGHTY CLOUDS OF JOY, THE
It's About Time. ABC 50177.

ROBERT MARTIN SINGERS
God Is Still on the Throne. Savoy MG 14031.

ROBINSON, REV. CLEOPHUS
The Unfolding of Life. Peacock 128.

ST. PAUL CHURCH CHOIR OF LOS ANGELES
On Revival Day. Capitol T791.

SALEM TRAVELERS
Everything's Going to Be All Right. Checker 10078.

SENSATIONAL CYMBALS
Peace Be Still. Jay Walking 1021.

STAPLE SINGERS, THE
Freedom Highway. Epic 24163.
The 25th Day of December. Riverside 93513.
Uncloudy Day. Vee-Jay 5000.
Will the Circle Be Unbroken. Buddah 7508.

WARD, CLARA
Gospel Concert Live with the Ward Singers. Roulette R 25233.

WOODS, MACEO
Amazing Grace. Vee-Jay 5001.

PROFESSIONAL GOSPEL MUSIC

Professional gospel music is a polished and often schooled music that derives from the nonprofessional tradition of Sanctified congregational singing. Certain individual artists are influenced, in addition, by yet another tradition, that of what might be called the concert spiritual performance. For a long time, the only outlet open to trained black concert singers, aside from the occasional and inevitable casting of a man as Verdi's Otello, was as concert performer of "Negro spirituals." The style of such performances was influenced by European art song, not only in the singer's approach to phrasing and tone production, but also in the approach to dynamics and the style of piano and organ accompaniment. The influence of this tradition is often felt in gospel music, but in recent years the influence of jazz, soul, and rock music has also been felt, since the black religious tradition does not necessarily care to separate itself stylistically from secular traditions.

It is not possible to list here the great number of available recordings by groups and soloists. Furthermore, the gospel market is such that many excellent performances are issued as singles but not necessarily on long-playing albums. In addition to Wesley Westbrooks' recommended list of favorite gospel recordings, given on the preceding pages, I have compiled a short list of stylistically and historically important recordings. For more comprehensive listings, I urge you to consult the catalogues of ABC (subsidiaries: Songbird and Peacock), Specialty, Columbia, and Nashboro (with subsidiaries Kenwood, Creed, Excello). A good mail-order source is J & F Southern Record Sales, 4501 Rising-hill Road, Altadena, Calif. 91001 (catalogue available).

BOATWRIGHT, McHENRY
Spirituals. Golden Crest RE 7024. A good example of the concert spiritual tradition, as performed by a trained singer-pianist.

BRADFORD, ALEX
A Lifetime Believing. Cotillion 057.
Black Man's Lament. Cotillion 061.

COOKE, SAM
Gospel Sound, vols. 1–2. Specialty 2116, 2127.
Two Sides of. . . . Specialty 2119. Gospel and pop selections; Cooke was the first singer to make a successful cross-over from gospel to commercial pop. He was lead singer with the Soul Stirrers, in addition to his solo work.

DORSEY, THOMAS A.
Precious Lord. Columbia KG 32151 (2-rec. set). One of the most important composers in the tradition, whose songs, as on these records, are performed by many prominent artists. Early in his career, Dorsey recorded many secular blues and ragtime novelty tunes under the name Georgia Tom; *see* Piano Blues section, page 25.

JACKSON, MAHALIA
The Great. . . . Columbia KG 31379 (2-rec. set).
The Life I Sing About. Caedmon TC 1413. Songs interspersed with comments and reminiscences.
See Columbia and Nashboro catalogues for comprehensive listings.

ORIGINAL FIVE BLIND BOYS OF ALABAMA, THE
_____. Specialty 2123.
Greatest Gospel Gems, vols. 1–2. Specialty 2144, 2145. A good introduction to the various artists available on the Specialty label; includes Sam Cooke, Alex Bradford, Dorothy Love Coates, Swan Silvertones, Bro. Joe May, Original Five Blind Boys of Alabama, and others.

WARD, CLARA
Gospel Soul. Nashboro 7098.

WILLIAMS, MARION
Gospel Now. Cotillion 053.
Blessed Assurance. Atlantic 7302.

ANTHOLOGIES AND COLLECTIONS
The Gospel Sound, vols. 1–2. Columbia G31086, G31595. Two two-record sets issued in conjunction with the publication of Tony Heilbut's book of the same name. A definitive documentary that takes in almost the whole spectrum of black religious music; the selections are of high musical quality. Blind Willie Johnson, Mitchell's Christian Singers, Mahalia Jackson, Marion Williams, Thomas Dorsey, and various gospel groups.
An Introduction to Gospel Song. RBF 5. Documentary recordings especially valuable for illustrating the formative period of the gospel quartet: Fisk Jubilee Quartet, Tuskegee Institute Singers, and others.

Clifton Chenier

CREOLE BLUES AND ZYDECO

Creole music is the music of the French-speaking black population of Louisiana and East Texas (in addition to other enclaves, one as far west as Richmond, California). Zydeco refers to an accordion or string band dance music, most often two-step, which is very close to the dance music of the French-speaking whites in the area. (*See* Cajun Music section, page 55.) There is a great deal of musical cross-fertilization between the two populations, and many—though not all—artists share a style that cannot be termed distinctly black or white. In most sections of this catalogue, it makes a certain amount of stylistic sense to distinguish between white and black music and musicians, since most of the music dealt with was recorded or originated when racial separatism was dominant. This is much less the case here.

ARDOIN, ALPHONSE "BOISEC"
La Musique Créole; Creole Cajun Blues. Arhoolie 1070.

CHENIER, CLIFTON A dynamic singer-accordionist and bandleader who, as these listings make obvious, is the preeminent exponent of the style. Recordings date mostly from the sixties.

Louisiana Blues and Zydeco. Arhoolie 1024.
Bon Ton Roulet. Arhoolie 1031.
Black Snake Blues. Arhoolie 1038.
King of the Bayous. Arhoolie 1052.
Recorded Live. Arhoolie 1059.
Out West. Arhoolie 1072. With younger white bluesmen Elvin Bishop and Steve Miller.
Very Best. Blue Thumb BTS 15. Selections from the first three Arhoolie albums.
Bayou Soul. Crazy Cajun 1002.
Bayou Blues. Specialty 2139.
Cajun Blues. Prophesy 1004.

FONTENOT, CANRAY, AND ALPHONSE ARDOIN
Les Blues du Bayou (1966). Melodeon 7330. Fiddle-accordion duets with percussion. While neither incompetent nor unpleasant, Fontenot and Ardoin do not possess a widely varying repertory; a few selections as part of an anthology might have been more appropriate. Their music is close to Cajun dance music; despite the title, they do not play blues.

Zydeco. Arhoolie 1009. An anthology; Paul McZeal, Willie Green, Amadé Ardoin, and others, along with relevant pieces by Leadbelly and Lightnin' Hopkins.

Retrospection

OTHER BLACK AMERICAN TRADITIONS AND GENERAL ANTHOLOGIES OF BLACK AMERICAN MUSIC

African and Afro-American Drums. Folkways 4502 (2-rec. set). An annotated set offering comparative examples of African, Caribbean, South American, jazz, and New York street drumming.

Afro-American Blues and Game Songs. AFS L4. 1933–41 Library of Congress field recordings; includes Sonny Terry and Muddy Waters.

Afro-American Music. Folkways 2692 (2-rec. set). An educational program edited and annotated by Dr. Willis James of Spelman College, which traces rhythmic and melodic themes from African sources on through field hollers, blues, spirituals, and work songs. Also discusses the retention of African rhythms and intonation patterns in Black American speech.

Afro-American Spirituals, Worksongs, and Ballads. AFS L3. 1933–39 Library of Congress field recordings.

COLEMAN, GEORGE
Bongo Joe. Arhoolie 1040. A Texas street entertainer who sings songs, mostly comic, of his own composition while accompanying himself on tuned steel drums. (*Note:* for other steel drum records, see The Caribbean section, page 130.)

Hard Times. Rounder 4007. Reissues of black social criticism songs.

LaRUE, MICHAEL
Songs of the American Negro Slaves. Folkways 5252.

Mississippi Folk Voices. So. Folklore SF-101. White and black blues, fiddle tunes, songs, sacred harp, and gospel music, recently collected in Mississippi, with fifty-five-page scholarly booklet. Collection compiled by William Ferris.

Music Down Home. Folkways 2691. The boxed collection is subtitled *An Introduction to Negro Folk Music, U.S.A.* Edited by Charles Edward Smith, it draws from the work of artists recorded on two larger Folkways collections, *Negro Folk Music of Alabama* and *Music from the South.*

Music from the South. 1940's Guggenheim Foundation field recordings in Alabama, Louisiana, and Mississippi, collected by Frederic Ramsey, Jr., in conjunction with his book *Been Here and Gone.* Everything here is valuable either musically or as a document; since few individuals will be able to buy the series, it makes special sense for librarians to consider it as an acquisition.
   Vol. 1. Folkways 2650. Country bands.
   Vols. 2–4. Folkways 2651, 2652, 2653. Songs and interviews with Alabama songster Horace Sprott, a gold mine of traditional lore.
   Vol. 5. Folkways 2654. Work songs, blues, play-party songs, instrumental blues and rags.
   Vols. 6–7. Folkways 2655, 2656. Spirituals in the older style.
   Vol. 8. Folkways 2657. Spirituals in the younger style.
   Vol. 9. Folkways 2658. Worship services.
   Vol. 10, *Been Here and Gone.* Folkways 2659.

Negro Blues and Hollers. AFS L 59. 1941–42 Library of Congress field recordings. Included on the blues side are three selections by Son House and four by William Brown, a great bluesman from Arkansas whose guitar parts are beautifully conceived.

Negro Folklore from Texas State Prisons. Elektra EKS-7296 (OP). Work songs, blues, spirituals, preaching, and rhyming toasts recorded by Bruce Jackson, probably about 1960. A valuable document that has been allowed to go out of print.

Negro Folk Music of Africa and America. Folkways 4500 (2-rec. set). Edited by Harold Courlander; presents examples of African music and of the survival of African style in Caribbean vocal and rhythm music and Black American vocal music.

Negro Folk Music of Alabama. Field recordings documenting the musical life of a regional culture, collected in 1950 by Harold Courlander in conjunction with his book; *see*

Part II, page 152. This is another valuable series that individuals may hesitate to acquire because of the expense; librarians should seriously consider it.

Vol. 1, *Secular Music.* Folkways 4417.
Vol. 2, *Religious Music.* Folkways 4418.
Vols. 3–4. Folkways 4471, 4472. Rich Amerson: A fine solo singer and a valuable informant for his large repertory of tales and secular and religious songs.
Vol. 5, *Spirituals.* Folkways 4473.
Vol. 6, *Ring Game Songs and Others.* Folkways 4474. *See also* Dock Reed, Religious Music section, page 33.

Negro Prison Camp Work Songs (1951). Folkways 4475. Field recordings of choral work songs from Texas penal farms, collected by Pete Seeger and others.

Negro Prison Songs. Tradition 1020. Work songs, hollers, and blues; solo and choral. Recorded at the Mississippi State Penitentiary (Parchman Farm) in 1947 by Alan Lomax. The prison work song tradition kept alive strong survivals of African tonal, rhythmic, harmonic, and polyphonic style. Selections on this recording are musically excellent.

Negro Songs of Protest. Rounder 4004. Selections from the important privately made field recordings collected by Lawrence Gellert and used as the basis for his books. (*See* Part II, page 144.) The entire collection is now housed in the Indiana University Archives of Traditional Music. The material ranges from unaccompanied songs and chain-gang choral singing to blues with guitar; all implicitly or, more rarely, explicitly protest social conditions. All are of high musical quality.

Negro Work Songs and Calls. AFS L8. 1933–40 Library of Congress field recordings.

Prison Worksongs Recorded at Angola. Arhoolie 2012. Unaccompanied solo and choral singing from the Louisiana State Penitentiary, recorded by Dr. Harry Oster in the late fifties.

Riverside History of Classic Jazz. BYG 529.061. Originally issued on the now-defunct Riverside label, this useful documentary collection emphasizes African and primitive Black American rhythm and vocal music, set next to examples of blues, ragtime, and early jazz.

Roots of Black Music in America. Folkways 2694. Musical selections, compiled and annotated by Sam Charters, that document the survival of African musical practices in Caribbean and Black American music.

SEA ISLANDS MUSIC The coastal islands of Georgia and the Carolinas have maintained a strong and independent tradition of Black American music making. One Sea Islands singer, Bessie Jones, has achieved national prominence as a performer.
John's Island, So. Carolina: Its People and Songs. Folkways 3840.
Sea Island Folk Festival: Moving Star Hall Singers. Folkways 3841.
Been in the Storm So Long: Spirituals and Shouts, Children's Game Songs, and Folktales. Folkways 3842.

Animal Tales Told in the Gullah Dialect, 3 vols. AFS L44, 45, 46.

J. B. Smith. Takoma B1009. Hollers and prison songs, unaccompanied solo voice. Smith is a good singer in this insufficiently documented tradition.

The Story of the Blues. Columbia G 30008. A well-organized two-record anthology that documents the blues tradition from African music through early blues on up to contemporary Chicago blues. The best design and production of any such anthology, with selections of generally high quality; but wider and better choices could have been made had the editors not been limited to the Columbia vaults.

Traveling Through the Jungle. Testament 2223. Examples of the rarely documented Black American fife and drum music that is played in rural Mississippi, Texas, and Alabama.

JAZZ: A FINAL WORD

Except for listing a few borderline cases in the ragtime section, I have tried to shy away from jazz. There is absolutely no question in my mind that the work of Johnny Dodds, Tommy Ladnier, and many other early jazzmen is more than tangentially relevant here; my only question is where to draw the line in a discussion of such figures. Perhaps someone will someday have the opportunity to compile a survey such as this one of early jazz resources. But it would be a disservice to exclude mention of the *Folkways History of Jazz Series.* This comprehensive documentary series is an essential resource for libraries and school music departments, as well as good listening for the individual.

History of Jazz Series. Folkways 2801–2811.
Vol. 1, *The South.* Primitive and folk origins.
Vol. 2, *The Blues.* Spirituals and hollers; country, classic, and early jazz blues.
Vol. 3, *New Orleans.* The earliest examples of New Orleans musicians, as recorded in Chicago during the twenties.
Vol. 4, *Jazz Singers.* A comprehensive survey ranging from Sonny Terry to Ella Fitzgerald.
Vol. 5, *Chicago #1.* Further changes in classic New Orleans ensemble style by black musicians of the late twenties.
Vol. 6, *Chicago #2.* Early white derivators of the Chicago–New Orleans style; they went on to develop the white Dixieland and swing styles.
Vol. 7, *New York* (1922–34). Black and white soloists and groups in the pre-swing style.
Vol. 8, *Big Bands Before 1935.* Lunceford, Henderson, Redman, and other great early arrangers: the changes in mood and musical panorama that these men could bring about within the space of one 78 rpm record should put many others who waste time to shame.
Vol. 9, *Piano.* A survey of blues, ragtime, Dixieland, and swing styles.
Vol. 10, *Boogie-Woogie, Jump, and Kansas City.*
Vol. 11, *Addenda.*
The series is edited by Frederic Ramsay, Jr.

NORTH AMERICAN INDIAN MUSIC

by David McAllester

Traditional American Indian music is almost entirely vocal, sung by men, in choruses with rattles, drums, or both as accompaniment. This singing ranges from the deep bass unison of the Pueblos to the piercing falsetto often used by the Indians of the plains and by the Navajos and Apaches in Arizona and New Mexico. In spite of great diversity from tribe to tribe, there are enough similarities in sound and use so that one can speak in general terms of American Indian music.

The nonharmonic melodic line descends in an arc from a high beginning to a strong repetitive use of the tonic, or base note, at the end of the song. There is often a rich use of grace notes, shouts, pulsations, and other melodic ornaments. Song speeds are moderate to fast, and single and duple meters are most common. The vocal timbre is robust and penetrating.

The number and variety of percussion instruments still used today is very great. Rattles and drums of many kinds are found all across the continent, including the unique water drum in which the membrane is wet and stretched over the mouth of an iron pot or other container with water inside. Rasps, conch shell trumpets, flutes, flageolets, whistles, and a few one-stringed fiddles are also characteristic Indian instruments, but all are rare compared with the ubiquitous drums and rattles.

Traditional social dances are still in wide use everywhere and, in fact, increasingly so with the growth of the powwow movement: the staging of public get-togethers featuring dance and song competitions as well as recreation. Most Indian dancing, however, is religious, as the Sun Dance of the plains and the Green Corn Dance of the eastern woodlands. The dancing may convey symbolic thanks to the deities, be part of a prayer for rain and fertile crops, or be an attempt to heal the sick or ward off danger. The specific function depends on the focus of the religion concerned. The text of a thanksgiving song may express appreciation to the three life-giving sisters, Corn, Beans, and Squash, for the blessing of food; a healing song of the Navajos may stress the restoration of harmony between a sick person and the forces of nature; a corn dance song of the Pueblos may mention rain deities and ask them to come bestow their bounty on the arid farmlands of the southwest. There are also highly individualistic songs which a religious seeker may learn in a vision; these bring spiritual power and the good things of life to the person who knows them. On the northwest coast, individuals or families often own songs and guard against their use by outsiders.

Though traditional music is still a vital art in modern American Indian life, there are many kinds of new music as well. New religious movements, such as the Native American Church, have a large literature of songs based on earlier native patterns. Christian groups, like many of the Cherokees in Oklahoma, have their own way of singing hymns in rich harmonies reminiscent of sacred harp singing in the deep south. Some genres of traditional dance songs may have some English words in the texts, and popular music from the Anglo-American culture is heard on records at such occasions as Indian high-school dances. It is also performed by Indian rock 'n' roll groups and country and western bands in many parts of the country.

A few Indians, like Ed Lee Natay and Buffy Sainte-Marie, have become popular folk singers and are known to wide audiences through their records. Natay sings his versions of traditional songs to a largely Indian audience; Sainte-Marie is a talented composer of a wide variety of folk songs in the Anglo-American tradition and is also noted for her Indian protest songs.

No written account can substitute for the actual sound of any music. Several hundred commercial records of American Indian music are now available. A few are listed as an introduction to a lively and still growing tradition among North America's many folk musics.

RECORDS

Iroquois Social Dance Songs (3-rec. set). Iroqrafts; Ohswegon, Ont.
War Songs of the Ponca (2-rec. set). Indian House 2001, 2002; Taos, N.M.
Indian Music of the Canadian Plains. Folkways 4464.
Navajo. Library of Congress. AAFS L41.
Music of the American Indians of the Southwest. Folkways P420.
Northwest (Puget Sound). Library of Congress. AAFS L34.

BOOKS

DENSMORE, FRANCES, *Teton Sioux Music,* Bureau of American Ethnology, Bulletin 61, 1918.
KURATH, GERTRUDE P., *Music and Dance of the Tewa Pueblos,* Museum of New Mexico, Research Records no. 8, Museum of New Mexico Press, 1970.
MCALLESTER, DAVID P., *Peyote Music,* Viking Fund Publications in Anthropology, no. 13, 1949.
MERRIAM, ALAN P., *Ethnomusicology of the Flathead Indians,* Aldine, 1967

NORTH AMERICAN INDIAN MUSIC AND TALES

On AFS Records:

Songs from the Iroquois Longhouse (1941). AFS L6.

Seneca Songs from Coldspring Longhouse (1941–45). AFS L17.

Songs of the Chippewa. AFS L22.

Songs of the Sioux. AFS L23. The latter two albums are from the Smithsonian-Densmore Cylinder Collection, recorded 1910–30.

Songs of the Yuma, Cocopa, and Yaqui. AFS L24.

Songs of the Pawnee and Northern Ute. AFS L25.

Songs of the Papago. AFS L31.

Songs of the Nootka and Quileute. AFS L32.

Songs of the Menominee, Mandan and Hidatsa. AFS L33.

The next eleven albums were recorded and edited by Willard Rhodes, 1940–52:
Northwest. AFS L34. Puget Sound tribes.
Kiowa. AFS L35.
Indian Songs of Today. AFS L36. Sung by children or youth.
Delaware, Cherokee, Choctaw, Creek. AFS L37.
Great Basin: Paiute, Washo, Ute, Bannock, Shoshone. AFS L38.
Plains: Comanche, Cheyenne, Kiowa, Caddo, Wichita, Pawnee. AFS L39.
Sioux. AFS L40.
Navajo. AFS L41.
Apache. AFS L42.
Pueblo: Taos, San Ildefonso, Zuni, Hopi. AFS L43.

On ARC Records:

The Ojibwa Choir: Directed by Chief North Star. ARC 254.

On Caedmon Records:

The Fire Plume: Legends of the American Indians Told by Jay Silverheels. Caedmon TC 1451. Edited by John Bierhorst.

Navajo Bird Tales As Told by Hosteen Clah Clee. Caedmon TC 1375. Edited by Franc Johnson Newcomb.

Pueblo Indians: Legends and Stories. Told by Swift Eagle. Caedmon TC 1327.

See also Caedmon's descriptive catalogue.

On Canyon Records:

American Indian Music for the Classroom. Canyon (no serial number). Four albums or cassettes with teacher's guide, duplicating masters of song transcripts, photos, map, and bibliography, compiled by Dr. Louis Ballard.

CASSADORE, PHILIP AND PATSY
Apache Songs. Canyon 6053.

CASSADORE, PHILIP
Apache Songs. Canyon 6056.
More Apache Songs. Canyon 6056.
Traditional Apache Songs. Canyon 6071.

WIND RIVER SINGERS
Social Songs of the Arapaho Sun Dance. Canyon 6080.
Arapaho War Dance Songs and Round Dances. Canyon 6092.

PONEMAH CHIPPEWA SINGERS
War Dance Songs for Pow-wow. Canyon 6082.

PARKER SINGERS
Cree Pow-wow Songs. Canyon 6091.

Hopi Butterfly Dance. Canyon 6072.

Kiowa Forty-nine and Round Dance Songs. Canyon 6087.

Songs from Laguna. Canyon 6058. (Pueblo.)

MESQUAKIE BEAR SINGERS
War Dance Songs. Canyon 6090.

NATAY, ED LEE
_____: *Navajo Singer.* Canyon 6160. Includes songs of other tribes.
_____: *Memories of Navajoland.* Canyon 6057.

Navajo Songs. Canyon 6055.

Traditional Navajo Songs. Canyon 6064.

Navajo Squaw Dance Songs. Canyon 6067.

Navajo Yei-bei-chai Chants. Canyon 6069.

Old-Time Navajo Songs. Canyon 8–6073 (8-track and cassette only).

LEE, ROBERT E.
_____: *Navajo Social Songs.* Canyon 6076.

My Beautiful Land. Canyon 6078. Contemporary Navajo songs.

Native American Church Peyote Ritual. Canyon 6054.

Chants of the Native American Church, vols. 1–3. Canyon 6063, 6068, 6074.

Native American Church Chants: Bright Morning Star Song. Canyon 6075.

Native American Church Religious Songs. Canyon 6083.

Peyote Healing Chants of the Native American Church. Canyon 6094.

Traditional Papago Music. Canyon 6084.

Chicken Scratch: Popular Dance Music of the Indians of Southern Arizona. Canyon 6085. This and the following recording represent dance band music of European derivation.

Chicken Scratch: Elvin Kelly y los Reyes; The Molinas. Canyon 6093.

AMOS RICHARDS
. . . and His Group: Songs from the Pima. Canyon 6066.

Pueblo Indian Songs from San Juan. Canyon 6065.

The Song of the Indian: A Collection. Canyon 6050.

Sioux Favorites. Canyon 6059.

Songs of the Sioux. Canyon 6062.

FORT KIPP SIOUX SINGERS
War Dance Songs. Canyon 6079.

HORNCLOUD, WILLIAM
Sioux Rabbit Songs. Canyon 6081.

Sioux Grass Songs and Round Dances. Canyon 6086.

Zuni Ceremonial Prayers. Canyon 6090.

Summer Songs from Zuni. Canyon 6077.

Great Plains Singers. Canyon 6052.

Plains Pow-wow. Canyon 6088.

Crow Celebration. Canyon 6089.

PAT KENNEDY AND SINGERS
From the Land of the Blackfeet. Canyon 6095.

The Denver Indian Singers. Canyon 6096.

Pezhin Wachipi (Sioux Grass Dance). Canyon 6097.

Papago Dance Songs. Canyon 6098.

Yaqui Music of the Pascola and Deer Dance. Canyon 6099.

Fort Kipp Singers: Montana Grass Songs. Canyon 6101.

PATSY CASSADORE
I Build the Wickiup. Canyon 6102. Apache social songs.

Kiowa Gourd Dance Songs. Canyon 6103.

Pow-wow Songs from Rocky Boy, Montana. Canyon 6104.

Stick Game Songs (Salish and Kootenai). Canyon 6105.

Chippewa Grass Dance Songs. Canyon 6106.

Hopi Social Dance Songs. Canyon 6107.

BALA-SINEM CHOIR (Colorado)
American Indian Songs and Chants. Canyon 6110.

Kyi-yo Pow-wow. Canyon 6111.

Sisseton-Wahpeton Songs (Sioux). Canyon 6112.

The following albums, not on the Canyon label, are available from Canyon:

BENNETT, KAY
Kaibah.
Songs from the Navajo Nation.

ORTEGA, A. PAUL
Two Worlds.

XIT An inter-tribal rock group whose songs are concerned with Indian awareness.
Plight of the Redman.
Silent Warrior.

See also Canyon's descriptive catalogue.

On Everest Records:

Authentic Music of the American Indian. Everest SDBR 3450 3/B (3-rec. set).
   Vol. 1, *War Dances and Honor Songs*.

Vol. 2, *Social and Folk Songs.*
Vol. 3, *Ceremonial Songs and Chants.*
This series represents the music of the following tribes: Cheyenne, Ponca, Sioux, Arikora, Omaha, Taos, Kiowa, Navajo, Crow, Pawnee, Shawnee, Tewa, Plains, Apache, Ute, Pima, Papago, Zuni, Hopi, Paiute.

On Folkways Records:

American Indian Dances. Folkways 6510.

Eskimos of Hudson Bay and Alaska. Folkways 4444.

Eskimo Songs from Alaska. Folkways 4069.

Healing Songs of the American Indians. Folkways 4251.

Hopi Children's Tales (in English). Folkways 7778.

Hopi Katcina Songs and Chants. Folkways 4394.

Indian Music of the Canadian Plains. Folkways 4464.

Indian Music of the Pacific Northwest Coast. Folkways 4523.

Indian Music of the Southwest. Folkways 8850.

Kiowa Music. Folkways 4393.

Kiowa Peyote Meeting. Folkways 4601 (3-rec. set).

Music of the Alaska Kutchin Indians. Folkways 4070.

Music of the Algonkians. Folkways 4253.

Music of the Pawnee. Folkways 4334.

Music of the Plains Apache. Folkways 4252.

Mushroom Ceremony of the Mazatec Indians. Folkways 8975.

Music of the American Indians of the Southwest. Folkways 4420.

Music of the Sioux and Navajo. Folkways 4401.

Nootka Music. Folkways 4524.

North American Indian and Eskimo Music. Folkways 4541 (2-rec. set).

Songs and Dances of the Flathead Indian. Folkways 4445.

Songs and Dances of the Great Lakes Indians. Folkways 4003.

Songs of the Seminole Indians. Folkways 4383.

War Whoops and Medicine Songs. Folkways 4381.

Washo Peyote Songs. Folkways 4384.

Yaqui Dances. Folkways 6957.

On Indian House Records:

Round Dance Songs of the Taos Pueblo, vols. 1–2. Indian House 1001, 1002.

Taos Round Dance, parts 1 and 2. Indian House 1003, 1004.

Ditch-Cleaning and Picnic Songs of Picuris Pueblo. Indian House 1051.

Turtle Dance Songs of San Juan Pueblo. Indian House 1101.

Cloud Dance Songs of San Juan Pueblo. Indian House 1102.

Zuni Fair. Indian House 1401.

Navajo Sway Songs. Indian House 1501.

Night and Daylight Yeibichei (Navajo). Indian House 1502.

Navajo Skip Dance and Two-Step Songs. Indian House 1503.

Navajo Round Dance. Indian House 1504.

Navajo Gift Songs and Round Dance. Indian House 1505.

War Dance Songs of the Ponca, vols. 1–2. Indian House 2001, 2002.

Ponca Peyote Songs, vols. 1–3. Indian House 2005, 2006, 2007.

Comanche Peyote Songs, vols. 1–2. Indian House 2401, 2402.

Handgame of the Kiowa, Kiowa Apache, and Comanche, vols. 1–2. Indian House 2501, 2502.

Kiowa Forty-Nine War Expedition Songs. Indian House 2505.

Kiowa Church Songs, vols. 1–2. Indian House 2506, 2507.

Songs of the Muskogee Creek, vols. 1–2. Indian House 3001, 3002.

Blackfoot A-1 Club Singers, vols. 1–2. Indian House 4001, 4002.

Old Agency Singers of the Blood Reserve, vols. 1–2. Indian House 4051, 4052.

Sounds of Indian America: Plains and Southwest. Indian House 9501.

Pueblo Songs of the Southwest. Indian House 9502.

See also the Indian House descriptive catalogue.

On Iroqrafts:

Iroquois Social Dance Songs, 3 vols. Iroqrafts.

On Redpath Records:

Taos Pueblo Round Dance. Redpath R-1.

Bad Lands Singers: Assiniboine-Sioux Grass Dance. Redpath R-2.

Ashland Singers. Redpath R-3.

Klagetoh Maiden Singers: Navajo Dances. Redpath R-4.

On Soundchiefs:

Songs of the Redmen. Soundchiefs (no number). Plains Tribes.

On TRP:

PETE CONCHA
Taos Indian Songs. Taos TRP-1 (7 inch LP).
More Taos Indian Songs. Taos TRP-7 (7 inch LP).

RAMOS, DURAN, AND PAT MARTINEZ
Picuris Indian Songs. TRP-5 (7 inch LP).
So These Won't Be Forgotten. TRP-121 (12 inch LP). Picuris dance songs and one fiddle instrumental.

See also TRP's descriptive catalogue.

Available from University of Washington Press:

Alaskan Eskimo Songs and Stories. University of Washington Press #902. Forty-two songs (in Eskimo) and stories (in English), collected in the field, 1950–64. Includes fifty-page booklet with background, texts, translations, and transcriptions.

CHICANO MUSIC
by Philip Sonnichsen

The term "Chicano" can be said to have two applications at the present time. The first, and perhaps most appropriate, refers to those Americans of Mexican descent who have a concern for their cultural heritage and their political and economic role in the United States. In the second definition, the term applies to all Mexican-Americans. A sizable proportion of Mexican-Americans, however, oppose ethnic labels and prefer to be regarded simply as Americans. Other individuals, usually more recent immigrants who for various reasons have had difficulty assimilating and adopting English as a functional second language, regard themselves as Mexicanos.

Because this discography is concerned with giving an overall impression of the music of the Mexican-American —as distinct from recordings of traditional or commercial Mexican music—the second definition will be the criterion

for inclusion. Although this volume is ostensibly devoted to folk traditions, I have chosen to mention certain commercial traditions, in part due to the problem of defining what is folk and what is not, and also to provide more of an overall view. Hence Chicano "salsa" as well as rock groups are included.

Mexican-Americans over the past fifty years have been quite prolific in terms of their recording output. Single records at 78 and 45 r.p.m. run well into the thousands. Many of these have been released on "one-shot" labels— labels that, for economic or other reasons, have been limited to the release of one or perhaps a very limited number of records in relatively small quantities. These have not been included here because of their general unavailability. With a few exceptions, this somewhat selective list has been limited to available long-playing, 33 r.p.m. recordings, although a few 45 r.p.m. recordings have been included because of their importance. A few out-of-print recordings have also been included because of their particular significance and the hope that they will be reissued.

Mexican-Americans comprise our second largest minority, and have located themselves in all fifty states. Their numbers in each state vary, depending on historical, political, and economic considerations. The roots of Chicano culture, however, are found along the *frontera,* the United States–Mexican border, and in those southwestern states with relatively heavy concentrations of Mexican-Americans. The heaviest concentrations are found in three regions: northern New Mexico and Colorado, the lower Texas–Mexican border from Del Rio to Brownsville, and the area frequently referred to as Aztlán—from El Paso west through southern New Mexico, southern Arizona, and the rich agricultural land of California—an area culturally centered in Los Angeles.

Of these three, the northern New Mexico area is the oldest and the one where a Hispanic way of life is frequently evident. Many residents of the area trace their heritage back to the Spanish settlement expedition of Juan de Oñate in 1598. This heritage is reflected in the recordings issued by Taos Recordings and Cantemos Records.

Cleofes Vigil has preserved the *alabado* (unaccompanied religious praise song) in *Buenos Días, Paloma Blanca, Five Alabados of Northern New Mexico* (Taos Recordings and Publications, Taos, N.M. 87571, with jacket notes) and in *New Mexican Alabados* (Taos Recordings, 7-inch LP, notes). *Meliton M. Trujillo sings Taos Spanish Songs* (Taos Recordings, 7-inch LP, notes) is a collection of folk songs of the area. Two instrumental recordings include *Bailes de Taos,* Spanish colonial dances played by Los Charros—Francisco Vallejos, violin, and Rafael Martinez, guitar (Taos Recordings, 7-inch LP, notes)—and *Taos Matachines Music,* Adolfo Fresquez, violin, and Tranquilino Lucero, guitar (Taos Recordings, 7-inch LP, notes).

Jenny Wells Vincent has issued two ten-inch long-playing records, voice and guitar, on the Cantemos label: *Spanish Folksongs of the Americas* (Cantemos Records, P.O. Box 246, Taos, N.M. 87571, notes) and the delightful *Folksongs for Children of All Ages* (Cantemos Records, notes).

The albums include songs from Argentina, Puerto Rico, Costa Rica, Peru, and Mexico as well as New Mexico and the southwest.

Vicente Saucedo, 10127 Paseo del Norte, N.W., Albuquerque, N.M. 87114, has released *Poemas de Luz y Sombra* and an instrumental album, *Vicente Plays.*

Alex J. Chávez, a music professor formerly with the University of New Mexico and presently teaching in Colorado, has released two recordings (voice and guitar) of folk material from northern New Mexico and Colorado: *Duermote Niño* (Century Records) and *El Testamento* (Century Records). Order from Alex J. Chávez, Fine Arts Department, Adams State College, Alamosa, Colo. 81101.

Of historical interest are two recordings issued by Folkways and one issued by the Library of Congress. Although these albums contain very worthwhile material, the recording quality is poor by contemporary standards.

Folk Music of New Mexico. Folkways FE 4426. Songs and dances of Mexican and New Mexican origin, with notes. Contains a variety of material recorded by J. D. Robb from 1946 through 1951. Included are "Matachines Dances," "Polka," "La luna se va metiendo," and others.

Folk Music U.S.A. Folkways FE 4530 (2-rec. set). A sampler of folk music from various sections of the United States, with introduction to the notes by Charles Edward Smith. Of interest here are two cuts: "Siete leguas" ("Seven Leagues"), the famous narrative of Pancho Villa's horse as sung by the well-known New Mexican artist Peter Hurd (recorded by J. D. Robb, 1956), and "Matachines Dance" (recorded by Robb in 1949).

Bahaman Songs, French Ballads and Dance Tunes, Spanish Religious Songs and Game Songs. AFS L5 (LP) or AFS 21–25 (5-rec. set, 78's). An interesting anthology edited by Alan Lomax. The last section contains the following: "Songs from Los Pastores," sung by Franquilino Miranda and a group at Cotulla, Texas, recorded by John A. and Alan Lomax in 1934; "Songs from El niño perdido," sung by Ricardo Archuleta at Cerro, New Mexico, recorded by Juan B. Rael in 1940; "El tecolote" (Spanish-American ring game), sung by Ricardo Archuleta at Cerro, New Mexico, recorded by Juan B. Rael in 1940; "La batalla del ojo de agua" (corrido), sung by José Suarez at Brownsville, Texas, recorded by John A. and Ruby T. Lomax in 1939; and "Mexican Children's Games," sung by Josephine Gonzáles, Aurora Gonzáles, Pearl Menchaco, Adela Flores, and Belia Trujillo at San Antonio, Texas, recorded by John A. and Alan Lomax in 1934.

The New Mexico area has, in recent years, become a growing force in the pop music industry, largely through the efforts of Al "Hurricane" Sanchez and his brothers, Tiny Morrie and Baby Gaby. The August 5, 1974, issue of *Newsweek* discussed *La Onda Chicana* (The Chicano Wave) in an article in which Albuquerque was described as the Nashville of Spanish-American music. Many Chicano pop artists have long resented what they feel is a negative attitude on the part of record promoters in Mexico toward supporting Spanish-language musical efforts north of the border. However, Tiny Morrie's single "No Hay Amor" made the "charts" in Mexico in mid-1974 in addition to selling over 90,000 copies in the United States. The San-

Fiesta in Taos, New Mexico

chez family's Hurricane label (1927 Mateo, N.E., Albuquerque, N.M. 87110) includes over seventy 45 r.p.m. singles (mostly Spanish, some English) and fourteen LP's. The albums are:

ARCHIBEQUE, MIGUEL
Miguel Archibeque canta sus favoritas canciones. Hurricane HS 10006.
La Voz Inolvidable. Hurricane HS 10011.
¡Aquí está!. Hurricane HS 10017.

GABY, BABY
Baby Gaby canta Pepito y otras. Hurricane HS 10013.

GARCIA, NENA
Nena García, La Rancherita con Los Reyes de Albuquerque. Hurricane HS 10005.

HURRICANE, AL
Mi Saxophone. Hurricane HS 10001.
Canciones del alma. Hurricane HS 10008.
Sigue cantando. Hurricane HS 10009.
Corridos canta Al Hurricane. Hurricane HS 10012.
Instrumentales con Al Hurricane. Hurricane HS 10014.
Para las madrecitas (with Tiny Morrie). Hurricane HS 10016.

MORRIE, TINY
Lonely Letters. Hurricane HS 10003.
Canciones tristes y alegres. Hurricane HS 10007.
Éxitos de Tiny Morrie. Hurricane HS 10010.
Para las madrecitas (with Al Hurricane). Hurricane HS 10016.
Más éxitos de Tiny Morrie. Hurricane HS 10018.

POHL, GLORIA
Gloria Pohl canta Malas Nuevas y otros éxitos. Hurricane HS 10015.

Bennie Martínez has issued five LP's on his MORE (Minority Owned Record Enterprises, 1205 Lester Drive, N.E., Albuquerque, N.M. 87112) label, three of these being devoted to his sixteen-year-old daughter, Debbie "La Chicanita" Martínez.

MARTINEZ, DEBBIE "LA CHICANITA"
Una pobre también. MORE 0835.
La Chicanita, Debbie Martínez, vol. II. MORE 0804.
Un retrato de Debbie. MORE 0806.

MARTINEZ, LORENZO, Y SUS VIOLINES
El redondo largo. MORE 0827.

STANLEY Y SU GUITARRA
————. MORE 0805. Spanish-English instrumentals.

G. G. Hardin oversees Christy and Casa Nova labels at 900 Fourth Street, S.W., Albuquerque, N.M. 87102. His LP releases on Christy are as follows:

BROWN, FREDDIE
Boracho perdido. Christy Records CR 5003.
El sensationál. Christy Records CR 5008.
El versátil. Christy Records CR 5012.

CHAPULTEPEC TRIO
Ground Explosion. Christy Records CR 5009.

CHAVEZ, NATO
El monarca del acordeón. Christy records CR 5014.

CHAVOS, LOS
Corazón vagabundo. Christy Records CR 5013.

DIMAS, EDDIE
El mosquito. Christy Records CR 5007.

GARCIA, NENA
Vuelve—La Rancherita. Christy Records CR 5006.

MANNY AND THE CASANOVAS
Otra vez. Christy Records CR 5010.

The following LP's are on Casa Nova Records:

CHAPULTEPEC TRIO
Una lágrima. Casa Nova Records LP 103.
Lloren guitarras lloren. Casa Nova Records LP 105.

CHAVEZ, GENOVEVA
Genoveva Chávez canta. Casa Nova Records LP 108.

HUAPANGUEROS, LOS
La Virgen Guadalupana. Casa Nova Records LP 109.

LITTLE RALPH'S COMBO
Los Moranitas. Casa Nova Records LP 102.

MAGOS, LOS
Echenle un quinto al piano. Casa Nova Records LP 104.

PURPLE HAZE, THE
Viejo el viento. Casa Nova Records LP 106.

TINO Y VANGIE
Corazón de mi vida. Casa Nova Records LP 107.

On Del Norte Records (P.O. Box 6021, Albuquerque, N.M. 87107), Bennie Martínez has the following LP's available:

GAVILANES, LOS TREMENDOS
————. Del Norte Records DN 1417.

MARTINEZ, BENNIE
Polkas y mas. Del Norte Records DN 793.

NICK AND JANE
Un regalo no mas. Del Norte Records DN 797.
Nick and Jane—Corridos y rancheras. Del Norte Records DN 1415.

Herman Martínez, a well-known recording engineer in Albuquerque, has recently begun his own label, Alta Vista Records (P.O. Box 6021, Albuquerque, N.M. 87107). His releases include:

CHAVOS, LOS
Para ustedes. Alta Vista Records AV 8889.
Alta Vista Presents Los Chavos. Alta Vista Records AV 8891.

COMPANIA, LA
La Compañía. Alta Vista Records AV 8892.

MANNY AND THE CASANOVAS
Manny and the Casanovas. Alta Vista Records AV 8890.

THE PURPLE HAZE
The Purple Haze. Alta Vista Records AV 8888.

Alta Vista has also released the following anthology:

The Artists of the Southwest. Alta Vista Records AV 8893.

Roberto Griego has released *Un pobre no mas* on his own label, RJG Records. This record, under number GL 2121, may be ordered from the artist at 2118 Anthony Lane, S.W., Albuquerque, N.M. 87105.

New Mexico's lieutenant governor, Robert Mondragón, has also recorded, but he has, thus far in his musical-political career, not released an LP album.

Two brothers, Rubén and Vicente Romero, have released an interesting pop-Latin–soft-rock album entitled *Pachuco* (Eagle LPS 3132), with a second scheduled for release in 1975 (through Eagle Record Company, P.O. Box 1102, Burbank, Calif. 91507).

In the Denver area, Victor Hernández has produced a number of LP's, including:

GARCIA, CLEM, Y SUS ESTRELLAS
Limoncito azucarado. Infal Records INL 2001.
Clem García y sus estrellas. Charro Records HRS–1005.

Lopez, Baltazar
Adiós a mi novia. Normex Records NX–6001.

Mendoza, Luisa
Luisa Mendoza con el Mariachi de Guadalajara. Charro Records HRS–1003.

Montoya, Eulogio
Polkas al estilo Montóya. Normex Records NX–6003. Order from Infal Records, Inc., 2144 Champa Street, Denver, Colo. 80202.

Populares del Norte, Los
Contrabando. Normex Records NX–6000.

Sauceda, Charlie
Charlie Sauceda y Los Flamingos. Charro Records HRS–1004.

Zuniga, Edelmiro
Amor de mis amores. Normex Records NX–6002.

Infal Records has also released *El Movimiento Chicano* (Infal Records INL 2002) as sung by Los Alvarados, Manuel, Emilia, y Ramón. Text and translations for the songs are included. Poetry copyrights and recording royalties go to Escuela y Colegio Tlatelolco (P.O. Box 18347, Denver, Colo. 80218). The recording may be ordered from Escuela y Colegio Tlatelolco or Infal Records, Inc. It is unfortunate that no writer credit is given for the lead song on the album, "Yo soy Chicano," frequently referred to as the theme song of the Chicano movement. The words were written by Juanita Domínguez (while riding on a bus to the Poor People's Campaign in Washington, D.C., in 1968) to the tune "La Rielera," a well-known Mexican folk song of railroad workers. La Familia Domínguez is planning an album, *Yo soy Chicano,* to be released in 1976. For further information, write La Familia Domínguez, 3246 Quitman Street, Denver, Colo. 80212.

Rudy García has developed his own label, Rayo Records. With his own modern group he has one LP available, *Rudy Garcia y Los Rayos* (Rayo 1003), from Rayo Record Co., 390 St. Paul Street, Denver, Colo. 80206.

The lower Texas Mexican border from Laredo south to Brownsville and from San Antonio to Monterrey, Nuevo León, is the home of a unique style known as *norteño* (from the north). The *norteño* style, which had its beginnings around the turn of the century, is, in the opinion of this writer, the only uniquely Chicano folk style as well as Mexico's last regional folk style. Borrowing the single-row button accordion from German and Bohemian immigrants, the Mexicanos in South Texas developed regional *conjuntos* known as Conjunto Polkeros, a name derived from the polka, the dance music which dominated their style (the waltz, mazurka, and schottische were also popular during the early years). Later the regional identification *(norteño)* became the identifying trademark. During the fifties contrasts in vocal and instrumental style became apparent; generally speaking, the groups below the border retained

the *norteño* identification while many of those above the border (usually the younger groups) became known as Tex-Mex. Although instrumentation remained the same on both sides of the border, in the *Tejano* style, there was more emphasis on instrumental technique and less on vocal style and text. By this time the single-row accordion had been replaced by a three-row button model, supported by bajo sexto, a large rhythm-bass guitar. These two instruments form the duo for which the region is famous. Larger groups include an upright bass (frequently with only three strings) and, for dances, a saxophone (usually an E alto) and a dance drum set. During the sixties many Tex-Mex musicians began looking to American popular music for new ideas. The electric organ replaced the accordion, the electric guitar took over the bajo sexto's role, and the electric bass replaced the acoustic stand-up model. As the groups expanded in size, brass instruments were added. Yet certain elements of the older style were retained, particularly the rhythmic stress on the off-beat.

Chris Strachwitz of Arhoolie and Folk-Lyric Records (Box 9195, Berkeley, Calif. 94709) has taken a strong interest in the historic development of this style. In the notes to his album *Texas-Mexican Border Music,* vol. 1, *An Introduction 1930–1960* (Folk-Lyric 9003), he describes the *norteño* as the music of ". . . a vast and remote region with its soul in Monterrey, Nuevo León, and its pocketbook in San Antonio, Texas! This is the music of the field hands who harvest the citrus crops, onions, carrots, and spinach along the rich bottomlands of the murky Rio Grande." This introductory album in Strachwitz's Folk-Lyric series is a reissue of old 78 r.p.m. recordings which give a historical overview of music along the border. Five albums are currently available in this series with additional albums planned:

Texas-Mexican Border Music, An Introduction: 1930–1960. Folk-Lyric 9003.
Texas-Mexican Border Music—Corridos, Part I. Folk-Lyric 9004. *Corridos* (ballads) of particular historic significance selected by Strachwitz, with a booklet by this writer; includes texts, translations, photographs, and considerable historical material.
Texas-Mexican Border Music—Corridos, Part II. Folk-Lyric 9005.
Texas-Mexican Border Music—Norteño Accordion. Folk-Lyric 9006. Reissues of the original 78 r.p.m. records made by the accordion players who created and developed the style from the 1920's through the 1950's.
Texas-Mexican Border Music—The String Bands. Folk-Lyric 9007. Reissues of a number of string styles using violin, mandolin, guitar, steel guitar, bajo sexto, and bass. The songs feature duet and group singing.

Strachwitz also plans an extended series on contemporary artists working within the tradition. Two albums have been released thus far:
Los Pingüinos del Norte. Arhoolie 3002. With accordion, six-string acoustic guitar, and bass. Singing *corridos* from the Rio Grande Valley, all recorded at a *cantina* (tavern) in Piedras Negras, Coahuila. Texts, translations, and notes are provided.
Trio San Antonio. Arhoolie 3004. A *conjunto* (group), fea-

turing accordion, bajo sexto, and bass, performs a variety of songs and dance tunes. Notes.

Over the past forty years, hundreds of *norteño* discs have been pressed and released. Many have had very limited pressings; others are practically impossible to obtain outside the lower border area. The following list of artists and labels is, therefore, at best a general guide largely based on a discography prepared by Strachwitz in his booklet to the *Texas-Mexican Border Music* introductory album (Folk-Lyric 9003). Many of the artists mentioned below are extremely prolific and have recorded for more than one label. With many labels record availability varies with the part of the country, and ordering by mail is not always satisfactory. It is frequently more expedient to work through a distributor. The following is a guide to the more popular groups.

Three of the most popular *conjuntos* are Los Relámpagos del Norte (Ramón Ayala and Cornelio Reyna—now disbanded: Ayala has joined Monterrey-based Los Bravos del Norte; Reyna has turned to acting and performing with a Mexico City *mariachi*); Los Tremendos Gavilanes (Juan Torres and Salomón Prado—they are also known as Los Gavilanes de Monterrey but should not be confused with other groups such as Los Famosos Gavilanes or Los Gavilanes del Norte); and Los Alegres de Terán (Euginio Ábrego and Tomás Ortíz). A good introduction to these well-known groups might be *Lo mejor de Los Alegres de Teran*, vols. 1–3 (Falcón GLP 01, 02, 03) (Falcón Records, 821 North 23rd Street, McAllen, Texas 78501). Other important artists include:

Conjunto Aguila *(norteño)*
Pedro Ayala *(norteño)*
Hermanos Banda *(norteño)*
Conjunto Bernal (Tex-Mex)
Los Bravos del Norte *(norteño)*
Los Broncos de Reynosa *(norteño)*
Carlos y José *(norteño)*
Los Costeños del Valle *(norteño)*
Los Cuatreros de Sonora *(norteño)*
Tony de la Rosa (Tex-Mex)
Los Donneños *(norteño)*
Los Dos Norteños *(norteño)*
Dueto Estrella *(norteño)*
Los Halcones del Salitrillo *(norteño)*
Los Huracanes *(norteño)*
Flaco Jiménez (Tex-Mex)
Santiago Jiménez (Tex-Mex)
Los Madrugadores *(norteño)*
Narciso Martínez (Tex-Mex)
Los Norteños de Nueva Laredo *(norteño)*
El Paloma y el Gorrión (Tex-Mex)
Los Pavos Reales (Tex-Mex)
Los Rancheros del Norte *(norteño)*
Los Rayos del Alamo *(norteño)*
Los Regionales de Texas (Tex-Mex)
El Conjunto Tamaulipas *(norteño)*
Los Tigres del Norte (Tex-Mex)

Lydia Mendoza dominates as the solo female singer of the lower border. Her recordings date from 1928, initially, with her parents, as the Cuarteto Carta Blanca. Two examples of her early work are available: "Pero hay que triste," a *canción* (song) originally recorded in San Antonio in 1934, has been reissued on the *Texas-Mexican Border Music* introductory album. Another example from 1934 is "María María," Lydia Mendoza and the Cuarteto Mendoza (María, Leonor, and Francisco), currently available on *Songs of Love, Courtship, and Marriage*, edited by Richard K. Spottswood, a Library of Congress recording (LBC–2). Spottswood is currently editing an RCA Bluebird disc to be devoted entirely to Lydia's early recordings. Release is scheduled for 1976. More recent recordings include *Lydia Mendoza, la alondra de la frontera* (Norteño no. 809), *Lydia Mendoza y su guitarra de oro* (Norteño no. 812), and *Lydia Mendoza* (Norteño no. 817). She shares an album with San Antonio singer Rita Vidaurrie, *20 Exitos de Siempre* (Norteño International NRC 204). Norteño Records are available from 2606 Ruiz Street, San Antonio, Texas 78228.

Perhaps the most prolific writer of *corridos* dealing with contemporary subjects is José Morante, known as "El rey del corrido." He is heard singing his own *corridos* (as well as traditional *corridos* and those of other writers) with his group, Los Conquistadores, in *Corridos y tragedias del siglo 20*, vol. 1 (Norteño no. 803); *Corridos y tragedias del siglo 20*, vol. II (Norteño no. 805); *El rey del corrido*, vol. III (Norteño no. 815); *Yo soy el corrido* (Norteño no. 820); and *Los Asesinos* (Sombrero SO–2009). Sombrero Records are also available from 2606 Ruiz Street, San Antonio, Texas 78228.

One Chicano singer stands alone in the country and western field, Johnny Rodríguez. Popular in both Chicano and Anglo circles, his albums include:

All I Ever Meant to Do Was Sing. Mercury SRM I-686.
Introducing Johnny Rodríguez. Mercury S-61378.
My Third Album. Mercury SRM I-699.
Songs About Ladies and Love. Mercury SR I-1012.
Just Get Up and Close the Door. Mercury SRM I-1032.

The one Tex-Mex singer who has broken into the Anglo market without losing his Chicano identity is a thirty-nine-year-old singer from San Benito, Texas, Freddy Fender. When asked why he changed his name from Baldemar Huerta, Fender replied, ". . . it was much easier for a gringo to drop a dime in the juke if the artist's name was Freddy Fender." (*Picking Up the Tempo*, no. 1, April, 1975.) Over the last twenty years Fender has cut seven albums and over one hundred singles, including the 1959 standard "Wasted Days and Wasted Nights." However, it took 1975 and a bilingual hit entitled "Before the Next Teardrop Falls" to make Freddy Fender a nationally known pop-country and western singer. That hit single has now been incorporated into an album, *Before the Next Teardrop Falls*, on ABC Dot Records (DOSD 2020).

Texas also abounds with a variety of contemporary Latin groups, generally with a Tex-Mex image, including Sunny and the Sunliners (Keyloc Records), Freddie Martínez (Freddie Records), Joe Bravo (El Zarape Records), The

Royal Jesters (G.C.P.—Guerra Company Productions), Little Joe and the Latinaires (El Zarape Records), and Little Joe and La Familia (Buena Suerte Records).

A young black singer creating a place for himself in the Spanish-speaking Chicano market is Bobby "El Charro Negro" Butler. Born in St. Louis, he moved to Texas, joining Little Joe's (Joe Hernández') Latinaires group in 1962. His own album, *El Papalote,* has been released on Buena Suerte Records (#1002).

The record industry in California dates from the twenties. But as is true of the record industry in Texas, countless early 78 rpm recordings (acoustic and electrical processes) have been broken or lost. Some documentation is presently available in the two volumes of *corridos* in the *Texas Mexican Border Music.*

During the thirties, forties, and fifties, one Chicano singer was unique among his contemporaries, partly because of his voice but largely because of his ideas and flexibility. His ability to adapt musical styles to changing musical tastes and the mood of his audience is perhaps unparalleled among Chicanos of his generation. Edward "Lalo" Guerrero began his career on record with the Trio Imperial (on Imperial Records) and later sang with a variety of *mariachi* and pop groups. Although he has issued well over one hundred singles and a number of albums, not all of his material is presently available. His *Christmas Songs with Lalo Guerrero* contains parodies and original material—"Pancho Claus," "Tacos for Two," "Mario from the Barrio," and "Elvis Pérez"—that are classics within the Chicano tradition (45 rpm, extended play available from L & M Records, P.O. Box 734, Monterey Park, Calif. 91754).

From a more contemporary perspective, no recording has had wider impact than *¡Viva la causa!—Songs and Sounds from the Delano Strike.* In 1965 the Mexicanos and Filipinos working in the vineyards around Delano, California, began the first *huelga* (grape strike), which led to the formation of César Chávez's United Farmworkers Union. The success of that first strike can, in part, be attributed to Luis Valdéz, his brother Danny Valdéz, Felipe Cantú, and Agustín Lira. Their farmworkers' theater (Teatro Campesino) and the songs that they wrote and sang generated the kind of response among farmworkers that made the term *huelga* synonymous with the principles for which Chávez has long fought. Today the plight of farmworkers is of national concern. The album *¡Viva la causa! —Songs and Sounds from the Delano Strike* presents the material—the songs that brought unity to a movement along with the sounds that resulted from that unity. The album is presently out of print, but may be re-recorded and re-released on the Menyah label by El Centro Campesino Cultural (parent organization for El Teatro Campesino), P.O. Box 1278, San Juan Bautista, Calif. 95045).

Two of the most effective Chicano songs ever recorded are "El Louie" and "The Ballad of Richard Campos." "El Louie," written in Spanish, English, and *calo* (something of a cross between Spanish and English with added words), is a setting of a poem by José Montoya which discusses the life of a Pachuco from Fresno, California. The music and highly effective arrangement are by Luis Valdéz. "The Ballad of Richard Campos," written and sung in English by Danny Valdéz, is an important statement on the Vietnam War. It tells the story of a young Chicano, killed in Vietnam, whose body was returned to the United States, where it remained unclaimed in the Oakland, California, railroad station.

Los Pingüinos del Norte

Danny was responsible for locating the next of kin (a farm-worker) and for telling the story. This recording is also out of print but is scheduled for reissue on the Menyah label.

Danny Valdéz has done one highly recommended album for A&M Records, entitled *Mestizo* (A&M SP–3622), which is available commercially or direct from El Centro Campesino Cultural. Eight of the songs are in English, three in Spanish. "Primavera" (the season of spring), written for his daughter of the same name, is one of the most beautiful songs in this writer's experience.

La Carpa de Rasquachis, music of the popular tent show of the Teatro Campesino, is scheduled for release on the Menyah label in the summer of 1975.

South American–born Suni Paz has become one of this hemisphere's most effective voices against oppression. Her album *Brotando del silencio* ("Breaking Out of the Silence") for Paredon Records (Box 889, Brooklyn, N.Y. 11202) contains fourteen protest songs, including "Corrido de Aztlán" by Danny Valdéz. Notes, text transcriptions, and translations are included in an enclosed booklet.

Miguel Barragan has recorded *¡Adelante!* ("Onward!") for Bronze Artists label. Each song is prefaced on the recording by a brief commentary in English. In addition, the record contains a booklet with texts and translations. The songs on side A relate directly to the Chicano struggle. In introducing side B, Barragan states that "La Raza preaches not ethnic racism but the promotion of human values and cultural worth to build a healthy multi-colored nation . . ." The songs on side B, including material by Phil Ochs and Bob Dylan, have been chosen to reflect "this spirit of true brotherhood." (Available from Manuel Barragan, 8747 Santa Fe Drive, Denver, Colo. 80229.)

California has produced a number of Latin-oriented groups, many with substantial followings. One of the most successful is that of Ray Camacho, originally with the Texas-based Falcón label, now recording on his own California Artists label (California Artists Corporation, P.O. Box 11474, Fresno, Calif. 93773).

The International Ray Camacho and the Teardrops. California Artists CAC 1001.
Los Reyes del Ritmo. California Artists CAC 1002.
Para los Chicanos. California Artists CAC 1003.
The International Ray Camacho. California Artists CR 1004.
Salsa Chicana. California Artists CR 1005.

Of the many Mexican regional styles, only the Jalisco *mariachi* has transcended regional and national boundaries. The Mexican *mariachi* has become world-famous, and dozens of *mariachis* (the term designates the style, the group, and the individual musician) have crossed the border and settled in urban and rural areas throughout the United States. By reputation, undoubtedly the most successful group of this type in the United States is Los Angeles–based Los Camperos de Nati Cano, which play nightly at their own nightclub, La Fonda de Los Camperos (2501 Wilshire Boulevard, Los Angeles, Calif. 90057). The group's records (not readily available outside the Los Angeles area) include:

Puro Mariachi—Los Camperos. Indigo Records IND-LP 501.
North of the Border. Cariño Records DBL 1–5117.
José Alfredo Jiménez (with Los Camperos). Aguila Records AM 1200.
Arriba. Listo Records SLP 2001.
El super mariachi Los Camperos. Discos Latin Internacional DLIS 2003.
Valses de amor de Silvestre Rodríguez. La Fonda Records LF 1001 (with notes by Manuel S. Acuña).

Four pop singers deserve mention. Although none of the four would be cast as Chicano, each is, at least in part, of Mexican extraction. Andy Russell has been singing the longest and presently has one album on the market. Vikki Carr has recorded fourteen albums, including songs in Spanish. Joan Baez is perhaps the most prolific, with twenty-nine albums to her credit, including one devoted exclusively to Spanish-language songs. Dallas-born Trini López made his mark in California and has recorded three albums to date.

Mexican-born composer Manuel S. Acuña has made Los Angeles his home for many years. He has written well over one hundred songs (all in Spanish), some of which have become standards in the Mexican popular repertory. Four of these songs are currently available on LP's. "Alma Angelina" (written for his daughter) is available on *David Reynoso con el trio Los Mexicanos* (Caytronics CYS 1321), and "Reconciliación" is sung by the late Javier Solis in the album *Y todavía te quiero* (Columbia EX 5196). Acuña's "Mis ojos me denuncian" is available on two albums, *Orquideas vocales por María Luisa Landin* (RCA MKS 2009) and an album by the popular vocal group Los Dandys, *Nosotros,* vol. 5 (RCA MKL 1574). "Solamente tu" is heard on *Miguel Archibeque canta sus favoritas canciones* (Hurricane HS 10006). A new album, devoted entirely to the songs of Acuña, is entitled *Canciones de Manuel S. Acuña* (Discos CSAN 61075) and features Los Angeles Mariachi Chapala on one side; a modern group on the other. Singers include Lalo Guerrero, Gloria Elva, Rosa Rodríguez and Rafael Rosales, Loreto Gamez, Pepe Rolón and Francisco Javier. The album is available from Círculo Social Amigos Nacozarenses, P.O. Box 734, Monterey Park, Calif. 91754.

Many Chicano artists have recorded rock music. The first to "hit the charts" in the sixties was Richie Valens, a very popular singer who died some years ago in a plane crash. His records have long been out of print, but some of his most popular hits have been reissued as part of the nostalgia craze. MGM Records has released the album *Ritchie Valens* (MONO GAS-117) as part of their Golden Archive Series. "La Bomba" (the southern Veracruz Jarocho *son* sung in Spanish, highly stylized) and "Donna" (sung in English) are both on an *Original Oldies,* vol. 11, disc by Springboard International Records, Inc. (1135 West Elizabeth Avenue, Linden, N.J. 07035), or commercially through a record dealer. *Super Oldies of the 60's,* vol. 10 (released by Trip Records through Springboard International), contains "Land of 1000 Dances" by one of East Los Angeles's most popular rock groups, Cannibal and the

Headhunters. "Land of 1000 Dances" also serves as the lead tune for *Thee Midniters on Whittier Blvd.* album. The group's other albums include *Thee Midniters Unlimited* and *Thee Midniters, Love Special Delivery* (all commercially available or from P.O. Box 7152, Los Angeles, Calif. 90022).

East Los Angeles produced a number of rock groups in the sixties. Three albums were released showcasing these groups (all out of print and extremely difficult to obtain): *East Side Review*, vols. 1 and 2 (Rampart Records), and *Chicanos Explode in Concert* (Mares Records). For many of the individuals in these groups, this was a formative period, a period in which individuals and ideas were intermixed. The outgrowth was the formation of a number of the major Chicano rock groups of the seventies, including Tierra, Tango, Yaqui, Macondo, Sapo, Azteca, and El Chicano.

Tierra has made a major statement for the Chicano with "Barrio Suite," perhaps the most significant number in the group's album for 20th Century Records (T-412) entitled *Tierra*. Additional albums are slated for release through Caytronics Corporation.

Tango, recently released through A&M, is the first album for Mark Guerrero (son of "Lalo" Guerrero) (A&M SP 3612). Yaqui is a highly commercial group with one album, *Yaqui*, released through Playboy Records (PB 127). *Macondo* is available on Atlantic Records (SD 7234) and *Sapo* on Bell Records (Bell 1301). Azteca has two records on Columbia, *Azteca* (KC 31776) and *Pyramid of the Moon* (KC 32451). The best-known and best-recorded group is El Chicano with six albums to date: *Viva Tirado* (Kapp KS 3632), *El Chicano Revolución* (Kapp KS 3640), *El Chicano* (MCA 69), *Celebration* (MCA 74), *Cinco* (MCA 401), and *The Best of Everything* (MCA 437). (El Chicano, a Los Angeles-based group, is not to be confused with Los Chicanos, a Mexican group presently recording for RCA.)

The name and dress of the group Redbone suggests an American Indian rock group; however, the four members are Chicanos. They have a number of albums currently available, including the album *Redbone*, which features the hit single "Come and Get Your Love."

Two other rock groups should be mentioned in this survey, the groups of two brothers, both Mexican-born and now living in the San Francisco area. Carlos Santana has developed an international reputation with six albums to date, all on the Columbia label, including:

Santana. Columbia CS 9781.
Santana Abraxas. Columbia KC 30130.
Santana's Greatest Hits. Columbia PC 33050.
Illuminations (with Alice Coltrane). Columbia PC 32900.
Carlos Santana and Buddy Miles Live. (Columbia KC 31308).
Santana Borboletta. Columbia PC 33135.

Carlos's brother, Jorge, has formed his own very well-known group, Malo. The group's four albums are:
Malo. Warner Brothers WBR 2584.
Dos. Warner Brothers WBR 2652.

Evolución. Warner Brothers WBR 2702.
Ascensión. Warner Brothers WBR 2769.

This article is, at best, an introduction to the rich and continuously evolving musical traditions of Mexican Americans. To an ethnomusicologist, much of the excitement in studying this music lies in watching the development of a new culture, a process we study in the historical past but do not associate with the present. Yet the seeds and early sprouts are there. Only time can tell us the general direction and impact Chicanos will have on the dominant Anglo culture.

Three published discographies should be mentioned in conclusion:

CHAVEZ, ALEX, "Recommended Sources for Commercially Available Discs and Field Tape Collections of Chicano Music," Music Library Association *Newsletter*, No. 14, September-October, 1973.

CHILDREN'S MUSIC CENTER, INC. (5373 West Pico Boulevard, Los Angeles, Calif. 90019; 213–937–1825), *Best Records and Books About Spanish Speaking Americans*, 1975 edition.

STRACHWITZ, CHRIS, "A Selected Discography of Currently More-or-Less Available LPs of Texas-Mexican Border Music," in the notes to *Texas-Mexican Border Music*, vol. 1.

A useful bibliography is:

HUERTA, JORGE A., ed., *A Bibliography of Chicano and Mexican Dance, Drama and Music,* 1972, published by Colegio Quetzalcoatl, 1401 Huntswood Way, Oxnard, Calif. 93030.

CANADIAN FOLK MUSIC

Most of the folk music of Canada comes from British and Irish tradition. This is true even of the music of French Canada in regard to instrumental music, for the French-speaking population absorbed the music of many English and Gaelic-speaking settlers. Their music persisted although their language did not, and there are families in Quebec and the Maritimes who carry Scots and Irish surnames but who have not spoken English for generations. The Celtic influence prevailed in instrumental music in particular, but there is an enclave of totally Celtic tradition on Cape Breton Island in northernmost Nova Scotia, rich in pipers and fiddlers, where Scots Gaelic is still sung and spoken.

The fiddle tradition remains strong in Canada, and the button accordion is also used. (Canadian fiddle records are not listed here, though, but in the Fiddle section, page 83.) French influence remains in rural dancing, continental quadrilles, and other circle and set dances rather than in the line dances of British and Celtic origin. But Celtic-derived clog dancing—the predecessor of modern-day tap dancing—is also practiced widely. It goes well with fiddle tunes, and many old-style fiddlers, especially when playing by themselves, sit in a chair and dance clog rhythms with their feet, providing an accompaniment that adds an exciting dimension to their music.

The French instrumental tradition was influenced and almost superseded by Celtic tradition, but did not die out entirely; in fact, it is enjoying a contemporary resurgence of interest due in part to French separatist political sentiments. There was also a French vocal tradition that persisted in a relatively pure form from the days of original French settlement in the 1600's, and this tradition is the subject of the remarkable *Acadie et Québec* recording discussed in Anthologies and Collections, page 54.

British and Irish songs and ballads are still sung in a very pure form, often from family tradition, in the English-speaking rural districts, particularly in Ontario and the Maritimes. In the United States such songs have been subjected to many influences; words persist with minimal change, but melody and style reflect the effects of the use of the guitar, of the development of rural string band style, and of Black American music. This has not been the case in Canada.

A separate section at the end of these listings (page 55) discusses the music of *les chansonniers*, the contemporary singer-songwriters of Quebec. For additional comments on Canadian folk music, see the article by Edith Fowke, page 156. Please note that there exists no Canadian trade catalogue equivalent to Schwann; some of the recordings listed may be out of print and cannot be verified.

ABBOTT, O. J.
Irish and British Songs from the Ottawa Valley. Folkways 4051. Field recordings made by Edith Fowke in 1957. Abbott is an older singer with an extensive repertory of traditional songs and ballads.

BARBEAU, MARIUS
My Life in Recording Canadian-American Folklore. Folkways 3501. A documentary account, with musical examples, of the work of one of the pioneer collectors of Canadian folk song.

BERARD, DENISE
Québec: La Belle Province. Monitor 714.

BLANCHETTE, LOUIS (d. 1969) Blanchette was a virtuoso harmonica player, specializing in up-tempo reels played literally and without much variation. It's most difficult to play this kind of music on the harmonica; Blanchette got an amazingly precise accordionlike sound. These recordings seem to be from about the forties.
Vingt grands succès d'hier. Coral (Canadian) 37008.
Reels. Carnaval 427.

BLONDAHL, OMAR
Famous Songs of Newfoundland. Can. Cavalcade 2001.
The Saga of Newfoundland in Song. Rodeo RLP 5.
Down to the Sea Again. Rodeo RLP 7.
A Visit to Newfoundland. Rodeo RLP 34.
The Great Seal Hunt of Newfoundland. Rodeo RLP 80.
The Roving Newfoundlander. Banff 1142.

LA BOLDUC (Mary Travers, 1894–1941) La Bolduc was a great and immensely popular vaudeville entertainer who used traditional melodies as vehicles for her wry, sarcastic French lyrics. One interesting feature of her strong performances, even for those who can't follow the French, is her use of a sort of French-Canadian equivalent of scat-singing (*see* "lilting," in the Glossary).
Vingt grands succès d'hier. Coral (Canadian) 37000.
Fêtons le mardi gras. Coral (Canadian) 33035.
Encore, encore. Carnaval 464.
Madame Bolduc. Carnaval 450.
Swing la bacquaise. Carnaval 518.
. . . chante La Bolduc. Carnaval 434.
Si vous avez une fille. Carnaval 505.
Le petit sauvage du nord. Carnaval 492.

BRANDON, TOM
The Rambling Irishman. Folk-Legacy FSC-10. Brandon is a Canadian despite the album title, which refers to the fact that he has learned his songs from tradition within his family, which is of Irish descent.

BRUNEAU, PHILIPPE
———— (1973). Philo 2003. French-Canadian dance tunes by a master of the button accordion, a virtuoso without flash. His interest seems to lie more in the French than in the Irish components of the dance music tradition, as reflected in a tendency to keep more to a level four-step time rather than to the livelier two-step time of Irish tradition.

CARTER, WILF
The First Five Sessions (1933–34). CMH 111. Recordings by Canada's first singer of American-style western music, who also recorded as Montana Slim. While his contemporary Hank Snow went on to achieve success in Nashville, Carter pursued a career in Canada; his later commercial recordings are widely available, as are those of other Canadian country-and-western style singers.

CHAMPOUX, PIERRETTE
Les bords du St-Laurent. Esoteric 536.

LES CHANTEURS D'ACADIE
Folklore acadien. Rodeo RLP 30.
Folklore du Canada français. Rodeo RLP 39.
Noël du Canada français. Rodeo RLP 41.

LA CHORALE DE L'UNIVERSITE DE ST-JOSEPH
Folklore canadien. Columbia (Canadian) FL-234.

CJON GLEE CLUB
Newfoundland Folk Songs, vols. 1–2. Rodeo RLP 83-84.

CLARKE, LARENA
A Canadian Garland. Topic 12T140. Ontario folk songs of British origin, from family tradition.

DINELLE, YVES
Les vielles danses à Québec. Dominion (Canadian) 48015. French-Canadian dances on button accordion.

DOBSON, BONNIE
————. Argo (British) ZFB 79. *See also* Contemporary Music section, page 99.

DOYLE, WILF
The Music of Newfoundland. Can. Cavalcade 2012. Smooth dance tunes by a commercial-style band, led by accordion.
Traditional Jigs and Reels of Newfoundland. Rodeo RLP 10.
A Selection of Favorite Newfoundland Old-Time Music. Rodeo RLP 49.

DUCHESNE, TOMMY Duchesne's career parallels that of fiddler Isidore Soucy: he began as a traditional-style accordion player, then moved into a more commercial way of playing as he achieved popularity as an entertainer during the forties.
Vingt grands succès d'hier. Coral (Canadian) 37002.
Dansons. Carnaval 506.

L'ENSEMBLE FOLKLORIQUE DE BAIE ST-PAUL
Portrait du vieux Kébec. Opus 212.

L'ENSEMBLE FOLKLORIQUE DU CANADA
Feux-follets. RCA (Canadian) PCS-1088.

GOELANDS, LES
Canadian Folklore. Select 398.516.

HARE, MARIE
————. Folk-Legacy FSC-9. Clear-voiced versions of unaccompanied ballads and songs, learned by an older singer from family and friends in New Brunswick.

HEMSWORTH, WADE
Folk Songs of the Canadian North Woods. Folkways 6821. Traditional and original songs. Hemsworth, an urban but unpolished singer, has the gift of writing songs that truly sound as if they come out of tradition.

IAN AND SYLVIA. *See* Contemporary Artists, Bands, and Songwriters section, page 122.

JAMES, KAREN. *See* Folk Song Revival section, page 105.

LES JOYEUX COPAINS D'HAWKESBURY
Au pays de l'érable. London (Canadian) MB 7.

KINES, TOM
An Irishman in North America. Folkways 3522.
Folk Songs of Canada. RCA (Canada) PCS 1014.

LABRECQUE, JACQUES Labrecque sings in a trained voice with a rather dramatized style of delivery. It's certainly not a traditional voice, but he's good at what he does; he avoids being obnoxious, a common pitfall for those who try to polish up folk songs.
Chansons populaires de France et du Canada. Folkways 3560. French and French-Canadian songs in solo voice.
Le Canada chante pour vous. Pathé 33AT1029.
Chansons populaires du Canada. London (Canadian) LB 959 (10 inch, OP). With orchestral background scores by a good commercial arranger.

WILLIAM MCCAULEY CHOIR
Canadian Folk Songs. Columbia (Canadian) FL 226.
Noël à Québec. Columbia (Canadian) FL 207.

MCCURDY, ED
Folk Songs of the Canadian Maritimes. Whitehall 850.

MACDONALD, C. F.
Cape Breton Pipe Music. Scheduled for release by Fiddler Records; serial number not available as this book goes to press.

MILLS, ALAN Mills is a polished performer with a nontraditional baritone voice who aims for straightforward but at times overdramatized performances—he's more of a performer than a musician.
Songs of the Maritimes. Folkways 8744.
. . . and Jean Carignan. Folkways 3532.
We'll Rant and We'll Roar: Sea Songs of Newfoundland. Folkways 8771.
French Canadian Folksongs. Folkways 6929.
Canada's Story in Song. Folkways 3000. A history of Canada in English, French, Indian, and Eskimo traditional music.
O Canada. Folkways 3001. A sequel to the above, conceived independently.
. . . with Hélène Baillargeon: Chansons d'Acadie. Folkways 6923.
. . . with Hélène Baillargeon: Duet Songs of French Canada. Folkways 6928.

MUNRO, WALDO
Honky Tonk Down East. Can. Cavalcade 2004.

NOLAN, DICK
I'se Da B'y What Catches Da Fish. Arc 694.

OKUN, MILT
I Sing of Canada. Stinson SLP 71.

OXNER, DIANE
Traditional Folksongs of Nova Scotia. Rodeo RBS 1142. Songs from the Helen Creighton collection.

PEACOCK, KEN
Songs and Ballads of Newfoundland. Folkways 3505.

PHILLIPS, STU
Folk Songs. Can. Cavalcade 2005.

ROY, RAOUL
Folklore, vols. 1–4. Select M298.068, M298.095, SSP24147, SSP24179.

ST. JOHN'S EXTENSION CHOIR OF MEMORIAL UNIVERSITY
Newfoundlanders Sing Songs of Their Homeland. RCA (Canadian) CC1024.

SEEGER, PETE
Champlain Valley Songs. Folkways 5210. Vermont and Quebec songs from the Marjorie Porter Collection of North Country Folklore.

SVEEN, OLAF
Western Canadian Polkas. Can. Cavalcade 2013.

THE TRAVELLERS
A Century of Song. Arc A261.

TRIGGS, STANLEY
Bunkhouse and Forecastle Songs of the Northwest. Folkways 3569. Traditional, revised, and original songs from British Columbia, with mandolin and guitar.

LA SOCIETE BACH CHORALE DE MONTREAL
Mon Canada. Vox 11860.

SULLIVAN, JOYCE, AND CHARLES JORDAN
Folk Songs of Canada. Waterloo CS 3.

WALL, MICHAEL T.
The Singing Newfoundlander. Banff 5416.

ANTHOLOGIES AND COLLECTIONS

Acadie et Québec. RCA (Canadian) CGP-139 (formerly LCP 1020). Field recordings made during the fifties by Roger Matton for the *Catalogue de la chanson folklorique française de l'Université de Laval, Québec.* The selections, mostly solo voice but with a few fiddle solos and with a few examples of lilting (*see* Glossary), are absolutely first-rate. The singers are from New Brunswick and rural Quebec; they sing in the old style, using beautiful archaic modal melodies. I don't think we'll hear much singing like this anymore; you have to grow up away from radios and machinery to sing like this. Most French immigration into Canada ended about 1675, just about the same time that the major and minor scales we know today were achieving dominance as the system of tonal organization in European music. The very oldest French-Canadian tradition, represented on this exceptional record, preserves the sounds that were current before the period of immigration came to an end. The recordings were apparently made on high-quality field equipment. If you care for this kind of music, buy this record; when it becomes unavailable, something will have passed from the world.

Canadian Folksongs. Columbia (Canadian) SL 211. Edited by Marius Barbeau from the collections of the National Museum and the National Film Board.
Canadian Folk Songs: A Centennial Collection. RCA (Canadian) CS-100. A nine-volume boxed set issued by Canadian RCA in association with Radio-Canada. The performers, who include Yves Albert, Hélène Baillargeon, Alan Mills, and Joyce Sullivan, are mostly rather polished nontraditional singers, but the series is an excellent representation of traditional material if not of traditional style.

Vol. 1, *Riddle Songs and Traditional Ballads.*
Vol. 2, *Legendary Ballads and Historical Songs.*
Vol. 3, *Romantic Adventures and Tragedies.*
Vol. 4, *Love Ballads.*
Vol. 5, *Love's Labors Lost.*
Vol. 6, *Songs of Courtship and Marriage.*
Vol. 7, *Songs and Ballads of the Lumber Camps.*
Vol. 8, *Worksongs.* Including sea songs.
Vol. 9, *Social Songs.*

Canadian Pipe Bands. Can. Cavalcade 2009.
Chantons un peu. Dominion (Canadian) 1221. French and French-Canadian songs for children.
Chants de noël du' Canada français. Folkways 6829.
Children's Game Songs of French Canada. Folkways 7214.
La danse traditionnelle à l'Isle d'Orléans. Opus 244. Quadrille sets in the old French manner with fiddles, accordion, and piano.
Folklore canadien. MBS 2915. Folk songs of the Gaspé Peninsula, collected by Carmen Roy of the Musée de l'Homme.
Folk Music from Nova Scotia. Folkways 4006. Field recordings by Helen Creighton, representing the surprising number of traditions active in that province: English ballads, a Gaelic song, a German tale, a black spiritual, an Indian war dance, French songs, fiddle tunes, lilting, hunter's animal calls, sea songs, and play-party songs.
Folksongs of Saskatchewan. Folkways 4312. Late fifties field recordings by Barbara Cass-Beggs, representing British, Welsh, German, Ukrainian, Icelandic, French, American, Cree Indian, and indigenous traditions active in the province.
An Irish Night in Canada. Banff 1230.
Lumbering Songs from the Ontario Shanties (1958–59). Folkways 4052. Field recordings by Edith Fowke, mostly from the Peterborough area. Singers include Tom Brandon and O. J. Abbott.
Maritime Folk Songs from the Collection of Helen Creighton (1948–54). Folkways 4307. Field recordings, issued in conjunction with Creighton's book of the same name. An interesting selection of material from the British, Gaelic, and French traditions, with some strong performances from the older informants in the English and Irish traditions.
Miramichi and Its Folksong Festival. Folkways 4053. Songs from the 1959 gathering of New Brunswick traditional singers.
Les musiciens de l'Isle d'Orléans, vols. 1–2. Opus 239 and 241.
Nova Scotia Folk Music from Cape Breton Island. Elektra EKL 22 (OP).
Ontario Ballads and Folk Songs. Prestige 25014 (OP).

Unaccompanied songs and ballads, mostly from English and Irish tradition, collected in the late fifties by Edith Fowke. Some valuable informants who are also good singers are represented, including O. J. Abbott, Tom Brandon, and Stanley Bâby.

Orainn Cheap Breatainn. Celtic CS 38. Gaelic songs from Cape Breton Island.

Salute to Cape Breton Island. Celtic CX 18. Fiddle tunes, songs in Gaelic, and lilting.

Songs and Ballads of Northern Saskatchewan and Northern Manitoba. Folkways 8764. Traditional and other songs, with a rather corny comic novelty feeling, as performed by a family band from the north.

Songs from Cape Breton Island. Folkways 4450.

Songs from the Outports of Newfoundland (1950–51). Folkways 4075. Field recordings by MacEdward Leach. A folk tale and various songs of Anglo-Irish descent, mostly sea songs.

Songs of the Great Lakes. Folkways 4018. Sixties field recordings by Edith Fowke; good performances of some interesting songs not heard elsewhere.

This Is Cape Breton. Celtic CX 16. A synthetic program with introductions by an emcee; piping, fiddling, readings, glee club Gaelic vocals, etc. Some of the music isn't bad if you can take the rest, but I think they produced this one for the tourist trade.

Twenty-four Cape Breton Pipe Selections. Celtic SCX 4.

Vingt succès souvenir des grands chanteurs western. RCA (Canadian) KTL2–7012 (2-rec. set). An anthology of major figures in *western québecois,* French-language country-and-western music, including Paul Brunelle and pioneer Willie Lamothe. This is a token listing for the many recordings available in this nontraditional genre.

Yukon and Other Songs of the Klondike Stamp. Quality ST3-5. An anthology of west coast revival singers and guitarists. Traditional and original songs by Ken and Melodie Stolz, Jigger Pine, and others.

LES CHANSONNIERS DU QUEBEC

Les chansonniers are a school of French-language singer-songwriters who work in a polished style reminiscent of French cabaret singing. Their work is not necessarily related to traditional music, but they deserve mention here for the honesty of their approach in writing about the big and little things that concern them: love, the weather, and French separatist politics are all acceptable subjects. A few select recordings are listed here by way of introduction; the first is an anthology that includes most of the major figures.

Les chansons d'or du Québec. Deram (Canadian) DEF-1000. Georges Dor, J-P Ferland, Gilles Vigneault, Raymond Lévesque, Felix Léclerc, Tex Lecor, Marc Hamilton, Claude Léveilée, Renée Claude, and Jacques Michel perform their compositions.

JULIEN, PAULINE
Suite québéçoise. Gamma 112. Compositions of Lévesque, Dor, Vigneault, Desrochers, and Ferland.

VIGNEAULT, GILLES
_____. Columbia (Canadian) FL 348.

CAJUN MUSIC

"Cajun" is a nonderogatory contraction of "Acadian," the name applied to the French settlers of the Maritime Provinces of Canada (Acadie) during the 1600's. Cajuns were forcibly uprooted from their settlements during the mid-1700's, as a result of their policy of nonalignment with British politics. They were expelled from their communities, and many were imprisoned. Later, they were resettled in Britain, France, and the American colonies. Later still, they regained their stability and reestablished their communities in New France, along the bayous and countryside in the area roughly between what are now Baton Rouge and the Louisiana–Texas border.

Traditional Cajun music reflects the European dance tradition, with an admixture of Creole (Hispanic and mainly Black American) elements. There is also a song tradition, not well represented on record, and a strong blues tradition borrowed from the black Creole population that also inhabits the area. (*See* Creole Blues and Zydeco section, page 37.) The typical dance music is played on fiddle or accordion or both together, the guitar serving mostly a rhythmic function in which it is assisted by triangle *(petit fer)* as the main percussion instrument. More recently, electric guitar, wood and electric bass, and drums have come into use in traditional bands, and sometimes piano and pedal steel as well. Vocals are most often produced toward the top of the singer's range, and funky harmonies predominate. Blue notes are typically used, and fiddle and vocal lines do not adhere to the well-tempered scale. Strong dance time-keeping, usually in two-step meter, is the rule. The number of musical conventions in the tradition is small, and only the best bands remain exciting for long to the non-Cajun ear—but they are very exciting.

The nontraditional "Cajun country music" shows the influence of the country swing, rockabilly, and Nashville traditions to varying degrees. The most popular exponent of the style, Doug Kershaw, is essentially a Nashville stylist at this point, and his recordings are not listed here. He usually makes a point of musically suggesting his Cajun credentials in his recordings. Nashville fiddlers have used the cliché Cajun shuffle stroke:

to conjure up images of bayous and Spanish moss on many a recording session, and the sound has been copied on guitar and pedal steel.

In addition to what is available on long-playing albums, a great deal of Cajun music has been recorded on 45 rpm singles. Good sources for further information about Cajun records and for mail-orders are Flat Town Music, J & F Southern Record Sales, Jive in the Hills, and Floyd's Record Shop (*see* page 4).

ABSHIRE, NATHAN An older singer-accordionist, especially strong as a blues singer.

Ardoin and Family, Cajun Country

. . . and Other Cajun Gems. Arhoolie 5013. From 78 rpm recordings originally issued on the Khoury label in the fifties. Includes several selections by others.
Pine Grove Blues. Swallow 6014.

BALFA BROTHERS
. . . Play Traditional Cajun Music. Swallow 6011. An exciting professional band. Playing triangle in a Cajun band is an art, and Burkeman Balfa is a master. Accordion, guitar, triangle, and two fiddles.
More Traditional Cajun Music. Swallow 6019.

BELTON, RICHARD
Modern Sounds of Cajun Music. Goldband 6013.

BERGERON, ALPHEE AND SHIRLEY
Sounds of Cajun Music. Lanor 1000.
Cajun Style Music. Lanor 1001.

BONSALL, JOE
Cajun Jamboree, vols. 1–2. Swallow 6008, 6012.

BRUCE, VIN
Cajun Country's Greatest. La Louisianne 134.
Jole Blon. Swallow 6002.
Greatest Hits. Swallow 6006.
Cajun Country. Swallow 6015.
Sings Country. Swallow 6016.

CHOATES, HARRY
Jole Blon. "D" 7000.

FALCON, JOE, AND HIS STRING BAND
Louisiana Cajun Music. Arhoolie 5005.

FORRESTER, BLACKIE
. . . and the Cajun Aces. La Louisianne 128.

GUIDRY, DOC
King of Cajun Fiddlers. La Louisianne 115.

HACKBERRY RAMBLERS
Louisiana Cajun Music (1963). Arhoolie 5003. A popular Cajun band led by Luderin Darbone. They mainly use guitar and fiddle, with some piano and steel guitar in addition to bass and drums. Accordion appears infrequently, thus giving their music a different texture from that of most Cajun bands, who depend heavily on the instrument.

LANDRENEAU, CYPRIEN AND ADAM: MAMOU CAJUNE BAND
Cajun Sole. Swallow 8001. Exciting two-steps, waltzes, and breakdowns with fiddle, accordion, triangle, and harmonica. This is the Cajun band best known to the general public, having played at the Newport and American Folklife festivals, in addition to having toured with the USIA.

LeBLANC, SHORTY
The Great. . . . Goldband 7742.

LeJUNE, IRY
The Legendary . . . , vols. 1–2. Goldband 7740, 7741. Breakdowns, reels, and waltzes by a flamboyant accordionist.

From 78 rpm recordings; some from masters, some from old discs; sound varies accordingly.

LOUISIANA ACES, THE
————. Rounder 6003. Modern Cajun country music.

MARCOTTE, MARION
Favorite Cajun Tales (in French). Swallow 6004.

MCGEE, DENNIS, AND S. D. COURVILLE
———— (1972). Morning Star 16001. Rather stiff fiddle duets by two older musicians.

MEAUX, PAPPY
Cajun Blues. Crazy Cajun 1001.

RAVEN, EDDIE
Cajun Country Sound. La Louisianne 127.

ROGER, ALDUS
King of the French Accordion. La Louisianne 114.
————. La Louisianne 122.

SONNIER, JO-EL
Hurricane Audrey. Goldband 7747.
Cajun Valentine. Goldband 7752.
Scene in Cajun Music. Goldband 7753.

THIBODEAUX, AMBROSE
French Music. La Louisianne 112.
More French Music. La Louisianne 119.
Acadian Sound. La Louisianne 133.

THIBODEAUX, RUFUS
Cajun Fiddle. La Louisianne 129.

VAN WEY, ADELAIDE
Street Cries and Creole Folk Songs of New Orleans. Folkways 2202 (10 inch).

ANTHOLOGIES AND COLLECTIONS

Allons au Fais Do-Do. Swallow 6009. An anthology of dance music played by some of the best bands, including Nathan Abshire, Mamou Cajune, and the Balfa Brothers. A *fais do-do* is a party.

Bahaman Songs, French Ballads and Dance Tunes, and Spanish Religious Songs and Game Songs. AFS L5. Library of Congress field recordings, the Cajun selections from 1934.

Best of the Cajun Hits, vols. 1–2. Swallow 6001, 6003. Blues, dance tunes, and Cajun country selections; mainly modern and country bands.

Cajun Country. Goldband 7762.

Cajun Country French Classics. La Louisianne 130.

Cajun Country's Greatest. La Louisianne 134.

Cajun Fais Do-Do (1966). Arhoolie 5004. Recordings by Nathan Abshire, Isom Fontenot, Landreneau Brothers, Breaux Brothers.

Cajun Music at Home. La Louisianne 110.

The Cajuns. RBF 21. Early dance music, mostly from the thirties, including the first Cajun recording, a 1928 concertina solo by Joe Falcon.

The Cajuns, vols. 1–2. Sonet SNTF 643, SNTF 644. Excellent music, recorded in 1972, and of far better sound quality than most Cajun recordings. Vol. 1, Balfa Brothers with Nathan Abshire, Ardoin Brothers. Vol. 2, Grand Mamou, Branch Playboys, Bessyl Duhon.

Cajun Songs from Louisiana. Folkways 4438. Mostly traditional songs and ballads, solo voice with guitar. There are also a few fiddle-accordion instrumentals, a children's song, and a chante-fable.

Folksongs of the Louisiana Acadians, vols. 1–2. Arhoolie 5009 (formerly Folk-Lyric A-4), Arhoolie 5015. Valuable recordings made by Harry Oster, between 1956 and 1959, that document other forms of Cajun music than that of the dance bands.

French Music and Folksongs from Southern Louisiana. La Louisianne 103.

J'étais au bal. Swallow 6020. Balfa Brothers, Clifton Chenier, Agnes Bourque, and others.

Louisiana Cajun Music
   Vol. 1, *The 1920's.* Old Timey 108.
   Vol. 2, *The Early 30's.* Old Timey 109.
   Vol. 3, *String Bands of the 30's.* Old Timey 110.
   Vol. 4, *The 30's to the Early 50's.* Old Timey 111.
   Vol. 5, *1928–38.* Old Timey 114.

That French Acadian Sound. La Louisianne 133.

ANGLO-AMERICAN MUSIC
THE SOUTH

Listings in this section on the south are divided into a rather odd set of categories, with a certain amount of overlap and ambiguity. The categories represent a compromise between the demands of the folklorist and the demands of the casually informed record buyer. I recommend browsing as the best approach. Sometimes artists are listed in one section when they could just as well, or almost as well, have been listed in another.

In all cases, except for instrumental records, the artists listed are traditional musicians and singers. For nontraditional artists (those who were not members of the musical culture, but learned the music from outside through media and fieldwork) consult The Folk Song Revival section, page 103.

TRADITIONAL SONGS AND SINGERS

This section includes the oldest traditions of Anglo-American music of the south. Most selections come from the Appalachian highlands, for it was in the remote mountain regions that the music brought over by the early English and Irish settlers flourished with the least interference from other influences. Most of the singers listed are advanced in years, and few are professionals; the younger singers and musicians, and the professionals, usually work in more modern and thus more lucrative styles.

The qualities most admired in the old-time ballad tradition are not at all those that are sought in contemporary commercial music, where values are often much closer to those of European art music. For one thing, the old music is rarely "performed" in any sort of show-business setting; the dynamic and dramatic devices typically used to enhance professional performances are shunned in this tradition as affected and inappropriate. In fact, the tradition is an extremely conservative one, and high values are *not* placed, as in some other musics, on originality or on the expression of unique, innovative, or eccentric personalities. Rather they are placed on a command of, and adherence to, tradition. In literary terms, this means an extensive knowledge of a ballad repertory that has persisted, with minimal variation, for hundreds of years. In musical terms, it means a clear and straightforward presentation of the melodic line. Creativity is manifested in a variety of possible ornamentations, within sanctioned limits, that can be given to a basically stable melodic line. The line itself, however, is not altered or varied in the way we expect it to be in jazz or classical music.

Some folklorists tend to value traditional singers as informants rather than as artists, and are more excited by an archaic or obscure repertory than by the technical, emotional, or musical quality of a performance. But the great singers—Horton Barker, Dillard Chandler, Aunt Molly Jackson—do display emotional qualities that cannot be imitated.

Technique is another question altogether. Diction is sometimes unclear, though often this has more to do with the singer's age than with the values of the style. Many recorded artists sing blatantly out of tune. Others sing very much in tune, but in accordance with archaic forms of the musical scale which are not used in European or contemporary pop music, and so they sound out of tune to the unsophisticated ear. A good example of this old style of singing in its purest form is to be found on the record by Sarah and Rita Keane listed in the England, Scotland, and Ireland section, page 127. For the uninitiated, I would recommend a preliminary acquaintance with the more "polished" singers in traditional style: Hedy West, Jean Ritchie, and Frank Proffitt (this section) and Frankie Armstrong and Ewan MacColl (section on England, Scotland, and Ireland, pages 126, 128). With the exception of Proffitt, these are all professional singers with traditional roots.

Other traditions are also represented here. One is the song (as opposed to ballad) tradition, which involves the use of instrumental accompaniment and may incidentally include ballads.

Ballad singers do without instrumental accompaniment for several reasons. One is that they prefer to sing in archaic scale patterns which can be realized vocally but not on fretted instruments. Another is that a nonprofessional singer with a large repertory of long songs sometimes has to stretch out syllables or leave irregular spaces in order to think of what comes next, and instrumental accompaniments don't allow a singer this freedom so easily. Finally, instrumental accompaniments profoundly limit a singer's opportunities to ornament a melody. For these and other reasons, instrumental accompaniments "sound wrong" and are not sanctioned by the tradition.

Songsters in the less ancient accompanied tradition, however, are often accomplished instrumentalists and even unique stylists. Few of them are guitarists. The guitar is a relative newcomer to the highlands, having achieved popularity only since the twenties. Furthermore, the guitar, much more than the banjo, tends to pull the singer's voice out of the traditional archaic scales and into the well-tempered scale of European classical music. (*See* Glossary.) For this reason, most of the instrumentalists listed here are banjoists. A few additional figures represent another tradition, that of the solo singer accompanying himself on fiddle. Since the fiddle is fretless and of variable pitch, it therefore lends itself to the playing of archaic scales more readily than the fretted instruments do.

Songsters in the instrumental tradition were much influenced, directly or indirectly, by black musicians. A large part of the creativity and innovation in this tradition was stimulated by contact with Black American music: mostly in tonality, rhythm, phrasing, and other aspects of style; less so in the influence of song structures (that is, the blues), and least so thematically.

Finally, one more category is represented in this section, that of the songwriter. This category cuts across stylistic lines: some singer-writers, like Molly Jackson and Sarah Gunning, belong to the unaccompanied ballad style; others, like George Davis and Dorsey Dixon, work in the style of the self-accompanied songster. Songwriters in this category also have a comprehensive knowledge of the traditional repertory.

BARKER, HORTON (b. 1889, d. late 1960's)
———. Folkways 2362. Moving, unpolished versions of songs and ballads in the old unaccompanied style, recorded in the sixties.

BOGGS, DOCK (1898–1971) A banjoist and singer of traditional (and a few original) songs. Boggs was active as a performer in the late twenties and made records during those years, some of which have been anthologized. The following albums, however, have all been recorded since 1963. Boggs is a good example of what makes for greatness in a folk artist. His instrumental technique is limited in the perspective of the total possibilities of the virtuoso banjo tradition, but his style is unique within those limits, and expresses a personal sound. His sense of arrangement and of interplay between vocal and banjo line is unlike that of any other player. His choice of repertory is not indiscriminate, but reflects a consistent and rather melancholy personal vision in which even gospel tunes seem pessimistic. *Legendary Singer and Banjo Player,* vols. 1–3. Folkways 2351, 2392, Asch 3903.
Excerpts from Interviews (1963). Folkways 5458. Selections from a long biographical interview with Mike Seeger.

CARSON, FIDDLIN' JOHN (d. 1935)
The Old Hen Cackled. Rounder 1003. An excellent Atlanta singer and writer of the twenties, accompanying himself on fiddle, with occasional other accompaniments. Sound quality of the original recordings not good.

CRISP, RUFUS (1880–1956)
———. Folkways 2342. A Kentucky singer with a personal approach to the banjo frailing style. These 1946 field recordings were not originally intended for public release, and are not of good sound quality. They were issued because they are the only surviving document, except for a

"Girl of Constant Sorrow": Sarah Ogan Gunning

few selections recorded by the Library of Congress, of a strong and unique musical personality, one credited as a major influence by Pete Seeger.

DAVIS, GEORGE

When Kentucky Had No Union Men. Folkways 31016. 1968 recordings by an eastern Kentucky radio entertainer. Some traditional songs, but mostly originals in traditional style; Davis writes well about coal mines and miners.

DIXON, DORSEY (b. 1897)

Babies in the Mill. Testament 3301. Dixon is the composer of some of the best topical, industrial, and social protest songs in southern tradition, and has composed or adapted many other mountain songs.

FERGUSON, HANK

Behind These Walls. Folk-Legacy FSA-13. Sixties recordings of prison songs, originals, and country songs, in a Nashville voice with guitar accompaniment.

GUNNING, SARAH OGAN (b. 1910)

Girl of Constant Sorrow. Folk-Legacy FSA-26 = Topic 12T171. Sixties recordings by an old-style singer of Appalachian songs, and one of the great composers of union-organizing songs of the twenties.

HOLCOMB, ROSCOE (b. 1913)

The High Lonesome Sound (sixties). Folkways 2368. Holcomb is an intense high tenor singer, who accompanies himself on guitar and on banjo in the two-finger style. His somewhat bluesy touch is unpolished and highly moving. *The Music of Roscoe Holcomb and Wade Ward.* Folkways 2363. Sixties recordings. Ward is a fine banjo frailer and fiddle player. (*See* Banjo section, page 81.) An excellent introduction to the work of two fine musicians.

JACKSON, AUNT MOLLY (1880–1960)

The Library of Congress Recordings. Rounder 1002. 1939 recordings of a strong Kentucky singer in the old unaccompanied style. She wrote many magnificent songs about the struggles of early union organizing in the Appalachian coal mines, and helped popularize Florence Reece's "Which Side Are You On?"
The Songs and Stories of. . . . Folkways 5474. Reminiscences and commentary; she was getting on in years at the time of this recording, and so her original songs, and some traditional songs from her repertory, are sung effectively by folklorist John Greenway.

KAZEE, BUELL (b. 1900)

Sings and Plays. Folkways 3810. Buell Kazee recalls his musical life in story and song on this enjoyable record. Kazee is a college-educated minister, who is also an excellent banjo frailer and singer. On the second side are six hymns sung without accompaniment. Kazee once wrote an extended choral work with Lewis Horton, based on one of the songs recorded here. Several songs from his repertory (such as "The Butcher's Boy") have become standards of the urban revival movement. (—D.W.)

LUNSFORD, BASCOM LAMAR (b. 1882)

Smokey Mountain Ballads (1947). Folkways 2040 (10 inch). A lawyer and promoter of traditional music in the Asheville, N. C., area, Lunsford is an authentic traditional singer and banjo player, in a sparse up-picking style.

OLD HARP SINGERS

———. Folkways 2356. Tennessee church music in the "shape note" style, a tradition of hymn notation in which pitch is indicated by the shape of the written notes. This tradition preserves many of the most archaic aspects of Anglo-American tonal, melodic, and harmonic practice, in addition to making for compelling performances.

Tobacco and Tradition: Frank Proffitt

PROFFITT, FRANK (1913–1969) A North Carolina tobacco farmer and banjo maker, who had a large repertory of songs learned from tradition, Proffitt sang in a clear, little-ornamented style without regional characteristics, and accompanied himself in a simple dulcimer and fretless banjo style. The recordings are from the sixties.

_____. Folk-Legacy FSA-1 = Topic 12T162.

Memorial Album. Folk-Legacy FSA-36.

Folk Songs. Folkways 2360.

RAMSEY, OBRAY

Folksongs from the Three Laurels. Prestige 13020 (OP). One of several now out-of-print records that Ramsey made during the sixties. A Tennessee singer, he accompanies his traditional Smoky Mountain songs and ballads with a pre-bluegrass three-finger banjo-picking style.

REED, BLIND ALFRED

How Can a Poor Man Stand Such Times and Live? Rounder 1001. An excellent songwriter and folk poet, accompanying himself on fiddle. Reed was an ordained Methodist minister, and many of his songs are religious or strongly moralistic. He performed on the streets of West Virginia towns, hawking printed copies of his songs which document the life-style and attitudes of his place and time. These 1927–29 recordings are of good sound quality for the period.

RIDDLE, ALMEDA

Ballads and Hymns from the Ozarks (1972). Rounder 0017. Although this recording is her only one currently available, Riddle has been known to folklorists and collectors for years as a prodigious source of traditional songs, some otherwise unknown.

RITCHIE, EDNA (b. 1910)

_____. Folk-Legacy FSA-3. Folksongs from early Kentucky tradition, recently recorded by a member of the Ritchie family.

RITCHIE, JEAN (b. 1922). Ritchie was born into a Kentucky mountaineer family; later she took a college education and moved to the New York City area. An excellent vocalist, she sings mountain songs and ballads, and more recently original songs as well, in a relatively polished manner, but still keeps the old mountain timbre and tonality. She often sings solo voice, or with dulcimer.

Singing Family of the Cumberlands. Riverside 12-653 (OP). One of a number of fine recordings that Ritchie made for the now-defunct Riverside label, this one in conjunction with her book of the same name. A vast amount of Anglo-American balladry and songs was handed down from generation to generation within her family.

Carols of All Seasons. Tradition 1031. Traditional and non-traditional songs, arranged with dulcimer, harpsichord, and recorder.

The Ritchie Family of Kentucky. Folkways 2316. A documentary record of songs transmitted within family and community culture. Old songs, sung by Ritchie, her family, and members of her Old Regular Baptist Church congregation. Selections are preceded by commentary or conversation. This is not a scholarly attempt to document the workings of folk song transmission. It does have an excel-

lent feel for the role of music as a cohesive activity in the life of the mountain family unit.

Children's Songs and Games from the Southern Mountains. Folkways 7054.

A Time for Singing. Warner WS 1592. Traditional and original songs with dulcimer, banjo, and guitar accompaniments.

Precious Memories. Folkways 2427. Early commercial country music songs of the thirties: an attempt to document the influence of early professional "hillbilly" music. With guitar, banjo, fiddle, mandolin.

Clear Waters Remembered. Geordie 101 = Sire SES 97014 (OP). Traditional and original songs and ballads with Eric Weissberg, fiddle; Dick Weissman, banjo; Happy Traum, guitar.

British Traditional Ballads in the Southern Mountains, vols. 1–2. Folkways 2301, 2302. Child ballads (*see* Glossary) in clear solo voice.

. . . and Oscar Brand. Ev. Arch. FS-207.

The Appalachian Dulcimer. Folkways 8352. *See* Instructional Books and Records, page 178.

As I Roved Out. Folkways 8872.

In Concert. Folkways 2428. Other selections by Oscar Brand and Dave Sear.

See also Doc Watson, below.

SMITH, BETTY

Songs Traditionally Sung in North Carolina. Folk-Legacy FSA-53.

SMITH, HOBART (1897–1965)

_____. Folk-Legacy FSA-17 = Topic 12T187. Excellent songs and instrumentals; Smith is a superb player of the fiddle, banjo, and guitar. He also plays several fiddle tunes and a banjo piece on the highly recommended anthology, *Instrumental Music of the Southern Appalachians.* Tradition 1007.

STEELE, PETE

Banjo Tunes and Songs. Folkways 3828. Steele recorded the classic versions of "Payday at Coal Creek" and the instrumental "Coal Creek March" for the Library of Congress in 1940; later the songs were learned and popularized by Pete Seeger. At the time of these late-fifties recordings, Steele had not played for several years, but he was still able to deliver a strong though grizzled performance of his classic pieces and others; his wife also sings several tunes. Steele plays in the frailing, up-picking, and two-finger styles.

TRIVETT, JOSEPH ABLE

_____. Folk-Legacy FSA-2. Traditional and original songs, recorded in 1961 by a rough-voiced Tennessee lumberman in his eighties.

WARD, WADE. *See* Banjo section, page 81, and Roscoe Holcomb, page 59.

WATSON, DOC (b. 1923) A unique figure, Watson might have been listed in any of several categories. He is best known as a clear and straightforward singer of songs and ballads learned from tradition around his native Deep Gap, North Carolina, and of early country music tunes learned from the recordings of such artists as the Delmore Brothers, who were clearly a major influence. The interplay between his guitar parts and his vocal line is particularly well conceived. He has also developed an exceptionally clean and fast flat-picking style, and is the leading exponent of the fiddle tune as adapted to flat-picked guitar. He also finger picks in a simpler style derived from the playing of Merle Travis, and occasionally plays banjo in the frailing style.

Watson's first exposure to the general public came when he appeared on the urban folk circuit in the late fifties with Clarence Ashley, Clint Howard, and Fred Price, in an old-time string band context. This is only one of the many styles Watson plays well; prior to his string band work, he had been playing in North Carolina as an electric guitarist in a country swing band. Recently, he has made several recordings in a commercial Nashville context, and he appears to be interested in breaking through to a career in more commercial music. For the time being he is a great favorite on the folk circuit, where he usually works with his son Merle, also a fine guitarist. Watson's recordings are models of clarity, good taste, and musical intelligence.

The following records have been recorded since 1961.

. . . and His Family. Folkways 2366. Old-time songs, ballads, hymns, and instrumentals by Watson, friends, and kinfolk including Gaither Carlton, fiddle.

———. Vanguard 79152.

. . . and Son. Vanguard 79170.

Southbound. Vanguard 79213.

Home Again. Vanguard 79239.

Ballads from Deep Gap. Vanguard 6576.

On Stage. Vanguard VSD 9/10 (2-rec. set). Live performances with Merle Watson; a well-rounded selection of his best and best-known songs and instrumentals.

The Essential. . . . Vanguard VSD 45/46 (2-rec. set). Another good representative collection, with various accompanists.

Good Deal: In Nashville. Vanguard 79276. This and the following recordings present Watson with good Nashville studio players who do not draw him out of his natural style.

Watson is less in the foreground on the following recordings, recorded and mixed in the full and rather busy "Nashville sound" style, and evidently oriented toward commercial air play.

Then and Now. Poppy PP LA022F. With Merle Watson, lead and slide guitar; Vassar Clements, fiddle; and Norman Blake, dobro; plus rhythm section.

Elementary, Doctor Watson. Poppy PYS-5703.

. . . and Jean Ritchie at Folk City. Folkways 2426. Solos by each, and a few duets, recorded in live performance. Not a bad record, but disappointing in view of the fact that they combine their talents infrequently and only in the most casual way.

Two Days in November. Poppy LA 210. With Merle Watson; many traditional songs. *See also* Clarence "Tom" Ashley, page 62.

WEST, HEDY (b. 1938) A clear-voiced Georgia singer and banjoist who, like Jean Ritchie, has a background that bridges the gap between rural origins and a sophisticated urban consciousness. Many of her songs are unusual or in unusual versions, as learned from her family's singing tradition. Recordings date from the mid-sixties on.

Old Times and Hard Times. Folk-Legacy FSA-32 = Topic 12T117.

Pretty Saro and Other Songs from My Family. Topic 12T146.

Ballads. Topic 12T163. With Bill Clifton.

Serves 'em Fine. Fontana STL 5432.

Getting the Folk Out of the Country. FV 12008. With Bill Clifton.

Volume 1. Vanguard 79124.

Volume 2. Vanguard 79126.

ANTHOLOGIES AND COLLECTIONS

Note: many of the AFS Library of Congress recordings in this section include material recorded in the south and other regions as well. In most cases, however, the selections from other regions have been recorded by émigrés from the south or at any rate represent a tradition that is essentially southern, and the recordings are therefore listed here. Also note that several items listed in the Midwest section reflect Appalachian tradition, as it was carried to the more heavily industrialized midwestern areas by Appalachian natives in search of work during the Depression and World War II.

Anglo-American Ballads: Library of Congress field recordings

——— (1934–41). AFS L1.

——— (1937–42). AFS L7. Kentucky, North Carolina, and Virginia. Justus Begley, Horton Barker, Texas Gladden, Hobart Smith, and others.

——— (1941–46). AFS L12.

——— (1941–46). AFS L14.

——— (1938–46). AFS 120. Rufus Crisp, Bascomb Lamar Lunsford, and others.

——— (1938–47). AFS L21. Crisp, Lunsford, Pete Steele, and others.

Anglo-American Shanties, Lyric Songs, Dance Tunes, and Spirituals. AFS L2. 1938–41 Library of Congress recordings; interesting songs and some good fiddling and banjo picking. Includes Pete Steele's poorly recorded but superbly played versions of "Coal Creek March" and "Payday at Coal Creek."

Ballads and Songs of the Blue Ridge Mountains: Persistence and Change. Asch 3831. Late sixties field recordings of singers, both unaccompanied and with guitar, fiddle, or string band. The recordings demonstrate the degree to which certain aspects of tradition persist in the music of older and slightly younger singers, ranging from the archaic solo style on up to styles influenced by instrumental accompaniments and by media music. An excellent album, with annotation; not necessarily for the casual listener, since selections are made for musicological, not musical, value.

Child Ballads Traditional in the United States, 2 vols. AFS L57, L58. 1936–50 Library of Congress field recordings.

Come All You Coal Miners. Rounder 4005. Appalachian miners' song, mostly original, by George Tucker, Hazel Dickens, Nimrod Workman, and Sarah Ogan Gunning.

Fa So La. Asch 4151. Shape-note hymn singing recorded in Mississippi by Frederic Ramsey, Jr.

Hammons Family: A Study of a West Virginia Family's Traditions, The. AFS L65–66 (2-rec. set). Stories, reminiscences, songs, banjo, and some excellent rough fiddle playing; with lengthy booklet. See *Shaking Down the Acorns,* listed below.

Instrumental Music of the Southern Appalachians. Tradition 1007. An excellent album, featuring the fiddle and banjo of Hobart Smith and the guitar of Etta Baker, in addition to other dulcimer, banjo, and guitar solos.

Mississippi Folk Voices. Southern Folklore SF-101. White and black music from rural Mississippi: songs, dances, fiddle tunes, blues. With lengthy booklet.

Mountain Music of Kentucky. Folkways 2317. Representative selections from a larger Library of Congress collection, recorded by John Cohen about 1960. Church singing, ballads, and dance tunes, solo voice and with banjo, guitar, or fiddle; includes selections by Roscoe Holcomb. An excellent document of the older music sung and played around Hazard, Kentucky, one of our richest sources of Appalachian music.

Old Love Songs and Ballads from the Big Laurel, North Carolina. Folkways 2309. Songs and ballads in solo voice, documenting the musical life and style of the older members of a small mountain community. Sung by Dillard Chandler and others.

Sacred Harp Singing. AFS L11. 1942 Library of Congress field recordings in Alabama. *See* comments on Old Harp Singers, Traditional Songs and Singers section, page 59.

Shaking Down the Acorns. Rounder 0018. Traditional stories, songs, banjo, and excellent rough fiddle playing by members and friends of the Hammons family of Pocahontas and Greenbrier counties, West Virginia. A superb stylistic documentary with much excellent music. Edited from the same source material that was used for *The Hammons Family* set listed above, but selections differ.

Songs and Ballads of the Anthracite Miners. AFS L16. 1946 Library of Congress field recordings.

Songs and Ballads of the Bituminous Miners. AFS L60. 1940 Library of Congress field recordings.

The Traditional Music of Beech Mountain, North Carolina
 Vol. 1, *The Older Ballads and Sacred Songs.* Folk-Legacy FSA-22. Mostly selections in solo voice.
 Vol. 2, *The Late Songs and Hymns.* Folk-Legacy FSA-23. Solo and group singing; some fiddle, guitar, dulcimer, and banjo accompaniments and instrumentals.

 Good recordings that represent the musical legacy of the older members of a mountain community. Music was an important function in the life of these communities, but the traditions will now survive only on records such as these.

OLD-TIME STRING BAND AND EARLY COUNTRY MUSIC

The music in this section comes mostly from the Appalachians, and much of it belongs to a category that sits on the boundary line between nonprofessional folk music and professional, cultivated pop entertainment music. Folklorist A. L. Lloyd calls music of this sort rural professional music.

The guitar's rise to popularity in the southern highlands during the first decade or two of this century made possible a new sort of ensemble music. Fiddle and banjo music had been played for years, but the guitar's ability to lay down a strong rhythmic foundation introduced another aspect to

the music. With the further addition of the mandolin, the rural ensemble was able to hang together in a new way. A typical string band might consist of guitar, banjo, one or two fiddles, and perhaps a mandolin. There was a particularly strong string band tradition in the area around Galax, Virginia, and it still persists today.

In addition to the string bands, there were other performers who were primarily vocalists. Some were working in styles influenced by jazzy or ragtimey novelty sounds of the twenties. One very important singer was Jimmie Rodgers, who worked mainly in a blues-derived vein, composing his own material. Another important act—and note the use of the word "act"—was the Carter Family, who arranged and adapted traditional and other material in an early commercial style. These are musicians whose roots are in traditional music, but who in the context of the early days of the broadcasting and recording industries became professionals.

The music of this time and place, and its contemporary derivatives, is generally known as old-time music.

ACUFF, ROY (b. 1903) Fiddler-singer Acuff was an important figure in the transition from early country music to the commercial sound we today associate with Nashville. Listed here is one representative recording of the many he has made over the years.

Great Speckled Bird. Harmony 11289.

ALLEN BROTHERS

The Chattanooga Boys (1927–34). Old Timey 115. Bluesy and ragtimey hillbilly songs, with tenor banjo, guitar, and kazoo.

_____. FV 12501.

ASHLEY, CLARENCE "TOM" (1895–1967) Ashley is a crusty old singer and fine banjo player, whose version of "The Cuckoo," first recorded in the twenties, has become an often-performed standard.

Old-Time Music at Clarence Ashley's, vols. 1–2. Folkways 2355, 2359. Spirited 1961–62 picking and singing session with fiddle, guitar, and banjo by Virginia and Carolina musicians Doc Watson, Clint Howard, Fred Price, Gaither Carlton, and others. Fine, casual music making among friends.

. . . and Tex Isley (1966). Folkways 2350. Isley plays guitar and autoharp. A good chance to hear Ashley's crisp frailing style on several tunes.

BALL, ESTIL C.

. . . and the Friendly Gospel Singers (1967). County 711. Good old-time gospel songs, with guitar and mandolin. This primarily vocal album is marred by apparent placement of the microphone too close to the guitar.

_____ (seventies). Rounder 0026. More old-time gospel songs, with mountain songs and guitar instrumentals in addition.

BLAKE, NORMAN Blake is a younger Georgia musician who presently enjoys a popularity on the collegiate folk circuit. He is most admired for his flashy flat-pick style; he also finger picks the guitar and plays mandolin, dobro, and fiddle. He doesn't concern himself enough with his singing, which obscures his considerable talent as a songwriter.

Roy Acuff and His Smoky Mountain Boys

Home in Sulphur Springs. Rounder 0012.
The Fields of November. Flying Fish 004.

BLUE SKY BOYS, THE (Bill Bolick, b. 1917; Earl Bolick, b. 1919)
The Sunny Side of Life (1947). Rounder 1006. Recordings by Bill and Earl Bolick, who along with fiddler Curly Parker were popular radio and recording artists of the thirties and forties. Their sound, which tends to be rather uniform from piece to piece, involves a close harmony pattern between tenor and high lead which is an important ingredient in the development of the classic bluegrass harmony singing style. The Everly Brothers, of recent popularity, seem to have derived their style from this one. The Bolicks' vocals, accompanied by Parker and their own guitar and mandolin, are satisfying in spite of static dynamic levels, a taste for cloyingly sentimental repertory, and some slight inaccuracies of pitch that would be hardly noticeable in a soloist but stand out in subtle harmony singing.
Together Again. Pine Mtn. 257.
Precious Moments (gospel, 1963). Pine Mtn. 269.
———. Pine Mtn. 305.
Bluegrass Mountain Music. Camden ADL2-0726 (2-rec. set).

BOGTROTTERS
The Original Bogtrotters. Biograph RC-6003. 1937–42 Library of Congress recordings by an influential Galax-area string band including Fields Ward and Eck Dunford, a popular fiddle soloist on records of the thirties. See *Early Country Music,* vol. 2, Anthologies and Collections, page 68.

BROWN'S FERRY FOUR A country gospel group that included the Delmore Brothers and Wayne Raney.
Sacred Songs. Pine Mtn. 250.
Old Gospel Favorites. Pine Mtn. 251.

BURNETT AND RUTHERFORD
———. Rounder 1004.

CAMP CREEK BOYS, THE
——— (sixties). County 709. Old-time string band music, including Kyle Creed and Fred Cockerham; a good band from North Carolina.

CARLISLE, BILL
Best of. . . . Hickory S-129.

CARLISLE, CLIFF. *See* Dobro section, page 82.

CAROLINA TAR HEELS, THE
——— (1962). Folk-Legacy FSA-24. The original band, including Clarence Ashley, was a popular recording band in the thirties. Dock Walsh and Garley Foster continue the tradition without his help in these recordings.

CARTER FAMILY, THE (Original) The original Carter Family consisted of A. P. Carter, his wife Sara, her sister Maybelle (who married A. P.'s brother), and later their children. They recorded from 1927 to 1941, attaining immense commercial popularity even though they did not perform on a large scale. Like many family groups, they attained a unique sound, marked by characteristic vocal harmonies, Sara's autoharp (Maybelle also plays autoharp), and Maybelle's guitar style. Her guitar style, commonly known today as Carter style, involves bass melody or har-

mony notes along with interspersed chords produced by brushing across the higher strings. A. P. Carter frequently traveled through the south in search of new songs for the family repertory and the Carters were responsible for the popularity of many songs regarded today as standards.
Old Family Memories (late twenties). CMH 107.
Original and Essential (late thirties). CMH 112.
_____. CMH 116, 118. Newly released 1928–41 recordings in the CMH reissue series, titles not available at time of compilation.
Famous Country Music Makers. RCA (British) DPM 2046 (2-rec. set). Represents the entire span from 1928 to 1941.
Lonesome Pine Special. Camden CAL-2473. 1927–34, and two selections from 1941, with much prominent autoharp.
The Original and Great. . . . Camden CAL-2473.
My Old Cottage Home. Camden ACL1-0047.
. . . on Border Radio. JEMF 101. Transcriptions intended for broadcast on Mexican radio, 1938–42, annotated by a comprehensive booklet.
_____, vols. 1–2. Ace of Hearts 58, 112.
Mid the Green Fields of Virginia. RCA LPM-2772.

CARTER FAMILY, THE (Later Versions)
Clinch Mountain Ballads. Pine Mtn. 206. A. P. Carter reunited with Sara, and their children Janette and Joe in 1956.
The Famous Carter Family. Harmony HS 13332.
I Walk the Line. Harmony HS 11392.
Best of. . . . Columbia CS 9119. Modern country music by Maybelle and daughters.
Three Generations. Columbia KC 33084. Older and modern songs by Maybelle, daughters, and grandchildren.
Travelin' Minstrel Band (1974). Columbia KC 31454. Listening to these sessions is like coming to the end of a Greek tragedy about the fall of a once-proud dynasty. Nobody would dispute the necessity of earning a living, but there are good and bad commercial songs, and these are bad ones, in highly competent but undistinguished versions by Maybelle and daughters, including Johnny Cash's wife, June Carter.
Mother Maybelle Carter. Columbia KG 32436/7 (2-rec. set). Apparently intended as a tribute, this rather roughly assembled set consists of some spoken reminiscences by Maybelle, a few autoharp solos, and a lot of good-natured casual jamming by an assembly of Nashville studio men.

CARTER, JANETTE
Howdayado. Traditional JC 573. Lesser-known Carter Family songs by the youngest of the daughters with autoharp, guitars, and fiddle.
Storms Are on the Ocean. Birch 1949.
Joe and Janette Carter. County 706.

COCKERHAM, FRED. *See* Camp Creek Boys and Oscar Jenkins, this section, page 63 and below.

COUSIN EMMY. *See* New Lost City Ramblers, String Band Revival section, page 113.

CREED, KYLE
. . . with Bobby Patterson: Virginia Reel. Leader 2053. Contemporary old-time string band music, rather polished.

Blue Ridge Style Square Dance Time. Mountain 301.
June Apple. Mountain 302.

DELMORE BROTHERS (Alton, 1908–64; and Rabon, 1916–52) Most of the brother acts in this idiom are distinguished by unique and well-conceived vocal harmony styles, the result of a childhood spent singing together. This is particularly true of the Delmores. Their music, coming out of the thirties and forties, favors a light, almost jazzy beat, influenced by country swing. The brothers were superb solo and rhythm players on guitar and tenor guitar, usually working with a band. In addition to the records listed below, watch for copies of their fine work on the now-defunct King/Starday label.
Early Recordings. County 402.
Memories of Yesterday. Pine Mtn. 218.
The Delmores Sing. Pine Mtn. 289. *See also* Brown's Ferry Four, this section, page 63.

FIVE HARMANIACS, THE
_____. Puritan 3004. A novelty band of the thirties, with banjos, harmonicas, and guitar.

GRAYSON AND WHITTER
_____ (1928). County 513. Old-time mountain songs with fiddle and guitar.

GREGORY, W. L., AND CLYDE DAVENPORT
Monticello. Davis Unltd. 33014.

HARRELL, KELLY
The Complete . . . , 3 vols. FV 12508/09/10.

HIGHLANDERS, THE
_____. Heritage 1. With Kyle Creed.

HOWARD, CLINT, FRED PRICE AND SONS
The Ballad of Finley Preston. Rounder 0009. Price and Howard (fiddle-banjo and guitar, respectively) are the two Tennessee singers and farmers in whose company Tom Ashley made his comeback and Doc Watson began his recording career. Howard does most of the singing, while Price shows how it is possible to be an excellent fiddler without being spectacular. Price's strength lies in phrasing, good funky intonation, and good musical sense when relating to the vocal line. This record offers an interesting selection of old-time songs and gospel tunes, with plenty of drive, good feeling, and fine harmony singing. Ensemble work is relaxed and effortlessly together, and Kenneth Price's occasional bluegrass-style banjo works perfectly.

ISLEY, TEX, AND THE NORTH CAROLINA BOYS
_____. Leader 4040. *See also* Clarence "Tom" Ashley, this section, page 62.

JARRELL, TOMMY. *See* Oscar Jenkins, this section, below.

JENKINS, OSCAR, TOMMY JARRELL, AND FRED COCKERHAM
Down to the Cider Mill. County 713. High-spirited old-time string band tunes on fiddle, guitar, and banjo by excellent older North Carolina players.
Back Home in the Blue Ridge. County 723.
Stay All Night. County 741.

JENKINS, SNUFFY

Carolina Bluegrass. Arhoolie 5011 (formerly on Folk-Lyric). Jenkins was a major contributor to the development of the three-finger roll that is the basis of the bluegrass banjo style, and both Earl Scruggs and Don Reno have cited him as an influence. His own style is a transitional one, and I feel that he is listed more appropriately here than in the Bluegrass section. The other featured performer is fiddler Homer "Pappy" Sherrill, likewise a transitional stylist. This record certainly emphasizes their roots in the old-time style and repertory, so the title is a misnomer. Sherrill is more prominent; Jenkins takes solos but is not dominantly recorded in the ensembles.

. . . and Pappy Sherrill: 33 Years of Pickin' and Pluckin' (1971). Rounder 0005. This album features traditional tunes as well as several western swing style tunes sung in an odd, somewhat Jolsonesque minstrel manner, along with a few originals and banjo solos. Of particular interest are the several solos where Jenkins alternates between the frailing, two-finger, and three-finger styles, providing a capsule history of the development of southern banjo technique.

JONES, GRANDPA (Louis, b. 1913)

A continuator of the rip-roaring Uncle Dave Macon tradition, though he isn't quite the banjoist Macon was. Jones updates his work with Nashville sidemen and excursions into the commercial country music style and repertory. He has been a favorite entertainer on the Grand Ole Opry and more recently on the *Hee-Haw* TV series.

Everybody's Grandpa. Monument 18083.
What's for Supper?. Monument 32939.
Gospel Album. Pine Mtn. 222.
Pickin' Time. Vocalion 73900E.
Hits from Hee-Haw. Monument 18131.

LEAKE COUNTY REVELERS

Saturday Night Breakdown (1927–30). County 532. Recordings by one of the most influential bands of the time.

LEDFORD STRING BAND

_____ (1971). Rounder 0008. Recordings of a trio led by fiddler Steve Ledford, with two guitarists. Ledford is a figure of some historical importance, having recorded in earlier days with Wade Mainer, Zeke Morris, and others. The present band is occasionally erratic and the vocal harmonies out of tune; but the feeling is good, and many of the songs are not well known.

MACON, UNCLE DAVE (1870–1953)

A popular fixture on the Grand Ole Opry radio broadcasts from Nashville from the earliest days until his death in the fifties, Macon did not become a professional entertainer until late in life. His specialties were rip-roaring, foot-stomping versions of hoedown, play-party, and comic tunes, and he was not above stereotyped hillbilly put-ons. His banjo style was essentially a frailing one, combined with other picking patterns to produce some of the most varied and rhythmically exciting right-hand work in the history of the instrument. His often-imitated "Cumberland Mountain Deer Chase," a descriptive monologue with banjo parts that imitate the braying of the hounds, the chase scene, etc., remains a classic.

Early Recordings (1925–35). County 521.
The Gayest Old Dude in Town. FV 12503.
_____. RBF 51. A good representative selection, spanning his career.
_____. Ace of Hearts 135.

MAINER, J. E. (1898–1971)

A popular showman and string band leader of the thirties, who continued recording into the sixties. In addition to the items below, a series of about twenty albums is available on the Rural Rhythm label from Uncle Jim O'Neal. (*See* mail-order listings, page 4.)

. . . and His Crazy Mountaineers. Old Timey 106. These thirties recordings effectively sum up the professional string show-band sound of the times. These bands had a tremendous impact not only in their own day but also on the urban revival string band concept and style.

Volume 2. Old Timey 107.

Mainer's Mountaineers (1963). Arhoolie 5002. Erratic performances by a band consisting essentially of Mainer and his sons.

Gospel Album. Pine Mtn. 224.

MAINER, WADE

_____ (1936–42). County 404. Recordings with Steve Ledford, fiddle, and Clyde Moody, vocals and guitar.
. . . and Mainer's Mountaineers. Old Homestead 9002.
Sacred Songs of Mother and Home. Old Homestead 9001.
Rock of My Soul. Old Homestead 90014.
Sacred Songs Mountain Style. Old Homestead 90016.

MCGEE BROTHERS (Sam, 1894–1975; and Kirk, b. 1899)
Pillars of the Grand Ole Opry. MBA 607.

MCGEE BROTHERS AND ARTHUR SMITH
Oldtimers of the Grand Ole Opry. Folkways 2379.
Milk 'em in the Morning Blues. Folkways 31007. The McGee Brothers (guitar, fiddle, and banjo) along with fiddler Smith were popular entertainers in the early days of the Grand Ole Opry radio broadcasts. These recordings, made in the sixties, are good examples of the good-timey and rather flashy kinds of traditional and homemade tunes that they were known for. Smith is a very good fiddler, who was well respected but whose influence, for some reason, was not felt as much as that of his peers.

MCGEE, SAM (as soloist). *See* Guitar section, page 91.

MORRIS BROTHERS AND HOMER SHERRILL
Wiley, Zeke, and Morris (1972). Rounder 0022. Old-time songs, many of a sentimental nature, with guitar, mandolin, fiddle, and bass. The emphasis is on trio harmony singing of the sort that Bill Monroe catalyzed into the classic bluegrass style.

NEAVES, GLEN
. . . and the Virginia Mountain Boys. Folkways 3830. A contemporary Galax-style string band, representing the more modern but still traditional-feeling style and repertory of the second generation of string band musicians from the area.

PATTERSON, RAY AND INA Bluegrassy harmony singing with guitar and mandolin, oriented toward a gospel and sentimental early country music repertory.
Old Time Ballads and Hymns. County 708.
Old Time Songs. County 715.
Songs of Home and Childhood. County 737.

PEGRAM, GEORGE
_____ (1970). Rounder 0001. Pegram is sometimes erratic but never without enthusiasm, singing old-time songs in a rough energetic way and accompanying himself on the banjo mainly in the two-finger style. With fiddle (Fred Cockerham), mandolin, and guitar.

PERRY COUNTY MUSIC MAKERS
Sunset Memories. Davis Unltd. 33009.

PHIPPS FAMILY, THE Imitators of the Carter Family style, the Phippses have numerous records on the Pine Mountain label.
Outstanding Gospel Church Songs. Pine Mtn. 130.
Echoes of the Carter Family. Pine Mtn. 132.
Southern Folk Songs. Pine Mtn. 195.

POOLE, CHARLIE (d. 1931) Banjoist Poole, who worked with various combinations of fiddle and guitar, was one of the most vital and popular string band leaders of the twenties, and many of the tunes recorded by his bands have become standards of the idiom. He was one of the earliest professional stars in the style.
. . . and the Highlanders (1927–29). Puritan 3002. An early band; not his major recordings. Poor sound quality on the original 78's; of interest mainly to specialists.
. . . and the North Carolina Ramblers, vols. 1–3 (1928–30). County 505, 509, 516. The first volume has many of his best-known songs.
. . . and the North Carolina Ramblers (1928–30). Biograph RC-6005.

POPLIN FAMILY, THE Recent old-time and newer country song recordings in a variety of styles; harmony vocals with guitar, mandolin, and banjo.
. . . of North Carolina. Folkways 2306.
Gwine Back to Sumter. Melodeon 7331.

PUCKETT, RILEY Puckett worked with the Skillet Lickers and other important string bands of the twenties. He accompanies himself in a rather basic guitar style distinguished by the well-conceived concept of bass runs that made him a great asset as a sideman. (He is probably the most influential back-up guitarist to have recorded.) Though he worked with countrified bands, his solo voice was rather a pop voice of the period, smooth, and influenced by both black and vodeodo-style singers and by the minstrel entertainment tradition.
_____. GHP 902. Ballads, gospel, and novelty songs.
The Riley Puckett Story (1924–41). Roots RL-701.

RED FOX CHASERS
_____. County 510. A late twenties string band.

REED, OLA BELLE
_____. Rounder 0021. Old-time, bluegrass, and gospel songs, helped by a backup band (banjo, fiddle, guitar) that consists mainly of family members in this seventies recording. Reed's voice is not always polished or centered, but full of feeling; she's the kind of singer who carefully chooses just what she'll sing, and then sings with guts. Her vocal style derives mainly from the male bluegrass singing tradition.

ROANE COUNTY RAMBLERS
_____. County 403. A late twenties string band.

RODGERS, JIMMIE (1897–1933) A Mississippi railroad brakeman before he started his recording career, Rodgers is regarded by many as the founder of commercial country music. His recorded repertory, consisting in great part of songs he composed himself, runs the gamut from blues through ragtimey tunes with an early jazz flavor on to corny pop and novelty tunes. The influence of black musicians was great, but his style was distinctly his own. There is a tradition in the critical and historical literature concerning American music in which white derivators of essentially black musical styles are condemned for their failure to grasp fully the rhythmic or tonal principles of their influences. Often, however, such a "failure" has resulted in the creation of a new and distinct idiom.

Rodgers' style is characterized by an archetypally twangy voice with frequent use of a yodeling falsetto, and a strong strumming guitar style with interesting accents and phrase structures. He often used accompanists, ranging from country-style string bands to small black jazz

The Stoneman Family

bands. Many Rodgers albums are available (consult the Schwann catalogue), and many of them overlap and repeat themselves. I recommend the first listing as a good introduction to his work.
This Is Jimmie Rodgers. RCA VPS 6091(e) (2-rec. set).
Never No Mo' Blues. RCA LPM 1232.
Train Whistle Blues. RCA LPM 1640.
Rough and Rowdy Ways. RCA LPM 2112.
Jimmie the Kid. RCA LPM 2213.
Country Music Hall of Fame. RCA LPM 2531.
Short But Brilliant Life. RCA LPM 2634.
Best of. . . . RCA LSP 3315(e).

SHADY MOUNTAIN RAMBLERS
Old Time Music from the Blue Ridge Mountains. Heritage 2.

SMOKEY VALLEY BOYS
_____. Rounder 0029. North Carolina string band music of the seventies.

STONEMAN, ERNEST (1893–1968)
. . . and His Dixie Mountaineers (1927–28). Historical 8004.

STONEMAN FAMILY
_____. Folkways 2315. *See* Schwann catalogue for other listings.

TANNER, GID (1885–1960), **AND THE SKILLET LICKERS**
One of the great string bands of the twenties and thirties, whose contributions to the style and repertory are still felt. This north Georgia band, with a "blacker" sound than that

of the eastern Appalachian band, included fiddlers Clayton McMichen and Lowe Stokes.
_____, vols. 1–2. County 506, 526.
_____. Rounder 1005.
A Corn Likker Still in Georgia. Voyager 303.

TARLETON, JIMMY. *See* Dobro section, page 83.

TENNEVA RAMBLERS
_____ (1927–28). Puritan 3001. String band recordings; this was Jimmie Rodgers' original backup band. Good songs.

WARD, FIELDS
Early Country Music. See Anthologies and Collections, page 68.
Fields and Wade Ward (1968). Biograph RC-6002. Good songs, with guitar, banjo, and fiddle. *See also* Wade Ward, Banjo section, page 81.
Bury Me Not on the Prairie. Rounder 0036.

WEST, HARRY AND JEANIE Old-time harmony and solo vocals with guitar, mandolin, and sometimes other accompanists.
Songs of the Southland. Folkways 2352.
Gospel Songs. Folkways 2357.
_____. Ev. Arch. FS-208.

WOLTZ, DaCOSTA
Southern Broadcasters (1927). County 524. String band and novelty tunes by early North Carolina radio entertainers; fiddle and banjos.

ANTHOLOGIES AND COLLECTIONS

Ballads and Songs. Old Timey 102. Tunes from the twenties and thirties by Bill Cox, Jimmy Tarleton, Wade Mainer, Blue Sky Boys, Grayson and Whitter, and others. Of special interest because there are many early versions of songs still well known today.

Band Music of Grayson and Carroll Counties, Virginia. Folkways 3832. Sixties recordings of musicians of different ages from one area, documenting changes in the string band style from generation to generation. Includes fiddlers Glen Smith, Charlie Higgins, and Glen Neaves, among other musicians. Good music as well as an interesting documentary.

Country Gospel Song. RBF 19. Religious music from southern recordings of the twenties and thirties; mostly representing white tradition.

A Day in the Mountains (1928). County 512. Comedy, vaudeville, and dialogue routines, as well as instrumentally accompanied monologues of the "Deer Chase" genre, by leading bands and instrumentalists of the late twenties.

Early Country Music, vol. 1. Historical 8001. 1929 recordings hitherto unissued, re-recorded from the original masters. Most of the selections are by Fields Ward, with the Buck Mountain Band including fiddler Eck Dunford. Guitarist-singer Ward is nephew of banjoist Wade Ward (*see* Banjo section, page 81), who originally led this band; later the band evolved into the Bogtrotters (*see* page 63), who recorded extensively for the Library of Congress in 1940. These selections document the formative years of the Virginia–North Carolina string band style, as played by some of the leading exponents of the time. There are several other selections by Ernest Stoneman.

Early Country Music, vol. 2. Historical 8002. 1928–31 recordings by Joe Evans, the Golden Melody Boys, and John Dilleshaw, one of the earliest white guitarists to assimilate the black finger-picking style. Poor original sound quality.

Early Rural String Bands. RCA LPV-552. 1922–49 recordings, giving a good sample of different idioms and their development. Includes some especially interesting items: an early fiddle solo by Eck Robertson, a 1926 medley of reels on hammered dulcimer, cymbalom, and tuba (!), and a 1940 recording by Snuffy Jenkins and Pappy Sherrill that straddles the boundary line between bluegrass and old-time music.

Echoes of the Ozarks, vols. 1–3. County 518–520. Arkansas string bands of the twenties and thirties.

High Atmosphere. Rounder 0028. Estil Ball, Fred Cockerham, Dillard Chandler, Wade Ward, Frank Proffitt, and others; compiled by John Cohen.

Maple on the Hill (thirties). Camden CAS 898-e. J. E. Mainer, Delmore Brothers, Carlisle Brothers, Uncle Dave Macon, Riley Puckett, Bradley Kincaid.

Mountain Ballads. County 502. Excellent performances of the twenties and thirties, including many definitive early recordings of well-known songs by Kelly Harrell, Clarence Ashley, Dave Macon, Grayson and Whitter, and others.

Music from the Ozarks (1958). Folkways 3812. Casual music making with fiddle, electric guitar, mandolin, etc., by various residents of Fayetteville, Arkansas. Nothing special in any way.

Native American Ballads (1927–39). RCA LPV-548. Story songs mostly from the southern Appalachians. Most of the songs are not traditional, but were contemporary at that time. Vernon Dalhart, Delmore Brothers, Kelly Harrell, Jimmie Davis, Mac McClintock, and others.

North Carolina Boys. Leader LEA 4040. Tex Isley and Craig Gray and the North Carolina Ramblers.

Old-Time Ballads from the Southern Mountains. County 522.

Old-Time Southern Dance Music: The String Bands, vols. 1–2. Old Timey 100, 101. Selections from the twenties and thirties. These albums encompass a wider variety of regional styles than most such anthologies, including even some Cajun material. Many of these selections are not easily accessible elsewhere; artists include Charlie Poole, the Hackberry Ramblers, Arthur Smith, Eck Robertson, Nathan Abshire, bluesman Bayless Rose.

Old-Time String Band Classics (1927–33). County 531. Recordings by Caplinger's Cumberland Mountain Entertainers, Alex Hood and His Railroad Boys, Aiken Co. String Band, Fox Chasers, and others.

Paramount Old-Time Reissues. JEMF 103.

Play and Dance Songs and Tunes. AFS L9. 1936–42 Library of Congress field recordings mainly from the south; includes string bands, banjo, and hammered dulcimer solos.

The Railroad in Folksong (1928–40). RCA LPV-532. A selection of good songs more or less about railroads and railroading, recorded by old-time performers and bands. Artists include the Carter Family, Mac McClintock, Monroe Brothers, Delmore Brothers, and others. The fine original recording of the fiddle showpiece "Orange Blossom Special" is here.

Smokey Mountain Ballads. RCA LPV-507. Fine 1934–38 recordings by Dave Macon, Mainer-Morris-Ledford, Dorsey Dixon, Monroe Brothers, Arthur Smith, Gid Tanner, J. E. Mainer, and the Carter Family.

Songs of the Railroad (1924–34). Vetco 103. String band and early country music selections.

String Ragtime. Yazoo 1045.

Traditional Country Classics. Historical 8003. Earl Johnson, Grayson and Whitter, Burnett and Rutherford, and others.

Traditional Music from Grayson and Carroll Counties (1961). Folkways 3811. Recordings of Virginia musicians Glen Neaves, Vester Jones, Wade Ward, Ed Spencer, and Glen Smith; the emphasis is on fiddle and banjo.

BLUEGRASS

Bluegrass is a specialized development of old-time string band music, as played and sung by mandolinist Bill Monroe and the musicians he has gathered around him, or otherwise influenced, over the years. The name of the style derives from Monroe's band, the Blue Grass Boys. Although Monroe himself comes from Kentucky, the Blue Grass State, most of the other great early musicians are from east Tennessee, Virginia, and North Carolina.

Monroe's early recordings with his brother Charlie and then with the Blue Grass Boys, beginning in the late thirties, reveal a personal approach to the old-time style characterized by strikingly gutsy high lead vocals, even higher tenor harmony sometimes going into the falsetto range, and a brilliantly original mandolin style clearly influenced by black music. With the Blue Grass Boys, Monroe developed a trio vocal harmony sound (high lead with baritone and higher tenor harmonies) that remains one of the most characteristic aspects of the original bluegrass sound. (When gospel songs are sung, and occasionally elsewhere in the repertory, it is conventional to add a bass part, recalling the four-part harmony tradition of church singing.) The band's use of a string bass also contributed to the emerging bluegrass sound. Old-time string band music, which was originally played for dancing in the two-step tradition, usually kept 2/4 time. The string bass made it easier for the new music to keep a more flowing 4/4 or cut time beat. In a useful, though superficial and somewhat dangerous analogy, one might say that the difference between old-time and bluegrass timekeeping roughly parallels the difference between Dixieland and swing band timekeeping.

Monroe's work through the early forties was unique and brilliant, but it was not until the middle and late forties that the definitive sound we immediately recognize today as bluegrass emerged. The band that created this sound featured guitarist Lester Flatt sharing vocal work with Monroe, fiddler Chubby Wise (whose roots are in western swing), and banjo player Earl Scruggs. Scruggs had developed a clear, brilliant three-finger picking style which in the ears of most people today—especially those only casually acquainted with the music—gives bluegrass music its most readily identifiable sound.

Bluegrass achieved some regional commercial success during the late forties and early fifties, and many of the sounds of the Monroe band, particularly the Scruggs banjo sound, were copied or adapted by Monroe's contemporaries. Most of the first-generation bluegrass players had musical roots independent of Monroe and Scruggs, and so were able to develop personal sounds of their own. This has tended to be much less the case with younger followers of the style.

Black music was a strong influence on the old-time string band sound. It seems that new forms of white American music develop out of new forms of interplay with black music, and this was true of bluegrass also. Monroe's trio harmonies are a bluesy transformation of white church harmonies, just as his mandolin style, for which he credits the influence of his fiddling Uncle Pen Vandever and of black guitarist Arnold Schultz, is a bluesy transformation of Irish-Appalachian fiddle tradition. Earl Scruggs and Chubby Wise, the two remarkable musical personalities he added to the Blue Grass Boys in the forties, were also influenced to varying degrees by black music. Out of their musical interactions they produced the classic bluegrass sound, and they owe much of the vitality and potency of that sound to the influence of Black American music.

After Flatt and Scruggs left Monroe to form their own band, they chose to add Buck "Uncle Josh" Graves, a bluesy dobro player who had made a stylistic break with the earlier Hawaiian-influenced country tradition on his instrument. Other contemporaries of Monroe had their own approaches. Don Reno's banjo playing, for example,

reflects elements of jazz banjo style, while Ralph and Carter Stanley always preferred to set themselves closer to white string band tradition.

Bluegrass passed through a period of economic doldrums during the late fifties, and few musicians found it possible to support themselves playing the music. Among the best known of those who struggled through these hard times were Monroe, Flatt and Scruggs, the Lilly Brothers and Don Stover, Reno and Smiley, and the Stanley Brothers. Other musicians with bluegrass roots, like the Osborne Brothers, Jim and Jesse McReynolds, and the Louvin Brothers (more of a country act), began to look toward Nashville. But interest in bluegrass music picked up again in the sixties, not only among the urbanites who were the backbone of the folk revival, but among rural southerners as well. Summer bluegrass festivals began to proliferate in the mid-sixties, and the music now has a following that extends from the original southern highlands on into the midwest and southwest.

Singing, and an evident joy in singing and in making harmony, were an important part of early bluegrass. But many second-generation musicians have chosen to concentrate instead on a narrow approach to instrumental virtuosity, with the emphasis mainly on speed and flash. These elements were always present in classic bluegrass, but not alone. Monroe can play at amazing tempos, and a banjoist, particularly in the Scruggs style, can easily outrun most guitarists, but no one would ever accuse Monroe of being a mere technician. He always plays with verve and feeling, and even his fast showpieces convey a sense of intrinsic joy in technique, rather than an outward-directed desire to impress. He shares with his contemporaries an excellent musical sense at slow tempos and in waltz time —areas of the repertory where some of today's speedy technicians just fall apart. I find it a real problem with contemporary bluegrass that many second-generation musicians adhere to hollow forms, with no sense of an emotional core.

Part of the problem, I think, stems from the fact that bluegrass is a fairly simple music, and yet has progressive tendencies. (In jazz, for example—a complex music with progressive tendencies—it is possible to conceive of a guitar tradition that begins with Charlie Christian in the late thirties and ends with Wes Montgomery in the late sixties. It took a good three decades of development by many fine players before Montgomery brought the tradition to its highest point. Now that he is dead, it seems that younger jazz guitarists should examine other influences and move in other directions to avoid winding up in a derivative and an inferior rut.) The first generation of bluegrass musicians achieved a consummate development of the genre early in their own playing careers, and the result is that younger musicians are faced with a choice either of being derivative or of striking out in such different directions that hard-core followers of classic bluegrass are reluctant to recognize their work as bluegrass at all. (A similar situation exists among traditional jazz fans, some of whom—known as "mouldy figs"—refuse to recognize as jazz any music played in a style later than that of the early thirties.)

Already in the sixties a number of musicians, loosely labeled as "progressive," had begun to move away from classic style or repertory. Many were urbanites, or urban-oriented. Among them were the Dillards, a band distinguished by the superb musicianship of banjoist Doug Dillard and competition-style fiddler Byron Berline. Within a traditional matrix, they were original stylists who adapted contemporary songs to their own style, sometimes meeting the contemporary material halfway. A Boston band, the Charles River Valley Boys, went so far as to put out an album of Beatles songs successfully adapted to bluegrass style. (That *Beatles Country* album and their other Elektra albums are now out of print.) New Yorker Roger Sprung, on the other hand, altered his Scruggs-based banjo style by experimenting with sophisticated jazz chords.

In the early seventies, Earl Scruggs and Lester Flatt separated, and Scruggs formed the Earl Scruggs Revue, incorporating the rock-oriented approach of his sons Randy and Gary. This band has set the pattern for a style which has come to be called Newgrass. The group has been hyped as a daring new synthesis of bluegrass, rock, and country forms, which it is not. (Though I don't mean by this to imply that the group's musicianship is inferior.) Their repertory is divided clearly into one category of tunes, in which Scruggs can make a solo statement in his personal style, and another category of tunes outside his style, in which he simply uses the banjo to provide a background texture suggestive of bluegrass. True, he has learned to adapt somewhat to the conventions of contemporary music; this is nothing more than what every working studio musician has to do every few years. Scruggs' original contribution to banjo style was immense, though so thoroughly imitated that we tend now to take it for granted. He's certainly entitled to rest on his past accomplishments, but let's understand that that's what he's doing, and simply changing with the times.

Bluegrass vocal style, with some adaptation and transformation, has become a major influence in contemporary pop recording, just as the black gospel harmony style to which it is closely related has. We can hear the echoes of bluegrass harmony in the work of such groups as Crosby, Stills, Nash and Young and the Eagles, as well as more obviously bluegrass-influenced groups like Country Gazette and Poco. And many of the back-up vocal harmonies in the recordings of singers like Linda Ronstadt come from bluegrass as well.

Bluegrass instrumental style has gone off in many exciting new directions. The spectacular playing of Buck Graves has been responsible for a resurgence of interest in the dobro, and younger players like Mike Auldridge have extended the Graves style into new areas. Doc Watson and the late Clarence White developed traditional guitar flat-

Gathered at the River

picking technique to new heights, and their instrument, which had mainly a rhythmic function in classic bluegrass, now has a solo voice. Fiddlers, following the lead of Vassar Clements and Richard Greene (two completely different stylists), are learning to play in a more modern offshoot of the western swing style, influenced as well by Nashville fiddlers like Johnny Gimble and Buddy Spicher. Clements is probably the most daring and versatile synthesizer in the new bluegrass. And among mandolinists, Dave Grisman and the sometimes erratic Frank Wakefield have developed new approaches rooted in Monroe but reflecting other influences as well.

Banjoists have sought out new approaches to their instrument too, based mostly on the Scruggs sound. Doug Dillard, studio musician Eric Weissberg of *Deliverance* fame, and TV comedy writer Marshall Brickman are among the urban stylists with a recognizably personal approach close to the Scruggs model. And thanks to Bobby Thompson and Bill Keith, there is a rather different approach as well, known as the "chromatic" style. The Scruggs style involves a variety of right-hand picking and accentuation patterns that bring out a melody line, surrounded by other chord tones, from comparatively stable left-hand fingering positions and chord shapes. The new style involves more complicated left-hand work, closely coordinated with picking patterns in order to emphasize a succession of single notes. It's possible to play the literal melody lines of fiddle tunes, for example, in "chromatic" style, whereas the Scruggs style would suggest a skeleton melody embedded in a texture of harmony notes and passing tones.

These new instrumental techniques are moving bluegrass away from the classic sound and into a new area as different from classic bluegrass as classic bluegrass was from old-time string band music. Diehard traditionalists will continue to play and support the classic style, keeping alive an important tradition in American music. And the best progressive and experimental players, now struggling with the sometimes uneasy accommodation of traditional bluegrass style and technique to the sounds of contemporary pop music may well survive their growing pains and work out an exciting new musical synthesis.

For other relevant record listings, *see also* the Banjo, Dobro, and Fiddle sections, pages 79, 81, and 83. Note that some of the best bluegrass of the fifties was recorded for the now-defunct King/Starday/Nashville label. These recordings are not listed here, but they can still be found in some shops; keep your eyes open for them.

ALLEN, LEE, AND THE DEW MOUNTAIN BOYS
Way Out Yonder: New Mountain Songs and Ballads. Old Homestead 90025.

ALLEN, RED, AND THE ALLEN BROTHERS
The Kentucky Story in Bluegrass. King Bluegrass 523.
Allengrass. Lemco 612.

ALLEN, RED, AND THE KENTUCKIANS
_____. Melodeon 7325.

Bluegrass Country, vols. 1–2. County 704, 710.
. . . with Frank Wakefield. Folkways 2408. Standard bluegrass tunes, and two originals by mandolinist Wakefield. The band is oriented toward the Monroe tradition, with innovative instrumental work by the two featured stylists: Wakefield and banjoist Bill Keith. Keith is a leading exponent of the modern "chromatic" style, while Wakefield tries to equal Monroe's rhythmic and harmonic freedom in his own way. An enjoyable casual session from 1964; historically important as an early recorded statement of Keith's work.

Apple Country Bluegrass. Orchard 1047.

BLAYLOCK, BILL
. . . with Clay Willis and the Travelling Band. JED 2935. A pleasant but undistinguished bluegrass record; some instrumentals. (—D.W.)

BLUEGRASS ALLIANCE, THE
_____. Amer. Her. LP 21 S. Mainly standard tunes, played without emotional commitment. With Dan Crary, lead guitar.
Newgrass. Amer. Her. 10–30 S. Contemporary and traditional songs in arrangements influenced by rock and Nashville ideas; rough in spots.

BLUEGRASS ASSOCIATION
Strings Today. Bluegrass Assoc. 42419. Bluegrass and contemporary country tunes.

BLUEGRASS BLACKJACKS
_____. Puritan 5004. A good Indiana band that adheres to classic vocal and instrumental style even in the arrangements of tunes from rock and country repertory that make up a good part of this album. Their original writing is good, too.
Let Us All Pray Together. Pine Tree 511. Original gospel tunes.
Blackjack's Country. Pine Tree 502. Original tunes, traditional-style arrangements.

BLUEGRASS CONNECTION, THE
Bluegrass français. Puritan 5006. A French bluegrass band.

BLUEGRASS GENERATION
Seven Bridges Road. Atteiram API-L-1505-A.

BLUEGRASS RAMBLERS
Live at the Kerrville Folk Festival. Folk Fest (no number).

BLUE RIDGE PARTNERS
Mountain Folks. GHP 901.

BLUE VELVET BAND, THE
Sweet Moments. Warner 1802. Bluegrass and country songs with Jim Rooney, vocals and guitar, and the superbly polished and homogeneous instrumental work of Richard Greene, fiddle, Eric Weissberg, banjo, and Bill Keith, pedal steel. They strike off in a new but not revolutionary direction in which good taste and excellent musicianship prevail.

BROWN, HYLO
Bluegrass Hits. Jessup MB 134.
_____. RR 168.
Folk Songs of Rural America. RR 176.
Legends and Tall Tales. RR 183.
Country Gospel. RR 187.
Sings the Blues RR 200.
Four Sessions (early fifties). CMH 301.

BRYSON, WALLY, AND THE BLAYLOCK BROTHERS
Bluegrass by. . . . Davis Unltd. 33011.

BUSBY, BUZZ, AND LEON MORRIS
Honkytonk Bluegrass. Rounder 0031.

CAIN, BENNIE AND VALLIE
_____. Rebel 1484.
More of. . . . Rebel 1537.

CARROLL COUNTY RAMBLERS, THE
_____. Zap 109.

CLIFTON, BILL
Blue Ridge Mountain Blues. County 740. Relaxed sessions originally recorded in the fifties for Mercury and Starday. Sidemen include Ralph Stanley, banjo, and Tommy Jackson, fiddle.
Happy Days. Golden Guinea GSGL 10476.
_____. With Paul Clayton. Stinson Recordings FV 12004.
See also Hedy West, in The South, Traditional Songs and Singers section, page 61.

COLLINS, RANDALL
. . . *with Curtis Blackwell and the Dixie Bluegrass Boys.* County 728.

CONNIE AND BABE AND THE BACKWOODS BOYS
Basic Bluegrass. Rounder 0042.
Backwoods Bluegrass. Rounder 0043.

COUNTRY COOKING Instead of following the more typical "Newgrass" approach of piling rock and Nashville clichés on top of bluegrass clichés, this band actually does come up with a new and original development of bluegrass style. The band's knowledge of traditional bluegrass and other idioms, especially country swing, is clearly indicated; the band members also have a fertile imagination that takes them beyond mere synthesis.
_____. Rounder 0006. Instrumentals, including originals.
Barrel of Fun. Rounder 0033. More standards and originals, with occasional pedal steel, synthesizer and odd saxophone; vocals not up to the level of the instrumental talent.

COUNTRY GAZETTE One might call this style Los Angeles bluegrass because of the influence of contemporary pop music, particularly in the vocal harmonies. Musicianship is excellent, centering around Byron Berline's fiddle.
A Traitor in Our Midst. United Artists UAS 5596. One of the worst-conceived record jacket designs of all time.
Don't Give Up Your Day Job. United Artists LA090-F.

COUNTRY GENTLEMEN, THE Personnel varies over the years; listings are approximately chronological beginning in the late fifties. The original band was traditionally oriented and very interested in speed. In general, this band provides a good example of an unfortunate tendency among second-generation bluegrass musicians to substitute speed, precision, and technical flash—however real those qualities are and however difficult they are to come by—for a more thoughtful development of the idiom.
_____, vols. 1–4. Folkways 2409, 2410, 2411, 31031.
Sing Bluegrass. Zap 101.
The Traveller. Rebel 1478.
Play It Like It Is. Rebel 1486.
New Look-New Sound. Rebel 1490.
Young Fisherwoman. Rebel 1494.
One Wide River to Cross. Rebel 1497.
Sound Off. Rebel 1501.
Award Winning. Rebel 1506.
Yesterday and Today, vols. 1–3. Rebel 1521, 1527, 1535.
Songs of the Pioneers. Pine Mtn. 248.
Remembrances and Forecasts. Vanguard 79349.
_____. Vanguard 79331.

COUNTRY GRASS
Livin' Free. Rebel 1532. Includes several members of the Shenandoah Cutups, with Herschel Sizemore, mandolin.

THE COUNTRY PALS
Your Bluegrass Favorites. Rich'r'tone 568.

COUNTRY STORE
_____. Rebel 1534.

CRAVENS, RED, AND THE BRAY BROTHERS
419 West Main (1964). Rounder 0015. With John Hartford, fiddle.

CROWE, J. D. Crowe is a particularly crisp banjo player, who came to prominence in Jimmy Martin's band. He favors good traditional vocal trios.
Bluegrass Holiday. Lemco 609.
The Model Church. King Bluegrass 611.
Ramblin' Boy. King Bluegrass 525.

DILLARD, DOUG
Douglas Flint Dillard. 20th Cent. 426.
Duelin' Banjo. 20th Cent. 409.

DILLARD AND CLARK
The Fantastic Expedition of. . . . A & M 4158. Dillard and Clark are part of the same bluegrass-country-rock fusion that later led to the kind of music played by the Nashville group Area Code 615. Doug Dillard is a superb banjo player, one of the few bluegrass pickers who uses different tones and attacks in his playing. Gene Clark was one of the original members of the Byrds, and cohort Bernie Leadon is one of the Eagles. An enjoyable record, with some fine picking and original songs by Clark, Dillard, and Leadon. (—D.W.)

DILLARDS, THE The original Dillards were a good bluegrass band, innovative within the limits of traditional bluegrass taste, and heavily dependent on Doug Dillard's fine banjo work. Such bands of the sixties, before the term "Newgrass" came into use, were called progressive.

Back Porch Bluegrass. Elektra 7232.
Pickin' and Fiddlin'. Elektra 7285. Essentially, a solo album by Byron Berline, featuring his well-executed versions of fiddle tunes with backup by the Dillards.
Live Almost. Elektra 7265.

The following albums were recorded after Doug Dillard left the band. Under the leadership of Rodney Dillard, the band turned increasingly toward a country-rock sound.
Wheatstraw Suite. Elektra 74035.
Copperfields. Elektra 74054.
Tribute to the American Duck. Poppy PP LA175-F.
Roots and Branches. Anthem 5901.

DIXIE GENTLEMEN
Blues and Bluegrass. Old Homestead 90024. With Tut Taylor, dobro; Vassar Clements, fiddle.

DIXIE TRAVELERS
Free Wheeling. Revonah 914.

EASTER BROTHERS
. . . and the Green Valley Quartet. County 716. Bluegrass gospel.

EMERSON AND WALDRON
Bluegrass Country. Rebel 1489.
Bluegrass Session. Rebel 1493.

FLATT, LESTER (b. 1914)
Best of . . . . RCA APL 1-0578.
Live with Bill Monroe. RCA APL 1-0588.
Flatt on Victor. RCA LSP-4495.
Kentucky Ridgerunner. RCA LSP 4633.
Foggy Mountain Breakdown. RCA LSP-4789.
Country Boy. RCA APL-0131.
Before You Go. RCA APL1-0470.
Flatt Out. Columbia CS-1006.

FLATT, LESTER, AND EARL SCRUGGS Of the following recordings, the first four are most highly recommended; they contain early work of an enthusiasm unmatched in later recordings.
_____. Collector's Classics CC 4. 1958–59 concert performances.
Foggy Mountain Chimes. Harmony 11401.
Flatt and Scruggs. Harmony 11314.
Sacred Songs/Great Original Recordings. Harmony 11202.
Songs to Cherish. Harmony 11265.
Changing Times. Columbia CS 9596.
Fabulous Sound. Columbia CS 9055.
Greatest Hits. Columbia CS 9370.
Hard Travelin'. Columbia CS 8751.
Bonnie and Clyde. Columbia CS 9649.
Wabash Cannonball. Harmony 30932.
See Schwann catalogue for additional listings; and *see also* Earl Scruggs, page 76.

FLATT, LESTER, AND MAC WISEMAN
On the Southbound. RCA LSP-4688. Country and traditional tunes in bluegrass settings.
Lester 'n' Mac. RCA LSP 4547.
Over the Hills to the Poorhouse. RCA APL1-0309.

FOOTHILL BOYS
Bluegrass in the Carolina Mountains. County 731.

GOINS BROTHERS
The Head of the Holler. Jessup MB 121.
A Tribute to the Lonesome Pine Fiddlers. Jessup MB 139.
God Bless Her, She's My Mother. Jessup MB146.

GREENBRIAR BOYS A good New York band of the sixties, who combined excellent muscianship with good taste and innovative ideas and repertory, including original songs. Centered around Bob Yellin's banjo and John Herald's guitar and vocals, other personnel variously included Ralph Rinzler or Frank Wakefield, mandolin; Jim Buchanan, fiddle; Fred Weisz, bass.
Ragged but Right. Vanguard 79159.
Better Late Than Never. Vanguard 79233.
Best of. . . . Vanguard 79317. Selections from previous albums.

GREEN VALLEY RAMBLERS
_____. Revonah 909.

HAGAN BROTHERS
Life, Liberty, Bluegrass Music. Kanawha 321.

HAMMONS, KEITH AND NORMA
Wings Over Jordan. Jalyn 151.

HENSLEY, WALTER
Pickin' on New Grass. Rebel 1488.
Three Days from Home. Revonah 912.

Lester Flatt

HICKORY HOLLOW RAMBLERS
_____. Revonah 907.

HIGH COUNTRY A traditionally oriented bluegrass band popular in the San Francisco area (1973–74 recordings).
_____. Warner WS 1937.
Dreams. Warner BS 2608.

HILL, WADE, AND THE BLUEGRASS PROFESSIONALS
_____, 2 vols. Revonah 502, 503.

HODGES BROTHERS
Watermelon Hangin' on the Vine. Arhoolie 5001. Sixties recordings; a countryish pre-bluegrass sound from Mississippi, with prominent fiddle and mandolin.

JIM AND JESSE (McReynolds; Jim b. 1927, Jesse b. 1929) The McReynolds brothers record both in the bluegrass style (featuring Jesse's mandolin) and in the commercial Nashville style (featuring Jim's tenor singing).
The Jim and Jesse Show. Prize 4. Bluegrass, with electric bass and some pedal steel.
Diesel on My Tail. Epic 26314. Truck-driving songs, Nashville style.
Superior Sounds of Bluegrass. Old Dominion 498–05.
Wildwood Flower. Harmony 11399.
Mandolin Workshop. Hilltop 202. Pop and country tunes with country band; many mandolin solos. Jesse McReynolds, a superb mandolin player, developed the unique "cross-picking" style, a flat-picked adaptation of bluegrass finger-picked banjo technique.
Saluting the Louvin Brothers. Epic 26465. A vocally oriented country album.

JONES BROTHERS AND THE LOG CABIN BOYS
The Old Time Way. Pine Tree 517.

KENTUCKIANS, THE *See* Red Allen, page 71.

KENTUCKY COLONELS, THE
_____. United Artists (British) UAS 29514. An English reissue of *Appalachian Swing*, originally put out by World-Pacific in the early sixties. Good bluegrass with fine contributions from all players, but especially valuable for presenting some of the best acoustic guitar work recorded by the late Clarence White. White, who played electric guitar with the Byrds from 1968 to 1972, brought to solo bluegrass guitar an unexcelled sense of touch and timing.

KENTUCKY GENTLEMEN
Headin' South. Pine Tree 518.

KING, CLINTON, AND THE VIRGINIA MOUNTAINEERS
_____. Revonah 905.

LEE, WILMA, AND STONY COOPER
Sunny Side of the Mountain. Harmony 11178. Excellent vocal work.

LILLY BROTHERS AND DON STOVER A good band with an original sound; these transplanted southerners were popular in the Boston area during the sixties.
Folk Songs from the Southern Mountains. Folkways 2433.

Early Recordings (1956–57). County 729.
What Will I Leave Behind. County 742. Gospel.
. . . in Japan, vols. 1–2. TOWA 101, 102.

LILLY, MIKE, AND WENDY MILLER
Newgrass Instrumentals. Old Homestead 90017.

The Lonesome Pine Fiddlers. Collector's Classics CC 3. An important band of the fifties.

LOUISIANA HONEYDRIPPERS
Bayou Bluegrass. Arhoolie 5010.

LUNDY, TED, AND THE SOUTHERN MOUNTAIN BOYS
_____. Rounder 0020.

MARCUM BROTHERS AND THE STANTON MOUNTAIN BOYS
_____. Jalyn 152.

MARTIN, ASA, AND THE CUMBERLAND RANGERS
_____. Rounder 0034.

MARTIN, JIMMY One of the many musicians who served an apprenticeship with Bill Monroe, Martin is an fine, expressive singer, who belongs stylistically somewhere between the bluegrass hills and Nashville. He favors a commercial country-music repertory and is reluctant to call himself a bluegrass singer, but in fact he chooses to be accompanied by a traditional style band, the Sunny Mountain Boys, through which some of the finest musicians have passed.
Big and Country Instrumentals. Decca DL 74891.
Sunny Side of the Mountain. Decca DL7-4643.
Widow Maker. Decca DL 74536. Truck-driving songs.
This World Is Not My Home. Decca DL 74360. Gospel.
Country Music Time. Decca DL7-4285.
Singin' All Day, Dinner on the Ground. Decca DL 75226. Gospel.
Good 'n' Country. MCA 81.
I'd Like to Be Sixteen Again. Decca DL7-5343.
. . . and the Sunny Mountain Boys. Decca DL7-4536.
Moonshine Hollow. Decca CB-20010.

MARTIN, MAC, AND THE DIXIE TRAVELERS
_____. County 743.

McCOURY, DEL McCoury is a good singer who has worked with some of the great bands but has never struck it rich on his own.
Sings Bluegrass (1967). Arhoolie 5006.
High on a Mountain (1972). Rounder 0019.

McGINNIS, ROY, AND THE SUNNYSIDERS
The Beautiful Hills of Kentucky. Jessup MB127.

McMILLAN, ROY
Up in the High Country. Rebel 1532.

McPEAKE BROTHERS
Bluegrass at Its Peak. RCA APL1-0587.

McREYNOLDS, JIM AND JESSE. *See* Jim and Jesse, above.

Bill Monroe

MILLER BROTHERS
The Bluegrass Sound of the. . . . Old Homestead 90039.

MONROE, BILL (b. 1911) A fine mandolinist and singer, and the originator of the classic bluegrass sound. *See* introduction to this section, for further comment, page 68.
The Father of Blue Grass Music. Camden CAL 719 (OP). Early 1940–41 sessions preceding the emergence of the definitive Monroe sound.
Sixteen All-Time Greatest Hits. Columbia CS 1065. Selections from his classic period, including the time when Lester Flatt and Earl Scruggs were in the band. It was the Scruggs banjo style that gave bluegrass its most characteristic instrumental trademark.
   The following two albums are also from this forties period.
The Great . . . . Harmony 11401.
. . . and His Blue Grass Boys. Harmony 11335.
Bluegrass Instrumentals. MCA 104 (formerly Decca DL7-4601). Recordings mainly from the fifties, including fiddlers Vassar Clements, Charlie Cline, and Kenny Baker. Such standards as "Rawhide," "Get Up John," and "Monroe's Hornpipe" are here.
The High Lonesome Sound. MCA 110 (formerly Decca DL7-4780). 1950–64 sessions including Charlie Cline and Vassar Clements (fiddle), Jim Smoak and Sonny Osborne (banjo), and Jimmy Martin and Carter Stanley (guitar-vocal).
Bluegrass Special. Decca DL7-4382.
I'll Meet You in Church Sunday Morning. Decca DL7-4537. Gospel.

Uncle Pen. Decca DL7-5348. A tribute to Monroe's uncle, whom he credits as a major influence. Kenny Baker is featured playing the traditional fiddle tunes Monroe heard from his uncle.
Greatest Hits. MCA 17 (formerly Decca DL7-5010). A good representative selection for starters.
Mr. Blue Grass. MCA 82.
Bluegrass Time. MCA 116.
Kentucky Blue Grass. MCA 136.
Country Music Hall of Fame. MCA 140.
Bluegrass Ramble. Decca DL7-4266.
A Voice from on High. Decca DL7-5135. Gospel.
I Saw the Light. Decca DL7-8769. Gospel.
. . . Sings Country Songs. Decca VL7-3702.
Blue Grass Style. Decca VL7-3870.
Road of Life. MCA 426.
Live Bluegrass Festival. RCA APL 1-0588. With Lester Flatt.

MONROE, BILL AND CHARLIE Monroe worked with his brother during the thirties. This music belongs more properly to the old-time music than to the bluegrass section, but the roots of the bluegrass harmony style are to be found here.
Early Blue Grass Music. Camden CAL-774.
_____. Decca DL7-5066.

MONROE, BILL AND JAMES Recently, Monroe has worked with his son, who sings more in a Nashville style.
Father and Son. MCA 310. With the Bluegrass Boys, including Kenny Baker.

MONROE, CHARLIE (b. 1903)
On the Noonday Jamboree (1944). County 538. This and the following recording are from transcriptions for radio broadcast.
. . . and the Kentucky Partners. County 539. Includes duets with Lester Flatt.
Lord Build Me a Cabin. Pine Mtn. 261.
. . . Sings Again. Pine Mtn. 272.
_____. REM 1003. Old-time and early bluegrass songs. Early sixties, with uncredited banjo, bass, fiddle.

MONROE DOCTRINE
_____. Falls River 002.

MOODY, CLYDE Moody is a good singer, who has never achieved the reputation he deserves.
Moody's Blues. Old Homestead 90013.

MOORE, CHARLIE Another good singer.
A Tribute to Clyde Moody. Old Homestead 90033.
Sings Good Bluegrass. Vetco 3011.
Gospel Time. Vetco 3013.

MORRIS, LEON
Walking Home to Pittsburgh. Folly 002.

MULESKINNER
_____. Warner BS 2787. A group consisting of some of the most talented and original younger players: Richard Greene, Bill Keith, David Grisman, Peter Rowan, and the late Clarence White. The emphasis is on traditional blue-

grass in a modern way, with banjo, mandolin, drums, electric bass, and acoustic and electric guitar. Clarence White had developed an electric guitar style, aided by a mechanical device, that enables him to imitate pedal steel sounds. (He plays acoustic guitar as well.) The fine standard of the instrumental work is marred at times by Peter Rowan's vocal affectations.

NEW SOUTH, THE
_____. Rounder 0044. With J. D. Crowe's fine banjo, Tony Rice's lead guitar.

O'DAY, MOLLY An excellent singer, who worked with gospel songs.
Heart and Soul. Mastertone 80313.
The Living Legend. Pine Mtn. 267.
. . . Sings Again. REM 1001.

OLD AND IN THE WAY
_____. Round 103. Modern songs by modern stylists with evident roots in the old way of playing: Vassar Clements, fiddle; Jerry Garcia, banjo; John Kahn, electric bass; Peter Rowan, guitar and vocals; and the highly imaginative mandolin of Dave Grisman.

OSBORNE BROTHERS (Bobby, b. 1931; and Sonny, b. 1937) Originally bluegrass players, the Osbornes have turned to country music and prefer not to be labeled as bluegrass, feeling, quite correctly, that it prevents them from being recognized as a commercial country act. Their original bluegrass sound of the fifties was marked by a unique approach to high vocal trio harmonies and the remarkable banjo work of Sonny Osborne, a player in the Scruggs-derived style who is unmistakably his own man. Their early work is listed below. *See* the Schwann catalogue for their later work.
Early Recordings, vols. 1–3. Gateway 101, 102, 103.
Bluegrass Instrumentals. MGM 4090.

PINE HILL RAMBLERS
Further Up the River. Revonah 501.
Red and Rusty. Revonah 911.

POOR RICHARD'S ALMANAC
_____. Amer. Her. 401–255. A band assembled especially to feature the banjo of Alan Munde and the mandolin and fiddle of Sam Bush, two highly regarded younger players; rather rough, however.

RECTOR, RED A good mandolin player. Like most first-generation bluegrass players, his style is distinctly his own.
Ballads and Instrumentals. Old Homestead 90023.
Mandolin Instrumentals. Old Homestead (new release, number not yet available).
. . . and Fred Smith. County 721. *Songs from the Heart of the Country.* With Kenny Baker.

RED, WHITE AND BLUE(GRASS)
Very Popular. General Recording Corp. GRC GA 5002. Good contemporary and original songs pleasantly sung and played, with bluegrass instrumentation but pop vocal styles and overdubbed string sections, etc. Really a country pop record with bluegrass roots.
Pickin' Up. GRC GA 10003.

RENO, DON, AND RED SMILEY Another of the first-generation musicians in the bluegrass style, Don Reno is an excellent player in a three-finger style influenced by jazz (four-string) banjo concepts who (especially in his earlier recordings) favors tunes with a blues and swing feel. His best-known work was with Red Smiley; some of their best recordings were on the now-defunct King/Starday label.
The Letter Edged in Black. Wango 111.
Reno and Smiley with Bill Harrell. Rome 1011.

RENO, DON, AND BILL HARRELL Since Smiley's death Reno has worked with Bill Harrell.
Bluegrass Favorites. Jalyn 108.
Most Requested Songs. Jalyn 119.
_____. RR 171.
Mr. Five-String Banjo on Stage. Viechi 1201.
Rivers and Roads. King Bluegrass 528.

RENO, DON, AND EDDIE ADCOCK
Sensational Twin Banjos. Rebel 1482.

RICE, TONY
. . . and Guitar. King Bluegrass 529. With J. D. Crowe, banjo.

RICHARDSON, LARRY
Blue Ridge Bluegrass. County 702.

ROONEY, JIM
_____. Rounder 3007.

ROSE, BUDDY
Down Home Pickin'. Dominion NR-3319. Traditional bluegrass with Hershel Sizemore, mandolin; Tater Tate, fiddle.

SCRUGGS, EARL (b. 1924) It was Scruggs who developed the three-finger banjo-picking style that has come to characterize bluegrass music, and which is usually called Scruggs-picking. He made his greatest impact while he was a member of Bill Monroe's band; *see* Bill Monroe, this section, page 75, for appropriate listings from this time. For many years after the end of his association with Monroe, he worked with Lester Flatt; recordings from this period are listed under Flatt's name above. Since the early seventies Scruggs has been involved with the Earl Scruggs Revue, essentially a country rock band, in which his sons are prominently featured. These are the recordings listed below.
I Saw the Light with a Little Help from My Friends. Columbia KC 31354. A pop and folk-rock band in which Scruggs does not play an especially important stylistic or instrumental role. Guest artists, who parade through the studio, making solid but not exceptional musical contributions, include the Nitty Gritty Dirt Band, Tracy Nelson, Arlo Guthrie, and Linda Ronstadt.
Live at Kansas State (1972). Columbia KC 31758. A strong band performance, featuring Gary Scruggs singing blues, rock, country, and bluegrass songs. Gary Scruggs is not really a good singer, but the instrumental work is excellent, especially from fiddler Vassar Clements.
Family and Friends. Columbia C 30584. From the sound track of an NET program. Friends include Doc Watson, the Byrds, Joan Baez, and the Morris Brothers. Recording quality is hardly professional.

Rockin' 'Cross the Country. Columbia KC 32943.
The Earl Scruggs Revue. Columbia KC 32426.

SECKLER, CURLEY
. . . Sings Again. County 712. Traditional standards favoring medium tempos, by the tenor singer known for his earlier work with Flatt and Scruggs. With elegant and not overbusy backup by the Shenandoah Cutups, a fine band in which Tater Tate's fiddling is prominent.

II GENERATION, THE
Head Cleaner. Rebel 1533.

SELDOM SCENE, THE
Act I. Rebel 1511.
Act II. Rebel 1520.
Act III. Rebel 1528. Old and new songs in bluegrass and newgrass arrangements, with vocal harmonies and solos on fiddle, dobro (Mike Auldridge), banjo, and mandolin.

SHENANDOAH CUTUPS
Bluegrass Autumn (1971). Revonah 904. An excellent traditional bluegrass album by ex-Reno and Smiley sidemen John Palmer, Billy Edwards, and Tater Tate, with fine mandolin from Herschel Sizemore. The band has a unique sound that comes about from a very sparse use of instrumental fills between vocal phrases. Perhaps this is because the men, though excellent players, are really concentrating on the very full harmonies in the vocal parts. It's a pleasure to hear this album.
. . . Sing Gospel. Revonah 908.
———. Revonah 910.
———. Rebel 1526.

SHENANDOAH VALLEY QUARTET Apparently an earlier version of the Shenandoah Cutups.
———. County 706. Good bluegrass gospel songs, with an emphasis on traditional-style vocal harmonies, and many mandolin solos by Herschel Sizemore. A lack of variations in tempo and arrangements detracts somewhat from the otherwise high quality of the music.
———. County 726.

SKYLINE PALS
Songs for Mom and Dad (1973). Skyline DD 104. Sentimental old-time songs.

SLONE FAMILY
Appalachian Bluegrass. Old Homestead 80002.

SMALLWOOD, BOB, AND THE SUNNYSIDERS
Have You Seen Papa's Coal Loading Hands?. Old Homestead 90021.

SMILEY, RED
Most Requested Gospel Songs. Rimrock 3001.
———, vols. 1–3. RR 160, 182, 211.
See also Don Reno, page 76.

SMOKEY MOUNTAIN BOYS
———. Rounder 0029.

SPARKS, LARRY, AND THE LONESOME RAMBLERS
Ramblin' Guitar. Pine Tree 500.
New Gospel Songs. Pine Tree 507.
Bluegrass Old and New. Old Homestead 90004.
Where the Sweet Waters Flow. Old Homestead 90035.
Lonesome Sound. Old Homestead 90041.

SPRUNG, ROGER Banjoist Sprung is well known in New York City bluegrass and old-time music circles. Featured on his recordings are mandolinist Jody Stecher, an excellent all-around musician on a number of instruments, and Jon Sholle, a remarkably versatile guitarist who has most recently recorded with soul singer Esther Phillips. Recordings date from the early sixties on. Sprung himself is an eccentric experimentalist, especially in the harmonic area; his excursions into jazz chords have won him strong enemies and admirers.
Progressive Bluegrass, vols. 1–3. Folkways 2370–2372.
Grassy Licks. Folkways 31036. Selections from the previous albums.
Bluegrass Blast. Folkways 31038. With Hal Wylie.

STANLEY BROTHERS, THE (Carter, 1925–66; and Ralph, b. 1927) The Stanleys are first-generation bluegrass men with a sound of their own. Ralph's banjo work, for example, is clearly in the Scruggs style but differently enough conceived to be regarded as a parallel development. The typical Stanley Brothers sound is sparse and clean, featuring high vocal leads and sometimes an even higher tenor harmony, without the baritone voice that completes the more usual trio. The roles of the instruments are strictly defined, with only one instrument playing solo or lead backup at a given time, even on fills. In the several years since Carter Stanley's death, Ralph Stanley has continued to lead the band under his own name *(see below).* Much fine material, not listed here, was recorded for the now-defunct King and Starday labels and can still be found in some record bins and mail-order catalogues.
Their Original Recordings. Melodeon 7322.
. . . of Virginia, vols. 1–2. County 738, 739.
The Legendary, vols. 1–2. Rebel 1487, 1495. Live performances, including songs not elsewhere recorded by them. Sound quality varies.
———, vols. 1–2. Collector's Classics 1, 2.
Beautiful Memorial Album. Pine Mtn. 213.
An Empty Mansion. Rimrock 153.
. . . and Jackie and Larry Dickson. Rimrock 200. One side of the Stanleys and one side of the Dicksons.
Together for the Last Time. Rebel 1512. Recordings from the 1966 Beanblossom Festival, augmented by several 1956 pieces also recorded in live performance.

STANLEY, RALPH
A Man and His Music. Rebel 1530. Stanley plays half the tunes on this record in the frailing style, and the rest with the more typical three-finger Scruggs roll. Because of its variety, this record can be listened to more times than many other bluegrass records can. Stanley is also an excellent singer and composer, and there are several examples of these aspects of his talent on this record. (—D.W.)
Old Time Music. Jalyn 118.
Bluegrass Sound. Jalyn 120.
Sing Michigan Bluegrass. Jessup MB 108.

"Bluegrass Sound": Ralph Stanley

Gospel Echoes of the Stanley Bros. Jessup MB 129.
The Stanley Sound. King Bluegrass 522.
Cry from the Cross. Rebel 1499.
Something Old, Something New. Rebel 1503.
Old Country Church. Rebel 1514.
I Want to Preach the Gospel. Rebel 1522.

STORY, CARL
. . . and the Original Rambling Mountaineers. Puritan 1001 (7 inch LP). Story is best known today as a country and bluegrass gospel singer. This album, originally recorded on amateur equipment in 1939, presents him at the beginning of his career, with banjoist Johnny Whisnant. They play essentially old-time music, but with the beat tending more toward an even four, and with several other hints of the transition toward bluegrass style. Only enough of this session survives to fill a 7-inch long-playing record, and the sound quality is quite poor; the record was issued for historical interest only.
Bluegrass Gospel Singing Convention. Jessup MB 116.
All Day Sacred Singing. Pine Mtn. 215.
'Neath the Tree of Life. Pine Tree 505.
. . . and the Brewster Bros. Rimrock 100.

STOVER, DON Although Stover developed his three-finger banjo style by studying the recorded work of Scruggs that first began to appear when Stover was a young man, he had already acquired the frailing and other pre-bluegrass styles. The independence that this prior knowledge would have given him may have contributed to his way of playing, which is personal and individual. It is also a rather warm style, much less mechanical than most offshoots of the Scruggs style. One of the relatively few banjo players to sing lead, Stover is also an excellent writer, with things to say.
Things in Life. Rounder 0014. Bluegrass and old-time songs, fiddle tunes and breakdowns, including five original pieces and one in frailing style. A very enjoyable and good-feeling record, with John Hall (fiddle) and Dave Grisman (mandolin) contributing to the good feelings.
. . . and the White Oak Mountain Boys. Rounder 0039.
West Virginia Coal Miner's Blues. Old Homestead 9011.
See also Lilly Brothers, page 74.

SUNNYSIDERS, THE
Motor City Bluegrass. Fortune 3010.

TAYLOR, EARL
. . . and the Stoney Mountain Boys. Vetco 3017.

TAYLOR, EARL, AND JIM McCALL
Bluegrass Favorites, vols. 1–2. RR 188, 242.
. . . with the Stoney Mountain Boys. RR 243.

TRISCHKA, TONY
Bluegrass. Rounder 0048. Trischka is a foremost experimentalist in the contemporary chromatic banjo style.

VAL, JOE, AND THE NEW ENGLAND BLUEGRASS BOYS
One Morning in May. Rounder 0003.
Volume Two. Rounder 0025.

VARNEY, LOWELL
Going Back to West Virginia. Jessup MB 131.

VERN AND RAY
Sounds from the Ozarks. Old Homestead 10001.

WALDRON, CLIFF
Right On. Rebel 1496.
Traveling Light. Rebel 1500.
Just a Closer Walk with Thee. Rebel 1505.
One More Step. Rebel 1510.
One More Mile. Rebel 1518.
Bluegrass Time. Rebel 1524.

WHITE, BUCK, AND THE DOWN HOMERS
————. County 735. Much mandolin from the leader, with fiddle (Kenny Baker), guitar, banjo, bass.

WHITEWATER
Springtime in the White Clouds. Amer. Her. 401–41D. Oregon musicians who play both typical bluegrass and what amounts to original bluegrass-rooted soft rock, with traditional instrumentation.

WILLIAMS, JIMMY
Summer's Gone. Jessup MB 132. Bluegrass gospel.

WISEMAN, MAC (b. 1925). Wiseman is more of a country singer, and would probably rather be known as such. But he has a great following among bluegrass audiences, and frequently works with bluegrass musicians. He's a fine, soulful singer, probably more suited to a bluegrass than a commercial country context.
Old Country Favorites. RR 158.
Concert Favorites. RCA LSP-4845.
See also Lester Flatt, page 73.

ANTHOLOGIES AND COLLECTIONS

Beanblossom. MCA 2–8002 (2-rec. set). From the proceedings of Bill Monroe's 1973 festival at Beanblossum, Indiana. Includes Bill and James Monroe, Jim and Jesse, Jimmy Martin, Lester Flatt, and Carl Jackson.
Bluegrass for Collectors. RCA APL1–0568. A misnomer; mostly includes old-time music by J. E. Mainer, Gid Tanner, and others, in addition to a few early pieces by Bill and Charlie Monroe, just on the verge of becoming bluegrass.
Blue Grass Special. Camden ADL2–0292. Rather slick recordings by recent studio groups: the Bluegrass Banjo Players, the Country Fiddlers, Living Guitars.
Early Bluegrass. RCA LPV-569. A first-rate selection of pre-bluegrass and bluegrass material, from 1936 to 1954. Performances are musically excellent, as well as of great documentary value. Bill Monroe, Charlie Monroe, Wade Mainer, Roy Hall, Blue Sky Boys, Lonesome Pine Fiddlers, Jimmy Martin, Osborne Brothers.
The Early Days of Bluegrass, vols. 1–7. Rounder 1013–1019. Scheduled for future release as this book goes to press; further information not available.
Mountain Music Bluegrass Style. Folkways 2318. Unaffected, noncommercial bluegrass by various musicians, mostly first-generation bluegrass players, but including urban revivalists. Compiled by Mike Seeger in the late fifties.
Oregon Territory. Grass Roots 001. Bands from the northwest: Tall Timber, Puddle City, Corn's Bluegrass Remedy, Muddy Bottom Boys, Sawtooth Mountain Boys.

Sound of Bluegrass, The. Camden ACL1–0535(e). Reissues from mostly out-of-print RCA albums, ranging from older recordings (Morris Brothers, Monroe Brothers, Blue Sky Boys) to recent studio groups.

INSTRUMENTAL ALBUMS

Records listed in this section are oriented primarily toward instrumental work, although they may include vocals also. In order to make the listings as useful as possible to the record buyer, I have not separated traditional and nontraditional performers, except in the Guitar section, which includes only traditional and Nashville guitarists. There are enough contemporary guitarists, either in traditional style or in modern styles that arise from traditional techniques and concepts, to justify separate listings. These may be found in the Blues Revival and Contemporary Guitarists sections, pages 109 and 117.

BANJO

Listings are of primarily instrumental albums. The singers and entertainers in the following list are all excellent banjo players, worthy of attention for their banjo work alone, but since they use the banjo mainly to accompany their own singing, they are listed in other sections.
1. Listed under Traditional Songs and Singers, page 57: Rufus Crisp, Roscoe Holcomb, Buell Kazee, Obray Ramsey, Hobart Smith, Pete Steele.
2. Listed under Old-Time String Band and Early Country Music, page 62: Uncle Dave Macon, Clarence "Tom" Ashley, Kyle Creed, Fred Cockerham, Tommy Jarrell, Snuffy Jenkins.
3. Listed under Bluegrass, page 68: J. D. Crowe, Doug Dillard, Don Reno, Earl Scruggs, Ralph Stanley, Don Stover, and many others.

ARONOFF, BENJI
The Two Sides of. . . . Prestige 7416 (OP). Vocals and instrumental solos, with guitar and banjo. Aronoff is one of the finest banjoists to have come out of the urban revival movement. He uses mainly the frailing style, making every note count melodically or harmonically, instead of using it as a rhythm style with a fairly low ratio of single-note-to-strum as in the work of most players. His tone is excellent and his sense of arrangement exceptionally clear, especially in regard to the use of unusual tunings. Out of print, but still turns up occasionally in the record stores.

BROWN, SULLIVAN, AND COMPANY
Magnum Banjos. Sequatchie (no serial number). Waltzes and other dance and fiddle tunes in the modern chromatic bluegrass style (*see* Glossary) on twin banjos, with bluegrass band.

CADWELL, PAUL, SHIRLEY KOLLER, AND CHARLIE WRIGHT
————. Twilight PSC 165. Side one contains banjo solos by Cadwell, with occasional piano accompaniments. Cadwell plays turn-of-the-century ragtime-influenced selections on the five-string banjo, in the style of Fred van Eps and Vess Ossman. Cadwell is a good player, but not in the van Eps

class. The second side features folk and pop songs in adequate but not particularly interesting arrangements by Koller and Wright. (—D.W.)

CAMP, A. L.
Plays the Banjo. Folkways 3525. Turn-of-the-century banjo music, with piano accompaniment, in a ragtime-influenced style. Camp has a liveliness in his playing that belies his age, eighty-four at the time of recording. A fascinating historical document despite occasional lapses in the performance. (—D.W.)

CAMPBELL, JEFF
Clawhammer Banjo and Old-Time Fiddle Songs. Vetco 3014.

FAIER, BILLY
The Art of the 5-String Banjo. Riverside 12–813 (OP). *Travellin' Man.* Washington 740 (OP, reissued from Riverside, OP). During his prime in the late fifties Faier made these two recordings. They present a triumphantly unique concept of the instrument, based on tasteful adaptations of traditional and original elements. He plays traditional American and European songs, fiddle tunes, original instrumentals, adaptations of Elizabethan lute music, etc. The second album includes more of his occasional vocal work, which is not exceptional, and some guitar playing. Frank Hamilton provides sympathetic guitar accompaniments on the first album.
Banjo. Takoma C-1037. Not up to the previous records; Faier seems to have lost interest in the kind of playing he was doing then; much loose improvisation here.

GEORGE, FRANKLIN
_____. Kanawha 307 (=Saydisc SDM=229). George, a fiddler and banjo picker from Virginia, has a fine sense for preserving the most archaic elements in the style of his instruments, though he is a relatively young man as far as mountain musicians go. He is assisted by John Summers, an excellent old fiddler from Indiana. While serving in Europe with the army, George became interested in the bagpipes, and he plays several tunes on them here. The recording quality is not good.

HALL, BARRY
The Virtuoso 5-String Banjo. Folkways 3533. Barry Hall has succeeded in making a pleasant and calm record of banjo music. Obviously influenced by Billy Faier and Pete Seeger, Hall has put their styles to his own use. He also has a pleasing and unaffected voice. (—D.W.)

JACKSON, CARL
Bluegrass Festival. Prize 2.
Banjo Player. Capitol ST-11166. Flashy country and bluegrass instrumentals in the modern chromatic style.

JARRELL, TOMMY
Come and Go with Me. County 748. North Carolina clawhammer banjo solos. *See also* Oscar Jenkins, Old-Time String Band and Early Country Music section, page 64.

JORDAN, VIC
Pickaway. Atteiram 1027. Bluegrass.

PARISH, PETE
Clawhammer Banjo. Tennvale 003. A whole album of banjo instrumentals in the style of Wade Ward, by a young Englishman who learned from Ward. It captures the essence of the style despite some rhythmic fluffs. Pretty and relaxed playing, never flashy. (—D.W.)

RESER, HARRY
Banjo Crackerjax (1922–30). Yazoo 1048. This listing represents a token bow in the direction of the four-string tenor banjo, an instrument used for the playing of pop, ragtime, jazz, and light classical music in the twenties. Reser was one of the greatest virtuosos on the instrument.

ROSENBAUM, ART
Five String Banjo. Kicking Mule 108 (European release: Kicking Mule/Sonet SNKF 101). A fine record by an excellent revivalist player of old-timey music. Art plays in a variety of tunings and styles on regular and fretless banjo; he is creative and true to tradition at the same time. There is a feeling of reality to these performances that makes you feel like a friend has come into your living room to trade stories and songs. (—D.W.)

ROSENBAUM, ART, AND AL MURPHY
_____. Meadowlands MS-2. Old-time songs and dance tunes on banjo, fiddle, and guitar; Rosenbaum, an art professor at the University of Iowa, is a fine frailer.

"The Gayest Old Dude in Town": Uncle Dave Macon

SMITH, ARTHUR, AND BOBBY THOMPSON
Battling Banjos. Monument Z 32259. This is Arthur "Guitar Boogie" Smith, not to be confused with Arthur Smith the fiddler. He recorded the original version of "Dueling Banjos" in the fifties—he called it "Feudin' Banjos" then and played it on the tenor banjo while Don Reno played five-string. This whole record is based on the same concept, and it wears a bit thin. But it does offer the rare opportunity to hear lots of picking by Bobby Thompson, a sensational and innovative player on the five-string. He gets off some breathtaking solos. (—D.W.)

WALLACE, HOWARD
Old-Time 5-String Banjo. Jewel 186.
When You and I Were Young. Jewel 219.
Early Sounds of the Mountain Banjo. Jewel 305.

WARD, WADE (1892–1971)
Uncle Wade. Folkways 2380. 1958–64 recordings—plus a selection from his 1938 Library of Congress recordings—by one of the greatest banjo players in the frailing style. Ward influenced both his Virginia neighbors and the urban imitators who studied his records. The banjo technique called frailing or clawhammer style (*see* Glossary) is a fairly simple basic gesture, which can be varied in any number of ways, with increasing degrees of rhythmic complexity. Some of the strongest southern musical personalities chose the style for their expression, but few developed it to the point Ward did. Also included are a number of tunes in his equally personal fiddle style. *See also* Roscoe Holcomb and Fields Ward, in the Traditional Songs and Singers, and Old-Time String Band and Early Country Music sections, pages 59 and 67, respectively.

ERIC WEISSBERG
. . . and Marshall Brickman: New Directions in Banjo and Bluegrass. Elektra 7238 (OP). With Clarence White, guitar.

WEISSBERG, ERIC, AND STEVE MANDEL
Dueling Banjos. Warner BS 2683. Only the title cut, which is from *Deliverance*, features Weissberg and Mandel. The rest of this album was released fifteen years before *Deliverance*, on an Elektra album, and was recorded by Weissberg and Marshall Brickman. The album represents one of the early attempts at playing fiddle tunes on the banjo, and both Weissberg and Brickman were at the forefront of the movement. (—D.W.)

WEISSMAN, DICK
The Things That Trouble My Mind. Capitol ST 2033 (OP).

WHISNANT, JOHNNIE
———— (1974). Rounder 0038. Country, ragtime, old-time, and bluegrass songs with vocals and band. Whisnant was one of the earliest banjo players to adapt the Carolina three-finger style to the bluegrass style later made popular by Earl Scruggs.

ANTHOLOGIES AND COLLECTIONS

American Banjo, Scruggs Style. Folkways 2314. An invaluable documentary, compiled by Mike Seeger, of various styles relating to the banjo picking of Earl Scruggs. Included are pieces by Earl's older brother Junie, and by Snuffy Jenkins, one of the chief influences on Earl's playing. A must for anyone interested in the development of modern banjo styles. (—D.W.)

Anthology of the Banjo. Tradition 2077. Erik Darling, Mike Seeger, Mason Williams, and others.

Clawhammer Banjo. Recently recorded solos in frailing style, as well as a few string band pieces. The players are personal stylists of varying degrees of proficiency, some excellent. It's interesting to observe the variety of approaches that can be taken within the limits of a regional style; all are older North Carolina players.

  Vol. 1. County 701. Wade Ward, Kyle Creed, Fred Cockerham, and George Stoneman.

  Vol. 2, *More Clawhammer Banjo Songs and Tunes.* County 717. Oscar Wright, Gaither Carlton, Tommy Jarrell, Willard Watson, and others.

Feuding Banjos. Olympic 7105. Eric Weissberg, Mike Seeger, Erik Darling, and others.

Five String Banjo Jamboree. Washington 704 (OP, formerly issued on Riverside, OP). Billy Faier, Eric Weissberg, and Dick Weissman.

Folk Banjo Styles. Elektra EKL 217 (OP). Tom Paley, Marshall Brickman, Eric Weissberg, Art Rosenbaum.

Kings of the Ragtime Banjo. Yazoo 1044. Early recordings by Fred van Eps and Vess Ossman. Both these men were virtuoso ragtime players on gut-strung five-string banjo. They were quite popular in the period 1900–25; unfortunately, recording quality at that time was poor, so some of the selections are hard to listen to, and one sometimes wishes for less flashy tempos. The recordings are of historical significance, however, and ragtime pianist David Jasen contributes informative notes. (—D.W.)

Mountain Banjo Tunes and Songs. County 515. An eclectic and uneven collection, which includes a sparkling "Coal Creek March" by Marion Underwood. Other artists include Buell Kazee, Uncle Dave Macon, Dock Walsh. (—D.W.)

DOBRO

See the About Guitars section, page 205, for a discussion of the dobro. I use the term loosely here to include several early Hawaiian-style guitarists who do not play the resophonic guitar, but do play a regular acoustic guitar in dobro style, with a steel slide.

AULDRIDGE, MIKE Auldridge is the foremost contemporary stylist on the instrument, having in recent years transcended the early influence of Josh Graves. Though his roots are in bluegrass—he has recorded with the Seldom Scene and Cliff Waldron—he is capable of dealing with areas of the contemporary pop repertory beyond the reach of most dobro players.
Dobro. Takoma D-1033. Excellent instrumentals, a few vocals. With David Bromberg, Vassar Clements, Josh Graves, and others.
Blues and Bluegrass. Takoma D-1041. With occasional vocals and many excellent sidemen, including David Bromberg, John Duffy, and Vassar Clements. If anything, too many sidemen, creating an ensemble sound too hectic at times. Blues, bluegrass, and more—Auldridge takes the dobro into new harmonic territory, where it's never been

before (for example, "Killing Me Softly"), and so plays it as it's never been played before.

BEVERLY, CHARLIE

Sounds of the Dobro. Starr 1050. Available from Rt. 2, Box 262, Pound, Va. 24279. A variety of old-time tunes, played well but accompanied by a spotty bluegrass backup group. Beverly plays in the older style that comes from the acoustic Hawaiian guitar tradition of the twenties: very full and busy, with the thumb moving in the finger-picking guitar style. The more modern style is sparser, leaving space for bass, drums, and other instruments of the contemporary ensemble.

BROTHER OSWALD, BASHFUL (Pete Kirby)

_____. Rounder 0013. Kirby is a great dobro player, best known for his work with Roy Acuff, though he appears here with suitably sparse accompaniment. His work, which bridges the gap between the twenties and today, is rooted in the old Hawaiian style, with little influence from the bluegrass developments of Josh Graves. Clarity of concept, execution, and tone are plentifully evident.
That's Country. Rounder 0041. With Charlie Collins.

Bottleneck Blues Guitar Classics. Yazoo 1026. Contains mostly country blues Spanish-style slide guitar work (*see* About Guitars, page 205), but also includes a spectacularly good twenties version of the "St. Louis Blues," Hawaiian-style.

CARLISLE, CLIFF

_____, vols. 1-2. Old Timey 103, 104. A popular country music entertainer of the thirties, who accompanied himself on steel guitar. It was from the playing of this school that the electric steel and pedal steel sounds of western swing came about.
Country Kind of Songs and Hymns. REM 1002.

CLINE, CHARLIE

Country Dobro. Adelphi 2001.

DARBY AND TARLETON

A popular duo, who helped shape the early country music sound; vocals with rhythm and Hawaiian guitar. *See also* Jimmy Tarleton, this section, page 83.
_____ (1927–32). Old Timey 112.
_____. FV 12504.

GABBARD, HARLEY

Tall Timber Man. Vetco 3006.

GRAVES, BUCK "UNCLE JOSH"

Alone at Last. Epic KE 33168. Country songs with studio arrangements, well-played by a passel of Nashville sidemen; the title is somewhat misleading.

GRAVES, BUCK "UNCLE JOSH," AND KENNY BAKER

Graves is the preeminent bluegrass dobro player, well-known for his work with Flatt and Scruggs, and more recently with the Earl Scruggs Revue. It was Graves who first developed a bluegrass style on the instrument, by applying a right-hand technique derived from Scruggs' banjo style, and not from the guitar finger-picking style which is more commonly applied to the dobro. Graves' work in that style is to be found on numerous Flatt and Scruggs albums. Here he plays in a deliciously economical, mainly single-note, style, possibly because Baker's guitar work is so full. But Graves' tone is so well centered, his notes so well placed, that he can say more with a few notes than other dobro players can with many. Baker is best known for his fiddling, which appears only on two cuts in the first album. He plays guitar in a busy finger-picking style or flat-picked in bluegrass rhythm style.
Something Different. Puritan 5001.
Bucktime. Puritan 5005.

GREEN, LLOYD

I have picked Lloyd Green as one select example of a Nashville-style pedal steel player who doubles on dobro; another good example might be Norm Hamlet from Merle Haggard's band. The characteristically twangy dobro sound is frequently used in Nashville recordings to introduce a funky or melancholy color to the background ensembles, or to suggest a down-home feeling. Green contributes simple and elegant backup parts to the following vocal albums by Don Williams, and pedal steel work as well.
Don Williams, vols. 1–2. JMI 4004, 4006.

HADDOCK, KENNY

Dobro and Fiddle. Zap 103. Old-time and bluegrass tunes in a very full style, with bluegrass backup band. Other side has Billy Baker, bluegrass fiddle.

The Hawaiian Steel Guitar (1920–40). Folk-Lyric 9008.

Hula Blues. Rounder 1012. Steel guitar instrumentals of the thirties and forties by Sol Hoopii, Frank Ferera, Jim and Bob, the Genial Hawaiians, and others.

JACKSON, SHOT

Hurting Side of Country. Arc 720.
Stealing with a Dobro. Arc 721.
. . . with David Musgrave and Paul Buskirk: Dobro, Shobro and Steel. Stoneway 444.

KING, BEVERLY

Drifting with the Dobro and *A Dobro Dozen.* Privately issued, available from King, Box 605, Revere, Pa. 18953.
Leave a Lot of Happy Tracks (1974). Old-time vocals and instrumentals, ali overdubbed by King herself on dobro, banjo, and guitar; rather rough.

KIRBY, PETE.

See Bashful Brother Oswald, above.

SHIPLEY, ROBBIE

In All Sincerity (1972). "D" 7009. Old-time and commercial country tunes played well in Nashville-style arrangements, with backup by various members of the Earl Scruggs Revue, including Josh Graves.

STEEL GUITAR CLASSICS

_____. Old Timey 113. Mostly instrumentals; a variety of styles by white and Hawaiian players and one black player of the twenties and thirties: Jimmy Tarleton, Sol Hoopii Cliff Carlisle, and others. Good selections and a good documentary of early styles.

TARLETON, JIMMY
Steel Guitar Rag (sixties). Testament 3302.

TAYLOR, TUT
Friar Tut (1971). Rounder 0011. A casual session by excellent musicians whose best work is on other records. Recording or mixing levels are erratic, especially in reference to Norman Blake's backup and solo guitar parts. Keep your eyes open for a now-out-of-print record that Taylor made several years ago on World-Pacific with Clarence and Roland White.

FIDDLE

In addition to American fiddlers, I have also included fiddlers from Ireland and the British Isles, since American fiddling is based on English and Celtic styles, combined with the continental influence of waltzes, polkas, schottisches, and set dances. Canadian fiddlers, whose roots are mostly Celtic, are also included here; a number of Canadian fiddlers represent the rich Scottish tradition of Cape Breton, Nova Scotia. For further comments on Canadian fiddling, *see* the Canadian Music section, page 156.

ALLEN, HAROLD
Fiddlin' Around. Amer. Her. 401–4.

ANDERSON, BOB, AND THE COUNTRY RAMBLERS
Indiana Hoedown. GHP 904 = Puritan 5003. Smooth midwestern versions of well-known fiddle tunes with bluegrass backup band.

ARBUCKLE, BOB
Square Dances with Calls. Folkways 8825.
Jigs and Reels. Folkways 8826.
Old Time Couple Dances. Folkways 8827. Tunes mostly of British and Irish descent, still in active use by dancers in Ontario. With accordion and piano.

ASHBY, JOHN
Old Virginia Fiddling. County 702.
Down on Ashby's Farm. County 745.

BAIN, ALY, AND MIKE WHELLANS
_____. Trailer LER 2022. Bain is the fine young Shetland Islands fiddler known for his work with the Boys of the Lough; Whellans plays guitar and sings.

BAKER, BILLY
Dobro and Fiddle. Zap 103. Standard fiddle tunes with bluegrass backup. Other side has Kenny Haddock, dobro.

BAKER, KENNY Baker is the leading bluegrass fiddler, known for his work with Bill Monroe and other major figures in the idiom, and like most bluegrass fiddlers he is well versed in standard fiddle tunes and the western swing style as well. The first record provides a particularly clear example of how his imagination works; it contains traditional tunes and originals as well. Baker's concept of an original fiddle tune actually constitutes a reworking and recombination of older tunes, so that the new tune is al-

most recognizable, but not quite. This is typical of the way innovation and change occur in this essentially conservative idiom.
A Baker's Dozen. County 730.
Portrait of a Bluegrass Fiddler. County 719.
Kenny Baker Country. County 736.
Dry and Dusty. County 744.
High Country. County 714. Twin fiddling with Joe Greene.
See also under Buck "Uncle Josh" Graves, Dobro section, page 82.

BEAUDOIN, LOUIS
_____. Philo 2000. Good French-Canadian fiddling, both older and newer tunes, by a Vermonter accompanied by piano, guitar, bones (wood percussion blocks), and his own clog dancing.

BELT, JAY
_____. Amer. Her. AH 401–510.

BERLINE, BYRON. *See* the Dillards and Country Gazette, Bluegrass section, page 72.

BLOCK, ALLAN, AND RALPH LEE SMITH
_____ (1971). Meadowlands MS-1. Old-time songs and fiddle tunes with most of the emphasis on Block's fiddle, but with plenty of excellent dulcimer work, and guitar and harmonica too, from Smith. One of the first urbanites to take up the fiddle, Block was a part of the old-time music scene in New York City for many years; until his recent

Just Fiddling

retirement, there was always a fiddle on the wall of his Greenwich Village sandal shop. This is a casual, good-feeling session, informally recorded, with some vocals not up to the standard of the instrumental work.

BOUDREAULT, LOUIS "PITOU"
Portrait du vieux Kébec. Opus 219. Joyful, thoroughly delightful fiddling from rural Lac St-Jean in Québec Province. Boudreault is a unique player in the old self-contained solo style, accompanying his own melodies with a judicious use of drones and double-stops, as well as with his own highly rhythmic clog dancing. He is *raconteur* as well as *violoneux.* About half the record is occupied with stories and introductions, but his voice and inflection are musical, and make pleasing interludes even if you can't follow the French.

BRIAND, ELMER
The Cape Breton Fiddle of. . . . Celtic SCX 56. A good strong fiddler, who preserves the Scottish sense of ornamentation. One side of rather tame waltzes, one of more spirited reels, jigs, strathspeys, and clog dances, with guitar and piano.

BRYSON, WALLY
Country Fiddling. Davis Unltd. 33006.

BURKE, JOE, ANDY MCGANN, AND FELIX DOLAN
A Tribute to Michael Coleman. Shaskeen OS 360. Jigs, reels, and a few beautiful airs for McGann's solo fiddle. Burke is an excellent accordionist; Dolan accompanies on piano.

CAMPBELL FAMILY
Champion Fiddlers. Fretless 101.

CARIGNAN, JEAN
Carignan's technique is amazing, but more so the joy and energy with which he applies it. There are few players in any music who reach his degree of virtuosity without sacrificing feeling or originality. Carignan had a taste of the life of the professional musician; now he prefers to drive a cab in Montreal and play on weekends. His favored repertory emphasizes the Celtic tradition in French-Canadian fiddling. Note that the last three records listed were issued under his nickname, Ti-Jean (*Ti-* is short for *petit,* "little").
_____ (1973). Philo 2001. His best-recorded album, and his first in a decade, it demonstrates continued growth. The freedom with which he varies and ornaments the tunes is so extravagant that it's reminiscent of a jazzman's approach to structure. A good deal of this freedom comes from the sympathetic support of pianist Gilles Losier, who is also a fiddler.
French-Canadian Fiddle Songs. Legacy 120 (originally issued on Elektra). With accordion (Philippe Bruneau), piano, and guitar; several selections feature Bruneau, who is a fine player.
Old Time Fiddle Tunes. Folkways 3531. Backup band includes Pete Seeger, banjo.
Songs and Dances of Québec. Folkways 6951 (10 inch). Canadian party songs and dance tunes by band with caller, featuring Carignan on several tunes.
Le violoneux. London (Canadian) MB 4 (OP).

Valses, reels, et gigues. With Philippe Bruneau. London (Canadian) 40032 (OP).
En hommage à l'atelier folklorique. London (Canadian) MB 52 (OP).
See also Alan Mills, Canadian Folk Music section, page 53; Pete Seeger, Folk Song Revival section, page 107; Newport Folk Festival, General Folk Anthologies and Folk Festival Recordings section, page 134.

CARSON, FIDDLIN' JOHN.
See Traditional Songs and Singers section, page 58.

CLEMENTS, VASSAR
Crossing the Catskills (1972). Rounder 0016. Clements is an accomplished bluesy bluegrass and western swing fiddler with a bagful of original hot licks and a good sense of how to extend the idioms and techniques he has mastered into new musical territory. Including overdubs, he plays fiddle, flat-picked fiddle, viola, cello, guitar, and mandolin in this polished selection of blues, fiddle tunes, old-time, pop, and original songs. David Bromberg, one of several accompanists, plays some of the best lead guitar he's ever recorded. An excellent album, full of enthusiasm that saves it from being almost too slick.
Southern Country Waltzes. RR 236. With pedal steel and rhythm section.
Hillbilly Jazz. Flying Fish 101.
_____ (1974). Mercury SRM-1-1022. With Nashville-style studio band.

CLINE, CURLY RAY
Chicken Reel. Rebel 1498. Fiddle tunes, blues, and bluegrass standards. Cline is best known as a member of Ralph Stanley's band, which usually accompanies him on his own records. On several tunes there are severe intonation problems, typical of amateur fiddlers but unexpected here.
My Little Home in West Virginia. Rebel 1515.
Fishing for Another Hit. Rebel 1531.
Kentucky Fox Hunt. Melody 17.
The Working Man. Jalyn 126.

COLEMAN, MICHAEL
Coleman is regarded as the great master of the up-tempo County Sligo dance style of Irish fiddling, although his greatest reputation was among Irish-Americans. On first hearing him, I found his playing stiff and rather mechanical. Later, as I learned more about fiddling and as my ear for bowings and ornamentation improved, I recognized in him a unique and influential stylist, and great technician.
The Heyday of Michael Coleman (1922–29). Intrepid IR 2.
Irish Jigs and Reels. Ace of Hearts AH 56. From the thirties.

CORMIER, JOSEPH
Scottish Violin Music from Cape Breton Island. Rounder 7001.

CRONIN, PADDY
Irish Fiddle. Fiddler 003. A good Boston fiddler originally from Ireland, Cronin also plays flute in a rather odd, breathy style; it sounds as if he uses his breath across the mouthpiece as a way of imitating the kinds of bowing attack that are available to him on the fiddle. Few Irish musicians are

Alabama Fiddling

accomplished on both these instruments; an interesting album in light of the relationship between Irish fiddle and flute and pipe music.

DACUS, JOHNNY
The Tennessee Mountain Fiddler. To be released by Old Homestead as this book goes to press; number not available.

DE JARLIS, ANDY
Fiddling Fantasies. London (Canadian) EBX-4167. A commercial fiddler, but with spirit, from western Canada, well known for his touch with waltzes.

DERRICK, VERNON
Cross-Country. Revonah 906. Bluegrass, led by fiddler Derrick.

DOUCET, TOM
The Down East Star. Fiddler 001. An excellent, gutsy Bos-

ton fiddler originally from Nova Scotia. Some recent recordings, some from old 78's.

DOUGLAS, BOB
Walden's Ridge: Old Time Fiddle Tunes from the Sequatchie Valley (1973). Tennvale 001S.

EAST, ERNEST, AND THE BLUE RIDGE MOUNTAIN BOYS
———. County 718.

EDMONDS, JIMMY, AND THE VIRGINIA-CAROLINA BUDDIES
———. Kanawha 318. Standard fiddle tunes, with backup band. Edmonds, who recorded this album at age fourteen, plays smoothly with a wide tone, sticking pretty much to the literal melody. Hopefully a distinct musical personality will emerge; certainly the basis is here.

EDMONDS, NORMAN
Old-Time Fiddling. Davis Unltd. 33002.

ENLOE, LYMAN
Fiddle Tunes I Recall. Bluegrass Assoc. 41308. Twenty-three tunes, some rarely recorded, by a good Missouri old-time fiddler with bluegrass backup.

EVANS, VIRGE
The Flying Fiddler. Amer. Her. 401-34.

FITZGERALD, WINSTON "SCOTTY" An excellent Canadian fiddler in the Scots Cape Breton style, strong and gutsy especially at slower and medium tempos, with his own style of phrasing and ornamentation. His versions of dance tunes are both polished and emotional.
It's New. Celtic CX 10.
The Music of Cape Breton. Can. Cavalcade 2002.

FORRESTER, HOWDY Forrester is preeminent among commercial competition-style fiddlers for his clear phrasing and execution and characteristic wide, hard tone. I'm surprised I could find only one of his records in print; look for others.
Howdy's Fiddle. Stoneway 127.

FOX, CURLY
Champion Fiddler, vols. 1–2. RR 251, 252.

FRALEY, J. P. AND ANNADENE
The Wild Rose of the Mountain (1973). Rounder 0037. A fine east Kentucky fiddler whose unusual playing is basically old-timey, with a lot of Irish in it and some more modern influences from bluegrass as well. Although accompanied by his wife Annadene on guitar, with occasional bass and spoons by his daughters, Fraley is a master of the old, essentially solo style, full of drones, double stops, and pedal points reminiscent of piping. His use of the style is sometimes very rich, both harmonically and in its occasional suggestions of moving voices.

FUREY, TED
Traditional Fiddle. Outlet 1020. Reels, jigs, and hornpipes well played by an Irish fiddler of great spirit and abandon. Most have a busy and sometimes eccentric bodhran (hand-drum) accompaniment.

GARNER, EARL
Cuttin' Bluegrass. Stoneway 113.
Bluegrass Fiddler. Stoneway 120.
Texas Bluegrass. Stoneway 122.

GEORGE, FRANKLIN. *See* Banjo section, page 80.

GILLIS, WILFRED
Arisaig: Violin Music of the Scot. Celtic CX 45.

GIMBLE, JOHNNY
Fiddlin' Around (1974). Capitol 11301. An excellent album in the jazzy country swing idiom (Gimble first came to prominence in Bob Wills' band of the thirties). Some flashy swing guitar from Troy Passmore, and smooth arrangements with all the polish of the Nashville studios to which Gimble has become accustomed. Excellent ensembles, arranging, and recording; produced, apparently with love, by Merle Haggard.

GRAYSON, G. B. *See* Grayson and Whitter, Old-Time String Band and Early Country Music section, page 64.

GREENE, JOE
Joe Greene's Fiddle Album (1969). County 722. Fine bluegrass fiddling; as testimony, Chubby Wise plays guitar, along with Roland White on mandolin, J. D. Crowe on banjo, Benny Williams on bass. *See also* Kenny Baker, page 83.

GUIDRY, DOC
King of the Cajun Fiddlers. La Louisianne 115.

HERDMAN, CURLY
_____. Saydisc SDM-242 (= Kanawha 310).

HOLLOW ROCK STRING BAND
_____. Rounder 0024. Old-time songs and dances. Essentially an outing for Alan Jabbour's excellent fiddle playing, with excellent banjo and guitar backup as well.

HOPKINS, E. J.
Championship Fiddlin'. Stoneway 101.
Championship Fiddler. Stoneway 102.
Contest Fiddlin'. Stoneway 133.

HUGHEY, RON
Country Fiddlin' Ozark Style. Amer. Her. 401–511. A few rarely recorded tunes and many standards, with banjo, guitar, bass, and sometimes second fiddle.

HUNTER, ERNIE
All About Fiddling. Stoneway 143.

HUTCHISON, DICK
Old Time Fiddlin'. Rimrock 120.

JOHNSON, HERMAN
Championship Fiddlin'. Amer. Her. 401–1.

JONES, RAMONA
Back Porch Fiddlin'. OFC (no number). Ramona Jones is best known for playing second fiddle to her husband, Louis "Grandpa" Jones, banjoist and popular Nashville entertainer. *See* Old-Time String Band and Early Country Music section, page 65.

KESSINGER, CLARK An excellent old-time fiddler from West Virginia, Kessinger was one of the smoothest and most advanced players to have recorded during the twenties. His recordings with his cousin Luches (billed as the Kessinger Brothers) were highly influential, and it seems to me they must have contributed to the development of the long-bow-stroke Texas style. His more recent recordings date from his rediscovery in the sixties.
The Kessinger Brothers (1928–30). County 536.
The Kessinger Brothers. Kanawha 600 (OP).
The Legend of. . . . Folkways 2336 (=County 733).
Sweet Bunch of Daiseys. County 747 (=Kanawha 306).
Live at Union Grove. Saydisc SDM 231 (=Kanawha 312).
Old Time Music. Rounder 0004. With excellent backup guitar by Gene Meade.

KIDWELL, VAN
————. Vetco 502.

KNUTH, RON
Fiddle Favorites. Stoneway 116.
Hoedown Wisconsin Style. Stoneway 119.

LANCASTER, BUDDY
Precious Memories. OFC (no number).

LONG, BILL
Mountain Music from Montana. Amer. Her. 401-14.

MacKENNON, MALCOLM
Scottish Fiddle Music. Scheduled for release by Fiddler Records as this book goes to press; serial number not yet available.

McGEE, DENNIS, AND S. D. COURVILLE
————(1972). Morning Star 16001. Rather stiff duets by older Cajun fiddlers.

McGUIRE, SEAN A fluent Irish championship fiddler who favors fast tempos, usually working with an accordionist and piano backup.
Two Champions. Outlet 1014. With Joe Burke.
Reels and Jigs. Outlet 1002. With Roger Sherlock.
At Their Best. Outlet 1008. With Roger Sherlock.
Best of. . . . Outlet 1006.

McREYNOLDS, JESSE
Me and My Fiddles. Atteiram API-1030. The great bluegrass mandolinist (*see* Jim and Jesse, Bluegrass section, page 74) here plays twin fiddle overdubs.

MEADOWS, JOE
Portrait of a Fiddler. Old Homestead 90036. With Larry Sparks and the Lonesome Ramblers.

MESSER, DON A commercial Canadian fiddler, skilled in both the western and the French-Canadian repertories, who achieved great popularity and influence in the fifties through his CBC radio broadcasts. His earliest recordings hold greatest interest for traditional fiddlers; Fiddler Records is planning a reissue as this book goes to press, but the serial numbers are not yet available.
The Don Messer Family. Can. Cavalcade 2003.
Very Best. MCA (Canadian) 2–4037 (2-rec. set).
Forty Years On. MCA (Canadian) 17018.
Canadian Gold. MCA (Canadian) 17002.
The Everlasting. MCA (Canadian) 17008.
Hello, Neighbor. Coral (Canadian) 35001.
Don Messer's Back. Coral (Canadian) 35004.

MITCHELL, BILL, AND MERLE "RED" TAYLOR
High Level Fiddling. Davis Unltd. 33012. One side of each Mississippi fiddler. Taylor's background includes recordings with both Bill Monroe (the original fiddle part on "Uncle Pen") and Hank Williams.

MOOREHEAD, ELEANOR
Canadian Queen of the Fiddle. Dominion (Canadian) 93071.

MOORING, JOHNNY
North American Fiddle Champion. Can. Cavalcade 20014.

MORRISON, FATE AND WILLIE
The Old Americans. OFC (no number).

MULLINS, MOON
————. Vetco 3004.

MURPHY, DENNIS, AND JULIA CLIFFORD
The Star and the Garter. Claddagh CC 5. Irish fiddle tunes from County Kerry.

NORTHCUTT, BILL
Old Time Hoedown. Stoneway 103.
Front Porch Fiddlin'. Stoneway 135.

PANCERZEWSKI, JOE
The Fiddlin' Engineer. Voyager 3068. Fiddle tunes in western competition style, with band.

PEERCE, LONNIE
Golden Fiddle Tunes. Amer. Her. 401–24.

PERKINS, J. T.
Just Fine Fiddlin'. Davis Unltd. 33007.

POSTON, MUTT
————, vols. 1–3. RR 130, 154, 157.
Country Waltzes. RR 173.
Blues Instrumentals. RR 156.

POTTER, DALE
Tribute to Bob Wills. RR 235.
Hoedown Fiddle Tunes. RR 179.

POTTS, TOMMY
The Liffey Banks. Claddagh CC 13. Airs, reels, jigs, and hornpipes; an exceptional record by an exceptional man. Potts is the most intensely original player I've encountered in folk music (outside of the great bluesmen). He has a way of searching out the essence of a tune (*getting inside* a tune, a jazz musician would say) and then making it his own by recasting it in terms of his own rhapsodically lyrical imagination. Many fiddlers judge their prowess by how many tunes they can learn, spongelike, from the playing of others, perhaps with a high degree of proficiency but with a minimum amount of the thought and reflection that leads to a personal style. Potts, who grew up in a musical family and learned from tradition, has evidently spent much time critically examining elements in the styles of others: accepting, reshaping, rejecting. It's especially interesting to set Potts' fiddling against the fiddling and other music supported by the institutionalized Irish folk music revival movement, Comhaltas Ceoltóirí Eirann. This movement has been a mixed blessing. Although it has certainly served to keep traditional music alive, it has done so, through competitions and an emphasis on large ensembles, only at the cost of discouraging individuality. Potts' playing is deeper and more personal than any you'll hear in a fiddler's contest.

*Fiddlin' Bob Haines
and His Four Aces*

Price, Fred. *See* under Clint Howard and under Clarence "Tom" Ashley, Old-Time String Band and Early Country Music section, pages 64 and 62.

Reed, Blind Alfred. *See* Traditional Songs and Singers section, page 60.

Richard, Ti-Blanc A highly competent French-Canadian fiddler in the commercial style, with Celtic roots but influenced also by American hoedown fiddling. He works mainly with dance-band ensembles, including rhythm section. His music can be taken as a good token example of this style of fiddling; many other Canadian fiddlers in this style are not listed in this book.
Vingt succès souvenir. RCA (Canadian) KTL2-7015 (2-rec. set).
. . . *à son meilleur.* London (Canadian) 5040.
_____. London (Canadian) 5086.
_____. London (Canadian) 5110.
_____. London (Canadian) 5133.
. . . *presente les meilleurs violoneux du Québec.* London (Canadian) 5165. A representative anthology of the commercial style, including the work of several other good players: Marcel Brisebois, J-M St-Louis, Lauréat Goulet, and Claude Lemarbre.

Riendeau Family, The
_____. County 725. New England French-Canadian fiddle standards; spirited, honest, sometimes rough.

Robichaud, Gerry A good French-Canadian fiddler now resident in Massachusetts. Robichaud, who has a lot of the Irish sound at times, draws from a repertory of the older

tunes as well as tunes from Don Messer and other modern fiddlers.
Down East Fiddling (1973). Voyager 310-S.
Traditional Dance Tunes from New Brunswick. Fiddler 002.

Rutherford, Leonard. *See* Burnett and Rutherford, Old-Time String Band and Early Country Music section, page 63.

Ryan, Buck
Fiddler on the Rocks. Rebel 1529. A bluegrass fiddler known for his work with Don Reno's band, which accompanies him on this album.

Schwarz, Tracy
Learn to Fiddle Country Style. See Instructional Books and Records, Fiddle section, page 179.

Sherrill, Homer "Pappy." *See* under Morris Brothers and under Snuffy Jenkins, Old-Time String Band and Early Country Music section, pages 65 and 66.

Simpson, Red
Old Time String Band Music. Calif. Condor CCLP-1.

Smith, Arthur
Old Time Fiddlin'. Pine Mtn. 202. *See also* under McGee Brothers, Old-Time String Band and Early Country Music section, page 66.

Smith, Hobart. *See* Traditional Songs and Singers section, page 60.

SMOKE, HERB
Mountain Fiddler (1973). Skyline DD 105. Old-time dance tunes, waltzes, and rags with banjo, guitar, and bass; a good feeling but with some intonation problems. Smoke recorded (as a banjoist) for the Library of Congress in 1940.

SOUCY, ISIDORE (1892?–1963) Soucy was the greatest of the French-Canadian commercial fiddlers and composed many original reels and other tunes which have entered into tradition. His earliest recordings, which seem not to be available, would be of greatest interest. Those listed below are in what I guess to be chronological order.
Dansons. Carnaval 520.
Années d'or. Carnaval 430.
Vingt grands succès d'hier. Coral (Canadian) 37008.
Chez Isidore. RCA (Canadian) CGP-128.

STARK, HARRY
Vermont Fiddling. Fretless 105.

ST-PIERRE, SIMON
The Joys of Quebec. Revonah 915. A good French-Canadian fiddler accompanied by a good bluegrass band, the Dukes of Bluegrass led by Walter Hensley. An unusual combination that succeeds very well; neither St-Pierre nor the Dukes make concessions, and they work well with each other. Needless to say, this record would make a good introduction to the riches of French-Canadian fiddling for hard-core bluegrassers.

STRIPLING BROTHERS, THE
The Lost Child and Other Original Fiddle Tunes (1928–36). County 401. Charlie Stripling (accompanied on guitar by Ira Lee Stripling) was a rather crude north Alabama fiddler with a knack for coming up with odd tunes involving abbreviated or asymmetrical phrase structures, skipped beats, and other interesting features.

SUMMERS, JOHN A fine Indiana fiddler in the old Appalachian solo style. *See* under *Fine Times at Our House*, Midwest Anthologies and Collections section, page 94, and under Franklin George, Banjo section, page 80.

SWARBRICK, DAVE
Rags, Reels and Airs. Polydor (British) 236.514. Swarbrick has become popular as the adventurous progressive electric fiddler and mandolinist with Fairport Convention. (*See* Contemporary Artists, Bands, and Songwriters section, page 121.) This album of British, Irish, and American tunes clearly establishes him as a virtuoso traditional fiddler and mandolinist. With Martin Carthy and Diz Disley, guitars.

TATE, TATER
Fiddle and Banjo Instrumentals. Rimrock 3000.
Fiddlin' Favorites of the U.S.A. and Canada. RR 193.
Country Favorite Waltzes. RR 213.
More Favorite Waltzes. RR 220.

THIBODEAUX, RUFUS
Cajun Fiddle. La Louisianne 129.

THOMAS, TONY
Old-Style Texas and Oklahoma Fiddlin'. Takoma A1013.

THOMASSON, BENNY A fine Texas-style player, in both the traditional and the swing idioms. The Texas way of playing is distinguished by smooth multinote bowings, with less dependence on drones and pedal points and on rhythmic bowing figures like the shuffle than Appalachian fiddling. The effect is even more legato than Irish or French-Canadian reel fiddling. Thomasson works with his son Jerry, a jazzy tenor guitarist.
Country Fiddling from the Big State. County 724.
A Jam Session with Benny and Jerry Thomasson. Voyager 309.

TOWNSEND, GRAHAM A smooth and polished player, with a more traditional sound and orientation than most commercial Canadian fiddlers. He usually works with rhythm section.
Old-Time Fiddle Favorites. Coral (Canadian) 30017.
Harvest Home. Coral (Canadian) 30020.
On Tour. Coral (Canadian) 30038.
Fiddlin' Favorites. Can. Cavalcade 2010.
By the Fireside. Point 372.
Old-Time Fiddle Favorites of Ward Allen. Point 328.
Swing Your Partner. Point 368.

WANZER, LOYD
Waltz Wonderland. Amer. Her. 401–9. Western-style waltzes, with second fiddle and guitar, played literally, without variation or ornamentation.

WARD, WADE. *See* Banjo section, page 81.

WHITE, BOB, AND CLYDE BREWER
Twin Fiddles. Stoneway 131.
Seven Come Eleven. Stoneway 141.

WILLS, BOB. *See* Western Swing section, page 98.

WISE, CHUBBY An excellent western swing player who was part of the Bill Monroe band of the forties that also included Lester Flatt and Earl Scruggs (*see* under Bill Monroe, Bluegrass section, page 75). Wise's role as a member of that band had an inestimable influence on the development of the bluegrass sound; his polished western fiddling with vibrato, long bow strokes, and elements of jazziness was one of the major catalysts in distinguishing the classic bluegrass sound from the older string band sound.
. . . and His Fiddle. Stoneway 104.
. . . Fiddles Around. Stoneway 105.
. . . Plays Uptown. Stoneway 106.
Hoedown, vols. 1–2. Stoneway 109, 130.
. . . Plays Bob Wills. Stoneway 110.
Precious Memories. Stoneway 112.
. . . Through the Years. Stoneway 114.
. . . Plays Polkas. Stoneway 118.
Waltzes. Stoneway 124.
. . . at His Best. Stoneway 125.

ANTHOLOGIES AND COLLECTIONS

American Fiddle Tunes. AFS L62. A selection of fiddle tunes mostly from the southern highlands or in the style of that region, compiled from Library of Congress field recordings made between 1934 and 1942. Many of the fiddlers were advanced in years, and some very old and beautiful sounds in the old solo style are represented. A few pieces have been chosen for documentary significance, but for the most part the level of the performances is superb. Edited with a comprehensive descriptive booklet by Alan Jabbour, beneath whose scholarly exterior lies the soul of a mountain fiddler.

Best of the Country Fiddlers. RCA (Canadian) KCL1-7004. Commercial fiddlers Al Cherry, King Ganam, and Ned Landry.

Cape Breton Fiddle Tunes. Fiddler 004. Angus Chisholm, Dan J. Campbell, and others, reissued from Celtic and Decca 78's of the thirties and forties.

Country Fiddle, The (film sound track). *See* Films section, page 244, and under Pete Seeger, Folk Song Revival section, page 107.

Country Fiddlers. Roots RL 316.

Fiddle Jam Session. Voyager 301. Byron Berline, Bill Long, Loyd Wanzer, and other competition fiddlers.

A Fiddler's Convention in Mountain City, Tennessee. County 525. String bands, featuring the fiddle of Dudley Vance, Charlie Bowman, G. B. Grayson, and Fiddlin' John Carson, as well as the banjo of Clarence "Tom" Ashley. Not actual convention recordings; the title is a rubric to encompass 1924–30 recordings by musicians who did attend that convention.

Fiddler's Grove. Recordings made at the Fiddler's Grove Convention from 1970 on are available from Fiddler's Grove Records, Box 11, Union Grove, N.C. 28689.

Fiddlers of the Tennessee Valley. Davis Unltd. 33004. Sam McCracken, Lena Hughes, Bob Douglas, Richard Blaustein, Frazier Moss, Bud Meredith, J. T. Perkins, Bill Mitchell, Bill Northcutt, and Texas fiddler Dick Barrett.

Fiddlin' Country Style. Pine Mtn. 242. Benny Martin, Chubby Wise, Tommy Jackson, and other modern players.

Flattops and Fiddles. Davis Unltd. 33010. Fiddle tunes for fiddle and flat-picked guitar, played by Claudie Holt, Algie Surratt, Roy Crawford, and J. T. Perkins.

Galax 1973. Tennvale 002. Old-time fiddle, string band, and banjo music casually recorded in live performance at the Old Fiddler's Convention.

Galax Old Fiddler's Convention. Folkways 2435. A selection of string band music casually recorded at the 1961–63 conventions; sound quality inconsistent.

Galax Old Fiddler's Convention. Selections recorded at the 1965–71 conventions are available from Box 665, Galax, Va. 24333.

Hell Broke Loose in Georgia. County 514. Fiddle-led Georgia string bands of the twenties and thirties.

Hoedown: Country Fiddlers. RR 253. Tater Tate, Dale Potter, Buck Ryan, and Vassar Clements.

More Fiddle Jam Sessions. Voyager 304.

Mountain Fiddle Music (1927–30). County 501. Old-time fiddle and string band music by Burnett and Rutherford, Lowe Stokes, Clayton McMichen, and other leading professionals of the day.

Old-Time Fiddling. Recordings of the Northeast Regional Old-Time Fiddling Contest, available from the Northeast Fiddler's Association, RFD 1, Stowe, Vt. 05672.

Old-Time Fiddling and Other Folk Music Recorded at the National Old-Time Fiddler's Contest at Weiser, Idaho. An annual anthology, available from American Heritage Records.

Paddy in the Smoke. Topic 12T176. Irish dance music, mostly fiddlers, recorded in London pubs.

Scottish Fiddlers to the Fore. BBC REB 84M. Winners of the 1969 Perth Fiddler's Competition.

Shetland Fiddle Music. Tangent 117.

Sop'n Up the Gravy. Log Cabin 8001. Informal recordings made at the 1973 First Annual Gathering of Traditional Indiana Fiddlers. Fiddlers of widely varying degrees of proficiency, mostly in the old Appalachian style, are represented. The best are very good; almost all are at least spirited and interesting. There are also some solos on autoharp, tin whistle, dulcimer, and ukelin, an odd turn-of-the-century fad instrument like a bowed zither.

Texas Farewells: Texas Fiddlers (1922–30). County 517.

Texas Fiddle Favorites. County 707. Early sixties recordings of traditional fiddle tunes by Major Franklin, Lewis Franklin, and Norman Solomon.

Texas Hoedown. County 503. Bartow Riley, Vernon Solomon, and Benny Thomasson.

Union Grove Fiddler's Convention. Annual anthologies are available from Box 38, Union Grove, N.C. 28689.

Vingt succès souvenir des grands violoneux. RCA (Canadian) KTL2-7017 (2-rec. set). Commercial French-Canadian players, recorded in the artificially full modern studio style so that it is a bit difficult to hear the fiddler over the rhythm section. Fiddlers include Isidore Soucy, Fernand Thibault, Victor Martin, Paul Cormier (Monsieur Pointu), Ti-Blanc Richard, and others, all good players.

Virginia Breakdown. County 705. Otis Burris, Sonny Miller, Buddy Pendleton.

The Wonderful World of Old-Time Fiddlers, vols. 1–2. Vetco 102, 104. Recordings by good and great fiddlers of the twenties and thirties: Bunt Stephens, Clayton McMichen, Arthur Smith, and others.

GUITAR

This is a sparse section for various reasons. The main one is that the guitar has only recently emerged as a solo instrument in white southern folk music. A few early white players acquired the black blues and finger-picking styles, adapting them to their own needs. But for the most part the role of the guitar in early white recordings was as a rhythm and backup instrument. Later, electric guitar emerged as a strong solo voice in country swing and rockabilly bands, in the hands of men like Tiny Moore, Les Paul, Thumbs Carllile, Roy Nichols, and Grady Martin, to name a few. But their work represents an application of jazz guitar technique, coming out of the Charlie Christian and Django Reinhardt traditions, to the simpler harmonic structures of country music. Fans of guitar music would do well to learn the work of these men, but they do not belong to the folk tradition and are not listed here.

Although Red Smiley and a few others have used the guitar to take solos in a bluegrass band, it is only recently that the bluegrass guitar solo has become commonly accepted and expected. Doc Watson's development of the flat-picking style has been a key factor, though Watson himself works primarily as a soloist or with second guitar. (He did make a record of instrumentals with Flatt and Scruggs on Columbia, now out of print; his own records are listed in the Traditional Songs and Singers section, page

"Granddad of the Country Guitar Pickers": Sam McGee

60.) A few guitarists in the bluegrass style are listed here.

Also listed here are a few Nashville guitarists—Merle Travis, Chet Atkins, and Jerry Reed. They are all technically spectacular players whose right-hand technique is derived from the black southeastern finger-picking style: melody notes produced by right-hand fingers on the treble strings, accompanied by bass arpeggio or ostinato figures produced by the right-hand thumb. Travis, the first of these guitarists, adapted the style to the "jazz four" beat of country swing, and incorporated a highly developed left-hand technique and concept involving sophisticated jazz chords, played on electric guitar. This opened the way to the exploration of sophisticated jazz and pop harmonies not found in folk music, and also to the use of moving bass and middle voices, an area which Atkins has explored more fully. Atkins, by the way, has done a great amount of work as a record producer, and is largely responsible for originating the contemporary Nashville pop sound, with its highly polished use of recording studio techniques and overdubbed backup parts. Jerry Reed's own recordings represent him as a somewhat manic singer and songwriter, but he's a spectacular finger-style hot-licks man as well. He prefers to work on nylon-strung guitar, as Atkins occasionally does. All these men have made many records. Travis' solo albums for Capitol are out of print, though still occasionally to be found in remaindered record bins. Only a few of the Atkins and Reed albums now available are listed here, by way of introduction.

Since the sixties old and new styles have been developed from black traditional techniques and concepts by young urban players. Consult The Blues Revival and Contemporary Guitarists sections, pages 109 and 117, for these listings.

ATKINS, CHET (b. 1924), **AND MERLE TRAVIS** (b. 1917)
The Atkins-Travis Traveling Show. RCA APL1-0479.

ATKINS, CHET, AND JERRY REED (b. 1937)
Me and Jerry. RCA LSP-4396.

BAKER, ETTA A superbly clean and original traditional finger-picking stylist. Her only recordings are several selections on the following record.
Instrumental Music of the Southern Appalachians. Tradition 1007.

BLAKE, NORMAN. *See* Old-Time String Band and Early Country Music section, page 62.

CRARY, DAN
Bluegrass Guitar. Amer. Her. 275. Fast and flashy guitar versions of traditional fiddle tunes, with a rough backup band.

HUTCHISON, FRANK (1897–1945)
The Train That Carried My Girl from Town (1927–29). Rounder 1007. Recordings by a white mountain guitarist who adapted the black southeast finger-picking style to hillbilly music. His style, superficially considered, sounds stiff beside the great black stylists like Blind Blake, as well as beside later white players like Merle Travis, who had the western swing tradition to rely on. But in a historical perspective, Hutchison can be seen as a unique stylist in his own right.

McGEE, SAM (1894–1975)
Granddad of the Country Guitar Pickers. Arhoolie 5012. Casual 1969–70 sessions. McGee was a longtime fixture on

the Grand Ole Opry radio broadcasts from Nashville, as soloist, with his brother Kirk and fiddler Arthur Smith, or as accompanist to Uncle Dave Macon. He was one of the early white assimilators of the southeastern black finger-picking style, and made important contributions to the style and repertory. His arrangements of "Buck Dancer's Choice" (here played on six-string banjo-guitar) and "Railroad Blues" have become oft-imitated standards. On this recording he plays finger- and flat-picking tunes and a few banjo tunes, with occasional vocals, second guitar, and bass. *Flat Top Pickin'*. MBA 606. *See also* McGee Brothers, Old-Time String Band and Early Country Music section, page 66.

Mister Charlie's Blues. Yazoo 1024. Recordings by early white blues and ragtime performers influenced by rural black guitar style, 1926–38. Dick Justice, Sam McGee, and others.

Mountain Blues. County 511. Vocal and instrumental blues recordings by white southern mountain string band musicians of the thirties; much guitar. Sam McGee, Jimmie Tarleton, Frank Hutchison, Dock Boggs, Burnett and Rutherford, and others.

Old-Time Mountain Guitar. County 523. Solo and duet blues, rags, and waltzes on guitar and steel guitar, 1926–30; Sam McGee, Frank Hutchison, and others. This represents the work of early white guitarists at a crucial point in musical history. Most of these men were not concerned with slavish imitation of the black guitarists from whom they learned the style; here, those stylistic divergences first appear that later result, at least in part, in an independent white tradition that includes the Delmores, Doc Watson, and Merle Travis.

WHITE, CLARENCE. *See* The Kentucky Colonels and Muleskinner, Bluegrass section, pages 74 and 75.

MANDOLIN

The mandolin is usually used as an integral part of the old-time and bluegrass string ensemble; yet there are relatively few records in which the mandolin is especially featured. It makes sense to single out the following listings, however. For some other fine mandolinists, consult the Bluegrass section, page 68: Red Rector and Bill Monroe under their own names; Jesse McReynolds under Jim and Jesse; Herschel Sizemore under Shenandoah Cutups and Shenandoah Valley Quartet; Dave Grisman under Don Stover, Muleskinner, and *Old and in the Way*. There is also a blues mandolin tradition; consult the Black American Music section for Yank Rachell (under his own name, page 11, and under Sleepy John Estes, page 9); for various string band listings (Jug Bands, String Bands, Country Ragtime and One-Man Bands, page 28); and for Johnny Young (Chicago Blues, page 24).

COUNTRY FIDDLERS, THE (featuring Wade Ray)
Down Yonder. Camden CAS-2145. Standard fiddle tunes, played by an anonymous Nashville pickup band including drums; Ray is the only musician credited by name. The mandolin player (probably Kenneth "Jethro" Burns) is su-

perb, taking many solos in a jazzy country swing style and combining imagination, good taste, and technical virtuosity of the highest order. The rest of the playing is competent and nondescript, but the record is worth having for the mandolin work alone. Burns has also recorded on many albums not listed here: with the hillbilly musical comedy act Homer and Jethro, on the RCA Nashville String Band recordings led by Chet Atkins, and on several square dance records with fiddler Tommy Jackson. The Jackson recordings are out of print, but are worth searching for.

HALL, KENNY Hall is an old-time mandolin player now resident in central California, and a great favorite at local clubs and festivals for his repertory of songs and fiddle tunes. He plays many Irish tunes, familiar to fiddler repertories but less often heard on the mandolin.
. . . and the Sweet's Mill String Band (1972). Bay TPH 727.
_____ (1974). Philo 1008. Hall plays fiddle tunes (some on fiddle as well as mandolin), old-time songs, and a few Irish tunes with clarity, precision, and a pristine simplicity. Backup parts by Holly Tannen (dulcimer) and Jim Ringer (guitar) are models of taste and sympathy. Hall also has a penchant for corny old-time songs with vocals, and a few are included.

LOWERY, BILL
Tennessee Valley Mandolin. Davis Unltd. 33005.
The Bald Headed Mandolin Picker. Davis Unltd. 33008.

SWARBRICK, DAVE. *See* Fiddle section, page 89, and Fairport Convention, in the Contemporary Artists, Bands, and Songwriters section, page 121.

WAKEFIELD, FRANK
_____. Rounder 0007. With backup from the progressive Country Cookin' bluegrass band, Wakefield shows the influence of jazz, blues, and classical music on a style derived from Monroe. Also includes some examples of his rather erratic autoharp style. *See also* under Red Allen and under Greenbriar Boys, Bluegrass section, pages 71 and 73.

DULCIMER, HAMMERED DULCIMER, AND AUTOHARP

The focus of these listings is on instrumental albums. Many other singers use the dulcimer for accompaniment. *See* Edna and Jean Ritchie, page 60; Holly Tannen (with Kenny Hall, this page, above); Andrew Rowan Summers, page 108; Paul Clayton, page 93; John Jacob Niles, page 106; Howie Mitchell, pages 106 and 177; Margaret MacArthur, page 105; Annie Grimes, page 94; Richard Fariña, page 122; and George and Gerry Armstrong, page 113. For hammered dulcimer, *see* Ed Trickett, page 108, and also Trickett with Sarah Grey, page 105, and with the New Golden Ring, page 104. For autoharp, *see* Mike Seeger, page 107; and the Carter Family and Maybelle Carter, page 63.

CLAYTON, PAUL
Dulcimer Songs and Solos. Folkways 3571. Well-known southern mountain songs with dulcimer accompaniments; a few solos.

ILA (Ila Anderson)
_____. Audicom (no number). Traditional and contemporary songs with dulcimer accompaniments.

MITCHELL, HOWIE In addition to his own record in The Folk Song Revival section (page 106), see *The Mountain Dulcimer: How to Make It and Play It*, Folk-Legacy FSI-19, reviewed in Part II, Instructional Books, Dulcimer section, page 177.

NICHOLSON, ROGER
Nonesuch for Dulcimer. Trailer LER 3034.

PARKER, CHET
The Hammer Dulcimer. Folkways 2381. Mid-sixties recordings of virtuoso pieces including reels, hoedowns, old-time dance tunes and gay nineties songs. Parker, a retired Michigan lumberman, has been playing since the turn of the century.

PRESNELL, EDD Several Presnell dulcimer solos are included on the following record.
Instrumental Music of the Southern Appalachians. Tradition 1007. This album also offers some excellent guitar, banjo, and fiddle work.

ROTH, KEVIN
. . . Sings and Plays Dulcimer. Folkways 2367.

ROUND, JAY
The Hammered Dulcimer Album. TurneRound 4054. Available from 6470 8th Ave., Grandville, Mich. 49418. Familiar tunes, with loose bluegrass band backup.

RUSSELL FAMILY, THE
_____. County 734. Old-time songs and dance tunes with dulcimers, guitar, and ukelele.

SCHILLING, JEAN
. . . and Lee Schilling: The Porches of the Poor. Traditional 617. Southern mountain songs, some little-known, with dulcimer, autoharp, recorder, harmonica, and mandolin.
Old Traditions. Traditional 5117. Well-known southern mountain songs on dulcimer, with second dulcimer, lead and rhythm guitar, and occasional vocals.

SMITH, RALPH LEE
Dulcimer (1973). Skyline 102. Traditional tunes well-played in an interesting variety of styles and tunings. Some vocals by Smith and by Mary Louise Hollowell. Fine music; marred by poor recording or mastering that results at times in some annoying instabilities of pitch and tempo, but worth hearing anyway. *See also* under Allan Block, Fiddle section, page 83.

SNOW, KILBY Snow is a fine old singer and excellent autoharp player from the southern mountains; he plays a variety of material reflecting the musical influences of the earlier part of the century.
Country Songs and Tunes (autoharp). Asch 3902.

SPENCE, BILL
The Hammered Dulcimer (1973). Front Hall FHR-01. Well-arranged and well-played string band recordings in which fiddle, banjo, and hammered dulcimer share lead roles, accompanied by guitar and/or piano in a variety of Irish and American folk songs and dance tunes. A most enjoyable album, clear and spirited.

STONE COUNTY DULCIMERS
_____. OFC (serial number not available).

YOUNG, LYNN
Little Log Cabin. Rimrock 281. Dance tunes and ballads with autoharp, fiddle, dulcimer, and guitar.

ANTHOLOGIES AND COLLECTIONS
All Around the Mountain. Available from Sweet Corn, 1335 Blakelee Ave., Kalamazoo, Mich. 49001. Bluegrass with hammered dulcimer.
Mountain Music Played on the Autoharp. Folkways 2365. Includes Kilby Snow.

ANGLO-AMERICAN MUSIC FROM OTHER REGIONS

The main emphasis in these recordings is on music and lore associated with areas of the country other than the south. Since the emphasis is on the literary content, regional origin, or collecting point of the material, rather than on musical style, the listings include both traditional and revivalist performers.

THE NORTHEAST

ALLISON, JOHN
Witches and War Whoops. Folkways 5211. Early New England ballads.

CANTERBURY COUNTRY DANCE ORCHESTRA
_____. F & W 3. Polished versions of New England contra-dance tunes, two-steps, reels, jigs, and a Baltic kolo for good measure. There are well-arranged parts for fiddles, mandolin, hammered dulcimer, accordion, piano, and bass; an unusual and enjoyable sound.
. . . Meets the F & W String Band. F & W 5.
Mistwold. F & W 4.
Swinging on a Gate. Front Hall FHR-03.

CLAYTON, PAUL
Bay State Ballads. Folkways 2106 (10 inch). As sung by a revivalist singer-scholar.

CLEVELAND, SARA
_____. Folk-Legacy FSA-33. A traditional ballad singer from New York State.

DILDINE FAMILY, THE
_____. Front Hall FHR-02. Ballads, laments, dances, and play songs.

F & W STRING BAND
_____, vols. 1–2. F & W 1–2. A twenty-five-piece Vermont

country dance ensemble who play exciting, well-made arrangements of line-dance and contradance tunes.

Folk Songs of the Catskills. Folkways 5311.

HARRINGTON, HAROLD
Songs of Old Vermont. Droll Yankee 107.

HUNTINGTON, E. G.
Folksongs of Martha's Vineyard. Folkways 2032 (10 inch).

IVES, SANDY
Folksongs of Maine. Folkways 5323.

MACARTHUR, MARGARET
Folksongs of Vermont. Folkways 5314.

OKUN, MILT
Adirondack Folk Ballads. Stinson SLP 82.

OLDER, LAWRENCE
_____. Folk-Legacy FSA-15. Adirondack songs, ballads, and fiddle tunes, learned from tradition.

OLD STURBRIDGE SINGERS
The New England Harmony. Folkways 2377.

ROGERS, GRANT
Songmaker of the Catskills. Folk-Legacy FSA-27.

SEEGER, PETE
Champlain Valley Songs. Folkways 5210.

The Southerners Plus Two. Available from Ralph Page, 117 Washington St., Keene, N.H. 03431. Music for New England contradancing.

Vermont Harmony. Philo 1000. Eighteenth-century fugue tunes and psalmody.

THE MIDWEST

BLUESTEIN, GENE
Songs of the North Star State. Folkways 2132 (10 inch). Minnesota songs as sung by a revival singer-scholar.

GIBSON, BOB
Folksongs of Ohio. Stinson SLP 76.

GRIMES, ANNIE
Ballads of Ohio. Folkways 5217.

JEMISON, EUGENE
Solomon Valley Ballads. Folkways 2023 (10 inch). Songs of the settlement of Kansas.

O'BRYANT, JOAN
Folksongs and Ballads of Kansas. Folkways 2134 (10 inch).

STORM, ARNOLD KEITH
Take the News to Mother. Folk-Legacy FSA-18. Traditional and old-time country songs learned from media and tradition by an Indiana singer, with guitar and harmonica.

ANTHOLOGIES AND COLLECTIONS

Fine Times at Our House. Folkways 3809. Ballads, tunes, and songs collected during the sixties from older Indiana musicians by Pat Dunford and Art Rosenbaum. Especially noteworthy are the many fine fiddle tunes in Appalachian style, played by John W. Summers and others. Many older inhabitants of Indiana are émigrés from Appalachia, and this record clearly demonstrates that they are a valuable source of old mountain tradition. Much of the music here is of good musical quality, aside from its documentary value.

Folk Music from Wisconsin. AFS L55. 1940–46 Library of Congress field recordings.

Folk Sounds of Iowa. Univ. of Iowa Press (number not available).

Green Fields of Illinois. Puritan 5007 (formerly CFC 201). Field recordings of traditional musicians from central and southern Illinois.

Missouri Folk Songs. Folkways 5324.

Songs of the Great Lakes. Folkways 4018.

Songs of the Michigan Lumberjacks. AFS L56. 1938–48 Library of Congress field recordings.

Sweet Nebraska Land. Folkways 5337.

Traditional Songs of the Midwest. Folkways 5330.

Wolf River Songs. Folkways 4001. Wisconsin lumber camp songs.

THE WEST, SOUTHWEST, PACIFIC NORTHWEST, AND ALASKA

AGINS, SAM
Singin' Sam's Saddlebag of Songs. Haywire 6419. Vocal with basic guitar accompaniment; thirteen cowboy songs, a few not well-known.

Authentic Cowboys and Their Western Folksongs (1925–30). RCA LPV-522.

CRITCHLOW, SLIM
Cowboy Songs. Arhoolie 5007.

FREDRICKSEN, DAVE
Songs of the West. Folkways 5259. As sung by a revival singer and anthropologist.

GUTHRIE, WOODY (1912–67) An Oklahoma sharecropper and dust-bowl refugee, Guthrie eventually settled into the company of left-wing intellectuals, where his natural talent as a songwriter flourished. His many songs about the Dust Bowl, travels through America, and social themes establish him as a major figure in American music. A strong, unpolished singer, he accompanied himself with basic guitar. Guthrie was a charismatic figure, and his recordings capture some of the fire.

Dust Bowl Ballads. Folkways 5212. The Dust Bowl experience stimulated some of Guthrie's very best writing. Moods here range from optimistic to wryly cynical. Good performances, about 1950.

Poor Boy. Folkways 31010.

Woody's Story. Folkways 2930. A biographical reminiscence with narrative read by Will Geer and Guthrie's songs performed by Dick Wingfield.

Sings Folk Songs. Folkways 2483. Traditional and original songs and instrumentals, with Leadbelly, Cisco Houston, Sonny Terry, and Bess Hawes.

. . . and Pete Seeger: Sacco and Vanzetti. Folkways 5485. Songs about Sacco and Vanzetti composed and sung by Guthrie, along with Seeger's setting to music of excerpts from Sacco's letters to his son.

Bound for Glory. Folkways 2481. Guthrie performs many of his best songs here. Sections from his autobiography, read by Will Geer, link the songs programatically.

Songs to Grow on. Folkways 31502.

Songs to Grow on for Mother and Child. Folkways 7015. Guthrie wrote some of the best children's songs ever.

The Library of Congress Recordings (1940). Elektra EKL 271/2 (3-rec. set; OP). Songs, interviews, and stories recorded by Alan Lomax for the Library of Congress.

————. Ev. Arch. FS-204.

The Immortal. Olympic 7101.

In Memoriam. Tradition 2058.

The Early Years. Tradition 2088.

Dust Bowl Ballads. RCA LPV-502.

The next three recordings are with Pete Seeger, Leadbelly, Sonny Terry, Alec Stewart, and others in various combinations.

American Folksay, vols. 1–3. Stinson SLPX 5, 9, 12.

Chain Gang. Stinson SLPX 7.

Southern Mountain Hoedowns. Stinson SLP 54.

The next two are with Cisco Houston.

Cowboy Songs. Stinson SLP 32.

Folk Songs, vols. 1–2. Stinson SLP 44, 53.

The following five albums contain performances of Guthrie songs by other artists:

ELLIOT, RAMBLIN' JACK

. . . Sings Woody Guthrie. Prestige 7453.

Talking Woody Guthrie. Topic 12T93.

. . . Sings Woody Guthrie and Jimmie Rodgers. Monitor MFS 380.

Songs to Grow On. Folkways 7020.

"Bound for Glory": Woody Guthrie

ENGLISH, LOGAN

Woody Guthrie's Children's Songs. Folkways 7503.

Greatest Songs. Vanguard VSD 35/36 (2-rec. set). Guthrie's songs performed by Guthrie, Cisco Houston, Joan Baez, the Weavers, Country Joe McDonald, Jack Elliot, the Babysitters, Odetta, and Jim Kweskin. Selected mostly from previously issued Vanguard and Folkways albums.

McDONALD, COUNTRY JOE

Thinking of Woody Guthrie. Vanguard 6546.

A Tribute to Woody Guthrie, vols. 1–2. Columbia KC 31171, Warner BS 2586. Excerpts from the 1968 and 1970 memorial concerts held in New York and Los Angeles; Guthrie's songs performed by the following artists: vol. 1, Judy Collins, Bob Dylan, Arlo Guthrie, Richie Havens, Odetta, Tom Paxton, Pete Seeger, and vol. 2, Joan Baez, Judy Collins, Jack Elliot, Richie Havens, Odetta, Arlo Guthrie, Joe McDonald, Tom Paxton, Earl Robinson, Pete Seeger.

IVES, BURL

Songs of the West. Decca DL7-4179.

JACKSON, HARRY

The Cowboy: His Songs and Brag Talk. Folkways 5723 (2-rec. set). Documentary of cowboy life and lore, interesting and well-conceived. An especially good aquisition for libraries and schools.

LOMAX, ALAN

Texas Folk Songs. Tradition 1029. As sung by a revival singer-scholar.

McCLINTOCK, HARRY K. ("Mac," 1882–1957)

Haywire Mac. Folkways 5272. Cowboy, union, rambling, and work songs recorded in the fifties by a colorful world traveler, IWW organizer, radio and recording entertainer of the twenties, and author of *The Big Rock Candy Mountain.*

McCURDY, ED

Songs of the West. Tradition 2061. As sung by a revival singer.

NEELY, BILL

Blackland Farm Boy. Arhoolie 5014.

NYE, HERMES

Texas Folk Songs. Folkways 2128 (10 inch). As sung by a revival singer-scholar.

OHRLIN, GLENN

The Hell-Bound Train. Puritan 5009 (formerly CFC 301). Cowboy and farmer's songs, solo voice and with basic guitar accompaniment.

REEVES, GOEBEL A late thirties singer of cowboy and hobo songs. An archetypal vagrant songster, the alienated son of a Texas politician, Reeves was once associated with the IWW, but later became disillusioned and turned to writing songs that became bitter to the point of offensiveness.

_____, vols. 1–2. CMH 101, 113.
The Drifter, vols. 1–2. FV 12513, 12514.
The Original Hobo's Lullaby. FV 12515.

ROSELAND, PAUL
Sourdough Ballads. Available from Alaska Folk Music, Box 4–1324, Spenard, Alaska 99503

SORRELLS, ROSALIE
Folksongs of Idaho and Utah. Folkways 5343. From a revival singer best known as a performer of her own songs; *see* Contemporary Artists, Bands, and Songwriters section, page 125.

SPRAGUE, CARL T. Sprague was the first cowboy singer to have recorded.
The Original Recordings (1925–29). FV 12506.
_____ (1972). FV 12001.

ANTHOLOGIES AND COLLECTIONS
Comin' 'Round the Mountain. Voyager 302. Sixties recordings by old-time musicians of the Pacific Northwest.
Cowboy Songs, vols. 1–2 (seventies). AFF 33-1, 33-2. Sung by working cowboys, ranchers, and vaqueros.
Cowboy Songs, Ballads, and Cattle Calls from Texas. AFS L28. 1941–48 Library of Congress field recordings.
Folk Songs of the Colorado River. Folkways 5333.

In an Arizona Town. AFF 33-3. A documentary of western and Anglo-American traditional music as played and sung in the seventies in the isolated mountain community of Clay Springs. Vocals and instrumentals with mandolin, guitar, banjo, and fiddle; very rough performances.
Mormon Folk Songs. Folkways 2036 (10 inch).
Songs of Texas. Folkways 5328. Performed by John A. Lomax, Jr., Ed Badeaux, Jim McConnell, and Howard Porper, all revival singer-scholars.
Songs of the Mormons and Songs of the West. AFS L30. 1938–49 Library of Congress field recordings.
Tenino Old-Time Music Festival. Voyager 308-S. Recordings from the 1970–72 festival of old-time musicians from the Pacific northwest.

SONGS OF THE SEA: BRITISH AND AMERICAN
American Sea Songs and Shanties, vols. 1 (1939–51) and 2 (1939–46). AFS L26, L27. Library of Congress field recordings.

BOK, GORDON. *See* Folk Song Revival section, page 103.

CLAYTON, PAUL
Foc'sle Songs and Chanties. Folkways 2429.
Whaling and Sailing Songs. Tradition 1005.

ESKIN, SAM
Sea Shanties and Logger's Songs. Folkways 2019 (10 inch).

KILLEN, LOU
Sea Chanteys. ESP 1085. An interesting collection of sea chanteys, ballads, and transport songs, sung in traditional British style, somewhat nasally, as often in that tradition. Mostly solo voice, with occasional harmony voice and concertina. Killen is a very good singer, with a good sense of ornamentation.
Farewell, Nancy. Topic 12T 110. Sea songs by a group led by Killen, with fiddle (Dave Swarbrick) and concertina.
50 Degrees North to 50 Degrees South. South St. Seaport Mus. 102.

LARNER, SAM
Now Is the Time for Fishing. Folkways 3507. Songs and reminiscences from an East Anglian fisherman in his eighties, a good singer with an interesting repertory. Larner also figures prominently in *Singing the Fishing*, below.

LLOYD, A. L.
Leviathan. Topic 12T174. British whaling songs with fine instrumental backup by Alf Edwards (concertina), Dave Swarbrick (fiddle), and Martin Carthy (mandolin). *See also* under A. L. Lloyd, England, Scotland, and Ireland section, page 128.
. . . and Ewan MacColl: Haul on the Bowlin', vols. 1–2. Stinson 80, 81.

LLOYD, A. L., EWAN MacCOLL, AND PEGGY SEEGER
Whaler Out of New Bedford. Folkways 3850.
Blow Boys Blow. Tradition 1026.

MILLS, ALAN
Songs of the Sea. Folkways 2312.

MORTON, CRAIG
Them Liverpool Judies. Philo 1002.

ROBERTS, JOHN, AND TONY BARRAND
Across the Western Ocean. Swallowtail ST-4. Songs of the transatlantic packet ships on the Liverpool-to-New York run of the 1800's; with booklet of background information.

Sea Shanties. Topic 12TS234. Sung by A. L. Lloyd, Roy Harris, and others.

Singing the Fishing. Argo (British) DA 142. One of the BBC "radio ballads," a series of documentary collages of song and written and field-recorded narrative. This one is a documentary of the British North Sea fishing communities.

The Valiant Sailor. Topic 12TS 232. British navy songs from the time of Nelson, sung by Frankie Armstrong, A. L. Lloyd, and others.

The X Seaman's Institute Sings at the South St. Seaport Museum. Folkways 32418. English and American sea songs and whaling songs.

WESTERN SWING, AND A NOTE ON NASHVILLE

The term "country and western music" means exactly what it says: a category of music that includes both "country" and "western" traditions. Country music is a commercial development of the old-time music listed in an earlier section. A good panoramic view of this style, including most of the later developments discussed in this section, is offered by the following two-record set:
Stars of the Grand Ole Opry (1926–74). RCA CPL2-0466. The term "western music" refers to a different set of traditions that came out of Texas and Oklahoma after the late twenties. The classic western sound synthesizes a number of influences, each important in varying degrees in the work of different individuals. One influence is Texas-style old-time fiddling, which differs from the eastern style in several ways. Eastern fiddlers tend to use shorter bow strokes, with relatively fewer notes per stroke. Texas fiddlers like to play more legato, more notes per stroke, and do not depend so highly on the two-beat shuffle stroke. The result is a style extremely receptive to the influence of jazz violin and jazz phrasing in general. It also happened that western guitarists developed a different style for accompanying fiddle music. Instead of using open chord strumming and carefully chosen bass notes and connecting runs, they played "sock style," using closed position chords that were easily muted by releasing left-hand pressure. This style tends to be played in 4/4 rather than 2/4 time and lends itself to jazzy shuffle rhythms—in fact, it became the favored style of big-band rhythm guitarists.

Commercial cowboy songs provide another influence. Early cowboy singers like Carl Sprague are listed in the section on the West, Southwest, Pacific Northwest, and Alaska, page 94. In addition, there is a more commercial tradition influenced by the bluesy work of Jimmie Rodgers, the most successful country singer of the late twenties. Gene Autry began his career as a singer in this style; his early recordings are listed below.

Then, there is the influence of the "territory bands," the black jazz bands like Alphonso Trent's that worked the southwest during the late twenties and early thirties. The best musicians tended to gravitate east to Kansas City, which developed a characteristic small-ensemble blues-based swing sound exemplified by the early bands of Bennie Moten, Jay McShann, Walter Paige, and Count Basie. Two of the musicians who laid down the basis for the development of bebop just after the end of the thirties came out of this important jazz tradition: altoist Charlie Parker, who had worked with McShann in Kansas City, and who always remained a superb blues player, and guitarist Charlie Christian, who worked with Benny Goodman from 1939 until he was disabled by tuberculosis in 1941. Before joining Goodman, Christian had already acquired a considerable reputation throughout the west as the first electric guitarist to develop a hornlike solo style, and the jazzy country swing guitar style shares its roots with Christian's work.

A final influence was the "Hawaiian" guitar sound, a novelty fad of the twenties. This involved the use of a steel or electrified steel guitar tuned not to a basic triad, but to

Weekend Entertainment

a chord including a sixth. The characteristic use of that sixth in chord harmonizations persisted in the development of the pedal steel guitar sound by Leon McAuliff of Bob Wills' band, and also affected the concept of melody line and of the harmonization of vocal and ensemble parts. It is still an influence on the contemporary pedal steel sound.

The early western swing bands ranged in size from trios to big bands. The small ensembles were close to being old-time string bands, but were distinguished by the looser and jazzier Texas fiddle sound. One of the largest bands was that of fiddler Bob Wills, who attained immense commercial popularity during the thirties and forties. Wills often used a second or third fiddle, several vocalists, piano, lead, steel, and rhythm guitar, bass and drums, and brass and reeds. By the late forties, it was no longer economically feasible to keep such large ensembles on the road, and smaller groups like those of Ernest Tubb (rhythm section, lead guitar, and steel) and Hank Williams (steel, fiddle, rhythm section, and sometimes lead guitar) became the rule. Country and western singers who record with diversified ensembles in the studio usually take a band this size on the road; Merle Haggard's band is a good contemporary example, consisting of first-rate musicians with roots in western swing.

Below are a few select listings for starters.

AUTRY, GENE
Young Gene Autry. Country Loon CSC-69.

BOYD, BILL (b. 1911) Boyd recorded through the thirties and forties and was a popular Dallas radio entertainer into the sixties.
Cowboy Ramblers. RCA AXM2-5503 (2-rec. set).

FRIZZELL, LEFTY (b. 1928) Like Hank Williams, Frizzell was a Texan whose musical inclinations contributed to the development of the Nashville sound; he is best known for his 1949 hit recording of "Long Black Veil." The influence of Frizzell and Williams on Nashville vocal styles has been great.
The Legendary. . . . ABC X-7999.
Greatest Hits. Columbia CS-9288.

GIMBLE, JOHNNY. *See* Fiddle section, page 86.

HAGGARD, MERLE (b. 1937) I have chosen the following instrumental album to show off the talents of Haggard's band, the Strangers, who offer some of the best small-ensemble music now being played with roots in the western swing sounds of the thirties and forties. Haggard himself is an excellent singer and writer who has recorded more than two dozen vocal albums, mostly excellent; consult the Schwann and *Phonolog* listings.
Totally Instrumental. Capitol ST-11141.

McAULIFF, LEON (b. 1917)
Mr. Western Swing. Pine Mtn. 271.
Take It Away. Stoneway 139.

SONS OF THE PIONEERS, THE
————. JEMF 102. A sextet who applied full vocal harmonies to original and other commercially written material on cowboy and western themes. Subject matter is treated rather romantically, and in general with an unreal viewpoint, as different from traditional cowboy songs as the Hollywood western is different from actual history. Their vocal harmonies used a "Hawaiian" sound, with sixths and major ninths, similar to the early pedal steel sound. These previously unissued recordings are taken from 1940 radio transcriptions.

TUBB, ERNEST
. . . *Story.* Decca DXSA7-159.

WILLIAMS, HANK (1923–53)
A Tribute. CMH 214. One side of rare recordings and radio transcriptions; the other side of song tributes by other country and western singers.
The Essential. . . . MGM 5-4651.

WILLS, BOB
. . . *Anthology.* Columbia KG 32416.
Best of. . . . MCA 153.
History of. . . . MGM 4866.
Merle Haggard: A Tribute to the Best Damn Fiddle Player in the World (*or, My Salute to Bob Wills*). Capitol ST-638. A 1970 session in which Haggard and his band, the Strangers, are joined by various original members of Wills' band in a re-creation of early tunes.

ANTHOLOGIES AND COLLECTIONS

Western Swing. Old Timey 105. Recordings mostly from the late thirties, documenting the development of the original western swing idiom and also of the Cajun country music that it influenced. Bob Wills and the Texas Playboys, the Light Crust Doughboys, Bill Boyd, Milton Brown, the Hackberry Ramblers, and Harry Choates.

Western Swing, vols. 2–3. Old Timey 116, 117. Includes thirties and forties recordings by Bill Boyd, Ft. Worth Boys, Tune Wranglers, Cliff Bruner, Lew Preston, W. Lee O'Daniel, Prairie Ramblers, Spade Cooley, Hank Penny, Texas Wanderers, Milton Brown, Shelley Lee Alley, Light Crust Doughboys, Adolf Hofner, Hy Fliers, and others.

ABOUT NASHVILLE

The commercial country music sound that began to come out of Nashville after the late forties represents a combination of eastern country music and western swing influences. The rise of the pedal steel as an original and creative medium, was a dominant characteristic. Later, in the fifties, less regionally defined pop sounds began to come out of Nashville. Largely developed by producer-guitarist Chet Atkins, the contemporary Nashville sound requires sophisticated recording techniques in order to accommodate overdubbed parts by string and horn sections, backup singers, pedal steel, very full rhythm sections, etc. Commercial country music is beyond the scope of this volume, just as jazz blues and soul music are. Country music fans need no exhortation of any sort, but many fans of traditional music share a kind of snobbism about Nashville that seems to have its roots more in bias and blind preconception than in an honest appraisal of the music. Granted, a great deal of commercial garbage comes out of Nashville; but some good music is also written and played there. A search for the best that Nashville has to offer in the way of songwriting, vocal performance, and especially musicianship will show that the best of Nashville can be excellent.

CONTEMPORARY MUSIC AND THE FOLK SONG REVIVAL

"Traditional" music, in the very strictest definition of the term, is a music that is transmitted within a continuous musical culture without the use of written or recorded media. It's often a very "natural" music in the sense that it's not studied. A young singer learns a lengthy ballad not by rote memory, but by having heard the song sung frequently over the years within his family or community; the song is just one of many cultural artifacts that he acquires in the process of growing up. A young instrumentalist learns to play not by formal study or technical discipline (except insofar as necessarily self-imposed), but by playing with his elders within the family or community, imitating them and perhaps receiving instruction in a casual way.

Music is rarely learned this way anymore. Traditional

social continuity has been disrupted; the effects of the media and of the star system, of the commercial necessity for fad and fashion, and of the professional necessity for cultivated technique and showmanship have all brought changes. Only a romantic would argue that they have been either for better or for worse; an individual school or style may be said to progress or degenerate, but there is no progress in the whole history of an art, only change. That change has occurred is indisputable, and it is time to rework the folklorists' old definition of traditional music so that we can deal with its course of development in the media age.

Music in traditional style, as played nowadays, is learned for the most part from records, often with some auxiliary use of books. The musicians are not from the older, fast-disappearing folk culture. In fact, they are likely to be the products of an urban and sometimes quite sophisticated background. Many have taken the trouble to develop an acquaintance or even friendship with older musicians from the folk culture, but their position is more like that of an anthropologist in the field than that of a genuine member of the culture. A few do come from the folk culture itself, and a very few of those who don't have gone through acculturative changes to bring themselves into psychological line with the folk culture. In my experience, this has been a dangerous undertaking, rarely successful and sometimes leading to insanity.

The term "folk music revival" is used to describe the phenomenon of younger singers and players from outside a traditional culture perpetuating its music. Attitudes of these younger performers vary greatly. Some take what is essentially an academic approach, imitating more-or-less exactly the work of the older traditional musicians; they regard change as irresponsible or improper, or as a process beyond their ability, preference, or concern. Their work is valuable, and its imitativeness does not necessarily prevent the artists from being entertaining and spirited performers. There are other musicians for whom the traditional styles remain vital and pliable processes, to be shaped according to their own needs. They are not imitators but continuators, original and innovative to the limits of their individual taste and compulsion. Some have assimilated the techniques and stylistic norms of a tradition so thoroughly that they can continue to develop and extend that tradition in its own terms. Others are eclectic synthesizers, drawing elements from different older traditions and combining them in new ways. And some are distinctly modernist, with definite stylistic roots in traditional music, but open to the influence of jazz, rock, soul music, Nashville, foreign music, classical music—all the gifts of the media, all the sounds of the cosmopolitan milieu. I have made entirely subjective judgments about whether to list such artists under Revival or Contemporary in the sections that follow.

Finally, there are revivalist singers whose concern is more with the folk song material than with the traditional musical style. Some sing in a polished manner, closer to

tional performers drawn into the early revival movement, including Josh White, Leadbelly, Woody Guthrie, Bill Broonzy, Brownie McGhee, and Sonny Terry.

During this period, urban audiences were most interested in the content and social significance of the folk song material. Except among folklorists and a few of the performers, there was not the interest in musical style and technique that there is today. In fact, there was a tendency on the part of some urban "sophisticates" to regard such integral aspects of traditional style as vocal timbre, phrasing, diction, and metrical "irregularities" as embarrassing mistakes caused by faulty education.

The importance of Pete Seeger cannot be overlooked or overstated. Even today, his audience casts him in the role of cheerleader, but his musical contribution has been great and influential nonetheless. The man's repertory and his acquaintance with a number of musical styles are awe-inspiring. He developed a personal banjo style, with Appalachian roots, and became the first instrumental virtuoso of the urban revival. This contribution to the understanding of traditional banjo technique, and later contributions on six- and twelve-string guitar, paved the way for later generations of revivalist players whose main interest was in style and instrumental technique.

The urban folk song movement, with its left-wing associations, did not thrive in the wake of the McCarthy period, but several notable instrumental talents emerged during those years. Peggy Seeger developed her own banjo style from Appalachian roots, while Mike Seeger, Pete's other half-sibling, along with mathematician Tom Paley, acquired a comprehensive *playing* knowledge of the old-time string band style. Between them, they covered guitar, fiddle, mandolin, autoharp, and banjo. By the end of the decade, Paley and Mike Seeger had joined with John Cohen to form the New Lost City Ramblers, whose enthusiastic imitations of old-time music in many urban and college concerts did much to spark the current resurgence of interest in traditional music.

By the late fifties, the second stage of the revival, characterized by a great interest in style and technique, was moving into full swing. That interest extended to the styles of the Appalachians, of the rural bluesmen, and of the bluegrass ensemble as well. The movement at this time was associated with a reemerging avant-garde cult on college campuses, and to a certain extent ran parallel to an involvement with the New York and San Francisco poets who came to be called the Beat Generation.

The young revivalists of the late fifties were the avatars of the hippie movement that blossomed half a decade later. Their interest in traditional music expressed a reaction to what the commercial music of the time had to offer, and was one of various manifestations of a desire to withdraw from urban consumer culture. Classical music was not an apt cultural form for the movement to seize upon; it had (and has) aristocratic overtones and is relatively inaccessible as a means of personal expression because of the necessity for long and devoted study.

European art song vocal production and phrasing than to the traditional style, which tends to be from the throat, speechlike in many ways. Others prefer to be unaffected and straightforward transmitters of the material, without calling attention to themselves through stylized devices. This is a common, though by no means uniform, attitude taken by many singers in traditional culture, particularly in the Anglo-American ballad tradition.

The revivalist movement itself can be divided into chronological stages. The first stage, beginning in the late thirties, was closely associated with left-wing politics. The interest of left-wing urban intellectuals in working class and rural folk music expressed itself in many ways: serious scholarship, collecting, and recording field work, a whole new genre of union and social songwriting, and performances by traditional musicians in front of sympathetic and receptive urban audiences. (Sometimes audiences were more responsive to a performer's ideological stance, real or imagined, than to the music itself.) There was also a patronizing romanticism: on the one hand, Leadbelly was forced to perform his songs in the striped uniform of the chain gang, while on the other, comfortable matrons tried to deliver equally intense versions of the same songs with bel canto vocal production.

Among the important performers from this time on into the early fifties were Pete Seeger, Lee Hays, Bess Lomax, Butch Hawes, Cisco Houston, Oscar Brand, Joe Glazer, and the groups centered around Seeger and Hays: the Almanac Singers and the Weavers. There were also various tradi-

Nor was jazz an apt medium, despite its use by the Beat poets. Though many white urban intellectuals were drawn to black jazz at that time, I believe they were more attracted by its mystique, both musical and racial, than by any understanding of the music itself. And jazz itself was in an amorphous state during those years, not able to provide much of a "handle" for the young white rebels to grab. The post-bop style had worked its way into a static, if not rigidly fossilized, condition, and Miles Davis was only beginning to work with the modal concepts that he developed through the sixties. The validity of Ornette Coleman's striking, and at the time alien, impact was still being debated, while Sonny Rollins' unique excursions out of time, phrase structure, and harmonic structure were too personal to be understood by many. John Coltrane was in his middle period, developing technique and extending previous harmonic concepts, but still several years away from the personal music that made him the most influential innovator of the late sixties. Funky jazz, like Cannonball Adderley's hit versions of Bobby Timmons' gospel-like blues, was commercially viable, but had little to offer that was musically progressive. There was at that time no center, no controlling ethos, that alienated white collegians could grasp as a way of expressing their dissatisfaction with their cultural milieu. In addition, jazz, like classical music, is an art music requiring years of careful study, and so is not an easy means of self-expression.

Meanwhile, the media culture was proffering Eddie Fisher and Perry Como as its finest musical expression. Rock and rhythm and blues had emerged at this time too, and black vocal groups, as well as Buddy Holly and the Sun label's early roster of rockabilly artists like Carl Perkins, Johnny Cash, and Elvis Presley, had made a national impact. Rock-and-roll was beginning to appeal to white youngsters from middle-class and suburban backgrounds; it seemed to express a vitality that was being expressed nowhere else in their culture. But the intellectuals, or even young collegians in general, were not picking up on the music the way they did a few years later. Partly it was because the music did not necessarily express their particular feelings or fantasies; partly it was out of class chauvinism. Also, a great deal of the music simply was not well done, which tended to obscure the fact that some of it was well done indeed. Alan Lomax included a street-corner rock group in his 1959 Carnegie Hall concert of folk music. The controversy it generated equaled in intensity, if not in numbers of participants, the controversy that Bob Dylan generated a few years later when he began to move into a rock format.

But folk music was something else; it was acceptable to the intellectuals if only for romantic reasons. The sound of traditional music hit the campuses like a chinook wind coming down off the mountains; at its best, it offered fresh enthusiasm as opposed to tired professionalism, an honest expression of individual and social feelings as opposed to show-biz theatrics, an elegant simplicity as opposed to gimmickry. Above all, it was relatively easy to understand and to play, and it carried with it associations, often romanticized, of a more honest and more personable culture.

It was harder to find out about folk and folk-based music then than it is now. Most of the recordings listed in this volume have been made, or reissued in accessible format, only since the sixties. Nowadays the buyer of traditional music recordings is virtually paralyzed by the variety of choice. In the late fifties it was very different. I can remember the excitement of encountering, in odd and out-of-the-way record stores in New York City, the old Starday records of the Stanley Brothers, the Vee-Jay records of John Lee Hooker, Chess records by Muddy Waters, and so on. The market was developing, but it was as hard to find sources in a cosmopolitan consumer-oriented environment then as it is now in the hinterlands. When Snooks Eaglin's first Folkways record came out, it was the subject of delighted conversation among blues enthusiasts for weeks, and every new revival singer whose recording was issued by Riverside or Vanguard or Elektra was discussed and debated. There were fewer records, and even on my limited student's budget, I had a sense then of being able to stay on top of the market situation. Listeners were less likely to have as specialized interests then, possibly because there was less information and it was easier to keep abreast. Reissues of the great music of the twenties and thirties, much less the more mediocre music that is also now available, were hard to come by then; you had to know someone who had tapes of the old 78's. The six-record *Anthology of American Folk Music* on the Folkways label was the most influential source of early recorded music, and it almost singlehandedly provided the touchstones of taste and historical judgment for the generation that came out of the late fifties.

From this period came a number of innovators and continuators who opened their ears to many styles of music, traditional and otherwise, or who gave their idiosyncracies full play. I think of banjoists Billy Faier, Dick Weissman, Bill Vanaver, Benji Aronoff, and Bill Keith, and guitarists Dick Rosmini, Dave Van Ronk, Rolf Cahn, Fred Gerlach, Bruce Langhorn, Jon Sholle, Happy and Artie Traum, John Fahey, Marc Silber, Stefan Grossman, Jerry Ricks, and Eric von Schmidt, and Erik Darling on both instruments, as some of the musicians important to my own development who either matured or cut their teeth during this period.

A bit later, many innovative talents were either co-opted or submerged by the mostly inferior music that arose from the commercial success of the Kingston Trio. The door to commercial acceptance was opened at a time when the newly emerging innovative styles, and possibly some of the players themselves, were not strong enough in their art to withstand the adulterating effects of commercialism. More mature styles and players are better equipped to survive when the necessary time for compromise arrives.

Many talents from the late fifties generation, along with many new talents, emerged in the mid-sixties, after the impact of the Beatles, the Rolling Stones, and Bob Dylan was felt. These were the most important of the performers industry that a contractual tie-in between recording and publishing rights could increase profits—some record executives now hesitate to consider performers who do not own original material that can be contracted. In addition, air play royalties are paid to composers but not to performers. This situation has compelled artists who are primarily writers to perform and artists who are primarily performers to write, with results that vary considerably in musical quality.

The traditionally rooted innovators and experimenters now have new avenues of expression open to them: rock, jazz, soul music, the various pop genres of the past, electric music, the commercial viability of original material, and the techniques of the modern recording studio, as well as a knowledge of one or many folk traditions. And then, there are many new writers and performers whose influences are one or several degrees removed from traditional music.

It seems to me that as a result of this liberalized climate, those new performers whose interests are solely in traditional music have grown more conservative than those who came out of the late fifties. They often tend to be more imitative and less willing to innovate within the tradition than their peers of a decade earlier, perhaps because it is now possible for innovative personalities to express themselves within the media culture. But it is still very difficult to emerge untainted from immersion in pop media; usually it's just a matter of the individual choosing the degree to which he will become implicated. For many of today's traditionalists, as for those of the fifties, the interest in folk music reflects an interest in folk life-styles as opposed to those of the media culture. There is also a new factor: the perception that the results of the generation gap of the sixties were as harmful as its causes, and that cultural bridges must be built to salvage those of the old ways that are valuable.

Three sections are devoted to revival recordings. The Folk Song Revival section is concerned mainly with imitators and continuators of the Appalachian song and ballad tradition, but also serves as a catch-all for artists with general interests as well. Then there are specialized sections for string band music and for blues. A striking characteristic of the blues revival is the small number of black musicians involved, particularly with country blues. The tendency of young white musicians has been to concern themselves mostly with instrumental styles. Blues vocal style is inextricably derived from black speech, phrasing, and stress and intonation patterns, and this has been a problem that few young white singers have solved. The most usual choices are either imitation, which runs the danger of being so artificial as to be grotesque or insulting, or a complete failure to face the problem. Some of the artists listed in the blues section might have been listed in the Contemporary Guitarists section, page 117, and vice versa.

In listing contemporary artists, bands, and writers, I have been selective and admittedly capricious. It's hard to deliver a generalized rationale for my selections and omissions, though I could do so case by case. No doubt I have

Bruce Langhorne

who completely revitalized the pop media at that time. The Beatles made it possible for popular artists to strike off in new musical directions. The Rolling Stones, who owe much to Muddy Waters, made the greatest impact of the various British and American bands and soloists who were important in repopularizing the blues. And Dylan's success made it commercially and artistically respectable for folk-rooted artists to use electric sounds, and for pop artists to use acoustic-folk sounds and to draw on traditional styles and materials. Dylan also made it possible for songwriters to express a whole range of emotions and social attitudes that previously had not been commercially viable.

These artists and their contemporaries helped to create a climate in which commercial acceptance no longer required as high a degree of artistic compromise as it formerly had. Dylan in particular made the greatest contribution to the commercial acceptance of the singer-songwriter. The singer-songwriter is not new to traditional music; aside from the many performers who have contributed one or a few songs to tradition, recent history has produced such figures as Sarah Ogan Gunning, Aunt Molly Jackson, Dorsey Dixon, Woody Guthrie, and a host of bluesmen with largely original repertories. But pop music, with its roots in Tin Pan Alley, had always tended to divide the musical labor between writers and interpreters.

The rise of the singer-songwriter genre was not, of course, accomplished by sheer force of the artists' personalities alone. It had become apparent to the recording left out artists that many readers feel should be included; economy of space and the consequent necessity for drawing arbitrary lines are my only apology. I have not hesitated to conserve space and energy by giving a token listing of very popular artists, with a suggestion that the commonplace trade catalogues be consulted. This means the Schwann catalogue or *Phonolog*, both easily accessible at larger record outlets.

Performers listed in the contemporary sections are connected with traditional music either in terms of musical influence or because of connections with the folk music scene. There is also a special section for contemporary guitarists, with its own introductory comments.

THE FOLK SONG REVIVAL

ADAMS, DERROLL
———. Village Thing VTS 17. *See also* Ramblin' Jack Elliot, page 104.

ARMSTRONG, GEORGE AND GERRY
Simple Gifts. Folkways 2335. Pleasant and unpretentious versions of Anglo-American songs.

BAEZ, JOAN
———. Vanguard 2077. Her first album, containing mostly traditional songs.
David's Album. Vanguard 79308. Typical of her later work; contains contemporary songs in Nashville settings. Some nice picking from the session men, featuring Grady Martin (guitar, mandolin, dobro).
See Schwann catalogue for other listings.

BEERS FAMILY, THE Bob "Fiddler" and Evelyn Beers developed a unique, sometimes mannered and overbearing

Bob Dylan

style centered around Evelyn's art song vocal approach and Bob's unusual command of the psaltery, an ancient instrument resembling the strings and sounding board of a piano on which the strings are plucked by the fingers. Bob Beers was also a country fiddler, though classically trained. Dulcimer, banjo, and guitar also appear on the family's recordings. Since Bob Beer's death in 1972, the family tradition has been carried on by Evelyn, daughter Martha, and son-in-law Eric Nagler.
Walkie in the Parlor. Folkways 2376. Bob and Evelyn Beers; features Evelyn's singing with psaltery accompaniment. Traditional and original songs.
The Golden Skein. Biograph 12045. Bob, Evelyn, and Martha. Pretty songs and a few fiddle tunes.
———. Biograph 12033. With Bob, Evelyn, Martha, Eric, and other singers joining in; some rough spots.
The Gentleness in Living. Philo 1010. 1973 sessions of new and old songs in the Anglo-American tradition. Several selections are marred by careless tuning.

BOK, GORDON Bok, a clear-voiced baritone singer, lives along the Maine coast and works on sailing and fishing vessels; his original songs and choice of traditional repertory are largely concerned with fishing and the sea. He has developed an interesting guitar style combining classical and traditional concepts.
A Tune for November. Folk-Legacy FSI-40. Sea songs, international songs, and fiddle tunes arranged for finger style guitar.
Peter Kagan and the Wind. Folk-Legacy FSI-44. Sea songs, fiddle tunes on guitar, and an original chante-fable.
Seal Djiril's Hymn. Folk-Legacy FSI-48. With Ann Mayo Muir. Side one is an evocation, through a cycle of original songs and poems, of the legend of the seal folk of the northern Scottish islands, the mythical gray seals who come up from the sea and turn into men. Side two is an international selection of songs concerned with the sea and sailing.
———. Verve FTS 3016 (OP).

BRAND, OSCAR
Best of. . . . Tradition 2053. *See* Schwann catalogue.

BROWN, FLEMING
———. Folk-Legacy FSI-1. Appalachian songs, many well-known, with banjo accompaniment.

CAHN, ROLF Cahn was active in the late fifties and early sixties, pursuing an interest in traditional and flamenco guitar techniques, mainly on nylon-strung guitar.
California Concert. Folkways 2416.
. . . with Eric von Schmidt. Folkways 2417.

CARAWAN, GUY
———, vols. 1–3. Folkways 3544, 3548, 3552.
The Telling Takes Me Home. Curnon CNL 722.

CARNS, BARBARA
Trouble in Mind. Living Folk (no number).

CLAYTON, PAUL
Cumberland Mountain Folksongs. Folkways 2007 (10 inch).

Bay State Ballads. Folkways 2106 (10 inch).
Folksongs and Ballads of Virginia. Folkways 2110 (10 inch).
Folk Ballads of the English-Speaking World. Folkways 2310.

COLTMAN, BOB
Lonesome Robin. Minstrel JD 200. Coltman sings simply and honestly, and plays banjo with a fine clear touch in picking and frailing styles, in addition to guitar and fiddle. Various friends join him, including Ed Trickett on guitar and hammered dulcimer, in a good selection of original and traditional songs not often heard. Sometimes uneven; always thoroughly enjoyable.
The Last Minstrel Show. Minstrel JD-202.

CONNOR, JIM
Connor is a young banjo and guitar player, who has respect for traditional styles, but modifies them for his own musical purposes. (—D.W.)
Traditional Old-Time Music from Alabama. HAFM II-002.

COONEY, MICHAEL
The Cheese Stands Alone. Folk-Legacy FSI-35. Songs and instrumentals by a leading revival performer and traditional purist. Perhaps it is having this self-conscious ax to grind that prevents these good performances from being great ones.

DANE, BARBARA
. . . and the Chambers Brothers. Folkways 2468.
Sings the Blues. Folkways 2471.
I Hate the Capitalist System. Paredon 1014. Traditional and contemporary songs of protest and social comment. A striking choice of material, in arrangements and performances that range from stimulating to very dull.
FTA. Paredon 1003. Militant songs of the GI anti–Vietnam War resistance movement, to which Dane made devoted contributions of time, talent, and energy. Recorded, with audience participation, in off-base coffeehouses near Ft. Hood, Ft. Benning, and Ft. Bragg. Sound quality varies.

DARLING, ERIK
Darling reached his widest audience during the late fifties and early sixties as a member of such commercial groups as the Tarriers, the Weavers, and the Rooftop Singers. As these three, unfortunately out-of-print, albums indicate, he is a unique and highly talented instrumentalist and rearranger of traditional material on guitar and banjo, in a variety of styles and idioms. He now teaches music privately in New York City.
Train Time. Vanguard 9131 (OP).
True Religion. Vanguard 9099 (OP).
_____. Elektra 154 (OP).

DARLINGTON, SANDY AND JEANNIE
_____. Folk-Legacy FSI-28. Little- and well-known Anglo-American and southern mountain songs.

DICKENS, HAZEL, AND ALICE GERRARD
Hazel and Alice. Rounder 0027. Traditional and original songs; some of the new songs are concerned with contemporary women's consciousness, in terms of the rural folk backgrounds of the singers. Although associated with the revival movement and sharing its attitudes, Dickens and Gerrard come from Appalachian culture. With guitars, bass, fiddle, banjo, mandolin, and dobro.
Won't You Come and Sing for Me? Folkways 31034.
Strange Creek Singers. Arhoolie 4004. Old-time and original songs by Mike and Alice (Gerrard) Seeger, Tracy Schwarz, Hazel Dickens, and Lamar Grier, recorded 1968–70. Most vocals in bluegrass harmony style, instrumental work in old-time style.

ELLIOT, RAMBLIN' JACK
Elliot sometimes calls himself the first of the Brooklyn cowboys. He was one of the pioneer singers who shed their urban ethnic roots and attempted to assimilate a folk life-style as well as musical style. Woody Guthrie was a major influence; Elliot in turn was a major influence on Dylan. Though in recent years he has been open to contemporary material, the core of Elliot's repertory consists of songs from tradition and from the early days of the urban movement. The first record listed below provides a sampling of the songs with which he is most often associated. No studio recording, though, can capture the impact of Elliot performing on a good night. He improvises on melodies and twists them around, singing free of commonplace phrase structure and of his own guitar rhythms. Taking great, crazy risks and usually succeeding, he generates a tremendous excitement of which his recordings offer a small glimpse.
_____. Prestige 7721. Accompanied by Ralph Rinzler and John Herald.
Country Style. Prestige 7804.
Sings Woody Guthrie. Prestige 7453.
Talking Woody Guthrie. Topic 12T93.
Muleskinner. Topic 12T106.
_____. Vanguard 79151.
_____. Ev. Arch. FS-210.
. . . and Derroll Adams. Topic 12T105.
Sings Woody Guthrie and Jimmy Rodgers. Monitor MFS 380.
Bull Durham Sacks and Railroad Tracks. Reprise 6387.
Young Brigham. Reprise 6284.

ESKIN, SAM
Sea Shanties and Logger's Songs. Folkways 2019 (10 inch). Eskin was a pioneer in the use of the tape recorder as a collecting tool, and collected many of these unusual songs himself.

GOLDEN RING
_____. Folk-Legacy FSI-16. Pleasant and harmonious singing by a group of friends including Howie Mitchell, George and Gerry Armstrong, and Ed Trickett. Most enjoyable versions of songs mainly from Anglo-American tradition.
The New Golden Ring: Five Days Singing, vols. 1–2. Folk-Legacy FSI-41, 42. An expanded ensemble, equally pleasurable.

GREENWAY, JOHN
Talking Blues. Folkways 5232. The talking blues (which does not use the blues form, strictly defined) is a rhymed and rhythmic spoken form with guitar or banjo accompaniment, usually used for comic, sarcastic, or social protest material. (Woody Guthrie wrote some of our best talking blues.) Greenway is a pleasant performer and well-known folklorist.

Frank Hamilton

GREY, SARA
———. Folk-Legacy FSI-38. An excellent selection, beautifully and simply sung, with some banjo accompaniments, of English, Scottish, and American songs and ballads. Ed Trickett makes occasional contributions with his vocal harmonies, guitar, and hammered dulcimer.

HALLMAN, NICK
Doublepicks. Gitfiddle ST 7310. Available from 114 W. Montclair Ave., Greenville, S.C. 29609. Original and traditional southern American songs with some flashy flat picking.

HAMILTON, FRANK
Sings Folk Songs. Folkways 2437. Original arrangements and rearrangements of traditional songs, by an influential urban singer and instrumentalist of the late fifties, who has a good sense of both tradition and independence. With guitar, banjo, and harmonica. *See also* Pete Seeger, page 107, and Billy Faier, Banjo section, page 80.

HAZEL AND ALICE. *See* Hazel Dickens, page 104.

HICKERSON, JOE
———. Folk-Legacy FSI-39. Songs and ballads—good ones not often heard or recorded—sung straightforwardly with guitar and sometimes with additional instruments and vocal harmonies. Hickerson, Director of the Archive of Folk Song of the Library of Congress, is known for his vast repertory.

HINTON, SAM
The Songs of Men. Folkways 2400.
Wandering Folk Songs. Folkways 2401.

HOUSTON, CISCO Best known as Woody Guthrie's sidekick, Houston sang with a clear, rather polished tenor voice. His repertory consisted mainly of western and some Appalachian songs. *See also* under Woody Guthrie, The West, Southwest, Pacific Northwest, and Alaska section, page 94.
———. Ev. Arch. FS-205.
900 Miles and Other Railroad Songs. Folkways 2013 (10 inch).
Cowboy Songs. Folkways 2022 (10 inch).
Hard Travelin'. Folkways 2042 (10 inch).
Songs of the Open Road. Folkways 2468.
American Folksongs. Folkways 31012.

HUNTER, MAX
Ozark Folksongs and Ballads. Folk-Legacy FSA-11. Songs collected from tradition, sung clearly with guitar accompaniment.

JAMES, KAREN A Canadian singer with a repertory of American, Canadian, and British songs.
Folk Songs, vols. 1–2. Folkways 3547, 3549.

JONES, DAVID
Easy and Slow. Minstrel JD-201.

KAHN, KATHY
The Working Girl: Women's Songs from the Mountains, Mines, and Mills. Voyager 305. Issued in conjunction with her Avon book *Hillbilly Women;* Kahn is a community organizer in rural Appalachia.

KAHN, SI
New Wood. June Appal (no number).

KOSSOY SISTERS
Bowling Green. Tradition 1018.

LaFARGE, PETER
Iron Mountain. Folkways 2531.
As Long As Grass Shall Grow. Folkways 2532. American Indian topical songs.
Cowboy Songs. Folkways 2533.
Love Songs. Folkways 2534.
On the Warpath. Folkways 2535.

LANGSTAFF, JOHN
American and English Folksongs and Ballads. Tradition 1009. Sung in a trained art song voice, solo and with piano.

LOMAX, ALAN
Collector's Choice. Tradition 2057.

LOMAX, JOHN A., JR.
American Folk Songs. Folkways 3508.

MacARTHUR, MARGARET, AND FAMILY
On the Mountains High (1971). Living Folk F-LFR-100. Songs from Anglo-American tradition, clearly sung solo

and with vocal ensembles in this recording with fiddle, dulcimer, harp, dobro, and banjo in various combinations. *See also* Northeast section, page 94.

McAdoo, Bill
_____, vols. 1–2. Folkways 2448, 2449.

McCurdy, Ed
Best of. . . . Tradition 2051.

Mitchell, Howie
_____. Folk-Legacy FSI-5. Tasteful, thoroughly enjoyable versions of Anglo-American songs mostly from the Appalachians, with guitar, banjo, autoharp, and virtuoso dulcimer solos and accompaniments.

Mud Acres
Music Among Friends (1972). Rounder 3001. Arrangements of traditional, contemporary, and original songs and instrumentals by musicians mostly from the Woodstock area. Tasteful, relaxed, and enjoyable examples of present-day revival music making. Happy and Artie Traum, Maria Muldaur, John Herald, Eric Kaz, and Bill Keith are among the performers featured in various combinations.

Nagler, Martha and Eric. *See* the Beers Family, this section, page 103.

New Golden Ring. *See* Golden Ring, this section, page 104.

Niles, John Jacob An older singer and collector from the south who sings in an eerie, nontraditional countertenor voice, sometimes moving but often discomfiting, with dulcimer accompaniment.
Folk Songs. Folkways 2373.
An Evening with. . . . Tradition 1036.
The Ballads of. . . . Tradition 1046/2 (2-rec. set).
Folk Balladeer. RCA LPV-513.

Odetta (Odetta Felious) Odetta sings with a big, husky voice that goes down to the bottom of the contralto range, and then some. Originally trained as an operatic singer, she sings clearly and with careful vocal production, but without bel canto affectations that would be alien to the folk repertory.
Ballads and Blues. Tradition 1010.
The Essential. Vanguard VSD 43-44 (2-rec. set). Thirty-one well-known songs often associated with the revival movement.
. . . at Carnegie Hall. Vanguard 73003.
_____. Ev. Arch. FS-273.
. . . Sings. Contemporary songs. Polydor 24.4048.
Best of. . . . Tradition 2052.
At the Gate of Horn. Tradition 1025.

Paley, Tom
Folk-Songs from the Southern Appalachian Mountains (1953). Elektra EKL-12 (10 inch, OP). This album, long out of print, was a classic of the revival movement. It was the first revivalist statement of virtuoso mountain guitar and banjo style.
. . . and Peggy Seeger: Who's Going to Shoe Your Pretty Little Foot? Topic 12T113 (formerly available on Elektra). Southern Anglo-American songs and ballads; a casual and enjoyable session by two fine musicians, but rough in a few spots.
See also New Lost City Ramblers and Old Reliable String Band, String Band Revival section, page 113.

Paton, Sandy and Carolyn
_____. Folk-Legacy EGO-30. The "EGO" serial number seems intended to express the Patons' whimsical embarrassment at recording themselves on their own record label. There is no need to be embarrassed about these pleasantly sung versions of traditional and contemporary songs in Anglo-American style.

Phillips, Utah
Good Though! Philo 1004. Philips, also known as Bruce or U. Utah, is a good songwriter in traditional style and an entertaining performer with a repertory of folk tales, dirty jokes, and excruciating puns to fill up the time between songs. This concept album, including original, contemporary, and traditional material, is centered around his favorite theme of railroads and hoboing, complete with railroad sound effects and guitar, bass, dobro, and vocal harmony accompaniments.

Roberts, Robin
Traditional Folk Songs and Ballads. Stinson SLP 77.

Rutherford, Betsy
Traditional Country Music. Biograph RC-6004. Although Rutherford claims both kinship and musical descent from a family of well-known old-time mountain musicians, only the kinship descent is undeniable. The accompanying string band is deadly dull.

Saletan, Tony, and Irene (Irene Kossoy)
_____. Folk-Legacy FSI-37. The Saletans sing in clear, strong, and unaffected voices, accompanying themselves with a great variety of idiomatic Appalachian guitar and banjo styles. Both were important figures in earlier days of the revival movement. The Saletans are now based in Boston, where Tony teaches music privately and does educational and documentary work.

Sandburg, Carl
The Great. . . . Lyrichord 766.
Flat Rock Ballads. Columbia Special Products AML 5339. An interesting selection of well- and little-known American folk songs, but despite his endearing position in American letters, Sandburg's vocal and guitar abilities are erratic at best.

Schneyer, Helen
Ballads, Broadsides and Hymns. Folk-Legacy FSI-50. A unique and wonderful record. Schneyer, who comes from Washington, D.C., and is not a natural singer, has chosen to work in what resembles one of the most mannered and difficult styles of British ballad singing. Her commitment to perfection in a difficult and alien style creates a tremendous tension that adds power to the performance; Schneyer constantly walks on the edge, harnessing potentially destructive energy and using it to enhance her art.

Like other perfectionists to whom perfection does not come easy, she knows that she must exercise great care in her selection of material (both British and American), which runs the entire spectrum of human emotions. The record is full of wit and courage and fun. Someone I know spilled coffee all over herself on first hearing "Beulahland." Mostly solo voice; on some selections Schneyer is aided by Jay Ungar's sympathetic fiddle or by excellent vocal harmonies from members of the Golden Ring circle of singers.

SCHWARZ, TRACY AND ELOISE
Home Among the Hills. FV 12007. Tracy Schwarz is known as a member of the New Lost City Ramblers.

SEEGER FAMILY (Peggy, Penny, Barbara, and Mike)
American Folk Songs. Folkways 2005 (10 inch). Many well-known songs (and others that should be) in traditional revivalist style.

SEEGER, MIKE
Old-Time Country Music. Folkways 2325. Imitations and occasional rearrangements of older music from the southern highlands, with fiddle, guitar, and banjo.
Tipple, Loom, and Rail. Folkways 5273. An historically oriented anthology of traditional songs of the industrialization of the south.
Music from True Vine. Mercury SRM 1-627. A superb album, mainly of traditional songs. Seeger plays very close to his sources, but always with an injection of his own vitality.
The Second Annual Farewell Reunion. Mercury SRM 1-685. Seeger is joined on each song by a different musical

"Perfection Does Not Come Easy": Helen Schneyer

friend: Ry Cooder, Peggy Seeger, Pete Seeger, Maria Muldaur, Elizabeth Cotten, and others.
See also Pete Seeger and Seeger Family, this page, and New Lost City Ramblers, String Band Revival section, page 113.

SEEGER, MIKE AND PEGGY
————. Argo (British) ZFB 62.

SEEGER, PEGGY
Seeger accompanies her clear soprano with guitar and banjo arrangements which are not necessarily in traditional style, but always reveal a superb sense of construction and seemliness in terms of traditional values. An original stylist, she sings and plays out of her total awareness of traditional and contemporary musical attitudes, and does not hesitate to extend traditional concepts. A good guitarist and superb banjo player, she does not find it necessary to avoid playing simply or to sing without accompaniment when it will enhance the song. In recent years, she has been involved in the British scene, and alone or in partnership with Ewan MacColl has made important contributions to contemporary style and repertory. (*See also* Tom Paley, Mike and Peggy Seeger, and Seeger Family, this section, and Ewan MacColl, England, Scotland, and Ireland section.) Not listed below are several excellent out-of-print Prestige records made in the early and mid-sixties, which may still be found in remainder bins in the shops.
Folksongs of Courting and Complaint. Folkways 2049 (10 inch).
American Folksongs for Banjo. Folk-Lyric 114 (OP). Good songs, excellent banjo accompaniments and a few instrumentals. Should be reissued.
. . . and Ewan MacColl: At the Present Moment. Rounder 4003. Original songs on social topics, ranging from doctrinaire to dramatic to humorous.
. . . and Ewan MacColl: The Folkways Record of Contemporary Songs. Folkways 8736.
Alone. Argo (British) ZFB 63. English and American songs and ballads with banjo, guitar, autoharp, and dulcimer; some in solo voice.
. . . and Ewan MacColl: The Angry Muse. Argo (British) ZDA 83. An historical survey of traditional British and American songs of protest.
. . . and Ewan MacColl: The Amorous Muse. Argo (British) ZFB 66. Traditional British and American love songs.
. . . and Ewan MacColl: The Wanton Muse. Argo (British) ZFB 67. Traditional British and American bawdy songs.
. . . and Ewan MacColl: The Paper Stage, vols. 1–2. Argo (British) ZDA 98, 99. Broadside ballads drawn from plays by Elizabethan dramatists.
. . . and Ewan MacColl: The Long Harvest, 10 vols. Argo (British) ZDA 66–75. Back-to-back variants of traditional ballads in the Scottish, English, and American versions, with extensive annotation. A likely candidate for library acquisitions.

SEEGER, PETE
American Industrial Ballads. Folkways 5251. A misleading title: the songs reflect the conditions of life of Americans in all lines of work: cowboys, miners, railroad men, farmers, factory hands. An excellent selection of material, with banjo accompaniment.

The Sea Islands Sound: Bessie Jones with Frank Warner

which became well-known standards in the urban revival because of this record. With banjo accompaniment.

The Rainbow Quest. Folkways 2454. A pastiche of songs or parts of songs, sung with banjo accompaniment, arranged in a manner suggestive of the thoughts and emotions a person generates in his passage through life.

Goofing Off Suite. Folkways 2045. A wonderful collection of short treatments of international folk, classical, and pop themes (but mainly American folk) on banjo, mandolin, guitar, and reed pipe.

. . . and the Almanac Singers: Talking Union and Other Union Songs. Folkways 5285.

. . . and Frank Hamilton: Nonesuch. Folkways 2439. Unaffected original, casual, and loose arrangements of songs and instrumentals from various American and international folk idioms, for six- and twelve-string guitar, guitarrón, banjo, harmonica, and recorder. Includes the finger-picking guitar instrumental "Singing in the Country."

. . . and Mike Seeger: Indian Summer. Folkways 3851. A film score based on impressionistic variations on folk themes, played on fiddle, guitar, banjo, and recorder; very pleasant listening. Also includes Seeger's sound tracks for *Horizontal Lines* and *The Many-Colored Paper,* and musical selections from the sound track of *The Country Fiddle* featuring Jean Carignan.

Banks of Marble. Folkways 31040. After ten years of often nondescript work for Columbia records, Seeger returns to the Folkways label in this 1974 recording. Recording quality goes down, musical quality goes up.

For additional listings, consult Schwann catalogue and *Phonolog. See also* under Mike Seeger (page 107), Big Bill Broonzy (Mississippi and Central Blues section, page 9), Woody Guthrie (the West, Southwest, Pacific Northwest, and Alaska section, page 94), and Jean Carignan (Fiddle section, page 84).

STEKERT, ELLEN
Songs of a New York Lumberjack. Folkways 2354. Now working mainly as a scholar rather than as a performer, Stekert was active in the New York revival movement in the late fifties.

STRANGE CREEK SINGERS. *See* Hazel Dickens, page 104.

SUMMERS, ANDREW ROWAN A revivalist singer of Anglo-American ballads with a clear nontraditional tenor voice, Summers usually accompanies himself on dulcimer.
Seeds of Love. Folkways 2021 (10 inch).
Lady Gay. Folkways 2041 (10 inch).
The Faulse Layde. Folkways 2044 (10 inch).
———. Folkways 2348.
Early American Hymns and Carols. Folkways 2361.
The Unquiet Grave. Folkways 2364.

TRICKETT, ED
The Telling Takes Me Home. Folk-Legacy FSI-46. Traditional and contemporary songs, clearly and enjoyably sung. Most songs are in a gentle ballad style, with vocal harmonies, guitar, and hammered dulcimer. The vocal ensembles, by singers associated with the Golden Ring, are excellent.

The World of Pete Seeger. Columbia KG 31949 (2-rec. set). Representative selections from his later work, culled from earlier Columbia releases, with an emphasis on audience-rousing live performances and topical songs.

Young vs. Old. Columbia CS 9873. Topical songs, some recorded in live performance, concerned with youthful rebellion, old people, Vietnam War resistance, etc.

. . . Sampler. Folkways 2043 (10 inch).

. . . with Brownie McGhee and Sonny Terry: Washboard Band Country Dance Music. Folkways 2201 (10 inch).

American Favorite Ballads, vols. 1–5. Folkways 2320/1/2/3, 2445. Especially well-known songs with banjo and guitar, available separately.

. . . Sings Woody Guthrie. Folkways 31002.

. . . Sings Leadbelly. Folkways 31022.

Little Boxes. Folkways 5302.

. . . Sings American Ballads. Folkways 2319. Good songs mostly from Appalachian tradition, with banjo accompaniment. For the typical Seeger vocal phrasing, for the absence of the purely showmanlike enthusiasm Seeger exhibits in his concert recordings, for the musical rather than programmatic or doctrinaire choice of material, this album equals the *Darling Corey* album below as a representation of Seeger at his best.

Darling Corey. Folkways 2003 (10 inch). A good selection of songs mostly from the southern mountains, many of

VANAVER, BILL
Coming Soon Here Now. Swallowtail ST-2. American, English, and Mediterranean songs and dances on banjo, guitar, and Balkan-Near Eastern instruments.

WARNER, FRANK Warner is an important collector-performer, with a vast knowledge of Anglo-American material. As this book goes to press, a multivolume series is being prepared by Minstrel Records. Many songs that we take for granted today, like Frank Proffitt's "Tom Dooley," were originally collected by Warner.

WEAVERS, THE The Weavers were a polished revival group, nontraditional in style, from which the Kingston Trio and other show groups of the early sixties derived. Originally, the group included Pete Seeger, Ronnie Gilbert, Lee Hays, and Fred Hellerman; after Seeger left, successive replacements included Frank Hamilton, Erik Darling, and Bernie Krause.
Best of. . . . Decca DXS-7173-e (2-rec. set).
Greatest Hits. Vanguard VSD 15/16 (2-rec. set).
At Carnegie Hall. Vanguard 6533E.
On Tour. Vanguard 6537E.
Reunion at Carnegie Hall, vols. 1–2. Vanguard 2150, 79161.
Songbag. Vanguard 73001.

WEILL, RITA
_____. Takoma A 1022. A continuator of the Anglo-American ballad tradition.

ANTHOLOGIES AND COLLECTIONS

Alabama Folk Music. HAFM II-001. Pleasant derivative vocal and instrumental versions of commonplace American tunes performed by younger Alabama musicians.
Berkeley Farms. Folkways 2436. An anthology of a wide variety of music, from jew's-harp to modern country, played by young Berkeley, California, musicians of the early seventies.
Colorado Folk, vol. 1. Biscuit City 1301 CF. Popular Denver-area performers: Dan McCrimmon, Mary Flower and Katy Moffat, Jim Ransom, and Grubstake.
Colorado Folk, vol. 2. Biscuit City 1302 CF. More from Denver: Vince and Kathy DeFrancis, City Limits Bluegrass Band, and the fine songwriters Ruthie Allen and Pete McCabe.
Folk Music of Washington Square. Folkways 2354. Through the fifties and into the sixties, New York City's Washington Square Park was a gathering place on warm Sunday afternoons for young revival singers and musicians to learn, compete, and play with each other.
Get Folked. Mountain Railroad GF-1. Live concert recordings by performers at Charlotte's Web coffeehouse, a haven for traditional and contemporary folk performances in Rockford, Illinois. Styles run from traditional blues and banjo songs to contemporary string band music and singer-songwriters.
Introducing Broadside. Broadside BR 301 (available from Folkways). Topical songs first printed in *Broadside* magazine, sung by Happy Traum, the New World Singers, and others including Bob Dylan under the pseudonym of Blind Boy Grunt. Excellent as a documentary of the urban topical song movement as it stood in 1963.
Lonesome Valley. Folkways 2010 (10 inch). Traditional songs, sung by Pete Seeger, Lee Hays, Tom Glazer, Woody Guthrie, and others. An excellent job of capturing the feeling of the revival movement of the forties.
Out West—Berkeley. Arhoolie 4001. Songs from various American traditions by the cream of the urban revival singers, who proliferated in Berkeley, California, in the mid-sixties. Janet Smith, Toni Brown, Pete Berg, Richmond (Steve T. A.) Talbott, Perry Lederman, and others.
Rackensack, vols. 1–2 OFC (numbers not available). Performers of the Rackensack Folklore Society of the Arkansas Ozarks, including Jimmy Driftwood.
Welcome to Caffé Lena. Biograph 12046. A sampling of the traditional and revivalist talent to be found at the well-respected coffeehouse in Saratoga Springs, New York. Michael Cooney, Bill Vanaver, Lou Killen, the High Level Ranters, Rosalie Sorrells, Mac Wiseman, Hedy West, and others are recorded in recent live performances.

THE BLUES REVIVAL

ALEXANDER, DAVE
The Dirt on the Ground. Arhoolie 1071. A younger Oakland singer-pianist, who plays mainly in the modern funky style, with many respectful bows in the direction of the older blues piano traditions. An individualist with a strongly two-handed concept, Alexander pays more attention to his playing than to his singing, which is adequate but not up to his piano work.
The Rattler. Arhoolie 1071.

"The Rattler": Dave Alexander

BACKWARDS SAM FIRK AND DELTA X
_____. Adelphi AD 1006S. Imitations of early rural blues by Michael Stewart and Stephan Michaelson. Inadequate vocals; satisfactory guitar work but sometimes out of tune, and lacking the spirit of the originals.

BOOKBINDER, ROY
Travelin' Man (1971). Adelphi AD 1017. Recordings of traditional blues and ragtime blues by a younger New York revivalist, whose strongest commitment is to the east and southeast guitar styles. He plays close to his sources, but with a clean, spirited, and swinging touch, and also sings well—a quality not often shared by other revivalist bluesmen with his degree of interest and competence in guitar work. An enjoyable album.

BUTTERFIELD, PAUL
East-West. Elektra EKS-7294. This album, featuring Butterfield's harmonica and Mike Bloomfield's electric guitar, made a tremendous impact in the mid-sixties. While most revivalists were concerned with older preelectric styles, a number of young white players in Chicago were learning the electric blues sounds; this album, representing a development of that style, paved the way for further use of electric sounds by traditionally oriented blues and rock players.
Better Days. Bearsville BR 2119. Later in the sixties Butterfield, who is also a good singer, got involved in a more commercial and rather stereotyped soul-band sound. This recent album reflects the greater originality of which he is capable, with no small help from guitarist Amos Garrett and from arrangers Geoff Muldaur and Howard Johnson. Garrett's electric guitar style, here as elsewhere, is polished, sensitive, and uniquely his own.
For other listings, *see* Schwann catalogue and *Phonolog.*

GERLACH, FRED
12-String Guitar. Folkways 3529. Gerlach, as a result of public appearances and especially because of this album, was a major influence in the revival of interest in virtuoso twelve-string guitar styles in the late fifties urban movement. Here he sings and plays Leadbelly arrangements and other traditional blues and songs in his own arrangements.
Songs My Mother Never Sang. Takoma C1028. Perhaps one reason she never sang them is that they are not melodic. These are instrumentals in the modern rambling, impressionistic, finger-picking style that concentrates mainly on developing sounds and textures, rather than melodic statements.

GROSSMAN, STEFAN Best known of the young New York guitarists who studied with Gary Davis in the early sixties, Grossman is also known for his many books of transcriptions of country blues virtuoso guitar stylists. His recorded repertory includes imitations of virtuoso country blues guitar pieces, contemporary guitar pieces, and numerous songs and instrumentals of his own composition in both traditional and contemporary style. Grossman plays acoustic guitar with a hard, bright touch, and favors the percussive string-slapping sounds used occasionally by rural stylists.

Yazoo Basin Boogie. Kicking Mule 102 (U.S.) = Transatlantic 217 (British). 1969–70 recordings of some of the most complex guitar instrumentals in Grossman's repertory; mostly original pieces, with a few rearrangements of older pieces and ragtime settings by Dave Laibman and Rory Block. This is an effective summary statement of what Grossman has learned from the older Black American guitarists; it's also a useful record to learn from in that many of the pieces have been transcribed in his books.
Aunt Molly's Murray Farm. Sonet SNTF 640. Original and contemporary blues, rags, and instrumental pieces for acoustic and bottleneck style guitar; occasional vocals and overdubs.
The Gramercy Park Sheik. Sonet SNTF 627. With an emphasis on original instrumentals in contemporary finger-picking style.
Acoustic Music for Body and Soul. Kicking Mule 105. Selections from the two above albums.
Live (1972). Transatlantic 264 (2-rec. set). Traditional and original pieces recorded in European and American concert performances.
The Ragtime Cowboy Jew. Transatlantic 223 (2-rec set). The title is an interesting historical allusion; it comes from the autobiography of Mezz Mezzrow, a Chicago Jew who learned the New Orleans clarinet style and chose to spend his life during the thirties and forties living in Harlem; later he became an expatriate in Europe, as Grossman himself has. Original and contemporary songs and guitar pieces, with occasional vocals and rhythm section.
Hot Dogs. Transatlantic 257. Old and new songs featuring finger picking, with rhythm section including Big Jim Sullivan, second guitar.
Memphis Jellyroll. Transatlantic 274 (= Kicking Mule 118). Original and other instrumentals on six- and twelve-string guitar, covering the ground from Mississippi to Nashville and on out into a space-age orbit somewhere.
Those Pleasant Days. Transatlantic 246.
How to Play Blues Guitar. See Instructional Books and Records, page 186.
Fingerpicking Guitar Techniques. Kicking Mule 112. Well-known traditional instrumentals, with tablature booklet.
. . . and Ton Van Bergeyk: Ragtime Guitar. Kicking Mule 115. Classic piano rags adapted for guitar, and early ragtime blues guitar solos; accompanied by tablature booklet. Not an instructional record for beginners, though; the material is difficult.

HAMMOND, JOHN Hammond has also recorded as John Hammond, Jr., and John Paul Hammond. He is not to be confused with jazz organist Johnny Hammond or with his father, John Hammond, Sr., the Columbia record producer who has been responsible since the late thirties for discovering a vast amount of important talent. Hammond favors a hard-driving electric rhythm-and-blues sound, marred by his rather grotesque vocal imitations of black style.
I'm Satisfied. Columbia KC 31318.
Source Point. Columbia C 30458.
Triumvirate. Columbia KC 32172.
Best of. . . . Vanguard VSD 11/12 (2-rec. set).
See Schwann catalogue and *Phonolog* for other listings.

HARPE, NEIL
_____. Adelphi 1013.

HINE, GRAHAM
Bottleneck Blues. Blue Goose 2002.

HUBBARD, ROGER
Brighton Belle Blues. Blue Goose 2005.

JOHNSON, LARRY
Fast and Funky. Blue Goose 2001.
Country Blues. Biograph 12028.

KELLY, JoANN
_____. Blue Goose 2009. A leading British singer, with guitarists John Fahey, John Miller, and others.

KIRKPATRICK, BOB
_____. Folkways 31032.

KOERNER, RAY, AND GLOVER "Spider" John Koerner, Dave "Snaker" Ray, and Tony "Little Sun" Glover, three younger musicians from the Minneapolis area, were popular for their enthusiastic blues performances on the college circuit through the sixties.
Blues, Rags and Hollers. Elektra 7267 (= Audiophile 78).
_____. Elektra 7305.
Live. Mill City 172.
Music Is Just a Bunch of Notes. Sweet Jane 5872 (Koerner).

KWESKIN, JIM The vodeodo-flavored Kweskin Jug Band was a college favorite during the sixties, and from it emerged such talents as those of Bill Keith and Geoff and Maria Muldaur. Kweskin's later records have been less interesting.
. . . and the Jug Band. Vanguard 2158.
Jug Band Music. Vanguard 79163.
Greatest Hits. Vanguard VSD 13/14 (2-rec. set.).
Best. Vanguard 79270.
Jump for Joy. Vanguard 79243.
See Reverse Side. Vanguard 79234.
Garden of Joy. Reprise RS 6266.
What Ever Happened to the Good Old Days at the Club 47? Paramount 6006.

MAHAL, TAJ One of the few younger black men to become involved with country blues styles, Taj also flirts with rock and soul music, and his strong husky voice is strongly affected by soul singing styles. He plays for the most part simple, highly rhythmic guitar and sometimes banjo parts, capitalizing on his strong internal rhythmic sense in his rousing performances.
Giant Step/De Ole Folks at Home. Columbia GP 18 (2-rec. set). Traditional, original, and contemporary songs. The *Giant Step* disc is oriented toward a contemporary sound, with rhythm section and electric lead guitar. The *Ole Folks* disc presents solo or acoustically accompanied vocals, and instrumentals with acoustic guitar, banjo, and harmonica; the songs are traditional or in traditional style.
Recycling the Blues. Columbia KC 31605. Side one was recorded in live performance. Side two offers an unusual variety of sounds, with various accompaniments by tuba and female gospel trio, and a flamenco fantasy on guitar.
The Real Thing. Columbia G 30619. An exuberant live performance recorded at the Fillmore West, with electric rhythm section and a strong bouncy bottom provided by four tubas.
Happy Just to Be Like I Am. Columbia C 30767. A great range of sounds, from acoustic guitar duets to soul vocals with large horn and rhythm sections.
The Natch'l Blues. Columbia CS 9698.
Ooh So Good 'n' Blues. Columbia KC 32600.
Mo' Roots. Columbia KC 33051.

MAYALL, JOHN Along with the Rolling Stones and the various members of the Yardbirds, Mayall was a primary figure in the British electric blues scene that later developed into hard rock. The following two of his many albums represent important stages of his career. The first, from the early sixties, is hard electric blues with Eric Clapton on lead guitar. (Mayall is also a guitarist, but confines himself on this album to piano, harmonica, and vocals.) The second represents his most recent work, with skilled jazzmen. For additional listings, *see* Schwann catalogue and *Phonolog.*
Bluesbreakers. London PS 492.
Jazz-Blues Fusion. Polydor 5027.

MILLER, JOHN
First Degree Blues. Blue Goose 2007.
How About Me? Blue Goose 2012. Miller's first record demonstrates his competence as an assimilator of country blues guitar style, with a capacity to inject original and synthesized elements. In his second album he begins to explore other forms in addition: forties pop ballads, Dixieland rags, Caribbean guitar à la Joseph Spence, all on finger-style acoustic guitar. He pays primary attention to his guitar work; his singing is barely adequate. Specialized enthusiasts of finger-style guitar will enjoy these records and recognize them as creative expressions of a distinct musical personality. Miller, however, has chosen not to develop his technique in such areas as tone, dynamics, and the elimination of fret noise; this will prevent a larger public from enjoying his considerable talents as a guitarist.
_____. Rounder 3002.

MUSSELWHITE, CHARLIE A young white southerner who has effectively assimilated the Chicago blues vocal and harmonica styles, with band.
Takin' My Time. Arhoolie 1056.
Tennessee Woman. Vanguard 6528.
Goin' Back Down South. Arhoolie 1074.

PERSSON, PEPS
The Week Peps Came to Chicago. Sonet SLPD-2532 (2-rec. set). Persson is a Swedish musician who has effectively cultivated a Chicago blues guitar and harmonica style as well as a vocal style that, all things considered, comes off rather well. He recently arrived in Chicago, with producer Sam Charters, to record one side each with the bands of Sunnyland Slim, Mighty Joe Young, Louis Meyers, and Jimmy Dawkins. All performances are smooth, well-arranged, and well-produced, suffering only from the same degree of sameness that would tend to be present in any four sides of contemporary Chicago blues by artists of similar schools. It looks at first glance like a vanity record, but it's not: unlike most vanity records, it's good.

RIEDY, BOB
Chicago Blues Band. Rounder 2005.

ROLLING STONES *See* Schwann catalogue and *Phonolog.*

RUCKER, SPARKY
Bound to Sing the Blues. Traditional SR 372. Original and traditional blues, spirituals, and folk songs pleasantly sung in a modern pop-influenced manner with basic guitar and harmonica backup.

RUSSO, MIKE
_____. Arhoolie 4003. An Oregon blues singer-pianist-guitarist in traditional style; his Leadbelly imitations on twelve-string guitar are particularly effective.

SOUCHON, EDMOND
Minstrel Days. Golden Crest CR 3065. Blues and vaudeville tunes by a New Orleans surgeon and a member of the Six and Seven-Eighths String Band. (*See* String Band Revival section, page 114.) Souchon was a respectful assimilator of black New Orleans tradition, which includes many songs that would not be fashionable among younger blues revivalists from the college environment—perhaps for their lack of soulful mystique.

VAN RONK, DAVE Long a favorite performer on the college circuit, Van Ronk was a central figure in the New York City revival scene of the late fifties. He was influential as a blues guitarist, and was one of the first white singers of his generation to cultivate a satisfactory and inoffensive black-derived vocal style.
Black Mountain Blues (formerly *Ballads, Blues, and a Spiritual*). Folkways 31020.
Van Ronk Sings. Folkways 2383.
Inside Dave Van Ronk. Prestige 7716. Anglo-American songs and ballads, mostly from the Appalachians, still sung in the characteristic gravelly voice Van Ronk developed for blues. With six- and twelve-string guitar, banjo, dulcimer, or autoharp.
In the Tradition. Prestige 7800.
_____. Fantasy 24710 (2-rec. set).
Ragtime Jug Stompers. Mercury 20864. Jugband.
. . . and the Hudson Dusters. Verve 3041. A venture into the world of rock and pop, not without self-parody.
Songs for Aging Children. Cadet 50044. Traditional and contemporary songs, some apparently chosen for commercial potential rather than a regard for Van Ronk's style. Undistinguished studio band arrangements.

VON SCHMIDT, ERIC
2nd Right, 3rd Row. Poppy 5705. Interesting original songs, from witty to serious, in the contemporary but traditionally rooted style associated with Geoff and Maria Muldaur and the other Woodstock sidemen on the album.
. . . Sings Von Schmidt. Prestige 7384.
Folk Blues (1963). Prestige 7717. Accompanied by Geoff Muldaur and others.

WINSLOW, TOM
_____. Biograph 12018.

ANTHOLOGIES AND COLLECTIONS
Blues Like Showers of Rain, vols. 1–2. Saydisc SDM 142, 167. British country blues stylists.
The Blues Project. Elektra 7264 (OP). Not a recording by the popular rock band of the sixties that took its name from this album, but an anthology of young white imitators and continuators of the country blues tradition: Dave Ray, John Koerner, Geoff Muldaur, Danny Kalb, Ian Buchanan, Mark Spoelstra, Eric von Schmidt, Dave van Ronk.
Some People Who Play Guitar Like a Lot of People Don't Kicking Mule 104 = Kicking Mule/Sonet (British) SNKF 102. An instrumentally oriented anthology of original and traditional blues and rags by young white guitarist-singers most of whom came out of New York City in the sixties, with two instrumentals by Rev. Gary Davis for good measure. Also included are Stefan Grossman, Woody Mann, Roy Bookbinder, and Larry Sandberg.
These Blues Is Meant to Be Barrelhoused. Blue Goose 2003. Graham Hine, Roger Hubbard, John Miller, and others.

THE STRING BAND REVIVAL

CRUMB, ROBERT
. . . and His Cheap Suit Serenaders. Blue Goose 2014. The well-known cartoonist turns out to be a fine tenor banjo player, playing with friends on guitar, mandolin, tuba, accordion, etc. The band re-creates early white string ragtime and vodeodo sounds, with period vocal stylings and some original songs.

DESERET STRING BAND
_____. Okehdokee (no number). Available from 370 West First Street South, Salt Lake City, Utah 84101. Irish songs, as well as songs collected in the band's native Utah, done in a graceful string band style influenced to varying degrees on various selections by Irish band style. Thoroughly enjoyable except by those for whom hi-fi sound quality is more important than the quality of the music.

FUZZY MOUNTAIN STRING BAND
_____. Rounder 0010. Old-time dance and fiddle tunes in the North Carolina style. The fiddle and banjo sound is dominant. The emphasis is on correct adherence to a limited number of styles and influences; the musicians are excellent at what they do, but sometimes there is the feeling that spontaneity and the spirit and energy that follow from spontaneous musical expression are lacking. The desire to preserve a tradition is commendable, but I don't think it's a sign of disrespect to inject a performer's personality into the music. These records are well-done and pleasurable, with moments of excitement, and serve as excellent sources for learning interesting and less well-known tunes from the dance and fiddle tune repertory.
Summer Oaks and Porch. Rounder 0035.

THE HIGHWOODS STRING BAND
Fire on the Mountain. Rounder 0023.
Volume Two. Rounder 0045.

HOLY MODAL ROUNDERS
_____. Fantasy 24711 (2-rec. set). Two younger urban

Bob Carlin and Mike Seeger

musicians, active as performers on the folk circuit through the sixties, play blues, mountain songs, comic songs, fiddle tunes, and some contemporary material with a good-time feeling, variously on banjo, fiddle, and guitar with vocals. From earlier Prestige label releases.
Alleged in Their Own Time. Rounder 3004.

IRON MOUNTAIN STRING BAND
_____. Folkways 2473. Correct performances of old-time tunes; vocals with banjo, fiddle, and guitar.

NEW LOST CITY RAMBLERS The original Ramblers included Mike Seeger, John Cohen, and Tom Paley, switching back and forth on guitar, banjo, mandolin, autoharp, dobro, and fiddle. Paley left in the early sixties and was replaced by Tracy Schwarz. The Ramblers have succeeded in copying not only the music but also the enthusiasm of early recorded string bands. Most of the following albums are also available on eight-track tape. The first four listings are with Seeger, Cohen, and Paley.
_____, vols. 1–5. Folkways 2396, 2397, 2398, 2399, 2395 in that order.
American Moonshine and Prohibition. Folkways 5263.
Songs from the Depression. Folkways 5364.
Old-Timey Songs for Children. Folkways 7064 (10 inch). The following six listings are with Seeger, Cohen, and Schwarz:
The New New Lost City Ramblers. Folkways 2491.
Instrumentals. Folkways 2492.
. . . with Cousin Emmy. Folkways 31015.
Modern Times. Folkways 31027.
Remembrance of Things to Come. Folkways 31035.
On the Great Divide. Folkways 31041.

Old Fashioned Dance Music. Union 1352 (OP). Instrumental re-creations of old-time string band dance tunes, including Ken Kosek's fiddle playing and the perfectionistic, pu-

ristic banjo playing of John Burke, which has earned both praise and condemnation.

OLD HAT BAND, THE
Concert. Voyager 307. Old-time standards by a Pacific Northwest band; vocals with fiddle (John Burke), banjo, and guitar.

OLD RELIABLE STRING BAND
_____. Folkways 2457. Re-creations and reinterpretations of old-time string band pieces by Tom Paley, Artie Rose, and Roy Berkeley. Rose and Berkeley are talented New York musicians who have never recorded much; this is a good chance to appreciate them.

PHILO GLEE AND MANDOLIN SOCIETY
_____. Puritan 5007 (formerly CFC 101).

POSSUM HUNTERS Enjoyable and solidly done versions of old-time tunes, with more emphasis on correctness than spontaneity. This band prefers a sparse, clear sound and moderate tempos, a refreshing change from the usual revivalist interest in the busier, up-tempo, and more hectic and showmanlike aspects of the Appalachian and string band repertory and style. Especially tasteful are the vocals with only fiddle accompaniment, a tradition that has interested very few revivalists. (Others include Mike Seeger, Jody Stecher, and Helen Schneyer.)
Death on Lee Highway. Takoma A 1010.
In the Pines. Takoma A 1025. Vocals with fiddle, guitar, and banjo in various combinations.

PUTNAM STRING COUNTY BAND
_____. Rounder 3003. Re-creations of old-time style and repertory, as well as modern reinterpretations of the style as applied to contemporary material. A good band, including New Lost City Rambler John Cohen, and fiddler Jay

Ungar, whose talent is being welcomed on more and more recording sessions as time goes on.

RED CLAY RAMBLERS
———. Folkways 31039.

SIX AND SEVEN-EIGHTHS STRING BAND
———. Folkways 2671. A white New Orleans quartet (guitar, Hawaiian guitar, mandolin, and bass) recorded in the fifties. They play a music that could only have come about in New Orleans, combining elements from the twenties Hawaiian novelty sound, string ragtime, the New Orleans jazz ensemble, and the old light classical string and mandolin ensembles that were popular a half century ago. The players are professional men but not professional musicians; rough spots stand out against the overall polish of their ensemble work. A unique and enjoyable sound.

SOUTHERN EAGLE STRING BAND
Old Timey Revival. FV 12005.
Doing That Nasty Swing. FV 12009.

SPARK GAP WONDER BOYS
Cluck Old Hen. Rounder 0002.

STECHER, JODY
Snake Baked a Hoecake. Bay 203. A young man from Brooklyn, Stecher has succeeded as well as anyone in preserving the sound and above all the feeling of traditional American music. Most of the selections capture his commitment; a few don't, and his accompanists are as much a hindrance on some selections as they are an asset on others. The best moments far overwhelm the worst. Stecher sings and plays old-time and Irish tunes on guitar, banjo, and fiddle, as well as one tune in Oriental style.

STRING BAND PROJECT
———. Elektra 7292 (OP). Early sixties recordings by eminent figures in the New York City revival movement, including Stu Jamieson.

ROOTS OF THE FOLK REVIVAL

by Ralph Rinzler

This short essay is a plea for some serious historical work on the roots of the folk revivals—music, dance, song, craft. Perhaps it can be viewed as an abstract of the longer study I wish I were writing now or as an outline from which others may draw sections for careful study.

The folk movements, which we take for granted today, have their roots in the romance of the pastoral. This idealization of the bucolic can only exist when there is an urban elite or privileged class which is separated from the idealized peasantry by education, social position, and economic resources. We find its earliest documented forms in the third century B.C. writings of Theocritus and two centuries later in Virgil's *Eclogues*. In *The Eclogues*, Theocritus' pastoral setting and characters are used effectively by Virgil's rustic shepherds, one blithely playing his pipe while the other mourns his eviction by governmental edict.

The direct influence of this stylized Virgilian use of the pastoral was not pervasive in Europe until the mid-fifteenth century, when the first printed edition of Virgil appeared in Rome. Moreover, the symbol of the prophet Jesus working as a carpenter and living humbly was used to encourage the separation of the sophisticated, materialistic life from the simple, monastic way. In Palestine, St. Jerome furthered this movement. It became fashionable among the wealthy and well-born to abandon rank and riches in the meritorious quest for monastic holiness.

This religious example, evident today in rural monasteries and convents, some of which were established in the Middle Ages, was supplemented by secular expression through the arts. Rustic pastoral songs—*pastourelles, chansons des trouvères*—were found throughout western Europe in the Middle Ages and early Renaissance. By the mid-fourteenth century, pastoral romances by Dante, Boccaccio, and Petrarch had appeared in Italy. Spenser's *Shepherd's Calendar*, 1579, marked the flowering of this tradition in England, while in France, Honoré d'Urfé's *L'Astrée* appeared in 1610. As writers were developing the use of the idyllic landscape of Arcady replete with shepherds playing their pipes, Shakespeare was evoking the pastoral in *A Midsummer Night's Dream* and *A Winter's Tale*. During this same period, the nobility took its pleasure in peasant dances, as noted in a letter from the Earl of Worcester to the Earl of Shrewsbury (1602): "We all frolic here at Court; much dancing in the Privy Chamber of country dances before the Queen's Majesty, who is extremely pleased therewith." Within a half-century of Worcester's communication, John Playford published the first printed collection of traditional dances (London, November 7, 1650).

In art music, Angelus Politianus' musical pastoral drama *Orfeo* (1475) is generally considered the earliest example of Italian musical drama or opera, yet by the seventeenth century Claudio Monteverdi and Jean Baptiste Lully were writing pastoral operas to be followed by André Grétry and Christoph Gluck in the eighteenth century. The strong impact of the pastoral in painting need not be discussed in detail: Jean Antoine Watteau, Jean Honoré Fragonard, François Boucher in the eighteenth century followed by Jean François Millet, J. M. W. Turner, and numerous others in the nineteenth attest to the ubiquity of the motif.

It is no surprise that the first comprehensive collection of English folk song texts, Thomas Percy's *Reliques* (1765), and the book that launched the Romantic movement, Jean Jacques Rousseau's *La Nouvelle Héloïse* (1761), appeared within four years of each other. The time was ripe for Rousseau's view of the noble savage, a philosophy which turned its back on the contrived, formal, and courtly in a back-to-nature movement. Thus, Marie Antoinette,

dressed as a milkmaid in her *bergerie* at the Petite Trianon, sought to capture the quality of the natural peasant by role playing. A century later the Russian *Narodniki* (radical students who felt a sense of debt to the peasantry) improved on the French court model by actually sharing the life of the people and carrying enlightenment and civilization to them. As Tolstoy took the role of a peasant in Russia, both Goethe and Thoreau in their native countries lived in rustic simplicity and isolation for sustained periods. Throughout the nineteenth century, composers of art music exploited the resource of folk music to the fullest extent possible: Beethoven, Brahms, Liszt, Schubert, Grieg, Dvorák, Borodin, Moussorgsky, and Tschaikovsky are but a few of the many who drew on the raw material of folk song.

It was during the nineteenth century that academic folklore studies developed both in Europe and in the United States. (For a thorough review of this movement, *see* Don Yoder's article, "The Folklife Studies Movement" in *Pennsylvania Folklife* magazine, July, 1963, vol. 13, no. 3, pp. 43–56.) With the publication of Sir Walter Scott's *Minstrelsy of the Scottish Border* in 1802–03 and of the brothers Grimm's *Children and House Tales* in 1812 followed by

J. Grimm's *German Mythology* (1835), a movement began. It developed from the popular antiquities approach of random collection to the systematic study of folklore in the context of the culture that produced it. The British Folk-Lore Society was established in London in 1877; the American Folklore Society in Cambridge, Massachusetts, in 1888.

In 1888 William Morris and his associates organized, in London, an Arts and Crafts Exhibition in order to encourage artists and the public to consider useful and decorative objects in the home with the same seriousness generally accorded the fine arts. The most influential thinker affecting this movement was John Ruskin, whose early Socialist philosophy integrated his aesthetic and sociopolitical views; he asserted that a satisfactory theory of art depended on a theory of society. (*See* his lectures, *The Political Economy of Art,* London, 1857.) Morris, susceptible to Ruskin's politics as well as his aesthetics, sold working class magazines on street corners, toured England lecturing, formed the Socialist League, and edited the organization's publication, *Commonweal,* from its inception in 1884 until 1890. Here, as with the *Narodniki,* we see elements of social and cultural idealism fostered by the elite for the benefit, as they saw it, of the working class. In his essay "The Decorative Arts," Morris extolled the simple and rustic way: "Simplicity of life, begetting simplicity of taste, that is, a love for sweet and lofty things is of all matters most necessary for the birth of the new and better art we crave for; simplicity everywhere, in the palace as well as the cottage." Morris also set in verse Icelandic folk tales and Norse legends as well as Virgil and other classic and medieval writings.

Morris and his craft exhibitions strongly influenced a Boston printer, Henry Lewis Johnson, who convened a meeting of prominent Bostonians on January 4, 1897. This led to the establishment in Boston of the Society of Arts and Crafts. Its first president was Ruskin's closest American friend, the eminent patrician Harvard professor of art history Charles Eliot Norton. The proliferation of this movement from Boston to other major American cities and its influence on the handicraft movement in Appalachia can be traced through the writings of Allen Eaton. (See Bibliography at end of this article.) Craft exhibitions were held with great regularity in Boston and other major urban centers well into the mid-twentieth century. The northern women who went south to work in settlement schools, Olive Dame Campbell among them, were aware of crafts and Morris' philosophy as a result of this movement. There was a tendency not only to identify with the working classes, but also to evince a moral concern for their well-being.

In the early twentieth century, Cecil Sharp, a Fabian Socialist and the most important English folk song collector, began his field work in Somerset (1903). From his august position as musical instructor to the Prince of Wales and to the royal children (1904–07), he turned in 1905 to teaching the folk dances he had collected to working class girls in Cumberland Market, London, at the Espérance Club. By 1911 he had established the English Folk Dance Society and three years later, at New York's brahmin stronghold, the Colony Club, he spoke before a group of women who soon organized American centers for the society in Boston, Chicago, and Pittsburgh. He was invited to return in 1915 by Mrs. James Storrow, a Boston patrician, at whose home he met Olive Dame Campbell. Mrs. Campbell arrived with transcriptions of folk songs she had collected in the southern Appalachians, and after an enthusiastic review, Sharp made plans to return to the United States to undertake a collecting trip in the field with Mrs. Campbell's assistance. The endeavor was funded by Mrs. Storrow in concert with the Russell Sage Foundation, and it led to the publication of the classic collection English Folk Songs from the Southern Appalachians.

On his visit in 1915 Sharp brought Lily Roberts (later Mrs. Richard Conant of Lincoln, Massachusetts) to teach dance. She remained in the United States as teacher and director of the Country Dance Society of America and was joined in 1927 by another English teacher, May Gadd, who only recently retired from her active role in the New York chapter. Originally, the society's membership consisted of socially prominent individuals seeking recreation in the rustic simplicity of peasant song and dance, not unlike the Earl of Worcester and his fellow Elizabethans, who preceded them by more than three centuries. Today's membership cuts across socioeconomic lines, and the Pinewoods Camp on Long Pond in Massachusetts, a gift of Mrs. Storrow to the society, is a rustic, woodland retreat where urbanites escape the summer heat to enjoy folk song and dance in an unspoiled "natural" setting.

Olive Dame Campbell and the Russell Sage Foundation played an important role in the crafts as well as the folk song movement. The foundation, established in 1907 "for the improvement of social and living conditions in the U.S.A." (Glenn and Andrews, Russell Sage Foundation, 1907–1946, p. 11), engaged theologian John C. Campbell to survey resources and conditions in the mountainous areas of the nine southern states east of the Mississippi and south of Ohio. After he and his wife completed the survey, Campbell became head of the Southern Highlands Division of the foundation, coordinating social, educational, cultural, and economic programs administered by private and government organizations in the area. After Campbell's death in 1919, his wife turned to a study of Danish folk schools and eventually established the John C. Campbell Folk School at Brasstown, North Carolina, which continues to function.

Through a meeting with Olive Campbell in 1926, Allen Eaton made his first trip to Appalachia, where he addressed the annual Conference of Southern Mountain Workers initiated by John Campbell years earlier. This speech led to the establishment, in 1929, of the Southern Highlands Handicraft Guild, which forty-five years later continues to hold two annual crafts fairs, one in Asheville, North Carolina, and the other in Gatlinburg, Tennessee. It is not surprising that Eaton quoted the influential English craftsman and philosopher, William Morris, in his second address to the conference: "Have nothing in your home which you do not know to be useful or believe to be beautiful" (Mountain Life and Work, July, 1930, p. 26).

As a result of his work in Appalachia, Eaton prepared the first comprehensive documentation of Appalachian craft traditions, Handicrafts of the Southern Highlands (1937), which he followed in 1949 with Handicrafts of New England, both published by the Russell Sage Foundation.

I have given only the barest sketch of the conception and idealization of "a folk" in its earliest forms and its persistence in the arts in Western civilization, tracing it through to contemporary revival movements. While the limitations of space have imposed a looseness which may lead one to accuse me of parlaying a molehill of facts into a mountain of surmise, I feel confident that the germs of several substantial studies are contained here:

1. The importance and persistence of the pastoral ideal, its relationship to the Christian ethic, and the influence of both the pastoral ideal and the Christian ethic on folklore as an academic discipline and on the folk revival.

2. The interrelationship between the British crafts movement and the American folk crafts revival.

3. Social philosophy, politics, and exoteric attitudes vis-à-vis the folk: from noblesse oblige to social consciousness.

4. The interrelationship of folk revival movements in the United States—crafts, dance, music.

The role of the urban elite in the folk song and craft movements is worthy of careful documentation and study, and attests, beyond any doubt, to the importance of socioeconomic distance and perspective in the understanding, appreciation, and exploitation of folk culture by those of us who have studied and popularized it. Mrs. George Washington Vanderbilt, who established folk craft projects on Biltmore, her Asheville, North Carolina, estate; the Rockefellers and van Alstynes, who amassed large collections of folk art; the son of a socially prominent merchant, Charles Seeger, organizer of the Society of Ethnomusicology, and, in turn, his son, Pete, who popularized the five-string banjo; John A. Lomax and his son, Alan, affluent Texans, and two of our greatest folk song collectors, are but a few of the notable figures. Of interest are the social values of the figures who have shaped these movements. Here is a challenge to scholars and lay people to document these revival movements by interviewing those who have given them form, direction, and meaning.

BIBLIOGRAPHY

BATE, WALTER JACKSON, *From Classic to Romantic: Premises of Taste in Eighteenth Century England,* Harper & Brothers, 1946. 197 pp.

BOTTOMORE, T. B., *Elites and Society,* Penguin, 1964. 160 pp.

BOWLES, ELLA SHANNON, *Homespun Handicrafts,* Lippincott, 1931. 251 pp.

BRIGGS, ASA, ed., *William Morris: Selected Writings and Designs,* Penguin, 1964. 309 pp.

CAMPBELL, JOHN C., *The Southern Highlander and His Homeland,* Russell Sage Foundation, 1921. 405 pp.

CAMPBELL, MRS. JOHN C. (OLIVE DAME), *The Southern Highlands* (bibliography), Russell Sage Foundation, 1920. Library bulletin, 3 pp.

CAMPBELL, MRS. JOHN C. (OLIVE DAME), *The Danish Folk School,* Macmillan, 1928. 359 pp.

CAMPBELL, MRS. JOHN C. (OLIVE DAME), *The Life and Work of John Charles Campbell,* College Typing and Printing Co., Madison, Wis. 1968. Mimeographed, 657 pp.

COURTHION, PIERRE, *Romanticism,* World, 1961. 136 pp.

EATON, ALLEN H., *Handicrafts of New England,* Harper & Brothers, 1949. 374 pp.

EATON, ALLEN H., *Handicrafts of the Southern Highlands,* Russell Sage Foundation, 1937. 370 pp.

EATON, ALLEN H., in *Mountain Life and Work,* July, 1926, pp. 17–22, 27–28. July, 1930, pp. 22–30.

GLENN, JOHN H., LILIAN BRANDT, and EMERSON ANDREWS, *Russell Sage Foundation, 1907–1946,* 2 vols., Russell Sage Foundation, 1947. 742 pp.

History of Christianity, Blackie and Son, 1929. 750 pp.

KARPELES, MAUD, and A. H. FOX-STRANGWAYS, *Cecil Sharp,* Oxford University Press, 1955. 225 pp.

KOHN, HANS, *The Mind of Modern Russia,* Harper & Brothers, 1955. 298 pp.

LLOYD, A. L., *Folk Song in England,* International Publishers, 1967. 483 pp.

MARX, LEO, *The Machine in the Garden: Technology and the Pastoral Ideal in America,* Oxford University Press, 1964. 394 pp.

MCNELLEY, PAT, ed., *John C. Campbell Folk School: The First 40 Years,* John C. Campbell Folk School, Brasstown, N. C., 1966. 81 pp.

MESSLER, ISAAC, "Our Co-worker," *Mountain Life and Work,* April, 1928, p. 7 ff.

RUSKIN, JOHN, *The Stones of Venice,* John Wiley, 1881. (This is the second American edition.)

SHARP, CECIL J., *A Book of British Song for Home and School,* John Murray, 1902.

SHARP, CECIL J., *Folk Songs from Somerset,* Wesson Press and others, 1904–1919.

SHARP, CECIL J., with Olive Dame Campbell, ed. by Maud Karpeles, *English Folk Songs from the Southern Appalachians,* Oxford University Press, 1938 (1960 reprint). 425 pp.

STEIN, ROGER B., *John Ruskin and Aesthetic Thought in America, 1840–1900,* pp. 240–259, for a discussion of the relationship between Norton and Ruskin.

THOREAU, HENRY DAVID, *Walden and Other Writings,* Modern Library, 1949. 714 pp.

WILGUS, D. K., *Anglo-American Folk Song Scholarship Since 1898,* Rutgers University Press, 1959. 466 pp.

WRITERS PROGRAM, New Hampshire, Works Progress Administration, *Hands That Built New Hampshire: The Story of Granite State Craftsmen Past and Present,* Stephan Daye Press, 1940. 288 pp.

YODER, DON, "The Folklife Studies Movement," *Pennsylvania Folklife,* vol. 13, no. 3, July, 1963, pp. 43–56.

CONTEMPORARY GUITARISTS

For the most part, the musicians in this section are acoustic guitarists with stylistic or technical roots in traditional blues and finger-picking styles who have developed and applied these styles and techniques for contemporary sounds and repertory. I have also included a few other guitarists from very different backgrounds, because I feel they are relevant and I want to promote an interest in their work. Other relevant players are listed in the Blues Revival section, page 109, and in the following Contemporary Artists, Bands, and Songwriters section.

Some of the individuals listed here can be grouped into schools with a minimum amount of injustice to their individuality. There is, for example, a ragtime style played by Dave Laibman, Rick Schoenberg, Stefan Grossman (Blues Revival section, page 110) and Bob Tryforos, among others. Their techniques are drawn from those of the great southeast ragtime blues guitarists, like Blind Blake and especially Gary Davis, and applied to the arrangement of classic piano or ensemble ragtime compositions for solo or duet acoustic guitar.

John Fahey is the figurehead of another group of guitarists who might be described as impressionists. They favor meandering structureless pieces intended to evoke a mood, and use the finger-picking style to generate sounds and textures, often quite busy, paying relatively little attention to melodic statement, development, or variation. Robbie Basho and Peter Lang belong to this school, and so does the earlier work of Leo Kottke. Kottke has achieved the greatest commercial success, although he is the least interesting guitarist of the school, and now finds himself equally at home working in a songwriter vein, with more emphasis on the song as a polished product, and less on the guitar work. To a certain extent, Gordon Giltrap and George Cromarty may be grouped along with Fahey.

Finally, there is a school of English guitarists who center around Bert Jansch and John Renbourn, best known for their work with the group Pentangle during the sixties. As far as I can see, the style has its origins in the work of Davy Graham (see page 119) and Martin Carthy, who is listed in the England, Scotland, and Ireland section, page 127. Carthy is primarily a singer of traditional British songs in the traditional British style, in which guitar accompaniment plays no part. But Carthy developed an accompaniment guitar style drawn loosely from American finger picking, and incorporating strongly syncopated dynamics and the jagged rhythms typical of some British dance traditions. Jansch and Renbourn developed a solo style also suitable for contemporary music; in their individual work, Jansch likes to play closer to the American finger-picking style, while Renbourn has incorporated a larger variety of influences ranging from sitar music to medieval and Renaissance lute and consort music. This style has been extremely influential in contemporary pop music, and represents on the guitar a larger series of developments that has resulted in the folk-rock styles of such bands and musicians as Steeleye Span, Fairport Convention, and Sandy Denny.

The records listed in this section are, with few exceptions, instrumentally oriented, though there may be occasional vocals.

BADEN POWELL Baden Powell is a brilliant and unique Brazilian guitarist, whose playing draws from the jazz, Brazilian folk and pop, and classical traditions. He plays finger style on a nylon-strung guitar, with a graceful and pleasing touch. Typically, his albums present his guitar work accompanied by rhythm section, perhaps with occasional flute and vocals. His repertory ranges from blues and jazz tunes through bossa nova and Brazilian folk tunes to adaptations of classical pieces.
Quartet, vols. 1–3. Barclay 80.428, 80.429, 80.430.
Aquarelle du Brasil. Barclay 80.416.
Le Monde Musical de . . ., vols. 1–2. Barclay 80.235, 80.385.
A Vontade. Barclay 820.092.
Os Afro-Sambas. Barclay 920.070.
Tristeza. BASF 29623.
Canto. BASF 25155 (2-rec. set).
Estudios. BASF 29194.
Images. BASF 29057.
Solitude. Columbia KC 32441.

BASHO, ROBBIE Basho plays rambling finger-style guitar pieces, consisting mainly of textures rather than melodies, that attempt to evoke moods drawn from Oriental and American Indian spiritual philosophies.

Guitar Soli. Takoma C 1005.
The Grail and the Lotus. Takoma C 1007.
Basho Sings. Takoma C 1012.
The Falconer's Arm, vols. 1–2. Takoma 1017, 1018.
Song of the Stallion. Takoma C 1031.
The Voice of the Eagle. Vanguard 79321.

BEBE, FRANCIS
Concert pour un vieux masque. Philips (French) 70.468L. Remarkable compositions for nylon-strung guitar by a native of Douala, Cameroon, whose background includes a formal European education. His music, reflecting the various forces in his life, might be described as a cross between Moreno Torroba, Baden Powell, and Joseph Spence.

BOSCO, JEAN MWENDA
_____. Gallotone 1586T. A Katanga singer with a fascinating and complex finger-picking style, an exciting style that other African guitarists also have developed.

BULL, SANDY Bull, who uses various western and eastern stringed instruments in addition to guitar, favors long and somewhat discursive improvisations drawing from various American, classical, and eastern folk sounds.
Demolition Derby. Vanguard 79119.
_____. Vanguard 6578.
E Pluribus Unum. Vanguard 6513.
Inventions. Vanguard 79191.
The Essential. Vanguard 6578.
Bulldog. Decca 75370.
Smasher. Buddah 5600.

CARR, ROB, AND BILL KAHL
Communication. Grotesque GS 101. Available from Denver Folklore Center, 608 E. 17th Ave., Denver, Colo. 80218, or from 649 Evergreen, E. Lansing, Mich. 48823. Mostly original guitar finger-picking duets, pleasantly done in the Jansch-Renbourn tradition, with occasional vocal and flute.

The Contemporary Guitar Sampler, vol. 1. Transatlantic TRASAM 14. A good introduction to the various styles of John Fahey and Englishmen Ralph McTell, Bert Jansch, John Renbourn, Pentangle, Gordon Giltrap, and John Pearse; mostly their earlier work.
_____, Vol. 2. Transatlantic TRASAM 15. Bert Jansch, John Renbourn, Gordon Giltrap, Mike Rogers, John James, Pentangle.

Contemporary Ragtime Guitar. Kicking Mule 107 = Kicking Mule/Sonet (British) SNKF 100. An anthology of the leading exponents of classic piano ragtime as adapted for finger-picked guitar, along with a few nonragtime pieces in a similar vein. Artists include Dave Laibman, Larry Sandberg, Eric Schoenberg, Leo Wynkamp, Woody Mann, Dale Miller, Tony Marcus, and Tom Gilfellon. The most comprehensive introduction to the style.

CROMARTY, GEORGE
Grassroots Guitar. Thistle 731. Pleasant and well-played impressionistic guitar pieces, more highly structured than the work of other guitarists in this vein. Folksy in feeling, but evincing an obvious knowledge of classical repertory and technique; equally good for late nights and bright

sunny mornings. *See also* Folk Songs for Children section, page 135.

DETLEFF AND FINGER (Detleff Durr and Peter Finger)
Guitar Instrumentals. Kicking Mule/Sonet SNKF 104 (European).

EVANS, DAVE
Sad Pig Dance. Kicking Mule/Sonet SNKF 107 (European). Evans plays the most original and exciting finger-picking instrumentals I've heard in years. He plays in the British finger-picking style, more legato than Americans play, with great control.

FAHEY, JOHN Fahey is more of a melodist than his various followers; mostly they pick up solely on the aspect of his style that uses traditional finger-picking techniques for the creation of harmonic textures rather than melodic statements. Although Fahey is an expert on the work of the early country blues guitarists, many of whom composed highly structured guitar parts, he prefers to use rambling or episodic forms for his own compositions, which frequently strike the ear as inchoate arrangements still in the experimental stage. This is especially true of his work on Takoma, which is of great interest to guitar players—since Fahey is a fine picker and bottleneck-style player—but which has not reached the members of a larger public with less specialized interests, who are more attracted to the total musical sound than to the quality of the guitar work. His work for Vanguard and Reprise is more carefully structured, possibly against his own creative inclinations, and probably as a concession to the larger public that major-label marketing must reach. The clear, elegant finger picking on the Reprise albums is marred by the presence of a rather mechanical Dixieland band accompaniment; the band idea is sound, but more spontaneous and less cliché-ridden musicians could have been used.
Blind Joe Death. Takoma C 1002.
Death Chants, Breakdowns, and Military Waltzes. Takoma C 1003.
Dance of Death. Takoma C 1004.
Great San Bernardino Birthday Party. Takoma C 1008.
Days Gone By. Takoma C 1014.
Transfiguration of Blind Joe Death. Takoma R 9015.
The Voice of the Turtle. Takoma C 1019.
The New Possibility. Takoma C 1020. Christmas songs.
America. Takoma C 1031.
Fare Forward, Voyagers. Takoma C 1035.
Requia. Vanguard 79259.
The Yellow Princess. Vanguard 79293.
Of Rivers and Religion. Reprise MS 2089.
After the Ball. Reprise MS 2145.

FAHEY, JOHN, PETER LANG, AND LEO KOTTKE
_____.Takoma C-1040. A good introduction to their work; four pieces each.

FINGER, PETER
Bottleneck Guitar Solos. Kicking Mule 110 (European release: Kicking Mule/Sonet SNKF 105).

GILFELLON, TOM
Loving Mad Tom. Trailer LER 2079.

GILTRAP, GORDON
A Testament of Time. Decca DL7-5296.
Portrait. Transatlantic 202. Original songs and instrumental solos in an energetic, sometimes bashing finger-picking style concerned mostly with textures. Giltrap thinks more about his playing than his singing.

GRAHAM, DAVY (b. 1940)
Folk, Blues and Beyond. Decca (British) LK-4649. Information on Graham's records has not been forthcoming; I'm sorry that this is the only one I know of to list. Graham is a remarkably versatile guitarist—the record includes several blues, English and American songs and ballads, a pop tune, and funky jazz pieces. His singing does not match his playing; he is an excellent guitarist whose influence on many of his better-known countrymen, like Carthy, Jansch, and Renbourn, has been great.

GROSSMAN, STEFAN. *See* Blues Revival section, page 110.

Guitars of Africa. Decca (British) LF1170.

HADLEY, BOB
The Raven. Kicking Mule 113. Guitar solos and some singing. Hadley sounds as if he began as a Fahey imitator, then grew into his own style, clean and melodic though busy.

JANSCH, BERT
Rosemary Lane. Reprise 6455. Traditional and original songs and instrumentals, with more emphasis on quasi-Elizabethan sounds than on his other recordings, where he favors a more American-sounding finger-picking style.
Moonshine. Reprise 2129. Traditional and original songs and guitar pieces, with accompanists.
Lucky 13. Vanguard 9212. Many original tunes, including six guitar instrumentals.
L.A. Turnaround. Charisma 109.
It Don't Bother Me. Transatlantic 132.
Jack Orion. Transatlantic 143.
See also under John Renbourn, this section, page 120, and Pentangle, Contemporary Artists, Bands, and Songwriters section, page 124.

KAHL, BILL. *See* Rob Carr, this section, page 118.

KOTTKE, LEO
Six- and Twelve-String Guitar. Takoma C 1024.
Circle 'Round the Sun. Symposium 2001 (available from Takoma).
Ice Water. Capitol ST 11262.
My Feet Are Smiling. Capitol ST 11164.
Dreams and All That Stuff. Capitol ST 11335.
Mudlark. Capitol ST 682.
Greenhouse. Capitol S 11000.
See also John Fahey, above.

LAIBMAN, DAVID, AND ERIC SCHOENBERG
The New Ragtime Guitar. Asch 3528. Seven duets and three solos by the two leading exponents of classic piano rags adapted for guitar.

LANG, PETER
The Thing at the Nursery Room Window. Takoma C 1034.

A clean finger picker in the Fahey mold, Lang is interested in developing textures by running picking patterns over chords.

McGrath, Suni
Cornflower Suite. Adelphi AD 1002. Finger-picked guitar impressions, without structure or economy.
Call of the Mourning Dove. Adelphi AD 1014.
Childgrove. Adelphi AD 1022.

Miller, Dale
Fingerpicking Delights. Kicking Mule 123. Many short, varied selections: ragtime, blues, fiddle tunes, jazz tunes, rock and classical pieces on acoustic guitar. Miller is a clean and proficient guitarist whose style is characterized by a great love for moving bass lines.

Miller, John. *See* Blues Revival section, page 111.

Renbourn, John
Another Monday. Transatlantic 149.
_____. Reprise 2RS 6482 (2-rec. set). Reissues of traditional British and American and original guitar pieces first recorded in 1965–66.
Faro Annie. Warner MS 2082. American songs and blues and a few English ballads, in new and often interesting arrangements. Whispered vocals with harmonica, electric guitar, sitar, fiddle, bass, and percussion in addition to Renbourn's finger-picked guitar.
The Lady and the Unicorn. Reprise RS 6407. Side 1: folk-flavored Renaissance dances for solo guitar and/or sitar accompanied by violin, viola, bells, percussion, and flute. Well-done arrangements imparting new and interesting textures to the older music; and unlike most versions of these tunes played by classically oriented musicians, these actually move like dance music. Side 2: original instrumental tunes and arrangements in a modernized Renaissance consort style influenced by contemporary rhythms; as enjoyable as side 1.
The John Renbourn Sampler. Transatlantic TRASAM 20.
_____ (1965). Transatlantic 135. His first solo album. The elements that persist in his later work are all here: the tendency toward strong accents, the eclectic mixture of elements from English, Anglo-American, and Black American traditions (later joined by Indian and Elizabethan traditions), and the willingness to take risks in order to work toward a personal style, often sacrificing accuracy and polish. Also present is the weakest aspect of his work, an excessive reliance on rather boring montuno figures as the sole structuring device. Renbourn's singing, like that of most performers in this idiom who are primarily guitarists, is barely adequate; his audience seems not to mind.
. . . and Bert Jansch: Stepping Stones. Vanguard 6506 (= *Bert and John,* Transatlantic 144). Duets on original and other themes; the two work well together, coming up with complementary parts, rather than dividing the music into lead and backup.

Rosmini, Dick
_____. Elektra EKS 7245 (OP). 1964 recording featuring flashy finger picking, sometimes along the lines that in the seventies brought fame and fortune to Leo Kottke. Ros-

mini, who now mainly works as a producer, was most active as a performer in the late fifties and early sixties, ahead of the time when the sort of work he was doing was to achieve popularity.

Ruskin, Richard
_____. Takoma C 1039. Ruskin, who does studio work in Los Angeles, here presents well-made arrangements, played with superb touch, tone, and dynamics, of a great variety of material: Gary Davis, Beatles, blues, a rag, original songs. Satisfactory vocals, and acoustic guitar with occasional acoustic and electric overdubs, rhythm section, and backup vocals. Ruskin is not an innovative stylist, but makes a striking impression by the excellence of his playing and of his arranging, in which he is assisted by Dick Rosmini.

Schoenberg, Eric. *See* David Laibman and *Contemporary Ragtime Guitar,* pages 119 and 118.

Tryforos, Bob
Scott Joplin, Composer. Puritan 5002. Successful versions of Scott Joplin rags adapted for acoustic guitar.

Van Bergeyk, Ton
Famous Ragtime Guitar Solos. Kicking Mule 114 (European release: Kicking Mule/Sonet SNKF 106). Piano rags adapted for guitar, with tablature booklet. *See also* Stefan Grossman, Blues Revival section, page 110.

Where the Guitar Is King. Kicking Mule/Sonet SNKB 300 (European). A sampler of the work of various contemporary guitar stylists, culled from other Kicking Mule releases. Includes Dave Evans, Ton Van Bergeyk, Stefan Grossman, Detleff and Finger, Woody Mann, Larry Sandberg, Dave Laibman, and Dale Miller. There are also selections by Rev. Gary Davis, and two banjo pieces by Art Rosenbaum.

CONTEMPORARY ARTISTS, BANDS, AND SONGWRITERS

Amram, David
Subway Night. RCA LSP-4820. Previously known as a classical composer and conductor and as a jazz French horn player, Amram in 1972 made his debut as a singer-songwriter in the contemporary pop mode. He writes with a combination of honesty and show-biz put-on; his musical arrangements draw eclectically from jazz, rock, classical, electronic, Near Eastern, and bluegrass music, ranging from cliché to highly innovative and interesting.

Andersen, Eric
Best. Vanguard VSD 7/8 (2-rec. set). Selections from his earlier work, as he emerged from a Dylan-influenced period.
Blue River. Columbia KC 31062. Contemporary soft pop songs that move beyond his roots in the urban folk songwriter's scene; this is indicative of greater maturity, growth, and independence.
See Schwann catalogue and *Phonolog* for other listings.

Ry Cooder

BAND, THE I like to think of The Band as truly modern folk musicians, approaching the resources of electric instruments and the modern recording studio with the same independent spirit that characterizes the great traditional stylists. Their music is mostly within modern folk-derived harmonic conventions, but with a unique and characteristic sense of texture and timbre.
Music from Big Pink. Capitol SKAO-2955.
The Band. Capitol STAO-132.
Cahoots. Capitol SMAS-651.
Stage Fright. Capitol SW-425.
Rock of Ages. Capitol SABB 11045 (2-rec. set). Live concert recording.
Moondog Matinee. Capitol SW-11214. A tribute to fifties rock and pop.

BLOCK, RORY
————. RCA APL1-0733.

BROCKETT, JAIME
Remember the Wind and the Rain. Oracle 701 (=Capitol ST-678).

BROMBERG, DAVID Like many performers who are primarily instrumentalists, Bromberg is really a nonsinger compelled to sing (he does get better at it with time), the strength of whose performances comes mainly from his instrumental work and arrangements. Although Columbia hypes him as an instrumental wizard, they in fact produce him as more of a middle-ground folk-rock performer and singer-songwriter; a good deal of his best instrumental work appears on other people's albums on which he is a sideman.
————. Columbia C 31104. Several blues with acoustic finger-picked guitar, a flat-picked fiddle tune duet with Norman Blake, and several murkily mixed band cuts.
Demon in Disguise. Columbia KC 31753. A variety of tunes including bluegrass, funky, and Irish fiddle pieces.
Wanted Dead or Alive. Columbia KC 32717.

COLLINS, JUDY
————. Elektra 7209.
In My Life. Elektra 7320. Collins came out of the late fifties as a singer of traditional songs; the first album is characteristic of her work in this stage. Later, with the second album listed, she moved into the realm of contemporary art song. *See* Schwann catalogue and *Phonolog* for other listings.

COODER, RY
————. Reprise RS 6402. A variety of traditional songs in addition to a thirties novelty tune, a Randy Newman song, and a Cooder original. Cooder's knowledge of previous musical traditions is great, but he makes each song uniquely his own, bringing wit, virtuosity (especially as a bottleneck-style guitarist), clarity, and intelligence to bear. Rarely does he choose merely to imitate, and then clearly as a sign of respect for the original, rather than through any lack of his own imagination. Folk music remains alive through such musicians.
Into the Purple Valley. Reprise 2052. Mostly traditional songs; Cooder brings them into rock-influenced arrangements without sacrificing the musicality or honesty of either the songs or himself.
Boomer's Story. Reprise MS 2117. The impeccable musicianship we expect; less interesting songs and arrangements than on his other albums.
Paradise and Lunch. Reprise MS 2179. Cooder's singing, which was certainly not bad to begin with, improves from record to record. This is primarily a vocal album; apparently he felt up to it by this time, and justly so. There are occasional glimpses of his guitar virtuosity, but the emphasis is mostly on the interesting and well-made arrangements, employing many studio musicians in a variety of settings of a superb choice of material.

DALTON, KAREN
In My Own Time. Paramount 6008. Dalton began her career in the fifties as a traditional singer; later she was associated with songwriters like Tim Hardin and Fred Neil. Her husky voice in this collection of pop, contemporary, and traditional songs reveals an interesting combination of influences, including Dave Van Ronk and Billie Holiday.

DOBSON, BONNIE
Dear Companion. Prestige 7801.
————. RCA LSP-4219.

DYLAN, BOB
John Wesley Harding. Columbia KCS 9825. A good example of the way Dylan can use traditional melodies for his own purposes. *See* Schwann catalogue and *Phonolog* for additional listings.

FAIRPORT CONVENTION A popular British electric folk-rock band whose first few albums, with singer Sandy Denny, offered mainly pop and rock versions of blues, English ballads, and contemporary songs, only suggesting what was later to come. Beginning with *Angel Delight*, the band began to achieve a definitive sound, with Simon Nicol, Dave Pegg, Dave Mattacks, and especially fiddler-mandolinist Dave Swarbrick: a heavy sound, strongly rooted in the English ballad and folk dance tradition, but brought into the twentieth century through the use of electric instruments and rock accents.

_____. A&M 4185.

Unhalfbricking. A&M 4206.

Leige and Lief. A&M 4257.

Rosie. A&M 4386. Mainly rock and pop material with a couple of tunes in electrified English folk dance style.

Angel Delight. A&M 4319.

Babbacombe Lee. A&M 4333. An original song cycle with narrative, concerning the story of murderer John Lee, for whom the scaffold refused to function.

Nine. A&M 3603.

A Moveable Feast. Island 9285. Live concert recordings.

FARINA, MIMI, AND TOM JANS
Take Heart. A&M 4310.

FARINA, MIMI AND RICHARD
Memories. Vanguard 79263.
Celebrations for a Grey Day. Vanguard 79174.
Best of. . . . Vanguard VSD 21-22 (2-record set).

GEREMIA, PAUL
Just Enough. Folkways 31023.
_____. Sire 4902.
Hard Life Rockin' Chair. Adelphi 1020.

GLAZER, TOM
Do Not Go Gentle. . . . CMS 167. Classic and contemporary poems, sung in a rather polished voice in folk song-like settings with guitar (Sam Brown and Dick Weissman), flute, and recorders.

GOODMAN, STEVE Goodman is the composer of "City of New Orleans" and many other good songs.
_____. Buddah 5096.
Somebody Else's Troubles. Buddah 5121.

GUTHRIE, ARLO
_____. Reprise MS 2141. A less talented performer, or one less grounded in a variety of traditional styles, would have gotten into an "Alice's Restaurant" rut and never have recovered. Guthrie's voice becomes increasingly centered and more free of affectation, while his writing continues to mature. This record presents a selection of original and other songs, written or arranged in a variety of traditional and pop styles. Mostly they are arranged in contemporary styles drawn from gospel, ragtime, bluegrass, and Nashville; a string section is even used on his father Woody Guthrie's moving "Deportees." Usually a hack device, this time it works, in a strange way. For other listings, *see* Schwann catalogue and *Phonolog.*

HARDIN, TIM
Live in Concert. Verve FTS-3049. Though the songs he writes—many excellent—are based on the simple harmonic structures of folk music, Hardin the performer is spiritually a jazz singer, and he strives toward a free and swinging vocal phrasing. Consequently, he is at his emotional, if not technical, best in this 1968 Town Hall concert performance unhampered by the rigid demands of studio arrangements. His best known song is "If I Were a Carpenter." For other listings, *see* Schwann catalogue and *Phonolog.*

HARTFORD, JOHN
Morning Bugle. Warner BS 2651. Contemporary string band music. Pleasant, original, low-keyed vocals with fiddle, guitar, dobro (Norman Blake), and bass.
Gentle on My Mind. RCA LSP 4068.
Aereo-Plain. Warner S-1916.
Iron Mountain Depot. RCA LSP-4337.

HAVENS, RICHIE
Mixed Bag. MGM S-4698. *See* Schwann catalogue and *Phonolog* for additional listings

HERALD, JOHN
_____. Paramount PAS 6043. Original songs with a good-time pop feeling, by a former member of the Greenbriar Boys bluegrass band.

HESTER, CAROLYN Like many singers in this section, Hester began as a singer of traditional songs and later moved into the contemporary pop field.
Folk Songs. Tradition 1043.
_____. RCA APD 1-0086.

HOLM, RON AND ANN
Song for Friends. Radex RHS 7303. Available from 10 N. Galena Ave., Freeport, Ill. 61032. Vocal duo with prominent violin accompaniment and small studio band; pleasant, mostly original tunes in a pop vein. These musicians are typical of the competent and enjoyable local talent who are increasingly turning toward local-label record production as a way of dealing with the grip of the star system on major-label record policies.

IAN AND SYLVIA
Northern Journey. Vanguard 79154. *See* Schwann catalogue and *Phonolog* for additional listings.

KAZ, ERIC A sensitive Woodstock songwriter, who often works out of a gospel-influenced musical bag. His songs, which have been recorded by Tracy Nelson, Bonnie Raitt, and Linda Ronstadt among others, are frequently concerned with the effort to survive in the face of a melancholy vision of life and relationships. Kaz has also worked as a sideman on various contemporary records, playing piano and harmonica. His own records express his songs in cold, well-conceived arrangements that expressively convey their melancholy.
If You're Lonely. Atlantic 7246.
Cul-de-Sac. Atlantic 7920.

McCRIMMON, DAN A Colorado poet and writer of songs ranging from introspective to dramatic.
Dreams, Lies and Whispers. Biscuit City 1304-CF.

McLEAN, DON
_____. United Artists 5651.
American Pie. United Artists 5535.
Homeless Brother. United Artists LA 315-G.
Tapestry. Mediarts 41-4.

McTELL, RALPH A good English guitarist and singer-songwriter, who may one day achieve greater popularity. The first three albums include his extraordinarily fine song "Streets of London."

Spiral Staircase. Transatlantic 177.
Revisited. Transatlantic 227.
Your Well Meaning Brought Me Here. Paramount 6015.
Not Till Tomorrow. Reprise 2121.

MITCHELL, JONI
Blue. Reprise MS 2038. *See* Schwann catalogue and *Phonolog* for complete listings.

MOTHER EARTH. *See* Tracy Nelson, this section, below.

MULDAUR, GEOFF AND MARIA
Sweet Potatoes. Reprise 2073. Original, traditional, and thirties pop tunes in a variety of well-arranged settings that are distinctly contemporary, yet reveal a respect for the past.
Pottery Pie. Reprise 6350.

MULDAUR, MARIA
————. Reprise MS 2148. Good pop and country tunes in arrangements based on various traditional and pop idioms, well-made and played by excellent musicians.
Waitress in a Donut Shop. Reprise MS 2194.

NEAR, HOLLY
Hang in There. Redwood (no number.) Original songs concerned with the Vietnam War and women's consciousness. Sung and arranged with a degree of talent not often found these days in the service of politically oriented art.
Live Album. Redwood 570. Both records available from 565 Doolin Canyon, Ukiah, Calif. 95482. More good songs, many more personal and more particular than on the previous album. Near has the gift for writing social and political songs free from imposition or mere didacticism. With piano and bass.

NEIL, FRED
The owner of a tender and spectacularly wide-ranged bass-baritone voice, Neil was associated with Tim Hardin in the New York songwriters' scene of the early sixties.
The Dolphins. Capitol ST 2665.
Sessions. Capitol ST 2862.
Everybody's Talkin'. Capitol ST 294.

NELSON, TRACY
Nelson grew up singing folk, blues, and country material in the early sixties, and these idioms remain strong influences in her current work in more commercially viable contexts. Her contralto is rich and exceptionally well controlled, apparently influenced by classic blues vocal style. Her band, Mother Earth, plays well-made arrangements with an emphasis on technical perfection rather than on swing or the graceful energy that comes from greater spontaneity, a problem with which Nelson too must come to grips. Her choice of material is careful and draws from the work of many of the best (if not widely known) contemporary writers.
Deep Are the Roots (1965). Prestige 7726. An early album of traditional blues and spirituals with guitar, piano, and harmonica. A good album for the time, but in retrospect, it reflects an early stage of development.
Mother Earth: Living with the Animals. Mercury SR 6 1194. An earlier version of the Mother Earth band, with Nelson in a lesser role.

Minding the Store: Arlo Guthrie and Pete Seeger

Mother Earth: Bring Me Home. Reprise S 6431. Contemporary songs from good writers, including Steve Young and Eric Kaz.
————. Reprise S 2054.
————. Atlantic 7310.
Poor Man's Paradise. Columbia KC 31759. Pop and country tunes by contemporary writers, including Eric Kaz's "Cruel Wind." The careful gospel-influenced arrangements are by members of Mother Earth.

NEWMAN, RANDY
Twelve Songs. Reprise 6373. A good pianist and singer-songwriter, who uses traditional forms for his clever, crazy, melancholy poems, stories, prayers, and confessions.
————. Reprise RS 6286.
Sail Away. Reprise MS 6286.
Good Old Boys. Reprise MS 2193. Portrait songs of the white south and southerners.

NITTY-GRITTY DIRT BAND
Uncle Charlie. Liberty LST-7942. An odd but entertaining combination of bluegrass and folk-rock songs, a classical banjo piece, and a monologue and songs from old-time Texas guitar picker Uncle Charlie.

In Concert. United Artists LA184-J2 (2-rec. set).
All the Good Times. United Artists 5553.
Will the Circle Be Unbroken. United Artists 9801 (3-rec. set). The Dirt Band is joined by numerous older folk and bluegrass musicians, including Doc Watson, Merle Travis, Earl Scruggs, Maybelle Carter, Vassar Clements, Brother Oswald, and Jimmy Martin, for pleasant and entertaining music making in a tribute to the older styles. The editing leaves in preliminary studio conversations, rough takes, etc.

OCHS, PHIL
I Ain't Marchin' Anymore. Elektra 7287. *See* Schwann catalogue and *Phonolog* for other listings.

PARSONS, GENE
Kindling. Warner BS 2687. Good contemporary songs and instrumentals that draw from American traditions. Accompanists include Cajun fiddler Gib Guilbeau and Clarence White on mandolin and guitar.

PAXTON, TOM
Ramblin' Boy. Elektra 7277. *See* Schwann catalogue and *Phonolog* for complete listings.

PENTANGLE An English group that enjoyed popular currency in the late sixties, Pentangle mainly used acoustic instrumentation, but helped develop a popular base for later English folk-oriented groups, like Steeleye Span, who favor an electric sound. They perform American blues, English ballads, and soft-rock jazzy instrumentals, featuring the guitar work of Bert Jansch and John Renbourn, in addition to Jacqui McShee (vocals), Danny Thompson (bass), and Terry Cox (percussion).
————. Reprise 6315.
Basket of Light. Reprise 6372.
Reflection. Reprise 6463.
Solomon's Seal. Reprise 2100.
Cruel Sister. Reprise 6430.
Sweet Child. Reprise 6334.

POST, JIM
Colorado Exile. Fantasy 9401.
Looks Good to Me. Fantasy 9451.
Rattlesnake. Fantasy 9425.
Slow to 20. Fantasy 9408.

RAITT, BONNIE Originally an adapter of country blues tradition, Raitt with the *Streetlights* album has moved into a sophisticated modern pop format that allows free play for her excellent vocal resources. She chooses her repertory from the work of the best contemporary songwriters.
————. Warner 1953.
Give It Up. Warner 2643.
Takin' My Time. Warner 2729.
Streetlights. Warner 2818.

RAMSEY, WILLIS ALAN
————. Shelter 8914. Possibly the most talented of the crop of Texas singer-songwriters who emerged from the Austin hills in the early seventies, Ramsey sings with a soft, interesting voice. The excellent traditionally rooted guitar work that enhances his live performances is obscured here by

Bonnie Raitt

the tasteful pop arrangements played by studio sidemen. His strong suit is in wry well-made songs about his life, attitudes, fantasies, and food.

RANSOM, JIM
Just Come Along for the Ride. Biscuit City 1303 CF. Original songs in a contemporary folk vein by a Denver-area performer.

REA, DAVID
Maverick Child. Capitol SKAO-548. Original and traditional songs in country-rock Nashville arrangements.
By the Grace of God. Capitol ST-826. Original, traditional, and country songs in various settings ranging from banjo and fiddle (with Mike Seeger) to hard rock.
Slewfoot. Columbia KC-32485.

RED STAR SINGERS
The Force of Life. Paredon 1023. Politically oriented songs, mostly message songs, by a popular Berkeley-area quartet associated with the radical political movement.

REYNOLDS, MALVINA (b. 1901) A heroine of the urban social protest song movement, Reynolds has been writing songs for most of her years; perhaps best known is "Little Boxes."
————. Century City CCR 5100. With Los Angeles-style studio band.
Malvina. Cassandra CFS 2807. With rhythm section; includes "Little Boxes."

RINGER, JIM
Waiting for the Hard Times to Go. Folk-Legacy FSI-47.
Good to Get Home. Philo 1012.

RODERICK, JUDY
Woman Blue. Vanguard 79197. Blues, folk, and contemporary songs by a fine singer who manages to combine gutsiness with a delicate, expressive reading of her material. Roderick, who is now working more in a country vein—often with her own first-rate original material—was popular on the folk circuit through the sixties. With Artie Traum, acoustic and electric guitar, and occasional rhythm section.

RUSH, TOM A soft-voiced singer, who began with traditional material and now works in a tasteful country pop vein; the two selections listed present the two aspects of his work. *See* Schwann catalogue and *Phonolog* for complete listings.
Blues, Songs, and Ballads. Prestige 7374.
Ladies Love Outlaws. Columbia C 33054.

SIEBEL, PAUL A writer who has emerged as his own man from the shadow of Dylan; many of his story songs and reflective songs have achieved general currency.
Woodsmoke and Oranges. Elektra 74064.
Jack-Knife Gypsy. Elektra 74081.

SKY, PATRICK
P.S. Vanguard 79179. Original and contemporary songs.
A Harvest of Gentle Clang. Vanguard 79207. Traditional songs.
Photographs. Verve FTS-3079. Original songs.
Songs That Made America Famous. Adelphi R 4101. But will they make Pat Sky famous? Social protest songs, mainly original, ranging in tone from comic-ironic-bawdy to merely silly-tasteless-obscene. Or maybe a parody of the social protest song movement, ranging in tone from. . . .

SMITH, JANET
The Unicorn. Takoma 1027. A pleasing singer of modern and traditional songs, popular in the San Francisco area, with interesting backup from swing guitarist Bob Wilson.

SORRELLS, ROSALIE Originally a singer of traditional songs, Sorrells has become, over the years, an intense and genuinely personal songwriter.
Folksongs of Idaho and Utah. Folkways 5343.
Travelin' Lady. Sire 5902.
Rosalie's Songbag. Prestige 13025 (OP).
If I Could Be the Rain. Folk-Legacy FSI-31.
What Ever Happened to the Girl That Was? Paramount 6072.

SPOELSTRA, MARK
State of Mind. Elektra 7307.
This House. Fantasy 8412.
Songs, vols. 1–2. Folkways 2444, 3572.
————. Kicking Mule 103.

STEELE, BILL
Garbage. Bay 202.

STEELEYE SPAN An English band that has tastefully adapted electric instrumentation, and the heavier rhythms that electric instruments engender, to the English ballad and country dance tradition.

Almanack (1969–72). Charisma CS 12 (available from B & C Records). Earlier, less electric versions of the band.
Following are other records that the band put out before it acquired its current American reputation. They reflect various personnel changes, but in all cases Tim Hart and Maddy Prior remain at the center.
Hark! The Village Wait. RCA (British) SF 8113.
Please to See the King. B & C CAS 1029.
Ten Man Mop. Peg 9.
Tim Hart and Maddy Prior: Summer Solstice. B & C CAS 1035.
The following records are of the band that achieved popularity.
Parcel of Rogues. Chrysalis 1046.
Below the Salt. Chrysalis 1008.

STUART, ALICE
All the Good Times. Arhoolie 4002.
Full Time Woman. Fantasy 8403.
Believing. Fantasy 9412.

TAYLOR, JAMES
Sweet Baby James. Warner 1843. This album really holds up well. *See* Schwann catalogue and *Phonolog* for other listings.

TRAUM, HAPPY AND ARTIE
————. Capitol ST-586.
Double-Back. Capitol ST-799. Both albums feature mostly original songs, with a couple of outside contributions apiece. The Traum brothers have a unique approach to songwriting and to instrumental styles that is distinctly contemporary, yet distinctly rooted in tradition.
Hard Times in the Country. Rounder 3008.
See also Mud Acres, Folk Song Revival section, page 106.

TURNER, JIM
The Well-Tempered Saw. Owl ORLP-22. Traditional, pop, and classical selections on musical saw. One plays the saw by drawing a violin bow across the untoothed edge while bending the blade in a certain manner; pitch variations are obtained by varying the degree of pressure with which the blade is bent. An eerie wavering tone, like that of the electronic instrument called the theremin, results. The instrument is impossible to play perfectly in tune; the problem is *relatively* minimal and inoffensive in Turner's playing. He is accompanied by various instruments ranging from musical glasses to the Boulder, Colorado, Philharmonic Orchestra.

WALKER, JERRY JEFF
Collectibles. MCA 450.
Viva Terlingua. MCA 382.
Driftin' Way of Life. Vanguard 6521.

WEISSBERG, ERIC, AND DELIVERANCE
Rural Free Delivery. Warner BS 2720. Original and country songs and instrumentals, influenced by both rock and bluegrass.

WILCOX, JON
Stages of My Life. Folk-Legacy FSI-45.

WINCHESTER, JESSE
_____. Ampex-Bearsville 10104.
Learn to Love It. Bearsville 6953.

YOUNG, STEVE
Rock Salt and Nails. A&M 4177.
Seven Bridges Road. Reprise 2081.

ZENTZ, BOB
Mirrors and Changes. Folk-Legacy FSI-51.

ENGLAND, SCOTLAND, AND IRELAND

So much of our music has its roots in British and Irish tradition that it is impossible to conceive of a survey of American music that omits reference to the British Isles. But Britain and Ireland have in recent years experienced a revival movement of their own, with the result that records have proliferated to such a degree that it is impossible to present a fair or comprehensive set of listings within the amount of space this volume permits. Please bear this in mind when referring to the following, a casual inventory of some of the best British and Irish albums, both traditional and revival, that have come to my attention. For fiddle records, consult the Fiddle section, page 83.

ANDERSON, ALISTAIR
. . . Plays English Concertina. Trailer LER 2074. Fiddle tunes, dance tunes, classical pieces, and a Scott Joplin rag, with occasional fiddle, whistle, guitar, and mandolin.
Concertina Workshop. Topic/Free Reed 12 FRS 501.

AR LEITHEIDI
The Ulster Outcry. Outlet SOLP 1019. Traditional Irish instrumental music, mainly dance tunes, recorded in live performance by a band comprising mainly members of the family of button accordion player Dinny O'Brian. A large ensemble, which includes whistles and flutes, uillean pipes, hand drum (bodhran), and several fiddles, in various combinations. The large Irish dance ensemble, called the ceili (pronounced "seeley") band, is not traditional, but dates back to the Irish revival movement of the twenties. Most ceili bands adopt the practice of playing strictly in unison throughout, with occasional turns at solos that usually have a minimum of variation or personal ornamentation. This band arranges and orchestrates its parts far more interestingly.

ARMSTRONG, FRANKIE
Lovely on the Water. Topic 12 TS 216. Armstrong, who prefers to work with the older ballads and modern material written in or adaptable to the old style, sings with a beautiful voice and great tastefulness.

BOYS OF THE LOUGH, THE Well-conceived and beautifully played instrumental arrangements of Irish, Shetland, Scot-

tish, and English songs and dances, with occasional vocals. Fiddle, flute, harp, concertina, mandolin, and bodhran.
———. Trailer LER 2086.
Second Album. Trailer LER 2090 = Rounder 3006 (U.S.).

CARTHY, MARTIN Carthy is a revivalist singer, who works mainly with traditional material and occasional contemporary material adaptable to traditional style. The guitar is not used in British tradition, but Carthy has developed a unique and influential guitar style based on American techniques. These listings do not completely represent his recorded work.
———. Fontana 5269.
Second Album. Fontana 5362. Accompanied on both albums by Dave Swarbrick, fiddle and mandolin.
Shearwater. Peg 12. Interesting arrangements of traditional songs and ballads; solo voice, with guitar or dulcimer, and vocal duet (with Maddy Prior).
Landfall. Philips 630.8049. Contemporary and traditional songs.
Prince Heathen. Fontana 5529.

CARTY, PADDY, AND MICK O'CONNOR
Reels and Jigs in the Galway Manner. Master Collector #1. Carty plays wood flute beautifully, accompanied by O'Connor on banjo. The Galway style is somewhat slower and softer, and better suited for listening, than the faster Sligo style, which is preferred by dancers.

CHIEFTAINS, THE Among the foremost revival virtuoso performers of Gaelic small ensemble music, they are a large ensemble (flutes, pipes, tin whistle, fiddle, concertina, and bodhran) who orchestrate traditional music in a non-traditional way, linking pieces in short suites and using harmonic and contrapuntal arrangements to express a music which traditional ensembles play in unison. The arrangements are beautifully conceived, at once polished and exciting. The Chieftains' approach represents one of the most successful solutions I have heard in British, Irish, or American music to the problem of how to play a traditional rural music—a music of simpler times, places, and people—in such a way as to preserve its essential spirit and at the same time satisfy the requirements of more sophisticated sensibilities.
———, vols. 1–4. Claddagh CC 2, 7, 10, 14.

COX, HARRY
Traditional English Love Songs. Folk-Lyric FSB-20. Solo voice songs and ballads, true and unpolished. Cox, an East Anglian farmer, has been known for many years as a valued informant to British folklorists.

EDWARDS, ALF
The Art of the Concertina. Prestige 13060 (OP). The concertina, a small accordion-like instrument, was immensely popular in England during the early part of the century. It was used not only for traditional music but also for dance music such as waltzes and schottisches, as well as marching music and light classical pieces. Many towns had large concertina orchestras in which bass, baritone, tenor, alto, and soprano concertinas were used. In the past few years, there has been a revival of interest in the instrument once more, kindled largely by the efforts of Neil Wayne, a hardworking

concertina monomaniac, who edits *Free Reed* magazine (*see* Periodicals and Serial Publications section, page 241); such fine players as Alistair Anderson (page 126) have risen to the fore. During the concertina's period of neglect, Alf Edwards was almost solely responsible for keeping the instrument in the public eye. This excellent record presents Irish, Scottish, and English songs and dances, with occasional vocals by Ewan MacColl and occasional guitar and banjo by Peggy Seeger. It would be a great service if someone could arrange to get it reissued; rights and the masters are now owned by Fantasy Records.

ELLIOTS OF BIRTLEY, THE
———. Folkways 3565. A documentary of music in the life of a northern English mining family.

ENNIS, SEAMUS
———. Leader LEA 2003. Ennis is one of the foremost players of uillean pipes, as well as a folklorist and collector. The Irish uillean (elbow) pipes are much smaller than the better-known Scottish war pipes, and differ in other features of construction as well as in style and repertory. The bag is inflated not by breath but by a bellows worked by the right elbow; the air pressure of the bag is controlled by the left elbow. The drone pipes are not of unvarying pitch as in the Scottish pipes; pitch is varied by working a set of so-called regulator keys by the right wrist. While all this is going on, the left- and right-hand fingers perform their usual chores on the melody ("chanter") pipe. In addition, staccato—inaccessible on the Scottish pipes—can be obtained on the uillean pipes by closing the bell of the chanter pipe against the thigh. As if all this isn't enough, the bellows' arrangement also permits the player to sing. Few modern players opt to do so; Ennis is one of them.
The Wandering Minstrel. Topic 12 TS 250.

FAIRPORT CONVENTION. *See* Contemporary Artists, Bands, and Songwriters section, page 121.

FUREY, FINBAR A young virtuoso player of the uillean pipes and tin whistle.
Traditional Irish Pipe Music. XTRA (Transatlantic) 1077.
. . . and Eddie Furey: Irish Pipe Music. Nonesuch H-72059.
. . . and Eddie Furey: The Dawning of the Day. Dawn 3037.

HEANEY, JOE
———. Topic 12 T 91. Excellent highly ornamented singing in English and Gaelic, without accompaniment.

HIGH LEVEL RANTERS
Lads of Northumbria. Trailer LER 2007. The leading traditionalist exponents of Northumbrian songs and instrumental music.

KEANE, SARAH AND RITA
Once I Loved: Songs from the West of Ireland. Claddagh CC4. Vocal solos and duets in English and Gaelic, without accompaniment. Unpolished, very beautiful singing in the old style, with great attention to the subtle variations in pitch and scale that characterize the style that survives from before the days of piano, guitar, and other equal-temperament instruments.

KILLEN, LOU
Ballads and Broadsides. Topic 12 T 126. Killen is a fine singer, with a fine sense of the ornamental manner.

KILLEN, LOU, AND JOHNNY HANDLE
Along the Coaly Tyne. Topic 12 T 189. Traditional and contemporary songs from Northumbria, with various instrumental accompaniment. For Killen, *see also* Songs of the Sea section, page 97.

LLOYD, A. L. A folklore scholar and wonderful singer, with a mirthful, unpolished manner sure to please those who appreciate honest music, and equally sure to displease those who insist that only a trained and polished voice is satisfactory. *See also* Ewan MacColl, this section, below, and Songs of the Sea section, page 97.
First Person. Topic 12 T 118. A 1966 selection of his favorite English and Australian songs and ballads, solo voice and with concertina and fiddle accompaniment by Alf Edwards and Dave Swarbrick.
The Foggy Dew. Tradition 1016. With Alf Edwards.

MacCOLL, EWAN A Scottish singer with a clear, well-centered voice; a leading figure in the English revival scene.
. . . and Dominic Behan: Streets of Song. Topic 12 T 41 = *The Singing Streets,* Folkways 8501 (U.S.). Songs and reminiscences of Glasgow and Dublin childhoods.
Chorus From the Gallows. Topic 12 T 16. A most interesting selection of ballads of crime and criminals, ranging from Child ballads and old broadsides to contemporary topical songs. Guitar and banjo accompaniments by Peggy Seeger.
Four Pence a Day. Stinson SLP 79. British industrial folk songs written during the past 150 years, including Mac-Coll's truck driver song "Champion at Keeping 'em Rolling."
. . . and Peggy Seeger: Classic Scots Ballads. Tradition 1015.
The Manchester Angel. Topic 12 T 147 = Tradition 2059 (U.S.). English songs and ballads, solo voice and with Peggy Seeger, guitar, dulcimer, and concertina.
The English and Scottish Popular Ballads, vols. 1–3. Folkways 3509, 3510, 3511. Selections from the Child collection.
In the late fifties, the now-defunct Riverside label issued an eight-volume series of Child ballads sung by MacColl and A. L. Lloyd; sadly, these records are no longer available, but are occasionally found in odd places. *See also* A. L. Lloyd, Songs of the Sea section page 97, and under Peggy Seeger, Folk Song Revival section, page 107. Many other MacColl records are not listed; *see* Schwann catalogue, *Phonolog,* and the catalogues of Folkways and Topic records.

MacLELLAN, JOHN A.
Scottish Bagpipe Music. Folkways 8814. A comprehensive survey of the various types of music commonly played on the Scottish pipes, as performed by a foremost army piper.

MacNEILL, SEUMAS, AND JOHN MacFAYDEN
Piobaireachd. BBC REB 48M. Piobaireachd (pronounced something like peebrahk) simply means "piping" in Scots Gaelic. It's the name for the classical way of playing the highland pipes, in which a melodic statement is followed by sets of variations, each using prescribed types of ornamentation. Ornamentation is extremely important in piping; staccato and variations in loudness are not possible on the pipes, leaving ornamentation as the most readily available dynamic device. This record is made from a set of BBC lectures on the art of the Scottish bagpipes; there is much talking and the presentation is orderly. Issued in conjunction with MacNeill's BBC Publications book of the same name.

MAKEM, TOMMY
Sings. Tradition 1044. The animated Irish singer and penny whistle player known through his association with the Clancy Brothers; a fine solo album devoid of the show-biz qualities the Clancys must resort to to survive.

McHAILE, TOM
All-Irish Champion Tin Whistle. Outlet 1001. Sometimes it's hard to believe the music that an Irishman can draw from a tin whistle.

NA FILI
Farewell to Connaught. Outlet SOLP 1010.
An Ghaoth Aniar. Mercier IRL 9.
Three. Outlet SOLP 1017. Traditional Irish songs, hymns, airs, and dance tunes, with occasional Gaelic vocals. Beautifully arranged and played on pipes, accordion, and fiddle; soulful enough to satisfy the traditionalist and polished enough for those who insist on polish.

PLANXTY
The Well Below the Valley. Polydor (British) 2383.232. Planxty are a young Irish revival quartet who work mainly with traditional material, but with some original material as well. They keep their music simple and tasteful. Vocals and instrumentals with pipes, guitar, tin whistle, various kinds of mandolins, and bodhran.

POWER, PEG CLANCY
_____. Folk-Legacy FSE-8. Traditional Irish songs by a member of the well-known Clancy family of professional entertainers; Peg Clancy chose to stay home and remain a traditional singer.

REDPATH, JEAN
_____. Folk-Legacy FSS-49. Traditional Scottish songs and ballads in solo voice, with personal ornamentation in traditional style. Redpath has a gentle, vital voice; a song from her is a living thing of beauty.

ROBERTS, JOHN, AND TONY BARRAND
Spencer the Rover. Swallowtail ST 1. English songs and ballads in two-part modal harmony; vocal duets.

ROBERTSON, JEANNIE
The Great Scots Traditional Ballad Singer. Topic 12 T 96. The Hollywood experience teaches us to beware of what we read in album notes and titles. This one, though, is absolutely accurate, for Robertson is mistress of a highly ornate style of solo singing.

ROWSOME, LEO (d. 1970)
Ri na bPíobairí (King of the Pipers). Claddagh CC 1. Uilean pipe solos. Rowsome was a superb and spectacular player, scion of a line of famous pipers. For a description of this difficult and beguiling instrument, see the caption for the record by Séamus Ennis, this section, page 127. Rowsome had an amazingly full concept of self-accompaniment on the regulated pipes; he got a lot of music out of them. Each tune is played with appropriate grace, wildness, or dignity.

STEELEYE SPAN. *See* Contemporary Artists, Bands, and Songwriters section, page 125.

TAYLOR, PADDY
The Boy in the Gap. Claddagh CC8. Airs and dance tunes from the Counties Limerick and Clare, lucidly played on wood flute with bodhran accompaniment.

TUNNEY, PADDY
The Man of Songs. Folk-Legacy FSE-7. Traditional Irish songs in solo tenor voice, finely ornamented.

WATERSONS, THE English songs and ballads with full, strongly conceived modal harmonies.
_____. Topic 12 T 142.
Frost and Fire. Topic 12 T 136. Ritual and ceremonial songs of the British Isles.
A Yorkshire Garland. Topic 12 T 167.

YOUNG TRADITION British songs and ballads, mainly traditional, in well-made vocal trio arrangements without accompaniment. Occasional solos; extensive use of modal harmonies.
_____. Transatlantic 155 (= Vanguard 79246).
Galleries. Vanguard 79295. Includes a Robert Johnson blues and several medieval songs with consort accompaniment.
The Young Tradition Sampler. Transatlantic TRASAM 13.
Galleries Revisited. Transatlantic TRASAM 30.

ANTHOLOGIES AND COLLECTIONS

The Borders. Folkways 8776. Songs recorded on a 1959 field trip along the Anglo-Scottish border by Sam Charters. Mostly vocal performances, with some selections on Northumbrian small pipes and fiddle.
English Folk Songs. Columbia Special Products AKL 4943. Folk songs and some instrumental music mostly by traditional performers, edited by Peter Kennedy and Alan Lomax from the BBC archives.
Field Trip: England. Folkways 8871.
Field Trip: Ireland. Folkways 8872. Recordings made by Kentucky singer Jean Ritchie in the late fifties. A wide sampling of the varieties of traditional instrumental and vocal music still a part of rural life. A few selections by professional artists, many by traditional informants well known to folklorists.
The Folksongs of Britain. A superb ten-volume collection, also available individually, of recordings made mostly in the field by Peter Kennedy and Alan Lomax during the fifties. England, Scotland and the Scottish islands, and to a lesser extent Ireland are well represented, Wales hardly at all. The emphasis is on solo English-language singing; occasionally, there appear instrumental accompaniments or solos, duet or ensemble singing, or songs in Gaelic. A few of the artists are professionals, most not; the quality of performance and of repertory is consistently high by musical as well as documentary standards. An especially valuable acquisition for libraries, since individuals may balk at the expense of a ten-volume series. Available from Caedmon in North America, from Topic in England.

Vol. 1, *Songs of Courtship.* Caedmon TC 1142 = Topic 12 T 157. Includes a stunning fiddle solo by Agnes Whyte, well worth the price of the record to lovers of Irish fiddle music.
Vol. 2, *Songs of Seduction.* Caedmon TC 1143 (= Topic 12 T 158).
Vol. 3, *Jack of All Trades.* Caedmon TC 1144 (= Topic 12 T 159). Songs of workers and craftsmen.
Vol. 4, *Child Ballads I.* Caedmon TC 1145 (= Topic 12 T 160).
Vol. 5, *Child Ballads II.* Caedmon TC 1146 (= Topic 12 T 161).
Vol. 6, *Sailormen and Servingmaids.* Caedmon TC 1162 (= Topic 12 T 194).
Vol. 7, *Fair Game and Foul.* Caedmon TC 1163 (= Topic 12 T 195). Songs of highwaymen and sportsmen.
Vol. 8, *A Soldier's Life for Me.* Caedmon TC 1164 (= Topic 12 T 196).
Vol. 9, *Songs of Christmas.* Caedmon TC 1224 (= Topic 12 T 198).
Vol. 10, *Animal Songs.* Caedmon TC 1225 (= Topic 12 T 198).

Irish Dance Music. Folkways 8821. Recordings from the late twenties through the early sixties; fiddle, pipes, accordion, banjo, flute, and tin whistle in various combinations or solo, and occasional piano accompaniments.
Irish Folk Songs. Columbia Special Products AKL 4941. English- and Gaelic-language songs and some instrumentals; field recordings from the western counties collected by Séamus Ennis, Alan Lomax, Robin Roberts, and Brian George.
Irish Jigs, Reels, and Hornpipes. Folkways 6819. Pipes, tin whistle, and fiddle (Michael Gorman), recorded in Ireland, with comprehensive notes on the dance steps and sets.
Irish Popular Dances. Folkways 6818. Jigs, reels, and hornpipes from 78's recorded in Ireland and in Boston, on pipes, accordion, jew's-harp, and fiddle in various combinations, with occasional guitar or piano accompaniment. Includes Leo Rowsome and Michael Coleman.
Gaelic Music from Scotland. OCORA OCR 45.
Songs and Pipes of the Hebrides. Folkways 4430.
Traditional Music of Ireland. Solo and ensemble music, mostly solo voice but also with fiddle, pipes, tin whistle, and accordion, recorded on a 1960 field trip by Sam Charters.
Vol. 1, *The Older Traditions: of Connemara and Clare.* Folkways 8781.
Vol. 2, *Songs and Dances from Down, Kerry and Clare.* Folkways 8782.
The Wheels of the World. Morning Star 45001. Traditional Irish reels and jigs, as recorded during the twenties and thirties by Irish and Irish-American musicians. Some standout fiddling and piping. Includes Patsy Touhey and Michael Coleman.

THE CARIBBEAN
(Including Puerto Rico)

A comprehensive survey of Caribbean music is outside the scope of this volume: following are selective and rather casual listings of some readily available material.

ESSO TRINIDAD STEEL BAND
_____. Warner WS 1917. Steel drums are actually closer to the vibraphone in musical principle; they are made by hammering out segments in the tops of steel barrels so that they will produce a precise pitch when struck. Caribbean bands use drums of various sizes in order to produce an orchestral range of sounds; repertory ranges from Caribbean music to American pop music to classical selections.

LORD INVADER
Calypso Travels. Folkways 8733.

SANCHEZ, PEPE Y FLORA
Tengo Puerto Rico en mi Corazón. Paredon 1005. Patriotic, militant, and sentimental songs associated with the Puerto Rican independence movement.

SPENCE, JOSEPH A great and unique guitarist, Spence is a popular hero on his home island of Andros. He works with simple melodies, embellishing them and breaking them up between bass and treble registers in order to generate intense and complex polyrhythms. His vocal lines, partly sung and partly mumbled, add yet another rhythmic dimension.
Music of the Bahamas, vol. 1 (1958). Folkways 3844.
Music of the Bahamas, vol. 4 (1958). Folkways 3847. Spence shares this album with two excellent Andros vocal groups led by John Roberts and Frederick McQueen.
Good Morning, Mr. Walker (1971). Arhoolie 1061. Has a greater emphasis on Spence's vocal work.
Happy All the Time. Elektra EKL-273 (OP).

TI RO RO AND VOODOO DRUMS
_____. Request 733. Many regard Ti Ro Ro as Haiti's most accomplished drummer.

WESTLAND STEEL BAND
The Sound of the Sun. Nonesuch H-72016.

ANTHOLOGIES AND COLLECTIONS

Anthems, Work Songs and Ballads from the Bahamas Islands (Music of the Bahamas, vol. 2). Folkways 3845. 1958 field recordings made on Andros Island by Sam Charters; most of the selections by fine singers John Roberts and Frederick McQueen.
Bahaman Songs, French Ballads and Dance Tunes, and Spanish Religious Songs and Game Tunes. AFS L5. Library of Congress field recordings, the Bahaman selections from 1935.
Caribbean Island Music. Nonesuch Explorer H 72047. From Haiti, Jamaica, and the Dominican Republic.
Cult Music of Trinidad. Folkways 4478.
Folk Music of Jamaica. Folkways 4453.

Appalachian "Jack Tales": Roy Hicks

Folk Music of Puerto Rico. AFS L18. 1946 Library of Congress field recordings.
Folk Songs of Puerto Rico. Asch 4412. Traditional vocal and instrumental music, in late-sixties field recordings by Henrietta Yurchenco.
Instrumental Music of the Bahamas (Music of the Bahamas, vol. 3). Folkways 3846. 1958 field recordings on Andros Island by Sam Charters.
Jamaican Cult Music. Folkways 4461.
Nueva York. Folkways 5559. A documentary in sound of the life of Puerto Rican immigrants in New York City by Tony Schwartz, a pioneer of tape documentary recordings.
The Real Bahamas in Music and Song. Nonesuch H-72013. The results of a 1965 field recording trip by Peter Siegel and Jody Stecher. Includes two selections by guitarist Joseph Spence; otherwise the emphasis is on the excellent polyphonic vocal style of the Bahamian spiritual tradition.
The Real Calypso. RBF 13. A collection of classic calypso pieces; fine songs and performances from 1927 to 1946, compiled by Sam Charters.

REGGAE. Reggae is a Jamaican popular music with Caribbean rhythmic roots, but strongly influenced by American soul music. The following two records serve as good introductions to commercial reggae music.
Jimmy Cliff: The Harder They Come. Mango SMAS-74000 (distributed by Capitol). Music from the movie sound track by Cliff and others.
This Is Reggae Music. Island 9251. Joe Higgs, Jimmy Cliff, Maytals, and others.

Rhythms of the Caribbean. Folkways 8811. Selections illustrating the rhythmic styles and usages in vocal and dance music on the island of San Andrés.
Songs and Dances of Haiti. Folkways 4432.

MUSIC OF THE WORLD

Readers are particularly urged to consult the catalogues of the following record companies for recordings of world-wide ethnic music: Bärenreiter-Musicaphon (UNESCO Series), CMS, Chant du Monde, Columbia Special Products (Columbia World Library of Folk and Primitive Music), Folkways, Lyrichord, Nonesuch (Explorer Series), Monitor, Request, and Tangent. As a very basic acquisition, especially for libraries, the following is recommended:

Music of the World's Peoples. Folkways 4504/5/6/7/8. A ten-record set of ethnic music from throughout the world, edited by Henry Cowell. Five volumes of two records each are available separately. The selections are arranged without regard to geographical sequence, which makes for varied and interesting casual listening.

FOLK TALES

See also North American Indian Music and Tales and Folk Songs for Children sections, pages 40 and 134.

Animal Tales Told in the Gullah Dialect. AFS L44/5/6.

CHASE, RICHARD
Three Jack Tales from the So. Appalachians. Folk-Legacy FTA-6.

HICKS, ROY
Four Jack Tales. Folk-Legacy FTA-14.

LEE, HECTOR
J. Golden Kimball Stories (from *Folklore of the Mormon Country*). Folk-Legacy FTA-25.

LONG, MAUDE
Jack Tales. AFS L47/8.

MARCOTTE, MARION
Favorite Cajun Tales. Swallow 6004.

RITCHIE, JEAN, PAUL CLAYTON, AND RICHARD CHASE
Folktales of the Southern Appalachians. Tradition 1011.

SOCIAL AND HISTORICAL DOCUMENTARIES AND ANTHOLOGIES

Almost all the recordings in this section are mentioned elsewhere as well. Most of these recordings, by both traditional and revival-scholarly performers, are suitable for educational use on many levels. This section has been assembled especially with that purpose in mind.

ALLEN, RED, AND THE ALLEN BROTHERS
The Kentucky Story in Bluegrass. King Bluegrass 523. A program in song and narrative.

American History in Ballad and Song, vols. 1–2. Folkways 5801, 5802. Each volume is a three-record program of songs designed to stimulate the study of American history, and ordered and annotated for that purpose. Vol. 1 is for junior high school, and vol. 2 is for high school.

Can't Keep from Crying: Topical Blues on the Death of President Kennedy. Testament S-01.

Come All You Coal Miners. Rounder 4005. Appalachian miners' songs, mostly original, by George Tucker, Hazel Dickens, Sarah Ogan Gunning, and others.

DIXON, DORSEY
Babies in the Mill. Testament 3301. Dixon is the composer of some of the finest topical, industrial, and protest songs from the southern highlands. He has composed or adapted many other mountain songs as well.

ENGLISH, LOGAN
The Days of '49. Folkways 5255. California gold rush songs.

Frontiers. Folkways 10003. An educational program providing support, through musical examples, for the study of America's westward colonization. A correlated teacher's manual is available.

GLAZER, JOE
The Songs of Joe Hill. Folkways 2039. Joe Hill was a songwriter, organizer, and martyred hero of the early days of the labor movement. Glazer's union background includes educational work for the CIO.
Sings Labor Songs. Collector 1918.

GLAZER, TOM
The Musical Heritage of America. Each volume is a four-record set with background notes; also available on tape cassette.
   Vol. 1, *Colonial Times to the Beginning of the Civil War.* CMS 650/4L.
   Vol. 2, *The Civil War.* CMS 660/4L.
   Vol. 3, *The Winning of the West.* CMS 670/4L. Guitar and banjo accompaniments are played by Dick Weissman.

GUTHRIE, WOODY
Dust Bowl Ballads. Folkways 5212.
Dust Bowl Ballads. RCA LPV-502.
Sacco and Vanzetti. Folkways 5485.

HOUSE, WALLACE
Songs of the War of 1812. Folkways 2163/4 (2-rec. set, 10 inch).

JACKSON, HARRY
The Cowboy: His Songs and Brag Talk. Folkways 5723. A two-record documentary of cowboy life and lore, interesting and well conceived. An especially good acquisition for schools and libraries.

KAHN, KATHY
The Working Girl: Women's Songs from Mountains, Mines, and Mills. Voyager 305. Issued in conjunction with her Avon book *Hillbilly Women;* Kahn is a community organizer in rural Appalachia.

KIRKPATRICK, REV. FREDERICK DOUGLASS
Ballads of Black America. Folkways 7751. With Pete Seeger.

KNIGHT, ELIZABETH
Songs of the Suffragettes. Folkways 5281.

LARUE, MICHAEL
Songs of the American Slaves. Folkways 5252.

LOMAX, JOHN A.
The Ballad Hunter, 5 vols. AFS L49/50/51/52/53. Lectures with musical examples on American folk music and collecting; it was Lomax who was responsible for the heydey of recording-collecting for the Library of Congress Archive of Folk Song. Available separately or as a set. *See* his book *Adventures of a Ballad Hunter,* Part II, Books about Folk Music, page 164.

McBEE, HAMPER
Cumberland Moonshiner. Prestige 14008 (OP). Songs and narratives from a Tennessee moonshiner, with guitar and banjo accompaniment by Guy Carawan.

MILLS, ALAN
Canada's Story in Song. Folkways 3000. A history of Canada in English, French, Indian, and Eskimo traditional music; with its sequel below.
O Canada. Folkways 30001.

Negro Songs of Protest. Rounder 4004. Selections from the privately made field recordings collected by Lawrence Gellert in the thirties, and used as the basis for his books. The entire collection is now housed in the Indiana University Archives of Traditional Music. The material ranges from unaccompanied songs and chain-gang choral singing to blues with guitar; all implicitly or explicitly protest social conditions; all are of high musical quality.

NEW LOST CITY RAMBLERS Exciting and well-played recreations of old-time string band songs.
American Moonshine and Prohibition. Folkways 5263.
Songs from the Depression. Folkways 5364.

NYE, HERMES
Ballads of the Civil War. Folkways 5004 (2-rec. set, 10 inch).

The Railroad in Folksong. RCA LPV-532. Old-time and early country music recordings.

Railroad Songs and Ballads. AFS L161. 1936–59 Library of Congress field recordings.

SEEGER, MIKE
Tipple, Loom and Rail. Folkways 5273. An excellent selection of songs that document the industrialization of the south.

SEEGER, PETE
American Industrial Ballads. Folkways 5251. Songs that reflect the conditions of life of Americans in various lines of work during the early part of the century and before: miners, railroaders, factory hands, farmers, and cowboys. An excellent selection of material.
Frontier Ballads
    Vol. 1, *The Trek.* Folkways 2175 (10 inch).
    Vol. 2, *The Settlers.* Folkways 2176 (10 inch). A well-chosen collection of traditional songs dating mainly from the early 1800's; pleasant for the listener and useful for the classroom teacher dealing with early America.
Songs of Struggle and Protest (1930–50). Folkways 5233.

Songs and Ballads of American History and of the Assassination of American Presidents. AFS L29. 1937–49 Library of Congress field recordings.

Songs and Ballads of the Anthracite Miners. AFS L16. 1946 Library of Congress field recordings made in Pennsylvania.

Songs and Ballads of the Bituminous Miners. AFS L60. 1940 Library of Congress field recordings.

Songs of the Civil War. Folkways 5717. Edited by Irwin Silber, in conjunction with his book of the same name.

Songs of the Railroad (1924–34). Vetco 103. String band and early country music recordings.

TERKEL, STUDS
Hard Times. Caedmon TC 2048. A collection of various plain folks' reminiscences of the Depression years, vivid and moving.

This Land Is My Land. Folkways 7027. Work and occupational songs performed by Pete Seeger, Woody Guthrie, Leadbelly, Cisco Houston, Mac McClintock, and others.

To Be a Slave. Caedmon TC 2066. Original slave narratives, compiled by Julius Lester and read by Lester, Ruby Dee, and Ossie Davis.

The Traditional Music of Beech Mountain, North Carolina
    Vol. 1, *The Older Ballads and Sacred Songs.* Folk-Legacy FSA-22. Mostly selections in solo voice.
    Vol. 2, *The Late Songs and Hymns.* Folk-Legacy FSA-23. Solo and group singing; some instrumental solos and accompaniments. Good recordings that represent the musical legacy of the older members of a mountain community, serving to illustrate the role of homemade music in the social life of the community.

GENERAL FOLK ANTHOLOGIES AND FOLK FESTIVAL RECORDINGS

AFS Anthology of American Folk Music. A fifteen-volume anthology of selections from the Archive of Folk Song of the Library of Congress, to be issued in conjunction with the 1976 Bicentennial. Further information is not available as this book goes to press.
Anthology of American Folk Music (three 2-rec. sets).
    Vol. 1, *Ballads.* Folkways 2951.
    Vol. 2, *Social Music.* Folkways 2952.
    Vol. 3, *Songs.* Folkways 2953.
    Often referred to as the "Harry Smith anthology" after its compiler, well-known in bohemian circles as an eccentric film maker, artist, and social and esthetic theorist. For a long time, this collection was the only easily accessible source of reissues of some of the great (and not great) recordings of the twenties and thirties, and it shaped the tastes and determined the influences of a whole generation. Including as it does tasteful and intelligent selections from every aspect of black and white American tradition, it still remains the best, most comprehensive, and most essential compact document of early recorded traditional music.
The Asch Recordings A four-volume series, available separately, of important recordings originally recorded at 78 rpm on the Asch label, precursor (now a part) of Folkways.
    Blues, Gospel and Jazz, vol. 1. Asch AA 1. Mainly blues: Leadbelly, Josh White, Bunk Johnson, McGhee and Terry, and others.
    Blues, Gospel and Jazz, vol. 2. Asch AA 2. Mainly traditional jazz and swing: Muggsy Spanier, Pee Wee Russell, James P. Johnson, Sidney Bechet, Art Tatum, Coleman Hawkins, Mary Lou Williams.
    Folk Singers, vol. 1. Asch AA 3. Leadbelly, Brownie McGhee, Pete Seeger, Josh White, Woody Guthrie, and others.
    Folk Singers, vol. 2. Asch AA 4. Hobart Smith, Gary Davis, Woody Guthrie, and others.

Folk and Bluegrass at Neusuedende, vols. 1–2 (1971–72). FV 12002, 12003. Bill Clifton, the Kentucky Mountaineers, and various European performers.
Folk Festival. Legacy 110. Judy Collins, Pete Seeger, Glen Campbell, Dillards, and others.
Folk Festival of the Smokies, vols. 1–2. Traditional FFS 528, 529. For the most part competent but undistinguished versions of commonplace tunes by revival performers; interesting selections by Hazel Dickens (vol. 1) and Babe Stovall (vol. 2).
Folk Music U.S.A. Folkways 4530 (2-rec. set). Selections from the Folkways catalogue, compiled by Harold Courlander in conjunction with his book of the same name. A thorough cross section including Anglo-American, Black American, Puerto Rican, Mexican-American traditions.
Greatest Folksingers of the Sixties. Vanguard VSD 17/18. Or, at any rate, the greatest folksingers of the sixties who happened to record for Vanguard; culled from earlier Vanguard and Newport Folk Festival releases.

Mississippi Folk Voices. Southern Folklore 101. Recent field recordings of black and white rural Mississippi traditions, with 55-page scholarly booklet by William Ferris.

NEWPORT FOLK FESTIVAL RECORDINGS:

1959
Volume 1. Vanguard 2053. Pete Seeger, Martha Schlamme, Leon Bibb, Tommy Makem, and Pat Clancy
Volume 2. Vanguard 2054. Joan Baez, Barbara Dane, Bob Gibson, McGhee and Terry, New Lost City Ramblers, Odetta.
Volume 3. Vanguard 2055. Oscar Brand, Cynthia Gooding, Frank Hamilton, Ed McCurdy, John Jacob Niles, Jean Ritchie, Earl Scruggs, Frank Warner.

1959 and 1960
Volume 1. Folkways 2431. Mike and Pete Seeger, Frank Hamilton, Butch Cage and Willie Thomas, and others.
Volume 2. Folkways 2432. McGhee and Terry, New Lost City Ramblers, and others.

1960
Volume 1. Vanguard 2087. Pete Seeger, John Lee Hooker, Alan Mills and Jean Carignan, Tommy Makem, Jimmy Driftwood, New Lost City Ramblers.
Volume 2. Vanguard 2088. Gibson and Camp, Cisco Houston, Ed McCurdy, Peggy Seeger and Ewan MacColl, Flatt and Scruggs.

1963
Newport Broadside. Vanguard 79144. Topical songs.
Country Music and Bluegrass. Vanguard 79146. Clarence Ashley, Clint Howard, Fred Price and Doc Watson, Jim and Jesse McReynolds, Tex Logan, Wiley and Zeke Morris, New Lost City Ramblers, Mac Wiseman.
Old Time Music at Newport. Vanguard 79147. Clarence Ashley, Dock Boggs, Maybelle Carter, Jenes Cottrell, Dorsey Dixon, and Clint Howard, Fred Price and Doc Watson.
The Evening Concerts I. Vanguard 78148. Joan Baez, Bob Dylan, Jack Elliott, Freedom Singers, Sam Hinton, John Hurt, Ian and Sylvia, Rooftop Singers.
The Evening Concerts II. Vanguard 79149. Bessie Johnson and the Sea Island Singers, Jackie Washington, Bob Davenport, Judy Collins and Theo Bikel, Dave Van Ronk, Jean Carignan, Jean Redpath, Pete Seeger.

1964
Blues I. Vanguard 79180. Fred McDowell, Dock Reed, Robert Pete Williams, Sleepy John Estes with Hammie Nixon and Yank Rachell.
Blues II. Vanguard 79181. Elizabeth Cotten, Willy Doss, John Hurt, Skip James, Robert Wilkins.
Traditional Music I. Vanguard 79182. Mamou Cajune, Gaither Carlton, Sarah Ogan Gunning, Fred McDowell, Hobart Smith, Doc Watson, and others.
Traditional Music II. Vanguard 79183. Séamus Ennis, John Hurt, Clayton McMichen, Frank Proffitt, Almeda Riddle, Edna and Jean Ritchie, and others.
Evening Concerts I. Vanguard 79184. José Feliciano, Jim Kweskin, Sleepy John Estes, Rodriguez Bros, Buffy Sainte-Marie, Pete Seeger.
Evening Concerts II. Vanguard 79185. Joan Baez, Theo Bikel, Jesse Fuller, Greenbriar Boys, Hamza el Din, Phipps Family, Staples Singers.
Evening Concerts III. Vanguard 79186. Mamou Cajune, Gaither Carleton, Koerner, Ray and Glover, Fred McDowell, Tom Paxton, Judy Roderick, Swan Silvertones, Hedy West, Doc and Merle Watson.

Roots of America's Music. Arhoolie 2001/2 (2-rec. set). Selections culled from the Arhoolie catalogue: a good cross section of traditional music as it was still being played in the sixties, and an excellent introduction to what the Arhoolie label has to offer. Statistically representative of Arhoolie's orientation: mostly blues with some gospel and spirituals, a smattering of country, bluegrass, and Cajun music, and a small and uneasy accommodation with old and new jazz and urban revival singers.
_____, vol. 2. Arhoolie 2021/2 (2-rec. set).

SOUTHERN FOLK HERITAGE SERIES 1959 field recordings
by Alan Lomax; the entire series is available as Atlantic HS-1, or individually as below:
Sounds of the South. Atlantic 1346.
Blue Ridge Mountain Music. Atlantic 1347.
Roots of the Blues. Atlantic 1348.
White Spirituals. Atlantic 1349.
American Folk Songs for Children. Atlantic 1350.
Negro Church Music. Atlantic 1351.
The Blues Roll On. Atlantic 1352.

Southern Journey. Prestige 25001–25012 (OP). A twelve-volume series of field recordings of white and black traditional music collected by Alan Lomax in 1959. The masters are now controlled by Fantasy Records, and it is hoped they will be reissued someday.

The Unexpurgated Folk Songs of Men. Arhoolie 4006. In 1959 folklorist Mack McCormick assembled an all-male group of white and black traditional performers, and some just plain folks, around a microphone, and asked them to turn loose their repertory of bawdy songs and routines. Names are not revealed; at least one well-known voice is recognizable.

The Unfortunate Rake. Folkways 3805. Sixteen variants, by different performers, of the widely disseminated Anglo-American ballad which in its best-known form is called "St. James Infirmary."

Versions and Variants of "Barbara Allen." AFS L54. 1933–54 Library of Congress field recordings. Like the previous album, a study in the "folk process" by which songs are varied and changed in the course of transmission.

FOLK SONGS FOR CHILDREN

These listings are for the most part concerned only with genuine folk songs of or for children, with a few other recommended records added as well. A comprehensive

The Leadbelly Legend

catalogue of all sorts of recorded material for children is available from the Children's Music Center, 5373 W. Pico Blvd., Los Angeles, Calif. 90019. In addition, the catalogues of Folkways Records and Young People's Records contain much valuable material for educators, parents, and children which is not listed here because it is not particularly concerned with folk music. A selection of folk-tale recordings follows the music listings. In addition to these listings, the catalogues of CMS and Caedmon Records offer a wide selection of traditional and nontraditional folk and fairy tales from around the world, recorded by excellent readers.

Some other relevant material for children may be found in the Folk Tales and Social and Historical Documentaries and Anthologies sections (page 131).

CROMARTY, GEORGE
The Only One. Thistle 732. Witty, hilarious, serious, and honest original songs for children; pleasing also to grown-ups.

GLAZER, TOM
Music for Ones and Twos. CMS 649; cassette 4649. Songs and games.
Activity and Game Songs, vols. 1 and 2. CMS 657 and 658; cassettes 4657 and 4658.

GUTHRIE, WOODY Our great songwriter (*see* page 94) wrote some of the best children's songs you can find; I grew up with these songs and still remember most of them and the delight they gave me.
Songs to Grow On. Folkways 31502.
Songs to Grow On for Mother and Child. Folkways 7015.
Songs to Grow On. Folkways 7020. Sung by Jack Elliot.
Woody Guthrie's Children's Songs. Folkways 7503. Sung by Logan English.

HINTON, SAM
I'll Sing a Story. Folkways 7548.

IVES, BURL
Animal Folk. Disneyland 3920.

JENKINS, ELLA Jenkins works with games, songs, and play instruments in a systematic way that helps develop a child's rhythmic sense and his ability to control motor activities in a rhythmic way. *See* the Schwann or Folkways catalogue for her other records.
Rhythms of Childhood. Folkways 7653.
Jambo and Other Call and Response Songs and Chants. Folkways 7661. Based on African songs and rhythms.

LEADBELLY (Huddie Ledbetter)
Negro Folksongs for Young People. Folkways 7533. Songs from the repertory of one of the greatest figures in the traditional music of Black America. (*See also* page 17.)

LORD INVADER
There's a Brown Boy in the Ring. Folkways 7262. Calypso songs for children, by one of the best singer-composers.

MACCOLL, EWAN, AND DOMINIC BEHAN
The Singing Streets. Folkways 8501 (=*Streets of Song,* Topic 12 T 41). Two eminent singers—Scottish and Irish—reminisce about their childhoods in the streets of Glasgow and Dublin; with songs, games, and stories.

MCCURDY, ED
Children's Songs. Tradition 1027. With Billy Faier, banjo.

MILLS, ALAN
Number, Letter and Animal Songs. Folkways 7545.

NEW LOST CITY RAMBLERS
Old-Timey Songs for Children. Folkways 7064. The Ramblers are among the foremost young urban exponents of the old-time string band style of the southern mountains.

PIUTE PETE
Play-Party Dances for Young Folks. Folkways 7672.

RICHARDSON, JOHNNY
Children's Songs. Folkways 7678.

RITCHIE, JEAN Ritchie is an urbanized singer of Kentucky mountain origins who still sings in the pure old mountain way. Her recordings (*see* page 60) are documents of the role of music in the family life of isolated mountain communities. Children's songs were a major aspect of that musical life, and they constitute an important part of her rich repertory.
Children's Songs and Games from the Southern Mountains. Folkways 7054.
Marching Across the Ocean and Other Game Songs. Folkways 7702.

SEEGER, PEGGY
Animal Folksongs for Children. Folkways 7051.
American Folk Songs for Christmas. Folkways 7053. With Barbara and Penny Seeger.

SEEGER, PETE
Song and Play Time. Folkways 7526.
Folk Songs for Young People. Folkways 7532.
American Folk Songs for Children. Folkways 31501.
American Playparties. Folkways 7604.
Games and Activity Songs for Children. Folkways 7674.
Abiyoyo and Other Songs for Children. Folkways 31500.
Birds, Beasts, Bugs and Little Fishes. Folkways 31504.
Birds, Beasts and Bigger Fishes. Folkways 7611.
Children's Concert at Town Hall. Columbia CS 8747.

VINCENT, JENNY WELLS
Spanish-American Children's Songs. Cantemos 101.

THE WAGONERS
Folk Songs for Camp. Folkways 7030.

ANTHOLOGIES AND COLLECTIONS

Alabama Ring Games. Folkways 7004.

American Folk Songs for Children. Atlantic SD-1350. 1959 field recordings by Alan Lomax of songs for, or associated with, children. Some of our best traditional performers and song informants are on this record: Hobart Smith, Bessie Jones, Almeda Riddle, and others.

American Indian Music for the Classroom. Canyon Records (no number). A multivolume set, also available on tape, comprising a complete educational program. Various teaching aids are also available.

Chantons un peu. Dominion (Canadian) 1221. French and French-Canadian songs for children.

Children's Game Songs of French Canada. Folkways 7214.

Children's Jamaican Songs and Games. Folkways 7250.

Golden Slumbers. Caedmon 1399. A collection of lullabies from around the world, sung by Pete Seeger, Oscar Brand, and others.

Head Start. Folkways 2690. Children's songs from Mississippi, sung by participants in Head Start programs in the mid-sixties.

Indian Songs of Today. AFS L36. American Indian songs performed by the children of various tribes.

One, Two, Three and-a Zing Zing Zing. Folkways 7674. Location recordings of New York City street games.

THE WORLD OF POPULAR MUSIC Two four-record boxed sets, with students' and teachers' books, compiled by Sidney Fox and Thomas MacCluskey and available from Follett Publishing Company. An educational program for junior and senior high schools, concerned with both folk and pop music.
The World of Popular Music: Afro-American (XL 11). African music, spirituals, blues, rags, gospel music, etc., in addition to pop music. Reissues of earlier recordings by Bessie Smith, John Lee Hooker, Lightnin' Hopkins, and others.
The World of Popular Music (XL 12). Performances by Pete Seeger, Jean Ritchie, Poco, and other folk and pop musicians; some new and some reissued. Includes demonstrations of various instruments and instrumental styles.

FOLK TALES AND STORIES

American Indian Tales for Children, vols. 1–2. CMS 500, 501; cassettes 4500, 4501. Narrated by Anne Pellowski.
American Tall Tales, vols. 1–4. Edited by Adrien Stoutenburg; narrated by Ed Begley.
    Vol. 1, *John Henry and Joe Magarac.* Caedmon 1318; cassette 51318.
    Vol. 2, *Davy Crockett and Pecos Bill.* Caedmon 1319; cassette 51319.
    Vol. 3, *Mike Fink and Stormalong.* Caedmon 1320; cassette 51320.
    Vol. 4, *Johnny Appleseed and Paul Bunyan.* Caedmon 1321; cassette 51321.

The Enchanted Spring. Folkways 7753. American Indian folk tales.
English Folk and Fairy Tales. CMS 504; cassette 4504. From the Joseph Jacobs collection; narrated by Anne Pellowski.
Hopi Children's Tales. Folkways 7778.
Paul Bunyan in Story and Song. Caedmon 1275; cassette 51275. Narration by Ed Begley; songs by Oscar Brand.
Uncle Bouqui of Haiti. Folkways 7107.

II
LEARNING

INTRODUCTION

The following pages include the most significant books that have been published in the thirteen years since the first edition of *The Folk Music Sourcebook,* and focus on what seem to be the most significant trends in scholarship.

Most of the scholarly collections of folk music that appear these days are regional: the blues of the Carolinas, for example, as opposed to a general "book of the blues." There is also increased interest in such areas, little explored previously, as Cajun music and cowboy songs and poems.

There has been an explosion of reference books. The *Music in American Life* series of the University of Illinois Press, for example, has expanded from the handful of books reviewed in our original edition to dozens of important titles.

Biographical and autobiographical works have proliferated as well. Books have appeared about Joan Baez, Judy Collins, Woody Guthrie, Lee Hays, and Pete Seeger. The ever-enigmatic Bob Dylan is a subject for many writers.

Instruction books have become more specialized. One can find reliable materials on such particular subjects as clawhammer banjo, melodic style bluegrass banjo, or mountain fiddle music. Although many excellent books have appeared, errors reported thirteen years ago still persist. Printing music and tab on separate pages, printing complete arrangements in tab but only melody lines in notation, failing to place chord symbols over *both* the tab and music lines, and reversing the accustomed order of tab and music lines, all make reading difficult for the student.

As I played through dozens of instruction books, I saw that certain writers consistently use intelligent, progressively ordered examples, enabling the student to learn steadily without undue discouragement. I've indicated the books which are easiest to follow, particularly in what is basically an "ear" sort of music. Learning from a book rather than from actually living a musical tradition is at best a difficult task.

Artists, publishers, folk music centers and instrument makers have appeared and vanished over the years, but it is my feeling that today's acoustic music is solidly grounded in the marketplace. The aspiring player can look forward to hours of pleasure working with even a few of the materials listed here. Our goal is to be a reliable guide to choosing from those which are currently available.

(—D.W.)

SONG BOOKS

COLLECTIONS OF SONGS

Most of the collections in this section have song texts with melody lines and chord symbols, except as noted.

ALLEN, LIND, *Washington Songs and Lore,* Melior, 1988, 186 pp.

BLOOD-PATTERSON, PETER, ed., *Rise Up Singing,* Sing Out!, 1988, 278 pp. A massive collection. Chords, no melodies.

BRIGHT MORNING STARS, World Around Songs, 1984, 72 pp. Handy vest-pocket format.

CANNON, HAL, ed., *Old-Time Cowboy Songs,* Peregrine Smith Books, 1988, 120 pp. Fifty favorite cowboy songs. Melodies and chords. Instrument-case format. A cassette by the Bunkhouse Orchestra contains enjoyable performances of twelve of the songs. Cannon is one of the folklorists specializing in this genre. *See* the *Cowboy Poetry and Song* section under REFERENCE BOOKS below.

CHEYNEY, THOMAS E. and WILLIAM I. KAUFMAN, ed., *The Mormon Pioneer Songbook,* Theodore Presser, 1980, 48 pp. Thirty-three songs, with chords and four-part vocal arrangements.

GETZ, C.L., ed., *The Wild Blue Yonder: Songs of the Air Force,* Redwood Press, 2 vols., 1981/1986. Cassette available.

HULLFISH, WILLIAM, *The Canaller's Songbook,* American Canal and Transportation Center, 1988, 88 pp. Attractive illustrations.

PANKAKE, MARCIA and JOHN PANKAKE, *A Prairie Home Companion Folk Song Book,* Viking-Penguin, 1988, 316 pp. Over 300 songs.

PETERS, HARRY B., *Folk Songs Out of Wisconsin: An Illustrated Compendium of Words and Music,* Wisconsin State Historical Society, 1977, 311 pp., Melodies, no chords.

SEEGER, PETE and BOB REISER, *Carry It On: A History in Song and Pictures of the Working Men and Women of America,* Simon & Schuster, 1985, 256 pp. A follow-up to Seeger's earlier *Hard Hitting Songs for Hard Hit People.*

WARNER, ANNE, *Traditional American Folk Songs from the Anne and Frank Warner Collection,* Syracuse University Press, 1984, 501 pp. Melody lines, no chords.

WENNER, HILDA E. and ELIZABETH FRELICHER, *Here's to the Women: 100 Songs For and About American Women,* Syracuse University Press, 1987, 352 pp. An important book, extensively annotated and illustrated.

REFERENCE BOOKS

GENERAL

American Folklore Films and Videotapes: An Index, Center for Southern Folklore, 1976, 338 pp. Huge and valuable. A video update is in preparation at this writing; a film update is needed too.

ANDERSON, GILLIAN B., ed., *Freedom's Voice in Poetry and Song: An Inventory of Political and Patriotic Hymns in Colonial American Newspapers,* Scholarly Resources, 1977, 1580 pp.

BARTIS, PETER T. and BARBARA C. FERTOG, eds., *Folklife Sourcebook: A Directory of Folklife Resources in the United States and Canada,* American Folklife Center, Library of Congress, 1986, 152 pp. Organizations, resources, archives, educational programs, etc. Invaluable.

BRUNNINGS, FLORENCE E., *A Comprehensive Guide to the Florence E. Brunnings Collection,* Garland, 440 pp.

CUTHBERT, JOHN, *West Virginia Folk Music: A Descriptive Guide to Field Recordings in the West Virginia and Regional Historical Collection.* West Virginia University Press, 1982, 185 pp.

DE LERMA, DOMINIQUE-RENE, *Bibliography of Black Music: Vol. 2, Afro-American Idioms,* Greenwood Press, 1981, 220 pp.

FEINTUCH, BURT, *Kentucky Folkmusic: An Annotated Bibliography,* University of Kentucky Press, 1985, 185 pp. Collections, studies, festivals, discographies, etc.

FLANAGAN, CATHLEEN and JOHN FLANAGAN, *American Folklore: A Bibliography 1950-1974*, Scarecrow, 1977, 412 pp.

FLOYD, SAMUEL A., JR. and MARSHA J. REISSER, *Black Music in the United States: An Annotated Bibliography of Selected References and Research Materials*, Kraus-Thompson, 1983, 234 pp.

HARRIS, SHELDON, *Blues Who's Who: A Biographical Dictionary of Blues Singers*, DaCapo Press, 1981, 775 pp. Bios, pictures, media listings; songs, and more. A must for blues scholars and fans.

HART, MARY L., LISA N. HOWORTH and BRENDA M. EAGLES, *The Blues: A Bibliographic Guide*, Garland, 1989, 500 pp.

HORN, DAVID, *The Literature of American Music in Books and Folk Music Collections: A Fully Annotated Bibliography*, Scarecrow, 1977, 556 pp.

KANAHALE, GEORGE S., ed., *Hawaiian Music and Musicians*, University of Hawaii Press, 1979, 543 pp.

KERSET, CATHERINE HIEBERT, *Ethnic Folklife Dissertations from the United States and Canada, 1960-1980: A Selected, Annotated Bibliography*. American Folklife Center, 1986, 69 pp.

KRUMMEL, D.W., *Bibliographical Handbook of American Music*, University of Illinois Press, 1987, 269 pp. An important resource.

LORNELL, KIP, *Virginia's Blues, Gospel and Country Records, 1923-1943*, University of Kentucky Press, 1989.

MILLER, TERRY, *Folk Music in America: A Reference Guide*, Garland, 449 pp.

OLIVER, PAUL, MAX HARRISON and WILLIAM BOLCOM, *The New Grove Gospel, Blues and Jazz with Spirituals and Ragtime*, W.W. Norton, 1986, 393 pp. Good general guide.

ROACH, HILDRED, *Black American Music: Past and Present*, Robert E. Krieger Co., 1985, 2 vols.

RUST, BRIAN, *The American Record Label Book: From the 19th Century through 1942*, Da Capo Press, 1984, 336 pp.

SEEGER, ANTHONY and LOUISE SPEAR, eds., *Early Field Recordings: Cylinder Collection of the Indiana University Archive of Traditional Music*, Indiana University Press, 1987. Mostly American Indian material.

SKOWRONSKI, JOHN, *Black Music in America: A Bibliography*, Scarecrow, 1981, 723 pp.

SMYTH, WILLIE, compiler, *Country Music Recorded Prior to 1943: A Discography of LP Reissues*, John Edwards Memorial Foundation, 1984, 83 pp.

STAMBLER, IRWIN and G. LANDUN, *Encyclopedia of Folk, Country and Western Music*, 2nd ed., St. Martin's Press, 1984, 902 pp.

SZWED, JOHN F. and ROGER D. ABRAHAMS, *Afro-American Folk Culture: An Annotated Bibliography of Materials from North, Central and South America and the West Indies*, Institute of Human Learning, 1978, 2 vols.

TAFT, MICHAEL, *Blues Lyric Poetry: A Concordance*, Garland, 1983, 3 vols.

TURNER, PATRICIA, *A Dictionary of Afro-American Performers: 78 RPM and Cylinder Recordings of Opera, Choral Music and Song, circa 1900 to 1949*, Garland, 1988, 200 pp.

WASSERMAN, PAUL and ALICE G. KENNINGTON, eds., *Ethnic Informa-tion Sources of the United States*, Gale Research, 1983, revised ed., 2 vols. Organizations, records and books.

WILLIAMS, BRETT, *John Henry: A Bio-Bibliography*, Greenwood Press, 1983, 175 pp.

WRIGHT, JOHN, *Ralph Stanley and the Clinch Mountain Boys: A Discography*, Evanston, IL, unpaged, 1983.

AMERICAN INDIAN MUSIC AND TALES

BIERHORST, JOHN, ed., collected by EDWARD CURTIS, *The Girl Who Married a Ghost and Other Tales from the North American Indian*, Four Winds Press, 1978, 110 pp. Includes photos by Curtis.

DE CESARE, RUTH, *Myths, Music and Dance of the American Indian*, Alfred, 1988, 51 pp. Material from 21 tribes, with suggested activities for children.

HANDBOOK OF NORTH AMERICAN INDIANS, 20-volume series, Smithsonian Institution, series began in 1978.

HINTON, LEANNE and LUCILLE WATAHOMIGIE, eds., *Spirit Mountain: An Anthology of Yuman Story and Song*, University of Arizona Press, 1984, 344 pp.

MCALLISTER, DAVID and SUSAN MCALLISTER, *Hogans: Navajo Houses & Songs*, Wesleyan University Press, 1980, 113 pp. Songs, stories and photos; beautifully designed.

SWEET, JILL D., *Dances of the Tewa Pueblo Indians*, School of American Research Press, 1985, 99 pp.

BLACK MUSIC

BARLOW, WILLIAM BROOK, *Voices from the Heartland: A Cultural History of the Blues*, UMI Research Press, 1986, 607 pp. The influence of the blues on other idioms.

BASTIN, BURCE, *Red River Blues*, University of Illinois Press, 1986, 379 pp. A meticulous scholarly study of the Carolina blues, a bit dry.

CHARTERS, SAMUEL, *Sweet as the Showers of Rain*, Oak, 1977, 178 pp. Biographies of blues artists, mostly based on secondary sources.

CHARTERS, SAMUEL, *The Legacy of the Blues: Art and Lives of Twelve Great Bluesmen*, Da Capo Press, 1977, 192 pp. Great may be an exaggeration for some of these artists.

CHARTERS, SAMUEL, *The Roots of the Blues: An African Search*, Perigee, 1982, 151 pp. A quest in search of blues roots, wherein Charters finds one great song about the early slave trade. Much detail about his odyssey in the hot sun.

DJEDJE, JACQUELINE COGDELL, *American Black Spiritual and Gospel Songs from Southeast Georgia: A Comparative Study*, Center for Afro-American Studies, University of California Press, 1978, 105 pp.

EPSTEIN, DENA J., *Sinful Tunes and Spirituals: Black Folk Music to the Civil War*, University of Illinois Press, 1977, 433 pp. An impressive work of scholarship.

EVANS, DAVID, *Big Road Blues: Tradition and Creativity in the Folk Blues*, Da Capo Press, 1988, 396 pp. Evans always sees the broader picture. He feels that creativity is often embodied in "links in the chain" rather than individual genius.

FERRIS, WILLIAM, *Blues from the Delta*, Da Capo Press, 1988, 226 pp.

Unpretentious, enjoyable book about Ferris's collecting experiences.

GARAN, PAUL, *Blues and the Poetic Spirit,* Da Capo Press, 1979, 178 pp. Garan sees the blues as subversive in a broad sense, and therefore aligned with surrealism.

GURALNICK, PETER, *The Listener's Guide to the Blues,* Facts on File, 1982, 134 pp. Brief, useful guide by a thoughtful, reliable writer.

HARRISON, DAPHNE DUVAL, *Black Pearls: Blues Queens of the 1920's,* Rutgers University Press, 1988, 295 pp. Song texts are interwoven with the narrative. Beautifully reproduced photos.

HAYDON, GEOFFREY and DENNIS MARKS, eds., *Repercussions: A Celebration of African-American Music,* Century Publishers, 1985, 182 pp. Mostly about African and West Indian music.

LEVINE, LAWRENCE W., *Black Culture and Black Consciousness,* Oxford University Press, 1977, 522 pp. An interpretation of black culture largely through music and folklore.

LIEB, SANDRA, *Mother of the Blues: A Study of Ma Rainey,* University of Massachusetts Press, 1981, 226 pp. Careful tracing of the rich life of a major blues artists.

LORNELL, KIP, *Happy in the Service of the Lord: Afro-American Gospel Quartets in Memphis,* University of Illinois Press, 1988, 171 pp. Many interesting details, yet somehow leaves you wanting more.

MCKEE, MARGARET and CHISENHALL, FRED, *Beale Black and Blue: Life and Music on America's Street,* Louisiana State University Press, 1981, 265 pp. A history of the Beale Street blues through the eyes of participants.

MURRAY, ALBERT, *Stomping the Blues,* Vintage, 1982, 264 pp. About jazz as well as folk blues. An impressionistic interpretation with fine, well-reproduced photos.

OAKLEY, GILES, *The Devil's Music: A History of the Blues,* Harvest, 1976, 287 pp. Useful, with attractive, relevant photos.

OLIVER, PAUL, *Blues Off the Record: Thirty Years of Blues Commentary,* Da Capo Press, 1984, 297 pp. Short pieces.

OLIVER, PAUL, *Songsters & Saints: Vocal Traditions on Race Records,* Cambridge University Press, 1984, 339 pp. Encyclopedic, useful discussion of blues and gospel. Many lyrics. Four correlated LP's available on the British Matchbox label.

PALMER, ROBERT, *Deep Blues,* Viking Press, 1981, 310 pp. An eloquent book on the Mississippi blues tradition and its successors.

SACRE, ROBERT, ed., *The Voice of the Delta: Charley Patton and the Mississippi Blues Traditions, Influences and Comparisons,* Liege, Belgium, Presses Universitaires, 1987, 2nd ed., 345 pp. Includes extensive research by David Evans on Patton's life, and articles by other scholars, several in French. An amazing book.

SMALL, CHRISTOPHER, *Music of the Common Tongue,* Riverrun Press, 1987, 495 pp. An outstanding interpretation of the meaning and emotional basis of Afro-American music.

TITON, JEFF TODD, *Early Downhome Blues,* University of Illinois Press, 1987, 296 pp. A worthwhile analysis.

WALKER, WYATT TEE, *Somebody's Calling My Name: Black Sacred Music and Social Change.* Judson, 1979, 208 pp. Useful charts, and a detailed analysis of themes in religious music.

CAJUN MUSIC

ALLAN, JOHNNIE, compiler, *Memories: A Pictorial History of South Louisiana Music, 1920's-1980's. Vol. 1: South Louisiana and East Texas Musicians,* Jadfel, 1988, 269 pp. This extensive picture book on the roots of Cajun and "swamp" music is clearly a labor of love.

ANCELET, BARRY JEAN, *The Makers of Cajun Music,* University of Texas Press, 1984, 160 pp. Text in English and French, beautiful color photos, interviews with important figures.

BROVEN, JOHN, *South to Louisiana: The Music of the Cajun Bayous,* Pelican, 1983, 368 pp. A detailed history: essential reading.

SAVOY, ANN, *Cajun Music: A Reflection of a People, Vol. 1,* Bluebird Press, 1984, 419 pp. Mostly a songbook, with interviews and background. An important book.

CANADIAN FOLKSONGS AND FOLKLORE

FOWKE, EDITH and CAROLE HENDERSON CARPENTER, *A Bibliography of Canadian Folklore in English,* University of Toronto Press, 1981, 272 pp.

FOWKE, EDITH, *Canadian Foklore,* Oxford University Press, 1984, 149 pp. A brief, useful survey.

HALPERT, HERBERT, ed., *A Folklore Sampler from the Maritimes,* Memorial University Division of Folklore, 1982, 273 pp.

KALLMAN, HELMUT, GILLES POTVIN and KENNETH WINTERS, eds., *Encyclopedia of Music in Canada,* University of Toronto Press, 1981, 1076 pp. Includes all idioms.

KURATH, GERTRUDE PROKOSCH, *Tutelo Rituals on Six Nations Reserve, Society for Ethnomusicology,* University of Michigan, 1981, 119 pp.

LEHR, GENEVIEVE, ed., *Come and I Will Sing You: A Newfoundland Songbook,* University of Toronto Press, 1985, 210 pp. 120 tunes, some not published in other collections.

MCGEE, TIMOTHY, *The Music of Canada,* Norton-Penguin, 257 pp. 1985. Includes social background.

MCGREGOR, ARTHUR, ed., *Coast to Coast Fever: A Collection of Canadian Songs for Guitar,* OFC Publications, 1981, 72 pp. Songs by Bruce Cockburn, Sylvia Tyson, Connie Kaldor, etc.

MERCER, PAUL, compiler, *Newfoundland Songs and Ballads in Print, 1842-1974,* Memorial University Division of Folklore, 1979. 343 pp. A directory.

O'DONNELL, JOHN, *The Men of the Deeps,* Waterloo Music, 1975, 62 pp. Melody lines and chords. An attractive collection of mining songs. Record available from the publisher.

QUIGLEY, COLIN, *Close to the Floor: Folk Dance in Newfoundland,* Memorial University Divsion of Folklore, 1985, 127 pp.

THOMAS, GERALD, compiler, *Songs Sung by French Newfoundlanders,* Memorial University Division of Folklore, 1978, 93 pp.

THOMAS, PHILIP J., *Songs of the Pacific Northwest,* Hancock House, 1979, 161 pp. 49 songs: melodies, chords and background information.

USHER, BILL and LINDA PAGE-HARPA, eds., *For What Time I Am in This World: Stories from Mariposa,* Peter Martin Associates, 1977, 226 pp. Stories, reminiscences, and thoughtful comments by performers at the Mariposa Folk Festival.

WHITE, NANCY, *Topical Punch: Saucy Songs by Nancy White,*

Methuen, 1986, 144 pp. Pithy satirical songs by the CBC songstress; only thirteen printed with tunes and chords.

HISPANIC-AMERICAN MATERIALS

PAREDES, AMERICO, *A Texas-Mexican Caneionero: Folksongs of the Lower Border.* University of Illinois Press, 1976, 194 pp. Old and contemporary songs with melodies and chords. An important book.

ROBB, JOHN DONALD, *Hispanic Folk Music of New Mexico and the Southwest: A Self-Portrait of a People,* University of Oklahoma Press, 1980, 891 pp. An essential book, representing a lifetime of work.

WEST, JOHN O., ed., *Mexican-American Folklore,* August House, 1988, 314 pp. Folklore, songs and games.

OTHER ETHNIC GROUPS

AMERICAN FOLKLIFE CENTER, *Ethnic Recordings in America: A Neglected Heritage,* Library of Congress, 1982, 269 pp. Essays and discography.

BURLINGAME, BURL and ROBERT D. KASHER, *Da Kine Sound: Conversations With the People Who Create Hawaiian Music,* Pacific Press, 1978, 174 pp. Interviews with twelve contemporary Hawaiian musicians.

GEORGE, LUVENIA A., *Teaching the Music of Six Different Cultures,* World Music Press, 1977, revised and updated, 126 pp. A must for teachers. Covers Black, Native American, Jewish, Hawaiian, Mexican and Puerto Rican music.

JESSUP, LYNNE, *World Music: A Source Book for Teaching World Music,* World Music Press, 1988, 64 pp. A wonderful resource for teachers: books, records, video and more.

KAEPPLER, ADRIENNE L., *Polynesian Dance,* Bishop Museum Press, 1983, 110 pp., cassette available.

MARTIN, PHIL, *Across the Fields: Fiddle Tunes and Button Accordion Traditional Norwegian-American Music from Wisconsin,* Old-Time Music Project, 1982, 48 pp. Includes material never before in print. Correlated LP available.

SILVERMAN, JERRY, *The Yiddish Song Book,* Saw Mill Publicatons, dist. by Theodore Presser, 1983, 204 pp. Melodies and chords, text in English and Yiddish, photos, some background.

SONGBOOKS AND OTHER MATERIALS FOR CHILDREN

CARLIN, RICHARD, *English and American Folk Music,* Facts on File, 1987, 118 pp. A brief but informative guide for secondary students. Photos and musical examples.

FOX, DAN, *Go In and Out the Window,* Metropolitan Museum of Art, 1987, 144 pp. Simple piano arrangements with chords and excellent reproductions of paintings.

FOWKE, EDITH, *Ring Around the Moon,* Prentice Hall, 1977, 160 pp. Canadian children's folklore with songs.

FULTON, ELEANOR and PAT SMITH, *Let's Slice the Ice: A Collection of Black Children's Ring Games and Chants,* Magnamusic-Baton, 1978, 56 pp.

HASKINS, JAMES, *Black Music in America: A History through Its People,* Thomas Y. Crowell, 1987, 198 pp. A good introduction to blues, jazz, and gospel music for secondary students.

HENRY, CAROL, *Very Favorites of the Very Young: Songs for 3-6 Year Olds,* World Around Songs, 1986, 71 pp. Melodies and chords. Convenient small format.

OPIE, IONA and PETER OPIE, *The Singing Games,* Oxford University Press, 1985. 148 songs, melodies, no chords. Includes descriptions of the games.

SNOW, BARBARA, *Index of Songs on Children's Recordings,* Staccato Press, 1988, 68 pp.

SURGE, FRANK, *Singers of the Blues,* Lerner Publications, 1981, 63 pp. Short biographies of seventeen blues singers.

BOOKS ABOUT FOLK MUSIC

ALVEY, GERALD R., *Dulcimer Maker: The Craft of Homer Ledford,* University of Kentucky Press, 1984, 186 pp.

BAEZ, JOAN, *And a Voice to Sing With,* New American Library, 1987, 378 pp. Many loose ends in this odd, flighty, yet occasionally deep life story.

BERMAN, LESLIE and HEATHER WOOD, eds., *Grass Roots International Folk Resource Directory,* Grass Roots Productions, N.Y., 1986, 232 pp. A wealth of information though no index.

BLAKE, BENJAMIN, JACK RUBECK and ALLAN SHAW, *The Kingston Trio on Record,* Kingston Korner, Inc., 1986, 272 pp. A history and appreciation of the trio by some avid fans and fellow musicians.

BOHLMAN, PHILIP J., *The Study of Folk Music in the Modern World,* Indiana University Press, 1988, 159 pp. A study of the origin, evolution and development of folk music. The author has a keen awareness of the role of key individuals in the shaping of unusual traditions.

BLACKWELL, LOIS S., *The Wings of the Dove: The Story of Gospel Music in America,* Donning, 1978, 173 pp. An important history of white gospel music.

BURTON, THOMAS, *Some Ballad Folks,* East Tennessee State University Press, 1978, 108 pp. Five female ballad singers from Beech Mountain, North Carolina. Cassette available.

BURTON, THOMAS G., ed., *Tennessee Traditional Singers,* University of Tennessee Press, 1981, 240 pp. Studies of Tom Ashley, Sam McGee and Bukka White, three important musicians.

COBB, BUELL E., JR., *The Sacred Harp: A Tradition and Its Music,* University of Georgia Press, 1978, 245 pp.

CAUTHEN, JOYCE H., *With Fiddle and Well-Rosined Bow: Old-Time Fiddling in Alabama,* University of Alabama Press, 1989, 282 pp. A history based on interviews. No music, many photos.

COLLINS, JUDY, *Trust Your Heart: An Autobiography,* Houghton Mifflin, 1987, 275 pp. More about her life than about music. Like Baez, Collins battles between her feminist desire to take charge of her own career and her need to be taken care of by others.

COUNTRY MUSIC FOUNDATION, *Country, the Music and the Musicians,* Abbeville Press, 1988. A massive book with many pictures.

DUNAWAY, DAVID KING, *How Can I Keep from Singing: Pete Seeger,*

McGraw-Hill, 1981, 386 pp. Some interesting social history, marred by the author's attempts to psychoanalyze his subject.

FERRIS, WILLIAM and MARY L. HART, eds., *Folk Music and Modern Sound,* University Press of Mississippi, 1982, 215 pp. Fifteen articles about the shape of folk music today by Anthony Heilbut, Charles V. Wolfe and others. Stimulating and sometimes opinionated.

GARLAND, JIM, edited by JULIA S. ARDERY, *Welcome the Traveler Home: Jim Garland's Story of the Kentucky Mountains,* University of Kentucky Press, 1983, 231 pp. A fascinating social history in the form of the life story of this ex-miner and protest singer.

GUNTHARP, MATTHEW G., *Learning the Fiddler's Ways,* Pennsylvania State University Press, 1980, 159 pp. Includes transcriptions without chords, and descriptions of styles. A fine book.

HAGGARD, MERLE, with PEGGY RUSSELL, *Sing Me Back Home, Time-scape Books, 1981, 287 pp.*

HIGH, ELLESA CLAY, *Past Titan's Rock: Journeys into an Appalachian Valley,* University of Kentucky Press, 1984, 183 pp. A colorful book about mountain culture, including extensive interviews with Lily Mae Ledford of the Coon Creek Gals.

HOOD, PHIL, *Artists of American Folk Music: The Legends of Traditional Folk, the Stars of the Sixties, the Virtuosi of New Acoustic Music,* William Morrow, 1986, 159 pp. Articles, interviews and pictures.

HOSKYNS, BARRY, *Say It One More Time for the Broken-Hearted: The Country-Side of Southern Soul,* Fontana/Collins, 1987, 239 pp. A fascinating study of the white roots of soul. Most work has been done in the opposite direction.

HUME, MARTHA, *You're So Cold I'm Turning Blue: Guide to the Greatest in Country Music,* Viking/Penguin, 1982, 202 pp.

IVES, EDWARD D., *Joe Scott: The Woodsman-Songster,* University of Illinois Press, 1978, 473 pp. Cassette available. Scott was a prolific poet-balladeer. Ives reconstructs his life and the backgrounds of his songs.

JONES, BESSIE, *For the Ancestors: Autobiographical Memories,* collected and edited by John Stewart, University of Illinois Press, 1983, 203 pp. From the great resource of Georgia Sea Island song and lore.

JONES, LOYAL, *Radio's Kentucky Mountain Boy: Bradley Kincaid,* Appalachian Center, Berea College, revised edition, 1988, 193 pp. Words, music, and chords to fifty songs.

JONES, LOYAL, *Minstrel of the Appalachians: The Story of Bascom Lamar Lunsford,* Appalachian Consortium Press, 1982, 249 pp. Lunsford, a lawyer-turned-musician, collector, and promoter, was a difficult but respected man. Includes several songs.

JONES, LOUIS M. "GRANDPA" with CHARLES K. WOLFE, *Everybody's Grandpa Fifty Years Behind the Mike,* University of Tennessee Press, 1984, 288 pp.

KIENZELE, RICH, *Great Guitarists: The Most Influential Players in Blues, Country Music and Rock,* Facts on File, 1985, 246 pp.

KLEIN, JOE, *Woody Guthrie: A Life,* Ballantine Books, 1980, 476 pp. The well-written, real story of a difficult and brilliant man.

KOCHMAN, MARILYN, ed., *The Big Book of Bluegrass,* Quill, 1985, 246 pp. Artists, history, many photos. An attractive book.

LEACH, ROBERT and ROY PALMER, *Folk Music in School,* Cambridge University Press, 1987, 162 pp. Using folksongs in the classroom.

LOMAX, JOHN III, *Nashville "Music City, USA,"* Harry N. Abrams, 1985, 224 pp. A large book, mostly photos.

LYLE, KATIE LETCHER, *Scalded to Death by the Steam: Authentic Stories of Railroad Disasters and the Ballads That Were Written about Them,* Algonquin, 1988, 212 pp.

MALONE, BILL C., *Southern Music, American Music,* University of Kentucky Press, 1979, 203 pp. Brief, well-informed.

MCCUE, GEORGE, eds., *Music in American Society; 1776-1976: From Puritan Hymn to Synthesizer,* Transaction Books, 1977, 201 pp.

MELLERS, WILFRED, *A Darker Shade of Pale: A Backdrop to Bob Dylan,* Oxford University Press, 1985, 255 pp. An interesting if odd attempt to bring Dylan into the scholarly mainstream, marred by questionable omissions and assertions. (I wouldn't describe Robert Johnson as "neurotic"!)

PARIS, MIKE and CHRIS COMBER, *Jimmie the Kid: The Life of Jimmie Rodgers,* Da Capo, 1977, 211 pp.

PORTERFIELD, NOLAN, *Jimmie Rodgers: The Life & Times of America's Blue Yodeler,* University of Illinois Press, 1979, 460 pp. The Paris-Comber book is a brief biography emphasizing black influences on Rodgers, while the Porterfield book is much more detailed.

RODNITZKY, JEROME L., *Minstrels of the Dawn: The Protest Singer as a Cultural Hero,* Nelson-Hall, 1976, 192 pp. An adequate if uninspired study of Baez, Dylan, Guthrie and Ochs.

ROGERS, JIMMIE N., *The Country Music Message: All About Lovin' and Leavin',* Prentice-Hall, 1983, 182 pp. Content analysis of country music lyrics.

ROSENBAUM, ART, *Folk Vision and Voices: Traditional Music and Song in North Georgia,* University of Georgia Press, 1983, 240 pp. A wonderful book: paintings by the author, photos by his wife, and songs and interviews with folk artists.

ROSENBERG, NEIL V., *Bluegrass: A History,* University of Illinois Press, 1985, 447 pp. A well-informed history.

SABLOSKY, IRVING, *What They Heard: Music in America 1852-1881, From the Pages of Dwight's Journal of Music,* Louisiana State University Press, 1986, 331 pp.

SCHWARTZ, ELLEN, *Born a Woman,* Polester Press, 1988, 158 pp. An interesting study of seven Canadian women singer-songwriters.

SEEGER, CHARLES, *Studies in Musicology, 1933-1975,* University of California Press, 1977, 357 pp. Difficult, far-reaching essays.

SHELTON, ROBERT, *No Direction Home: The Life and Music of Bob Dylan,* William Morrow, 1986, 573 pp. Shelton was a friend and early supporter of Dylan.

SIEGEL, DOROTHY SCHAINMAN, *Glory Road: The Story of Josh White,* Harcourt Brace Jovanovich, 1982, 160 pp. An affecting story, from the blues singer's impoverished childhood to his appearance before the Un-American Activities Committee and his repudiation by the radical movement.

TAWA, NICHOLAS, *A Sound of Strangers: Musical Culture, Acculturation and the Post-Civil War Ethnic American,* Scarecrow, 1982, 318 pp.

TOWNSEND, CHARLES R., *San Antonio Rose: The Life and Music of*

Bob Wills, University of Illinois Press, 1976, 395 pp. Detailed and well-documented.

TSAMURA, AKIRA T., *Banjos: The Tsamura Collection,* 1984, and *Guitars: The Tsamura Collection,* 1987, Kodansha International, dist. by Harper and Row. Two beautiful photo books of a major collection.

THOMSON, RYAN J., *The Fiddler's Almanac,* Captain Fiddle Publications, 1985, 138 pp. Tips on learning, buying, contests, etc.

TRIBE, IVAN M., *Mountaineer Jamboree: Country Music in West Virginia,* University of Kentucky Press, 1984, 223 pp. The first book to detail the influence of radio on country music.

VON SCHMIDT, ERIC and JIM ROONEY, *Baby Let Me Follow You Down: The Illustrated History of the Cambridge Folk Years,* Anchor, 1979, 314 pp. An entertaining if somewhat superficial book about the folk revival. Mostly it's wine, women, drugs, and song.

WEBB, ROBERT LLOYD, *Ring The Banjer! The Banjo in America: From Folklore to Factory,* MIT Museum, 1981, 101 pp. Articles on the history of the banjo with thirty pages of photos. Delightful.

WILLENS, DORIS, *Lonesome Traveler: The Life of Lee Hays,* W. W. Norton, 1988, 281 pp. An informed and sympathetic biography of a difficult, important figure in the folk music revival.

WILLOUGHBY, LARRY, *Texas Rhythm Texas Rhyme: A Pictorial History of Texas Music,* Texas Monthly Press, 1984, 144 pp.

WOLFE, CHARLES K., *Kentucky Country Folk and Country Music,* University of Kentucky Press, 1982, 199 pp. An entertaining history. Correlated Rounder Records album available.

WOLFE, CHARLES K., *Tennessee Strings: The Story of Country Music in Tennessee,* University of Tennessee Press, 1977, 118 pp.

WOLLIVER, ROBBIE, *Bringing It All Back Home: 25 Years of American Folk Music at Folk City,* Pantheon, 1986, 258 pp.

WRIGHT, JOHN, ed., *It's the Hardest Music in the World to Play: The Ralph Stanley Story in His Own Words,* Beaver Valley Press, 1988, 24 pp. Sincere and revealing life-history of the bluegrass musician.

COWBOY POETRY AND SONG

In the late nineteenth century the work of cowboy poets like Badger Clark, D.J. O'Malley, and (somewhat later) Bruce Kiskadoon was popular all over the west. During the 1970's, folklorists discovered that cowboys were still writing poetry, and an artist/fieldworker named Sarah Sweetwater arranged for some of her subjects to recite at a small folklife festival in Elko, Nevada.

Soon Hal Cannon and other folklorists of the western states were concentrating on the preservation of cowboy poetry and song. During the 1980's the small Elko festival became the large Cowboy Gathering. Cowboys and fans come from all over the west during four days in January, and smaller versions are held in other states as well. Some of the poets have had success giving performances elsewhere, publishing their own books, or mixing their poems with songs on cassettes.

I've tried in a short space to give the reader a taste of what is available. The best source of material is the Western Folklife Center, P.O. Box 81005, Salt Lake City, UT, 84108. In addition, cassettes of performances at the Cowboy Gathering are available

Only cowboys sit like this.

through Worldwide Communications, 320 Stewart Street, Reno, NV 89502.

BLACK, BAXTER, *Coyote Cowboy Poetry,* Coyote Cowboy Co., 1986, 202 pp. A well-designed and illustrated collection by perhaps the most professional of the cowboy poets.

BLACK, BAXTER, *Croutons on a Cow Pie,* 1988, Coyote Cowboy Co., 58 pp. A more modest collection. Cassettes of Black reading and singing are available from the same source.

CANNON, HAL, ed., *Cowboy Poetry: A Gathering,* Peregrine Smith Books, 1985, 199 pp. The best introduction to the idiom, from the nineteenth century to today. Extensive bibliography.

CLARK, BADGER, *Badger Clark Ballads: Selected Works of a Cowboy Poet, with Music by J.E. Morhardt,* Westerners International, 1982, 55 pp.

COOLIDGE, DANE, *Texas Cowboys,* University of Arizona Press, 1981. Reprint of 1937 book, 162 pp. Stories about the west with two chapters on songs, no music.

DARY, DAVID, *Cowboy Culture: A Saga of Five Centuries,* Knopf, 1981, 384 pp.

EDWARDS, DON, *Guitars and Saddle Songs,* Sevenshoux Publishing, no date, 64 pp.

EDWARDS, DON, *Songs of the Cowboy,* Sevenshoux Publishing, 1986, 69 pp. Small guitar-case sized collections of original and traditional songs. Cassettes available. A good singer with a pleasant, straightforward voice.

FLETCHER, CURLY, *Songs of the Sage: The Poetry of Curly Fletcher,* Peregrine Smith Books, 1986, 74 pp. By one of the classic writers, with a well-informed introduction by Hal Cannon.

HUGHES, STELLA, ed., *Hashknife Cowboy: Recollections of Mack Hughes,* University of Arizona Press, 1985, 234 pp.

HORSE SENSE, *Fences, Barbed Wire and Walls.* Kicking Mule cassette or album 338. Horse Sense are a duo who perform polished versions of cowboy and western songs.

JORDAN, TERESA, *Cowgirls: Women of the American West: An Oral History,* Anchor, 1982, 301 pp.

KISKADOON, BRUCE, *Rhymes of the Ranges,* ed. by Hal Cannon, Peregrine Smith, 1987, 136 pp. The influential Kiskadoon was an authentic cowboy, yet most of these poems were later in life, when he was a bellhop in Los Angeles.

LEE, KATIE, *Ten Thousand Goddam Cattle: A History of the American Cowboy in Song, Story and Verse,* Northland Press, 1976, 257 pp. Entertaining tales of the author's quest for the ghost town of Delores. Lots of stories, song texts, illustrations, and some tunes.

MARSHALL, HOWARD W. and RICHARD E. AHLBORN, *Buckaroos in Paradise: Cowboy Life in Northern Nevada,* University of Nebraska Press, 1981, 95 pp.

MCRAE, WALLACE, *Up North Is Down the Crick,* Museum of the Rockies, 1985, 59 pp.

MCRAE, WALLACE, *It's Just Grass and Water,* Oxalis Group, 1986, 44 pp. McRae is a polished performer and poet. His work has a hard edge that comes from long reflection and evident sincerity.

TINSLEY, JIM BOB, *He Was Singin' This Song: A Collection of Forty-Eight Traditional Songs of the American Cowboy, with Words, Pictures and Stories,* University of Florida Press, 1981, 255 pp. Melody lines, chords, and background. A fine collection.

Note: Hal Cannon's *Old Time Cowboy Songs,* listed in the *Collections of Songs* section, has an extensive bibliography. The group Riders in the Sky is a sort of wacky modern Sons of the Pioneers, with a radio theatre show on PBS, and a number of albums. Randy Erwin is a smooth cowboy-style singer on Four Dots Records. Excellent cowboy music reissue albums are: Historical Records' *The Plains of Alberta* and Morning Star Records' *When I Was A Cowboy.* The National Council for the Traditional Arts has an excellent cassette called *The Cowboy Tour,* with songs and poetry by several performers.

SCHOLARLY COLLECTIONS

BAYARD, SAMUEL P., ed., *Dance to the Fiddle, March to the Fife: Instrumental Folk Tunes in Pennsylvania,* Pennsylvania State University Press, 1982, 628 pp. 651 tunes collected over 35 years. No chords.

BETHKE, ROBERT D., *Adirondack Voices: Woodsmen and Woods Lore,* University of Illinois Press, 1981, 148 pp.

BRONNER, SIMON J., *Old-Time Music Makers of New York State,* Syracuse University Press, 1987, 252 pp. Forty-five songs: melodies, no chords.

BROWNE, RAY B., *The Alabama Folk Lyric: A Study in Origins and Media of Dissemination,* Bowling Green University Popular Press, 1979, 480 pp. 192 songs, no chords. Mostly collected in the 1950's.

CAZDEN, NORMAN, HERBERT HAUFRECHT, and NORMAN STUDER, *Folk Songs of the Catskills, with a Study of their Formation and Relationships,* SUNY Press, 1982, 650 pp. Annotation available in a separate volume.

CHEYNEY, THOMAS, *Mormon Songs from the Rocky Mountains: A Compilation of Mormon Folksong,* University of Utah Press, 1981 reprint of 1968 book, 166 pp.

COHEN, NORMAN, *Long Steel Rail: The Railroad in American Folksong,* University of Illinois Press, 1981, 710 pp. A rich study, extensive discography and bibliography, songs with chords and melodies.

CHRIST-JANER, ALBERT, CHARLES W. HUGHES and CARLETON SPRAGUE SMITH, *American Hymns Old and New,* Columbia University Press, 1980, 838 pp. 17th to 20th century; four-part vocal arrangements.

CHRISTESON, R.P., *The Old Time Fiddler's Repertory, Vol. 2,* University of Missouri Press, 1983, 169 pp.

Engine 8444 of the Union Pacific.

MCNEIL, W.K., compiler, *Southern Folk Ballads,* August House, 1987/88, 217/224 pp. Unusual in that the bulk of the materials was collected after 1955. Texts and tunes, no chords.

ROBERTS, JOHN STORM, *The Latin Tinge: The Impact of Latin American Music on the United States,* Oxford University Press, 1979, 246 pp. Two chapters on roots; the rest on popular music and dance.

SLOBIN, MARK, *Tenement Songs: The Popular Music of the Jewish Immigrants,* University of Illinois Press, 1982, 213 pp.

WALKER, WILLIAM, ed. by GLENN C. WILCOX, *Southern Harmony and Musical Companion: Containing a Choice Collection of Tunes, Hymns, Psalms, Odes and Anthems,* University of Kentucky Press, 1987, 342 pp. The most popular shape-note hymnbook, reprinted from its 1854 edition.

BOOKS ON FOLKLORE

ABERNATHY, FRANCIS EDWARDS, ed., *Hoein' the Short Rows,* SMU Press, 1987, 238 pp. Mostly folklore. Includes an excellent survey of cowboy poetry by Guy Logsdon.

ABRAHAMS, ROGER D., ed. and selector, *Afro-American Folktales: Stories from Black Traditions in the New World,* Panetheon, 1985, 352 pp. 107 tales classified by type.

ABRAHAMS, ROGER D., KENNETH S. GOLDSTEIN and WAYLAND D. HAND, eds., *By Land and by Sea: Studies in the Folklore of Work and Leisure Honoring Horace P. Beck,* Legacy Books, 1985, 225 pp.

BAUMAN, RICHARD and ABRAHAMS, ROGER D., eds., *And Other Neighborly Names: Social Process and Cultural Image in Texas Folklore,* University of Texas Press, 1981, 321 pp.

BRONNER, SIMON J., *American Folklore Studies: An Intellectual History,* University of Kansas Press, 1986, 213 pp.

DORSON, RICHARD M., ed., *Handbook of American Folklore,* Indiana University Press, 1983, 584 pp.

FIFE, AUSTIN E., *Exploring Western Americana,* ed. by ALTA FIFE, UMI Research Press, 1988, 279 pp.

GILLESPIE, ANGUS K., *Folklorist of the Coal Field: George Korson's Life and Work,* Penn State University Press, 1980, 200 pp.

GOLDSTEIN, KENNETH S. and NEIL V. ROSENBERG, eds., *Folklore Studies in Honour of Herbert Halpert,* Memorial University Division of Folklore, 1980, 395 pp.

GRIFFITH, JAMES S., *Southern Arizona Folk Arts,* University of Arizona Press, 1988, 234 pp.

IVES, EDWARD M., *The Tape-Recorded Interview: A Manual for Field Workers in Folklore and Oral History,* University of Tennessee Press, 1980, reprint of 1974 ed., 130 pp. An important book.

JACKSON, BRUCE, *Fieldwork,* University of Illinois Press, 1987, 311 pp. Excellent exposition of ethics and research procedures, well-written and amusing.

JAHN, ROBERT, *Down Barnegat Bay: A Nor'easter Midnight Reader,* Beachcomber Press, 207 pp.

Long Journey Home: Folklife in the South, Southern Exposure, 1977, 224 pp. Collected articles from the journal *Southern Exposure.*

ZUMWALT, ROSEMARY LEVY, *American Folklore Scholarship: A Dialogue of Dissent,* Indiana University Press, 1988, 186 pp. A

Bonnie Phipps: Autoharp power.

study of the schism between anthropologists and folklorists in the American Folklore Society.

INSTRUCTIONAL BOOKS AND RECORDS

Since the first edition of this book, Big 3 has been bought by Columbia Pictures Publications and Hal Leonard has become a major publisher in the folk area and has taken over the distribution of Centerstream Publications. More and more books are appearing with soundsheets or cassette tapes.

I have included new titles of particular importance and focussed on the most consistently reliable writers.

AUTOHARP

PHIPPS, BONNIE. *Beginning Autoharp Instruction Book,* Alfred, no date, 88 pp., cassette available. Good method by a fine player.

BANJO

Banjo Tabs: Jeep Watson (Banjo Sheet Music) has published a large list of tabs for Earl Scruggs, J.D. Crowe, Allen Shelton and Ben Eldridge.

BRODY, DAVID, *The Banjo Picker's Fakebook,* Oak, 1986, 215 pp. Tab only. Repertoire book of tunes in bluegrass and clawhammer styles, arranged by Bob Carlin, Marty Cutler, Ken Perlman and Hank Sapoznik.

CARLIN, BOB, *Fiddle Tunes for Clawhammer Banjo,* Centerstream, dist. by Hal Leonard, 1983, 48 pp. Many interesting tunings, taken from Carlin's Rounder records. Tab only.

DAVIS, JANET, *Mel Bay's Back-Up Banjo*, Mel Bay, 1981, 238 pp. Excellent ideas and patterns for intermediate and advanced players. Music and tab.

DEERING, JANET, ed., *World-Wide Banjo Resource Directory*, Deering Banjo Company, 1988, 80 pp. Planned as an annual directory.

HATFIELD, JACK, *Bluegrass Banjo Method*, Hatfield, 1984, 2nd ed. Good beginning method; unique material on picks. Cassette also available. Tab only.

JACKSON, CARL, *The Carl Jackson Banjo Book*, Mel Bay, 1981, 75 pp. Jackson is a fine player. For advanced players. Music and tab.

KEITH, BILL, *Bill Keith Banjo,* by TONY TRISCHKA and BILL KEITH, Oak, 1978, 71 pp., tab only. An important book of solos for advanced players.

MUNDE, ALAN, *Banjo Solo Series,* and tab for the *The Banjo Kid Rides Again.* Munde is an excellent player. *See* MAIL-ORDER BOOKS for ordering information.

PERLMAN, KEN, *Clawhammer Style Banjo*, Prentice Hall, 1981, 194 pp. Large and useful. Tab only.

PERLMAN, KEN, *Melodic Clawhammer Banjo*, Oak, 1979, 96 pp. A better choice for beginners because it comes with a soundsheet. Tab only.

ROSENBAUM, ART, *The Art of the Mountain Banjo*, Centerstream, dist. by Hal Leonard, 1981, with soundsheet, 84 pp. Solos from this fine player's Kicking Mule records, using a variety of tunings. Tab only.

SOKOLOW, FRED, *Bluegrass Banjo Inventions,* Kicking Mule, 1977, 17 pp. Tabs from his innovative album.

SOKOLOW, FRED, *Foggy Mountain Breakdown Plus 12 Great Solos,* Columbia Pictures Publications, 1983, 50 pp. Excellent, intelligent solos; music and tab.

SOKOLOW, FRED, *Gospel Banjo Bluegrass, Vols. I and 2,* Columbia Pictures Publications, 1984, 87 and 72 pp. Easy-to-play and logical; music and tab. Cassettes available.

SOKOLOW, FRED, *Ragtime, Blues and Jazz Banjo,* Mel Bay, 1983, 53 pp. Tab only. Good collection including Scott Joplin tunes. Cassette available.

TRISCHKA, TONY, *Melodic Banjo,* Oak, 1976, 127 pp. Soundsheet. Some wonderful tab transcriptions of solos by Bill Keith, Eric Weissberg, and Bobby Thompson. I feel that this is the best of Trischka's books, all of which are interesting. Look for them from Oak Publications.

TRISCHKA, TONY and PETE WERNICK, *Masters of the 5-String Banjo,* Oak, 1988, 413 pp. An immense book, recommended for all bluegrass fans. Tab only.

WEISSMAN, DICK, *5-String Banjo Chord Dictionary,* Alfred, 1982, 48 pp.

WEISSMAN, DICK, *Banjo Chord Dictionary Handy Guide,* Alfred, 1978, 48 pp. The above book is larger; both contain chords in various tunings.

CONCERTINA

BUTLER, FRANK, *The Concertina,* Oak, 65 pp.

CARLIN, RICHARD, *The English Concertina,* Oak, 64 pp.

CONVERSE, FRANK J., *Concertina Book,* Mel Bay, 52 pp. Simple method for 20-key concertina.

WATSON, ROGER, *Handbook for Anglo-Chromatic Concertina; Handbook for English Concertina; Handbook for Melodeon;* all published by Music Sales.

DOBRO

PHILLIPS, STACY, *Traditional Tunes for Contemporary Dobro,* Mel Bay, 1983, 101 pp. Music, tab and chords. Worthwhile.

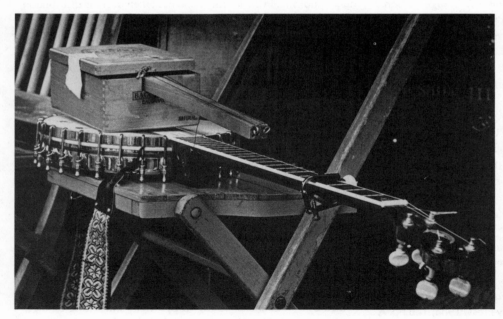

Vega and cigar-box banjos belonging to Cathy Fink.

DULCIMER AND HAMMERED DULCIMER

CAROL, BONNIE, *Dust Off That Dulcimer and Dance*, Alfred, no date, 168 pp. A huge tome.

FORCE, ROBERT and D'OSSCHE, ALBERT, *The Wild Dulcimer Songbook*, Centerstream, dist. by Hal Leonard, 1981, 107 pp.

HELLMAN, NEIL, *Dulcimer Chord Book*, Gourd Music, dist. by Hal Leonard, 1981, 59 pp.

HELLMAN, NEIL, *Dulcimer Method for Beginning-to-Intermediate Players*, Hal Leonard, 71 pp. Cassette available.

HORNSTOBEL, LOIS, *Anthology for the Fretted Dulcimer*, Mel Bay, 1982, 188 pp. Chords, tab and notes. Includes pieces by European and Japanese players.

REILLY, LUCILLE, *Striking Out and Winning: An Unabridged Guide to the Hammered Dulcimer*, Shadrach Productions. Cassette also available.

ROTH, KEVIN, *Kevin Roth Anthology, Dulcimer Songbook: Folkways Years, 1974-1982*, Centerstream, dist. by Hal Leonard, 1983, 120 pp. Music, chords, no tab.

FIDDLE

BOS, MARILYN, *Beginning Country Fiddle*, Oak, 1984, 95 pp. Many useful tips.

CARLIN, RICHARD, *The Master Collection of Dance Music for Violin*, Mel Bay, 1984, 189 pp. Tunes, with chord symbols, from Canada and Britain.

DUNLAY, K.E., *Traditional Celtic Fiddle Music of Cape Breton*, Fiddlecase Books, 1986, 113 pp. 86 tunes, no chords.

GREENBLATT, DEBOARH, *Fiddlescapes*, Centerstream, dist. by Hal Leonard, 1981, 55 pp. A good introductory method.

GREENBLATT, DEBORAH, *The Cajun Fiddle Tune Book*, Centerstream, dist. by Hal Leonard, 1985, 39 pp. Cassette available.

KRASSEN, MILES, *Masters of Old Time Fiddling*, Oak, 1983, 139 pp. with soundsheet. 49 transcriptions of southeastern fiddlers; no chords.

LIEBERMAN, JULIE LYON, *Blues Fiddle*, Oak, 1986, 110 pp. From classic blues to modern jazz.

MESSER, DON, *Anthology of Favorite Fiddle Tunes*, Mel Bay, 1980, 135 pp. 190 tunes, with chords, by the Canadian favorite.

PHILLIPS, STACY and KENNY KOSEK, *Bluegrass Fiddle Styles*, Oak, 1978, 112 pp. Music and chords. Bluegrass fiddlers from the roots to today.

ROCHE, FRANCIS, *The Roche Collection of Traditional Irish Music*, Ossian Publications, dist. by Music Sales. 566 tunes; no chords.

THOMSON, RYAN J., *Captain Fiddle's Tunebook*, Captain Fiddle Publications, 1988, 45 pp. Music and chords. Good cassette available.

GUITAR

Blues, Bottleneck And Ragtime

GROSSMAN, STEFAN, *Ragtime Guitar*, Mel Bay, 1986, 117 pp. Includes Scott Joplin and Elizabeth Cotton tunes. A good book. Grossman now places music and tab together so they can be easily followed.

GROSSMAN, STEFAN, *Texas Blues*, Oak, 1984, 144 pp. with soundsheet. See comments above.

Improvising Blues Guitar, Vols. 2 and 3, Green Note Publications, ea. 34 pp. plus 17 pp. appendix, with soundsheets. This book deals with pick-style electric blues. When giving lead parts, it doesn't list the chords from which the solos are coming.

SOKOLOW, FRED, *Best of Blues Guitar*, Mel Bay, 1987, 41 pp. Music and tab. Nice solos in the style of various blues artists.

SOKOLOW, FRED, *Bo Diddley Guitar Solos*, Hal Leonard, 1988, music and tab.

Chords, Scales And Theory

DARLING, ERIK and TOM RIKER, *Over 300 Chords for Guitar*, G. Schirmer, dist. by Music Sales, 1980, 223 pp. Pocket-size book.

FOX, DAN and DICK WEISSMAN, *Fretboard Theory for Guitar*, Schirmer, 1977, 48 pp. Relates music theory to the physical layout of the guitar.

HANSON, MARK, *Alternate Tunings Guide for Guitar*, Accent on Music, 8 pp., 1986. Chord diagrams and record references.

SANDBERG, LARRY, *Chords and Tunings for Fretted Instruments*, Oak, 1977, 71 pp.

WILLIAMS, CHARLES, *The Nashville Number System*, Charles Williams, 1988, 40 pp. Explains the notation system used by Nashville session players.

The face of fiddle music: Delaware fiddler Slim Ricksell at a local fiddlers' convention

Flatpicking

BRODY, DAVID, *The Guitar Player's Fakebook,* Oak, 1984, 191 pp. Tab only. Useful for building repertoire.

CRARY, DAN, *The Flatpicker's Guide,* Centerstream, dist. by Hal-Leonard, 1986, 110 pp., cassette available. Music and tab. An excellent book. The cassette is at performance speed — a bit difficult to follow, though nice to listen to.

Folk Guitar

AXELROD, DAN, *The "Axelrod Axe" System of Improvising Harmonized Leads for 12-String Guitar,* Warner Brothers, 1984, 55 pp. with soundhseet. An interesting idea; tunes pairs of strings in thirds.

BAKER, DUCK, *Irish, Scottish, English and American Fiddle Tunes for the Fingerpicking Guitarist,* Centerstream, dist. by Hal Leonard, 1981, 123 pp. with soundsheet. Difficult pieces; a good source for advanced players.

BENSUSAN, PIERRE, *The Guitar Book,* Hal Leonard, 1985, 187 pp., tab and music. Great solos by a master of fingerstyle guitar, though tab and music are printed in the reverse of their usual relative positions.

FLACKE, RAY, *Solos,* Centerstream, dist. by Hal Leonard, 1986, 26 pp. Cassette available. Hot solos by Ricky Skaggs's lead player. Cassette is at performance speed, but each solo is repeated several times. Challenging.

FLINT, TOMMY, *Anthology of Fingerstyle Guitar,* Mel Bay, 1978, 161 pp. Music, tab and chords; an excellent book by a fine player.

GROSSMAN, STEFAN. Stefan has a series of *Fingerpicking Guitar Exercises and Hot Licks* published by Mel Bay, each 32 pages long and covering a different area. Stefan has written other useful books on fingerpicking published by Mel Bay with music, tab, and chords.

HANSON, MARK, *The Art of Contemporary Travis Picking,* Accent on Music, dist. by Music Sales, 67 pp. At last: a good, easy-to-follow and logical book on Travis picking, with an excellent cassette.

HANSON, MARK, *Solo Style Contemporary Travis Picking,* Accent on Music, 1988, 80 pp., cassette available. A fine advanced method. Details role of wrist and hand positions. Nicely constructed solos.

KOTTKE, LEO, *Eight Songs,* Hal Leonard, 1986, 94 pp., ed. and transcribed by JOHN STROPES. Music and tab, no chords. Tunes written in the early part of Kottke's career.

PERLMAN, KEN, *Fingerpicking Fiddle Tunes: Traditional Dance Music Arranged for Fingerstyle Guitar,* Chappell, dist. by Hal Leonard, 1978, 72 pp. Music and tab, no chords.

PERLMAN, KEN, *Fingerstyle Guitar,* Centerstream, dist. by Hal Leonard, 1985, 242 pp. Some pieces with chords, some without. A fine book.

RENBOURN, JOHN, *Original Guitar Solos: The Nine Maidens, The Hermit, Stefan and John,* Hal Leonard, 1986, 96 pp. The music and tab printed separately; no chords. Renbourn is a fine player.

SMITH, JANET, *Fingerstyle Guitar Solos,* Centerstream, dist. by Hal Leonard, 1983, 75 pp., cassette available. Fifteen pieces: music, tab, and chords. Cassette and book are both good.

SOKOLOW, FRED, *Great Country Hits,* Hal Leonard, 1986, 55 pp.

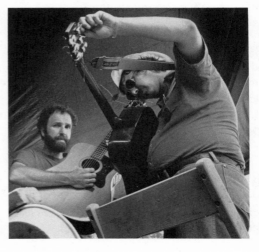

Tuning up

Cassette available. Arrangements are both finger and pick style. Music and tab.

SOKOLOW, FRED, *The Complete Country Guitar Book,* Mel Bay, 1983, 96 pp., cassette available. Music and tab.

STROPES, JOHN and PETER LANG, *20th Century Masters of Fingerstyle Guitar,* Stropes Editions, 1982, dist. by Hal Leonard, 98 pp. A beautifully-designed book with music and tab, although they are printed separately.

HARMONICA

BAKER, DON, *The Harmonica,* Walton's Manufacturing, dist. by Music Sales, 48 pp. book, with a cassette. Easy to follow, good cassette.

GINDICK, JON, *Rock n' Blues Harmonica,* Cross Harp Presses, 1982, dist. by Music Sales, 223 pp.

GINDICK, JON, *The Natural Blues and Country Western Harmonica: A Beginner's Guide,* 1977, Cross Harp Press, dist. by Music Sales, 128 pp. I find them funky and folksy but a bit hard to follow, and too chatty.

NELSON, GEORGE-HEAPS and BARBARA MCCLINTOCK KOEHLER, *Folk and Blues Harmonica,* Mel Bay, 1976, 136 pp. Excellent guide. Record also available.

MANDOLIN

BRODY, DAVID, *The Mandolin Player's Fakebook,* Oak, 1983, 192 pp. Tabs and chords. Excellent for developing repertoire.

DEL GRASSO, RICH, *Hal Leonard Mandolin Method,* Hal Leonard, 1986, 62 pp., cassette available. A good method. Music and chords, no tab. Many duets.

HAYTH, GENE and KEN EDISON, *Mel Bay's Old Time Mandolin Solos,* Mel Bay, 1979, 80 pp., music, chords and tab. A nice book of solos.

MOORE, TINY, *The Tiny Moore Mandolin Method: Country, Western Swing, Jazz,* Charles Anderson, 1982, 48 pp. Music, tab and chords. Not for the beginner. Good material by an outstanding player.

Note: Look into other Mel Bay mandolin books as well, particularly those which involve the late Jethro Burns.

Maíre Ní Chathasaigh: Dance tunes on the courtly harp.

PIANO

JOPLIN, SCOTT, *Piano Music,* Carl Fischer, 1985, 132 pp.

LINDEMAN, CAROLYNN, compiler, *Women Composers of Ragtime,* Theodore Presser, 1985, 39 pp.

MORATH, MAX, *Cripple Creek: A Ragtime Suite for Piano,* Mel Bay, 1986, 30 pp. A suite in eight parts by the renowned ragtimer. Record available.

OLSON, LYNN FREEMAN, *First Favorite Folk Songs,* Alfred, 1986.

SHAFTEL, PAUL, *Folk Songs from Around the World,* Alfred, 3 vols., each 32 pp. Easy arrangements.

SILVERMAN, JERRY, *Blues Piano,* Saw Mill Music, dist. by Theodore Presser, 1983. 6 vols., each 31 pp. Blues classics arranged for voice and piano.

MISCELLANEOUS INSTRUMENTS

Sylvia Woods has published a number of attractive harp books, some with videos.

Captain Fiddle offers a pennywhistle tape for beginners, and Geraldine Coter has written *Traditional Irish Tin Whistle Tutor* for Ossian Publications. (Distributed by Music Sales, 102 pp. with two soundsheets.) An actual whistle is included with *The Clarke Tin Whistle* by Bill Ochs (Pennywhistler's Press, 1988, 80 pp.) It deals with scales, tonguing, etc.

Jerry Silverman has writtern the useful *How To Sing Higher and Lower* (Saw Mill Music Corp., dist. by Theodore Presser, 1983, 96 pp.) It groups songs according to the vocal range required to sing them.

INSTRUCTIONAL AUDIO AND VIDEO TAPES

Captain Fiddle Publications, 4 Elm Court, New Market, NH 03857. Books, cassette tapes.

Andy Cushing, 4202-A Park Ave., Nashville, TN 37209. Bluegrass tape with solo instrument on separate channel.

Stefan Grossman's Guitar Workshop, Box 802, Sparta, NJ 07871.

Hatfield Music, Box 6263, Knoxville, TN 37914. Bluegrass banjo tabs.

Hot Licks Productions, Box 337, Pound Ridge, NY 10576. Harmonica, banjo and guitar videos.

Homespun Tapes and Videos, Box 694, Woodstock, NY 12498. Send for their large catalog of audio and video products. I've found the products I've gone through well-done and generally easy to follow, though the more advanced tapes are trickier.

Al Munde's Banjo College, Box 8240, Levellend, TX 79338.

Rhythm Productions, Box 34485, Los Angeles, CA 90034. Folk dance albums and cassettes; also children's music.

Ridge Runner Home Lessons, Box 122115, Fort Worth, TX 76121. Send for their large catalog of bluegrass and country tapes and videos.

Fred Sokolow, 5034 Pickford Way, Culver City, CA 90230. Cassettes for many of his excellent instruction books.

Barry Solomon, 423 Ashland Ave., Suite D3, Santa Monica, CA 19405. Bluegrass cassettes with solo instruments on a separate channel.

Specialty Music Productions, Box 37395, Pensacola, FL 32506. Bluegrass videos.

Harold Streeter, Le Walt Publishing, N. 190 Highland Ct., Post Falls, ID 83854. Bluegrass videos, cassettes, books.

The Video Educator, 8400 Secor Rd., Lambertville, MI 48144. Videos.

BOOK AND MUSIC PUBLISHERS

In addition to the addresses of traditional book and music publishers, this section includes addresses of individuals who publish their own books or music folios.

Abbeville Press, 488 Madison Ave., New York, NY 10022

ABC Clio, Riviera Campus, 2040 Alameda Padre Serra, Santa Barbara, CA 93103

Abingdon Press, 201 Eighth Ave. S., Nashville, TN 37202

Abrams, Harry N., Inc., 100 Fifth Ave., New York, NY 10011

Acadian Publishing Enterprises, Rt. 3, Box 362, Church Pt., LA 70525

Accent on Music, Box 417, Palo Alto, CA 94302

Afro-Am Publishing Co. Inc., 819 S. Wabash Ave., Chicago, IL 60605

Alaska Folk Music Co., Box 4-1324, Spenard, AK 99503

Alfred Music Co., 16380 Roscoe Blvd., Box 10003, Van Nuys, CA 91406

Algonquin Books of Chapel Hill, Box 2225, Chapel Hill, NC 27515

American Canal & Transportation Center, 809 Rathton Rd., York, PA 17405

American Christian Press, Box 328, New Knoxville, OH 45871

American Folklore Society, Dist. by University of Texas Press

AMSCO, Dist. by Music Sales

AMSCO School Publications, 315 Hudson St., New York, NY 10013

AMS Press, 56 E. 13th St., New York, NY 10003

Anchor, Dist. by Doubleday & Co.

Anderson, Charles, Music Publications, Box 4296, Mountain View, CA 94040

Appalachian Consortium Press, University House, Appalachian State University, Boone, NC 28608

Archon Books, Shoe String Press, 995 Sherman Ave., Hamden, CT 06514

Arlington House, Dist. by Crown Publishers

Avon Books, 105 Madison Ave., New York, NY 10016

August House Publishers, Box 3223, Little Rock, AR 72203

Ballantine Books, Division of Random House

Banjo Newsletter, Box 364, Greensboro, MD 21639

Bantam Books, 666 Fifth Ave., New York, NY 10019

Basic Books, 10 E. 53rd St., New York, NY 10022

Beachcomber Press, Box 42, Mantoloking, NJ 08738

Beaver Valley Press, Box 282, Chimacum, WA 98235

Belwin-Mills Publishing Co., Dist. by Columbia Pictures Publications

Berea College, Appalachian College Center, Box 2336, Berea, KY 40404

Berkeley Publishing Corp., 200 Madison Ave., New York, NY 10016

Berklee Press Publicàtions, 1140 Boylston St., Boston, MA 02215

Bernandel Music Ltd., 651 Progress Ave., Scarborough, Ontario, Canada

Big 3 Music Corp., Dist. by Columbia Pictures Publications

Bishop Museum Press, Box 19000A, Honolulu, HI 96817

Blaylock, Bill, Box 25, Marietta, GA 30061

Bluegrass Bookshelf, Academy of Bluegrass, Box 537, Lake Butler, FL 53054

Blues Unlimited, 38A Sackville Rd., Bexhill on the Sea, Sussex, England

Bonanza Books, Dist. by Crown

Boston Music Co., Dist. by Frank Music

Bowling Green University, Dist. by Popular Press, 101 University Hall, Bowling Green, OH 43403

Broadcast Music, Inc., 40 W. 57th St., New York, NY 10019
    Broadman Press, 127 Ninth Ave. N., Nashville, TN 37203

Broadside Press Publications, Box 48204, 4734 Sturtevant, Detroit, MI 48204

Brumley, Albert E., & Sons, Powell, MO 65730

Bucknell University Press, Lewisburg, PA 17837

Cambridge University Press, 32 E. 57th St., New York, NY 10022

Canadian Folk Music Society, Michael Cass-Beggs, 15 Julien St., Pointe Claire 72P, Quebec, Canada

Captain Fiddle Publications, 4 Elm Ct., Newmarket, NH 03857

Castle Publishing Co., Box 188, Portland, ME 04112

Center for Southern Folklore, 1216 Peabody Ave., Box 4081, Memphis, TN 38104

Caxton Printers Ltd., 312 Main, Caldwell, ID 83605

Century Publications, 1536 4th St., Ste. 61A, San Rafael, CA 94901

Chappell & Co., Dist. by Hal Leonard

Chilton Book Co., Sales & Service Dept., Chilton Way, Radnor, PA 19089

Clarkson Potter, Dist. by Crown

CMF Press, see Country Music Foundation Press

Cole, M.M., 251 E. Grand Ave., Chicago, IL 60611

Collier, see Macmillan Publishing Corp.

Collins, Dan, 1375 Crosby Ave., Bronx, NY 10461

Columbia Music Co., Dist. by Theodore Presser

Columbia Pictures Publications, 16353 N.W. 54th Ave., Miami, FL 33014

Columbia University Press, 562 W. 113th St., New York, NY 10025

Consolidated Music Publishers, Dist. by Music Sales

Cooper Square Publishers, Inc., 81 Adams Dr., Totowa, NJ 07512

Cornell Maritime Press, Inc., Box 456, Centreville, MD 21617

Cornell University Press, 124 Roberts Place, Ithaca, NY 14580

Council of the Southern Mountains, Box 2307, Berea, KY 40403

Country Music Foundation Press, 700 16th Ave. S., Nashville, TN 37203

Coward, McCann & Geoghegan, Inc., c/o Putnam

Coyote Cowboy Co., Box 190, Brighton, CO 80601

Criterion Music Corp., 17 W. 60th St., New York, NY 10023

Crowell, Thomas Y., c/o Harper & Row

Crown Publishers, Inc., 225 Park Ave. S., New York, NY 10003

Da Capo Press, 233 Spring St., New York, NY 10013

Davis, Sandy, RD #1, Weston Rd., Lincoln, MA 01773

Dent, J.M. & Sons, Ltd., Aldine House, 10-13 Bedford St., London WC2, England

Ditson, Oliver, Dist. by Theodore Presser

Dodd, Mead & Co., 71 Fifth Ave., New York, NY 10003

Donning Co., 5969 Virginia Beach Blvd., Norfolk, VA 23502

Dorchester Press, Dist. by Grove Press

Doubleday & Co., 501 Franklin Ave., Garden City, NY 11530

Dover Publications, 180 Varick St., New York, NY 10014

Duke University Press, 6697 College Station, Durham, NC 27708

Dulcimer Shoppe, The, Drawer E, Highway 9 N., Mountain View, AR 82560

Dunkelberger, A.C., Box 188, Madison, TN 37115

Dutton, E.P. & Co., 2 Park Ave., S., New York, NY 10016

East Tennessee State University Press, Johnson City, TN 37601

Eddison Bluesbooks, Eddison Press Ltd., 2 Greycoat Pl., London SW1, England

Edwards, John Memorial Foundation, Middle Tennessee State University, Murfreesboro, TN

Emerson Books, Inc., 121 N. Hampton Dr., White Plains, NY 10603

Facts on File, 460 Park Ave. S., New York, NY 10016

Fawcett World Library, c/o Ballantine Books - Random House

Faxon, F.W. Co., 15 Southwest Pack, Westwood, MA 02090

Fiddlecase Books, c/o Captain Fiddle.

Fischer, Carl, 62 Cooper Square, New York, NY 10003

Flash Books, Dist. by Music Sales

Fluharty, Russell, RD #3, Box 119, Mannington, WV 26582

Folklore Associates, Dist. by Gale Research

Folklore Society of Greater Washington, Box 19303, 20th Street Station, Washington, DC 20036

Forster Music Pub., 216 S. Wabash Ave., Chicago, IL 60604

Four Winds Press, Dist. by Macmillan

Frank Music, 119 W. 57th St., New York, NY 10019

Free Press, Dist. by Macmillan

Funk & Wagnalls, Dist. by Harper & Row

Gage Educational Pub. Ltd., Box 5000, 164 Commander Blvd., Agincourt, Ontario, Canada

Gale Research Co., Book Tower, Detroit, MI 48226

Garland Publishing Co., 136 Madison Ave., New York, NY 10016

Gollancz, Victor, Ltd., 14 Henrietta St., Covent Garden, London WC2 E8A, England

Gordon Publishers Press, Box 459, Bowling Green Station, New York, NY 10004

Gospel Publishing House, 1445 Boonville Ave., Springfield, MO 65802

Grass Roots Productions, 444 W. 54th St., New York, NY 10019

Gray, H.W., Co., Dist. by Belwin-Mills (Columbia Pictures Publications)

Green Note Publications, Box 4187, Berkeley, CA 94704

Greenwood Press, 51 Riverside Ave., Westport, CT 06880

Gregg Press, 491 S. Main, Plymouth, MA 48170

Grisman, David, Box 373, Mill Valley, CA 94941

Grossman Press, Dist. by Viking Press

Guthrie, Woody, Publications, Inc., 200 W. 57th St., Room 1304, New York, NY 10019

Hancock House, Saanichton, British Columbia, Canada

Hansen Publications, 1824 West Ave., Miami Beach, FL 33139

Harcourt Brace Jovanovich, 1250 Sixth Ave., San Diego, CA 92101

Harper & Row, 10 E. 53rd St., New York, NY 10022

Harvard University Press, 79 Garden St., Cambridge, MA 02138

Harvest Press, Dist. by Slawson Communications, 165 Vallecitos de Oro, San Marcos, CA 92069

Haskell House Publications, Inc., Box 420, Blythbourne St., Brooklyn, NY 11219

Hill & Range Music, Dist. by Big3, Columbia Pictures Publications

Holcomb, Dave, 548 E. Campbell Ave., Campbell, CA 95008

Holt, Rinehart & Winston, 111 Fifth Ave., New York, NY 10003

Houghton Mifflin Co., 1 Beacon St., Boston, MA 02108

Hudson River Sloop Restoration, Box 25, Cold Spring, NY 10516

Huntington Library Publications, 1151 Oxford Rd., San Marino, CA 91108

Hutchison, 3 Fitzray Sq., London W1 TA, England

Immediate Music Pub., now Lorimar Pub. Ltd., 47 Dean St., London W1V 5HL, England

Indiana University Press, 10th & Morton Sts., Bloomington, IN 47401

Industrial Workers of the World (IWW), 752 W. Webster, Chicago, IL 60614

Interbook, 131 Varick St., New York, NY 10013

International Folk Music Council, Dept. of Man, Queens University, Kingston, Ontario, Canada

Jadfel Publishing, 204 Kevin Dr., Lafayette, LA 70507

Johns Hopkins Press, Baltimore, MD 21218

Johnson Publishing Co., Box 217, Murfreesboro, NC 27855

Johnson Reprint Corp., c/o Harcourt Brace Jovanovich

Judson Press, Box 851, Valley Forge, PA 19482

Kelley, Augustus M., Pub., 1140 Broadway, Room 901, New York, NY 10001

Kent State University Press, Kent, OH 44240

Kenyon Publications, 17 W. 60th St., New York, NY 10023

Kingston Korner, 6 S. 230 Cohasset Rd., Napierville, IL 60540

Kjos, Neil, Music Co., 4382 Jutland Dr., San Diego, CA 92117

Knopf, Alfred A., Inc., Subsidiary of Random House, Inc.

Kodansha International USA, 10 E. 53rd St., New York, NY 10022

Kountry Korral, Box 8014, 72008 Vasterias 8, Sweden

Kratt Publishing Co., 988 Johnson Place, Union, NJ 07083

Kraus Reprint Co., Div. of Kraus-Thompson Organization, Ltd., Millwood, NY 10546

Krieger, Robert E., Box 9542, Melbourne, FL 32901

Leonard, Hal, Pub., 7777 W. Bluemound Rd., Box 13819, Milwaukee, WI 53213

Lerner Publications Co., 241 First Ave. N., Minneapolis, MI 55401

Le Walt Pub., Box 164, Coeur D'Alene, ID 83814

Lewis Publishing Co., 262 Veterans Blvd., Carlstadt, NJ 07072

Library of Congress, Washington, DC 20540

Lippincott, J.B., Co., E. Washington Sq., Philadelphia, PA 19105

Little, Brown & Co., 34 Beacon St., Boston, MA 02106

Liveright Publishing Co., c/o W.W. Norton Co.

Living Blues Magazine, Center for the Study of Southern Culture, University of Mississippi, University, MS 38977

Louisiana State University Press, Baton Rouge, LA 70803

Macmillan Publishing Co., Inc., 866 Third Ave., New York, NY 10022

Magnamusic Distributors, Inc., Sharon, CT 06069

Marks, Edward, Dist. by Belwin-Mills, Columbia Pictures Publications

Martin , Peter, 280 Bloor West, Toronto, Ontario M58 1W1, Canada

Mauer & Co., Box 94743, Schaumburg, IL 60194

MCA Music, Dist. by Belwin-Mills, Columbia Pictures Publications

McClain Printing Co., 212 Main St., Parsons, WV 26287

McClelland & Stewart Ltd., 25 Hollinger Rd., Toronto, Ontario M45 3G2, , Canada

McGraw-Hill Book Co., 1221 Avenue of the Americas, New York, NY 10036

McKay, David Co., c/o Random House

McKinney, J.P., 2010 Conejo Dr., Santa Fe, NM 87501

Mel Bay Publications, 4 Industrial Dr., Pacific, MO 63069

Melior Publications, Box 1905, Spokane, WA

Memorial University Division of Folklore, St. Johns, Newfoundland , Canada

Mercury Music Corp., Dist. by Theodore Presser

Methuen & Co., 11 New Fetter Lane, London EC4, England

Metro Books, Inc., Arlington Heights, IL 60004

Metropolitan Museum of Art, c/o Henry Holt & Co., 521 Fifth Ave., New York, NY 10175

Michigan State University Press, 1405 S. Harrison Rd., 25 Manly Miles Bldg., E. Lansing, MI 48823

Mills Music, Dist. by Belwin-Mills, Columbia Pictures Publications

MIT Museum, Cambridge, MA 02142

MIT Press, 55 Hayward St., Cambridge, MA 02142

Mogull, Ivan, Music Corp., 33 W. 60th St., New York, NY 10023

Morris, Edward H., & Co., 31 W. 54th St., New York, NY 10019

Morrow, William, & Co., 105 Madison Ave., New York, NY 10016

Murphy Method, Box 2498, Winchester, VA 23601

Museum of the American Indian, Heye Foundation, Broadway at 155th St., New York, NY 10032

Museum of New Mexico Press, Box 2087, Santa Fe, NM 87501

Museum of the Rockies, Montana State University, Bozeman, MT 59717

Music Educators National Conference, 1201 16th St. N.W., Washington, DC 20036

Music Minus One, 50 S. Buckhout St., Irvington, NY 10533

Music Sales Corp., 24 E. 22nd St., New York, NY 10010

National Museum of Man, Ottawa, Ontario, K1A OM8, Canada

Naturegraph Publishers, Box 1075, Happy Camp, CA 96039

Nelson-Hall Publishers, 111 N. Canal St., Chicago, IL 60606

Neo Press, Box 32, Peaks Island, ME 04108

New American Library, c/o Pearson, 1633 Broadway, New York, NY 10019

New World Artist Corp., see Le Walt Publishing

New York Public Library, Room 50A, Fifth Ave. & 42nd St., New York, NY 10018

No Limit Books, Dist. by Book People, 2940 Seventh St., Berkeley, CA 94710

Northland Press, 2900 N. Forest Valley Rd., Flagstaff, AZ 86001

Norton, W.W., & Co., Inc., 500 Fifth Ave., New York, NY 10036

Norwood Editions, Box 38, Norwood, PA 19074

Oak Publicatons, 24 E. 22nd St., New York, NY 10010

Ohio Historical Society, 1985 Velma, Columbus, OH 43211

Ohio University Press, Scott Quadrangle, Athens, OH 45701

Old Time Music, 24 Upper Tollington Park, London N4 3EL, England

Outerbridge & Lazard, Dist. by E.P. Dutton

Oxalis Group, W. 428 27th Ave., Spokane, WA 99203

Oxford University Press, 200 Madison Ave., New York, NY 10016

Pan American Union (Organization of American States), 17th St. & Constitution Ave. NW, Washington, DC 20006

Panjandrum Press, 11321 Iowa Ave. Ste. 1, Los Angeles, CA 90025

Pantheon Books, 201 E. 50th St., New York, NY 10022

Pedlar Press, 53 Whitemore Rd., Sturbridge, MA 01566

Peer-Southern Publicatons, 1740 Broadway, New York, NY 10019

Pelican Publishing Co., 1101 Monroe St., Gretna, LA 70053

Penguin Books, Inc., c/o Viking Press

Pennsylvania State University Press, 215 Wagner Bldg., University Park, PA 16802

The Pennywhistle Press, 22244 Pacific Coast Hwy., Malibu, CA 90265

People's Folk Dance Directory, Box 8575, Austin, TX 78712

Peregrine Smtih, Box 667, Logan, UT 84041

Perigee Books, 200 Madison Ave., New York, NY 10016

Pierian Press, Box 1808, Ann Arbor, MI 48106

Polestar Press Ltd., RR1, Winlaw, British Columbia VO6 2JO, Canada

Praeger Publishers, Div. of Greenwood Press

Premier Books, see Fawcett World Library

Prentice Hall, One Gulf & Western Plaza, New York, NY 10023

Press Pacifica, 1230 Kainui Dr., Kailua, HI 96734

Presser, Theodore, Presser Place, Bryn Mawr, PA 19010

Presses Universitaires Laval, 28 Rue St., Famille, Quebec, Canada

Progressive Music, Dist. by Big 3/Columbia Pictures Publications

Putnam's, G.P., & Sons, 200 Madison Ave., New York, NY 10016

Quick Fox, Dist. by Oak

Quill, Dist. by William Morrow & Co.

Random House, Inc., 201 E. 50th St., New York, NY 10022

Redwood Press, Box 776, Inverness, CA 94937

Revell, Fleming H., Co., Old Tappan, NJ 07675

Riverrun Press, 1170 Broadway, Room 807, New York, NY 10001

Rutgers University Press, 109 Church St., New Brunswick, NJ 08901

Ryerson Music, Dist. by Oak

Ryerson Press, McGraw-Hill & Reyerson, Ltd., 330 Progress Ave., Scarborough, Ontario, Canada

St. Martin's Press, 175 Fifth Ave., New York, NY 10010

Scarecrow Press, 52 Liberty St., Metuchen, NJ 08840

Schirmer, G., Inc., Subsidiary of Macmillan

Schirmer Music, Dist. by Music Sales

Schocken Books, Inc., 201 E. 50th St., New York, NY 10022

Scholarly Book Services, Div. of Scholastic Magazine, 730 Broadway, New York, NY 10003

Scholarly Resources, 104 Greenhill Ave., Wilmington, DE 19805

School of American Research, 660 Garcia, Santa Fe, NM 87501

Screen Gems Publications, see Columbia Pictures Publications

Seeger, Pete, Box 431, Beacon, NY 12508

Seneca Books, Grantsville, WV 26147

Sevenshoux Music, Rt. 4, Box 92-05, Weatherford, TX 76086

Shadrach Productions, Box 712, Moorestown, NJ 08057

Shoe String Press, see Archon Books

Sierra Club Books, 730 Polk St., San Francisco, CA 94109

Simon & Schuster, 1230 Ave. of the Americas, New York, NY 10020

Singing Tree Press, Dist. by Gale Research Co.

Sing Out!, Box 5253, Bethlehem, PA 18015

Smithsonian Institution Press, Washington, DC 20560

Society for Ethnomusicology, Room 513, 201 S. Main St., Ann Arbor, MI 48108

Southern Exposure, c/o Institute for Southern Studies, Box 531, Durham, NC 27702

Southern Illinois University Press, Box 1774, Edwardsville, IL 62026

Southern Methodist University Press, Dallas, TX 75222

Southern Music, 1100 Broadway, Box 329, San Antonio, TX 78292

Staccato Press, 278 Hambletonian Dr., Eugene, OR 97401

Stackpole Books, Cameron & Keller Sts., Harrisburg, PA 17105

Stamm, G.W., Stamm Industries, 471 W. South, Kalamazoo, MI 49001

Stanford University Press, Stanford, CA 94305

Sterling Publishing Co., 2 Park Ave., New York, NY 10016

Storyville Publ., 63 Oxford Rd., London E17, England

Studio Vista Books, Blue Star House, Horizon Hill, London N19 5NY, England

Sunny Mountain Records, Box 14592, Gainesville, FL 32604

Sunstone Press, Box 2321, Santa Fe, NM 87501

Syracuse University Press, 1600 Jamesville Ave., Syracuse, NY 07642

Tara Publishing Co., Box 314, Hillside, NJ 07642

Taylor Museum, 30 W. Dale, Colorado Springs, CO 80903

Texas Eastern Press, University of Texas, El Paso, TX 79968

Texas Monthly Press, Box 1569, Austin, TX 78767

Tidewater District Council, Dist. by Cornell Maritime

Timescape Books, Div. of Simon & Schuster

Topsail Music, 22283 Cass Ave., Woodland Hills, CA 91364

Transaction Books, Rutgers University, New Brunswick, NJ 08903

Traum, Happy, Homespun Tapes & Video, Box 694, Woodstock, NY 12498

TVegas Songs, Dist. by Hansen Publications

UMI Research Press, Box 1346, Ann Arbor, MI 48106

Ungar, Frederick, Publishing Co., 370 Lexington Ave., New York, NY 10017

Union Grove Old Time Fiddle Contest, Box 36, Union Grove, NC 28669

University of Alabama Press, Box 2877, Tuscaloosa, AL 35487

University of Arizona Press, 1230 N. Park Ave., Suite 102, Tucson, AZ 85719

University of California Press, 2120 Berkeley Way, Berkeley, CA 94720

University of Chicago Press, 5801 Ellis Ave., Chicago, IL 60637

University of Florida Press, 15 NW 15th St., Gainesville, FL 32601

University of Georgia Press, Terrell Hall, Athens, GA 30601

University of Hawaii Press, 2840 Holowalu St., Honolulu, HI 96825

University of Illinois Press, 54 E. Gregory Dr., Champaign, IL 61820

University of Maine Press, Orono, ME 04473

University of Massachusetts Press, Box 429, Amherst, MA 01002

University of Minnesota Press, 2037 University Ave. S.E., Minneapolis, MN 55414

University of Missouri Press, 200 Lewis, Columbia, MO 65211

University of Nebraska Press, 901 N. 17th St., Lincoln, NE 68508

University of New Mexico Press, Albuquerque, NM 87131

University of North Carolina Press, Box 2288, Chapel Hill, NC 27514

University of Oklahoma Press, 1005 Asp Ave., Norman, OK 73019

University of Tennessee Press, Communications Bldg., Knoxville, TN 37996

University of Texas Press, Box 7819, University Station, Austin, TX 78712

University of Toronto Press, 63A St. George St., Toronto, Ontario, M5S 1A6, Canada

University of Utah Press, University Service Bldg., Salt Lake City, UT 84112

University Press of Kansas, 329 Carruth, Leavenworth, KA 66045

University Press of Kentucky, 663 S. Limestone St., Lexington, KY 40506

University Press of Mississippi, 3825 Ridgewood Rd., Jackson, MS 39211

University Press of Virginia, Box 3608, University Station, Charlottesville, VA 22903

University Presses of Florida, 15 NW 15th St., Gainesville, FL 32603

Viking Press, Inc.-Penguin Books, 40 W. 23rd St., New York, NY 10010

Vintage Books, Div. of Random House

Vista Music, 15 Alta Vista Circle, Irvington, NY 10533

Vitali Import Co., 5944 Atlantic Blvd., Maywood, CA 90270

Wadsworth Publishing Co., 10 Davis Dr., Belmont, CA 94002

Walker & Co., 720 Fifth Ave., New York, NY 10019

Wallo, Joseph, 1319 F St., Washington, DC 20004

Warner Brothers Publications, 75 Rockefeller Plaza, New York, NY 10019

Warner Paperback Library, 666 Fifth Ave., New York, NY 10103

Waterloo Music, 3 Regina St. N., Waterloo, Ontario, Canada

Watts, Franklin, Inc., Subsidiary of Grolier, Inc., 387 Park Ave. S., New York, NY 10016

Wayne State University Press, 5959 Woodward Ave., Detroit, MI 48202

Wentworth Corp., Box 666, West Columbia, SC 29169

Wesleyan University Press, 110 Mt. Vernon St., Middletown, CT 06457

West Virginia University Library, Morgantown, WV 26506

Westerners International, Box 3485, Tucson, AZ 85772

Williams, Charles, Box 290342, Nashville, TN 37229

Wisconsin State Historical Society, 816 State St., Madison WI 53706

World Around Songs, 5790 Highway 80 S., Burnsville, NC 28714

World Music Press, Box 2565, Danbury, CT 06813

Wright, John, 1137 Noyes St., Evanston, IL 60201

Yale University Press, 302 Temple St., New Haven, CT 06520

Yellow Moon Press, Box 1316, Cambridge, MA 02238

Yorktown Music Pub., Dist. by Oak

MAIL-ORDER

RECORDS AND NON-INSTRUCTIONAL VIDEOS

Alcazar Productions, Inc., Box 429, Waterbury, VT 05676

Andy's Front Hall, Box 307, Voorheesville, NY 12186

Appalshop, Box 743, Whitesburg, KY 40403

Capritaurus Music, 5497 Highway 9, Felton, CA 95018

Carthage Records, Inc., Box 667, Rocky Hill, NJ 08553

Central Sun Videos, Box 3135, Reston, VA 22091

Country Music Hall of Fame and Museum, 4 Music Sq. E., Nashville, TN 37203

Down Home Music, 10341 San Pablo Ave., El Cerrillo, CA 94530

Elderly Instruments, 110 N. Washington, Box 14210, Lansing, MI 48901

Mandolin Bros., 629 Forrest Ave., Staten Island, NY 10310. Mostly instruments, some books, etc.

CATALOGS OF BOOKS, RECORDS AND INSTRUMENTS

Banjo Sheet Music, 1102 Over brook Rd. Baltimore, MD 21239

Theodore Front, 16122 Cohasset St., Van Nuys, CA 91406

Hobgoblin Music, Box 5311, S. San Francisco, CA 94080. Concertinas, etc.

House of Musical Traditions, 7040 Carroll Ave., Takoma Park, MD 20912. Books and records.

Lark in the Morning, Box 1176, Mendocine, CA 95460. Many instruments.

Legacy Books, Box 494, Hatboro, PA 19040. A wonderful supplier for books on folk music and folklore.

Mountain Song Music, Box 4502, Estes Park, CO 80517

Musician's Friend, Box 869, Eagle Point, OR 97524

The New Boston Co., Box 14, Avon, MA 02322

Note-Ably Yours, 6865 Scarff Rd., New Carlisle, OH 45344. A large book and record catalog.

Irene Rouse, Box 310, Mt. Wharton Farm, Atlantic, VA 12202. Out-of-print books on folklore and folksong.

The Library of Congress publishes many bibliographies. Among them are lists of books on banjo, dulcimer, fiddle, guitar and mandolin. They are all available free by writing to them at Washington, DC 20540.

SONGBOOKS

INTRODUCTION

I've included two kinds of songbooks: artists' songbooks and collections of songs.

Artists' songbooks are, obviously enough, compilations of songs composed or recorded by particular artists. These songbooks tend to go in and out of print rather quickly; some of the ones below may already be unavailable. The decision as to which artists are "folk" and which are not has been made arbitrarily—that is, on the basis of my taste and experience. Bob Dylan is "folk," because his songs influence the course of folk music. An artist like Tony Bennett does not have such an effect. Some of the artists included here are not included in the record section. Since we're not dealing with a rigid academic definition of folk music, Larry Sandberg and I occasionally disagree about how much "folk" is in the music of a performer—Laura Nyro, for example.

Collections of songs vary greatly in size, format, readability, method of organization, etc. They almost always include music (as do artists' songbooks), either as melody lines with chords or as piano or guitar arrangements. I played through most of the music or tablature in the banjo, guitar, and piano books I've reviewed. After several weeks of playing through review materials, I got more and more involved with the question of what keys arrangements ought to be written in.

Most music publishers don't understand that folk and country styles of playing guitar and banjo use the keys of C, D, E, G, and A major and D, E, or A minor most of the time. When folk musicians use keys like F sharp or D flat, they are almost always using a capo. An artist like Dylan doesn't play or think in a key like D flat; he is actually playing and thinking in the key of C, while using a capo at the first fret, or in the key of A with a capo at the fourth fret, etc. The sound of open strings is an essential ingredient for a folk guitarist or banjoist. Open strings ring in a way that differs from the sound of a stopped string. To a jazz guitarist, the opposite effect is desirable; most jazz guitarists will go to great lengths to play chord positions somewhere on the neck, thereby enabling them to avoid open strings. Open string chords are also easier to play. The D flat chord is a lot harder to finger than a C chord with a capo on the first fret.

When a folk or country songbook includes a number of songs in difficult guitar or banjo keys without capo directions, the arranger is probably a piano player or a jazz guitarist who doesn't understand all of these stylistic details about open string chords. The better modern sheet music arrangers, like Dan Fox, give capo directions when they print folk or country songs that have been transcribed from a record in a capoed key. In discussing songbooks, I have indicated when a book includes a number of songs in impractical keys without capo directions.

When the information has been available, I have given titles, publishers, date of publication, the number of songs, whether songs are arranged for piano and/or guitar, and some of the songs printed. I have chosen not to include prices because of the frequency with which they change. The term "lead sheet" means that only the melody line of a song is printed; no piano or guitar arrangement. "PB" stands for "paperback," "HB" for "hardback," "dist." for "distributed." The term "chord frames" means that the guitar chord diagrams are actually drawn where the chord symbols are shown. The date listed for publication denotes the latest edition, unless otherwise indicated. "OP" stands for out of print—I have listed a few out-of-print books that are not too hard to find in libraries and cover something I feel is important.

When chord symbols are printed, the songs will be playable on the guitar, contingent, of course, on your knowledge of chords. If you play five-string banjo, you will have to change the chord symbols into the key in which you are playing, probably C, D, or G, depending on which tuning you are in. On page 217, you'll find a transposition chart which will help you to play some of these songs on the banjo, or in easier keys with the use of a capo on the guitar. At the moment, there is very little music written specifically for the five-string banjo.

ARTISTS' SONGBOOKS

Songs of Eric Anderson, The, Deep Fork Music, dist. by Big 3, 1969. 19 songs, 96 pp. Piano arrangements and chord symbols. Includes "Thirsty Boots" and "Violets of Dawn."

Joan Baez Songbook, The, Ryerson Music, dist. by Oak, 1964. 66 songs, 189 pp., PB and HB. Piano arrangements and guitar chords. Good piano arrangements by Elie Siegmeister. This book has also been published as three separate paperbacks, entitled *British Ballads and Folk Songs, Noel,* and *Songs for Our Time.* All of these books are selected from Baez' repertory.

Johnny Cash at Folsom Prison. Southwind Music, dist. by Big 3, 1969. 13 songs, 40 pp. Piano arrangements and guitar chords.

CASH, JOHNNY, *Hello, I'm Johnny Cash,* Crescendo.

CASH, JOHNNY, *Motion Picture Songs,* Hill & Range, dist. by Big 3, 1970. 18 songs, 43 pp. Piano arrangements and guitar chords.

CASH, JOHNNY, *Song and Picture Folio #1,* Southwind Music, dist. by Big 3, 1959. 12 songs, 40 pp. Piano arrangements and guitar chords.

CASH, JOHNNY, *Song and Picture Folio #2,* Southwind Music, dist. by Big 3, 1960. 12 songs, 40 pp. Piano arrangements and guitar chords.

Songs of Johnny Cash, Oak. Over 50 songs, 239 pp.

CASHMAN AND WEST, *A Song or Two,* Blendingwell Music, dist. by Big 3, 1972. 12 songs, 64 pp. Piano arrangements

Hedy West

and guitar chords. Songs by the duo that produced Jim Croce's records.

Songs of Leonard Cohen, Oak, dist. to bookstores by Collier, 1969. 24 songs, 96 pp. Lead sheets with guitar tablature and chords. Many photos.

Songs of Love and Hate/Leonard Cohen, Oak, 1969. 96 pp.

Judy Collins Songbook, The, Grosset & Dunlap, music dist. by Oak, 1973. 55 songs, 255 pp. Piano arrangements and chord symbols, most in good guitar keys, no capo directions for others. Songs by various composers, including Billy Edd Wheeler, and Tom Paxton, with several autobiographical articles. An attractive collection.

CROCE, JIM, *His Life and Music*, Blendingwell Music and American Broadcasting Music, dist. by Big 3, 1974. 44 songs, 255 pp.

CROCE, JIM, *I Got a Name*, Blendingwell Music, dist. by Big 3. 11 songs, 64 pp. Piano arrangements with chord symbols. Good guitar keys.

CROCE, JIM, *Life and Times*, Blendingwell Music, dist. by Big 3, 1973. 13 songs. 64 pp. Piano arrangements and chord symbols. No capo directions.

CROCE, JIM, *You Don't Mess Around with Jim*. Blendingwell Music, dist. by Big 3. 12 songs, 64 pp. Piano arrangements, chord symbols, no capo directions.

DAVIS, REV. GARY, *The Holy Blues*, ed. by Stefan Grossman, Chandos Music, dist. by Big 3, 1970. 80 songs, 120 pp. Lead sheets with chord symbols. Many songs from Davis' unique repertoire.

DENVER, JOHN, *Aerie*, Cherry Lane Music, dist. by Crite-

rion, 1971. 12 songs. Piano arrangements, chord symbols, capo directions included.

DENVER, JOHN, *Back Home Again*, Cherry Lane Music, dist. by Warner Bros., 1974.

DENVER, JOHN, *Farewell Andromeda*, Cherry Lane Music, dist. by Warner Bros., 1973. 11 songs, 80 pp. Piano arrangements and chord symbols. Includes capo directions.

DENVER, JOHN, *Rocky Mountain High*, Cherry Lane Music, dist. by Warner Bros. 12 songs, 79 pp.

John Denver Songbook, The, Cherry Lane Music, dist. by Criterion, 1971. 23 songs, 112 pp. Includes piano arrangements and chord symbols. Includes "Take Me Home Country Roads," "I Guess He'd Rather Be in Colorado," and others. All of the above John Denver books are lavishly illustrated and have sensible piano arrangements. The songs are in good guitar keys or have capo directions.

Great Gospel Songs by Thomas A. Dorsey, Aberbach Group, dist. by Big 3. 37 songs, 80 pp. Piano arrangements and chord symbols. Dorsey is an important writer of gospel tunes, formerly a blues writer and performer. Appropriate piano arrangements.

DURST, JAMES, *Just Dreams and Journey*, Phoenix Songs, 1974. 128 pp., PB. A double book bound in two different directions. The author has played all over the world, and these are original songs and poems with lead sheets and chord symbols.

Richard Dyer-Bennet Song Book, Simon & Schuster, 1971. HB. Dyer-Bennet has been an important and somewhat neglected figure in the folk song revival.

Bob Dylan, Warner Bros., 1974. 71 songs, 180 pp. Piano arrangements and chord symbols. Mostly songs from 1963 to 1968, including "Blowing in the Wind," "Don't Think Twice," and others. No capo directions and many in bad guitar keys.

DYLAN, BOB, *Blonde on Blonde*, Bob Dylan Words & Music, dist. by Big 3, 1966. Piano arrangements and chord symbols, no capo directions.

DYLAN, BOB, *John Wesley Harding*, Bob Dylan Words & Music, dist. by Big 3, 1968. 12 songs, 40 pp.

DYLAN, BOB, *Nashville Skyline*, Bob Dylan Words & Music, dist. by Big 3, 1969. 10 songs, 48 pp.

DYLAN, BOB/THE BAND, *Before the Flood*, Warner Bros. 21 songs, 86 pp. Pictures, plus piano arrangements, chord frames for guitar, and chord symbols. Selections from the 1974 tour.

Songs of Richard Fariña, The, Warner Bros., OP. 15 songs. Piano arrangements and chord symbols. Includes "Pack Up Your Sorrows," "Another Country," and others. Has guitar chord frames.

Fat City Songs, Cherry Lane Music, dist. by Criterion, 1971. 18 songs, 64 pp. Piano arrangements and chord symbols. Fat City—Bill Danoff and Taffy Nivert—has written a number of songs for and with John Denver, including his first hit, "Take Me Home Country Roads."

Lester Flatt and Earl Scruggs, Peer-Southern, 1962. 23 songs and instrumentals, including "Foggy Mountain Breakdown."

Memories of Stephen Foster, Edward Marks, dist. by Belwin-Mills. 16 songs, 48 pp. Piano arrangements and chord symbols.

Steve Goodman Song Book, Buddah Music, dist. by

Cimino, 1973. 80 pp. Piano arrangements, chord symbols, and guitar frames. Includes "City of New Orleans."

Arlo Guthrie Book, AMSCO, dist. by Collier. 26 songs, 96 pp. Some piano arrangements, chord symbols, and some guitar tablatures for introductions. Includes "Alice's Restaurant" and "The Motorcycle Song."

Nearly Complete Woody Guthrie Songs, TRO, 1967, OP. 189 songs, 264 pp., PB. Lead sheets, almost all with chord symbols. Many little known songs.

GUTHRIE, WOODY, *The Woody Guthrie Songbook,* Grosset & Dunlap, 1975. 256 pp., HB. This is sort of (but not exactly) the successor to the Woody Guthrie songbook mentioned above.

Tribute to Woody Guthrie, A, TRO, 1972. 29 songs, 72 pp. Lead sheets and chord symbols. A nice tribute. Contains songs, narrative material drawn from Woody's writings, and photos. Part of this concert tribute was recorded on Warner Brothers and Columbia records.

Best of Tom T. Hall, The, Hallnote Music, dist. by Chappell. 13 songs, 64 pp. Piano arrangements and chord symbols. No capo directions.

HALL, TOM T., *The Storyteller,* Hallnote Music, dist. by Chappell. 11 songs, 48 pp. Piano arrangements and chord symbols. No capo directions.

HARDIN, TIM, *Songs and Poetry,* Faithful Virtue Music, dist. by Big 3, 1968. 26 songs, 96 pp. Piano arrangements and guitar chords, no capo directions. Piano arrangements are bad. Hardin deserves better.

John Hartford Song Book, Glaser, dist. by Big 3, 1971. 24 songs, 64 pp. Guitar music in notation, no tablature. Capo directions included.

Richie Havens Anthology, Big 3, 1972. 24 songs, 96 pp. Piano arrangements and chord symbols.

HOUSTON, CISCO, *900 Miles,* Oak, 1965. 70 songs. Traditional and topical songs from his repertoire.

IAN, JANIS, *Stars,* April Blackwood and Frank Music, dist. by Big Bells. 10 songs, 64 pp. Piano arrangements, chord symbols, and chord frames. Capo directions included.

IVES, BURL, *Favorite Folk Ballads,* vol. 2, MCA Music, dist. by Belwin-Mills. 36 pp. Piano arrangements and chord symbols, no capo directions.

Favorites of Mahalia Jackson, Aberbach Group, dist. by Big 3. 15 songs. Piano arrangements and chord symbols.

JANSCH, BERT, *The Bert Jansch Song Book,* London, 1967. 20 songs. Available from Legacy Books. (See Mail-Order Books section, page 196.)

Louisiana Man, The Doug Kershaw Songbook, Collier, dist. to music trade by Oak, 1971. 30 songs, 144 pp. Includes material about Kershaw's life.

KRISTOFFERSEN, KRIS, *Artist/Composer,* Screen Gems Columbia Publications, 1972. 28 songs, 85 pp.

KRISTOFFERSEN, KRIS, *The Silver Tongued Devil and I,* Chappell. 25 songs, 100 pp. Includes "Me and Bobby McGee," "The Silver Tongued Devil and I," and others.

KRISTOFFERSEN, KRIS, *Spooky Lady's Sideshow,* RESACA Music, dist. by Warner Bros., 1974. 12 songs, 62 pp. Chord frames for guitar.

KRISTOFFERSEN, KRIS, *Sunlight and Shadows,* Chappell. 26 songs, 72 pp. Includes "Me and Bobby McGee," "Sunday Mornin' Comin' Down," and others. All the above Kristoffersen books have piano arrangements, guitar frames, chord symbols, but no capo directions.

LEDBETTER, HUDDIE, *The Leadbelly Legend,* ed. by John and Alan Lomax, TRO, 1965. 79 songs, 96 pp. Lead sheets and chord symbols. Many classic tunes that deserve greater popularity.

LIGHTFOOT, GORDON, *Anthology,* vol. 1, Warner Bros. 39 songs, 120 pp. Piano arrangements and chord symbols. Includes "Early Morning Rain," "Ribbon of Darkness," and others.

LIGHTFOOT, GORDON, *Don Quixote,* Warner Bros., 1972. 11 songs, 68 pp. Piano arrangements and chord symbols. No capo directions.

LIGHTFOOT, GORDON, *Sundown.* Warner Bros., 1974. 10 songs, 64 pp. Piano arrangements and chord symbols. Includes capo directions.

LONZO and OSCAR, *Folio of Mountain Ballads and Comedy Songs,* Ernest Tubb Music, dist. by Big 3, 1948. 15 songs, 39 pp. Piano arrangements and chord symbols.

Mary, Warner Bros., 1971. 12 songs, 48 pp. Piano arrangements and guitar chords, with capo directions. This is Mary Travers, of Peter, Paul, and Mary.

Songs of Don McLean, The, Big 3, 1972. 17 songs, 110 pp. Piano arrangements and chord symbols.

Ralph McTell, Essex Music Ltd., England only. 20 songs, 48 pp. Mostly guitar arrangements, some have nice piano arrangements by McTell. Includes capo directions. McTell is a good writer and singer, who has never made much impact in the United States.

MELANIE, *Songs from "Born to Be,"* Big 3. 32 pp. Piano arrangements and chord symbols, no capo directions.

Golden Songs of Roger Miller, The, Hansen. 103 songs. Piano arrangements and chord symbols. Good collection by a somewhat neglected figure.

MITCHELL, JONI, *Songbook,* vol. 1, Siquomb Music, dist. by Warner Bros., 1966–70. 32 songs, 120 pp.

MITCHELL, JONI, *Songbook,* vol. 2, Crazy Crow Music, dist. by Warner Bros. 32 songs, 190 pp. Both Mitchell books have chord frames, chord symbols, piano arrangements, and guitar tunings. The second book includes material dating from the *Blue* album. Joni Mitchell is a superb songwriter, and these are important collections.

Van Morrison, Warner Bros., 1974. 108 pp. Piano arrangements and chord symbols.

The Music of Laura Nyro, Tuna Fish Music, dist. by Warner Bros. 44 songs, 251 pp. Piano arrangements and chord symbols. Many fine songs.

OCHS, PHIL, *The War Is Over,* Barricade Music, dist. by Big 3, 1968. 32 songs. Lead sheets and chord symbols. Good guitar keys.

Tom Paxton Anthology, UA Music, dist. by Big 3, 1971. 25 songs, 64 pp. Piano arrangements and chord symbols. Uses practical guitar keys.

PHILLIPS, U. UTAH, *Starlight on the Rails and Other Songs,* Wooden Shoe, 1973. 44 songs, 96 pp. Good songs and stories. Includes "Rock, Salt and Nails" and "If I Could Be the Rain." Lead sheets and chord symbols.

John Prine, Cotillion Music, dist. by Warner Bros., 1972. 15 songs, 96 pp. Piano arrangements and chord symbols.

RAMBO, DOTTIE, *More Great Gospel Songs,* Hansen. 23 songs, 56 pp. Piano arrangements and chord symbols with guitar chord frames. Dottie Rambo is a member of the Rambos, one of the leading white gospel groups.

Jerry Reed Songbook, The, Ivan Mogull Music, OP. 15 songs, 60 pp. Lead sheets and guitar arrangements in music. No tablatures. Includes "Guitar Man," "Alabama

Wild Man," and others. An important book; Reed is a fine Nashville guitar picker.

REYNOLDS, MALVINA, *Little Boxes and Other Handmade Songs*, Oak, 1964. 54 songs, 95 pp. Lead sheets and chord symbols. Songs include "Little Boxes" and "What Have They Done to the Rain?"

REYNOLDS, MALVINA, *The Malvina Reynolds Songbook*, Schoeder Music Co., 1974. 98 pp. Lead sheets and chord symbols. Includes "Little Boxes," "What Have They Done to the Rain?" and "Turn Around."

REYNOLDS, MALVINA, *The Muse of Parker Street*, Oak. 56 songs. Lead sheets and chord symbols.

RITCHIE, JEAN, *Celebration of Life*, Geordie Music, dist. by Big 3, 1971. 78 songs, 128 pp. Lead sheets and chord symbols. A beautiful book, traditional songs from the Ritchie family, new songs by Jean, many photos by George Pickow.

RITCHIE, JEAN, *Folk Songs of the Southern Appalachians*, Oak, 1965. 77 songs, 96 pp. Lead sheets and chord symbols. A collection of songs from the Ritchie family with notes on the songs.

RODGERS, JIMMIE, *Blue Yodel.* Peer Int'l., 1943. 39 songs, 64 pp. Piano arrangements and guitar chords, no capo directions. Includes 12 of the blue yodels.

RODGERS, JIMMIE, *Supreme Edition*, Peer-Southern, 1943. 36 songs, 64 pp. Lead sheets and chord symbols, no capo directions.

ROSELAND, PAUL, *Alaska Sourdough Ballads.* Alaska Folk Music, 1969. 52 songs, 70 pp. Lead sheets and chord symbols. Some traditional songs, some composed by the author. Sixteen of the songs are available on a record by the author (*see page 96*).

The Buffy Sainte-Marie Song Book. Belwin-Mills/Grosset & Dunlap, 1971. 61 songs, 224 pp. With lead sheets and chord symbols. Some songs have guitar introductions, and suggested accompaniments in tablature. Includes "Universal Soldier," "Codeine," "Now That the Buffalo Has Gone."

John Sebastian Anthology, Faithful Virtue Music, dist. by Big 3, 1970. 37 songs, 112 pp. Piano arrangements and chord symbols. Best-known songs by the composer, who was founder of the Lovin' Spoonful.

Folk Songs of Peggy Seeger, Oak, 1964. 88 songs. Lead sheets and chord symbols. Peggy Seeger has a huge repertoire of folk songs. This collection whets the appetite for future songbooks.

SEEGER, PETE, *American Favorite Ballads*, Oak, 1961. 83 songs, 96 pp. Lead sheets and chord symbols. Mostly familiar songs.

SEEGER, PETE, *The Bells of Rhymney and Other Songs and Stories*, Quick Fox, 1964. Over 80 songs.

Pete Seeger on Record, TRO. 17 songs, 40 pp. Piano arrangements and chord symbols. Vocal edition.

SILVERSTEIN, SHEL, *Dirty Feet.* TRO, 1969. 115 songs, 140 pp. Lead sheets and chord symbols.

Songs of Paul Simon, The, Knopf, 1973. 59 songs, 329 pp., PB. Piano arrangements and chord symbols, no capo directions. Songs written 1963–72, with a few earlier works.

SKY, PATRICK, *Clear.* Oak, 1970. 20 songs, 48 pp.

Stephen Stills, Gold Hill Music, dist. by Warner Bros. 22 songs, 128 pp. Lead sheets and chord symbols, 1 guitar arrangement, others have piano arrangements. Includes

"Love the One You're With" and "Change Partners."

WATERS, MUDDY, *Music for Groups*, Arc Music, dist. by Warner Bros., 1970. 12 songs, 36 pp. Piano arrangements and chord symbols. Dull piano arrangements, some nice songs, including "Honey Bee," and "Standing 'Round Crying."

Songs of Doc Watson, The, Oak, 1971. 32 tunes, 128 pp. Guitar and banjo music and tablatures. In 13 of the arrangements, the music notation doesn't acknowledge the use of the capo, but the tablature does. Some nice tunes here—"Train That Carried My Girl from Town," "Southbound," and others. Three banjo arrangements are included. Let's hope the music will be corrected in future editions.

The Weavers' Song Book, Harper & Row, 1960. 77 songs, 177 pp. Most with piano arrangements and chord symbols.

Travelling on with the Weavers. Harper & Row, 1966. 59 songs, 165 pp. Piano arrangements and chord symbols. The Weavers were a vital part of the folk song revival. In both of the Weavers books, foreign-language songs are printed in English and the original language.

WELLES, MEG, *Just Plain Folk Songs*, Rosarita Music, dist. by Big 3, 1964. 35 songs, 77 pp. Piano arrangements and chord symbols. Very nice piano arrangements. Many rewrites by the author of traditional songs, with some original songs.

Hedy West Song Book, Verlag Rolf Gekeler, 1968, OP. 39 songs, 143 pp. Lead sheets and chord symbols. Songs in English and German, text in German. Good songs, composed or collected by the author.

WHEELER, BILLY EDD, *Honey in the Horn*, vol. 1, Hargail, 1963. 15 songs, 28 pp. Lead sheets and chord symbols.

WHEELER, BILLY EDD, *Honey in the Horn*, vol. 2, Hargail, 1963. 17 songs, 23 pp. These two Wheeler books include both original and traditional material.

WHEELER, BILLY EDD, *The Songs and Poetry of Billy Edd Wheeler*, Big 3, 1971. 40 songs, 128 pp. Lead sheets and chord symbols. Billy Edd Wheeler is one of the best composers of folk-related music. This is a fine book and includes a number of poems as well as such songs as "Winter Sky," "Coal Tattoo," and "Coming of the Roads."

Josh White Song Book, The, ed. by Robert Shelton, Quadrangle, 1963, OP. 57 songs, 191 pp. Piano arrangements and chord symbols. Includes a long and interesting biographical section. Josh is a neglected figure. If there is another edition of this book, perhaps it will include guitar arrangements.

Tony Joe White Song Book, The, Hansen. 19 songs, 55 pp. Much good material from this underrated writer. Includes "Polk Salad Annie," "Willie and Laura Mae Jones," and others. Piano arrangements and chord symbols.

Songs of Hank Williams, Hansen, 1974. A number of other Hank Williams folios are available from Acuff-Rose Publishing Company.

WILLIAMS, MIKE, *Songs*, Athena Enterprises, 1974. 25 songs, 37 pp., PB. With lead sheets and chord symbols. Besides the songs, written by Mike Williams, this book contains additional poems and songs by Charles John Quarto.

WILLS, BOB, *Songs from San Antone*, Hill & Range, dist. by

Big 3, 1946. 20 songs. Piano arrangements and chord symbols. Songs featured by the king of Texas swing.

YOUNG, NEIL, *Complete Music*, vol. 1., Warner Bros., 1974. 28 songs, 191 pp. Piano arrangements with chord symbols and capo directions. These are songs from the period 1966–69; they are from his early solo albums and his work with the Buffalo Springfield.

YOUNG, NEIL, *Harvest*, Warner Bros., 1972. 10 songs, 62 pp. Lead sheets and chord symbols.

COLLECTIONS OF SONGS

All Top Hits, Arc Music, dist. by Warner Bros., 1970. 41 songs, 111 pp., PB. Piano arrangements with chord symbols. Songs by Willie Dixon, Sonny Boy Williamson, and others. Includes "Going Down Slow," "Back Door Man," and others. No capo directions; but blues keys are easy, and the necessary transpositions use the same chords repeatedly.

American Cowboy Songs, Big 3. 67 songs, PB. Piano arrangements and guitar chords. Old favorites with a few modern ringers thrown in.

ASCH, MOSES, JOSH DUNSON, and ETHEL RAIM, eds., *Anthology of American Folk Music*, Oak, 1973. 48 songs, 118 pp., PB. This book contains many songs from the Folkways 6-record set of the same name. Lead sheets and chord symbols, banjo tunings, etc. It also has Mike Seeger's interview with Frank Walker, a man who recorded many important country artists in the twenties and thirties. A must.

"Ballads from Deep Gap": Doc Watson

ATTAWAY, WILLIAM, *I Hear America Singing*, Li-on, 1967. Book and record.

BABAD, HARRY, ed., *Roll Me Over*, Oak, 1972. 130 songs, 144 pp., PB. Lead sheets with guitar chords. Some very bawdy, some not so bawdy.

Ballad of Ira Hayes and Other New Folk Songs, Edward Marks, dist. by Belwin-Mills. 19 songs, 32 pp., PB. Lead sheets and guitar chords. Songs by Peter La Farge and others.

BEST, DICK and RUTH, *Song Fest Deluxe*, Hansen, 1948, then revised, 1955. 330 songs, 192 pp. Three hundred of the songs are traditional, 30 contemporary. Lead sheets and chord symbols over the music, but unfortunately music and words are printed apart from each other. Good collection, though.

Best of Modern Folk Music, The, Cherry Lane Music, dist. by Criterion, 1972. 32 songs, 64 pp., PB. 20 songs lead sheets and chords only; first section of 12 songs with piano arrangements and chord symbols. Includes "Leaving on a Jet Plane," "Country Roads," and others.

Blues for Today. Aberbach Group, dist. by Big 3, 1970. 28 songs, 63 pp., PB. Piano arrangements and chord symbols. The repertoire of the great Robert Johnson credited to a mythical composer. Tasty piano arrangements, fine songs.

BONI, MARGARET, and NORMAN LLOYD, *Fireside Book of Favorite American Songs*, Simon & Schuster, 1952. 131 songs, 359 pp., HB. Nice piano arrangements, melody and chord symbols, no capo directions. Mostly folk songs with some early American pop tunes. Attractive illustrations.

BONI, MARGARET, and NORMAN LLOYD, *The Fireside Book of Folk Songs*, Simon & Schuster, 1947. 147 songs, 323 pp., HB. Piano arrangements, lead sheets, and chord symbols, no capo directions. A classic collection, intended mostly for piano and voice.

Book of the Blues, The, Hansen, PB. Piano arrangements with guitar chords and frames. Eclectic collection, tunes by Duke Ellington, Morton, Tin Pan Alley-ites.

BRACE, GEOFFREY, *Something to Sing*, vol. 2, Cambridge University Press, 1965. 85 pp. Lead sheets, most with chord symbols.

BRAND, OSCAR, *Bawdy Songs and Backroom Ballads*, Dorchester Press, dist. by Grove Press, 1960. 41 songs, 95 pp. Piano arrangements and chord symbols.

BRAND, OSCAR, *Folk Songs for Fun*, TRO, 1961. 150 songs, 192 pp., PB. Lead sheets and guitar chords.

BRAND, OSCAR, *Songs of '76*. Evans, dist. by Lippincott, 1972. 63 songs, 178 pp., HB. With lead sheets and chord symbols. Each song is accompanied by a page of text explaining the song and its historical significance.

BRODERICK, RICHARD, ed., *100 Great Country Songs*, Quadrangle, 1974. 320 pp., PB and HB. Piano arrangements, chord symbols, and guitar chord windows. Some great songs and some dull ones in adequate piano arrangements.

BRUMLEY, ALBERT E., *Olde Time Camp Meetin' Songs, Lamplitin' Songs, The Best of Albert E. Brumley, Songs of the Pioneers, and All Day Singin' and Dinner on the Ground*, Albert E. Brumley Music. All PB. A series of collections of folk, religious, and sentimental songs.

Campus Sing, TRO. 26 songs, 64 pp., PB. Piano arrangements and chord symbols. Arrangements are dull.

CARAWAN, GUY and CANDIE, *Freedom Is a Constant Struggle*, Oak, 1968. 58 songs, 224 pp., PB. Lead sheets and guitar chords, many photos. Documents the struggle for black freedom in the southern United States.

CARMER, CARL, *America Sings*, Knopf, 1950, HB.

CHARTERS, ANN, *The Ragtime Songbook*, Oak, 50 songs, PB. Lead sheets and chords, a few piano arrangements. Many different composers.

CHARTERS, SAMUEL, *Robert Johnson*, Oak, 1973. 29 songs, 87 pp., PB. Songs have lead sheets and chord symbols. A combination songbook and biography. Valuable for gathering these great songs and for Charters' notes on the songs.

CHASE, RICHARD, *American Folk Tales and Songs*, New American Library, 1951, OP. 48 songs, 210 pp., PB. Lead sheets, no chords.

COHEN, MIKE, *To Hell with Skiing*. Oak, PB. Songs of Oscar Brand, Ray Conrad, Bob Gibson, and others.

COLERIDGE-TAYLOR, S., *Twenty-Four Negro Melodies*, Oliver Ditson, dist. by Theodore Presser, 1905. 127 pp., PB. Piano arrangements in the form of art song setting. Sixteen songs from the United States, others from Africa and the West Indies.

CRAY, ED, *The Erotic Muse*, Oak, 1969. 138 songs, 272 pp., HB. Lead sheets, no chord symbols. The songs range from mildly bawdy to outrageous.

CYPORYN, DENNIS, *The Bluegrass Songbook*, Collier, 1973. 88 songs, 154 pp., PB. Lead sheets and chords. A number are in bad guitar keys with no capo instructions. Some articles. Songs by Bill Monroe, A. P. Carter, and others. Cyporyn includes some classics that have seldom been printed before.

DALLIN, LEON and LYNN, *Folk Songster*, Wm. C. Brown Pub., 1967. HB and PB.

DE TURK, DAVID, and A. POULIN, JR., *American Folk Songs*, Dell. PB.

DOWNES, OLIN, and ELIE SIEGMEISTER, *A Treasury of American Song*, Knopf. 1943. 195 songs, 412 pp., HB; Consolidated Music, PB. Nice piano arrangements, no chord symbols. A nice collection, not quite scholarly, not quite "popular."

EDWARDS, JAY, and ROBERT KELLEY, *The Coffee House Songbook*, Oak, 1966. 239 pp. Lead sheets and chord symbols. Chords printed over the music, but not the words. A good collection, some unusual songs collected from semiprofessional folk singers all over the United States.

GLOVER, TONY, and PAUL NELSON, eds., *The Festival Songbook*, Quick Fox, 1973. PB.

Folk Blues, Arc Music, dist. by Warner Bros., 1965. 104 songs, 144 pp. Lead sheets and chords. Songs by Chuck Berry, Willie Dixon, and others.

40 Country and Western Hits of Our Times, book 4, MCA Music, dist. by Belwin-Mills, 1965. PB. Piano arrangements and guitar chords. Songs from the thirties, forties, and fifties; many forgotten tunes.

FOSTER, STEPHEN, *The Social Orchestra*, Da Capo Press, 1973 reprint of 1854 book. 83 pp., HB. For flute, violin, etc. Solos-quartet pieces by Foster and others. A fascinating glimpse into the kind of music played in the American living room around 1854.

FREY, HUGO, *25 Selected Negro Spirituals*, Big 3, 1924. 47 pp., PB. Piano arrangements with melody lines, no chords.

GAMSE, ALBERT, *The Best of Folk Music*, Lewis Publishing Company, 1968. 97 songs, 232 pp., PB. Piano arrangements and chord symbols. These are mostly folk songs, with a few composed songs.

GELLERT, LAWRENCE, and LON ADOMIAN, *Me and My Captain*, Hours Press, 1939, OP. 24 songs, 31 pp., PB. Piano arrangements by Elie Siegmeister, no chord symbols.

GELLERT, LAWRENCE, *Negro Songs of Protest*, American Music League, 1936, OP. 24 songs, 42 pp., PB. Both of the above books are valuable. They represent black protest material collected by Gellert. Rounder Records has issued the field recordings (*see* page 39), although the books themselves are out of print. Gellert's collections are the most explicit black protest material that has ever been collected and published.

GLAZER, TOM, *A New Treasury of Folk Songs*, Bantam Books, 9th printing, 1973. 81 songs. Lead sheets and chords. A good general collection which includes some guitar instruction for beginners in the back of the book.

GLAZER, TOM, *Songs of Peace, Freedom and Protest*, Fawcett, 1972. 172 songs, 362 pp., PB. Lead sheets and chords. Some songs in bad guitar keys with no capo information. Everything from Josh White to Tom Lehrer. A good collection.

Golden Encyclopedia of Folk Music, The, ed. by Clarkson N. Potter. 185 songs arranged for piano, voice, guitar.

Gospel Melodies, Gospel Pub. House. 255 hymns. Round and shaped notes.

GRAHAM, BILL, *Live at Fillmore*, Warner Bros. 28 songs, 124 pp., PB. Piano arrangements, chord symbols, and guitar diagrams. A general collection compiled by the ex-proprietor of the Fillmore Auditoriums. Songs by Lightfoot, Stills, Elton John, and others.

Great Folk Songs of the 60's, TRO. 35 songs, 112 pp., PB. Piano arrangements and guitar chords with suggested strums. Songs are by Pete Seeger, Lee Hays; some are traditional. A useful book.

GROSSMAN, STEFAN and HAL, and STEPHEN CALT, eds., *Country Blues Songbook*, Oak, 1973. 136 songs, 208 pp., PB. Lead sheets and chord symbols. A unique collection; songs of Blind Boy Fuller, Skip James, Charley Patton, and others. Also has long musical and historical introductions of value.

HANCOCK, EUGENE W., *13 Spirituals*, H. W. Gray, dist. by Belwin-Mills, 1973. 48 pp. For voices in unison and two parts. Some unaccompanied, some with organ. No chord symbols. Nice arrangements.

HANSEN, CHARLES, ed., *Song Fest #2*, Hansen, 1973. 400 songs, 213 pp. With lead sheets and chord symbols. Folk songs and some old pop songs. A reasonably good collection, but the chords and music are not printed over the words.

HAUFRECHT, HERBERT, ed., *Folksing* TRO, 1960. 165 songs, 192 pp., PB. Lead sheets and guitar chords. Some traditional, some new. Also a Berkeley paperback.

HILLE, WALDEMAR, ed., *The People's Song Book*, Oak, 1971. 105 songs, 128 pp., PB. Piano arrangements and chord symbols. Folk and protest songs, American and foreign. One of the first collections to emphasize songs of protest.

HOLM, RON, *Charlotte's Web School of Folk Music Song Book*, Charlotte's Web School of Folk Music. 24 songs, PB. Lead sheets and chords. Used in classes at the school.

IWW Songbook, IWW (Industrial Workers of the World). Songs of Joe Hill, T-Bone Slim, and others.

JOHNSON, J. ROSAMUND, *Album of Negro Spirituals*, Edward Marks, dist. by Belwin-Mills, 1940. 26 songs, 56 pp., PB. Piano arrangements and melody lines, no chords. Concert arrangements, piano parts difficult.

JORDAN, PHILLIP, and LILLIAN KESSLER, *Songs of Yesterday*, Doubleday, 1941, OP. 96 songs, 392 pp., HB. Piano arrangements, no chords. Composed songs—the popular music that paralleled American folk music.

KINSCELLA, HAZEL, *Folk Songs and Fiddle Tunes of the U.S.A.*, Carl Fischer, 1959. 42 songs and 7 fiddle tunes, 48 pp. Piano arrangements and chord symbols. The piano arrangements are pleasant and easy to play.

LANDECK, BEATRICE, *Git on Board*, Edward Marks, dist. by Belwin-Mills, 1964. 63 songs, 79 pp., PB. Piano or vocal arrangements, guitar chords.

LANDECK, BEATRICE, and E. CROOK, *Wake Up and Sing*, Morrow, 1969. HB.

LAWRENCE, DOROTHEA, *Folklore Songs*, George Briegel, 1959 OP. 109 songs, PB. Piano arrangements and chord symbols, no capo directions. A kitchen-sink collection; authors throw in a little bit of everything.

LEISY, JAMES, *Good Times Songbook*, Abingdon, 1974. PB.

LEISY, JAMES, ed., *Songs for Pickin' and Singin'*, Fawcett, 1971. PB.

Little Book of Cowboy Songs and Sea Chanties, Pyramid, PB.

LOMAX, ALAN, *The Penguin Book of American Folk Songs*, Penguin, 1964. 111 songs, 150 pp., PB. Piano arrangements and chord symbols. These are nice piano arrangements by Elizabeth Poston, imitating what the banjo or guitar would do. Capo directions given.

LOMAX, JOHN and ALAN, *Best Songs from the Lomax Collections*, TRO, 1966. 85 songs, 96 pp., PB. Lead sheets and guitar chords. Some nice, uncommon songs.

LYNN, FRANK, *Songs for Singin'*, Chandler Publishing, dist. by Belwin-Mills, 1961. 195 songs, 263 pp. Lead sheets and chords.

LYNN, FRANK, *Songs for Swinging Housemothers*, Oak. 350 songs, PB. Lead sheets and chord symbols. A good collection despite the jive title.

McLEAN, DON, ed., *Songs and Sketches of the First Clearwater Crew*, Hudson River Sloop Restoration, 1970. 43 songs, 95 pp., PB. Old and new songs, by McLean, Pete Seeger, Len Chandler, and others.

Memories of the Gay Nineties, Edward Marks, dist. by Belwin-Mills. 15 songs, 48 pp., PB. Piano arrangements, some with chord symbols. Includes "Preacher and the Bear."

Mess of Blues, A, Progressive Music, dist. by Big 3, 1968. 14 songs, 36 pp., PB. Piano arrangements and chord symbols. Includes good fifties songs by Ray Charles, Doc Pomus and Mort Shuman, and others.

MONROE, MINA, *Bayou Ballads*, Schirmer, 1921. 12 songs, 55 pp., HB. With piano arrangements and no chord symbols. French and English texts. Monroe grew up on a plantation in Louisiana, and these are songs that she heard sung by blacks who worked there.

Country Blues: Blind Boy Fuller

MOSS, JAMES, and NANCY MATTHEWS, eds., *Sierra Club Survival Song Book*, Sierra Club. PB. Songs by Eric Anderson, Tom Paxton, and others.

NEWMAN, HAROLD, *Folksongs and Ballads*, Hargail Press, 1963. 39 songs, 24 pp. Lead sheets and chord symbols.

Newport Festival Songbook, The, ed. by Jean Ritchie, Alfred Music, 1965. 57 songs, 128 pp., PB. Lead sheets and chord symbols. One song selected by each of 57 performers at the festival.

NYE, PEARL, *Scenes and Songs of the Ohio-Erie Canal*, Ohio Historical Society, 1971. 8 songs, PB. Lead sheets only. Brief descriptions of the songs.

OKUN, MILT, ed., *New York Times Great Songs of the Sixties*, vols. 1–2, Quadrangle, 1974. 328 and 286 pp., respectively, HB and PB. Piano arrangements, chord symbols, guitar frames. Volume one contains 82 songs, volume two, 64. This is a good overall survey of the songs of the period. Authors included are Jim Webb, Bob Dylan, Tom Paxton, Bachrach and David, and others. All in all, volume one is a more attractive selection; volume two is marred by the inclusion of such dull pop hits as "Young Girl," and "You're Sixteen." There are many songs of merit included, folk and pop.

OKUN, MILT, *Something to Sing About*, Macmillan, 1968. 76 songs, 241 pp., HB and PB. Piano arrangements and chord symbols. Personal choices by well-known folk artists, with biographies of the artists.

100 All Time Country Hits, Acuff-Rose, dist. by Walter Kane. A fine collection of songs by Don Gibson, John D. Loudermilk, Mickey Newbury, Hank Williams, and others. Mediocre piano arrangements, along with chord symbols and guitar chord frames.

100 Favorite Gospel Songs, vols. 1–2, Hill & Range, dist. by Big 3. Vol. 1, 220 pp. Vol. 2, 221 pp. Piano arrangements and chord symbols. Black and white gospel songs by various composers.

100 Great Country and Western Songs, vols. 1–3, Aberbach Group, dist. by Big 3. 215, 228, and 215 pp., PB. Each book has 100 songs, piano arrangements, and guitar chords. Vol. 1 includes Ernest Tubb, Hank Snow; vol. 2, Johnny Cash, Hank Snow; vol. 3, Marty Robbins, Merle Travis, and others. Mostly hits of the forties and fifties.

100 of the Greatest Country Hits, Big 3. 256 pp., PB. Piano arrangements and guitar chords. Songs by Joe South, Merle Haggard, and others.

104 Folk Songs on Folkways Records, Big 3, 1964. 96 pp., PB.

124 Folk Songs on Folkways Records, Big 3, 1965. PB. Both of these two books have lead sheets and chord symbols. Suggested strums, chord charts for guitar and banjo.

RAIM, ETHEL, and JOSH DUNSON, *Grass Roots Harmony*, Oak, 1968. 42 songs, 95 pp., PB. Raim and Dunson have put together a collection of vocal arrangements for two-part singing, with chord symbols for accompaniment. Most of the existing songbooks concentrate on vocal solos or instrumental accompaniments; this book is a valuable addition to folk song publications.

RAINEY, LEO, *Songs of the Ozark Folk*, Ozark Mountaineer, 1972. 55 pp., PB. Lead sheets and chord symbols. Includes biographies of the singers.

Reprints from the People's Songs Bulletins, ed. by Irwin Silber, Oak, 1961. 71 songs and articles, PB. Folk and protest songs. Silber includes a good deal of material not available elsewhere.

Reprints from Sing Out, vols. 1–12, Oak, 1960–70. PB. All with lead sheets and chord symbols. Songs from the pages of *Sing Out!* magazine.

RING, LYLE R., ed., *10 New England Folksongs*, E. C. Schirmer. 17 pp. Nice piano arrangements of mostly unfamiliar songs, with a few old favorites.

RITCHIE, JEAN, *Singing Family of the Cumberlands*, Oak, 1963. 258 pp., PB. Lead sheets, some with guitar chords.

RITCHIE, JEAN, *Swapping Song Book*, Henry Z. Walck, 1952. 21 songs, 93 pp., HB. Piano arrangements and chord symbols. Very nice piano arrangements, unfortunately many in bad guitar keys with no capo directions. This is an excellent introduction to folk music for children, placing the songs in the context of their environment.

ROBINSON, EARL, ed., *Young Folks Song Book*, Simon & Schuster, 1963. PB.

SANDBURG, CARL, *The American Songbag*, Harcourt Brace, HB, reprint of 1927 book, 1970; Harvest Books, PB. Current edition of one of the oldest popular collections. An outstanding collection. The piano arrangements are by 15 different people and tend to be rather arty and complicated.

SANDBURG, CARL, *New American Songbag*, Broadcast Music, 1950, OP. 59 songs, 109 pp. Piano arrangements with guitar chords. No capo directions. Some of the songs come from Sandburg's first book.

SEEGER, MIKE, and JOHN COHEN, *The New Lost City Ramblers Song Book*, Oak, 1964. 256 pp. Lead sheets and chords. Some instrumental breaks and vocal arrangements. The Ramblers have a large and unusual repertoire, and this sampling of their song bag contains many songs that have not been printed before or are currently unavailable elsewhere.

74 Super-Giant Gospel Songs including Songs from "Godspell," Hansen, 1973. 174 pp., PB. Includes piano arrangements and chord symbols. A collection of white gospel songs, mostly composed by Dottie Rambo and William and Gloria Gaither, with one George Harrison song and 8 songs by Stephen Schwartz from the musical "Godspell."

SHARP, CECIL, and MAUD KARPELES, *80 English Folk Songs from the Southern Appalachians*, M.I.T. Press, 1968. 109 pp., PB. Lead sheets and chords, some sample piano and guitar accompaniments. Notes and sources on the songs.

SHELLAN, HERBERT, *Folk Songs of the Blue Ridge Mountains*, Oak, 1968. 96 pp., PB. Lead sheets and chord symbols. These songs were collected in the late fifties.

SHIRLEY, KAY, and FRANK DRIGGS, eds., *The Book of the Blues*, Crown, 1963, OP. 100 songs, HB. Lead sheets and chord symbols, no capo directions. Includes songs by Leroy Carr, Big Bill Broonzy, Tampa Red, and others.

SIEGMEISTER, ELIE, *American Legends*. Edward Marks, dist. by Belwin-Mills, 1945. 6 songs, PB. These are original songs for voice and piano based on American legends. Lyrics by Lewis Allan, Rosemary Benet, and others.

SIEGMEISTER, ELIE, *Songs of Early America, 1620–1830*, Edward Marks, dist. by Belwin-Mills, 1944. 16 songs, 56 pp., PB. Four-part vocal arrangements with piano accompaniment. No chord symbols. Very nice arrangements.

SILBER, IRWIN, *The Great Atlantic and Pacific Song Book*, AMSCO. 144 songs, 160 pp., PB. Lead sheets and chord symbols.

SILBER, IRWIN, *Hootenanny Song Book*, Consolidated Music, dist. by Oak, 1963. 165 songs, 160 pp., PB. Lead sheets and chord symbols.

SILBER, IRWIN, ed., *Lift Every Voice*, Oak, 1964. 77 songs, PB. Piano arrangements and chord symbols; this is the second *People's Songbook*. More emphasis on composed songs than the first book, which had more traditional folk songs.

SILBER, IRWIN, *Soldier Songs and Home Front Ballads of the Civil War*, Oak, 1964. 48 songs, 96 pp., PB. Lead sheets and chords.

SILBER, IRWIN, *Songs America Voted By*, Stackpole Books, 1971. 320 pp., HB. Lead sheets and chord symbols. An informative tableau of American politics. The songs are accompanied by descriptions of the elections described.

SILBER, IRWIN, *Songs of the Civil War*, Columbia University Press, 1960. HB.

SILBER, IRWIN, ed., *This Singing Land*, AMSCO, 1965. 144 songs, 160 pp., PB. Lead sheets and chord symbols. Some guitar instructional material by Happy Traum.

SILBER, IRWIN and FRED, *The Folksinger's Wordbook*, Oak, 1973. 413 songs, 431 pp., PB. Words and chord symbols only. If you can't quite remember a song or are unsure of the chords, this book will provide you with the necessary information. A songbook without any printed melodies should have a large bibliography. The one printed here is inadequate, and consists mostly of earlier books by Irwin Silber.

SILVERMAN, JERRY, *Folk Song Encyclopedia*, 2 vols., Chappell Music Co., music trade dist. by Walter Kane, 1975. 431 pp. each. Lead sheets and chord symbols. Silverman has put together the largest and most ambitious collection of folk songs available. It is an excellent source for tracking down unfamiliar or half-remembered songs. Over 1,000 songs appear in these two large volumes. Most of the songs are American, but there is one group of 83 songs from other parts of the world.

SILVERMAN, JERRY, *Folk Songs for Schools and Camps*, Big 3, 1970. PB. Lead sheets and chord symbols. Familiar favorites.

SILVERMAN, JERRY, *The Liberated Woman's Songbook*, Macmillan, 1971. 77 songs, 146 pp., HB and PB. Silverman includes some unusual songs in the historical sections. Quite a number of the songs in other parts of the book have female protagonists, but have nothing to do with women's liberation. (It seems only fitting that a male critic should review a liberated women's songbook compiled by a man!)

Songs from Broadside, vol. 2, Oak, 1968. 100 songs, 96 pp., PB; vol. 3, Oak, 1970. 97 songs, PB. Songs by Len Chandler, Phil Ochs, and others. Lead sheets and guitar chords.

Songs of the Gay Nineties, AMSCO, 1943. 72 songs. Piano arrangements and chord symbols. Many classics of the period, such as "The Band Played on."

SPAETH, SIGMUND, *Read 'Em and Weep*, Arco Publishing Co., 1945, revised ed. 259 songs, 248 pp., HB. Lead sheets, no chords. This is pop material; it provides a useful adjunct to studying folk materials of the period.

STAVIS, BARRIE, and FRANK HARMON, *Songs of Joe Hill*, Oak. PB. Complete collection of the IWW songster.

STUDENT PEACE UNION, *Songs for Peace*. Oak, 1966. 95 songs, 112 pp. Lead sheets and chord symbols. Songs from England and the United States.

Super Country, MCA Music, dist. by Belwin-Mills, 1971. PB. Piano arrangements and chord symbols. Songs of Bill Anderson, Joe South, and others, mostly covering the years from 1950 to 1970.

TRAVIS, DAVE, *103 Folk Songs*, Hansen. 129 pp., PB. Includes lead sheets and chord symbols. A fine general collection by an English folk singer.

VINSON, LEE *The Early American Songbook*, Prentice-Hall, 1974. 159 pp., HB. A fine collection of eighteenth-century American songs, mostly unfamiliar. The piano arrangements are intelligent, and the guitar chords are in reasonable keys for easy playing. The printing and layout are particularly well done, with drawings throughout.

VON SCHMIDT, ERIC, *Come for to Sing*, Houghton Mifflin, 1963. HB.

WILKINSON, CHARLES, *Sing 'Em Cowboy*, AMSCO. 61 songs. Piano arrangements and chord symbols.

RECOMMENDED COLLECTIONS

Below are the thirteen books I recommend most highly from the list of collections. All of these are paperbacks. For further details about each book, *see* the main listings.

When you buy a songbook, consider whether you are looking for complete versions of partly remembered songs or for new material. Also consider whether the music is readable, chord symbols are included, the binding will hold up, and the price is reasonable.

ASCH, MOSES, et al., *Anthology of American Folk Music.*

BEST, DICK and RUTH, *Song Fest Deluxe.*

CARAWAN, GUY and CANDIE, *Freedom Is a Constant Struggle.*

EDWARDS, JAY, and ROBERT KELLEY, *The Coffee House Songbook.*

GLAZER, TOM, *A New Treasury of Folk Songs.*

GROSSMAN, STEFAN, et al., *Country Blues Songbook.*

LOMAX, ALAN, *The Penguin Book of American Folk Songs.*

LYNN, FRANK, *Songs for Swinging Housemothers.*

Newport Festival Songbook, The.

RITCHIE, JEAN, *Swapping Song Book.*

SEEGER, MIKE, and JOHN COHEN, *The New Lost City Ramblers Song Book.*

SILBER, IRWIN. Any one of the general collections, some listed under his name, some under *Folk Songs on Folkways Records.*

SILVERMAN, JERRY, *Folk Song Encyclopedia*, 2 vols. The most complete songbook of its kind.

REFERENCE BOOKS

The following section is a potpourri; it includes reference works and bibliographies, books about the music of particular ethnic and foreign groups, books about folk music and its history, etc.

Many of the books listed in this section are scholarly rather than popular (that is, songbooks) in orientation. Often, they are available only in hardback. They may or may not include music; when they do, it is usually in the form of a melody line without chord symbols. Scholarly books almost always give extensive notes on the songs and sources of the songs and texts that have been compiled.

GENERAL

The works listed here include bibliographies, discographies, and various catalogues or encyclopedias containing substantial material on American folk music.

AHRENS, PAT, *A History of the Musical Careers of Dewitt "Snuffy" Jenkins and Homer "Pappy" Sherrill*, Wentworth, 1970. 18 pp., PB. Biography and discography.

ASSOCIATION FOR RECORDED SOUND COLLECTION, *A Preliminary Directory of Sound Recordings Collections in the U.S. and Canada*, New York Public Library, 1967. 157 pp., PB.

BAND, R. W. I., ed., *Directory of Institutions and Organiza-*

tions Concerned Wholly or in Part with Folk Music. International Folk Music Council, 1964. 40 pp.

BOARD OF MUSIC TRADE OF U.S.A., *Complete Catalogue of Sheet Music and Musical Works*, Da Capo Press, 1973 reprint of 1870 book. HB.

BRIEGLEB, ANNE, *Directory of Ethnomusicology Sound Collections in the U.S. and Canada*, Society for Ethnomusicology, 1971. 45 pp., PB.

CASH, JOHNNY, *Discography and Recording History*, John Edwards Memorial Foundation, 1969. 48 pp., PB. Mostly a discography, with some biographical material.

CHASE, GILBERT, *Bibliography of Latin American Folk Music*, Library of Congress, Division of Music, 1942. 141 pp. Pages 117–24 cover Spanish-American music, with a bibliography, history, and criticism, and a description of music and texts. The same section deals with American Indian music.

Check List of Recorded Songs in the English Language in the Library of Congress to July, 1940, Arno Press, 1971. HB.

DE CHARM, DESIREE, and PAUL BREED, *Songs in Collections*, Information Service Ltd., 1966. An index to 411 volumes.

DENISOFF, R. SERGE, *Songs of Protest: War and Peace*, ABC Clio, 1973. 88 pp., PB. A bibliography and discography.

FERRIS, WILLIAM, JR., *Mississippi Black Folklore*, University Press of Mississippi, 1971. 61 pp., PB. Bibliography and discography; the bibliography is more complete.

Folk Music. A Catalogue of Folk Music and Folktale Holdings of the Archive of American Folksong, Library of Congress, Division of Music.

FRASER, NORMAN, ed., *International Catalogue of Recorded Folk Music*, UNESCO, in association with Oxford University Press, London, 1954.

GENTRY, LINNELL, *A History and Encyclopedia of Country, Western and Gospel Records*, Scholarly Reprints, 1972 reprint of 1961 book. HB.

GILLIS, FRANK, and ALAN MERRIAM, *Ethnomusicology and Folk Music Dissertations*, Wesleyan University Press, 1966. 148 pp. An international bibliography of theses.

GODRICH, J., and R. M. W. DIXON, *Blues and Gospel Records, 1902–1942*, Storyville, 1967. 912 pp.

HAYWOOD, CHARLES, *A Bibliography of North American Folklore and Folksong*, vols. 1–2, Dover, 1961. 1301 pp., HB. Includes folk dance, folk song, folklore, regional collections, music of various nationalities, recordings, sheet music, etc. Vol. 2 deals with American Indian materials. This is a valuable work, though badly in need of revision.

HAZLUND, URBAN, and GILES OLSSON, *A Listing of Bluegrass LP's Up to 1971*, Kountry Korral.

JASEN, DAVID, *Recorded Ragtime, 1897–1958*, Archon Books, 1973. 155 pp., HB. Includes a history of ragtime. Pieces are listed by title, composer, and artist. An excellent reference work.

JONES, F. O., ed., *A Handbook of American Music and Musicians*, Da Capo Press, 1971 reprint of 1886 book. 182 pp. Mostly lists "serious" musicians; a piano player named Blind Tom and George Dobson of Dobson banjos are mentioned.

LANGRIDGE, DEREK, *Your Jazz Collection*, Archon Books, 1970. 162 pp., HB. Tells how to establish and catalogue a record collection. Deals mostly with jazz, but some blues and ragtime items are mentioned.

LAWLESS, RAY, *Folksingers and Folksongs in America*, enlarged ed., Hawthorn, 1965. 750 pp., HB. An enormous listing of professional folk singers, collectors, etc., with biographies.

LEADBITTER, MIKE, and NEAL SLAVEN, *Blues Records, 1943–1966*, Oak, 1968. 381 pp., HB. An invaluable discographical work on postwar blues.

LOMAX, ALAN, and SIDNEY ROBERTSON COWELL, *American Folk Song and Folk Lore*, Progressive Education Association, 1942, OP. 59 pp., PB. Listing and review of works available at that time. An intelligent and well-organized compilation.

LUMPKIN, BEN GRAY, *Folksongs on Records*, vol. 3, Swallow, Denver, 1950, OP. 98 pp. Reviews and listings of many records that are now out of print. Although this book is out of print, it is still available through the Denver Folklore Center. Many 10-inch LP's are listed.

MUNN, ROBERT F., *The Southern Appalachians: A Bibliography and Guide to Studies.* West Virginia University Library, 1961.

O'NEAL, JIM and AMY, "Chicago Blues Label Guide," *Living Blues* magazine, no. 12, Spring, 1973. We have not generally listed magazine articles, but this one is of exceptional value.

REUSS, RICHARD, ed., *A Woody Guthrie Bibliography, 1912–1967*, Woody Guthrie Publications, 1968.

RINZLER, RALPH, and NORMAN COHEN, *Uncle Dave Macon: A Bio-Discography*, John Edwards Memorial Foundation, 1970. 50 pp., PB. A biographical and discographical study of the first big star of the Grand Ole Opry. There are articles by the editors and others, pictures, and reminiscensces by fellow musicians. An important study.

RORRER, CLIFFORD, *Charlie Poole and the North Carolina Ramblers*, published by the author, PB. Charlie Poole was one of the founders of the southern string band style that preceded bluegrass. This book describes his life and career and contains a discography.

ROSENBERG, BRUCE, *Folksongs of West Virginia*, University Press of Virginia, 1969. A checklist of WPA holdings at the library of the University of Virginia.

ROSENBERG, NEIL, ed., *Bill Monroe and His Blue Grass Boys*, CMF Press, 1974. 120 pp., PB. A thorough discography with a biography and pictures.

RUSSELL, TONY, designer and producer, *The Carter Family: Old Time Music Booklet #1*, Old Time Music, 1973. 62 pp., PB. An enjoyable collection of biographical, historical, and other articles, profusely illustrated. Included is an article by Lesley Riddle, a black guitarist and early traveling companion of A. P. Carter.

SCHOLES, PERCY, *A List of Books About Music in the English Language*, Scholarly Reprints, reprint of 1940 book.

SHESTACH, MELVIN, ed., *Country Music Encyclopedia*, Crowell, 1974. HB.

STAMBLER, IRWIN, and GRELUN LANDON, *Encyclopedia of Folk, Country and Western Music*, St. Martin's Press, 1969. HB and PB.

STANDIFER, JAMES and BARBARA REEDER, *Source Book of African and Afro-American Materials for Music Educators*, Music Educators National Conference, 1972. 147 pp. Books, articles, readings.

Ralph Stanley Discography, Biography, Ralph Stanley Fan Club. PB. The career of the famous bluegrass singer-banjoist.

STICHESON, ANNE and ANTHONY, *Classified Song Directory*, Criterion, 1961.

TIERNEY, JUDITH, ed., *A Description of the George Korson Archive in the Leonard Corgan Library of Kings College, Wilkes Barre, Pa.*, 1973

TULLY, MARJORIE, and JUAN RAEL, eds., *Annotated Bibliography of Spanish Folklore in New Mexico and Southern Colorado*, University of New Mexico Press, 1950.

ULLOM, JUDITH, *Folklore of the North American Indians: An Annotated Bibliography*, Library of Congress, 1969.

WACHSMANN, K. P., ed., *International Catalog of Published Records of Folk Music*, International Folk Music Council, 1960. 37 pp. Some American items, a worldwide listing.

WALKER, EDMUND and STEVEN, *English Ragtime, A Directory*, Walker, 1971. Unpaged, PB.

ZIEGLER, ELSIE, *Folklore: An Annotated Bibliography and Index.* Faxon, 1973.

AMERICAN INDIAN MUSIC

AUSTIN, MARY, *The American Rhythm, American Indian Songs*, Cooper Square 1970 reprint of 1930 book.

BIERHORST, JOHN, *Songs of the Chippewa*, Farrar, Straus, & Giroux, 1974. 17 songs, 47 pp., HB. With piano arrangements and chord symbols. These songs are taken from the Densmore and Henry Schoolcraft collections.

COLLAER, PAUL, *Music of the Americas*, Praeger, 1973. 207 pp., HB.

CRONYN, GEORGE, *American Indian Poetry: An Anthology of Songs and Chants*, Liveright, 1970, HB and PB.

CURTIS, NATALIE, *The Indians' Book*, Dover, 1968 reprint of 1923 book. 149 songs, 584 pp. PB. Lead sheets, no chords. This attractive book covers a number of tribes and regions. Drawings, stories, legends, and songs.

DAVIS, CAROL, *Songs of the Totem.* Empire Printing Co., 1939, OP.

DENSMORE, FRANCES, *American Indians and Their Music*, Johnson Reprints, reprint of 1936 original. 150 pp. Dances, games, ceremonies, musical instruments, and types of songs.

The following ten books are by Frances Densmore, and are reprinted by Da Capo Press from earlier editions. All are hardbound.

Music of Acoma, Isleta, Cochiti, and Zuni Pueblos, 1972 reprint of 1957 book. 82 songs, 117 pp.

Chippewa Music, vol. 1, 1972 reprint of 1910 book. 200 songs, 216 pp.; vol. 2, 1972 reprint of 1913 book. 180 songs, 341 pp.

Choctaw Music, 1972 reprint of 1943 book. 65 songs, 88 pp.

Mandan and Hidatsa Music, 1972 reprint of 1923 book. 192 pp.

Menominee Music, 1972 reprint of 1932 book. 140 songs, 230 pp.

Northern Ute Music, 1972 reprint of 1918 book. 110 songs, 213 pp.

Papago Music, 1972 reprint of 1929 book. 167 songs, 229 pp.

Pawnee Music, 1972 reprint of 1929 book. 86 songs, 129 pp. Densmore heard Peyote songs, but didn't print them because she thought they were too modern!

Seminole Music, 1972 reprint of 1956 book. 243 songs, 223 pp. In the Seminole collection, 153 songs come from Billy Stewart. This is the largest number of songs Densmore got from any Indian informant; she actually collected 200 songs from Stewart.

Teton Sioux Music, 1972 reprint of 1918 book. 600 songs, 561 pp.

All of these books were originally published by the Bureau of American Ethnology. I find it hard to conjure up a picture of this incredible woman collecting folk songs on remote Indian reservations over a fifty-year period. Densmore traveled alone, or with a sister or companion, all over the United States and Canada collecting and transcribing this body of music.

These recordings are housed in the Folk Song Archive of the Division of Music of the Library of Congress. There is a complete book devoted to Frances Densmore, entitled *Frances Densmore and American Indian Music,* by Charles Hofmann, published by The Museum of the American Indian.

FLETCHER, ALICE, *Indian Games and Dances with Native Songs,* AMS, 1970 reprint of 1915 book. 130 pp. Includes 25 melodies.

FLETCHER, ALICE, *Indian Song and Story,* AMS Press, 1970 reprint of 1900 book. 30 songs with piano accompaniment.

GLASS, PAUL, *Songs and Stories of the American Indian,* Grosset & Dunlap, OP. 31 songs, 61 pp., PB. Lead sheets and chord symbols. Songs from various tribes.

HOFMANN, CHARLES, *American Indians Sing,* John Day, 1967, OP. 96 pp. HB. 11 melodies, no chords.

HOFMANN, CHARLES, *Frances Densmore and American Indian Music,* Museum of the American Indian Foundation, 1968. 127 pp., HB. Includes photos and a bibliography.

HOFMANN, CHARLES, *War Whoops and Medicine Songs,* Boston Music, dist. by Frank Music, 1952. 34 pp. Lead sheets, no chords to 16 songs. A good introductory book. Also has information about dances that go with the songs.

KILPATRICK, JACK F. and ANNA G., *Muskogean Charm Songs Among the Oklahoma Cherokees,* Smithsonian Press, 1967. 10 songs, PB. This pamphlet is extracted from *Smithsonian Contributions to Anthropology,* vol. 2, no. 3, pp. 29–40. Lead sheets only. Songs of medicine and magic among the Oklahoma Cherokees.

KURATH, GERTRUDE, and ANTONIO GARCIA, *Music and Dance of the Tewa Pueblos,* Museum of New Mexico Press, 1973. 309 pp., PB. Many music transcriptions (melody lines only), photos, and descriptions of the dances.

MCALLESTER, DAVID P., *Indian Music in the Southwest,* The Taylor Museum, 1961. 15 pp., PB. A brief pamphlet, discussing music of the Apaches, Navajos, and various Pueblo groups.

MCALLESTER, DAVID, *Peyote Music,* Johnson Reprint, 1964 reprint of 1949 book. 104 pp. of text, followed by 84 melodies in lead sheet form, PB. The music of 14 tribes is included, together with a rhythmic and melodic analysis of the songs, and descriptions of Peyote ceremonies.

MERRIAM, ALAN P., *The Anthropology of Music,* Northwestern University Press, 1964. 358 pp., HB. An absorbing attempt to tie music to the social structure in numerous primitive tribes and societies. Merriam deals at some length with the Flathead Indians of Montana. He discusses musicians, problems of composition, the integration of music with the culture, etc.

MERRIAM, ALAN P., *Ethnomusicology of the Flathead Indians,* Aldine, 1967. 138 songs, 403 pp., HB. Includes musical analysis and background of songs.

NETTL, BRUNO, *North American Indian Musical Styles,* American Folklore Society, University of Texas Press, 1954. 51 pp., PB. This book contains 28 musical examples. It divides North America into 6 musical areas and describes the different musical traits in these areas.

PAIGE, HARRY, *Songs of the Teton Sioux,* Westernlore Press, 1969. 216 pp., HB. Texts, no melodies.

PIETROFORTE, ALFRED, *Songs of the Yokuts and Paiutes,* Naturegraph Publishers, 1965. 25 songs, 64 pp., HB. Tapes also available. Lead sheets, no chord symbols. Music of the California Indians, collected in 1959 and 1960, with notes on the songs and the singers.

ROBERTS, HELEN, *Form in Primitive Music,* W. W. Sutton, 1933, OP. 180 pp. A musical analysis and comparative study of the music of the Indians of southern California, especially the music of the Luiseño.

SPINDEN, HERBERT J., *Songs of the Tewa,* Sunstone Press, 1975, new edition of 1933 original. 144 pp., HB. Contains a new supplementary introduction by Margaret D. Ortix and Sandra P. Edelman, and a new foreword by Alice Marriott.

UNDERHILL, RUTH, *Singing for Power,* University of California Press, 1938. HB. 158 pp., texts only. Songs of the Papago Indians. Highly recommended in Lomax–Cowell discography for its description of songs in the context of their culture.

BLACK MUSIC

I have included materials on blues, spirituals, and gospel music. Jazz is discussed only occasionally and only insofar as it relates to folk materials. Early jazz music evolved out of the folk tradition, especially out of the blues. Later, jazz required formal music training and involved such matters as orchestration and large-scale composition, which places it outside of the folk idiom.

There are a number of interesting controversies and unresolved questions about black music. Many of the books listed deal with these problems. One such question involves the relationship between blues and country music, and just how interrelated these forms were. We do know that a number of important white musicians, including Bill

Monroe and Merle Travis, were strongly influenced by black musicians. Another thorny problem is whether Negro spirituals derive from white hymns or independently of them. A number of the books reviewed here present rather strong, opposing views on this question.

ABRAHAMS, ROGER, *Deep Down in the Jungle*, rev. ed., Aldine, 1970. 278 pp., HB and PB. Stories, tales, "dirty dozens," collected in the Philadelphia ghetto. Excellent book.

ABRAHAMS, ROGER, *Positively Black*, Prentice-Hall, 1970, 177 pp., PB. A brilliant interpretation of contemporary black culture through black folklore and music.

ALBERTSON, CHRIS, *Bessie Smith*, Stein & Day, 1972. 253 pp., HB. This is an excellent biography of the great singer; most of the information came from Ruby Walker, Smith's niece by marriage. Carmen Moore's book, on the other hand, used Smith's ex-husband, Jack Gee, as a primary source.

ALLEN, WILLIAM, CHARLES WARE, and LUCY GARRISON, *Slave Songs of the United States*, Peter Smith, 1951 reprint of 1867 original. 136 songs, 153 pp., HB and PB. Lead sheets, no chord symbols. An invaluable collection; one of the first collections of black music in the United States.

The Greatest Classic Blues Singer: Bessie Smith

ARMSTRONG, MAY, and HELEN LUDLOW, *Hampton Institute and Its Students*, Metro Books, 1874 original. 50 songs, HB.

BASTIN, BRUCE, *Crying for the Carolinas*, Studio Vista, 1971. 112 pp., PB and HB. Describes Piedmont blues style, including artists such as Blind Boy Fuller, Gary Davis, and Brownie McGhee. Includes some texts.

Beale St. USA, Blues Unlimited, 12 pp. Theaters, bars. Numerous photos.

BELL, BERNARD, *Folk Roots of Afro-American Poetry*, Broadside, 1974.

BLESH, RUDI, *Eight Lives in Jazz*, Hayden, 1971, 240 pp., PB; Chilton, 1971, HB. One chapter on Eubie Blake, the ragtime pianist, gives an excellent glimpse into the ragtime era. Others covered are jazzmen.

BLESH, RUDI, and HARRIET JANIS, *They All Played Ragtime*, Oak, 1971. PB. 356 pp. *The* book on ragtime, includes 15 rags for piano. Includes history, biographies, discography, and bibliography.

BOOM, FRANK, *Laughing to Keep from Crying*, Studio Vista, 1971. An essay on satire in the blues. Written in the mid-forties.

BOTKIN, B. A., *Lay My Burden Down*, University of Chicago Press, 1945. 284 pp., HB. Fascinating narratives by dozens of ex-slaves describing their lives.

BRADFORD, PERRY, *Born with the Blues*, Oak, 1965, OP. HB and PB. Bradford's life and hard times; as he sees it, he's one of the world's only honest men. Includes some of his songs.

BRADFORD, ROARK, *John Henry*, music by Jacques Wolfe. Harper, 1939, OP. 90 pp. A play, including 8 songs. The original cast included Paul Robeson and Josh White.

BREWSTER, J. MASON, *American Negro Folklore*, Quadrangle, 1968. 47 songs, 386 pp. Lead sheets, no chord symbols.

BROONZY, WILLIAM (BIG BILL), As Told to Yannick Bruyoghe, *Big Bill Blues*, Cassell & Co. (England), Oak (U.S.), 1955, OP in U.S. 139 pp., PB. Texts to 10 songs. Broonzy tells the story of his life. Included is a wild story about a blues contest he lost to Memphis Minnie. Broonzy ran off with the prize, a bottle, anyway. Broonzy was an important bluesman, and this is a fascinating memoir.

BROVEN, JOHN, *Walking to New Orleans*. HB and PB. Story of postwar blues and rhythm-and-blues scene in New Orleans.

BUERKLE, JACK V., and DANNY BARKER, *Bourbon Street Black*, Oxford University Press, 1973. 244 pp., PB. What it's like to be a black jazzman in New Orleans.

CARAWAN, GUY and CANDIE, *Ain't You Got a Right to the Tree of Life*, Simon & Schuster, 1966. 21 songs, 191 pp., HB. Lead sheets, no chords. The speech of the black Sea Island informants is transcribed. An attractive book, with good photos.

CARAWAN, GUY and CANDIE, *Freedom Is a Constant Struggle*, Oak. PB and HB. Documentary of the freedom movement through its songs.

CARAWAN, GUY and CANDIE, *We Shall Overcome!* Oak, 1963. 112 pp., PB. A valuable social history through songs and some additional texts.

CHAMBERS, H. A., *The Treasury of Negro Spirituals*, Emerson Books, 1963. HB. 30 spirituals, 6 modern compositions.

CHAPMAN, MARIA WESTON, compiler, *Songs of the Free, and Hymns of Christian Freedom,* Original edition, 1836, Books for Libraries. HB.

CHAPPELL, LOUIS W., *John Henry: A Folk-Lore Study,* Kennikat, 1968 reprint of 1933 book. 144 pp., PB. Detailed study, largely in disagreement with Guy Johnson's book on the same subject.

CHARTERS, ANN, *Nobody,* Macmillan, 1970. 157 pp., HB. Words and music to 10 songs. A study of the black comedian and singer Burt Williams.

CHARTERS, SAMUEL, *The Bluesmen,* Oak, 1967. 223 pp. A musical and environmental analysis of regional blues styles. Chapters on Blind Lemon, Charley Patton, Son House, and others. Tends to be episodic and superficial; still a useful book. Includes some musical transcriptions and analyses.

CHARTERS, SAMUEL, *The Country Blues,* Rinehart, 1959, HB, OP; Da Capo, PB. One of the first books on the subject. This book inspired later and more careful research by Charters and others. It is overliterary and not too accurate.

CHARTERS, SAMUEL, *Poetry of the Blues,* Oak, 1963; Avon, 1970. PB. A superficial book, Charters' poorest.

CONE, JAMES, *The Spiritual and the Blues,* Seabury. PB and HB.

COOK, BRUCE, *Listen to the Blues,* Scribner's, 1973. 263 pp., HB. An excellent popular study of the blues. Cook visited many blues singers, and his affection and understanding for the blues carries over to the reader. I would have been happier with less material and more detail.

COURLANDER, HAROLD, *Negro Folk Music USA.* Columbia University Press, 1963. HB and PB. 324 pp. Lead sheets to 43 songs, no chords. A good general introduction to black music, with chapters on blues, work songs, spirituals, Creole music, etc.

COURLANDER, HAROLD, *Negro Songs from Alabama,* Oak, 1963. 67 songs, PB. Lead sheets, no chords. Some of the songs are in his other book. This music has been recorded on Folkways records in a 6-set LP series called *Negro Folk Music of Alabama.*

CRITE, ALLAN, *Were You There When They Crucified My Lord?* McGrath, 1969 reprint of 1944 book. HB.

CUNEY-HARE, MAUD, *Negro Musicians and Their Music,* Da Capo Press, 1974 reprint. HB.

DE LERMA, RENE-DOMINIQUE, ed., *Black Music in Our Culture,* Kent State University Press, 1970. 263 pp., HB.

DE LERMA, RENE-DOMINIQUE, *Reflections on Afro-American Music,* Kent State University Press, 1973. 271 pp., HB. Both of the De Lerma books are symposiums on black music. The *Reflections* book has an interesting article by Thomas A. Dorsey, the father of black gospel music. *Black Music* lists many sources of materials on black music.

DETT, R. NATHANIEL, ed., *Religious Folk Songs of the Negro,* AMS Press, reprint of 1927 original. HB.

DIXON, ROBERT, and JOHN GODRICH, *Blues and Gospel Records 1902–1942,* Stein & Day, 1970. 112 pp., HB and PB. A history of blues recording until 1945. Informative.

EVANS, DAVID, *Big Road Blues,* Studio Vista, 1971. Mississippi singers and their blues.

EVANS, DAVID, *Tommy Johnson,* Studio Vista, 1971. 112 pp., PB. A good biography of the Delta singer. Includes texts of songs and a description of his guitar style.

FAHEY, JOHN, *Charley Patton,* Studio Vista, 1970. 112 pp., PB. 31 texts and tunes, 12 additional texts. This is a rather formal work, concentrating on such matters as scale analysis. More biographical material and some analysis of the lyrics would have been useful.

FERRIS, WILLIAM, JR., *Blues from the Delta,* Studio Vista, 1970. 111 pp., PB. Emphasizes the interplay in live music which cannot be captured in the comparatively sterile world of recording.

FISHER, MARK MILES, *Negro Slave Songs in the United States,* Cornell University Press, 1953; Citadel Press, 1969, PB. Emphasizes longings for Africa in the spiritual, argues that Negro spirituals are older than white ones.

GARON, PAUL, *The Devil's Son-in-Law,* Studio Vista, 1971. 112 pp., PB. A history of Peetie Wheatstraw and the St. Louis blues scene.

GERT ZUR HEIDE, KARL, *Deep South Piano,* Studio Vista, 1970. 67 pp., PB. A biography of Little Brother Montgomery and the musicians he played with. Includes a number of song lyrics.

GLASS, PAUL, *Songs and Stories of Afro-America,* Grosset & Dunlap, 1971. PB.

GRISSOM, MARY, *The Negro Sings a New Heaven,* Dover, 1969. PB. A collection of spirituals.

GROOM, BOB, *Blind Lemon Jefferson,* Blues World, 1970. PB.

GROOM, BOB, *The Blues Revival,* Studio Vista, 1971. 112 pp., PB. Study of the blues revival and the rediscovery of many old bluesmen.

GROOM, BOB, *Robert Johnson,* Blues World, 1969. PB.

GURALNICK, PETER, *Feel Like Going Home,* Outerbridge, dist. by Dutton, 1971. 224 pp., PB. A sensitive and intelligent study of several of the author's favorite bluesmen, with chapters on Muddy Waters, Johnny Shines, Robert Pete Williams, Howlin' Wolf, and the Sun and Chess record companies. Guralnick also includes some less interesting material on rockabilly music. The chapter on Charlie Rich, written before his recent comeback from obscurity, is an accurate portrait of the life of a working musician.

HANDY, W. C., ed., *Blues: An Anthology,* rev. ed., Collier, 1973. 53 songs, 224 pp., PB. Music revised by Jerry Silverman. Piano arrangements, capo directions when necessary, and chord symbols. A good book, long historical introduction by Abbe Niles, some tunes by Handy, some traditional, some by other composers.

HANDY, W. C., *Father of the Blues,* ed. by Arna Bontemps, Collier, 1970 ed. of 1941 book. 333 pp. PB and HB. The life story of Handy, a key link in the history of folk blues, ragtime, and jazz.

HARALAMBOS, MICHAEL, *Right On: From Blues to Soul in Black America,* Edison Bluesbooks. HB.

HATFIELD, EDWIN, *Freedom's Lyre,* Books for Libraries, reprint of 1840 ed. HB.

HAVERLY JOHN *Negro Minstrels: A Complete Guide,* Gregg Press, 1969 reprint of 1902 book. HB.

HEILBUT, TONY, *The Gospel Sound,* Simon & Schuster, 1971, HB, 350 pp.; Anchor, PB. The author paints a vivid picture of the hard life of a gospel performer. Too many singers are covered; nevertheless this is the only book of its kind. There is a useful discography. The author is weakest when commenting about music, when he degenerates into comments about "far out chords."

At Home in the Evening

History of the Blues, The. With an introduction by Leonard Feather, no author listed, Hansen, 1972. 200 pp., PB. Piano arrangements with chord symbols. An eclectic group of tunes by such writers as B. B. King, Jimmy Rushing, Leonard Feather.

HURSTON, ZORA, *Mules and Men*, Negro Universities Press, 1969 ed. of 1935 book. 10 songs, HB. A pioneer study in black folklore.

JACKSON, BRUCE, *The Negro and His Folklore*, University of Tennessee Press, 1967. 374 pp. Mostly folklore, a few songs.

JACKSON, BRUCE, *Wake Up Dead Man*, Harvard University Press, 1972. 65 songs, 326 pp., HB and PB. Lead sheets, no chords. A valuable collection that describes the relationship between the singers' lives and music. The songs were collected from black prisoners in Texas.

JACKSON, J., *The Colored Sacred Harp*, Paragon, 1973 ed. of 1934 book. 77 songs, 96 pp. Lead sheets and shaped notes.

JACKSON, MAHALIA, and EVAN WYLIE, *Movin' on Up*, Hawthorn, 1966. The singer's autobiography.

JOHNSON, GUY, *John Henry*, University of North Carolina Press, 1929. 155 pp., HB. Johnson's book includes tunes as well as texts.

JOHNSON, JAMES W., and J. ROSAMUND, *The Book of American Negro Spirituals*, vols. 1–2, Viking, 1937. 121 songs, 576 pp. These are piano arrangements for concert performance; there are no chord symbols.

JOHNSON, JAMES W. and J. ROSAMUND, *Lift Every Voice and Sing*, Hawthorn, 1970.

JOHNSON, ROBERT, *King of the Delta Blues Singers*, Immediate Music. Words and music to 29 blues.

JONES, BESSIE, and BESS LOMAX HAWES, *Step It Down*, Harper & Row, 1972. 69 songs, 233 pp. Lead sheets, no chords.

JONES, HATTIE, *Big Star Fallin' Mama*, Viking, 1973. HB. A novel.

JONES, LE ROI, *Blues People*, Morrow, 1963. 244 pp., HB and PB. A good introduction to black music, where it comes from and why. The author is overly fond of generalizing.

KATZ, BERNARD, ed., *The Social Implications of Early Negro Music in the U.S.*, Arno Press and New York Times, 1969. 146 pp., HB and PB. Many early articles with songs. Texts and music (lead sheets) included.

KEIL, CHARLES, *Urban Blues*. University of Chicago Press, 1966. HB and PB. Keil focuses on the modern urban blues singer and his life and music. There are extended sections on B. B. King and Bobby Blue Bland. Keil suggests areas for further study, and makes a number of insightful points. He is somewhat reluctant to admit that the modern blues is much closer to the grab bag of commercial manipulation than to the anguished cries of a folk blues artist like Robert Johnson.

KIMBALL, ROBERT, and WILLIAM BOLCOM, *Reminiscing with Sissle and Blake*, Viking, 1973. 254 pp. HB.

KREHBIEL, HENRY, *Afro-American Folk Songs*, Frederick Ungar, 1971 ed. of 1913 book. 176 pp., HB. This book contains musical analyses of 500 songs, and includes material on African and Creole music. A basic book.

LANDECK, BEATRICE, *Echoes of Africa in Folk Songs of the Americas*, McKay, 1969, 2nd rev. ed. 184 pp. This is mostly a collection of Latin American songs, but Landeck includes a few Creole songs, and a fair number of black work songs, spirituals, blues and minstrel songs from the United States. Lead sheets and chord symbols included.

LANG, IAN, *Jazz in Perspective: Background of the Blues*, Hutchinson, 1947.

LEADBITTER, MIKE, *Crowley, Louisiana Blues*, Blues Unlimited. 32 pp., PB. Story of the Excello record label.

LEADBITTER, MIKE, *Delta Country Blues*, Blues Unlimited, 1968. 37 pp., PB. Some articles from the magazine, some new work.

LEADBITTER, MIKE, ed., *Nothing but the Blues*, Oak, 1971. 278 pp., HB. This is an invaluable reference work; a virtual encyclopedia of the blues drawn from old articles in *Blues Unlimited* magazine. Much biographical and historical information about blues artists, both famous and obscure.

LEADBITTER, MIKE, and EDDIE SHULER, *From the Bayou*, Blues Unlimited, 1969. 62 pp. The story of Goldband Records. Shuler has recorded Cajun music, blues, pop hits, and country music on the Goldband label.

LEISER, WILLIE, *I'm a Road Runner Baby*, Blues Unlimited. 38 pp., PB. An entertaining description of the author's American tour. Leiser met and talked with many blues and gospel singers. Includes many photos.

LOCKE, ALAIN, *The Negro and His Music*, Arno Press, 1969 reprint. HB and PB. A history of black music in the United States. Locke deals with musicians, spirituals, jazz, serious music, etc. He was one of the first writers to take black music seriously.

LOMAX, ALAN, *Mister Jelly Roll*, Grove Press, 1950. 302 pp. Contains 20 pages of piano arrangements. A fascinating study of Jelly Roll Morton, an important figure in ragtime and early jazz.

LOMAX, ALAN, *The Rainbow Sign*, Duell, Sloan & Pearce, 1959, OP. 204 pp., HB. The lives of a black singer and a minister. Reprints a sermon recorded in northern Mississippi. Interesting and well-written.

LOMAX, JOHN and ALAN, *Negro Folk Songs As Sung by Leadbelly*, Macmillan, 1936, OP. 242 pp., HB. Numerous songs with lead sheets, no chords. A valuable study, but essentially John Lomax's side of the Leadbelly–John Lomax dispute in their rather thorny relationship.

LOVELL, JOHN, JR., *Black Song: The Forge and the Flame*, Macmillan, 1972. 686 pp., HB. An extremely detailed history of black spirituals, which Lovell sees as being original and not derived from white music. This is an essential book, and its only drawback is the endless number of quotations which the author throws into almost every paragraph.

LYDON, MICHAEL, *Boogie Lightning*, Dial Press, 1974. HB.

MARSH, J. B. T., *The Story of the Jubilee Singers with Their Songs*, Greenwood, reprint of 1881 ed. 128 songs, 243 pp., HB. A collection of spirituals.

MCILHENNY, E., *Befo' De War Spirituals*, Christopher Pub., 1933, OP. 123 songs, 251 pp., HB.

MITCHELL, GEORGE, *Blow My Blues Away*, Louisiana State University Press, 1971. 208 pp., HB. The lives of various obscure Delta singers; tape-recorded interviews and photos. Some lyrics are transcribed. Two Arhoolie LP's have been released in conjunction with this book. A worthwhile glimpse into real life; after all, most Delta singers did not become superstars.

MOORE, CARMEN, *Somebody's Angel Child: The Story of Bessie Smith*, Crowell, 1970, 121 pp., HB; Dell Books, 1975, PB. Carmen Moore is a sympathetic interpreter of the life and work of Bessie Smith. This book is really intended for teenagers, and it tends to oversimplify what is really a very complicated life story. Since the book was written with the aid of Jack Gee, Bessie's ex-husband, it tends to be very gentle in dealing with their marital relationship, in comparison with the Albertson book.

MURRAY, ALBERT, *The Hero and the Blues*, University of Missouri Press, 1973. 120 pp., HB. A work of literary criticism with a bit of material on black music.

NAPIER, SIMON, ed., *Back Woods Blues*, Blues Unlimited, 1968. 55 pp., PB. Reprints from *Blues Unlimited* and some other articles.

NATHAN, HANS, *Dan Emmett and the Rise of Early Negro Minstrelsy*, University of Oklahoma Press, 1972. 496 pp., HB. Now published by Detroit Reprints In Music. Interesting materials on early minstrels, and on nineteenth-century banjo tunes. Many musical examples including 66 tunes by Dan Emmett. These are piano arrangements, with no chord symbols. Some of the early minstrels were white and some black, but all of their work was based on black music.

NICHOLAS, A. Y., *Poetry of the Blues*, Bantam Books, 1973. PB. Includes lyrics only.

NILES, JOHN JACOB, *Singing Soldiers*, Singing Tree Press, reissue of 1927 book. 171 pp., HB. 32 texts and melodies, some with piano arrangements, some with melody lines. No chord symbols. These are songs that Niles collected while serving with the air force in World War I. This book gives a glimpse of how a new blues song is written.

ODUM, HOWARD, *Rainbow Round My Shoulder, Wings on My Feet, and Cold Blue Moon*, Bobbs-Merrill, HB. These three out-of-print novels, published from 1928 to 1931, are based on the life of Left Wing Gordon, who was a singer that Odum and Guy Johnson encountered while collecting songs. Some of the dialogue seems stilted today; but this was a notable attempt for its time, in an area that is still relatively untouched by novelists.

ODUM, HOWARD, and GUY JOHNSON, *The Negro and His Songs*, Greenwood, reprint of 1925 ed. 306 pp. There are 210 texts in this collection, but no music. The songs included are both religious and secular. A pioneering work; bawdy texts are somewhat expurgated.

ODUM, HOWARD, and GUY JOHNSON, *Negro Workaday Songs*, Greenwood, reprint of 1927 book. 278 pp., HB. There are 248 texts here, no music. There is a chapter on Left Wing Gordon, the character on whom Odum based his three novels.

OLIVER, PAUL, *Aspects of the Blues Tradition*, Oak, 1970. 294 pp., HB. In England this book is called *Screening the Blues*. Oliver is a perceptive critic, and he raises a number of interesting questions, such as whether recordings accurately reflected what a singer would do in his normal setting. Chapters on Joe Louis, pornography, and other topics. Oliver is open-minded, but seems to lack a sense of humor and an awareness of possible inconsistencies or contradictions in the songs or attitudes of the artists.

OLIVER, PAUL, *Bessie Smith*, A. S. Barnes, 1959. PB.

OLIVER, PAUL, *Blues Fell This Morning*, Horizon Press,

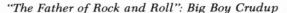

"The Father of Rock and Roll": Big Boy Crudup

1960. 355 pp., HB. Backgrounds of the blues, includes 305 partial or complete texts. Also available in paperback, under the title *The Meaning of the Blues,* Collier, 1972.

OLIVER, PAUL, *Conversations with the Blues,* Horizon Press, 1965. 217 pp., HB. Biographies of various singers extracted from tape-recorded interviews. Includes 80 photographs.

OLIVER, PAUL, *Savannah Syncopators: African Retentions of the Blues,* Stein & Day, 1970. 112 pp., HB and PB. This book deals with the routes of slaves across Africa and suggests that the slaves came from more areas than we've realized.

OLIVER, PAUL, *The Story of the Blues,* Chilton, 1969. 176 pp., HB. A comprehensive history of the blues with many pictures to set the scene. 11 musical examples, bibliography and discography.

OLSSON, BENGT, *Memphis Blues,* Studio Vista, 1970. 112 pp. Mostly biographies. A panorama of the Memphis blues scene. Includes 14 texts.

OSTER, HARRY, *Living Country Blues,* Folklore Associates, dist. by Gale, 1969. 464 pp., HB. 221 texts, 22 tunes. Discography and bibliography. An excellent collection of Louisiana blues, including songs by Robert Pete Williams. Contains excellent material on how blues are constructed and what the songs say. It would have been nice to have more music.

PAGET, M., *Spirituals Reborn,* Cambridge University Press. Lead sheets and chords.

PARRISH, LYDIA, *Slave Songs of the Georgia Sea Islands,* Gale, reprint of 1942 book. 85 songs, 256 pp. Lead sheets, no chords. An invaluable book; among other subjects this book deals with the survival of African traits in America. Many artistic photographs.

PARSONS, ELSIE W., *Folk-Lore of the Sea Islands.* Kraus Reprint, 1969 ed. of 1923 book. Folklore, with 18 songs at the end of the book.

PIKE, GUSTAVUS, *The Singing Campaign for Ten Thousand Pounds; or The Jubilee Singers in Great Britain,* Books for Libraries, reprint of the 1875 ed. HB. The appendix contains slave songs.

RAMSEY, FREDERIC, JR., *Been Here and Gone,* Rutgers University Press, 1969. 177 pp., HB and PB. An excellent book on black music and life in the rural south in the 1950's. Many fine photos, an essential book for understanding black music in the south. People in the photographs recorded a 10-set LP series on Folkways.

REDD, LAWRENCE, *Rock Is Rhythm and Blues.* Michigan State University Press, 1974. 167 pp., HB. Interesting data on how copyrights and tunes were stolen from black artists. Interviews with B. B. King, Big Boy Crudup, Jerry Butler, and Jesse Whitaker, the former baritone of the Pilgrim Travelers gospel group.

ROACH, HILDRED, *Black American Music,* Crescendo, 1973. HB and PB. A history of black music from African survivals to present-day composers. Seventy musical examples. Roach includes material on modern African and American jazz composers.

ROBERTS, JOHN, *Black Music of Two Worlds,* Praeger, 1972. 286 pp., HB. An adequate survey of the relationship between African and American music. Tries to cover a great deal of ground in a short book.

ROONEY, JAMES, *Bossmen: Bill Monroe and Muddy Wa-* ters, Hayden, 1972, PB; Dial Press, 1971. 159 pp., HB. The section on Muddy Waters is not too valuable; I don't have the feeling that Rooney got close to him. The section on Bill Monroe, the father of bluegrass, is excellent. For further information *see* the Books about Folk Music section, page 165.

ROWE, MIKE, *Chicago Breakdown,* Eddison Press Ltd., 1973. 226 pp., HB. A comprehensive and fascinating history of Chicago blues styles. Rowe includes biographies and career descriptions of dozens of musicians, famous and obscure.

RUSSELL, TONY, *Blacks, Whites and the Blues,* Stein & Day, 1970. 112 pp., HB and PB. A fascinating account of musical cross-fertilization. Has discography and bibliography.

SACKHEIM, ERIC, *The Blues Line,* Grossman Publishers, dist. by Viking, 1969. 500 pp., HB. This book consists mostly of blues lyrics and drawings by Jonathan Shahn. The last 50 pages give an impressionistic picture of the artists through a collage of interviews and quotations from many nonblues poems. No discography, unfortunately.

SCARBOROUGH, DOROTHY, *In the Land of Cotton,* 1923, OP. HB. A novel, which includes some songs.

SCARBOROUGH, DOROTHY, *On the Trail of Negro Folk Songs,* Harvard University Press, 1929. 289 pp. Includes 108 melodies with no chord symbols, and some additional texts. Includes work songs, blues, etc. One of the earliest collections of black music.

SCHAEFER, WILLIAM J., and JOHANNES REIDEL, *The Art of Ragtime,* Louisiana State University Press, 1973. 249 pp., HB. A history, with 6 rags, including 1 for banjo.

SIDRAN, BEN, *Black Talk,* Holt, Rinehart & Winston, 1971. 201 pp., PB and HB. Another exploration of black music in terms of the cultural differences between whites and blacks. The most interesting part of the book is the opening section on the character of an oral culture as opposed to a written one. The rest of the book is somewhat like the Le Roi Jones book reviewed previously.

SILVERMAN, JERRY, *Folk Blues,* Macmillan, 1960. 110 songs, HB and PB. Piano arrangements and chord symbols. A worthwhile collection. Could use some guitar arrangements, but at the time of the original edition in 1958, there probably wasn't enough interest to justify them. Everything from Blind Lemon to Jelly Roll Morton.

SOUTHERN, EILEEN, *The Music of Black Americans,* W.W. Norton, 1971. 557 pp., HB and PB. A complete history of black music in the United States—folk, jazz, and "serious." An essential book.

SOUTHERN, EILEEN, *Readings in Black American Music,* W.W. Norton, 1971. 302 pp., HB and PB. Many informative articles by numerous authorities on slave music, black music of today, etc.

STEWART BAXTER, DERRICK, *Ma Rainey and the Classic Blues Singers,* Stein & Day, 1970. 112 pp., PB and HB. A history and description of Ma Rainey and many lesser-known blues singers, including Mamie Smith, Edith Wilson, Lucille Hegamin, and Victoria Spivey.

TALLEY, THOMAS, *Negro Folk Rhymes,* Macmillan, 1922, OP. 347 pp., HB. Mostly texts, with a few tunes.

THOMAS, WILL, *Some Current Folksongs of the Negro,* Southern Methodist University Press, 1912. 19 pp.

VESCHER, WILLIAM L., *Black Mammy,* Books for Libraries, reprint of 1885 ed.

WALTON, ORTIZ, *Music: Black, White and Blue,* Morrow, 1973. 180 pp., HB and PB. The use and misuse of Afro-American music.

WHITE, NEWMAN, *American Negro Folk Songs,* Gale, reprint of 1928 book. HB. 73 songs complete, 800 fragments, 15 tunes, others have texts only. Tunes have lead sheets, no chords. One of the early and important collections.

WILLIAMS, MARTIN, *Jelly Roll Morton,* A.S. Barnes, 1962. PB.

WILSON, BURTON, *Burton's Book of the Blues,* self-pub., 1971. PB. An attractive book of photos of old bluesmen, with a few rock-and-rollers thrown in.

WORK, JOHN, *American Negro Songs and Spirituals,* Bonanza Books, dist. by Crown, 1940. 230 songs. Mostly spirituals with piano arrangements, no chord symbols. Includes some work songs.

WORK, JOHN, *Folk Songs of the American Negro,* Greenwood, reprint of 1915 book. 131 pp., HB.

WORK, JOHN, *Jubilee,* Holt, Rinehart & Winston, 1963. PB.

CANADIAN MUSIC

CANADIAN FOLK SONGS

by Edith Fowke

The largest number of Canadian folk songs came to Canada with the early settlers from France and Britain and were handed down through many generations. The French habitants, who tilled their farms along the St. Lawrence, and the voyageurs, who pushed their way inland, sang hundreds of ballads from medieval France, often adapting them to new purposes. As Marius Barbeau wrote, "Threshing and winnowing in the barns moved to the rhythm of work tunes as did spinning, weaving, and beating the wash by the fireside," and the voyageurs sang romantic tales of knights and princesses as they dipped their paddles in Canada's many rivers.

Ernest Gagnon published the first substantial collection of French-Canadian songs, *Chansons populaires du Canada,* in 1865. For a long time this was thought to represent the entire French-Canadian repertoire, but when Marius Barbeau joined the National Museum of Canada in 1911, he soon discovered that the people of Quebec had preserved literally thousands of songs. From the collection he assembled for the National Museum, he published an important series of books, including *Folk Songs of French Canada* (1925), *Folk Songs of Old Quebec* (1935), *Romancero du Canada* (1937), *Alouette* (1946), *Jongleur Songs of Old Quebec* (1962), and *Le Rossignol y chante* (1962).

Meanwhile in the Maritimes, Father Anselme and Brother Daniel collected Acadian songs and published three small folios of *Chansons d'Acadie* (1942–48). Later important collections include Marguerite and Raoul d'Harcourt's *Chansons folkloriques françaises au Canada* (1956) and Russell Scott Young's *Vieilles chansons de nouvelle France* (1956).

In addition to the large collection at the National Museum, Les Archives de Folklore at Laval University in Quebec City contain thousands of songs which scholars are studying and classifying.

Dr. Barbeau estimated that nineteen out of twenty of the French-Canadian songs came originally from France, but the smaller number composed on this continent most truly reflect the Canadian culture. Some of the best known of these are "Petit rocher de la haute montagne," the lament of the trapper Cadieux; "Vive la Canadienne," a lively toast to the Canadian girl; "Un Canadien errant," about a lad exiled to the United States after the Papineau Rebellion; "Le Bal chez Boule," about a lively country dance; "Youpe, Youpe, sur la rivière," about a habitant lad who goes courting; and "Dans les chantiers" and "Les raftsmen," which describe life in the lumber camps.

Similarly, when people of the British Isles began to settle in Canada, they brought with them thousands of the songs then current in their homeland. Many of *The English and Scottish Popular Ballads* catalogued by F. J. Child survived in Canada, the most popular being "Barbara Allen," "The Gypsy Laddie," "The Cruel Mother," "Young Beichan," "The Sweet Trinity," "Sweet William's Ghost," "Lady Isabel and the Elf Knight," and "Hind Horn." An even greater supply of broadside ballads crossed the ocean, along with many old-world love songs.

Of the native English-Canadian ballads, the largest number were composed by men who worked on the sea or in the woods. People along the coasts of Newfoundland and Nova Scotia composed and sang hundreds of songs of whaling, sealing, or cod-fishing trips and about ships and men who were lost at sea. In the lumber woods of New Brunswick and Ontario, the shantyboys composed hundreds of songs describing their work in the camps and telling of their companions who died in the woods or on the rivers.

The first important collector in English Canada was W. Roy Mackenzie, who found many colorful folk singers in Nova Scotia early in this century. In 1919 he described his adventures in a delightful book, *The Quest of the Ballad,* and in 1928 he published *Ballads and Sea Songs of Nova Scotia.* Helen Creighton followed him, reaping a rich harvest of Maritime songs in the next thirty years, and publishing a series of books: *Songs and Ballads from Nova Scotia* (1932), *Traditional Songs from Nova Scotia* (1950), *Maritime Folk Songs* (1962), *Gaelic Songs in Nova Scotia* (1963), and *Folksongs from Southern New Brunswick* (1971).

Other collections from the Maritimes include *Songs of Miramichi* by Louise Manny and Reginald Wilson (1968), *Twenty-one Folksongs from Prince Edward Island* by Edward D. Ives (1963), and *Folk Ballads and Songs of the Lower Labrador Coast* by MacEdward Leach (1965).

In Newfoundland the first important collection was made by two young Americans, Elisabeth Bristol Greenleaf and Grace Yarrow Mansfield, who published *Ballads and Sea Songs of Newfoundland* in 1933. Maud Karpeles of the English Folk Dance and Song Society visited the island about the same time and published thirty of the old British songs she found there as *Folk Songs from Newfoundland* in 1934; thirty-seven years later she published a more complete edition of her collection under the same title.

Gerald S. Doyle, a St. John's businessman, helped to preserve the native Newfoundland songs by publishing several editions of a small paperback booklet, *The Old-Time Songs and Poetry of Newfoundland* (1927, 1940, 1955, 1966), and Kenneth Peacock spent several summers on the island collecting for the National Museum, from which came his massive three-volume *Songs from the Newfoundland Outports* (1965).

Collecting in Ontario started later than on the east coast, and has been less extensive. Samples of British songs appear in my *Traditional Singers and Songs from Ontario* (1965), and songs composed by the shantyboys make up my *Lumbering Songs from the Northern Woods* (1970). Father Germain Lemieux has done extensive collecting among the French-Canadians in northern Ontario and has published a number of small songbooks.

Comparatively little collecting has been done in the four western provinces. Margaret Arnett MacLeod's *Songs of Old Manitoba* (1960) contains some interesting Métis songs, and Barbara Cass-Beggs has published two small pamphlets, *Eight Songs of Saskatchewan* (1963), and *Seven Métis Songs* (1967). P. J. Thomas is preparing a book from his collection of British Columbia songs.

In addition to these regional collections, I have compiled several anthologies giving a broader selection of songs from across the country: *Folk Songs of Canada* (1954), *Canada's Story in Song* (1960), *More Folk Songs of Canada* (1967), and *The Penguin Book of Canadian Folk Songs* (1973).

Folkways has issued a number of records by traditional Canadian singers: *Folk Songs of Ontario* (FM 4005), *Folk Music in Nova Scotia* (FM 4006), *Songs of the Great Lakes* (FM 4018), *Irish and British Songs from the Ottawa Valley* (FM 4051), *Lumbering Songs from the Ontario Shanties* (FM 4052), *Songs of the Miramichi* (FM 4053), *Maritime Folk Songs* (FE 4307), *Folk Music of Saskatchewan* (FE 4312), and *Songs from the Outports of Newfoundland* (FE 4055). In addition, Folk-Legacy has produced two Canadian records of *Marie Hare* (FSC 9) and *Tom Brandon* (FSC 10).

A Canadian issue of *Ethnomusicology*, September, 1972, gives more detailed information on Canadian folk music, and the first issue of the *Canadian Folk Music Journal* (1973) contains a fuller bibliography and discography.

THE FOLK MUSIC OF CANADA

In compiling this section, we leaned heavily on the Canadian Folk Music Society publication, *A Reference List on Canadian Folk Music*, by Edith Fowke and Barbara Cass-Beggs. Many of the books mentioned here are difficult or impossible to find in the United States. Since our book is oriented toward people who sing and play the guitar rather than simply toward scholars, we have tried to describe where chords are marked with the music, whether the music is only a melody line, a piano arrangement, etc. When using the Folk Music Society's listings, we usually could not get this information, and therefore it is not included in some of our listings.

ANSELME, PERE, and FRERE DANIEL, *Chansons d'Acadie*, 3 vols., Pointe aux Trembles: La Réparation, 1942–48.

BAILLARGEON, HELENE, *Vive la Canadienne*, Les Editions du Jour, 77 songs, PB. Lead sheets, no chords.

BARBEAU, MARIUS, *Chansons Populaires du Vieux Québec*. Musée National du Canada, Bulletin 75, 1936.

BARBEAU, MARIUS, *Folk Songs of Old Quebec*, National Museum of Canada, Bulletin 75, 1935. (This appears to be the same as the above, but in English.)

BARBEAU, MARIUS, *Jongleur Songs of Old Quebec*, Rutgers University Press, 1962. 42 songs. Lead sheets, no chords.

BARBEAU, MARIUS, and EDWARD SAPIR, *Folk Songs of French Canada*, Yale University Press, 1925.

BLONDAHL, OMAR, *Newfoundlanders, Sing!* E. J. Bonnell, 1964.

Canadian Folk Songs and Handicrafts Festival, National Museum of Canada, 1927. 32 pp., HB. Includes 8 folk songs with lead sheets, 3 with piano accompaniments. French and English texts.

CARLISLE, ROXANNE, *Folk Music in Canada*, Canadian Centre for Folk Culture Studies, National Museum of Man, 1974. 7 pp. With bibliography and a brief discussion.

CREIGHTON, HELEN, *Folksongs from Southern New Brunswick*, National Museum of Man, 1971. 118 songs, 239 pp. Lead sheets, no chords.

CREIGHTON, HELEN, *Maritime Folk Songs*, Michigan State University Press, 1962. 167 songs, 210 pp. In Canada published by Ryerson Press. A record of some of these songs is available from Folkways (FE 4307): *Maritime Folk Songs*, which are songs from the collection of Helen Creighton.

CREIGHTON, HELEN, *Songs and Ballads from Nova Scotia*, Dover, 1966, reprint of 1932 book. 150 songs, 334 pp., PB. Lead sheets, no chords. Many nice and unusual tunes.

CREIGHTON, HELEN, and CALUB MACLEOD, *Gaelic Songs in Nova Scotia*, National Museum of Canada, Bulletin 198, 1964.

CREIGHTON, HELEN, and DOREEN SENIOR, *Traditional Songs from Nova Scotia*, Ryerson Press, 1950. 137 songs, 284 pp. Lead sheets, no chords.

CRESTON, PAUL, *French Canadian Folk Songs for Voice and Piano*, Colombo, dist. by Belwin-Mills, 1968. 31 pp. French lyrics with English translations. A model of intelligent piano arrangements; not difficult to play but stimulating.

Fais Do-Do Cajun Orchestra

DENSMORE, FRANCES, *Music of the Indians of British Co-lumbia,* Da Capo Press, 1972 reprint of 1943 book. 98 songs, 99 pp., HB.

DZIOBKO, J., *My Songs: A Selection of Ukrainian Folksongs in English Translation,* Ukrainian Canadian Pioneers' Library, 1958.

Ethnomusicology magazine, September, 1972, vol. 16, no. 3, pp. 329–516. This issue was devoted to Canada, with articles on minority groups, French-Canadian music, bibliographies, etc.

Folksinger's Passport to Canada, The, BMI Canada. 39 songs, 50 pp. Lead sheets and chords. These are composed songs based on Canadian themes by Alan Mills, Stu Phillips, and others.

FOWKE, EDITH, *Lumbering Songs from the North Woods,* University of Texas Press, 1970. 65 songs, 232 pp., HB. Songs from Ontario and Quebec with notes on the singers and the songs.

FOWKE, EDITH, ed., *Penguin Book of Canadian Folk Songs,* Penguin, 1974. 82 songs, 224 pp. PB. Lead sheets and chords; French material in French with English translation.

FOWKE, EDITH, *Sally Go Round the Sun. See* Songbooks for Children, page 161. This is such a fine book we have listed it in two sections.

FOWKE, EDITH, *Traditional Singers and Songs from Canada,* Folklore Associates, dist. by Gale, 1965. 62 songs, 198 pp. Lead sheets, no chord symbols. With notes on the songs and biographies of the singers.

FOWKE, EDITH, and BARBARA CASS-BEGGS, *A Reference List on Canadian Folk Music,* rev., Canadian Folk Music Society, 1973. 12 pp. A valuable reference guide. Includes many magazine articles which we have not listed here.

FOWKE, EDITH, and RICHARD JOHNSTON, *Chansons de Québec,* Waterloo Music, 1957. Piano accompaniment.

FOWKE, EDITH, and RICHARD JOHNSTON, *Folk Songs of Canada,* Waterloo Music, 1954. 77 songs. Piano arrange-

ments and chords. Also published in a choral edition and a piano solo edition. Accompanying record by Joyce Sullivan and Charles Jordan also available.

FOWKE, EDITH, and RICHARD JOHNSTON, *More Folk Songs of Canada,* Waterloo Music, 1967. 78 songs, 207 pp.

FOWKE, EDITH, and ALAN MILLS, *Canada's Story in Song,* W. J. Gage, 1965. 72 songs, 229 pp., HB. A beautifully compiled book; nice piano arrangements with chord symbols and capo directions when necessary, notes on the songs and sources, bibliography and discography. Two Folkways LP's, with many of the songs in this book performed by Alan Mills, are available.

GAGNON, ERNEST, *Chansons Populaires du Canada,* Beauchemin, 1947 reprint of 1865 book. 105 songs, 350 pp. Lead sheets only, no chords. All material in French only.

GAUTHIER, CONRAD, *40 Chansons d'Autrefois,* Archimbault, 1947.

GIBBON, JOHN M., *Canadian Folk-Songs Old and New,* Dent, 1927. 105 pp. Lead sheets and piano arrangements. English or French texts.

GREENLEAF, ELIZABETH, and GRACE MANSFIELD, *Ballads and Sea Songs of Newfoundland,* Folklore Associates, dist. by Gale, 1968 reprint of 1933 book. 189 songs, 395 pp., HB. Lead sheets, no chords. Includes Child ballads, lumberjack ballads, dance tunes, etc.

GRIGGS, MARY ANN, *Le Chanson Folklorique dans le Milieu Canadien-Français Traditionnel* (The Folk Song in the Traditional Society of French Canada), La Société Historique du Nouvel Ontario, Sudbury, 1969.

D'HARCOURT, MARGUERITE and RAOUL, *Chansons Folkloriques Françaises au Canada,* Presses Universitaires Laval, 1956. 186 songs, 449 pp., HB. French text only.

IVES, EDWARD, *Larry Gorman, The Man Who Made the Songs,* Indiana University Press, 1964.

IVES, EDWARD, *Lawrence Doyle: The Farmer Poet of Prince Edward Island,* University of Maine Press, 1971. About 20 songs, 219 pp. Lead sheets, no chords.

JOHNSTON, RICHARD, *Chansons Canadiennes Françaises*, Waterloo Music. 531 choral arrangements, French only.

KARPELES, MAUD, *Folk Songs from Newfoundland*. Archon Books, 1970. 89 songs, 3 dances. Lead sheets, no chords. Mostly Canadian versions of English songs. Good tunes and texts.

KLYMASZ, ROBERT, *The Ukrainian-Canadian Immigrant Folksong Cycle*, National Museum of Canada, Bulletin 234, 1970.

KLYMASZ, ROBERT, *The Ukrainian Winter Folksong Cycle*, National Museum of Canada, Bulletin 236, 1970.

LAFORTE, CONRAD, *Le Catalogue de la Chanson Folklorique Française*, Presses Universitaires Laval, 1958.

LEACH, MacEDWARD, *Folk Ballads and Songs of the Lower Labrador Coast*, National Museum of Canada, Bulletin 201, 1965. 138 songs, 332 pp.

LEMIEUX, GERMAINE, *Chanteurs Franco-Ontariens et Leur Chansons*, La Société Historique du Nouvel Ontario, Sudbury, 1963–64.

LEMIEUX, GERMAINE, *De Sumer au Canada Français*. La Société Historique du Nouvel Ontario, Sudbury, 1968.

LEMIEUX, GERMAINE, *Folklore Franco-Ontarien*, 2 vols., La Société Historique du Nouvel Ontario, Sudbury, 1949–50.

LEMIEUX, GERMAINE, *Les Jongleurs du Billochet*, La Société Historique du Nouvel Ontario, Sudbury, 1972.

MacKENZIE, W. ROY, *Ballads and Sea Songs from Nova Scotia*, Folklore Associates, dist. by Gale, 1963 reprint of 1928 book. 162 texts, 42 tunes. Lead sheets, no chords.

MacKENZIE, W. ROY, *Nova Scotia Ballad Hunting*, Haskell House, 1966 reprint. 242 pp. No music.

MacLEOD, MARGARET, *Songs of Old Manitoba*, Ryerson Press, 1960.

MANNY, LOUISE, and JAMES WILSON, *Songs of Miramichi*, University Press of New Brunswick, 1968. 101 songs, 330 pp. Lead sheets, no chords; songs 1–50 are native to New Brunswick. This is an interesting collection, with many lumberjack songs. A recording of unaccompanied songs from the Miramichi River is available on Folkways (FM 4053), with notes by Louise Manny.

MILLS, ALAN, *Favorite French Folk Songs*, Oak, 1963. 65 songs, 96 pp. Lead sheets and chords. French and French-Canadian songs are included.

PEACOCK, KENNETH, *A Garland of Rue: Lithuanian Folksongs of Love and Betrothal*, National Museum of Canada, Bulletin 2, 1971.

PEACOCK, KENNETH, *Songs of the Doukhobors*. National Museum of Canada, Bulletin 231, 1970.

PEACOCK, KENNETH, *Songs of the Newfoundland Outports*, 3 vols., National Museum of Canada, Bulletin 197, 1965. 321 songs. Lead sheets, no chord symbols.

PEACOCK, KENNETH, *A Survey of Ethnic Folkmusic Across Western Canada*, National Museum of Canada, Anthropology Paper 5, 1965.

PEACOCK, KENNETH, *Twenty Ethnic Songs from Western Canada*, National Museum of Canada, Bulletin 211, 1966.

ROBERTS, HELEN H., "Songs of the Nootka Indians of Western Vancouver Island," *Transactions of the American Philosophical Society*, vol. 45, part 3, 1955.

YOUNG, RUSSELL S., *Vieilles Chansons de Nouvelle France*, Presses Universitaires Laval, 1956.

SPANISH-AMERICAN MATERIALS

BOATWRIGHT, MODY, ed., *Mexican Border Ballads*, Southern Methodist University Press, 1967 reprint of 1946 book. 143 pp., HB. Includes one long article on border ballads with 9 songs, lead sheets, no chords.

BLOCH, PETER, *La-Le-Lo-Lai: Puerto Rican Music and Its Performers*, Plus Ultra Educational Pub., 1973. 197 pp., PB. The only book in the English language that I have found on the pop, folk, and classical music of Puerto Rico. There is some occasional confusion as to what is indigenous to Puerto Rico, and what has been added in New York. But all in all this is an indispensable book.

CAMPA, ARTHUR LEON, *Spanish Folk Poetry in New Mexico*, University of New Mexico Press, 1946. 224 pp., HB.

CAMPA, ARTHUR LEON, *The Spanish Folksong in the Southwest*, University of New Mexico Press, 1933. 67 pp.

CAMPA, ARTHUR LEON, *Spanish-American Folksongs*, Independent Music, 1946.

DURAN, GUSTAVO, transcriber, *14 Traditional Spanish Songs from Texas*, Pan American Union, 1942. 20 pp. Unaccompanied melodies transcribed from Texas field recordings made in 1934–39 by John, Ruby, and Alan Lomax.

FISHER, REGINALD GILBERT, *The Way of the Cross: A New Mexico Version (Four Principal Alabados)*, School of American Research, 1958.

HAGUE, ELEANOR, *Spanish American Folksongs*, Kraus, 1969 reprint of 1917 book published by American Folklore Society. 95 songs, 111 pp. From California, Mexico, etc. Texts in Spanish and in English translation.

LEA, AURORA, *Folk-Dances of the Spanish-Colonials of New Mexico*, Examiner Pub. Co., 1937.

LEA, AURORA, *Literary Folklore of the Hispanic Southwest*, Naylor Co., 1953. A collection of folk dramas, ballads, stories, and folkways from New Mexico in Spanish and English.

LUMMIS, CHARLES F., *Spanish Songs of Old California*, pub. by author, 1923, OP. 14 songs, 35 pp. Piano arrangements, no chord symbols. Texts in Spanish and English.

PAREDES, AMERICO and GEORGE FOSS, *The Décima on the Texas-Mexican Border*, University of Texas, Institute of Latin-American Studies, 1967. A reprint from the *Journal of Folklore Institute*, August, 1966, vol. 3, no. 2.

PAREDES, AMERICO, *With His Pistol in His Hand*, University of Texas Press, 1958; PB 1973. 262 pp. The story of a Spanish-American rancher who lived in Texas. Paredes tells the story, the legend, and prints texts of the ballad while showing its evolution.

RAEL, JUAN, *The New Mexico Alabado*, Stanford University Press, 1951. 154 pp.

ROBB, JOHN, *Hispanic Folk Songs of New Mexico*, University of New Mexico Press, 1953. 15 songs, 83 pp., PB. Texts in English and Spanish, piano arrangements with no chord symbols. Robb has collected 1300 Spanish popular and folk tunes in the Southwest. This book is a tiny sampling of that collection. The texts are in Spanish and English, some of the songs are religious, some are secular. All of the tunes are housed in the University of New Mexico Library on records or tapes.

RYAN, HELEN C., supervisor, *Spanish American Folk Songs of New Mexico,* 2 vols., WPA, Federal Music Project, 1940.

SEDILLO, MELA, *Mexican and New Mexican Folkdances,* University of New Mexico Press, 2nd ed., 1938. Instructions, music, and costumes for many popular dances.

STARK, RICHARD, compiler, *Juegos Infantiles Cantados en Nuevo Mexico* (Spanish American Singing Games of New Mexico), Museum of New Mexico Press, a revised edition of the 1940 WPA book.

STARK, RICHARD, *Music of the Spanish Folk Plays in New Mexico,* Museum of New Mexico Press, 1969. 359 pp., PB. Music from the folk plays; mostly from New Mexico. Hundreds of tunes, melodies only. Spanish texts, and one complete play text in Spanish.

TAICHERT, RUTH, *Sante Fe Folksongs and Dances,* Mills Music dist. by Belwin-Mills, 1940. 48 pp.

VAN STONE, MARY, *Spanish Folk Songs of New Mexico.* Ralph F. Seymour, publisher, 1928, OP. 23 songs, 40 pp. Spanish and English texts.

VAN STONE, MARY, *Spanish Folk Songs of the Southwest,* Academy Guild Press, 1963 ed. of 1928 original. 25 songs, 44 pp. Piano arrangements, no chord symbols. Spanish texts, with English translations in the back of the book.

An exceptionally valuable and detailed booklet accompanies Folk-Lyric Record 9003, *Texas-Mexican Border Music,* vol. 1. For a review of the record, *see* page 47.

OTHER ETHNIC GROUPS

This is a cursory listing of some English, Irish, and West Indian materials; a few books of English language material from different American ethnic groups are also included.

ABRAHAMS, ROGER, *Deep the Water, Shallow the Shore,* University of Texas Press, 1974. HB. Bahamian songs.

BEHAN, DOMINIC, *Ireland Sings,* Essex Music, 1965. 100 songs. Lead sheets, most have chords. Includes notes on the songs.

BERGMAN, MARION, *Russian-American Song and Dance Book,* A. S. Barnes, 1947. 19 songs, 95 pp., HB. Piano arrangements, no chords. Texts of songs in Russian and English.

BLEGEN, THEODORE, and MARTIN RAND, *Norwegian Emigrant Songs and Ballads,* University of Minnesota Press, 1937. 60 songs of old- and new-world origin.

BOYER, WALTER, *Songs Along the Mahantonga,* Gale, 1964. 231 pp. More than 60 Pennsylvania Dutch folk songs. Music and English translations included.

Clancy Brothers and Tommy Makem Song Book, Oak, 1964. 50 songs, PB.

EDWARDS, CHARLES, *Bahama Songs and Stories.* Kraus, 1964. 111 pp.

ELDER, J. D., *Song Games from Trinidad and Tobago,* American Folklore Society, University of Texas Press, 1964, PB.

GALVIN, PATRICK, *Irish Songs of Resistance,* Oak, 1962. 50 songs, PB. From the twelfth century to the present day.

HAUSMAN, RUTH, *Sing and Dance with the Pennsylvania Dutch,* Edward Marks, dist. by Belwin-Mills, 1953. 49 songs, 112 pp., PB. Piano arrangements and chords. Lyrics in German and English.

JACOBS, GERTRUDE, *The Chinese-American Song and Game Book,* A. S. Barnes, 1966. 96 pp.

JOSEPH, NATHAN, and ERIC WINTER, eds., *New English Broadsides,* Oak, 1967. 80 songs, 96 pp., PB. Lead sheets and chords. Songs by Ian Campbell, Sydney Carter, Bert Jansch, and others.

KELLEY, JOHN M., JR., *Folk Music Festival in Hawaii,* Boston Music, dist. by Frank Music, 1965. 65 songs, 96 pp. Lead sheets and chords. Songs in original languages and English translation. Songs from the United States, China, Hawaii, Japan, Korea, Philippines, and Samoa.

LLOYD, A. L., *Folk Song in England,* International Publishers, 1967. 433 pp., PB and HB. An extensive history of English folk songs with musical examples.

LLOYD, A. L., and ISABEL ARETZ DE RAMON Y RIVERA. *Folk Songs of the Americas,* Oak, 1966. 150 songs. Lead sheets, no chords. Spanish lyrics with English translation.

LOCHLAINN, COLIN, *Irish Street Ballads, Sign of the Three Candles,* Dublin, 1952. 102 songs. Lead sheets, no chords.

MacCOLL, EWAN, and PEGGY SEEGER, *I'm a Freeborn Man,* Oak, 1968. 45 songs. Lead sheets and chords. Mostly radio ballads written for the BBC.

Ewan MacColl and Peggy Seeger Songbook, Oak, 1963. 51 songs, 91 pp. Lead sheets and chords. Mostly topical songs composed by the authors.

NETTL, BRUNO, *Folk and Traditional Music of the Western Continents,* 2nd ed., Prentice-Hall, 1973. HB and PB.

PATTERSON, MASSIE, and SAMMY HEYWARD, *Calypso Folk Sing,* TRO. 142 songs. Lead sheets and guitar chords. Probably the most complete collection of calypso songs.

PERDEIRA, JOSE ENRIQUE, ed. and arranger, *Puerto Rico Sings,* Edward Marks, dist. by Belwin-Mills. 11 songs. Piano arrangements and chords. Includes an informative introductory discussion of Puerto Rican music, printed in Spanish and English.

ROBERTS, HELEN, *Ancient Hawaiian Music,* Dover, n.d. PB. 401 pp. A scholarly book about song and dance forms.

RUBIN, RUTH, *A Treasury of Jewish Folksong,* Schocken, 1950. 224 pp., HB and PB. 111 songs. Piano arrangements, no chords. Texts in Yiddish and English. The author is an authority in this field.

WILLIAMS, RALPH VAUGHAN, and A. L. LLOYD, eds., *The Penguin Book of English Folk Songs,* Penguin, 1959. 70 songs, 128 pp., PB. Lead sheets, no chords. A nice collection, with some excellent melodies. Includes notes on the songs.

WRIGHT, ROBERT, *Swedish Emigrant Ballads,* University of Nebraska Press, 1965. 209 pp., 19 tunes, many texts.

YODER, DON, *Pennsylvania Spirituals,* Finch Press, 1961 reprint. These are Pennsylvania Dutch songs.

SONGBOOKS FOR CHILDREN

BLEY, EDGAR, *The Best Singing Games for Children of All Ages,* Sterling, 1973. 96 pp., HB. Piano arrangements of 50 tunes, no chords.

BOTKIN, B. A. *American Play-Party Songs,* Frederick Ungar, 1963 reprint of 1937 book. 400 pp.

CASS-BEGGS, MICHAEL and BARBARA, *Folk Lullabies,* Oak,

1969. HB and PB. A worldwide collection, original language and translation given.

CHALLIS, EVELYN, *Fun Songs, Rounds, and Harmony,* Oak, 1974. 109 songs, 142 pp., PB. Foreign songs in original language and translation are emphasized more than in her other books.

CHALLIS, EVELYN, *Jumping, Laughing and Resting,* Oak, 1974. 97 songs, 132 pp., PB. Traditional songs, and songs by Guthrie, Seeger, and others.

CHALLIS, EVELYN, *Love, Work and Hope,* Oak, 1974. 105 songs, 176 pp., PB. Emphasis on contemporary songs; composers include Paxton, Sainte-Marie, MacColl, and others. All three Challis books have lead sheets and chord symbols.

CHROMAN, ELEANOR, *Songs That Children Sing,* Oak, 1969. HB and PB. 60 songs. Piano arrangements and chords. Songs are in the original language and in English translations.

COLLIER, JAMES, *Jug Bands and Handmade Music: A Creative Approach to Music Theory and the Instruments,* Grosset & Dunlap, 1973. For grades 5–9.

FOWKE, EDITH, *Sally Go Round the Sun,* McClelland & Stewart (Canada) 1969; Doubleday (U.S.), 1970. 160 pp., 300 songs and rhymes. Piano arrangements and guitar chords. An attractive and delightful book. In Canada it comes with a very nice record of children singing the title song. Beautiful printing and layout, drawings by Carlos Marchiori.

GLASS, PAUL, *Songs and Stories of Afro-Americans.* Grosset & Dunlap, 1971. 21 songs, 161 pp., HB. With lead sheets and chord symbols. A good introduction for children of junior high school age and older. There are sections on Duke Ellington, W. C. Handy, Leadbelly, and others.

GLAZER, TOM, *Eye Winker Tom Tinker Chin Chopper: Fifty Musical Fingerplays,* Doubleday, 1973. 50 songs,

91 pp. Piano arrangements and chords. An attractive book with directions for finger play. A few in bad guitar keys, but the transpositions are fairly simple.

GLAZER, TOM, *Treasury of Folk Songs for Children,* Grosset & Dunlap, dist. by Belwin-Mills, 1964. 131 songs, 253 pp., HB. Simple piano arrangements with guitar chords. Some guitar keys bad, no capo directions. Mostly old favorites.

GOMME, ALICE, ed. and collector, *Children's Singing Games,* Dover, 1967 reprint of 1899 original. 70 pp., PB. 8 songs with piano arrangements and no chords. Has directions for the games. Many charming pictures with the songs.

JENKINS, ELLA, *Songbook for Children,* Oak, 1966. 27 songs, 72 pp., PB. Piano arrangements and chord symbols. Some traditional songs, some composed by the author.

JONES, BESSIE, and BESS LOMAX HAWES, *Step It Down.* Harper & Row, 1972. 233 pp., HB. Bessie Jones is a black singer from Dawson, Georgia. This book contains songs, stories, and games. The melodies are printed without chords, because they are generally sung without instrumental accompaniment. There is quite a bit of background material on the songs.

LANDECK, BEATRICE, *Songs to Grow On,* Morrow, 1950. 125 pp., HB.

LANDECK, BEATRICE, *More Songs to Grow On,* Morrow, 1954.

LANDECK, BEATRICE, and ELIZABETH CROOK, *Wake Up and Sing.* E. B. Marks, dist. by Belwin-Mills, 1969. 128 pp., HB. Piano arrangements, with chord symbols.

LANGSTAFF, NANCY and JOHN, *Hey Ho the Rattling Bog,* Harcourt Brace.

LANGSTAFF, NANCY and JOHN, *Jim Along Josie,* Harcourt Brace, 1970.

MYRUS, DONALD, *Ballads, Blues and the Big Beat,* Macmillan, 1966. 136 pp., HB. An adequate, somewhat simplistic history of contemporary professional folk singers, intended for teenagers. Some of the artists included are Pete Seeger, Phil Ochs, and Joan Baez.

NASH, GRACE C., *Today with Music,* Alfred Music Co., 1973. 64 pp., PB. There are two methods of teaching music to children which utilize folk music. The Orff method uses rhythm instruments and folk melodies that employ simple scales, often 5-note. Grace Nash has written a number of books that illustrate the Orff method, and this is a good introduction to the system for the general reader. Includes material on simple rhythm instruments, music reading, games, etc. The other method that utilizes folk music is the Kodaly method. It concentrates more on vocal music than the Orff system. (Thanks to Rita Davis, music teacher from Hartford, Connecticut, for some background material that helped explain the two methods to me.)

NELSON, ESTHER, *Dancing Games,* Sterling, 1974. HB. 36 songs, no chords, piano arrangements. Includes directions for the games.

NEWELL, WILLIAM, *Games and Songs of American Children,* Dover, 1963 reprint of 1883 book. 289 pp., PB. A scholarly study; some texts, some melodies, no chords. All the games include directions.

NILES, JOHN JACOB, and HELEN L. SMITH, *Folk Ballads for Young Actors,* Holt, Rinehart & Winston, 1962.

NILES, JOHN JACOB, and HELEN L. SMITH, *Folk Carols,* Holt, Rinehart & Winston, 1962. These two Niles books are intended for grades 1–6.

RUNGE, JOHN, *Songbook for Children of All Ages,* Hargail, 1961. 13 songs, 16 pp. Includes lead sheets and chords. Some of the songs are in bad keys for guitar. A chord chart is included with the book.

SEEGER, PETER and CHARLES, *The Foolish Frog,* Macmillan, 1973. 40 pp., HB. Pete's famous adaptation of the children's story song. Attractive illustrations.

SEEGER, RUTH, *American Folk Songs for Children,* Doubleday, 1948, OP. 94 songs, 190 pp., HB. Piano arrangements and chords. Good guitar keys and nice piano arrangements. An outstanding book, includes instructions for the games.

SEEGER, RUTH, *American Folk Songs for Christmas,* Doubleday, 1953. For children in grades 1–6.

SEEGER, RUTH, *Animal Folk Songs for Children.* Doubleday, 1950, OP. 43 songs, 80 pp., HB. Piano arrangements and guitar chords.

SLOTE, GIL, *Songs for All Year Long,* Oak, 1964. PB. Songs recorded on Folkways records. Piano arrangements, chords. Original songs about holidays, seasons, and particularly geography.

VAN DER HORST, BRIAN, *Folk Music in America,* Franklin Watts, 1972. A history and biography written for young children.

WINN, MARIE, and ALLAN MILLER, *Fireside Book of Children's Songs,* Simon & Schuster, 1966. HB.

Tony Saletan has recorded two LP's for Western ITV Records, 1549 N. Vine, Los Angeles, Calif. They are *Let's All Sing* (WV 1102) and *The Song Bag* (WV 1103). Each is taken from two sets of 32 programs intended to help teach music to children. The records come with a songbook that contains words, lead sheets, and chord symbols for the songs. Each song demonstrates various aspects of music, and projects are suggested to accompany the songs. Video cassettes of the programs are also available from the same source. The records are well recorded and performed, and should be a stimulating classroom tool. The singing and playing are by Tony Saletan, with additional accompaniments by Irene Saletan and Sandy Davis, on banjo, dulcimer, guitar, etc.

BOOKS ABOUT FOLK MUSIC

ABRAHAMS, ROGER, and GEORGE FOSS, *Anglo-American Folksong Style,* Prentice-Hall, 1968. 242 pp., HB. This book has a number of sensible observations about folk song style and types, notation of tunes, etc., combined with the seemingly inevitable scholar's need for classification in the form of various diagrams. Also includes 60 texts, 55 tunes; lead sheets only.

AHRENS, PAT, *Union Grove: The First Fifty Years,* Union Grove Old Time Fiddle Convention, 1975. 243 pp., PB. A history of the famous old-time fiddler's gathering, with many pictures, biographies of outstanding players, a list of the winners since 1968, and assorted memorabilia. A picturesque and satisfying memoir.

AMES, RUSSELL, *The Story of American Folksong,* Grosset & Dunlap, 1960. HB. A good brief introduction to American folk song.

ARTIS, BOB, *Bluegrass,* Hawthorn Books, 1975. 182 pp. HB. Bob Artis has written an intelligent and well-balanced book detailing the history of bluegrass, and the key figures in its development. The author is well aware of the roots of the music and its emotional aspects. The evolution of musical styles can be a painful process, and Artis does not gloss over the growing pains that bluegrass is experiencing today, nor does he back away from evaluating the creative and fallow periods that many of the prominent figures in bluegrass have experienced in the overall perspective of their careers. A lengthy and useful discography and lists of bluegrass radio programs, periodicals, and organizations are included in the book's appendix.

ATKINS, CHET, with Bill Neely, *Country Gentleman,* Regnery, 1974. The autobiography of Mr. Nashville.

BAEZ, JOAN, *Daybreak,* Dial Press, 1968. Her autobiography.

BART, TEDDY, *Inside Music City,* Aurora, 1970 PB. The music business in Nashville.

BLUESTEIN, GENE, *The Voice of the Folk,* University of Massachusetts Press, 1972. 170 pp., HB and PB. Sometimes stimulating, sometimes ponderous attempt to connect folklore and American literary theory.

BOATWRIGHT, MODY C., *Gib Morgan: Minstrel of the Oil Field,* Southern Methodist University Press, 1965 reprint of 1943 book.

BOATWRIGHT, MODY C., WILSON M. HUDSON, and ALLEN MAXWELL, eds., *A Good Tale and a Bonny Tune,* Southern Methodist University Press, 1964. 274 pp., HB. Several articles on folk song and folk song scholarship, one by D. K. Wilgus calling for more attention to commercial recordings by scholars.

BOATWRIGHT, MODY C., WILSON M. HUDSON, and ALLEN MAXWELL, eds., *Singers and Storytellers,* Southern

Methodist University Press, 1961. 298 pp., HB. Articles on Mexican canciones, Arkansas variants of Texas folk songs, and an interesting article by MacEdward Leach calling for more attention to aesthetic values in collecting.

BONTEMPS, ARNA, *Chariot in the Sky*, rev. ed., Holt, Rinehart & Winston, 1971. A fictional story, based on the life of one of the Fisk Jubilee Singers.

BOULTON, LAURA, *The Music Hunter*, Interbook, 1969. HB. Autobiography of one of the early ethnomusicologists.

BRAND, OSCAR, *The Ballad Mongers*, Funk & Wagnalls, 1961. HB and PB. Deals with folk songs and American politics. Sensible, but Brand has a way of writing about history twenty-five years later and patting himself on the back for the correctness of his views. His ideas about the copyrighting of public domain songs are fair and intelligent.

BRONSON, BERTRAND, *The Ballad As Song*, University of California Press, 1969. 324 pp. HB.

BRONSON, BERTRAND, *The Ballad as Song*, University of California Press, 1969. 324 pp., HB. Essays on Cecil Sharp, modes, George P. Jackson, the Frank Brown collection, etc.

CARAWAN, GUY and CANDIE, *Voices from the Mountains.* Knopf, 1975. 256 pp., PB and HB. Guy and Candie Carawan present a realistic picture of mountain life today through the media of interviews, songs, and photographs. The songs include lead sheets and chord symbols, and are by some relatively unfamiliar writers and by better-known writers like Hazel Dickens, Jean Ritchie, and Billy Edd Wheeler.

COHEN, ANNE, *Poor Pearl, Poor Girl*, University of Texas Press, 1973. 131 pp. A discussion of murdered-girl ballads.

CONN, CHARLES, *The New Johnny Cash*, Fleming H. Revell, 1973.

COOK, HAROLD, *Shaker Music: A Manifestation of American Folk Culture*, Bucknell University Press, 1972. 197 songs, 312 pp. Lead sheets, no chords.

DENISOFF, R. SERGE, *Great Day Coming: Folk Music and the American Left*, University of Illinois Press, 1971; Penguin Books, 1973. 221 pp., HB and PB. Much material about folk music and the American left, as well as the rightist attitude toward folk music. Denisoff has a poor writing style; a hodgepodge of sociological theory. It is always disturbing to see how closely the American left followed Russian ideology during the thirties and forties, and Denisoff makes this point forcefully. One wishes that Denisoff could accept the music for its own sake rather than tieing it inextricably to politics. The better protest singers, like Pete Seeger, seem capable of it. Why not the scholars?

DENISOFF, R. SERGE, *Sing a Song of Social Significance*, Bowling Green University, 1972. 229 pp., HB. A discussion of protest material. Sometimes Denisoff confuses the ideology of the artist with the orientation of his record producer or songwriter. A commercial protest song is still a commercial song.

DUNKELBERGER, A. C., *King of Country Music—The Life Story of Roy Acuff*, self-pub., Williams Printing Co., 1971. 137 pp., PB. A friend and fan's biography of the Nashville star.

DYLAN, BOB, *Writings and Drawings*, Knopf, 1973. 315 pp., HB. No music, but drawings, poems, album notes. Nicely designed.

FOX, WILLIAM, *Ruby Red*, Lippincott, 1971. A country and western music novel.

GILBERT, DOUGLAS, *American Vaudeville: Its Life and Times*, Dover, 1963 reprint of 1940 book. PB. Contains some half-dozen melodies.

GLASSIE, HENRY, EDWARD D. IVES, and JOHN F. SZWED, *Folksongs and Their Makers*, Bowling Green University, 1971. 170 pp., PB. This book concludes that the song maker is a person somewhat at odds with his community, a loner. The book has an interesting study of a racist upstate New York songwriter.

GRAY, MICHAEL, *Song and Dance Man—The Art of Bob Dylan*, Dutton, 1973. 337 pp.

GREEN, ARCHIE, *Only a Miner*, University of Illinois Press, 1972. 502 pp., HB. Music has lead sheets, no chords; 12 tunes and many additional texts are included. A magnificent book, balancing music, anthropology, politics, and literature to produce a brilliant study of mining songs. Green has a great rapport with his informants and an obvious warm feeling toward them.

His Master's Voice

GUITAR PLAYER PUBLICATIONS, *Guitar Notables,* Guitar Player Pub., 1975. 63 pp., PB. Interviews with guitar players concerning technique, tunings, etc. A few of the players are country and folk musicians: Jack Elliott, Taj Mahal, Paul Simon, etc.

GUTHRIE, WOODY, *American Folksong,* Oak, 1961 ed. of 1947 book. 18 songs, 53 pp. With chord symbols and lead sheets in back. A remarkable book; Woody tells stories about Leadbelly, the Almanac Singers; includes drawings. Probably the most interesting of all the Guthrie books.

GUTHRIE, WOODY, *Born to Win,* Macmillan, 1965. 250 pp., HB. An uneven collection of stories, letters, and some song texts, edited by Robert Shelton.

GUTHRIE, WOODY, *Bound for Glory,* Dutton, 1968 reprint of 1943 book, HB; New American Library, 1970, PB. Colorful autobiography, takes Woody up to 1943.

GUTHRIE, WOODY, *Woody Sez.* Grosset & Dunlap, 1975. 172 pp., PB. Selections from Woody's column in the west coast radical paper, *People's World.* There are occasional song lyrics and some drawings. In this book Woody comes off like a radical Will Rogers.

HEINRICH, ANTHONY P., *The Dawning of Music in Kentucky* and *The Western Minstrel,* De Capo Press, 1970 ed. of 1820 musical works. 308 pp. Heinrich was a German who came to this country and tried to write the great American folk symphony. Interesting, though the music isn't too good. There is a Vanguard recording of these works.

HEMPHILL, PAUL, *The Nashville Sound: Bright Lights and Country Music,* Simon & Schuster, 1970. 289 pp. This is an excellent guide to the music business in Nashville; it deals with the styles of today and is not a history book.

HOOD, MANTLE, *The Ethnomusicologist,* McGraw-Hill, 1971. HB. Includes 3 plastic records. Deals with music notation, field methods, film, etc.

HORN, DOROTHY, *Sing to Me of Heaven,* University of Florida Press, 1970. 212 pp., HB. 159 musical examples in melody form, a musicological work about white religious music.

KARPELES, MAUD, *Cecil Sharp, His Life and Work,* University of Chicago Press, 1967. 228 pp., HB. A biography and tribute to the man who almost single-handedly initiated the folk song revival on a scholarly level. Karpeles was his friend and devoted collaborator.

KARPELES, MAUD, *The Collecting of Folk Music and Other Ethnomusicological Materials: A Manual for Field Workers,* International Folk Music Council, 1958. 44 pp.

KOLINSKI, M., ed., *Studies in Ethnomusicology,* vol. 1, Folkways Records, dist. by Oak, 1964. 76 pp. Various technical articles about such subjects as classification of tonal structures in American Indian, African, and Black American music.

LAWS, MALCOLM, *American Balladry from British Broadsides,* American Folklore Society, University of Texas Press, 1957. 315 pp., PB. Traces ballads to their broadside origins; 290 songs are traced.

LEACH, MacEDWARD, and TRISTRAM P. COFFIN, eds., *The Critics and the Ballad,* Southern Illinois University Press, 1973. PB.

LIGERRA, LANAYRE, ed. *Feminist Folksongs,* Boston Feminists, 1972. PB.

LOMAX, ALAN, *Folk Song Style and Culture,* American Association for the Advancement of Science, 1968. 363 pp., HB. Lomax's work in cantometrics, dividing the world into different culture areas and analyzing song styles, dances, the use of the throat, etc.

LOMAX, JOHN, *Adventures of a Ballad Hunter,* Macmillan, 1947, OP. 302 pp. Lomax's adventures as a ballad hunter, in prisons, on the road, etc.

LORD, BOBBY, *Hit the Glory Road,* Broadman Press, 1969. 143 pp., PB. Interviews with Nashville figures like Bobby Bare, Skeeter Davis, and Tex Ritter.

MALONE, BILL, *Country Music, USA,* American Folklore Society, University of Texas Press, 1968, HB; 1974, PB. 422 pp. Excellent and detailed introduction to country music. Not too sympathetic to contemporary practitioners, but a gold mine of historical details.

MARTIN, DEAC, *Book of Musical Americana,* Prentice-Hall, 1970. 243 pp., HB. A handful of songs, lead sheets, no chords. Additional texts and discussion.

McALLESTER, DAVID P., ed., *Readings in Ethnomusicology,* Johnson Reprint, 1971. PB and HB.

McGREGOR, CRAIG, *Bob Dylan: A Retrospective,* Morrow, 1972.

MERRIAM, ALAN P., *The Anthropology of Music,* Northwestern University Press, 1964.

MIDDLETON, RICHARD, *Pop Music and the Blues,* London, 1972.

MITSUI, TORI, *Bluegrass Music: Traditional Music,* Traditional Song Society, Toyohashi, Japan, 1968. 159 pp. Illustrated. The *Bluegrass Music* book will be revised with a record list, and will be published by the Bronze Co.

MITSUI, TORI, *A History of Country Music.* Ongaku-no-Toma Co., Tokyo, 1971; rev. ed., 1974. 383 pp. Illustrated.

MITSUI, TORI, *The Instruments of Anglo-American Traditional Music.* Traditional Song Society, Kanazawa, Japan, 1970. 141 pp. Illustrated.

MOORE, RUTH, *Cold As a Dog and the Wind Northeast,* Gordon Bok, dist. by Folk-Legacy Records, 1958. 62 pp. This is a book of poetry in the form of ballads about the sea.

MOORE, THURSTON, ed., *Hank Williams the Legend,* Heather Enterprises, Inc. Sentimental, maudlin, and occasionally lively material.

NETTL, BRUNO, *Folk and Traditional Music of the Western Continents,* Prentice-Hall, 1965. 213 pp., HB. There is one chapter on American Indian music, one on Negro music in the New World, and one on foreign language folk music in the Americas.

NETTL, BRUNO, *An Introduction to Folk Music in the United States,* Wayne State University Press, 1972. 126 pp., PB. A reasonably good overall introduction to American folk music, which will lead you to other sources for more detailed information.

NETTL, BRUNO, *Theory and Method in Ethnomusicology,* Free Press, 1964.

NETTL, REGINALD, *Social History of Traditional Song,* Augusta M. Kelley, 1954.

NOEBEL, DAVID, *The Marxist Minstrels,* American Christian Press, 1974. 346 pp. The right wing view.

PAVLAKIS, CHRISTOPHER, *The American Music Handbook,* Free Press, 1974. 836 pp., HB. Information on everything from music publishers to fellowships in music.

Muddy Waters

Nothing special about folk music, but a valuable reference work.

PICKERING, STEPHEN, ed., *Dylan: A Commemoration*, No Limit Books, 1971. PB.

PRICE, STEVEN D., *Old as the Hills: The Story of Bluegrass Music.* Viking, 1975. 110 pp. HB. An adequate though unexceptional introduction to bluegrass music for the initiate. Although Price covers the basic background and history of bluegrass, this book lacks any real depth, and somehow doesn't succeed in conveying the feeling of the music.

PRICE, STEVEN D., *Take Me Home*, Praeger, 1974. 184 pp., HB. An impressionistic history of country music for those who don't have the patience for Malone or Shelton. The author has a tendency to generalize and oversimplify. The discography is odd; it lists Charley Mingus but not Jerry Reed.

RIDDLE, ALMEDA, *A Singer and Her Songs*, ed. by Roger Abrahams, Louisiana State University Press, 1970. 52 songs, 191 pp. HB. Story of the Arkansas singer and song collector; with notes and musical analysis of her songs. Useful for placing the songs in a real life context.

RIVERS, JERRY, *Hank Williams from Life to Legend*, Heather Publications, 1967. 40 pp., PB. His story told by one of his sidemen.

RODGERS, MRS. JIMMIE, *My Husband, Jimmie Rodgers*, Southern Literary Institute, 1935, OP. PB. Sentimental to the core, but of historical value.

ROONEY, JAMES, *Bossmen: Bill Monroe and Muddy Waters*, Dial Press, 1971, HB; Hayden, 1972, PB. 159 pp. The section on Monroe is an excellent historical sketch

of bluegrass music. Good insights into the music and the man.

ROSEN, DAVID, *Protest Songs in America*, self-pub., Westlake Village, Calif., 1972.

SCADUTO, ANTHONY, *Dylan*. Grosset & Dunlap, 1971, HB; Signet Books, 1971, PB. 351 pp. Scaduto tries hard to do an intelligent job. Yet Dylan always seems brighter and more complex than his biographers and critics. How much can someone write about Dylan's relationship with Al Grossman, his ex-manager, when neither of them wants to talk about it? Scaduto does penetrate some of the masks, but the reader comes away more frustrated than informed. A final bizarre touch is supplied by a copyrighted discography of private tapes and bootleg records by Dylan.

SEEGER, PETER, *Henscratches and Flyspecks*, Putnam's, 1973, HB; Berkeley, 1974, PB. 256 pp. A method for learning to sight-sing music through the use of folk songs. Useful for instrumentalists also.

SEEGER, PETER, *The Incompleat Folksinger*, ed. by Jo M. Schwartz, Simon & Schuster, 1972. 596 pp., HB. A fascinating glimpse into Seeger's life, thought, and travels. Material on steel drums, his battles with the House Un-American Activities Committee, copyrights, songwriting, etc.

SHARP, CECIL, *English Folk Songs: Some Conclusions*, Methuen, 1954. 143 pp., HB. Sharp wrote this book in 1907. He feared that the folk song tradition was dying and called for its revival.

SHELTON, ROBERT, and BURT GOLDBLATT, *The Country Music Story*, Castle, 1971. 256 pp., HB. An excellent book with many rare photos which help to give the flavor of the music. This book has a balanced viewpoint on commercialism versus authenticity.

SHEPHERD, MURIEL, *Cabins in the Laurel*, University of North Carolina Press, OP. About the southern Appalachians.

SILBER, IRWIN, *Folksong Festival*, Scholastic Book Services, 1969.

SORRELS, ROSALIE, ed. *What, Women and Who*, Wooden Shoe, 1974. 84 pp. An excellent collection of songs and poetry by and about women. Some of the songwriters represented include the author, Jean Ritchie, and Toni Brown, along with such poets as Anne Sexton and May Swenson. The music includes lead sheets and chord symbols. Liz Schoeberlein contributes attractive color illustrations throughout the book.

STRACHWITZ, CHRIS, and PETE WELDING, *American Folk Music Occasional*, Oak, 1970. 80 pp., PB. Articles and interviews; the subjects include Hank Williams, Muddy Waters, and others. Several articles on Cajun music.

THOMPSON, TOBY, *Positively Main Street: An Unorthodox View of Bob Dylan.* Coward-McCann, 1971, HB; Warner Paperback Library, 1972, PB. 187 pp. An enjoyable book about Dylan's early years in Minnesota, marred by the author's pretentious hip new journalese.

TOLL, ROBERT, *Blacking Up the Minstrel Show in 19th Century America*, Oxford University Press, 1974. 310 pp., HB. Some interesting material on black and white musical interaction. Extensive bibliography of songbooks.

TURNER, MARTHA, *The Yellow Rose of Texas: The Story of a Song*, Texas Western Press, 1971. 19 pp., PB. A history of the song, including interesting details about David Guion, who composed symphonic arrangements of folk songs and believed that the original composer of this Confederate classic was black.

VOSMEK, J., *Rise of the American Nation in Poetry and Song,* Country Beautiful, 1973.

WILGUS, D. K., *Anglo-American Folksong Scholarship Since 1898,* Rutgers University Press, 1959. HB. An excellent study of folk song scholarship. Includes bibliography and discography.

WILLIAMS, ROGER, *Sing a Sad Song: The Life of Hank Williams,* Ballantine, 1973. 276 pp., PB. A good biography, without tears.

WREN, CHRISTOPHER, *Winners Got Scars Too: The Life of Johnny Cash.* Ballantine, 1974. 252 pp., PB. Good insights into Cash's early life. Shows just how hard it is to be a country star. The last part of the book degenerates into countless episodes of breaking up motels and pill addiction. Too many events, not enough explanation.

YURCHENKO, HENRIETTA, *A Mighty Hard Road,* McGraw-Hill, 1970. A biography of Woody Guthrie.

SCHOLARLY COLLECTIONS OF SONGS

American Songster: As Sung in the Iron Days of '76, The, Norwood Editions, n.d. HB.

ARNOLD, BYRON, *Folksongs of Alabama,* University of Alabama Press, 1950. One of the important regional collections.

BAILEY, R., and H. ROTH, *Shanties by the Way,* Lawrence Verry, 1968.

BARRY, CECILIA, *Folk Songs of Old Vincennes,* H. T. Fitzsimons Co., OP. 37 songs, 95 pp., HB. Piano arrangements, no chord symbols. French text and English translation.

BAYARD, SAMUEL, *Hill Country Tunes,* Kraus, reprint of 1944 book. 95 tunes, HB. Instrumental music of southwest Pennsylvania.

BELDEN, HENRY, *Ballads and Songs Collected by the Missouri Folklore Society,* University of Missouri Press, 1955. 530 pp., HB and PB. A massive and valuable collection.

BISHOP, SELMA, *Isaac Watts' Hymns and Spiritual Songs,* Pierian Press, 1974 reprint of 1707 book. HB.

BOETTE, MARIE, *Singa Hipsy Doodle,* McClain, 1971. Folk songs of West Virginia. Over 100 songs.

BOND, CARRIE J., *Old Melodies of the South,* Gordon Press.

BRAND, OSCAR, *Songs of '76: A Folksinger's History of the Revolution,* Evans, 1972. HB.

BRONSON, BERTRAND, *The Traditional Tunes of the Child Ballads,* vols. 1–4, Princeton University Press. All HB. Vol. 1, Ballads 1–53, 1959, 465 pp.; Vol. 2, Ballads 54–113, 1962, 565 pp.; Vol. 3, Ballads 114–243, 1966, 496 pp.; Vol. 4, Ballads 245–299, 1972, 516 pp. Index to the entire collection is printed in Vol. 4. A classic study; Bronson prints tunes, texts, and sources of the tunes. Lead sheets only, no chords. Some one thousand tunes are included.

BROWN, FRANK C., *Collection of North Carolina Folklore,* vols. 2–5, Duke University Press. Vol. 2, *Folk Ballads,* ed.

by Newman White, 1952, 207 texts, 747 pp.; Vol. 3, *Folk Songs,* ed. by Henry Belden and Arthur Hudson, 1952, 658 texts, 710 pp.; Vol. 4, *Music of the Ballads,* ed. by Jan Schinhan, 1957, 420 pp; Vol. 5, ed. by Jan Schinhan, 639 pp. Lead sheets, no chords. With musical analysis of the tunes and 26 additional texts. There are seven volumes in the collection; the others contain folklore. This entire collection of folklore and folk song is housed in the Duke University library (*see* Folk Music Archives, page 248).

Bulletin of Folksong Society of the Northeast, Kraus, 1960. 264 pp., PB.

BURTON, THOMAS, and AMBROSE MANNING, eds. *Collection of Folklore: Folksongs,* vols. 1–3, East Tennessee State University, Institute of Regional Studies. Vol. 1, 2nd ed. 1970, 94 songs, PB. Vol. 2, 1969, PB; a collection of songs from four informants; the authors should have printed the banjo tunings. Vol. 3, 1971, PB. These three books are good local collections.

CAREY, G. G., *Maryland Folk Legends and Folksongs,* Tidewater District Council, dist. by Cornell Maritime, 1971. PB.

CAZDEN, NORMAN, *Abelard Folk Song Book,* Abelard-Schuman, 1958. 102 songs, HB. Piano arrangements and chord symbols, no capo directions. Folk music of the Catskill Mountains. A good collection.

CHAPPELL, LOUIS, *Folk Songs of Roanoke and the Albemarle,* Ballad Press, 1959, OP. 203 pp. 117 songs, most with tunes. Lead sheets, no chords.

CHASE, RICHARD, ed. and compiler, *Old Songs and Singing Games,* Dover, 1972 reprint of 1938 book. 49 pp., PB. 21 songs and 7 singing games, some well-known, some obscure.

CHEYNEY, THOMAS, ed., *Mormon Songs from the Rocky Mountains,* University of Texas Press, 1968. 221 pp., HB. 100 texts, most with tunes, no chord symbols. Much material about Mormon history and music.

CHILD, FRANCIS J., *English and Scottish Popular Ballads,* 5 vols., Dover, 1965. PB. The classic collection of English ballads.

COFFIN, TRISTRAM P., *The British Traditional Ballad in America,* American Folklore Society, 1950; 1963 rev. ed.

COHEN, LILY, *Lost Spirituals,* Books for Libraries, reprint of 1928 original. HB.

COLEMAN, SATIS, and ADOLPH BREGMAN, eds., *Songs of American Folk,* Books for Libraries, 1942. HB. There is a 1968 ed of the 1942 original. 47 songs, 128 pp., HB. Piano arrangements, no chord symbols.

COLLINGS, HENRIETTA, *Georgia's Heritage of Song,* University of Georgia Press, 1955.

COMBS, JOSIAH, *Folk Songs of the Southern United States,* ed. by D. K. Wilgus, American Folklore Society, University of Texas Press, 1967. 60 songs, texts only. 325 additional texts classified from Combs' collection in back.

COMBS, JOSIAH, and H. G. SHEARIN, *A Syllabus of Kentucky Folk Songs,* Norwood Editions, n.d.

COX, JOHN, *Folk Songs of the South,* Dover, 1967, reprint of 1925 book, PB; Peter Smith, HB. 545 pp., 185 texts, 26 tunes. Lead sheets, no chords. An early and basic work.

COX, JOHN, *Traditional Ballads and Folksongs Mainly from West Virginia,* American Folklore Society, University of Texas Press, 1964. 218 pp., PB.

DAVIS, ARTHUR, JR., *Traditional Ballads of Virginia,* University of Virginia Press, 1969 ed. of 1929 book. HB.

The Cumberland Ridge Runners

DEAN, MICHAEL, *Flying Cloud*, Norwood Editions, 1973 reprint of 1922 book. 146 pp., 150 songs of outdoorsmen, lumberjacks, sailors, etc.

DOERFLINGER, WILLIAM, *Shantymen and Shantyboys*, Macmillan, 1951, OP. 156 songs, 374 pp., HB. Lead sheets, no chords.

DOLPH, EDWARD, *Sound Off*, Farrar & Rinehart, 1942, OP. 329 songs, 621 pp., HB. Piano arrangements, a few with chords. Songs of America's wars.

DWYER, RICHARD, and RICHARD LINGENFELTER, *Songs of the Gold Rush*, University of California Press, 1964, OP. PB. Guitar arrangements by David Cohen. 88 songs with lead sheets and chord symbols. A fine collection.

ECKSTROM, FANNY, and MARY SMITH, *Minstrelsy of Maine*, Gale, reprint of 1927 book. HB. Over 125 Maine ballads and folk songs with essays.

EDDY, MARY BAKER, *Ballads and Songs from Ohio*, Folklore Associates, dist. by Gale, 1964 reprint of 1939 ed. 153 songs, 330 pp. Lead sheets, no chords. Includes 6 songs about Indians and whites. A very broad collection.

FIFE, AUSTIN, *Songs of Saddle and Sage*, Peter Smith, 1956.

FIFE, AUSTIN and ALTA, *Cowboy and Western Songs*, Clarkson Potter, dist. by Crown, 1969. 128 songs, 372 pp., HB. Lead sheets and chords, no capo directions.

FINGER, CHARLES, *Frontier Ballads*, Doubleday, 1927, OP. 65 songs, 181 pp. Lead sheets, no chords. Sea shanties, outlaw ballads, and cowboy songs.

FLANDERS, HELEN, *Vermont Chap Book*, Books for Libraries, reprint of 1941 ed.

FLANDERS, HELEN, and GEORGE BROWN, *Vermont Folk Songs and Ballads*, Folklore Associates, dist. by Gale, 1968 ed. of 1931 book. 120 texts, most with tunes. Lead sheets, no chords.

FLANDERS, HELEN, and MARGUERITE OLNEY, *Ballads Migrant in New England*, Books for Libraries, 1953. Helen Flanders was the foremost collector of folk songs in Vermont. Her collection is now housed at the Middlebury College library, and these books comprise part of the collection.

FONER, PHILIP, *American Labor Songs of the Nineteenth Century*. University of Illinois Press, 1975. 600 pp. More than 550 texts, no music. A gigantic collection of 19th-century labor songs. This book is useful for the sociologist, historian, singer, etc. Many of the songs are parodies using well-known melodies, such as "Old Dan Tucker."

FOWKE, EDITH, and JOE GLASER, *Songs of Work and Protest*, Dover, 1973 ed. of 1960 book. 100 songs, 209 pp., PB. Piano arrangements and chord symbols.

FRIEDMAN, ALBERT, *Viking Book of Folk Ballads of the English-Speaking World*, Viking, 1974. PB. Mostly texts with a few tunes.

FROTHINGHAM, ROBERT, *Songs of the Sea and Sailors' Chanteys*, Books for Libraries, Reprint of 1928 book. HB.

GARDNER, EMELYN, and GERALDINE CHICKERING, *Ballads*

and Songs of Southern Michigan, Folklore Associates, dist. by Gale, 1967 ed. of 1939 book. 201 songs, 501 pp. Most with tunes. Lead sheets, no chords. Details about informants and notes on the songs, and a list of additional songs not included.

GRAY, ROLAND, *Songs and Ballads of the Maine Lumberjacks,* Gale, 1969 reprint of 1924 book. Songs collected in early part of the twentieth century.

GREENWAY, JOHN, *American Folksongs of Protest,* Octagon, reprint of 1953 book. 225 songs, 31 with melodies. 348 pp., HB. Lead sheets, no chords. An excellent history, weak on black protest music but a lot of interesting analysis of American history through song.

GROVER, CARRIE, *A Heritage of Songs,* Norwood Editions, 1973 reprint. HB. 140 folk songs from the repertoire of a traditional singer born in Nova Scotia and raised in Maine.

HEAPS, WILLARD and PORTER, *The Singing Sixties,* University of Oklahoma Press, 1960. 423 pp. HB. A complete Civil War songbook, including hundreds of texts and 23 musical examples. Many of the songs use tunes of other songs.

HEATON, PETER, and MARIE BIRD, *Songs Under Sail,* Crescendo, 1971. Work songs and shanties sung by crews of sailing ships.

HUBBARD, LESTER, *Ballads and Songs from Utah,* University of Utah Press, 1961. 475 pp., HB. Lead sheets, no chords. 46 local songs, 264 found in Canada and parts of the United States other than Utah.

HUGILL, STAN, *Shanties from the Seven Seas,* Dutton, 1961, OP. 446 songs, 609 pp., HB. Lead sheets, no chords. This is a huge collection.

HUNTINGTON, GALE, *Songs the Whalemen Sang,* Dover, reprint of 1963 book. 331 pp., PB. Over 175 songs, lead sheets and no chords. Many good tunes.

JACKSON, GEORGE P., *Down East Spirituals and Others,* J. J. Augustin, OP. 300 songs, HB. Lead sheets, no chords.

JACKSON, GEORGE P., *Spiritual Folk Songs of Early America,* Peter Smith, n.d.

JACKSON, GEORGE P., *White Spirituals in the Southern Uplands,* Dover, 1965 reprint of 1943 book. PB. Jackson believed that black spirituals were taken from earlier white hymns. These three books contain many songs and his attempts to support his beliefs.

JACKSON, GEORGE S., *Early Songs of Uncle Sam,* Gale, 1971 reprint of 1933 ed. 297 pp., PB. 202 songs, texts only. These are songs in popular collections, printed in the United States from 1825 to 1850.

JOINER, CHARLES, *Folk Song in South Carolina,* University of South Carolina Press, 1971. 45 songs, 112 pp., PB. Lead sheets and chords. Some songs from collections, some from recordings, some collected by the author.

KARPELES, MAUD, ed., *Cecil Sharp's Collection of English Folk Songs,* 2 vols., Oxford University Press, 1974. Songs collected from 1903 to 1924 in England. Most of them have never been published before.

KENNEDY, ROBERT, *Mellows,* Greenwood, reprint of 1925 book.

KORSON, GEORGE, *Minstrels of the Mine Patch,* Gale, 1964 reprint. HB. Folk songs of Pennsylvania coal miners.

LEACH, MacEDWARD, *The Ballad Book,* Harper & Row, 1955, OP.

LEVY, LESTER, *Grace Notes in American History,* University of Oklahoma Press, 1967. 410 pp., HB. Lead sheets, no chords. A collection of pop sheet music 1820–1900. There are 77 songs.

LINGENFELTER, RICHARD, and RICHARD DWYER, *Songs of the American West,* University of California Press, 1968.

LINSCOTT, ELOISE, *Folk Songs of Old New England,* Archon Books, 1974 reprint of 1939 book. 158 songs and dances, 344 pp., HB. Tunes have lead sheets and no chords, or piano arrangements with no chords. Sources and notes on the songs.

LOMAX, ALAN, *The Folk Songs of North America,* Doubleday, 317 songs, 623 pp. 1960, HB; 1975, PB. A huge collection. All songs with chord symbols; 100 of them also have piano arrangements. There are notes on the songs, a discography, and a bibliography.

LOMAX, JOHN and ALAN, *American Ballads and Folk Songs,* 8th ed., Macmillan, 1964. 268 songs, 625 pp., HB. No chords. A great variety of songs from the Lomax collections.

LOMAX, JOHN and ALAN, *Best Loved American Folk Songs,* Grosset & Dunlap, 1947. 111 songs, HB. Piano arrangements and chords. More familiar songs than in most of the Lomax books.

LOMAX, JOHN and ALAN, *Cowboy Songs and Other Frontier Ballads,* Macmillan, 1969. 208 songs, 431 pp. Lead sheets, no chords. Not all texts have tunes. The first John Lomax book, originally published in 1910. An essential work in American folk song.

LOMAX, JOHN and ALAN, *Our Singing Country,* Macmillan, 1941, OP. 416 pp., HB. A valuable collection. Music edited by Ruth Crawford Seeger.

LOMAX, ALAN, WOODY GUTHRIE, and PETE SEEGER, eds., *Hard Hitting Songs for Hard Hit People,* Oak, 1967. 196 songs, 367 pp., HB. Lead sheets and chords. Songs of the Depression and New Deal periods. This is a good companion to the Greenway book, and the present volume is much stronger on black material.

MacDOUGALL, HAMILTON, *Early New England Psalmody,* Stephan Daye Press, 1940. 179 pp., HB. These are not folk songs, but the religious works of various New England composers are analyzed. Musical examples are included; main periods covered are the eighteenth and early-nineteenth centuries.

McCURRY, JOHN G., *The Social Harp,* ed. by Daniel Patterson and John Garst, University of Georgia Press, 1973, reprint of the 1855 edition. 294 pp., HB. Words and music to over 200 songs. Vocal arrangements only.

McINTOSH, DAVID, *Folk Songs and Singing Games of the Illinois Ozarks,* Southern Illinois University Press, 1974.

MELLINGER, HENRY, *Folk Songs from the Southern Highlands,* Finch Press, reprint of 1938 book. HB. A basic work.

METCALF, FRANK J., *American Psalmody,* Da Capo Press, 1968 ed. of 1917 original. HB. This book lists the titles of songbooks printed in America from 1721 to 1820.

MOORE, ETHEL and CHAUNCEY, *Ballads and Folk Songs of the Southwest,* University of Oklahoma Press, 1966. HB. Lead sheets, no chords, over 200 songs. This is only part of a huge collection made by the Moores. Notes on the songs and sources.

MOROSCO, W. T., and HAROLD GLEASON, *Music in America from the Landing of the Pilgrims to the Close of the Civil War,* W.W. Norton, 1974. PB.

National Society of Colonial Dames of America, *American War Songs*, Gale, reprint of 1929 book. 202 pp., 136 patriotic songs.

NILES, JOHN JACOB, *The Ballad Book of John Jacob Niles*, Dover, 1970 reprint of 1960 ed. 110 songs, 369 pp., PB. Piano arrangements and chords. Lots of entertaining material on the histories of the songs and how Niles collected them. He places his informants in a real and colorful setting.

OHRLIN, GLENN, *The Hell Bound Train*, University of Illinois Press, 1973. 291 pp., HB. Lead sheets, no chords. 100 cowboy songs, almost all with tunes. Includes a song sheet with 6 songs on a paper record sung by Glenn Ohrlin.

POUND, LOUISE, *American Ballads and Folk Songs*, Scribner's, 1972 reprint of 1922 book. PB. 120 texts. English, cowboy, and mountain songs collected by the noted scholar.

RABSON, CAROLYN, *Songbook of the American Revolution*, Neo Press, 1974. 43 songs, 112 pp., HB and PB. Lead sheets and chords. A meticulous book; should be used in every American school when students are studying the American Revolution.

RANDOLPH, VANCE, *Ozark Folksongs*, 4 vols., State Historical Society of Missouri, 1946, OP. Lead sheets, no chords. One of the most important regional collections. Contains 883 songs.

REND, JAN, ed., *Sing Me a Texas Song*, Heidelberg Publishers, 1974.

RICKABY, FRANZ, *Ballads and Songs of the Shantyboys*, Harvard University Press, 1926, OP. This is considered the classic collection of lumberjack songs.

ROBERTS, LEONARD, *Sang Branch Settler*, American Folklore Society, University of Texas Press, 1974. 100 songs, 401 pp., HB. Lead sheets and chords, no capo directions. The book also includes 61 folk tales and riddles. All of this material was collected from a single family. Previously published in two books, *Up Cutshin and Down Greasy*, and *Tales and Songs of the Couch Family*.

SCARBOROUGH, DOROTHY, *A Song Catcher in the Southern Mountains*, AMS Press, reprint of 1937 book. HB.

SCHEIPS, PAUL, *Hold the Fort*. Smithsonian Press, 1971. 57 pp., PB. A history of the song, from the Civil War through its uses in labor struggles. Includes the tune and many texts.

SCOTT, JOHN A., *Ballad of America*, Bantam Books, 1972, PB; Grosset & Dunlap, HB. The history of the United States in song and story.

SHARP, CECIL, *English Folk Songs from the Southern Appalachians*, vols. 1–2, Oxford University Press, 1952. 274 songs, 436 and 411 pp. Lead sheets, no chords. First published in 1932, this is the classic collection of American folk songs of English origin.

SHAY, FRANK, *American Sea Songs and Chanteys*, Books for Libraries, 1948.

SHAY, FRANK, *My Pious Friends and Drunken Companions* and *More Pious Friends and Drunken Companions*, Dover, 1961 reprints of 1927 and 1928 books. 132 songs, 235 pp., PB. Sort of a 1920's version of *Song Fest*. Many texts are printed without tunes.

SILBER, IRWIN, ed., *Songs of Independence*, Stackpole Books, 1973. 97 songs, 243 pp. HB. Lead sheets and chords.

SMITH, REED, *South Carolina Ballads*, Books for Libraries, reprint of 1928 ed.

SMYTHE, AUGUSTUS, and ten others, *The Carolina Low Country*, Macmillan, 1931, OP. 327 pp., HB. 49 songs and numerous articles. Lead sheets, no chords. The songs are printed in dialect.

SWAN, HOWARD, *Music in the Southwest, 1825–1950*. Huntington Library, 1952. 316 pp., HB. Swan includes material on the music of the Mormons, mining camp songs, and he touches on Indian and Spanish music. He concludes with an extensive section on serious music in California, to midcentury. A number of Mormon song texts are included, without music.

THOMAS, JEAN, *Ballad Makin' in the Mountains of Kentucky*, Oak, 1964 ed. of 1939 book. 268 pp. Piano arrangements, no chords.

VESCHER, WILLIAM, *Blue Grass Ballads*, Books for Libraries, reprint of 1900 ed.

WELLS, EVELYN K., *The Ballad Tree*, Ronald Press, 1960. 370 pp., HB. 60 British and American ballad texts and tunes.

WHEELER, MARY, *Steamboatin' Days*, Books for Libraries, 1944. 66 songs, 121 pp.

WHITFIELD, IRENE, *Louisiana French Folk Songs*, Dover, 1969 ed. of 1939 book. 171 pp., PB. Lead sheets, no chords. Divided into French, Creole, and Cajun sections.

BOOKS ON FOLKLORE

Since this book is about folk music, the following listing of folklore books does not pretend to be complete or comprehensive. It is intended as a starting point for the reader's own investigations.

BOATWRIGHT, MODY, *Folk Travellers: Ballads, Tales and Talk*, Southern Methodist University Press, 1953.

BOTKIN, B. A., *Folksay*, 1929–30. *Folksay*, 1931. *Folksay*,

A Smoke and a Song

1932. 473 pp., 354 pp., and 296 pp., respectively. Johnson Reprint, 1970. Folklore, songs, tales, etc.

BOTKIN, B. A., *A Treasury of American Folklore,* Crown, 1944. 66 songs, 932 pp. Lead sheets, no chords. Folk humor and tales.

BOTKIN, B. A., *A Treasury of Mississippi River Folklore,* Crown, 1955.

BOTKIN, B. A., *A Treasury of New England Folklore,* Crown, 1963.

BOTKIN, B. A., *A Treasury of Railroad Folklore,* Crown 1953.

BOTKIN, B. A., *A Treasury of Southern Folklore,* Crown 1949.

BOTKIN, B. A., *A Treasury of Western Folklore,* Crown, 1953. The last five Botkin books all include some songs but focus on folk humor and tales.

BREWSTER, PAUL G., ARCHER TAYLOR, BARTLETT JERE WHITING, GEORGE P. WILSON, and STITH THOMPSON, *North Carolina Folklore, Vol. 1: Games and Rhymes, Beliefs and Customs, Riddles, Proverbs, Speech, Tales and Legends,* Duke University Press, 1952. 712 pp.

BROWN, FRANK C., *Collection of North Carolina Folklore,* vols. 1, 6, 7, Duke University Press. Vol. 1: *Games and Rhymes, Beliefs and Customs, Riddles, Proverbs, Speech, Tales and Legends,* ed. by Paul Brewster, Archer Taylor, Bartlett Jere Whiting, George P. Wilson, and Stith Thompson, 1952, 712 pp. Vol. 6: *Popular Beliefs and Superstitions, 1–4873,* ed. by Wayland D. Hand, 1961, 664 pp. Vol. 7: *Popular Beliefs and Superstitions, 4874–8569,* ed. by Wayland D. Hand, 1964, 677 pp. Superstitions of North Carolina. (*See* Scholarly Collections of Songs, page 166, for other books in the series.)

BRUNVAND, JAN, *The Study of American Folklore: An Introduction,* W. W. Norton, 1968.

CLARKE, KENNETH and MARY, *Introducing Folklore,* Holt, Rinehart & Winston, 1963. PB.

COFFIN, TRISTRAM, *Our Living Traditions: An Introduction to American Folklore,* Basic Books, 1968.

COFFIN, TRISTRAM, *Uncertain Glory: Folklore and the American Revolution,* Gale, 1971. Songs, legend, and lore.

COFFIN, TRISTRAM, and HENNIG COHEN, *Folklore in America,* Doubleday, 1970, PB; 1966, HB. 256 pp. Folk tales, superstitions. Includes 24 songs, lead sheets only.

COOPER, HORTON, *North Carolina Folklore and Miscellany,* Johnson Publishing Company, 1972.

DAIGLE, PIERRE, *Tears, Lore and Laughter. The Story of the Acadians,* Acadian Publishing Enterprises, 1972. 135 pp. A history of the Acadians and a listing of musicians. Includes lead sheets to 5 songs.

DAVIDSON, LEVETTE, *A Guide to American Folklore,* Greenwood, 1969 reprint of 1951 book.

DOBIE, J. FRANK, *Coffee in the Gourd,* Southern Methodist University Press, 1969. HB.

DOBIE, J. FRANK, *Follow De Drinkin' Gourd,* Southern Methodist University Press, 1965 reprint.

DOBIE, J. FRANK, *Southwestern Lore,* Southern Methodist University Press, 1965 reprint of 1951 book. One article on Mexican vaquero songs. Includes lead sheets to 5 songs.

DOBIE, J. FRANK, *Texas and Southwestern Lore,* Southern Methodist University Press, 1967 reprint of 1927 book. 259 pp. Includes some songs in lead sheet form and some

texts. Dobie was an outstanding folklorist of the southwest.

DORSON, RICHARD, *America in Legend,* Pantheon Books, 1973. 336 pp., PB. Cowboys, miners, lumberjacks, and others wind their way through these fascinating pages. The book is essentially an interpretation of American history through folklore. It is a beautifully done book, with many pictures and woodcuts, and is as current as the section on the folklore of drugs.

DORSON, RICHARD, *American Folklore and the Historian,* University of Chicago Press, 1971.

DORSON, RICHARD, *American Negro Folktales,* Premier Books, 1967. 378 pp., PB. A collection drawn from two previous hardback books by Dorson.

DORSON, RICHARD, *Buying the Wind. National Folklore in the U.S.,* University of Chicago Press, 1972. PB. Mostly folklore, includes 12 songs.

DORSON, RICHARD, *Folklore and Folklife: An Introduction.* University of Chicago Press, 1972. HB.

DORSON, RICHARD, ed., *Folklore Research Around the World,* Kennikat, 1973 reprint of 1961 book.

DUNDES, ALAN, *The Study of Folklore,* Prentice-Hall, 1965.

EMRICH, DUNCAN, *American Folk Poetry: An Anthology.* Little, Brown, 1974. 831 pp., HB. Emrich has gathered a huge collection of song texts without melodies, many compiled by the Library of Congress Archive of Folk Song. Included are love songs, children's songs, work songs, etc. There is an extensive and current bibliography by Joseph Hickerson. Emrich is the former head of the Library of Congress folk song archive, and Hickerson its current director.

EMRICH, DUNCAN, *Folklore on the American Land,* Little, Brown, 1972. 707 pp., PB. Sections on language, proverbs, street cries, tall tales, etc. Includes 86 songs with lead sheets, no chords. An enjoyable book.

FIFE, AUSTIN and ALTA, *Folklore Among the Mormons,* Indiana University Press, 1956. 367 pp., HB. Mostly a folklore study, this book includes 17 song texts, most with music, lead sheets, no chords.

GOLDSTEIN, KENNETH, *A Guide for Field Workers in Folklore,* Gale, 1964, OP. 199 pp.

GREENWAY, JOHN, *Folklore of the Great West,* American West, 1969. 453 pp. A collection from 83 years of the *Journal of American Folklore.* Some song texts are included.

HAND, WAYLAND D., ed. *North Carolina Folklore, Vol. 6: Popular Beliefs and Superstitions 1–4873,* Duke University Press, 1961, 677 pp. *Vol. 7: Popular Beliefs and Superstitions, 4874–8569,* Duke University Press, 1964.

HUDSON, ARTHUR, *Folklore Keeps the Past Alive,* University of Georgia Press, 1962.

HUGHES, LANGSTON, and ARNA BONTEMPS, *The Book of Negro Folklore,* Dodd, Mead, 1958. 677 pp., HB and PB.

Journal of American Folklore, vol. 84, no. 332, April-June, 1971, pp. 221–29. This is an article on undergraduate folklore programs. Graduate folklore programs are offered by the University of California at Berkeley and Los Angeles, University of Indiana, University of North Carolina, University of Pennsylvania, University of Texas, Western Kentucky University, and the State University College of Oneonta at Cooperstown, N.Y.

KORSON, GEORGE, ed., *Pennsylvania Songs and Legends,* Johns Hopkins Press, 1960.

POST, LAUREN, *Cajun Sketches,* Louisiana State University Press, 1962. The economy, sociology, folklore, and music of the Cajuns.

THOMPSON, STITH, *Motif Index of Folk Literature,* rev. ed., 6 vols., Indiana University Press, 1955–59.

THOMPSON, STITH, *Round the Levee,* Southern Methodist University Press, 1932.

WHITNEY, ANNIE, and CAROLINE BULLOCK, *Folk Lore from Maryland,* Kraus, reprint of 1925 book.

INSTRUCTIONAL BOOKS AND RECORDS

Since I started work on this catalogue I have played through hundreds of guitar and banjo instructional books. In many respects, seeing what so many others have done has clarified my own approach to teaching.

The first question you need to ask in looking at a book is whether it teaches a method or is a collection of solos. A method book starts at a certain point, often at the very beginning, and leads you gradually through various styles and techniques. The first part of a method book is always much easier than the last part. A collection of solos is just that, a series of instrumental solos in one or more styles that are not necessarily progressive in degree of difficulty. A particular solo in such a book may inflict a great deal of new material on the reader because the author plays a song in some especially complicated way.

The main problem is that most books are not clearly identified as either a method book or a collection of solos. For example, Stefan Grossman has written a number of interesting books on blues. They appear to be method books, but they are really collections of solos by various artists. Sometimes they are in progressive order of difficulty, but sometimes they are not. If you know little or nothing about blues, these books are hard to follow. On the other hand, Barry Kornfeld's banjo solo collection appears to be a collection of solos, and in a way it is. However, he starts off with relatively simple material, and most of the solos are graded progressively. Therefore it does make sense to go through this book from beginning to end. Grossman's books are more like encyclopedias or catalogues; it is best to use what interests you specifically rather than to play through a Grossman book from A to Z.

Unfortunately, there are other problems in trying to learn to play from books. One of them is the use of traditional music notation versus the system called tablature. Tablature is a way of identifying notes through the use of string and fret numbers. Most tablature systems follow the one Pete Seeger uses in his banjo book, but other writers, like Bob Baxter, use their own systems of tablature. Reading *any* form of notation can be confusing enough, but being subjected to more than one system of tablature seems an unfair punishment for the average reader; I know it is for me.

Some authors seem to be emotionally and intellectually committed to opposing traditional musical notation. John Burke, in his banjo book, develops all kinds of complex and pseudo-intellectual reasons for his anti-intellectualism. Peter Wernick doesn't print any written notes of music, but does refer to fairly complex matters of music theory, which is, after all, based on notation.

In my view, all folk guitar and banjo books should be printed with both music and tablature. Those who already know how to read music will find it easier and faster to follow, and many people can be taught to read music without as much trouble as Burke takes to attack the use of written music. Tablature can be useful to people who do not want to read music; it is also helpful when playing in different tunings on guitar or banjo. When you retune an instrument, all of your carefully nurtured reading skills and shortcuts become useless, because all of the left-hand fingering patterns are now changed. Some people experience this problem in changing from guitar to banjo. I have only experienced it when changing tunings on the same instrument. When I change instruments, my mind makes the adjustment for the different tuning.

Still another problem in the use of tablature is achieving some sort of rhythmic notation that is understandable. According to *Bluegrass Unlimited,* a midwestern banjo player, Harold Streeter, is doing his tablatures in eight subdivisions for each measure. A little box represents each eighth note. This probably works fine for a lot of the Scruggs eighth and sixteenth note patterns, but it might get a little crowded with thirty-second notes, or dotted sixteenths or whatever. Yet it represents a step forward from the rhythmic vagueness of quite a bit of tablature. (Dan Fox, in his article on page 217, also discusses some of these problems.)

Is it worthwhile to learn to read music, and if so, how does one go about it? The answer to the first part of the question depends to a great extent on what you want to do with your instruments and what styles of music interest you. For example, if the music of Ernest Tubb is the only kind you care to play, then I would say no, don't bother learning to read music. But what if you decide to play one of the numerous easy pieces in the classic guitar repertoire, or a Burt Bachrach song, or whatever? You *can* do this entirely by ear if you have the talent of a Wes Montgomery or a Josh White. (Neither of them could read music.) Most of us don't have ears that sharp, and we need all the help we can get.

Another reason for learning to read is to play with piano players, trumpet players, or other musicians. It helps to read music when trying out new tunes, and when establishing a form of dialogue with other players. Learning to read music is not a substitute for playing it; it is simply another tool to be used in approaching an instrument.

At the present moment, there is no one book on learning to read music that I would recommend to guitar or banjo players. Some books at least deal with the problem, such as Griffin's banjo method; and I hope to publish some relevant materials in the near future. For now, try to keep an open ear. Learn as much about music as you can, listen to everything around you, and play whatever you can. You can learn from records, instructional books, teachers, and your own playing experiences.

Instructional records and tapes pose different problems from the ones that come up when learning from a book. Ideally, a record should present the material at a slow and a medium tempo; the first for the beginner, and the second for use when the learner begins to assimilate the material. On most records and tapes that I have reviewed, the tempos are either much too fast to begin with, or they ignore the intermediate level. For example, Pete Seeger's banjo instructional record presents each piece in a slow, easy-to-follow tempo. Then the next presentation is lightning fast, as though Seeger is unaware that between learning a technique and mastering it comes an intermediate step. This is what I mean when I refer to tempos on an instructional record or tape as being too fast for a beginning or intermediate student.

In the following section, instructional materials are arranged alphabetically, by instrument.

AUTOHARP

The autoharp is probably the world's easiest stringed instrument to play. All you have to do is brush across the strings with the right hand, while the left hand presses down on the chord bars. Folk and country musicians, like Maybelle Carter, Mike Seeger, and Brian Bowers, have applied a number of guitar picking techniques to the autoharp, giving the instrument a richer and more colorful sound.

There are numerous instruments similar to the autoharp, which are harder to play because they do not have any chord bars. Among these are different kinds of zithers and the ukelin. They often turn up in attics and antique shops, especially in the eastern United States.

The Carter Family

Autoharp is a trade name of the Oscar Schmidt Company; similar instruments are marketed under the names Chromaharp and Cythaharp.

I have included here both a comprehensive and then a selected list of autoharp books.

BAY, MEL, *Fun with the Autoharp*, Mel Bay, 1971. 49 songs, 32 pp. Melodies and chord symbols. This is a songbook with chord symbols. No autoharp instruction is included except for information on how to hold the instrument.

BLAIR, ELIZABETH, *Autoharp Accompaniment to Old Favorite Songs*, Summy-Birchard, 1958.

DIERS, ANN, *21 Folk Songs Arranged for Autoharp, Guitar, and Zither*, Boston Music, dist. by Frank Music, 1964. 16 pp.

HALL, FRANCIS, *Favorite Folksongs, Ballads and Spirituals for Autoharp*, Boston Music, dist. by Frank Music, 1965. 35 songs, 47 pp. This book includes some autoharp instruction and has chord symbols for guitar or other accompanying instruments.

HOLM, ANN, *Picking Styles for the Autoharp*, Charlotte's Web School of Folk Music. 8 pp. A collection of right-hand techniques.

LUDWIG, ALICE and LOUIS, *Colors and Chords for the Autoharp*, Carl Van Roy, dist. by Peripole. A beginner's method which transposes all songs into the key of G.

MCLAUGHLIN, ROBERTA, and MURIEL DAWLEY, *Making Music with the Autoharp*, Carl Van Roy, dist. by Peripole.

NULL, CECIL, *Autoharp Instruction Book*, Cedarwood, dist. by Hansen, 1969. Songs and instructions.

NULL, CECIL, *Pickin' Style for the Autoharp*, Hansen, 1963. 32 pp. This book has no right-hand instructions.

NYE, ROBERT, and MEG PETERSON, *Teaching Music with the Autoharp*, MEG, 1973. 119 pp. A method for teaching music in the classroom. It uses strums, pitch identification, scales, simple orchestrations, etc., all centered around the autoharp. Numerous songs are included, each with a melody line and chord symbols. A practical and innovative idea for teachers.

PETERSON, MEG, *Autoharp Parade:* vol. 1, *Songs for Young People*, vol. 2, *100 of the World's Best Love Songs*, and vol. 3, *100 Hymns and Spirituals*, Oscar Schmidt, 1967. 50, 64, and 56 pp., respectively. All three volumes have chords, symbols, and text, no music or instructional materials; these are really songbooks.

PETERSON, MEG, *The Many Ways to Play the Autoharp*, vol. 1, Oscar Schmidt, 1966. 28 pp. A good book for beginners, particularly those who haven't played other instruments. It concentrates on right-hand strums and doesn't deal with melody playing.

PETERSON, MEG, *The Many Ways to Play the Autoharp*, vol. 2, Oscar Schmidt, 1966. 32 pp. This is an introduction to melody playing. It is easier to follow than the Taussig book, and uses a number system so that music reading is not essential. Near the end of the book, the author tries to cover a variety of musical styles in very little time, and she doesn't quite make it.

PETERSON, MEG, *Tuning the Autoharp*, Oscar Schmidt. 12-inch LP record. If you do not have access to a piano, this is a useful tool.

TAUSSIG, HARRY, *Folk Style Autoharp*, Oak, 1973. 80 pp. An intelligently constructed method, especially if you already play guitar or banjo. The section on music reading is inadequate, considering how dependent this method is on music reading. The transposition chart is also not as clear as it should be. There is a lengthy history of the autoharp by A. Doyle Moore at the beginning of the book.

WALDROP, EVELYN, *Sing 'n' Strum Autoharp*, Wm. J. Smith, 1953. 44 songs, 31 pp. Lead sheets and chords, and right-hand directions. A collection of familiar tunes with autoharp accompaniment.

RECOMMENDED AUTOHARP BOOKS

PETERSON, MEG, *The Many Ways to Play the Autoharp*, vol. 1, A good beginners' book.

TAUSSIG, HARRY, *Folk Style Autoharp*. For those who already play guitar or banjo.

BANJO

Listed below are most of the instructional books for the five-string banjo which I have encountered in my research. At the end of this section, I have listed separately those books that I recommend most highly. I have tried to be as comprehensive as possible, within the limits of books and records available to me. The designation "self-pub." means that the author has published the book himself.

BAY, MEL, *Riverboat Banjo*, Mel Bay Pub., 1973. 40 pp. A collection of ragtime and twenties tunes arranged for tenor and plectrum or five-string banjo. Good reading practice (notation only) but essentially a series of plectrum banjo solos. (Note: The plectrum banjo is tuned like the five-string, but has no fifth string and is played with a pick.)

BLAYLOCK, BILL, *Bluegrass Banjo Course*, Self-pub., 1968. Three books of 10, 12, and 21 pp. and two 7-inch LP records. Tablature and diagrams only. Fairly easy to follow. Skimpy for its price. Tempos on the records are too fast.

BORCHELT, DON, *15 Fiddle Tunes for Five String Banjo*, Self-pub., 1974. 16 pp. Tablature only, tape available. Some nice arrangements utilizing Bobby Thompson techniques with a dash of Billy Faier. Printing hard to read.

BRADBURY, FRANK, *Five String Banjo Method*, vols. 1–2, Mel Bay, 1967. 64 pp. each. All material in music notation, no tablature. These volumes deal extensively with music reading. They are logically and sensibly written, but of minor value to the folk player. Their approach to the instrument is similar to that of a classical guitar instructional book.

BROWN, ABE, *Solid Bluegrass Banjo Lessons*, Self-pub. Includes tablature, cassette and instructions.

BURKE, JOHN, *John Burke's Book of Old Time Fiddle Tunes for Banjo*, AMSCO, 1968. 96 pp. Tablature only. Burke's method of using the thumb to play part of the melody rather than percussively is an interesting idea. His tablature is hard to follow and rhythmically disastrous. His choice of obscure tunes further complicates matters. In other words, if you have no access to his recommended records, forget it. Some of the arrangements in this book are nice, but Burke doesn't give you many clues to unscramble them. For example, some of his tunings may result in broken strings if you don't retune the banjo to a lower pitch.

CARBO, JOHN, *How to Play the 5 String Banjo*, Hansen, 1965.

CHAMPION, PAUL, *Kingston Trio Presents an Introduction to Bluegrass Five String Banjo Three Finger Style*, Hansen, 1964. 64 pp. Champion uses his own, rather confusing, style of tablature without any music notation. Too much space is spent on details, too little on the actual playing of songs. A song sheet (paper record) accompanies the book. The fast tempos are way beyond the reach of the average player.

CLAYTON, BOB, *Old Timey Banjo Book*, Self-pub., 1972. 32 pp. Tablature, no music. Moves too fast for beginners. Clayton does include some pleasant arrangements.

Country Banjo: Sensational 70 for the 70's. Screen-Gems Columbia, 1973. 200 pp. Contains strums and chords. (No editor credited.)

CUNNINGHAM, BILL, *Ad Lib Bluegrass Banjo*, Self-pub., 1974. 32 pp. Tablature only. Some nice competent arrangements, but the tablature is hard to read because of poor printing.

CUNNINGHAM, BILL, *Ad Lib Frailing Banjo*, Self-pub., 24 pp. Tablature only. This method is not progressive in difficulty. It does have some interesting insights into such techniques as choking the strings and right-hand picking patterns.

ELIOT, LEE, *Bluegrass Five String Banjo Method*, Self-pub., 1974. 22 pp. Tablature only; 12 songs with words, but no chords printed over the words. The tablature consists of sequences of rolls with the chords. A cassette can be bought with the book. The book alone is fair, but the cassette is excellent. It is thorough, and the tempos are slow.

ERBSEN, WAYNE, *How to Play the Five String Banjo*, formerly self-pub., to be published by Carl Fischer. 52 pp. Tablature and music. The music isn't too useful because it is a summary of what's in the tablature rather than a complete transcription. There is some good material in this book, especially in the GCGCD and GCGCE flat tunings. This is a good book for someone who comes away from other books wondering how you play the melody and the strums together. The author also has a forthcoming bluegrass book, and a cassette is available with the *How to Play* book.

Billy Faier's Banjo Book, Hargail, 1958. 12 pp. This book has 6 very nice solos from Faier's out-of-print record *The Art of the Five String Banjo*. There is music notation only, with some position diagrams, no tablature. Solos are in a style akin to classical guitar, and quite a bit of technique is required to play them; but they're worth the struggle.

FORD, MIKE, *How to Play Bluegrass Banjo*, Hargail, 1972. 64 pp. Music and tablature. This book is a useful reference tool, with a good section on introductions, fills, and licks. The arrangements are adequate but not stimulating.

GREATHOUSE, ALFRED, *Finger Pickin' Good Tunes: 5 String Banjo*, Hansen, 1974. 80 pp. Music and tablature.

A poorly organized and confusing method book. Greathouse doesn't seem to fully understand the instrument. Most of the arrangements are awkward versions of three-finger picking in a sort of quasi-Scruggs style. The only things of value in this book are the diagrams of movable chords.

GRIFFIN, NEIL, *Mel Bay's Deluxe Bluegrass Banjo Method*, Mel Bay, 1974. 128 pp. This is the first bluegrass banjo method I found that works reasonably well without a private instructor. It contains music and tablature. There is a good section on integrating hammering on and pulling off with the Scruggs rolls. Griffin does not cover the whole neck of the banjo, but a future volume is intended for that purpose. There are many playable and well-thought-out solos here.

GRIMSHAW, EMILE, *How to Excel on the Banjo*, Clifford Essex. 51 pp. An English classical banjo method which also has a section on pick-style playing.

HARING, LEE, *The Gypsy Laddie*, Hargail, 1961. 27 pp. Music and tablature. A collection of solos for the advanced player. Some nice arrangements and particularly useful insights into the unusual style of Billy Faier.

HOLCOMB, DAVE, *Banjo Lessons by Mail*, Self-pub. This is not a book, but Mr. Holcomb has available 19 Scruggs solos and 9 Bill Keith-style solos. Each tune is in music and tablature and comes with a thorough tape at slow and faster tempos. The author also has general style analyses for sale. It is all well done and expensive.

JONES, LOUIS "GRANDPA," *Method of Old Time Southern Style Five String Banjo*, Self-pub., 1954, OP. Not a very complete book, but does have some information on Grandpa's frailing sound, including the fact that he tunes his banjo a whole tone higher to get a brighter sound.

JOPLIN, SCOTT, *Great Scott! Songs and Solos for Banjo*, Hansen, 1973. 32 pp. This is really a plectrum banjo book. There are lead sheets and chord frames for five-string or plectrum banjo.

KORNFELD, BARRY, *Blue Grass Banjo in Scruggs and Other Three Finger Picking Styles*, Hargail, 1965. 31 pp. A well-done and coherent collection for intermediate players. Music and tablature; the solos are intelligently progressive in difficulty.

KRASSEN, MILES, *Clawhammer Banjo*, Oak, 1974. 88 pp.

KURTH, KARL, *Banjo Pickin' Solos*, Mel Bay, 1973. 32 pp. Music and tablature. A good collection of solos. Has section on scales used in chromatic playing, and combines some Seeger and Scruggs techniques. For intermediate and advanced players.

Langey–Carl Fischer Tutor for Banjo, rev. ed., Carl Fischer, 1950. 112 pp. Mostly unplayable because it uses early twentieth-century banjo notation, with the whole banjo tuned a minor third below today's C tuning.

LEE, RONNY, *Beginner's Five String Banjo Book*, Alfred Music. Starts out slowly, then tries to jam a great deal of information into a very small space.

LEE, RONNY, *Chord Chart for Five String Banjo*, Alfred Music, 1964. A 3-page chart. Very useful and economical. Chords in the C, G, and D tunings, but no movable chords or chords up the neck.

LOMBARD, NEIL, *Pocket Dictionary of Banjo Chords*, Kenyon.

MEADOWS, REUBEN, *A Comprehensive Approach to Bluegrass and Folk Style 5 String Banjo*, Bluegrass Bookshelf,

Academy of Bluegrass. Some music, some tablature, not very complete.

Mel Bay's Encyclopedia of Banjo Chords, Mel Bay, 1972. 111 pp. More chords than you'll ever use, but none in D tuning.

MIDDLEBROOK, RON, *Five String Banjo Chord Chart*, Mel Bay, 1973. 3 pp. Covers only the G tuning.

Modern Five String Banjo Method, M. M. Cole.

MULLER, ERIC, and BARBARA KOEHLER, *Frailing the Five String Banjo*, Mel Bay, 1973. 96 pp. An excellent and attractive book on frailing, and it's easy to follow. Unfortunately, there is not a note of music in the book; it is all tablature. The authors also never really explain how to play chords, or in what way chords relate to these solos. There are a number of really attractive solos in a variety of tunings. This is a good book if you already have an idea of what chords are about from playing Seeger or Scruggs style and would like to discover frailing. The tablature is exceptionally easy to follow because of good layout and printing. A record to accompany the book is also available, but it is badly organized, and the tempos are too fast. It is very pleasant to listen to for entertainment rather than instruction, however.

NATHAN, HANS, "The Early Banjo Tunes and American Syncopation," *Musical Quarterly*, vol. 13, no. 4, October, 1956, pp. 455–472. This is a magazine article with valuable examples of nineteenth-century styles not readily obtainable elsewhere. Notation only.

OSBORNE, SONNY, *Bluegrass Banjo*, Mel Bay, 1964. Music and tablature. Includes only 7 solos. Poor editing; notation and tablature often disagree. The solos are nice, but the book has too many details about the notes on each string, and the like.

PALMER, W. A., III, *How to Play Folk and Bluegrass Banjo*, Alfred Music, 1965. 48 pp. Not a good beginners' book, but a useful collection of solos in music and tablature. Has some nice Bill Keith-style "Cripple Creek" variations. This is really a collection of solos, not a method book.

RENO, DON, *Five String Banjo Instruction Book*, Self-pub., 1974. 79 pp. Don Reno is a terrific banjo player, but this is a bad book. It has 35 pages of chords, mostly the same chords moved up a fret for each new key, before the right hand is even discussed.

RESER, HARRY, *Let's Play the Five String Banjo Folk Style*, Remick, dist. by Warner Bros., 1964. Reser was a great tenor banjo player. There isn't anything here of much interest for the folk player.

RICHARDSON, PETER, *Advanced Bluegrass Instruction Manual*, self-pub., 1971. 17 pp. Tablature, no music. Very little information.

RICHARDSON, PETER, *Bluegrass Five String Banjo*, Self-pub., 1964. 28 pp. Tablature only. Only 2 real solos in the whole book. Too many directions, not enough songs.

RICHARDSON, PETER, *Chromatic Five String Banjo*, Self-pub., 1971. 20 pp.

RIGHTMIRE, RICHARD, *Introduction to the Five String Banjo*, Clef Music, 1967.

ROSENBAUM, ART, *Old Time Mountain Banjo*, Oak, 1968. 88 pp. This is a poor book for beginners, with 3 different tunings in the first 3 lessons. The book is 95 percent tablature with minute doses of music; but it's a gold mine of information on various mountain styles, including frailing and two- and three-finger pre-bluegrass styles.

SCRUGGS, EARL, *Earl Scruggs and the Five String Banjo*, Peer-Southern, 1968. 156 pp. PB and HB. Detailed music and tablature. This is not a good book for beginners, but if the intermediate or advanced player has patience, it will teach him how to play exactly like Earl Scruggs. A record, which is helpful—essential in fact for really understanding this book—is available from the author.

SEEGER, PEGGY, *The Five String Banjo: American Folk Styles*, Hargail, 1960. 52 pp. Music, no tablature. This book has a nice collection of songs, and good chord diagrams presented in the form of chord families. The songs are presented without any instructions under them, so you have to do a lot of page turning to figure out what is happening. Some of Peggy Seeger's dulcimer-like banjo tunings are interesting.

SEEGER, PETE, *The Goofing Off Suite*, Hargail, 1959. 29 pp. Music and tablature. There are 15 tunes here, of which 11 are for banjo. They vary in difficulty; but this is a collection of solos from the record of the same name, not an instructional book.

SEEGER, PETE, *How to Play the Five String Banjo*, self-pub., dist. by Oak, 1962. 72 pp. Music and tablature. This is a confusing book for beginners, because it moves too fast and starts in the C tuning. For the advanced player, though, it's a fascinating collection of material which can keep you busy for several years. Seeger sees the banjo in a larger frame than most players do, and so he includes materials on blues, calypso, flamenco music, etc. There is too much type on the page, which makes the book hard to read. A Folkways LP record (FI8303) is available, with most of the material in the book recorded at slow and faster tempos. Unfortunately, the fast tempos are much too fast to be useful.

SHARPE, A. P., *Complete Guide to the Instruments of the Banjo Family*, 36 pp. Originally published in England, issued here by Mills, available from Vitali Import Company.

SHEALY, ALEXANDER, *Picture Chords Five String Banjo*, Lewis Publishing Company, 1974. 80 pp. No attention is paid to the right hand; for all practical purposes, this could be a plectrum banjo method.

SILVERMAN, JERRY, *Beginning the Five String Banjo*, Macmillan, HB; Collier, PB, 1974. 150 pp. Music only. This book starts out too fast, then spends 125 pages on Seeger style before mentioning anything else. A good book for learning the finger board in Seeger style, but there is almost no material on frailing and very little on bluegrass. It would have been better to devote the whole book to the Seeger style.

SIMINOFF, ROGER, *Five String Banjo Bluegrass Style*, vol. 1, Colonial Press, 1973. 32 pp. Tablature only. The author has a different and confusing way of writing tablature. There is little instruction for the right hand here. The most informative part of the book concerns technical matters such as bridges and tailpieces.

SMECK, ROY, and MEL BAY, *Ragtime Banjo*, Mel Bay Pub., 1974. 32 pp. A series of Scott Joplin pieces arranged for tenor and plectrum or 5-string banjo, together with some Roy Smeck solos. The Joplin pieces work fairly well on five-string, the Smeck pieces are really pick-style solos.

Smith's Banjo in the Blue Grass, Wm. J. Smith, 1965.

Mike Seeger and Earl Scruggs

SMOAK, JIM, *The Five String Banjo Technique*, Experience Pub. Ltd., dist. by Chappell, 1972. 60 pp. Music and tablature. There is some good music in this book, but Smoak has been done in by his editor. Four of the 21 solos are unplayable because the author gives capo directions and then writes the music and tablature as if the capo weren't there. This is a reasonably good collection of solos, though not really a method book.

Jim Smoak's 360 Chords for Five String Banjo, Experience Pub., dist. by Chappell, 1973. 46 pp. This book is rather useless because all the chords shown are for the G tuning.

STOLLS, BERNARD, and PETER MORRIS, *Choice Folksongs for Five String Banjo*, Hargail, 1965. 47 pp. Music and tablature. Interesting combination of Seeger and Scruggs styles. The book owes a lot to Seeger in terms of songs and arrangements.

STREETER, HAROLD, *5 String Banjo Improvisations for 3 Finger Picking*, New World Artists Corp., 1974. 94 pp. An intelligent three-finger approach for the intermediate player. Streeter uses a system of tablature that represents rhythmic values by dividing each bar into 8 parts. Each box represents an eighth note. Unlike most bluegrass players, Wheeler plays in tunings besides G and D, and incorporates chromatic-style playing with Scruggs style in some of his arrangements. There is a detailed section on intros, fills, and endings.

SWEENY, PAT, *Five String Banjo Chromatic Style*. Self-pub.

Traditional Folk Collection for Banjo, M. M. Cole.

WEISSBERG, ERIC, arranger, *Dueling Banjos, arr. for banjo and guitar*. Warner Bros., 1973. 11 pp. The hit song from the *Deliverance* movie, written by Arthur Smith and arranged by Eric Weissberg for guitar and banjo in music and tablature.

WEISSMAN, DICK, *Five String Banjo: vol. 1, For Beginners Only*, Big 3, 1973. 48 pp. A beginner's method that teaches the G and C tunings, simple chord changes, and Pete Seeger's Basic Strum.

WEISSMAN, DICK, *Five String Banjo: vol. 2, Frailing, Bluegrass and Melody Playing*, Big 3, 1974. 48 pp. A continuation of volume 1, teaching melody playing and the basic right-hand techniques most commonly used in folk and bluegrass banjo.

WEISSMAN, DICK, *Five String Banjo: vol. 3, For Advanced Players Only*, Big 3, 1976. 112 pp. An advanced method dealing with playing up the neck, chord progressions, reading music for the banjo, and a variety of advanced techniques.

WERNICK, PETER, *Bluegrass Banjo*, Oak, 1974. 143 pp. With song sheet. Tablature only. An excellent book for the intermediate player who is already fairly familiar with the basics of bluegrass style. There is good material on up-the-neck playing, chromatic style, single-string style, and other matters not covered in Scruggs' or other books. Although the book is presented as an introductory text, it moves much too quickly for the beginning player. It is unfortunate that the author has not included a single note of music; he goes into matters of music theory which are dependent upon a knowledge of chord structure, so he could have dealt with the music itself, at least for those who already do read notation.

WERNICK, PETER, *Bluegrass Banjo*, 1974, MMO 180. This is a long-playing record of a bluegrass band, Wernick's Country Cooking. If you are an intermediate or advanced player without access to a bluegrass band, you will find this record quite useful. The banjo is recorded on a separate channel, so you can play with or without the banjo tracks. The tempos are much too fast for beginners. In each tune one solo is transcribed in tablature form; the idea is that you are to improvise the rest of the solos with the band. This is a nice idea, but Wernick does not explain how you do this. So if you don't grasp this concept, the record isn't going to help you much. Once again, no music is provided to go with the tablature.

YATES, JEFF, *Mel Bay's Folklore Banjo Method*, Mel Bay, 1974. 40 pp. Music and tablature. This book tries to cover everything in a very short space. It doesn't work unless you already know most of the banjo.

RECOMMENDED BANJO BOOKS

BORCHELT, DON, *15 Fiddle Tunes for Five String Banjo*. A good book of three-finger style solos.

Billy Faier's Banjo Book. A good book of solos in Faier's individualistic banjo style.

GRIFFIN, NEIL, *Mel Bay's Deluxe Bluegrass Banjo Method*. The best book for the beginning bluegrass player.

HOLCOMB, DAVE, *Banjo Lessons by Mail*. Various transcriptions and a style analysis booklet. Expensive but good.

KORNFELD, BARRY, *Blue Grass Banjo in Scruggs and Other Three Finger Picking Styles*. A sensible collection of bluegrass solos.

KURTH, KARL, *Banjo Pickin' Solos*. Another good collection of bluegrass solos.

MULLER, ERIC, and BARBARA KOEHLER, *Frailing the Five String Banjo*. Well-done and coherent.

ROSENBAUM, ART, *Old Time Mountain Banjo*. Not very well organized, but a valuable encyclopedia of banjo techniques in traditional styles.

SCRUGGS, EARL, *Earl Scruggs and the Five String Banjo*.

This is the book that really will teach you how to play like Earl Scruggs.

SEEGER, PETE, *How to Play the Five String Banjo*. For all its faults—and they are many—a gold mine of new ground to explore for the person who is not hung up on any one style.

STREETER, HAROLD, *5 String Banjo Improvisations for 3 Finger Picking*. An intelligent book, easy to follow.

WEISSMAN, DICK, *Five String Banjo: vol. 1, For Beginners Only*.

WEISSMAN, DICK, *Five String Banjo: vol. 2., Frailing, Bluegrass, and Melody Playing*.

WERNICK, PETER, *Bluegrass Banjo*. An excellent book if you are already familiar with the basic bluegrass style. Happy Traum has three sets of banjo instruction tapes or cassettes available in his Homespun Tapes series (Box 694, Woodstock, N.Y. 12498). *Five String Banjo, Series I and II* were recorded by Happy, and a set of *Bluegrass Banjo* tapes were made by Bill Keith. I played through some of the Keith tapes, and they are exceptionally clear and coherent, with very sensible tempos. All come with tablature sheets. Each of these sets contains six tapes or cassettes.

DOBRO

The Dobro Company is only one of the companies that make the kind of guitar used to play the music described in this section; but it is the instrument most players choose, and the name has come to be used generically. The instrument has a characteristic tone, produced by an aluminum resonator cone within the body. Occasionally, resonator guitars are played like any other guitar, for sound effect. But the term "Dobro" usually means a resonator guitar played Hawaiian-style, tuned to an open chord, with raised action, held flat on the lap, and fretted not with the fingers but with a steel bar that in effect constitutes a movable fret. Standard Dobro tuning is GBDGBD, from low to high.

(—L.S.)

CUNNINGHAM, BILL, *How to Play the Dobro*, Self-pub., 1971. 30 pp. Tablature only. This is a collection of solos, without progressive arrangement. Cunningham deals with technique in the most minimal fashion. He also ignores the relationship between double and triple stops and chord configurations, which is possibly the most important knowledge to acquire in playing the dobro. The printing and layout of the book are sloppy and cheap.

EDISON, KEN, and TOM SWATZELL, *Country Dobro Guitar Styles*, Mel Bay, 1974. 72 pp. 27 tunes, using GBDGBD tuning only. A good method, easy to follow, with music and tablature. Tapes of the songs are available from Ken Edison, 2121 Linneman St., Glenview, Ill. 60025.

KING, BEVERLY, *Country and Bluegrass Dobro*, Self-pub., 1973. Book 1, 33 pp. Book 2, 27 pp. A collection of pieces with instructional notes, arranged in a more or less progressive order of difficulty. The pieces are notated in a tablature that fails to represent rhythmic values, and many of the tunes are not well known. As a result, it is impossible to use these books without buying the accompanying tapes or cassettes. King gives a certain amount of useful technical and theoretical information in these books. The student will find much of benefit in these volumes, but he will also experience some confusion and frustration.

KING, BEVERLY, *Thirty-Six Songs for Dobro,* typed offset, 8 × 11 inches, 44 pp. Tablatures of arrangements (with some variations) of some well- and little-known songs, with minimal instructions and explanations. Not graded in order of difficulty.

TAYLOR, TUT. As this book goes to press, *Guitar Player* magazine is planning to publish an instruction method by Taylor. Further information not available.

TOTH, STEPHEN F., *Dobro Techniques for Bluegrass and Country Music,* vol. 1, Colonial Press, 1975. 8 × 11, 60 pp. The best dobro method I've seen, with good photos, line drawings and diagrams, background information, comprehensible tablature, instructions on the use of the steel, etc. It always seemed to me that the dobro, of all American folk instruments, is least likely to be learned from a book. But if you do need a book, this is the one.

TYLOR, KEITH, and PETER RICHARDSON, *How to Play Bluegrass Dobro by Ear,* Bluegrass Bookshelf, 1971.

DULCIMER AND HAMMERED DULCIMER

Steve Weincrot's initials follow reviews by him.

DAVIS, SANDY, *Hammered Dulcimer List,* self-pub., 1975. A list of makers, articles, records, etc.

EACHMAN, LEN and MAC, *Dulcimer by Ear and Other Easy Ways,* Here, Inc. Tuning, strums, modes.

FORCE, ROBERT, and ALBERT D'OSSCHE, *In Search of the Wild Dulcimer,* Vintage, 1974. 109 pp., PB. An enjoyable essay on the dulcimer, not terribly concerned with traditional music, but more with adapting the instrument to any music the authors enjoy. Not exactly an instruction book; rather, an exploration of possibilities.

FRENCH, DOROTHY, and LYNN MCSPADDEN, *Brethren We Have Met; Traditional Hymns and Carols for the Dulcimer,* The Dulcimer Shoppe, 1970. 44 pp. 30 songs, with music and fret numbers. This book includes brief

Jean Ritchie

but instructive notes on playing styles, modes, and chords.(—s.w.)

GAMSE, ALBERT, *The Best Dulcimer Method Yet.* Lewis Publishing Company, 1974. 97 pp. A collection of 139 songs with music and fret numbers. Very little information on right-hand techniques. (—s.w.)

HELLMAN, NEAL, and SALLY HOLDEN, *Life Is Like a Mountain Dulcimer,* TRO, 1974. 56 pp. With sound sheet for most of the 33 songs and tunes. All materials are written in tablature for fingering melody, drone, and bass strings simultaneously. There are sections on right-hand techniques, chords, and embellishments. The book is clear and entertaining; the recording plays the tunes at normal tempos only.

HICKERSON, JOE, *A Bibliography of Hammered and Plucked Dulcimers and Related Materials,* Folklore Society of Greater Washington, 1972.

HUGHES, VIRGIL, *Fun with the Dulcimer,* Mel Bay, 1972. 32 pp. This book is designed to get you started by giving general instructions, and then becomes a songbook. There is music and a number form of tablature. The instructional material is basic and doesn't go very far at all.

JEFFREYS, A. W., JR., *Tuning and Playing the Appalachian Dulcimer,* self-pub., 1964. 22 pp. Includes music and tablature, simple instructions, tunings, etc. Concise and easy to follow.

MASON, PHILLIP, *The Dulcimer Players' Bible, and Supplement Book,* self-pub., 1975. 52 pp. (supplement book, 24 pp.), PB. Dulcimer strings, tunings, instruction techniques, scales, chords, etc. The supplement includes 4 songs, a discography, and a list of dulcimer makers. A good compilation for dulcimer players and fans.

MCSPADDEN, LYNN, and DOROTHY FRENCH, *Four and Twenty: Songs for the Mountain Dulcimer,* The Dulcimer Shoppe, 1970. 24 songs, 44 pp. The songs are written in music and tablature. Different sections describe traditional strumming, modes, tunings, etc. (—s.w.)

MITCHELL, HOWARD W., *The Hammered Dulcimer,* Folk-Legacy Records. 12 inch LP Folk-Legacy FSI 43 and 57 p. booklet. The booklet is enclosed in the record, but is also available separately. It tells how to build and play the instrument, and the music included is on the record. The record is educational as well as enjoyable listening. It includes material on tuning and general information about the instrument. Five styles of playing are explained and demonstrated. An enticing selection of tunes.

MITCHELL, HOWARD W., *The Mountain Dulcimer: How to Make It and Play It,* Folk-Legacy Records. 49 pp. Book available with or without a record. Mitchell deals with the four-string dulcimer, discussing tunings, modes, chord playing, and includes information on dulcimer building. Mitchell covers the three-, four-, and six-string dulcimer, the double dulcimer, and the double psaltery. The record is of particular value in exploring and creating new musical dimensions on the dulcimer. For advanced players.

PATE, JASON, *Some Available Albums Featuring the Dulcimer,* self-pub. Four pages with a 1-page supplement listing albums that employ the dulcimer. Useful for the dulcimer fan, though expensive for the price.

PUTNAM, JOHN F., *The Plucked Dulcimer and How to Play It*, Council of the Southern Mountains, 1969. 30 pp. A good little guide; Putnam's directions are easy to follow. The book includes a list of dulcimer makers, 7 songs, and material on chords and tunings.

RITCHIE, JEAN, *The Appalachian Dulcimer*, Folkways LP FI 8352. This is a companion record to *The Dulcimer Book*, reviewed below, although it can be used independently from the book. Side 1 has spoken tuning instructions and 8 song examples. Side 2 contains 9 songs with dulcimer accompaniment by 9 different artists. A practical instruction tool. (—s.w.)

RITCHIE, JEAN, *The Dulcimer Book*, Oak, 1964. 44 pp. This book is most effective when used with the record. It includes 16 songs written in music and with fret numbers. Ritchie includes her own recollections of the dulcimer in her Kentucky childhood, 6 tunings, strumming, and finger picking. (—s.w.)

RITCHIE, JEAN, *Dulcimer People*, Oak, 1975.

SIMMONS, TOMMY and JEAN, *Simmons Family Songbook. Folksongs and Tunes for Guitar, Autoharp, and Dulcimer*, self-pub., 1974. 40 pp. A pleasing collection of 33 traditional songs and tunes with music and fret numbers. There are sections on various tunings. Nine of the songs are on the *Stone County Dulcimer* recording, and 7 more are on *Wandering Through the Rackensack*, reviewed below. (—s.w.)

SIMMONS FAMILY, *Stone County Dulcimer*, LP, The Dulcimer Shoppe. A recording with 18 traditional songs and tunes. The accompanying instruments include dulcimer, guitar, and dancing doll. (—s.w.)

SIMMONS FAMILY, *Wandering Through the Rackensack*, Rodney Pepperhorst Productions. LP, available from The Dulcimer Shoppe. 16 more traditional songs and tunes accompanied by dulcimer, guitar, and autoharp. (—s.w.)

FIDDLE

As a rule, the word "fiddle" is used of the instrument in folk music, "violin" in classical music. Fiddle-like instruments are found throughout the world, and the fiddle itself has a strong folk tradition throughout Europe. The tradition is especially strong in Ireland and Great Britain, and it is from the Anglo-Irish tradition that our North American ways of playing the instrument come.

Most fiddles played by folk musicians throughout America today are German-made instruments of the period 1880–1937, built in small factories. These and similar instruments are frequently available from used-instrument shops, from individuals, or from fiddle collectors for $50 to $200, and most of them do just fine. It's hard for a beginner to appraise a fiddle, since there are no standard brand names and model numbers in this price-quality range, as there are with guitars and banjos. But there should be absolutely no need to buy a new factory-made fiddle; most are inferior, anyway. If you're having trouble buying a fiddle, browse through our Organizations section in Part IV (page 227) for your nearest fiddlers' association; the association can almost certainly recommend someone to

help you. Fiddle collectors are shrewd horse traders among themselves, but it should be possible to find one who will do right by a beginner. Having a good bow—unwarped, well-balanced, and well-haired—will be extremely important to your progress. Try to get expert advice in selecting one, and don't be surprised, particularly if you have to get a new one, if you're asked to pay almost as much for it as for the fiddle itself. A classical violinist might pay many hundreds of dollars for a fine old bow. Satisfactory new ones can be had from music stores for $18 to $50.

American fiddle styles make use of a systematic variety of rhythmic bowing patterns. These comprise an ordered body of knowledge, just as guitar and banjo picking patterns do. If you read through a fiddle tune without knowing how to use the idiomatic bowings, you'll be playing the right notes, but will still wonder why you don't *sound* right. For this reason, comments on bowing play an important part in the following reviews.   (—L.S.)

CHRISTESON, R. P., *The Old Time Fiddler's Repertory*, University of Missouri Press, 1973. 208 pp., HB. A varied collection including rags, blues, waltzes, quadrilles, etc. There are occasional piano accompaniments, but unfortunately no chord symbols are included. (—D.W.)

CUNNINGHAM, BILL, *How to Play Hoe-Down Fiddle*, self-pub., 1971. 31 pp. Typed photo-offset. This book has much to commend it in its detailed attention to idiomatic bowing technique, an important aspect of fiddling neglected by other methods. Sometimes Cunningham moves too fast and will confuse you, but this is a worthwhile method if used in conjunction with a book of fiddle tunes. Recommended in spite of bad layout and printing.

DUNHAM, NELLIE, *50 Fiddlin' Dance Tunes*, Carl Fischer, 1926. PB. A good selection of tunes: waltzes, schottisches, hornpipes, jigs, reels, polkas, and hoedown tunes. Representative of the older professional fiddlers' total repertory, many aspects of which are no longer fashionable among revival fiddlers; includes familiar and little-known tunes. Dunham was a Maine championship fiddler in the twenties.

FELDMANN, PETER, *How to Play Bluegrass Fiddle: Volume One*, Sonyatone Records. A record with a 16-page booklet.

ISAAC, BURTON, *Bluegrass Fiddler*, Mel Bay, 1974. 48 pp. Many of the tunes in this book have no connection with bluegrass. No bowing instructions are given, but Isaac does include additional variations of the tunes, which are useful for showing how a fiddler's imagination works.

ISAAC, BURTON, *Folk Fiddle*, Mel Bay, 1964. 32 pp. Really an intermediate and advanced student's guide to the fiddle; many of the pieces are fairly difficult. This is essentially a collection of solos.

KENNEDY, PETER, ed., *The Fiddler's Tune Book*, English Folk Dance and Song Society, dist. by Hargail. 100 traditional tunes for melody instruments.

KINSCELLA, HAZEL, *Folk Songs and Fiddle Tunes of the U.S.A. See* Collections of Songs section, page 145.

KRASSEN, MILES, *Appalachian Fiddle*, Oak, 1973. 87 pp. A well-assembled and intelligently ordered book with a gratifying selection of tunes. Unfortunately, Krassen does not deal with the problem of bowing, and it is necessary to go to other sources, such as the Cunningham book or Schwarz's record, to get this information. This book is highly recommended in conjunction with other materials that cover bowing more thoroughly.

LOWINGER, GENE, *Bluegrass Fiddle*, Oak, 1974. 29 tunes, 88 pp. A good introduction to the style, but not for beginners.

O'NEILL, JAMES, *O'Neill's Music of Ireland*, Dan Collins, 349 pp. A massive collection, 1,850 fiddle tunes.

1000 Fiddle Tunes, M. M. Cole, 1967. 128 pp. Enough tunes for months of playing.

SCHWARZ, TRACY, *Learn to Fiddle Country Style*, Folkways LP FI 8359. An invaluable record for its attention to bowing. It should be used slowly in conjunction with a tune book, or a method such as that in the Miles Krassen book. The booklet that goes with the record is adequate, but it could be longer.

THEDE, MARION, *The Fiddle Book*, Oak, 1967. 160 pp., HB and PB. Thede is a classically trained violinist who later became interested in traditional fiddling. There are over 150 tunes in this book, transcribed from the playing of country fiddlers. This is not a beginners' book, but it is entertainingly written and can teach anyone a great deal about what it is like to be a fiddler. It will increase the more advanced player's repertoire and extend his concept of variations on a tune.

WELLING, WILLIAM, *Welling's Hartford Tunebook*, self-pub., 1974. 16 pp. A collection of 55 fiddle tunes, clearly printed, with metronome markings, occasional double stops, and a bare but useful minimum of bowing instructions. The tunes vary considerably in difficulty and popularity. They are from the northern and southern United States, French-Canadian, Irish, and Scottish traditions. A good collection, well worth buying.

What Is Old Time Fiddling? American Fiddler News. A two-track reel-to-reel tape at 3¾ ips available from *American Fiddler News*.

A number of the books listed under Miscellaneous Instruments (page 190) contain songs that can be played on the fiddle, as well as on other melody instruments.

From the Adirondacks: Lawrence Older

GUITAR

In order to make it easier for you to find what you are interested in, I have placed the guitar instructional materials in four separate categories: (1) blues, bottleneck, and ragtime, (2) chords, scales, and theory, (3) flat picking, and (4) folk guitar. Folk guitar includes general method books, books of solos, etc.

BLUES, BOTTLENECK, AND RAGTIME

ANDERSON, CHUCK, *An Improvisational Approach to Rock and Blues Guitar*, Theodore Presser, 1973. 32 pp. A worthwhile idea, improvisation taught through the use of the blues and pentatonic scales, and scales utilizing the dorian and mixolydian modes.

Art of Ragtime Guitar, The, Green Note, 1974. 96 pp. Includes sound sheet. This is a nice book, about the only ragtime book I've seen which is playable without extensive knowledge of the finger board. Tempos on the record are too fast for the student.

BAXTER, BOB, *Finger-Picking Blues and Ragtime Manual*, AMSCO, 1969. 122 pp. Baxter uses his own type of tablature, and it is confusing, even though he also prints the pieces in music notation. With only 11 arrangements, this is a rather skimpy book.

BERRY, CHUCK, *Easy Guitar*, Arc Music, dist. by Warner Bros., 1974. 48 songs, 88 pp. Melody line and easy guitar chords, no tablature. A good songbook for Chuck Berry fans, but it doesn't include much interesting guitar music.

BLOCK, CLAUDIA, *Gospel and Blues Guitar*, TRO, 1972. Music only. Fair arrangements, not too useful.

BLOCK, CLAUDIA, *Ragtime for Guitar*, Edward Marks, dist. by Belwin-Mills, 1974. 16 pp. This includes 7 Joplin tunes and 4 others. Music notation and chord symbols are used, no tablature. You need a fairly good knowledge of the finger board to play these arrangements. Sometimes the voicings are not very clear or interesting.

BORELLO, PIERRE, *Guitar Improvisation: The Blues*, Hansen, 1971. 48 pp. This is not a bad book for learning the finger board through chord arpeggios. It can help a beginning blues player by introducing passing tones and blue notes. No right-hand instruction.

CHARLES, RONNIE, *The Sting. Arranged for Two Guitars*, MCA Music, dist. by Belwin-Mills, 1974. 10 tunes, 35 pp. The lead parts are difficult and require lots of finger board knowledge and rhythmic expertise. The accompaniments are of medium difficulty. This book contains music only, and will help sharpen your sight-reading.

DICKLER, PAUL, *Bottlenecking and Blues Guitar*, Tara Publishing Company, 1974. 72 pp. Contains paper record (sound sheet). This book has good material on open tunings, especially D tuning. Tablature only, no music, although the tablature is easy to follow. Very little information on bottlenecking in regular tuning. The record is good, but the tempos are too fast for the student.

GARWOOD, DONALD, *Masters of Instrumental Blues Guitar*, Oak, 1968. 78 pp. Tablature and music. Good, clear

Sonny Terry

arrangements and rewrites in styles of John Hurt, Mance Lipscomb, and others. Music should be printed larger.

GROSSMAN, STEFAN, *Contemporary Ragtime Guitar*, Oak, 1972. 112 pp. Music and tablature. The following remarks apply to all of the Stefan Grossman books, and will not be repeated in the reviews of each one. In all of his books, Grossman includes music and tablature. However, the books are set up so that the music reader must also follow the tablature and the tablature player must follow the music. This is because the written music contains no guitar position markings, and the tablature contains no rhythmic time values. Grossman does have a system for marking the chord positions you are playing out of, but this is often on a third set of pages. So to play one arrangement, you have to shuttle your eyes back and forth like a spectator at a tennis match. Furthermore, Grossman's books are not progressive in difficulty. In sum, they are books of solos, rather than method books, despite what the titles indicate. If you pick and choose the solos you like, they are very useful; they constitute kind of an encyclopedia of blues and ragtime playing. Grossman does have tapes that go with the books, and some of the performances are available on records. However, you may have difficulty finding the records, or you may not want to invest in the tapes.

GROSSMAN, STEFAN, *The Country Blues Guitar*, Oak, 1968. 120 pp. Tunes by John Hurt, Furry Lewis, Robert Wilkins, and others. Includes music and tablature.

GROSSMAN, STEFAN, *Delta Blues Guitar*, Oak, 1969. 136 pp. Includes music and tablature. Pieces by Charley Patton, Son House, and others.

GROSSMAN, STEFAN, *Ragtime Blues Guitarists*, Oak, 1970. 132 pp. Music and tablature. Tunes by Blind Blake, Blind Boy Fuller, Blind Lemon Jefferson, and others.

GROSSMAN, STEFAN, *Rev. Gary Davis Blues Guitar*, Oak, 1974. 128 pp. A fine introduction to the Davis guitar style. There are several articles by Stefan and others, all written with evident love and appreciation for Gary

Davis. Tablature and music to 20 tunes are included; as is usual with Stefan's books, you need to follow both music and tablature to play the arrangements. But it's well worth the time and trouble in this instance.

HARLEY, JAMES, *Instant Blues Funky Style*. Playback Music Publishing Co., 1973. 40 pp.

Improvising Blues Guitar, Green Note, 1973. 84 pp. Includes sound sheet. This book deals with pick-style electric blues. When giving lead parts, it doesn't list the chords from which the solos are coming.

KING, B. B., *Blues Guitar*, Edward Marks., dist. by Belwin-Mills. These are Hampton Reece arrangements of jazz standards in the Marks catalogue. Nice stuff, jazzy and difficult. Not much to do with B. B., really.

KING, B. B., *Blues Guitar—A Method*, ed. by Jerry Snyder, Hansen, 1973. 64 pp. Music and tablature. Has sound sheet with nice, slow-tempo playing by B. B. This is a description of the various techniques and devices that B. B. uses in his playing, not a book of solos.

B. B. King, AMSCO, 1970. 60 pp. Contains music and tablature for 15 songs. Each song is followed by a guitar solo. Songs are co-written by B. B., V. Josea, S. Ling, and J. Taub. The printing is clear and easy to read.

MANN, WOODY, *Six Black Blues Guitarists*, Oak, 1973. 28 songs, 112 pp. Music and tablature. A good book, includes pieces by Blind Blake, Memphis Minnie, Gary Davis, and others. Mann neglects to print position markings with the music. Sometimes the music and tablature are printed parallel; sometimes they are not.

MOORE and WILLIAMS, *18 Patterns for the Blues*, M. M. Cole.

NANCE, FRED, and MARY ANN GODIA, *Blues 'n' Bottleneck Guitar*, Neil A. Kjos, 1973. 23 pp. Music and tablature. Not a bad beginners' guide. Could use more detailed treatment of each tuning, but a good start.

NUNES, WARREN, and JERRY SNYDER, *Jazz Guitar Series: The Blues*, Hansen, 1974. 48 pp. With sound sheet. When modern jazz players use the term "blues," they do not mean folk blues, but rather tunes based on folk blues that employ a more advanced harmonic structure. This is a useful book for the advanced player who is interested in that style of playing, which includes minor 7th chords, 9th chords, major 7th chords, etc. The tempos on the sound sheet are fairly fast.

PEARSE, JOHN, *Fingerpicking Guitar Method*. B. Feldman, London.

PEARSE, JOHN, *Flatpicking Guitar Method*, B. Feldman, London.

ROBINSON, MARCEL, ed. and transcriber, *Guitar Workshop*, dist. by Theodore Presser, 1974. The following solos are available: Joseph Lamb, "Reindeer"; Scott Joplin, "The Entertainer," "Maple Leaf Rag," and "Weeping Willow." Music only. For advanced players with a knowledge of the fingerboard. Some of the voicings are cloudy because of overuse of the bass strings. I thought Lamb's rag came out the best, "The Entertainer" the worst.

SEEGER, PETE, and JULIUS LESTER, *The 12 String Guitar As Played by Leadbelly*, Oak, 1965. 80 pp. Music and tablature. A good description of Leadbelly's style with numerous examples from his repertoire and a few of Seeger's own tunes.

SILVERMAN, JERRY, *The Art of the Folk Blues Guitar*, Oak, 1964. 71 pp. Not bad for the intermediate guitarist who wants to learn about blues. Many examples of breaks, but no real explanation of what is going on or why. Silverman is one of the few teachers who has studied and transcribed Josh White's techniques.

Slide Guitar, Green Note, 1972. 81 pp. Includes sound sheet. The section on imitation pedal steel playing is poor, and there is not much information here about open tunings. The most useful material is on playing bottleneck style in standard tunings (the first section on electric blues). Not much material here, and the typeface is ridiculously large. The record is not very good, and the tempos are too fast. Music and tablature included.

SNYDER, JERRY, transcriber, *"The Entertainer," "Maple Leaf Rag," "The Easy Winners," Guitar Arrangements of 3 Scott Joplin Piano Pieces*, Hansen, 1974. 7 pp. Reasonably interesting arrangements of these rags, at a medium level of difficulty.

TRAUM, HAPPY, *The Blues Bag*, Consolidated Music, 1968. 95 pp. Music and tablature. Partly a songbook, partly a book of solo breaks, this is not a very satisfying collection.

TRAUM, HAPPY, ed., *Guitar Styles of Brownie McGhee*, Oak, 1971. 102 pp. Music and tablature. A good book which clearly analyzes how Brownie plays and deals with his improvisations. Brownie has written a fascinating autobiographical foreword of some length.

CHORDS, SCALES, AND THEORY

ALLEN, J. WORTH, *Revelation Chord Book for All Fretted Instruments*, Forster Music, 1936. 32 pp. Allen includes chords for numerous string instruments, such as guitar, mandolin, and tenor and five-string banjo. This is a good general guide but is necessarily limited to basic materials.

BAY, BILL, *Guitar Chord Chart*, Mel Bay, 2 pp. Common chords in first position. Handy for beginners.

BERG, KNOTH and DAVID, *Learning Music with the Guitar*, Wadsworth, 1973.

BERLE, ARNIE, *Handbook of Single String and Bar Chord Studies*, AMSCO, 1974. 100 pp. Good position studies, weaker in its use of chord progressions and tunes.

BOBRI, VLADIMIR, *The Segovia Technique*. MacMillan. HB. Many illustrations of correct hand positions for classical guitar playing.

CARCASSI, MATTEO, *Classical Guitar Method*, Carl Fischer, rev. ed., 1962. 128 pp. One of the basic classic guitar texts.

CLEMENT, A. P. B., *The Chord Board*, Edward Schuberth. 6 fold-out pp. Good detailed chord chart for the guitar.

FILIBERTO, ROGER, *Guitar Position Studies*, Mel Bay, 1973. Good for finger board comprehension. Most of the tunes are boring.

FODEN, WILLIAM, *Chords for the Guitar*, rev. by George Roberts, Wm. J. Smith, 1955. 40 pp. This old book (originally published in 1919) is still just about the best chord book for guitar. There is a good section on movable chords.

GALBRAITH, BARRY, *Bach Two Part Inventions Adapted for Guitar*, Vista Music, 1972. 31 pp. These are the Bach inventions transcribed for two guitars, pick-style. Fingerings and positions are marked. These are invaluable technical studies. A cassette is also available from the publisher.

GREENE, TED, *Chord Chemistry*, Dale Zdenek Publications, 1971, dist. by Chappell. 109 pp. An excellent book for the player who gets deeply involved with chords and wants to know variations and the reasons behind them. Material on chord progressions, substitutions, etc.

GUITAR, REMO, *4400 Guitar Chords*, Big 3, 1963. 160 pp. 4,400 chords is more than you will ever need.

HANLON, ALAN, *Kreutzer for Guitar*, Edward Marks, dist. by Belwin-Mills. These are excellent pick-style studies transcribed for guitar from the famous violin studies.

HIGGINS, RALPH, and RICK GUIDO, *Introduction to Guitar Notation*, Belwin-Mills, 1973. 32 pp. Not bad for learning to read music for the guitar.

KOENIG, CHARLES, *Chord Finder Dictionary, Guitar*, Artcom Co., 1970. 24 pp. A good introduction to jazz chords, with a fairly detailed analysis of music theory for such a small publication.

LILIENFELD, ROBERT, and BASIL CIMINO, *The Guitarist's Harmony*, Colombo, dist. by Belwin-Mills, 1965. 79 pp. It is easier to deal with the subject of harmony on a piano, but if you don't have access to a piano, or can't play it, you may find this book useful. It covers chords, inversions, modulation, scales, etc.

Mel Bay Deluxe Scale Book, Mel Bay, 1973. 72 pp. Too many scales on bass strings, not enough covering the whole finger board.

OWEN, TOM, *Chord Coloring Book*, Chappell, 1974. 72 pp. Gives chords on each note of major and minor scales. Also includes progressions and inversions. Good for learning the finger board.

OWEN, TOM, *Scaling the Fretboard*, Chappell, 1974. 63 pp. Major and natural, melodic and harmonic minor scales in notation and diagram form.

PAPWORTH, KEITH, *500 Chords for the Guitar*, Big 3, 1963.

25 pp. Each chord diagram has 2 higher position inversions. Includes 8 standards with melody and chords. This is a good way to present chord inversions.

RICE, HOWARD, *Guitar Chords,* Kenyon.

SEGOVIA, ANDRES, *Diatonic Major and Minor Scales,* Columbia Music, 1953. 8 pp. Major and minor scales. This is for finger-style playing and uses seven different right-hand finger patterns.

SILVERMAN, JERRY, *A Folksinger's Guide to Note Reading and Music Theory,* Oak, 1972. 64 pp. A solid introduction to note reading and music theory. It covers a bit too much ground for a small book.

TRAUM, HAPPY, *The Guitarist's Chord Book,* AMSCO, 1967. 46 pp. Includes some simple chord progressions. Adequate.

VAN FEGGELEN, CARL, *Complete Scale Book for Guitar,* Berandol Music, 1969. 25 pp. A good scale book, includes major and relative minor scales. It also groups melodic and harmonic minors together.

WATKINS, RAY, *The Original Country Music Blue Book #1,* self-pub., 1974. 89 pp. Has some reasonable material on music theory. Fairly sketchy sections on guitar, dobro, pedal steel guitar, banjo, mandolin, and harmonica. Most useful for the chord diagrams for each instrument. Also includes material on fiddle, bass, and songwriting.

FLAT PICKING

This section deals with country flat picking; some of the blues books discussed, such as those by B. B. King, utilize flat picking in blues playing.

BALL, GEORGE, *Baxter's Flat-Picking Manual,* AMSCO, 1967. Tablature only. This uses Baxter's own tablature system, which I find confusing.

CRARY, DEACON DAN, *Flat-Picking Guitar Technique,* Experience Music, dist. by Chappell, 1974. 61 pp. Music and tablature. A very useful book for flat pickers. The music printing is exceptionally clear. Includes 15 arrangements.

Dave Holcomb's Guitar Tabs, self-pub. 16 flat-pick pieces and a style analysis booklet are available. Each tune comes with a tape. Music and tablature for each song. Well-done, though not cheap.

FLINT, TOMMY, *Flat Pickin' Styles,* Mel Bay, 1973. 23 tunes, 32 pp. Music and tablature. Good, clear book. Could have included more material on how chords are integrated into flat-pick leads.

LIEBERSON, RICHARD, *Old Time Fiddle Tunes for Guitar,* AMSCO, 1974. 128 pp. 40 tunes in music and tablature with chord symbols. Nice for improving flat-pick technique, but doesn't explain how to use the chords with the solos. Music doesn't include position markings, and the music and tablature are not always printed parallel to one another.

SILVERMAN, JERRY, *Flat-Picker's Guitar Guide,* Oak, 1966. 97 pp. Some nice advanced things, especially the George Shuffler arrangement of "Mountain Dew." Some of the arrangements don't clearly show where you are supposed to strum the chords.

TRAUM, HAPPY, *Bluegrass Guitar,* Oak, 1974. 127 pp., with sound sheet (record). Music and tablature to 30 tunes. A

clear and logical explanation. There are no position markings in the music, but it is usually lined up with the tablature for easy reading. You should have a basic knowledge of chords before tackling this book. The record is well-done, with slow as well as faster tempos for the various examples.

TRAUM, HAPPY, *Flat-Pick Country Guitar,* Oak, 1973. 111 pp. Good arrangements in music and tablature. For some reason, the arrangements in the first part of the book are in tablature, and the music shows only the melody. This book does explain the use of chords with flat-pick leads.

FOLK GUITAR

American Folk Style for Guitar, M.M. Cole.

ATKINS, CHET, *Play Guitar Like Chet Atkins,* Big 3, 1965. 32 pp. 11 songs in music notation only. The songs are pop standards. Includes chord symbols.

AXTON, HOYT, *Guitar,* Lady Jane Music, dist. by Warner Bros. 25 songs, 92 pp. Guitar arrangements in music only, with chord symbols. Includes "Greenback Dollar," "Joy to the World," and others. Really a songbook; but for guitar, not piano.

BAY, MEL, *The Chet Atkins Style for Guitar,* vols. 1–2, Mel Bay, 1952, 1964. Each 40 pp. Music only. These books tell a bit about the Atkins style, but don't cover right-hand technique adequately.

BAXTER, BOB, *Baxter's Guitar Workshop,* AMSCO, 1974. 146 pp. Some music, some tablature, but not both together. Some interesting discussions with Ry Cooder, Fred Gerlach, Clarence White, and others concerning their technique and ideas about music.

BAXTER, BOB, *Baxter's Magic Flip Book and Right Hand Style Manual,* AMSCO, 1971. 93 pp. one way, 97 the other (book printed in two directions). Not bad, the pictures help. I like the Goldberg–Walls book better for the same purpose.

BAXTER, BOB, *Finger-Picking Manual,* AMSCO, 1967. 53 pp. Tablature only. Uses his own confusing tablature.

BAXTER, BOB, *Kid's Guitar Manual,* AMSCO, 1973. 82 pp. This book is too cute for me. Starts off with no notation, then suddenly prints a lot of songs with notation.

BLOCK, CLAUDIA, *Blue Grass Guitar,* Edward Marks, dist. by Belwin-Mills, 1970. 10 songs, 16 pp. Not really bluegrass, but Travis picking. No use of the flat pick, which is what we usually link to the words "bluegrass guitar." Music only, no tablature.

BLOCK, CLAUDIA, *Pete Seeger on Record,* TRO, 17 songs, 32 pp. Music only, no tablature. Finger-style arrangements of no particular interest.

CAMPBELL, GLEN, *Guitar Method,* Crown.

Classic American Folk Songs for Voice and Guitar, ed. and pub. by Guitar Workshop, dist. by Theodore Presser, 1970. 16 pp. Three complex and worthwhile arrangements for classic guitar. No tablature. Not for the beginner.

DAVIS, BOB, and JOHN ADAMS, *The 50 Cent Guitar Book,* Flash Books, dist. by Oak, 1974. 920 pp. Entertaining but of little instructional substance. Introducing the A chord as the student's first chord is a poor idea.

ELLIOTT, HELEN, *Guitar Magic,* Selmer Guitars. 128 pp.

This is a teacher's manual that goes with a 33-lesson junior high guitar course.

FAVA, JOE, and MORRIS LAST, *Folk Guitar Instruction Book,* CRS, 1964.

FILIBERTO, ROGER, *Folk Guitar Styles,* Mel Bay, 1967.

FLINT, TOMMY, *Authentic Bluegrass Guitar,* Mel Bay, 1972. 32 pp. Not really bluegrass, but 22 arrangements which constitute an advanced guide to Travis picking. Only 1 flat-pick tune in the book. Music and tablature.

FLINT, TOMMY, *Country Blues Guitar,* Mel Bay, 1974. 40 pp. Music and tablature. Not really country blues, but nice solos of advanced difficulty in the style of Merle Travis. In other words, white blues.

FLINT, TOMMY, *Dueling Guitars,* Mel Bay, 1973. 15 solos, 32 pp. Music and tablature with suggested banjo strums and chords. Enjoyable duets, but makes an awful lot of mileage on "Dueling Banjos." The banjo parts are really just chords with Scruggs rolls.

FLINT, TOMMY, *Guitar Tunings: Folk, Country and Bluegrass,* Mel Bay, 1973. 40 pp. Music and tablature. This is an excellent guide to tunings for someone who knows little about them. Each tuning is covered in detail; including open G, high third-string tuning, open D tuning, open C tuning, and high bass tuning. A number of other tunings are listed at the back of the book.

FOX, DAN, *Songs, Strums, and Chords for Beginning Folk Guitar,* TRO, 1971. 34 songs, 64 pp. Songs include melody lines, chords, and a recommended strum. There is a strum chart at the back of the book. A good beginners' book, easy to follow. The strums would be easier to follow if the songs were on adjoining pages, at least in the beginning.

GOLDBERG, STUART, and BYRON WALLS, *The Compleat Book of Right Hand Strums for Folk and Electric Guitar,* Marina Music, 1968. 93 pp. This is a good collection of strums, especially in its use of Latin-American right-hand styles. It doesn't include the Merle Travis style of picking.

GREEN, RON, *Folk Guitar Strums,* self-pub., 1971. Tape also available from the author. Not a bad book; besides strums, it has information about chord construction, tuning the guitar, etc.

GROSSMAN, STEFAN, *Book of Guitar Tunings,* AMSCO, 1973. 96 pp. Music and tablature in G, D, open E, E minor, and 8 other tunings. A valuable guide with some of the same deficiencies mentioned in discussing Grossman's other books.

HARRISON, RICHARD, *Choice Folk Songs,* Hargail, 1966. 25 songs, 32 pp. Guitar notation only, no tablature. Does include chord symbols.

HARRISON, RICHARD, *Choice Folk Songs Encore,* Hargail, 1974. 27 songs, 40 pp. Harrison's two books are based on arpeggio patterns and are adequately done.

HELMS, JIM, *The Big 12 String Guitar,* Hansen, 1965. 21 tunes, 24 pp. Music and chord symbols only. Helms' book is a series of transcriptions from a recording originally issued on World Pacific, and now available on Olympic, a budget label distributed by Everest Records. Included are solos by Glen Campbell, Frank Hamilton, Roger McGuinn, Dick Rosmini, and others. These are difficult solos to sight-read. Some of them are valuable studies; some are of routine interest.

HIGGINS, RALPH, *Introduction to Finger Picking Guitar,* Belwin-Mills, 1973. 32 pp. Music and tablature. The arrangements are stiff and a bit dull, but the explanations are clear and well-done.

HOLTMAN, ROGER, and ROGER ERB, *Twelve String Guitar Styles,* Mel Bay, 1967. Some tablature, all with music. Dull arrangements.

Jerry Silverman Plays Johnny Cash Hits, Big 3, 48 pp. Music notation for guitar, no tablature.

KORNFELD, BARRY, *Finger Picking Guitar,* Hargail, 1965. 11 songs, 32 pp. Music and tablature. Well thought out; nice arrangements of progressive difficulty. The layout is bad—for some songs you have to turn the page.

KORNFELD, BARRY, *The Folk Guitarist's Manual,* Hargail, 1964. 27 pp. Very clear right-hand directions, but not too much else of value.

LANGILL, ROXANNE, *Anyone Can Play the Guitar,* Scribner's, 1973. 154 pp., PB. The organization of this book—music reading, chords, then right-hand techniques—is in opposite sequence to the easiest way to teach folk guitar. The information is solid but its presentation too hard to follow.

LEE, RONNY, *Folk Strums for Guitar,* Sam Fox, dist. by Carl Fischer, 1961. 40 pp. Record available. A fair introduction to finger-style playing. 53 strums included.

LEE, RONNY, and HOWARD DAVID, *More Folk Strums for Guitar,* Sam Fox, dist. by Carl Fischer, 1963. 48 pp. Record available. There are some interesting combinations of various patterns here, but the lack of Travis or blues strums seriously detracts from the value of the book.

Ed Collins, Ira Mullins, and Merle Travis (on guitar)

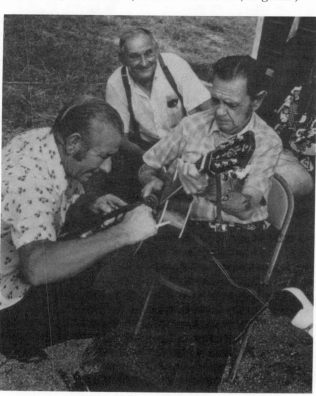

MAIRANTS, IVOR, *Method for 12 String Guitar*, Belwin-Mills, 1965. 50 pp. Notation with some tablature. Some nice things using the flat pick, and Chet Atkins' finger-style solos. Many of the arrangements don't seem especially designed for the twelve-string.

MAIRANTS, IVOR, and STEVE BENBOW, *Folk Music Accompaniment for Guitar*, Southern Music.

MANDELBLATT, ABE and MALKA, *100 Guitar Accompaniment Patterns for Guitar*, Oak, 1974. 208 pp. With sound sheet (record). An extensive strum guide, with lists of recommended songs for each strum pattern. The accompanying record has demonstrations of the strums, usually played too fast.

McKEOWN, BEVERLY, *Guitar Songbook with Instruction*, Houghton Mifflin, 1975. 196 pp. A book for the music teacher who does not play guitar, for use in learning the instrument and teaching it in the classroom. McKeown introduces too many keys and chords without adequate repetition of previous materials.

MILLER, JIMMY, *Nashville Guitar*, Alfred Music, 1970. 49 pp. Music and tablature. A good introduction to finger picking in the Merle Travis–Chet Atkins styles.

MILLER, JOHN, and MICHAEL CROMIE, *Folk Guitar*, Quadrangle, 1968.

MORGAN, DAN, *Playing the Guitar*, Bantam Books, 1967. This is really a plectrum guitar method (pick-style). It covers a great deal of ground, too much in fact. Chapters on bass guitar, classic guitar, etc.

MULLEN, FRANK, *Guitarfest*, Theodore Presser, 1967. 160 pp. Notation and chord symbols. These are finger-style solos in first position. Includes hymns, folk songs, instrumentals, etc.

NANCE, FRED, and MARY ANN GODIA, *Folk Guitar*, Neil A. Kjos, 1973. 35 pp. Music and tablature. Not a bad beginning for finger-style playing. The tablature is sometimes in disagreement with the music.

NANCE, FRED, and MARY ANN GODIA, *Gospel Guitar*, Neil A. Kjos, 1974. 47 pp. Music only. This book makes good use of the finger board, although it could have better chord diagrams or position markings for the chords up the neck of the guitar.

NANCE, FRED, and MARY ANN GODIA, *Mariachi Mexican Guitar*, Neil A. Kjos, 1974. 22 pp. Solos and duets.

NANCE, FRED, and MARY ANN GODIA, *Music Through the Guitar*, Neil A. Kjos. This includes volumes covering 4 levels of instruction. Also available are 4 books of solos and a book of chamber music for guitar and strings, all graded at level 5, and 3 flamenco books and a Christmas guitar book graded level 6. I have not gone through all of these books, but the folk books, which I have played through, are intelligently graded and easy to follow.

New Big 75 Easy Guitar, The, Warner Bros., 1974. 76 songs, 176 pp. Music, no tablature. Songs by Dylan, Mitchell, Elton John, and others. Not much of a guitar book, but a good collection of songs. Includes melody line and easy chords.

John Jacob Niles Song Book for Guitar, Schirmer, 1963. 28 songs, 32 pp. Guitar arrangements in notation with chord symbols. Easy but uninteresting arrangements of such Niles classics as "Ribbon Bow" and "Go Way from My Window."

PAZ, ELENA, *Illustrated Folk Guitar*, Frank Music, 1965.

PEARSE, JOHN, *First Guide to Guitar*, AMSCO, 1970. 58 pp. This is an oddly constructed book. At first, Pearse writes in notation, but then switches to tablature. They never appear together.

PERNECKY and RABY, *Sing and Play Folk Songs*, vol. 1, M. M. Cole.

RENBOURN, JOHN, *Guitar Pieces*, Warner Bros., printed in England, OP in U.S. 48 pp. Appealing medieval and original dance tunes for nylon- or steel-string guitar. These solos are beyond categorization, and of great interest. Music notation only, some in other guitar tunings.

ROBINSON, EARL, *Play Guitar in Ten Sessions*, AMSCO, 1965. 72 pp. Too much text, and he introduces too many chords too quickly.

SEEGER, PEGGY, and ALAN LOMAX, *American Folk Guitar*, Big 3, 1957. 22 pp. A practical guide. 15 songs with chords and texts. Chords are organized in terms of families, or chords that often go together.

SILVERMAN, JERRY, *Beginning the Folk Guitar*, Oak, 1973. 96 pp. A good general beginners' method. The layout is not too good; there is too much on a page for easy reading.

SILVERMAN, JERRY, arranger, *Cavalcade of Country Hits*, Big 3, 1972. 57 songs, 128 pp. Notation only. The arrangements are of no particular interest.

SILVERMAN, JERRY, *Chord and Music Writing Book*, Big 3, 1971. 63 pp. This book contains 19 pages of songs and instruction, and 45 pages of manuscript paper and chord diagrams.

SILVERMAN, JERRY, *Folksinger's Guitar Guide*, Oak, 1962. 80 pp. Based on Pete Seeger's instructional record. It is a good beginners' book, although it moves along a bit too fast for my taste.

SILVERMAN, JERRY, *Folksinger's Guitar Guide: Vol. 2, Advanced*, Oak, 1964. 96 pp. Tablature and notation. Bass runs, chord progressions, up-the-neck playing. Lots of useful information, which might have been better organized in two books rather than one. The finger-picking solos are clumsy.

SILVERMAN, JERRY, *A Folksinger's Guide to Chords and Tunings*, Oak, 1967. 96 pp. This is a chord book for guitar, banjo, and mandolin. The guitar chords are shown in the D and G tunings, as well as standard tuning. The banjo chords are in G, C, D, G minor, and G "mountain minor" tuning. A good book.

SILVERMAN, JERRY, *How to Play Better Guitar*, Doubleday, 1972.

SMITH, ELIZABETH, *The Highwayman and 12 Other Folk Songs*, Columbia Music, dist. by Theodore Presser, 1973. 22 pp. Music only. These are pleasing intermediate level finger-style arrangements. They are a good introduction to note reading, especially to reading the notes that actually constitute chords.

TAUSSIG, HARRY, *Folk-Style Guitar*, Oak, 1973. 126 pp. Music and tablature. Not a bad book for finger-picking techniques. Lacks a sense of direction.

TAUSSIG, HARRY, *Instrumental Techniques of American Folk Guitar*, Oak, 1968. 91 pp. Good material on the Carter Family and finger-picking styles. Includes G and D tuning. The student needs to know how to change chords before starting this well-organized book.

TAUSSIG, HARRY, *Teach Yourself Guitar*, Oak, 1971. 150 pp. Music and tablature. A good book for people who are really poor singers; Taussig's format is to teach you a melody, then show you a guitar solo for that melody. I feel that starting with the C and G7 chords is a mistake; other chords are easier. The book never gets beyond the C, F, and G7 chords, which is too slow a pace.

TRAUM, HAPPY, *Children's Guitar Guide*, Oak, 1968. 80 pp. Starts out with his own diagram system, which is easy to follow. The melodies are written in notation form at the back of the book. The printing is exceptionally clear.

TRAUM, HAPPY, *Finger Picking Styles for Guitar*, Oak, 1966. 64 pp. Music and tablature. A good clear book about finger picking. It assumes the ability to change chords quickly.

TRAUM, HAPPY, *Guitar Finger Picking Styles*, Oak, 1969. 71 pp. Music and tablature. A more venturesome book than the one reviewed above. It includes some John Hurt, some African guitar pieces, etc. Nicely printed and easy to read.

TRAVIS, MERLE, and TOMMY FLINT, *The Merle Travis Guitar Style*, Mel Bay, 1974. 48 pp. Music and tablature. A good book on the style of a master. It is clear and informative, and describes Travis' unusual chord playing, using the left thumb but no barre chords.

WHITE, HY, *Folklore for Guitar*, MCA Music, dist. by Belwin-Mills, 1959. 48 songs, 56 pp. Music and chord symbols. A good beginners' book, teaches chords and some strums, and moves along at a nice slow pace.

RECOMMENDED GUITAR INSTRUCTIONAL BOOKS

BLUES, BOTTLENECK, AND RAGTIME

Art of Ragtime Guitar, The. Nice arrangements, easy to follow.

GROSSMAN, STEFAN, *Rev. Gary Davis Blues Guitar*. An essential presentation of the style of a master guitarist.

KING, B. B., *Blues Guitar—A Method*, ed. by Jerry Snyder. Particularly recommended if you want to play electric blues.

MANN, WOODY, *Six Black Blues Guitarists*. This is the easiest book of its kind to follow.

NANCE, FRED, and MARY ANN GODIA, *Blues 'n' Bottleneck Guitar*. Recommended for newcomers to these styles.

CHORDS, SCALES, AND THEORY

FODEN, WILLIAM, *Chords for the Guitar*. Clear and pragmatic.

GALBRAITH, BARRY, *Bach Two Part Inventions Adapted for Guitar*.

HANLON, ALAN, *Kreutzer for Guitar*. The Galbraith and Hanlon books are both excellent studies for left-hand and pick-style technique.

OWEN, TOM, *Chord Coloring Book*. Good for learning the finger board.

VAN FEGGELEN, CARL, *Complete Scale Book for Guitar*. The most intelligently assembled book of its kind.

FLAT PICKING

CRARY, DEACON DAN, *Flat-Picking Guitar Technique*.
FLINT, TOMMY, *Flat Pickin' Styles*.

Dave Holcomb's Guitar Tabs.

TRAUM, HAPPY, *Bluegrass Guitar*. Excellent; and so is the record.

TRAUM, HAPPY, *Flat-Pick Country Guitar*.

All of the above are good; Holcomb's materials include good tapes, but are also the most expensive.

FOLK GUITAR

FLINT, TOMMY, *Guitar Tunings*. A good introduction.

FOX, DAN, *Songs, Strums and Chords for Beginning Folk Guitar*. For beginners only.

GOLDBERG, STUART, and BYRON WALLS, *The Compleat Book of Right Hand Strums for Folk and Electric Guitar*. The best of the strum books.

GROSSMAN, STEFAN, *Book of Guitar Tunings*. Much of the material in this book is unavailable elsewhere. Like Grossman's other books, this book is not always easy to follow, but this one is worth extra patience.

KORNFELD, BARRY, *Finger Picking Guitar*. An excellent book.

MANDELBLATT, ABE and MALKA, *100 Guitar Accompaniment Patterns for Guitar*. An exhaustive treatment of the right hand.

RENBOURN, JOHN, *Guitar Pieces*. An important book by an innovative player.

SEEGER, PEGGY, and ALAN LOMAX, *American Folk Guitar*. A useful organization of chords and strums.

SILVERMAN, JERRY, *Folksinger's Guitar Guide*. A good beginners' book.

SILVERMAN, JERRY, *A Folksinger's Guide to Chords and Tunings*. The best single book of chord diagrams.

TRAUM, HAPPY, *Finger Picking Styles for Guitar*. Well-organized and easy to follow.

TRAUM, HAPPY, *Guitar Finger Picking Styles*. A good follow-up to the above book.

WHITE, HY, *Folklore for Guitar*. Another good, easy beginners' book.

GUITAR INSTRUCTIONAL RECORDS AND TAPES

BADEAUX, ED, *American Folk Guitar*, Folkways LP FG 3534. Purportedly a documentary study and exposition of the major American folk guitar styles, this album, though well-conceived, is rendered ineffectual because Badeaux does not play well enough to have undertaken such a project. (—L.S.)

BARENBERG, RUSS, *Bluegrass Country*, MMO 185. With Country Cooking band. A record to buy if you are already a good flat-pick guitarist and need a band to practice with. The tempos are very fast, and the booklet with the record has tablature only. These are two major disadvantages; otherwise a nice record. (—D.W.)

D'AUBERGE, ALFRED, and MORTON MANUS, *The New Guitar Course*, Blaine-Worthington Enterprises. 2 12-inch LP's and 2 48-p. books. This is an easy method to follow. The record, by Dan Fox, is intelligently put together with nice slow tempos. The books contain no tablature and are slanted heavily toward the learning of notes on each string. (—D.W.)

GROSSMAN, STEFAN, *A Study in Blues and Ragtime Guitar*,

Kicking Mule 112. A sequel to *How to Play the Blues Guitar,* this record comes with a tablature book.

GROSSMAN, STEFAN, and AURORA BLOCK, *How to Play Blues Guitar,* Kicking Mule 109. The title is somewhat misleading; in fact, this record doesn't teach a method and a beginning player will have trouble with it. Instead, it presents re-creations of classic country blues guitar solos recorded without vocals and in a modern studio, making these versions easier to hear than the original recordings. The accompanying booklet includes instructions and tablature. The tablature does not include rhythmic values. This record has value as pleasant listening, or for the intermediate player who is already somewhat familiar with the blues. (—L.S.)

MARAVILLA, LUIS, *Lección Guitarra Flamenco,* HispaVox HH 10–297. LP, available from Spanish Music Center, 319 W. 48th Street, New York, N.Y. 10036. Maravilla is a fine player. The spoken material on the record is in Spanish, but the text is in English, French, German, and Spanish. Tempos are rapid; this record is best used by a good player who wants to know about flamenco. (—D.W.)

SEEGER, PETE, *The Folksinger's Guitar Guide,* Folkways LP FQ 8354. There is some good material here, but the tempos are too fast, and the book progresses too quickly. There is a booklet with the record, but the record is better used with the more complete Jerry Silverman Oak book. (—D.W.)

SILVERMAN, JERRY, *The Art of the Folk Blues Guitar,* Folkways F 18355. 1 12-inch LP. The booklet here is an abridged version of an Oak book. A good basic record with easy tempos. (—D.W.)

SILVERMAN, JERRY, *Beginning the Folk Guitar,* Folkways FS 8353. 1 12-inch LP. The booklet enclosed inside the record album is also an abridged version of a larger Oak book. A reasonable method that moves a bit too fast for the total beginner. (—D.W.)

SILVERMAN, JERRY, *The Folksinger's Guitar Guide,* vol. II, Folkways CRB 5. 1 12-inch LP. Another booklet enclosed, abridged version of a larger Oak book. A sound explanation of integrating melody-playing with strums. Good material on foreign songs, rare in this method. The description of finger picking is inadequate, though. (—D.W.)

THOMPSON, ERIC, *Ten Fiddle Tunes for the Guitar,* self-pub. Tape or cassette from the author at Box 628 Cloverdale, Calif. 95425. Creative arrangements of traditional tunes for flat-pick style guitar. The tempos on the tape are very fast and should only be attempted by advanced players. The intermediate player can work from the accompanying booklet and build his technique in order to play with the tape. Tablature only in the booklet. (—D.W.)

TRAUM, HAPPY (Box 694, Woodstock, N.Y. 12498). Happy Traum has sets of six tapes or cassettes with the following titles: *Flatpick Country Guitar, Fingerpicking Series I, Fingerpicking Series II, Blues Guitar Series I.* All of the tapes come with tablature sheets. I have played through a number of them; they are clear and easy to follow, and the tempos on the cassettes are slow and easy to play. Another tape series by Artie Traum, also available from Happy, deals with lead guitar. The tempos are a bit too fast; for more advanced players only. Also available from

the same source is a tape series on bottleneck-slide guitar by Arlen Roth. (—D.W.)

TUFT, HARRY, and DICK WEISSMAN, *Favorite Folk Songs Minus Guitar,* MMO LP 160. A collection of songs with simple guitar accompaniments and a booklet instructing the student in a variety of right-hand techniques and basic chords used on the record. The performances are arranged in order to facilitate playing along. (—L.S.)

WEISSMAN, DICK, and DAN FOX, *How to Play the Blues,* MMO LP 140. A uniquely useful record in that it is really a record for beginners, but differs from other beginners' records in that the repertory and techniques have to do exclusively with blues and related materials. The record provides examples of songs and techniques printed in an accompanying booklet. A form of tablature is used; additional standard notation of guitar parts and melody lines would have been useful. The bottleneck is held in precisely the opposite direction from the one illustrated in the booklet. (—L.S.)

WEISSMAN, DICK, and DAN FOX, *How to Play Folk Guitar,* MMO 50. 2 12-inch LP's. A set for beginners, with a comprehensive booklet that presents over 30 songs that can be accompanied with basic chords. The main orientation is toward right-hand techniques for rhythmic song accompaniments. (—L.S.)

Stefan Grossman and Happy Traum have a number of guitar instructional tapes available. Traum also has banjo and blues piano tapes. For further information *see* page 176.

CLASSICAL AND JAZZ GUITAR INSTRUCTION

The purpose of this book is not to discuss classical or jazz guitar in any detail, but here is some information for people interested in pursuing those directions.

CLASSICAL GUITAR

The Carcassi method, published by Carl Fischer, is a basic tool. A good beginners' book is *Learning the Classic Guitar* by Arai, published by Schirmer. The Aaron Shearer methods, published by Belwin-Mills, are also good. Most players do not realize that many of the Renaissance guitar solos are not very difficult to play. There are many anthologies of solos, in addition to books on individual composers, that the student will find beneficial.

JAZZ GUITAR

For chords try the *Ronny Lee Jazz Guitar Method,* books, vols. 1–2, published by Mel Bay. The *William Leavitt Berklee Jazz Guitar Method,* vol. 1, Berklee Press, is a good overall method. Anytime you're getting complacent about your playing, try the George Van Eps *Guitar Method,* published by Plymouth Music. It deals with finger board harmony and provides many technical challenges for the advanced player. Another idea is to play jazz trumpet or saxophone solos on the guitar, especially the works of Louis Armstrong, Bix Beiderbecke, and Charlie Parker.

If finger-style jazz and bossa nova interest you, try the Jack Marshall book, *Authentic Brazilian Bossa Nova Guitar Arrangements* (MCA Music, dist. by Belwin-Mills). It represents still another direction in guitar, combining jazz harmonies with finger-style playing.

HARMONICA

Two kinds of harmonicas are in general use, although some other types are also made. The single reed harmonica, which is also called the diatonic harmonica, cannot play sharps or flats. The chromatic harmonica plays sharps and flats. In folk and blues playing, the marine band-style harmonica is the more common instrument. It is also cheaper and easier to play. Because of this, we have listed only the few chromatic methods or records that seem to relate specifically to folk-style playing (as opposed to the music of The Harmonicats or other pop groups).

ARNOLD, KEN, *Amazing Grace and Other Gospel Sounds for Harmonica*, Edward Marks, dist. by Belwin-Mills, 1972. 30 songs. Arnold's book contains words and music, chord symbols, and correct hole numbers (sort of the harmonica equivalent of tablature) for chromatic and marine band harmonicas. It is easy to follow.

Blues Harmonica (no author listed), Barran Music Company, 1970. 16 pp. A beginners' method only, with emphasis on blues playing. For marine band harmonica.

CHAM-BER HUANG, *The Blues and All That Jazz*, MMO 1048. 1 12-inch LP with booklet. A blues method for chromatic harmonica only. Side 1 has folk blues solos, and side 2 has more modern swing-style blues. First you hear the solo on harmonica, then you get several choruses to play your own solo with a rhythm section. A constructive method, with music notation only.

CHAM-BER HUANG, *Folk Song Fest for the Hohner Chordomonica II*, Mills Music, dist. by Belwin-Mills, 1965. 32 songs. This book is for still another kind of harmonica, designed by the author. There are melody lines and chord symbols for American and foreign folk songs.

CHAM-BER HUANG, *Learn to Play the Harmonica*, MMO 1014. 1 12-inch LP with booklet. The author teaches you how to play melodies on the marine band or chromatic harmonica through music reading only.

GLOVER, TONY, *Blues Harp*, Oak, 1973. 72 pp. Glover analyzes the blues of such players as Sonny Terry, Sonny Boy Williamson 1 and 2, and Little Walter, and gives good instruction on the various aspects of blues playing. The writing style is strictly out of the Jack Kerouac beatnik era. Some music notation would have been helpful.

GLOVER, TONY, *Blues Harp*, Folkways LP 9358. A booklet is enclosed with the record, but it's sketchy. It is better to use the record along with the book above. Glover's recorded text is delivered in a deadpan style.

GLOVER, TONY, *Blues Harp Songbook*, Oak, 1975. With sound sheet.

KRATT, WILLIAM, *Harmonica Course*, Kratt Publishing, 1927. 200 songs, 64 pp. Kratt's book is typical of the dozens of marine band methods available; it uses well-known songs that are easy to play.

MORGAN, TOMMY, *Blues Harmonica*, Gwyn Publishing, 1971. 49 pp. Morgan covers many musical examples with

Johnny Young and Big Walter Horton

music, chord symbols, and hole numbers. A cassette is available from the publisher. For marine band harmonica only.

RECOMMENDED HARMONICA INSTRUCTIONAL BOOKS AND RECORDS

CHAM-BER HUANG, *The Blues and All That Jazz*. A good method; for chromatic harmonica only.

GLOVER, TONY, *Blues Harp*. Book and record. The best all-around blues method if you can stomach the overcool text and narration.

MORGAN, TOMMY, *Blues Harmonica*. A more general guide than Glover's with less reference to specifics of the styles of various bluesmen.

MANDOLIN

In the twenties and thirties, there were many mandolin orchestras in the United States. They included mandolins, mandolas, mandocellos, and mandobasses. The range and tuning of these instruments corresponded to that of a normal string quartet. The typical repertoire consisted of light classics and popular songs of the day. The mandolin itself was probably the most popular "courting" instrument of the twenties.

Many old mandolins were pear-shaped. The instrument used most often today is flat-backed. In bluegrass it can be a solo or rhythm instrument, and it can play the earlier pre-bluegrass string band music of the twenties and thirties in combination with a banjo and guitar.

Guitar, banjo, and fiddle techniques have been adapted to the mandolin by such virtuoso players as Bill Monroe and Jesse McReynolds.

Steve Wiencrot's initials follow reviews by him in this section.

ALLEN, CHARLES, *Mandolin Chords*, Kenyon.

DE CRISTOFARO, F., *Music for Mandolin*, books 1–2, Carl

Fischer, 1891 and 1895. 88 pp. and 106 pp. These books contain music only, and teach music reading through solos and exercises. The second book has more difficult solos and some playing in higher positions. Both books have some duets. This is not a folk method, but teaches how to play popular and classical music.

FODEN, WILLIAM, *Chords for the Mandolin*, Wm. J. Smith, 1947 ed. of 1919 book. 39 pp.

GRISMAN, DAVID, *10 Tunes in 9 Keys*, self-pub. Cassette tape and Xerox booklet with tablature only. The tape is clearly recorded in stereo with a metronome on one track and the solos on the other. There are 10 fiddle-style tunes, some original and some traditional, and each tune is played at 3 different speeds. A very useful collection. (—S.W.)

LANGEY-CARL FISCHER, *Tutor for Mandolin*, Carl Fischer. 94 pp. Music only. This book contains numerous exercises, material on music reading, solos and duets.

LEE, RONNY, *Chord Chart for the Mandolin*, Alfred Music, 3 pp. Practical and concise.

TOTTLE, JACK, *Bluegrass Mandolin*, Oak, 1975. 160 pp. with sound sheet. Tottle's book is an excellent overall survey of bluegrass mandolin. The sound sheet is useful because everything is played at reasonable tempos for the students. The only weaknesses of the book are that it takes Tottle far too long to print any music—there is an awful lot of preliminary explanatory material—and nowhere does he adequately cover simple chord accompaniments. (—S.W.)

VALLA, RAY, *Bluegrass Mandolin Method*, Sunny Mountain Records. 1 12-inch LP. Valla performs 29 songs from his book on this record. The mandolin is on one track and guitar accompaniment on the other, so that you can play with or without the lead parts. This is a pleasant record, but dependent upon your purchase of the book for much instructional value. (—S.W.)

VALLA, RAY, *Deluxe Bluegrass Mandolin Method*, Mel Bay, 1974. 64 pp. Valla includes 30 fiddle tunes in music and tablature together with 10 scale exercises. He also has short sections on tuning, chords, and rhythms. This is not really a bluegrass mandolin method, but a book about playing fiddle tunes on the mandolin. A clear and well-organized book. (—S.W.)

WIENCROT, STEVE, *Country and Folk Style Mandolin*, self-pub., available at the Denver Folklore Center. I have seen an advance copy of this manuscript and found it to be an excellent method, especially for beginners. All material is in music and tablature, and Wiencrot covers chords, strums, runs, and bluegrass chords, and finishes up with some very difficult solos in the style of Jesse McReynolds. There is so much material in this book that it might have been better presented in two volumes, the second one for intermediate and advanced players only.

FOLK OR FOLK-BASED MUSIC FOR PIANO

AGAY, DENIS, *The Joy of Ragtime*, Yorktown Music, dist. by Oak, 1974. 80 pp. A collection of classic piano rags.

BLESH, RUDI, ed., *Classic Piano Rags*, Dover, 1973. 364 pp. An invaluable collection of 81 rags. The composers represented include Joplin, Joseph Lamb, Tom Turpin,

and others. The clarity of printing and the degree of difficulty among the rags varies greatly.

BOLCOM, WILLIAM, *Grace Ghost Rag*, Edward Marks, dist. by Belwin-Mills, 1971.

BOLCOM, WILLIAM, *Seabiscuits*, Edward Marks, dist. by Belwin-Mills, 1971. Bolcom's two books are for advanced players only.

CHARLES, RAY, *Instrumental Folio*, Progressive Music, dist. by Big 3, 1963. 13 tunes, 43 pp. These solos are not easy, but they are still a good introduction to the blues-soul-gospel-jazz amalgam that is the music of Ray Charles.

DAHL, INGOLF, *Quodlibet on American Folk Tunes*, C.F. Peters, 1957. 22 pp. Pieces for 2 pianos and 8 hands based on "Boston Fancy," "Arkansas Traveler," "Devil's Dream," "Turkey in the Straw," "California Joe," and "Deep Blue Sea."

DENNIS, MATT, *Blues Piano Styles*, Mel Bay, 1973. 40 pp.

DENNIS, MATT, *Ragtime Piano Styles*, Mel Bay, 1973. 40 pp. Dennis' two books contain 14 blues and 12 rag solos. They are excellent for the intermediate player, and the blues book includes everything from boogie to band style. All solos are Dennis' compositions.

HOEFER, GEORGE, ed., *Jelly Roll Morton's Folio: Blues Stomps, and Ragtime*, Melrose Music Corp., 1949, probably OP. 20 tunes, 49 pp. Good tunes, not for the beginner.

HOLLANDER, ARTHUR, *Indian Drum Beats for Piano*, Belwin-Mills, 1956. 32 pp. These are good rhythm studies for piano, drawn from the famous collections of Frances Densmore.

JOHNSON, JAMES P., *Piano Solos*, Clarence Williams, 1945, probably OP. Johnson was one of the greatest pianists of the Harlem ragtime school and an excellent composer.

JOPLIN, SCOTT, *Piano Music*, vol. 1, and *Vocal Music*, vol. 2, New York Public Library, dist. by Dover to book trade, by Belwin-Mills to music stores. Vol. 1 has 305 pp., 50 tunes, and 6 exercises, a discography and piano rollography. There is an excellent biography of Joplin by Rudi Blesh in the opening part of the book.

JOPLIN, SCOTT, *Piano Rags*, book 2, Hansen, 1973. 20 tunes, including 6 songs with lyrics.

Best of Scott Joplin, The, Hansen, 1972. 13 tunes, 65 pp.

Note: Since the music of Scott Joplin is in the public domain, there are dozens of other Joplin folios by various publishers.

KAIL, BOB, *How to Play Blues Piano for the Advanced Pianist*, Hansen, 1974. 33 pp. Mostly arrangements and compositions by the author, with some instructional details.

KAIL, BOB, *How to Play Ragtime Piano for the Advanced Pianist*, Hansen, 1974. 32 pp. Arrangements and compositions by the author, with three rags by Billy Taylor, and some instructional details on ragtime techniques by Kail.

KNORR, FREDERICK, and LLOYD SHAW, *Cowboy Dance Tunes*, Caxton Printers, 1949. 24 pp. This booklet includes 33 tunes with simple piano arrangements and chord symbols. It accompanies Shaw's larger book of cowboy dances.

KRISS, ERIC, *Barrelhouse and Boogie Piano*, Oak, 1974. 112 pp. An excellent collection of works by pianists, some famous, some obscure, with details about the background of the music. The book is not progressively graded, but is divided into sections according to different piano styles, such as boogie woogie, barrelhouse, etc. There is an accompanying plastic song sheet (record) which has fragments of the brilliant original performances. These would be more useful if Kriss had recorded the tunes himself, at slower tempos for the student.

KRISS, ERIC, *Six Blues Roots Pianists*, Oak, 1973. 104 pp. This is a nice book, but you need to be a reasonably good sight-reader to use it. There are some exercises to help master specialized blues techniques. Included are pieces by Jimmy Yancey, Little Brother Montgomery, and others. The solos are not particularly graded; that is, some of the harder solos appear early in the book. An excellent book for the competent classical pianist who wants to check out the blues.

LAMB, JOSEPH, *Ragtime Treasures*, Belwin-Mills. 13 rags, 64 pp. This is a nice collection by a protégé of Joplin's who lived quietly for years in Brooklyn. Printing is very clear.

Leeds Music Piano Folios. Each of these folios has 5 tunes, and they include books by Albert Ammons, Pete Johnson, Meade Lux Lewis, Sammy Price, and Pine Top Smith. As far as I know, they are all out of print.

MORATH, MAX, *Giants of Ragtime*, Edward Marks, dist. by Belwin-Mills. 13 rags, 64 pp. These are playable versions of rags by Joplin, Eubie Blake, Luckey Roberts, and others.

MORATH, MAX, ed., *Ragtime Guide*, TRO, 1972. 43 songs, 126 pp. A good book for beginners in ragtime. Many composers are included; some songs by the editor. Some of the type is too small.

POWELL, JOHN, *Five Virginian Folk Songs for Voice and Piano*, J. Fischer & Co., 1938. 37 pp. Piano arrangements and lead sheets, no chord symbols. These are piano settings by a composer. There are extensive notes on the songs and the rationale behind each arrangement.

Rag Classix, Warner Bros., 1973. 144 pp. This collection has only a handful of real rags; it's mostly Tin Pan Alley stuff.

Ragtime Piano, Belwin-Mills, 1963. 16 rags. The tunes here vary greatly in difficulty. The printing is good. Chord symbols are included.

RAPHLING, SAM, *American Album*, Mercury Music, dist. by Theodore Presser. 8 pieces, 30 pp. Original piano pieces on American folk themes. They are interesting and difficult.

SCHAUM, JOHN, *The Ragtime Book*, Belwin-Mills. 13 tunes. Works by Johnson, Joplin, Botsford, and others.

SIEGMEISTER, ELIE, *Folksongs*, books 1–5, Theodore Presser. Book 1, 1954, 40 songs, 30 pp. Book 2, 1955, 27 songs, 30 pp. Book 3, 1958, 15 songs, 32 pp. This is an excellent piano method, developed through the use of American folk songs. I was unable to obtain books 4 and 5.

SMALL, ALLAN, *Blues and "How": A Method of Teaching Blues for the Pianist*, Claire Music, dist. by Alfred Music, 1968. 64 pp. A well-graded blues piano book. All tunes included are originals. There are 22 solos. The book includes little material on chord structure.

SMALL, ALLAN, *Ragtime Piano Solos*, Easy Piano, dist. by Alfred Music, 1974. 48 pp. Easy and playable versions of Scott Joplin piano solos. One of the few ragtime books that really is easy to play.

STAIRS, LOUISE, *An American Folk Tune*, Theodore Presser, 1962. A pleasant tune, written for the black keys.

TOWNSEND, DOUGLAS, *Four Fantasies on American Folk Songs. Piano Duets for 4 Hands.* C. F. Peters, 1960. 48 pp. These are duets based on the 5 folk tunes "Follow the Drinkin' Gourd," "The New River Train," "Johnny Has Gone for a Soldier," "Old Joe Clark," and "Sourwood Mountain."

WATSON, DICK, *Let's Play Player Piano Style*, Warner Bros., 1966. 12 songs, 32 pp. A nice book for intermediate or advanced players; includes Limehouse Blues, Charleston, and others.

WESTERVELT, MARIE, *The American Traveler*, Oliver Ditson, dist. by Theodore Presser, 1952. The folk song arranged for piano.

Two series of six tapes or cassettes have been recorded by David Cohen for Happy Traum's Homespun Tapes. One series deals with blues and rock piano, the other with ragtime piano.

RECORDER

There is a huge amount of literature available for the recorder, in the form of both method books and books of solos. There is also quite a number of recorder duets, trios, and quartets available. Here's a very brief listing, mostly without comment, of some recorder music books. We have also indicated where more complete listings of recorder music can be obtained. Although the recorder is not primarily a folk instrument, it is being used in the Orff system of teaching children music through the use of simple folk tunes. It is also quite suitable for playing duets with the guitar.

BERGMANN, WALTER, *Casey Jones,* Hargail, 1971. 23 pp. For voices, alto and soprano recorders, and Orff school orchestra. A work based on the famous folk song.

BERGMANN, WALTER, *Sixteen Easy Folksongs for Soprano Recorder,* Hargail, 1973. 15 pp. Includes easy piano accompaniments.

BERGMANN, WALTER, *Two American Suites: American Indian Suite and Peruvian Suite for Soprano Recorder and Piano,* Hargail, 1973. 15 pp.

GIESBERT, FRANZ J., *Method for the Treble Recorder,* Schott, dist. by Belwin-Mills. 79 pp. A method book with solos, duets, trios, and exercises for the alto recorder.

MANABE, RICHIIRO, *Folk Tunes of Japan for Recorder and guitar.* Academica Music, dist. by Hargail, 1967.

NITKA, ARTHUR, *Traditional Folk Songs,* Anfor no. 15 and no. 16. Solos, duets, and trios with chord symbols.

NITKA, ARTHUR, and JOHANNA KULBACH, *The Recorder Guide,* Oak, 1965. 128 pp. With record. The authors teach soprano and alto recorder by using the folk melodies of numerous cultures. The record is intelligently organized, with separate instruction for soprano and alto recorder, followed by duets for alto and soprano.

TOBEY, CLIFF, *A Guide to Playing the Recorder,* AMSCO, dist. by Oak, 1970. 71 pp. A simple and well-constructed method for the beginning player. It is particularly designed for those who have not previously read any music.

TRAPP FAMILY SINGERS, THE, *Enjoy Your Recorder,* Magnamusic. Book M-1 for C-Soprano or C-Tenor, Book M-2 for F-Alto, F-Soprano, or F-Bass. Both books have 48 pp. These are method books, starting from the very beginning.

WEBER, LAURA, *All the Pretty Little Horses,* Hargail, 1960. 24 pp. For soprano recorder with chord symbols for accompanying instruments.

WEBER, LAURA, *I Know Where I'm Going,* Hargail, 1960. 24 pp. For soprano recorder with chord symbols for accompanying instruments.

Both Hargail and Schott (the latter distributed by Belwin-Mills) publish considerable amounts of recorder music and have catalogues available. Many other publishers print some recorder music, and Music Minus One offers instructional records for recorder.

MISCELLANEOUS INSTRUMENTS

The following list includes such items as material for concertina, choral music, and collections of melodies playable on various instruments.

BUTLER, FRANK, *The Concertina: A Handbook and Tutor for Beginners on the "English" Concertina,* Free Reed Press.

Concertina Workshop, Topic Records, England. Book and record set available together or separately, from Free Reed Press.

DARR, A., *Method for Zither,* Carl Fischer, 1950. 50 pp. English and German text. Includes tuning, exercises, scales, and solos. Music only.

EDWARDS, ALFRED, *Wheatstone's Instruction for the English Concertina,* C. Wheatstone, London, 1960. 52 pp. Edwards is the acknowledged master of folk-style concertina, and has played on many recordings with Ewan MacColl and Peggy Seeger.

GROSS, arranger, *American Folk Suite,* Edward Marks, dist. by Belwin-Mills. 3 songs for chorus, guitar, and banjo.

HORTON, LEWIS, *An Appalachian Nativity,* H. W. Gray, dist. by Belwin-Mills, 1955. 48 pp. For solo and mixed chorus with piano accompaniment. This nativity is based on shape note hymns. It is enjoyable and not too difficult.

HORTON, LEWIS, and BUELL KAZEE, *The White Pilgrim,* H. W. Gray, dist. by Belwin-Mills, 1940. 43 pp. For mixed voices, soli, and piano accompaniment. String parts are also available. Buell Kazee is a famous banjo player who recorded in the 1920's and has a relatively recent LP out on Folkways. *The White Pilgrim* is based on the true story of an itinerant preacher and uses traditional religious songs. This work should be performed in schools and churches.

JOPLIN, SCOTT, *The Red Book,* ed. by Gunther Schuller, Belwin-Mills. There are arrangements of 8 tunes, and parts for flute, A and B flat clarinets, string quartet, and rhythm section.

KARPELES, MAUD, and KENWORTHY SCHOFIELD, *100 English Folk Dance Airs for Melodic Instruments,* English Folk Dance and Song Society, dist. by Hargail, 1951. 61 pp.

O'NEILL, JAMES, *O'Neill's Music of Ireland.* For review *see* The Fiddle section, page 179.

Ragtime String Quartet, MMO 48. 12-inch LP including booklet with music. These string quartets are available as an instructional record with one part missing, or as a listening record, with all parts included. There are 10 tunes by Scott Joplin, Luckey Roberts, Tom Turpin, and others.

RIGHTMIRE, RICHARD, *Folk Music for the Accordion,* Belwin-Mills, 1960. 29 songs, 28 pp. Music, chord symbols, and fingering are included. Playable on all accordions.

Robbins Collection of 200 Jigs, Reels and Country Dances, Robbins Music, dist. by Big 3, 1961. 64 pp. For piano, violin, flute, mandolin, and other instruments. No chord symbols. A useful collection, for the most part playable on five-string banjo because many tunes are in the keys of C and G.

SEEGER, PETE, *The Steel Drums,* Oak, 1964. 40 pp. Seeger includes many details on construction, and some arrangements for steel drum orchestra, including bass and additional rhythm.

SHARP, DON, *Mel Bay's Pedal Steel Guitar,* Mel Bay, 1972. 47 pp. No music, includes number system and chords. Sharp includes a lot of original material for a book with no music notation.

Wolf's Concertina Method, M. M. Cole.

III
PLAYING

The most wonderful gift our language makes to musicians is to let us use the word "play" to describe what we do. It's too bad that social, economic, and professional pressure so often causes us to lose sight of the original meaning of the word; our music would be better if we could remember it more often. For me, the most vital aspects of folk music come from its nonprofessional social context—a context in which the musician is granted the freedom to be truly playful. Within this context, any musician's qualities of perfectionism, integrity, and originality are free to develop under the compulsion of no pressures except those of his own conscience and personality. (—L.S.)

AN ELEMENTARY GUIDE TO THE CARE OF THE FIVE-STRING BANJO

by David Ferretta

This article is meant only as a general reference, not as a complete history. Finer points of description, detail, and history of these instruments may be obtained by writing the author in care of Ferretta Music in Denver. I shall deal primarily with banjos used for frailing and related styles, although some of the details for setting up bluegrass banjos may be similar.

Since the primary reason for choosing a particular banjo is its quality of sound, let us consider the different types of rims made in years past:

The first type of rim is that found on most very old banjos (1890–1920). It is a very thin wooden rim covered by a thin sheet of metal which is curled at the top, over which the head is fitted. These banjos have a very plunky or mellow sound, and should only have a skin head, since a more modern plastic head tends to make them sound thin or tinny. Some of the more common brands of this type are S. S. Stewart, Fairbanks & Cole, and Schall; many others are made for mail-order houses.

The second type of rim is all wood and has a small brass ring between the rim and the head or sometimes no ring at all. These rims are thicker and somewhat louder than the first style, and generally sound better with plastic heads, since skin heads mute them. Some of the most common simple wood-rimmed banjos include the Vega Little Wonder, Bacon Peerless, Weymann Keystone, Regal, and among present-day banjos, the Ome X, Gibson RB-170, and the Vega Wonder model.

The third (my own choice) type of rim is similar to the second in that the entire rim is wood, but it is fitted with any one of several styles of tone rings. These devices add a sound of their own to that of the vibrating head and act as resonating chambers. All of these tend to make the sound crisper, but the tone varies with each. My favorite is the old Vega Tu-ba-phone, which is no longer made in the true old style. This and the Vega Whyte Laydie both use a bracket band to which all the brackets, or hooks, are attached. It is slipped onto the rim from the bottom, so that no holes are drilled through the wood. This solid rim design, along with the tone ring, which is a square chamber with holes in it, gives the Tu-ba-phone a unique clear sound, along with substantial volume.

Some other banjos with fairly elaborate tone rings are the Dobson, which is the original tone ring banjo, the Gibson trap door, called that because of a hinged resonator back, Orpheum, Epiphone, some of the fancier model Washburns and Bacons, and a few modern open-back banjos, such as the Ome XX and XXX and, most recently, the Alvarez Silver Princess. The Silver Princess is an almost exact reproduction of the old Vega Tu-ba-phone rim, and it is well done.

Necks vary in design and ornamentation, but the most important feature is playability, which is usually a function of the straightness of the neck. Necks needn't be perfectly straight; they tend to play much cleaner (that is, with fewer buzzes) when there is a slight upward bow in them. Usually, even necks with substantial warps can be straightened to a reasonable degree with a heating process that bends the neck to its original profile. This should only be done by a competent repairman, however, since it's very easy to ruin a neck doing this.

The neck should also be in correct alignment with the rim. With a plastic head, the action is higher than with a skin head because the bridge does not sink into the head; so when you change from a skin to a plastic head you should push the neck back with a shim of wood or leather between the finger board and the rim. In extreme cases, let a repairman do the work, as this operation puts a lot of pressure on the rim stick, which extends through the body. Worn frets should be replaced.

Old tuners often need to be replaced, since they are usually friction pegs and frequently slip, or at best, such tuners need to be adjusted often. Friction pegs never tune as accurately or as easily as geared ones.

SETTING UP THE BANJO

The head should be fairly tight, but not so tight that the banjo sounds tinny. This is only a problem with plastic heads, since skin heads break before they are tight enough to sound tinny. To safeguard against breaking the head, tighten it slowly and test it with the thumb. It should sink only slightly under a moderate amount of pressure. Tighten the head in a circular motion, from one bracket to the next, until an even tension all around the head is obtained. After the banjo is strung, the tone can be changed by loosening (for a mellower tone) or tightening (for a brighter tone) the head. This adjustment will also affect the action, so you may need to compensate with a different size bridge, or shim.

Set the bridge using the twelfth fret as a reference point, but do *not* set it exactly twice the distance from the nut as the twelfth fret. Play the first string open (unfretted) and then fret the string at the twelfth fret. These two notes should sound exactly one octave apart. If the octave is flat, the bridge should be moved forward toward the neck. If the octave is sharp, the bridge should be moved back toward the tail piece. This can also be done using the harmonic at the twelfth fret instead of the open string. To get the harmonic, simply touch the string above the twelfth fret and pick it, producing a chimelike sound, then check this with the note fretted at the twelfth fret. Repeat this with the fourth string, and the banjo will play as much in tune as possible. You will notice that the bridge is slanted. Although it may look strange, it is correct. The third string never seems to play exactly in tune all the way up the neck. This is the nature of the instrument.

Changing the strings often is important if you are to keep the banjo playing in tune. After you have played out of tune too long, playing in tune sounds bad.

ACCESSORIES

Here's a list of optional accessories for the banjo. Some of them are useful, but none is essential:

Fifth-string capo: cumbersome and unattractive, but helpful if you capo the banjo past the second fret.

Tension tail piece: puts pressure on the strings and gives a brighter sound.

Geared fifth-string peg: probably the most helpful invention in the past two hundred years. Herman Kroll invented it, and he still makes the best one.

Mute: nice for damping the sound, so as not to disturb others, but as Pete Seeger says, a diaper in the back of the rim does just as well.

Armrest: keeps a skin head sweat-resistant, and also positions the arm higher for a better attack on the strings.

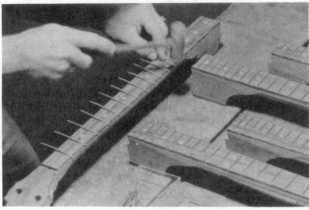

BANJO MANUFACTURERS AND BUILDERS

Currently there are virtually no banjos available that are both playable and fall into a moderate (under $300) price range. The following companies currently make banjos (as best as I am able to tell).

(— D.W.)

Allen, 392l Milton, Houston, TX 77005

Alvarez, St. Louis Music Supply, 1400 Ferguson Ave., St. Louis, MO 63133

Deering, 7936 D Lester Ave., Lemon Grove, CA 92045 (many models).

Epiphone (Gibson's less expensive line).

E. Lowell Jacobs, 951 Devon Dr., Newark, DE 19711

First Quality Banjos, 5303 Galaxie Dr., Louisville, KY 40238

Gibson, 641 Massman Dr., Nashville, TN 37219. Medium to high priced models.

Goose Acre Banjos, 2175 Cornell, Cleveland, OH 44106

Bill Graham, Madison Mills, VA 22963

Hondo International Music Co., 1316 E. Lancaster, Ft. Worth, TX 76113

The New Boston Co., Box 148, Avon, MA 02322

Ome Banjos, 5680 Valmont, Boulder, CO 80301. Does a lot of custom work.

Bart Reiter, 5910 E. Sleepy Hollow Rd., E. Lansing, MI 48823

Stelling Banjo Works, Rt 2, Box 302, Afton, VA 22920

Washburn, 230 Lexington Dr., Buffalo Grove, IL 60089

Wildwood Banjos, Actata, CA

BANJO PARTS AND ACCESSORIES

BD Products, Box 412B, Murphys, CA 96247. Mutes, parts, pick holders.

Beacon Banjo Co., RFD #3, Box 254, Putney, VT 05346. Keith tuners.

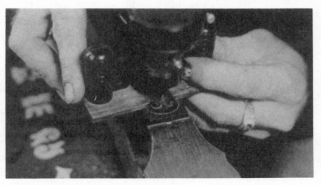

Ome Banjo under Construction

Bucks County Folk Shop, 40 Sand Rd., New Britain, PA 18901. Various parts.

Exotic Wood, 444 Erial Williamstown Rd., Sicklerville, NJ 08081. Inlay.

Geiger Banjo Bridges, 190 Berwick Dr. NE, Atlanta, GA 30328. Bridges.

Paul Gudelsky, 341 W. Broadway, Ste. 329, San Diego, CA 92101. Wood.

Intermountain Guitar and Banjo, 712 E. 100 St., Salt Lake City, UT 84117. Various parts, necks.

Kalamazoo Music Laboratory, 2618 Portage St., Kalamazoo, MI 49001. Stainless steel finger picks.

Stewart McDonald, Box 900 C., Athens, OH 45701. Large catalog of parts.

Minalco Products, Box 36, Free Union, VA 22940. Parts.

Northern Musical Instrument Supplies, Rt. 2, Box 158, Oakcrest Dr., Bunduel, WI 54107. Wood, tone rings, flanges.

Pearl Works, Rt. 3, Box 122, Mechanicsville, MD 20659. Inlay.

Stockwell Moon Bridge, Box 09141-N, Columbus, OH 43209. Bridges.

REMEMBERING GARY DAVIS

by Dick Weissman

Winter, 1954. I was a nineteen-year-old college junior. Philadelphia-born, living in New York City, not knowing too much about myself or the world. Spending most of my time playing the five-string banjo. Bob Harris, who ran Stinson Records out of a hole-in-the-wall store on Union Square said I ought to go by Tiny Ledbetter's house at 414 E. 10th Street on Tuesday night, and see Gary Davis.

I did. I could hear the guitar music floating down the stairwell as I climbed up the stairs. Tiny Ledbetter was Leadbelly's niece. She loved to dance, smiled a lot, played a little guitar, and was Gary's host. For six weeks I went to the place, and each time was a little different from the last, sometimes the same people, sometimes others. One night Woody Guthrie was there with his last wife, I think her name was Arnica. I remember his singing "which way does

that blood red river run, it runs straight from my house, straight to the rising sun." A little man, must have weighed ninety-five pounds, drinking beer, soon after to go into the hospital for the last time.

John Gibbons was usually there. He was probably the first of the young white pickers who wanted to learn Gary's tricks, and he kind of apprenticed himself to Gary. Some years later came Stefan Grossman, Barry Kornfeld, and others. John, Tiny, and I would sit still for hours listening to Gary, drinking wine and beer, and sometimes playing a little bit ourselves. I'd never heard any of the songs before, except "Oh What a Beautiful City." Most of them were spirituals or gospel tunes, and once in a while John would pursuade Gary to play a ragtime guitar piece or the "Ice-pick Blues."

There's no way I can describe the music. At the time, I'd been playing banjo for about two years, and I knew only a little guitar. Playing with Gary was like a college course in ear training. He made lots of chords by draping his left thumb halfway over the finger board, so I had to listen rather than look at what he was doing. One night we played a tune called "Oh Lord Search My Heart," and it was one of the finest musical moments of my life. (Others

"When I Die I'll Live Again":
Rev. Gary Davis

were: listening to Stu Jamieson playing his banjo near Albuquerque, watching Mississippi John Hurt at the Newport Folk Festival, seeing Wes Montgomery sit in with John Coltrane after a Monterey Jazz Festival, and hearing Jean-Pierre Rampal and Robert Veyron-Lecroix play flute and harpsichord duets in Town Hall.) That night at Tiny's I was playing too. Looking back on it, I know I wasn't a good player. I was playing out of Gary's head and heart rather than my own.

A few years later I was back in New York again, and I saw Gary a few times. Sometimes at blues parties at my apartment on W. 106th Street, which were attended by Brownie McGhee and Sonny Terry, Bruce Langhorne, Erik Darling, and lots of people I'd never met, as well as John Lee Hooker, who tried to plug his AC amplifier into the DC current of my wall. Tiny moved to Brooklyn about this time, and I never did get to play with Gary again.

Shortly after this, Gary began to achieve a modest degree of financial success. Peter, Paul, and Mary recorded a couple of his songs; his reputation spread nationally and into Europe because of records he made and the work of some of his students, like Stefan Grossman and Barry Kornfeld. Gary did some touring, all over the United States and in Europe. Robbins Music published a book of his songs, and Gary no longer had to walk the streets of New York City with his guitar and a tin cup.

One day in 1971 I was sitting in my house in Roosevelt, New Jersey, and I wrote a song about Gary Davis, most of it in about ten minutes. It was all sketched out in my mind in an instant, as though somebody else had taken the trouble to organize it for me. It took me about a week to write the last verse to tie the whole thing together. A year later Gary died, and my only regret is that I never got to play it for him. Here it is.

BLIND GARY

Words and Music by
RICHARD WEISSMAN

Cathy Fink: Mastery of many traditions.

ABOUT GUITARS, PICKS, AND STRINGS

by Larry Sandberg

KINDS OF GUITARS

Few musical instruments are available in as many different styles and models as the guitar. In fact, it's virtually meaningless to talk about "the guitar" as a single instrument, for although there's a certain amount of borrowing and crossing over from one style to another, each kind of guitar is designed to produce a specific kind of music, and each kind of guitar is disposed to accept specific touches and techniques of playing.

Classical and flamenco techniques rely on the specific virtues of nylon-strung guitars. The classical and flamenco nylon-strung guitars are customarily built following canonical models of size and shape established by Antonio Torres, a great Spanish guitar maker of the nineteenth century. Classical players prefer the tone that rosewood back and sides generate, while flamenco players prefer cypress.

Both the classical and flamenco models are constructed with a rather wide finger board that sits well under the touch and hand positions of those styles. The techniques and hand positions of virtuoso American folk guitar styles don't work as well on nylon-strung instruments. Beginners and nonvirtuoso or nontraditional players might do well with such instruments, and a few stylists, such as Nashville guitarists Chet Atkins and Jerry Reed, do favor them for bringing out certain aspects of style. In general, however, the instrument is unsatisfactory for the typical sounds and techniques of blues, folk, and country music.

In addition to the standard classical and flamenco models, many nondescript nylon-strung models are also available. Some have a finger board width more suitable for folk

playing, but nylon-strung guitars still can't produce idiomatic sounds. Moreover, nonstandard nylon-strung models tend to be bad guitars.

The typical folk guitar is known as the round-hole acoustic flat-top guitar. The internal bracing is heavier and its design is different from the classical model in order to withstand the greater pressure of steel strings. There's no standard model. Different sizes and shapes are available, and each tends to be best suited to a particular style or manner of playing. I'll discuss these qualities later on.

The word "acoustic" is used to describe nonelectric guitars. Of course, it's easy enough to mount an electric pickup on an acoustic guitar, but it is still basically an acoustic guitar. A few guitarists—jazzman Gabor Szabo is a notable example—like that sound and use it effectively, but the general opinion is that this method does not produce the most desirable electric sound.

The cellolike arch-top f-hole model is another kind of steel-strung acoustic guitar. There are two f-shaped sound holes in an arched body top, as opposed to a single round hole in the flat body top of folk guitars. Jazz players prefer the tonal and dynamic qualities of the f-hole guitar; folk players, with a few notable and a few special-purpose exceptions, don't. Maybelle Carter, for example, plays an f-hole guitar.

The first electric guitars were simply f-hole guitars with pickups added. (F-hole guitars respond much better to electrification than round-hole guitars do.) These are the electric guitars that are favored by jazz players who seek a clear, wide, mellow tone. Charlie Christian, Kenny Burrell, Wes Montgomery, and George Benson are among the guitarists who use or have used these instruments.

Once you electrify a guitar, it no longer has to possess the qualities of good acoustic sound, though you may prefer it to. In fact, you can get a more characteristically "electric" sound from an instrument that possesses little or no acoustic sound at all. In order to minimize acoustic sound, highly electric-sounding guitars are constructed out of solid pieces of wood and are therefore called solid-body guitars. A slightly different tone and dynamic response can be obtained if the guitar body is basically solid, but with a small hollow air space; such an instrument is called variously a semi-acoustic, semi-solid-body, or semi-hollow-body guitar. The solid- and semi-solid-body guitars produce the characteristic sounds of modern electric music.

The resophonic guitar is yet another kind of creature, an odd one indeed. In a resophonic guitar, the tone is produced by the interaction of string vibration not with wood, but with an aluminum resonator cone set inside the body of the guitar. The Dobro and National companies first developed resonator guitars during the twenties, and these guitars are referred to generically as dobros no matter what the particular brand, just as cellophane tape is casually called Scotch tape. Dobros and their imitations have wood bodies that generate a tone favored by bluegrass players, but the old-time bluesmen liked the sound of metal-bodied Nationals better. The patented Dobro cone design produces an inimitable tone. The original purpose of the resonator was to produce nonelectric amplification, but tone differences also result. Resonator guitars produce a very thick tone, musty or twangy depending on the model. Guitarists often play resonator guitars in the usual manner in order to achieve special tonal effects. But for those players who go after the blues and bluegrass sounds involving the use of a glass or metal slide (or bottleneck) to fret the strings, resonator guitars are especially desirable.

The term "Spanish guitar" has caused no end of confusion. It actually has nothing to do with Spain or Spanish music. It refers merely to any guitar—usually a steel-strung one—that's held vertically in the lap, in the usual manner. The opposite of "Spanish guitar" is "Hawaiian guitar," which refers to an instrument with raised strings, held flat across the lap and fretted with a steel bar. You can play any old guitar this way. All you need is an extender nut to raise the height of the strings so you won't press them down to the frets with the steel bar, and the steel bar itself acts as a movable fret. Beat-up old guitars with warped necks are especially good to learn on; if the neck is badly enough out of line, you won't even need the extender nut. But the most favored sound in this style is to be gotten from a Dobro. Solid-body electric Hawaiian guitars are called lap-steel guitars; they often have seven or eight strings.

The term "steel guitar" can refer to any guitar played Hawaiian-style with a steel bar, but most often it's used as a shortened term for pedal steel guitar. The pedal steel is an electrified Hawaiian guitar mounted on a stand and equipped with a combination of pedals and knee levers which alter the pitch of the various strings, eight to twelve in number. The pedal steel is an extraordinarily difficult instrument to play creatively and well, and few instruments have been so misunderstood in this respect.

The twelve-string guitar, acoustic or electric, is simply an ordinary guitar with six *pairs* of strings instead of six individual ones, so you play it as you would a six-string. The four lowest sets of strings are tuned in octaves, creating a unique and very full sound. Except for novelty, its virtues as a solo instrument are limited, but it produces some powerful rhythm and accompaniment sounds.

Finally, let me mention the so-called high-string guitar. This is simply an ordinary guitar on which any or all of the lower strings are strung an octave higher than usual. The crisp, ringing quality of the high-strung rhythm guitar is a basic ingredient in the Nashville sound.

QUALITIES OF GUITARS

I'll be talking mainly about folk guitars—steel-strung, acoustic, round-hole, flat-top guitars—from now on, but much of what I say is relevant to other kinds of guitars, too. My generalities may not apply to given individual instruments, if they are very good and great guitars. Such guitars have unique and personal characteristics, and like great personalities, they may also have striking defects of character which must be ignored or forgiven.

In judging the sound of a guitar, do not be misled by volume. It's relatively easy to build a guitar that's loud but has other defects which only an experienced ear will notice: harsh tone or improper balance.

Balance refers to the relative tone, volume, clarity, and sustaining power of the different strings. Inexpensive guitars that boom usually produce most of the volume in the bass, at the expense of the high notes. They're fine for strumming and bluegrass backup, but try a jazz or finger-picking solo, and you'll find yourself sounding muddy and obscure. Volume is important in ensemble playing, but good balance and pleasing tone will give you more satisfaction in your hours alone with the instrument.

Volume is not to be confused with responsiveness, or the ease with which a guitar is said to "speak." What this means, basically, is that you should not have to pound the strings into oblivion in order to produce a tone that sounds satisfying and full. Note, *full*, not necessarily loud. With an unresponsive instrument, you won't be able to learn how to achieve delicacy, economy of right hand movement, or control of dynamics. Of course, there are some styles, like bluegrass, where the guitar is customarily played quite hard—but then again, bluegrass dynamics are achieved mainly through ensemble interplay and the use of the vocal ensembles, not by individual instruments.

The size of the guitar is another factor in how it sounds. Remember to consider the size of the instrument in relation to your own size, posture, and comfort requirements. Very large-bodied guitars, of the so-called dreadnought or jumbo shapes, have become the standard professional workhorses because of their great carrying power in ensembles and in acoustically poor performing situations. This does not mean that they are the best guitars in all circumstances. As a rule (with many exceptions), they're built to be played relatively hard and to produce a bass-heavy balance. Flat-picked or strummed, especially in ensembles, they are usually superior. In other styles—the solo finger-picking style, for example—they rarely achieve the clarity of a good smaller guitar. Bigger means different, not better.

You must also consider the shape, width, and length of the guitar neck. The length, or scale, of the neck is not uniform among folk guitars. The scale can be any length as long as the frets and bridge are placed in their mathematically correct positions, and typical guitars of different models may vary a noticeable ¾ inch in scale length. The width and depth of the guitar neck, with scale, should be considered in relation to the size and musculature of your hands and to the particular requirements of the style you wish to cultivate. As a general rule, narrow necks (with the strings closer together) lend themselves to being flat picked, and wider necks (with the strings farther apart) lend themselves to being finger picked.

The action of an instrument is another important factor. Action refers to the relative ease with which a string can be depressed by the left hand. It is a function of both the amount of string tension and the distance that the string must travel before it presses against the fret. Even though heavier or lighter strings can be used, some guitars just seem to feel as if they create more string tension than others: the scale, the presence or absence of a tail piece, the height of the frets, and (I think) just plain magic are 'among the factors. But the main factor is the height of the strings from the finger board. Strings may be too high or too low for any of the following reasons:

1. The neck of the guitar may be warped. A good repairman can perform amazing surgery on a warped neck, but it ain't cheap.

2. The guitar may not be well set up. Being "well set up" refers to a number of factors. One is the angle at which the guitar neck joins the body; problems here are expensive, too. Another is the height of the strings as determined by the height of their resting places: the nut (at the peg-head end) and the saddle (set into the bridge). These problems are quite easy to cure.

Overly high action makes a guitar difficult or impossible to play. Overly low action, on the other hand, causes poor tone, fret noise, and string buzzing. Many seasoned players like their action a bit stiff; the guitar can assert itself more that way.

WOODS

The kind and quality of the wood is important. Cheaper instruments (and some surprisingly expensive ones, too) may be made of laminated wood. This is a fancy way of saying "plywood," but the wood is better than the lumberyard stuff and is not easily detectable. Some guitar manufacturers have a habit, which should be outlawed, of saying "spruce" or "mahogany" when they should be saying *"laminated* spruce" (or "mahogany"). But many cheap laminated instruments provide perfectly adequate balance, tone quality, and responsiveness up to a certain level, and they should by no means be eliminated from consideration. Some guitar makers have even experimented with high-quality lamination in serious instruments—though such experiments are often looked on with disfavor.

Almost all guitars of quality have solid spruce tops. Occasionally, mahogany is used, with satisfactory results, in some cheaper guitars. As spruce becomes increasingly rare, other woods are being used experimentally. Canadian and Sitka spruce are about standard; German spruce, now rare, is considered superior.

Various hardwoods, especially maple, are used for the back and sides of medium-range instruments, but mahogany is standard. Rosewood, considered to provide maximum projection, sustaining power, and tonal brilliance, is traditionally used for the back and sides of the instruments of highest quality. Brazilian rosewood, increasingly rare, is regarded as superior to Indian. Of course, design and individual craftsmanship are variable factors that can override the question of wood. I've played many mahogany guitars with excellent balance and sweet tone, and many rosewood guitars with excessive boom and harsh tone. But the best mahogany guitars don't equal the best rosewood guitars.

Guitar necks are best made of Honduras mahogany, which seems to be least likely to warp. Some instruments use maple, another stable wood. And then there are devices that can be used to keep a neck stable: cross-grained laminations or a built-in steel rod.

The best-made guitar of the finest woods will be superior, but the factors are so complex that an impressionistic judgment may be just as trustworthy as a careful analysis of the woods. I haven't even gone into subtleties, such as wood grain, finish, and so on, but guitar makers nowadays are very busily advertising what woods they use, so I've furnished this guide even though I realize a little knowledge can be dangerous.

YOUR FIRST GUITAR

I've been teaching guitar on and off for about a dozen years now, and I can tell you from hard experience that a troublesome situation can arise when a beginner makes a great economic commitment to an inappropriate instrument. Please consider the following points:

1. Under no circumstances should you spend a lot of money.

2. Seek the advice of the most experienced player you can find, but *only* on these questions: Is the guitar you have in mind easy to play? And is it free of gross defects such as buzzing or other strange noises? It may be prudent to accept a small amount of buzzing. Don't expect the instrument to sound great; you haven't earned the right to a great-sounding one yet, anyway. It should sound, well, adequate.

3. If possible, *rent* or borrow a playable guitar. Then you'll have some experience under your belt when it comes time to make a purchase decision. Remember, though, that most rental guitars are in bad condition.

4. Think of your first guitar as a temporary instrument you will outgrow. Look for something you will able to sell after a while at minimal loss.

5. To avoid some common dumb mistakes: Do *not* feel you must play the same model guitar your favorite player uses. Do *not* set your heart so blindly on a particular model that you must have one, even though the individual instrument in question may be a poor one of its type. And do *not* assume that a more expensive instrument is necessarily better. You may be in for a bad shock when you learn more. Judge each instrument individually; as with people, you'll then be able to enter into a more satisfying relationship.

PICKS

With picks, it's every man for himself. I can only tell you about my own tastes and experiences, and those of my friends.

Finger picks and thumb picks, metal or plastic, are available in a large variety of shapes and sizes. You'll just have to mess around till you find what you like. I will put in a word, though, for the Jim Dunlop Company, which makes metal picks in a variety of thicknesses and with flanges that are a little more comfortable than those of other companies. Dunlop picks are nationally merchandised and should be widely available.

I like to use thumb and finger picks when I play dobro, which is an instrument that requires a pretty hard touch. Even then, I leave them off when I'm fooling around casually or playing electric steel (dobro) guitar. I like to use a thumb pick and bare fingers on a twelve-string guitar; I find that I need the pick to articulate the bass strings. I don't care for picks on a six-string guitar at all. They can be used effectively for some kinds of rhythm playing, but I don't mind saying, bluntly and categorically, that I have never met a finger-style guitar player who achieved a respectable control of right-hand touch, clarity, and dynamics using anything but bare fingers. I know that this excludes some very well known players, but I'll stick by it.

The size, shape, and thickness of the best flat pick for you will also be a matter of experiment. Here are a few typical shapes reduced from actual size:

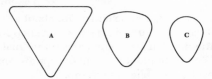

Beginners love shape A. It's big, easy to grab, and you don't have to worry so much about losing it from your grip. Most experienced players hate it; they find it cumbersome and clumsy. On the other hand, one of the best flat pickers I ever met uses one, which just goes to show something.

Size B is the most commonly used. I like to use it on rhythm electric and on acoustic guitar in all styles. Sometimes for chuck-chuck rhythm, I'll turn it around and use the rounded edge.

Size C is especially favored by electric guitarists with a soft touch. I use it in that style. Its main virtue is that you don't have to use more than the first joint of the index finger to hold it against your thumb. That way you can finesse the pick very gracefully, using the movement of just the thumb and index-finger first joints, by themselves or in conjunction with other finger, wrist, and arm movements. A few very sensitive guitarists I know buy these picks and then cut them down even smaller. Larger picks tend to overlap the first joint, making localized control impossible and requiring wrist and/or forearm movement exclusively.

It's even harder to give advice about the thickness of the pick, since you have to base your decision in part on what gauge strings you use and in part on the tone and touch of your individual instrument.

Beginners often feel most comfortable with very thin picks. You can grab a thin pick firmly, and it'll give easily when you drag it across the strings, producing a bright tone and a comforting rhythmic slapping sound. The problem comes later on, when you've gotten sick of the same tone, the same slapping sound, and just about the same dynamic level all the time, no matter how much you try to alter your touch. It makes some sense to use a thin pick if you favor extremely light strings that give as much as the pick does. Otherwise it's time to get used to a medium or hard pick, and reserve the thin one just for times when you want that special-effects slapping tone.

The medium pick asks more of you. It won't give as you move it across the strings, so you'll have to learn to relax your grip, distinguishing between loud hard tones with the pick held tightly, and soft tones and brushes with the pick held loosely. It might take you a year to become good at this, and you can expect to drop your pick inside the guitar more than once during the early stages.

Many players alternate between a medium and hard pick, depending on what guitar or style they're playing, what mood they're in, or perhaps what they had for breakfast. In general, guitarists like to use a hard pick for playing either extremely loud or extremely soft. For very loud

playing, if you care for it, grasp the pick firmly and use plenty of forearm. For soft playing, hold the pick loose and relaxed, and use the fingers or delicate wrist movements with your wrist arched out. Oddly enough, I've found that once I learned how to control the tightness and looseness of my grip, I found myself liking a softer pick for harder playing, a harder pick for softer playing.

STRINGS

There are three main categories of strings: nylon, compound, and steel.

Nylon strings sound best on guitars that were built for them. They are not strong enough to make any but the most delicately built folk guitars respond effectively. Some manufacturers use slightly different materials and processes than others; you'll have to experiment to see what brand sounds best. My experience has been that the most expensive brands are not necessarily the best. Some brands are heavier in gauge and tension than others, and some manufacturers offer strings of different gauges. Inexpensive nylon-strung guitars tend to be overbalanced in the bass; this can be partially remedied by using heavy-gauge strings in the treble, lighter-gauge strings in the bass.

The term "gut-strings" is often used as a synonym for nylon strings, which have replaced them. I haven't heard of a set of real gut strings in years. Fifteen years ago I bought a set, perhaps the last in the world. One broke immediately, and the other five sounded terrible.

Compound strings are also called silk-and-steel strings. The first and second (unwound) strings are stainless steel, as in a set of regular steel strings. The wound strings consist of a thin metal winding around a core of nylon (formerly silk) thread. Compound strings are effective on extremely delicate steel-strung guitars, but dangerously strong for nylon-strung guitars; they might pull one apart. They don't sound very good on guitars meant to be driven by heavier strings, but it makes sense for beginners to use them because they're much easier to play.

The term "steel strings" is used casually to describe a class of strings actually composed of many different metals. In most cases, the unwound first and second strings are actually stainless steel. The wound strings are more often of other metals, usually wound around a thin steel core. Bronze windings are typical on acoustic guitar strings, while nickel–steel alloys are favored on electric guitar strings for their responsiveness to the pickups. Then there is a category of Monel alloy strings, less bright-sounding than bronze, but longer-lasting.

Steel strings are available in a number of gauges. The extremely light rock-and-roll gauge strings are usually used on just electric guitars. They're so light that few acoustic guitars will respond effectively to them, though occasionally they are used on responsive acoustic guitars for special effects. Their main virtue is that they bend easily, permitting slurs and microtones. Their virtue is also their defect; they give so easily that they're very hard to keep in tune. Many players opt for slightly heavier strings, where almost all the same effects are possible with greater exertion but less danger of putting the string out of tune. Extra-light strings are also used on very small or delicate guitars by players who might otherwise prefer light-gauge strings.

Light- and medium-gauge strings might be considered standard. Choice would depend on how hard the guitar has to be driven, the individual player's touch and tonal preference, whether he plays with picks or bare fingers, and so on. Many people shy away from medium strings, since they are noticeably stiffer to play than light ones and require greater strength. But their virtue lies in their stiffness; they're especially good for fast flat picking because they don't give much and the pick comes off them very fast. Heavy strings are extremely difficult to play, and suitable only for the strongest guitars and the heaviest touches. They are rarely used.

GUITAR MAKERS
(Including some recommendations)

The Martin and Guild companies make professional-quality steel-strung acoustic guitars and have maintained a consistent level of quality in sound and construction. Gibson guitars continue to be well made, but their sound quality over the past decade has been inconsistent. In the less expensive price range, if you choose carefully, the various Yamaha models deliver the best sound and durability for the money. Takamine guitars can also have an excellent sound but don't do well in drier climates.

In many ways used guitars and especially older ones are more desirable than new ones. The older Martins and Gibsons were more finely made, sometimes designed slightly differently because of lower production-quantity factors, and often used better woods. And the sound of a wooden instrument improves with age. Unfortunately, the used market has been widely exploited by collectors, investors, and fanatics to a degree that calls for great expertise, greater than I could hope to develop in this short space.

There have been some interesting changes in the guitar world since our book first appeared. The Martin Guitar Company is still in business, and more willing to experiment with new styles and techniques. Guild guitars has recently been bought by Randall. Gibson has not been concentrating on the acoustic guitar market to any extent, but a number of its former employees have opened up a factory in Kalamazoo, and are marketing their work under the name Heritage Guitars. Taylor Guitars, in the San Deigo area, has emerged as one of the leading Martin competitors, and Santa Cruz is a small quality maker in Northern California, as is Pimentel in Albuquerque.

Yamaha, Takamine and Washburn make fairly good, fairly reasonably-priced guitars.

We refer you to Farrell's *Directory of Contemporary American Musical Instrument Makers* for details on those making guitars by hand.

(— D.W.)

DULCIMERS

The instrument called the dulcimer has three or four strings. There is another instrument, known as the hammered dulcimer, which has a great many more strings and is much more difficult to play. To further complicate matters, there is also an instrument called the psaltery, which is similar to the hammered dulcimer but has longer, thinner strings. The psaltery is plucked with the fingers, and the hammered dulcimer is usually played with mallets.

There is an incredible amount of dulcimer building going on at the present time. Rather than list makers, we refer you to Susan Caust Farrell's book, *Directory of Contemporary American Musical Instrument Makers*. The makers listed below are two makers known to me, and two manufacturers who ship dulcimers to other stores, or sell direct. (—D.W.)

Carol, Bonnie, c/o Krimmel, Salina Star Route, Boulder, CO 80302. Makes good mountain dulcimers.

London, Dale, 2639-1/2 N. 48th, Lincoln, NE 68504. Makes quality hammered dulcimers.

Dusty Strings Dulcimer Co., 3406 Fremont Ave. N., Seattle, WA 98103

Leo Instruments Co., 1907 S. Pearl, Denver, CO 80210

THE MANDOLIN AS A FOLK INSTRUMENT

by Steve Wiencrot

A mandolin is a fretted, stringed instrument of the lute family. It is roughly the size of a violin, with its four pairs of strings similarly tuned by fifths (that is, GDAE). There are five common styles: (1) the Neapolitan has the familiar gourdlike shape and is often called roundback, appleback, or tater bug; (2) the Milanese is also round-backed, but much shallower; (3) the English, or flatback, has a pear-shaped front silhouette and a flat back; (4) the Gibson A style is pear-shaped with face and back arched like a violin; and (5) the Gibson artist or F style is similar to the A style with the addition of two "points" on the treble rim and a scroll on the bass rim.

The popularity of the mandolin rose around the turn of the century and continued into the 1920's. During that time mandolin clubs and orchestras were in vogue. These groups played all members of the mandolin family: mandolin, mandola (corresponding in size and tuning to the viola), mando-cello (corresponding to the cello), and mando-bass (corresponding to the double bass). In various combinations these instruments were played with standard guitars, Hawaiian steel guitars, harp guitars, Irish harps, banjos, flutes, violins, cellos, and ukeleles. The 1921 Gibson catalogue, reproduced by the Country Music Foundation, has dozens of pictures of mandolin ensembles from the early part of this century. The catalogue shows a wide variety of groups, from the tuxedoed, fifty-eight-member Chicago Symphony Mandolin Orchestra to the five Musical Middletons, who played all four members of the mandolin family and dressed like Gypsies. These pictures seem to indicate that although the music played by such groups was varied, it was probably classical, light classical, and "standards." The association of mandolins and country music is not evident in this catalogue.

Before Bill Monroe and his bluegrass music aroused interest in the mandolin, the instrument occupied a relatively small role in country music. The *New Lost City Ramblers Song Book*, a representative collection of old-timey music, includes a mandolin part in a dozen or so of its 125 songs. The Ramblers, however, have documented fine examples of early country music played on the mandolin, both as faithful reproductions of the original recordings and as their own arrangements of tunes in the idiom of old-time string bands. During the 1960's, they offered some of the only available music in this style. Since that time, and due in large part to their devotion to reviving interest in such music, other recordings have become available. Of these, mandolin is featured on records by the Monroe Brothers, the Blue Sky Boys, the Lilly Brothers, Kenny Hall and the Sweets Mill String Band, Ray and Ina Patterson, the Old Reliable String Band, and some of the recordings by Woody Guthrie, Cisco Houston, and Pete Seeger. Kenny Hall is particularly noteworthy for his unique playing style; he holds the instrument vertically on his knee and picks the strings with his fingers only.

Mandolins have long been played by immigrants, who brought with them their native music and styles of playing. Many people are familiar with the characteristic tremolo played with Italian ballads. Greeks use the mandolin with the bouzouki for dance tunes and folk music such as that played in *Zorba the Greek*. Russian and Balkan peoples play a four-stringed mandolin, called a domra, as the lead in balalaika groups for dance tunes and folk music such as that heard in *Dr. Zhivago*. In the British Isles, the use of the mandolin is much like our own. In this music can be heard familiar dance tunes, with the mandolin often playing note-for-note the fiddle or pipe lead, as on the albums of the Boys of the Lough. Recordings of the Ian Campbell Folk Group, the Incredible String Band, and Dave Swarbrick and Martin Carthy have numerous fine examples of the mandolin used for song accompaniment.

Ragtime and blues have also been played on the mandolin, although there are not many recordings of such music. The Folkways anthology *Ragtime 2: The Country* has some nice ragtime tracks, as do some of the records by the New Lost City Ramblers, Jim Kweskin and the Jug Band, the Even Dozen Jug Band, and Carl Martin (playing with Ted Bogan and the Armstrong Brothers). At present, live ragtime mandolin is occasionally played in "gay nineties" pizza or ice cream parlors. Yank Rachell, Johnny Young, and Ry Cooder have all recorded blues albums featuring mandolin.

The largest group of mandolin players by far play bluegrass, the music started and standardized by mandolinist Bill Monroe, who began recording in the mid-1930's with his brother Charlie on guitar. By the mid-1940's, he had arrived at his usual ensemble of mandolin, guitar, fiddle, banjo, and bass. The musical idiom he developed combined the dance tunes, blues, and white gospel tradition from his rural background; with the addition of Chubby Wise on fiddle and especially Earl Scruggs on banjo, he defined the "bluegrass sound." Like Miles Davis and Muddy Waters, Monroe has been the band leader and teacher for many of the finest musicians to follow. Even those who have not played with him have spent hours listening to his playing and imitating his lines, phrasing, attack, and settings. He has consistently set the highest standards for the singing and playing of his whole band as well as for himself.

Monroe favored playing tunes high, to suit his voice. The result was playing in virtually new keys, like B and B , thus teaching country mandolin players to play in closed positions—involving few if any open strings. He introduced highly embellished and syncopated, bluesy improvisations that often went high up the fret board. He also popularized the use of chords that covered all the strings, as opposed to chords with open strings. He could thus lessen pressure on all the strings at once and so produce a clearly defined, choppy backup, one that utilized the high range of the instrument to contrast with and cut through the low rhythmic backup of the guitar and bass.

Monroe considers bluegrass his music and has therefore defined its boundaries, regarding both technique and repertoire. Many groups have followed his lead almost religiously, but there is currently a schism in bluegrass between the traditionalists and those who wish to modernize this music. The modernists, as it were, include such groups as the Seldom Scene and the New Grass Revival, who retain the overall sound and spirit, as well as groups like the Earl Scruggs Revue, who may not be identifiably bluegrass to the traditionalists, but who definitely acknowledge their roots. A select listing of bluegrass and related groups include Bill Monroe and the Bluegrass Boys, Jim and Jesse and the Virginia Boys, the Stanley Brothers or Ralph Stanley and the Clinch Mountain Boys, Country Gazette, Kentucky Colonels, Bluegrass Alliance, Flatt and Scruggs, Earl Scruggs Revue, Seldom Scene, New Grass Revival, Osborne Brothers, the Greenbriar Boys, Lilly Brothers, the Dillards, J. D. Crowe and the Kentucky Mountain Boys, Red Allen and the Kentuckians, and the Country Gentlemen.

Of special interest to mandolin players is Jesse McReynolds, of Jim and Jesse and the Virginia Boys. McReynolds has popularized the technique of cross picking the mandolin. This involves playing the melody within rolls or string patterns that duplicate the finger patterns of Scruggs-style bluegrass banjo. Like its banjo counterpart, McReynolds'-picking (as it is called) achieves a high degree of syncopation.

Recently, the mandolin has been used more in contemporary music. Some artists and groups to listen to include Ry Cooder, the Incredible String Band, Seals and Crofts, the Nitty Gritty Dirt Band, and Rod Stewart and Faces. The Charles River Valley Boys have a record of Beatle tunes played in bluegrass style featuring Joe Val on mandolin. In a very different vein is Jethro Burns, of Homer and Jethro fame. His music has often been obscured by their focus on humor, but for me his playing is among the finest. His jazzy style can be heard on the out-of-print album *Playing It Straight.* (*See also* Mandolin record section, page 92.)

SOME THOUGHTS ON STARTING TO PLAY

If you are a beginner, start with an inexpensive instrument. You can learn on any style, as long as the instrument is not so shoddy that it is unplayable. Inexpensive mandolins can be made more playable in several ways:

1. Check the tuning pegs. If they are worn or have some play in them, replace them. The Harmony Company manufactures tuning machines with a 24:1 gear ratio. That's "twice as precise" (their name) as the standard 12:1 machines. They cost $4.00 and allow you to achieve more precise tuning. If these pegs don't fit your instrument, a repairman may be able to redrill the peg head to accommodate them. Most music stores can order Harmony parts.

2. With a straight-edge, check the straightness of the finger board. Generally, the straighter the board is, the lower the strings can be, and the easier it is to play. If the board is not too bowed (lengthwise) or warped (widthwise), a repairman may be able to make some simple, inexpensive alterations, like filing the fret wires evenly or adjusting the truss rod if your instrument has one. More radical deviations in the neck can also be rectified, but at greater cost.

3. Make sure that the bridge is placed so that the twelfth fret wire is exactly halfway between the nut (the plastic piece at the peg-head end of the finger board) and the bridge. Check this with a ruler or by a harmonic note. This note is sounded by plucking the string while touching it lightly, then immediately removing the finger. You should hear a bell-like tone similar to the note regularly sounded when the string is plucked without being fretted. When the bridge is properly placed, the harmonic will sound precisely over the twelfth fret wire.

4. Check the height of the strings from the fret board. In general, you want them as low as possible without causing them to rattle. If the strings are uncomfortably high near the nut, you can file the grooves that hold them deeper. If the problem is at the bridge, you can file its grooves, or replace the original bridge with one that is adjustable for about $4.00. If the strings are so low as to rattle, you can raise the action (height of the strings) with paper shims appropriately placed under the nut or bridge. When you adjust the action, remember that the bass (G) strings have wider vibrations than the treble (E) strings, and so should be slightly higher off the board.

Good, new strings will improve the sound of your mandolin. Strings are available in Monel (nickel–steel) round-wound and flat-wound (usually played on electric instruments) and in bronze round-wound. Whether to use Monel or bronze is a matter of personal preference, although bronze is favored more by country and bluegrass players. Strings can be kept bright sounding longer if you wipe them off when you are finished playing. This retards deterioration due to sweat and grease. If you are a beginner, change the strings when one breaks or appears corroded. Mandolin strings are manufactured by the following companies: Gibson, Martin, GHS, D'Merle (D'Angelico), Ernie Ball, National Musical String Company (Bell brand), and Black Diamond. Gibson and Martin strings are probably the most popular. I have found that GHS strings last longer than the others.

Good mandolins are expensive. New Gibsons, favored by most bluegrass players, cost between $500 and $1,200. Older Gibsons, especially prized for their craftsmanship, tone, and volume, sell for $200 to $4,000 plus. The C. F. Martin Company makes only one instrument, for about $350. Although not particularly well suited for bluegrass, it is a fine instrument for old-timey music, ragtime, and contemporary sounds.

Autoharp

Dobro and Nineteenth-Century German Guitar

MISCELLANEOUS INSTRUMENT MANUFACTURERS

Dobros or Dobro parts:

Richard Jacks, 601 34th Place, Ft. Madison, IA 52627

Melody Music, 11110 Los Alamos Blvd., Ste. 204, Los Alamitos, CA 90720

National Resophonic Co., 3950 Atlantic Ave., Ste. 12, Long Beach, CA 90807

Barbara Sinclair, Box 2104, Costa Mesa, CA 92628

Harps

Sylvia Woods Harp Center, Box 29521-F, Los Angeles, CA 90029. An excellent source for folk harps or instructional materials for harps.

Wood

Roger Siminoff details sources for wood in his book *Constructing a Bluegrass Mandolin.*

BOOKS ABOUT MUSICAL INSTRUMENTS, CONSTRUCTION, REPAIR

DUCHOISSIR, A.R., *Guitar Identification, How to Date the Guitars Made by Fender, Gibson, Gretsch, Martin,* Media Press, 1985, dist. by Hal Leonard. Serial numbers, markings, etc.

FARRELL, SUSAN CAUST, *Directory of Contemporary American Musical Instrument Makers,* University of Missouri Press, 1981, 216 pp. A large list of instrument makers, what they make, and the extent of their production.

HARTMAN, ROBERT CARL, *Guitars and Mandolins in America, Featuring the Larsens' Creations,* Hoffman Estates, 1988, 181 pp. revised ed. Concerns Euphon, Prairie State and Stahl instruments.

SIMINOFF, ROGER, *Constructing a Five String Banjo,* Hal Leonard, 1985, 63 pp. A very comprehensive book with pictures and construction diagrams.

SIMINOFF, ROGER, *Constructing a Bluegrass Mandolin: A Complete Technical Guide,* Hal Leonard, 1981, 54 pp. Many pictures and charts.

Note: George Gruhn, of Gruhn Guitars in Nashville, is compiling data on the history and development of fretted instruments for future publication.

BAILEY, JOHN, *Making an Appalachian Dulcimer,* English Folk Dance and Song Society. 55 pp., PB. Photos, diagrams. Available from Vitali.

BAILEY, JOHN, *Making a Folk Guitar,* English Folk Dance and Song Society, 1965. 64 pp. Available from Vitali.

BAINES, ANTHONY, ed. *Musical Instruments Through the Ages,* Walker, 1974, HB; Penguin, 1961, PB.

BELLOW, ALEXANDER, *The Illustrated History of the Guitar,* Franco Colombo, dist. by Belwin-Mills, 1970. 216 pp., HB.

BONE, PHILIP, *The Guitar and Mandolin,* Scholarly Reprints, enlarged ed., reprint of 1954 ed. 388 pp., HB.

BROSNAC, DONALD. *The Steel String Guitar; Its Design and Construction.* Panjandrum Press, 1974. 104 pp., PB. 132 photos, 10 pp. of schematics. Available from Vitali.

BROWN, H. E., *Classic Guitar Maker's Guide,* 1967. 44 pp. Step-by-step diagrams and photos. Available from Vitali.

BROWN, H. E., *How to Build Your Own Electric Guitar,* H. E. Brown Company, 1966. Available from Vitali.

BUCHNER, ALEXANDER, *Folk Music Instruments of the World,* Crown, 1972. 300 illustrations, usually demonstrating how the instrument is played.

COOPER, ROBERT, *Lute Construction.* 31 chaps. Available from Vitali.

DENSMORE, FRANCES, *Handbook of the Collection of Musical Instruments in the U.S. National Museum,* Da Capo Press, 1971 reprint of 1927 book.

FLUHARTY, RUSSELL, *The Dulcimer Story,* Self-pub., 1964.

GILLMORE, LEE, *Folk Instruments,* Lerner Publications, 1962. PB.

GRUNFELD, FREDERICK, *The Art and Times of the Guitar,* Macmillan, 1969. 340 pp., HB. A history of the guitar through paintings and photos. No musical examples.

GUITAR PLAYER MAGAZINE, *Guitar Repair Manual*, Oak, 1972. 311 pp.

HILL, THOMAS A., *The Guitar*, Franklin Watts, 1973. 116 pp., HB. A children's book, for grades 5 up.

HINES, CHET, *How to Make and Play the Dulcimore*, Stackpole Books, 1973. 160 pp. Includes detailed instruction on making and playing the dulcimer, many attractive photos, and a detailed history of the instrument.

HUTTING, H. E., *Guitar Construction from A to Z*. Diagrams and photos. Available from Vitali.

HUYN, P., G. LEIS, and DANIEL MARI, *A Guitar Manual*. Background, repair, history. Available from Vitali.

JOHNSON, BRIAN, *Guitar Fret Position Calculator*. No publishing information available.

KAMIMOTO, HIDEO, *Complete Guitar Repair*, Oak, 1974. 192 pp.

KIMBALL, DEAN, *Constructing the Mountain Dulcimer*, David McKay, 1974. 192 pp. Diagrams, photos, etc.

LONGWORTH, MIKE, *Martin Guitars: A History*. Colonial Press, 1975. 219 pp., HB. The Martin guitar is the Stradivarius of the folk and country picker. Longworth has compiled an absorbing history for the musician or guitar collector. There are complete details on all of the various Martin models, including experimental models and custom guitars, a history of the Martin company, and numerous fascinating details. Unfortunately the photos are not too good, and the book could use an index. Nevertheless this is a valuable and unique book.

MANDELL, MURIEL, and ROBERT E. WOOD, *Make Your Own Musical Instruments*. Sterling, 1957. 128 pp., HB. A great idea for children—making and playing all kinds of musical instruments, including castanets, bells, rhythm sticks.

MCKINNEY, J. P. *How to Rehair Bows*, Self-pub.

MCLEOD, DONALD, and ROBERT WELFORD, *The Classical Guitar—Design and Construction*, Marina Music. 107 pp., HB. Guitar construction guide with diagrams and photos.

OBERHOLTZER, ARTHUR, *Classic Guitar Making*, Lawrence A. Brock, 1974. 323 pp. Illustrated. Available from Vitali.

POLLACK, RICHARD, and IRVING SLOANE *Guitar Repair*, Dutton, 1973. 95 pp., HB. Contains many pictures, and includes sections on glue, tools, cracks, re-fretting, etc.

REEVES, WILLIAM, *Catalog of Books on the Violin—Making, Repairing, History, Technique*, William Reeves, Publishers.

RIDGE, ERIC V., *Making a Concert Guitar*, H. L. Wild. 27 pp., PB. Plans for the guitar available separately from the same source.

SEEGER, PETE, *How to Make a Chalil*, self-pub.

SHARPE, A. P., *Complete Guide to the Instruments of the Banjo Family*, Mills Music, 1966.

SHARPE, A. P., *Make Your Own Spanish Guitar*, 1957. 32 pp. HB. Available from Vitali.

SLOANE, IRVING, *Classic Guitar Construction*, Dutton, 1966. 95 pp., HB. Photos and texts.

STAMM, G. W., *How to Make a Banjo and a Banjo Guitar*, Self-pub., 1971. 24 pp. Includes full-sized finger board plans and list of companies that supply parts. A good method if you are already experienced in the use of tools. (Reviewed with the help of Steve Crook.)

TEETER, DON, *The Acoustic Guitar: Adjustment, Care, Maintenance and Repair*, University of Oklahoma Press, 1974. 200 pp. Teeter is recognized as one of the outstanding guitar repairmen in the United States. This book is an extremely informative guide to the repair of the steel string guitar, with drawings and photos. There are chapters on cracks, re-fretting, glues, etc.

TURNBULL, HARVEY, *The Guitar from the Renaissance to the Present Day*, Scribner's, 1974. 168 pp., HB. A history with many photos of old guitars and musical examples.

WAKE, H. S., *The Technique of Violin Making*, self-pub.

WALLO, JOSEPH, *Flat Top Guitar Plans*, 1973.

WALLO, JOSEPH, *Twelve String Guitar Plans*.

WHEELER, TOM, *The Guitar Book*, Harper & Row, 1974. 269 pp., HB. Acoustic and electric guitars, amps, strings, sound systems, etc. There are sections on Fender, Gibson, and Martin guitars, with numerous pictures.

WILD, GEORGE F., *Guitar Plans for Steel String Guitar, and for Classic Guitar*. Available from H. L. Wild.

Note: Many of the guitar-making books are not listed anywhere but in the Vitali catalogue, and therefore we do not know the actual publishers. The Vitali catalogue is available from Vitali Import Company, 5944 Atlantic Boulevard, Maywood, Calif. 90270.

For the addresses of publishers and self-published authors in this section, see the Book and Music Publishers section in Part II, page 191.

REPRINTS OF OLD INSTRUMENT CATALOGUES AND PUBLISHERS' ADDRESSES

B&D "Silver Bell" Banjo Family, The, repr. by Banjo Newsletter. 48 pp. A reprint of the Bacon banjo catalogue with biographies and pictures of many early players.

Mandolin-Banjo, or Cithern

1902 Gibson Guitar and Mandolin Catalog, The, Mugwumps.

Gibson, The, Country Music Press facsimile edition of 1921 catalogue, ed. by William Ivey. 120 pp. Includes many pictures. The cover is the same as *The Gibson Story* by Julius Bellson, but this is a different book.

1927 Gibson Banjo Catalog, The, Mugwumps.

1927 Gibson Inc. Catalog, Mugwumps. Includes guitars, harp guitars, mandolins, tiples, and ukes.

1956 Gibson Catalog, The, Northern Prairie Music, 28 pp.

Gibson Story, The, by Julius Bellson, The Gibson Company, 1973. 96 pp. This is not a catalogue, but a history of The Gibson Company with pictures of instruments, artists, etc.

Martin String Instruments, Mugwumps, 47 pp. 1924 catalogue of guitars, mandolins, and ukeleles.

Martin String Instruments, John Gima, 1974. Reprint of 1937 catalogue. 32 pp. Guitars, mandolins, ukes, etc.
Note: Gima has recently reprinted a National and Dobro catalogue of the 1936–7 period.

1940 Martin Catalog, The, Country Music Foundation Press. 39 pp. Includes guitars, mandolins, tiples, and ukes.

Paramount Banjos Catalog, Mugwumps. 1920's catalogue. 80 pp. Many pictures of players and five-string, tenor, plectrum, and guitar banjos (six-string banjos).

Progressive Musical Instrument Corp., GTR. 1931 musical instrument catalogue of a music wholesaler. Includes banjos, guitars, mandolins, violins, etc. This catalogue includes various manufacturers, such as Bacon, Gibson, Martin, and National.

Stewart, S. S., Banjo Catalog, Mugwumps. 1896 catalogue. 56 pp. Mostly banjos with a few guitars and mandolins.

Vega Banjos, Mugwumps. 1923 catalogue. 32 pp. With photos of the famous Whyte Laydie and Tu-ba-phone models, guitar banjos, etc.
Note: All of these reprints are paperbacks.

The publishers' addresses are as follows:

Country Music Foundation Press, 700 16th Avenue S., Nashville, Tenn. 37203

Gibson Company, The, 225 Parsons Street, Kalamazoo, Mich. 49007

GTR, 111 4th Avenue N., Nashville, Tenn. 37219

Mugwumps Instrument Herald, 12704 Barbara Road, Silver Springs, Md. 20906

Northern Prairie Music, 277 Greenbay, Wilmette, Ill. 60011

TRANSPOSITION AND A SMALL DOSE OF MUSICAL THEORY

by Dick Weissman

In many of the reviews in previous pages, we have criticized books for having songs printed in "bad" guitar keys. A bad guitar key is one that requires the extensive use of barres, or closed position chords. An E flat chord as opposed to a G chord, for example. How do you transpose a song from one key to another? The first step is to find out what key the song is in. You do this by looking at the key signature, which appears at the beginning of each line of music. For example, turn to page 203, where we have printed the song "Blind Gary." You will notice one sharp that is printed # at the beginning of each line. This tells you that this song must be in either the key of G major or the key of E minor. We will not discuss the relationship between sharps and flats, and keys here—but below is a complete list of keys with the identifying number of sharps and flats.

0 sharps or flats, key of	C major or A minor.
1 sharp	G major or E minor
2 sharps	D major or B minor
3 sharps	A major or F# minor
4 sharps	E major or C# minor
5 sharps	B major or G# minor
6 sharps	F# major or D# minor
7 sharps	C# major or A# minor
1 flat	F major or D minor
2 flats	B♭ major or G minor
3 flats	E♭ major or C Minor
4 flats	A♭ major or F Minor
5 flats	D♭ major or B♭ Minor
6 flats	G♭ major or E♭ Minor
7 flats	C♭ major or A♭ Minor

Your next problem is to determine whether the song is in a major or minor key. The last note and chord of a piece *usually* name the correct key. Turning back to "Blind Gary" again, you will see that this rule holds true. The last note and chord are G and G major, respectively. If that note and chord had been E and E minor, that would have been the correct key of the song. If you follow the chart below, you can transpose a song from the original key to any key you choose.

	I						IV	V			
Key or Note	C	C#	D	D#E	F	F#	G	G#A	B	A#
	C#D	D#E	F	F#G	G#A	A#C	B			
	D	D#E	F	F#G	G#A	A#B	C#C			
	D#E	F	F#G	G#A	A#B	C	D	C#		
	E	F	F#G	G#A	A#B	C	C#D#	D		
	F	F#G	G#A	A#B	C	C#D	E	D#		
	F#G	G#A	A#B	C	C#D	D#F	E			
	G	G#A	A#B	C	C#D	D#E	F#F			
	G#A	A#B	C	C#D	D#E	F	G	F#		
	A	A#B	C	C#D	D#E	F	F#G#G			
	A#B	C	C#D	D#E	F	F#G	A	G#		
	B	C	C#D	D#E	F	F#G	G#A#A			

Remember that D$\flat$ is the same as C#, E$\flat$ is the same as D#, G$\flat$ is the same as F#, A$\flat$ is the same as G#, and B$\flat$ is the same as A#.

In order to use the chart on the previous page you need to follow the chart vertically. In going from the key of G to the key of C, for example, your eye needs to go back and forth between the line with the letter G on the far left and the line marked C on the far left. (The C line happens to be the first line on the chart.) Any added number or symbol must be retained in the new key; that is, a G7 chord in the key of G will become a C7 chord in the key of C. Minor chords follow the same rule; an A minor chord in the key of G becomes a D minor chord in the key of C. Let's suppose that you want to play "Blind Gary" in the key of C, instead of in G. The G chord becomes a C chord, the C chord becomes an F, the E minor an A minor, and the B7 an E7.

Using the same system, you can transpose any melody from one key to another.

Before concluding this discussion, I'd like to take up the subject of chords. If you've ever played the piano, you know that a C scale contains the notes CDEFGABC. If this is new to you, ask someone to show you a C note on the piano. The rest of the notes in the C scale are all the white keys until you hit the next C, an octave higher than the first one. A major chord uses the first, third, and fifth notes of the scale. Thus a C major chord contains the notes CEG. Below are the spellings for C chords, through sevenths.

C major, CEG

C minor, CE$\flat$G

C augmented (written aug. or C+), CEG#

C diminished (written dim. or C°), CE$\flat$G$\flat$

C dim. 7 is C E$\flat$ G$\flat$ B$\flat\flat$ (double flat). B$\flat\flat$ is a fancy way of saying A, but necessary for theoretical reasons.

C6, CEGA

C minor 6, CE$\flat$GA

C7, CEGB$\flat$

C major 7 or maj. 7 or C$^{\triangle 7}$, CEGB

C minor 7, CE$\flat$GB$\flat$

C minor major 7 CE$\flat$GB

Finally, there is another chord called C half-diminished 7 or C min. 7$\flat$5, which is CE$\flat$ G$\flat$B$\flat$.

One last thought about chords: The C major chord contains the notes CEG. This is called the root position of the chord; that is, C is the bass note. When the notes appear in the order EGC, the C chord is said to be in first inversion. When the note sequence is GCE, the chord is said to be in second inversion. When you see someone playing up the neck of a guitar or banjo, he or she is playing inversions of chords that you have probably played on the lower positions of the finger board.

If you want to learn more about harmony, I suggest you read either Walter Piston's *Harmony*, published by W. W. Norton, or Elie Siegmeister's two-volume *Harmony and Melody*, published by Wadsworth. In order to get through the exercises in these books, however, you really have to play the piano. Some guitar books deal with harmony, but they aren't of much use and don't progress very far.

LEARNING TO PLAY FOLK MUSIC ON BANJO AND GUITAR

by Dan Fox

Instrumental technique as applied to folk music has become a highly developed art. Unlike playing the piano, where both hands do similar things, a musician playing a fretted instrument must make totally different movements simultaneously with his right and left hands. The left hand not only fingers single notes and chords consisting of anywhere from two to six notes, but also plays special effects such as hammering on, pulling off, slides, bends, and smears. Each of these effects uses a different finger motion. The right hand strikes the strings (and sometimes the body of the guitar) with a variety of techniques including strumming with the thumb, hand, or flat pick, brushing across the strings with the fingernail of one or more fingers, finger picking with a combination of thumb and fingers, sometimes while wearing picks on the thumb and fingers. With the five-string banjo, a player uses all these devices plus frailing, which consists of striking the strings with a sharp downward movement of the nail of the index finger.

A good notational system must have symbols for all these techniques as well as the actual notes and chords being played. But many, perhaps most, folk musicians are not oriented toward reading music. They prefer learning directly from the playing of other musicians, either in person or on record.

Learning from another player in a person-to-person situation, whether he is a teacher in the formal sense or not, has the advantage of allowing the learner to hear exactly how the music should sound. In addition to this and just as important, it lets him see exactly what the right and left hands are doing to create a given musical sound. However, learning this way is very slow, and it's not always easy to find good players who are willing to spend the many hours required. And, of course, in the case of such deceased greats as Robert Johnson or Leadbelly, the aspiring player must do the best he can using only the recordings.

Learning from records presents many difficulties. Recording techniques during the first thirty or forty years of this century were primitive, and with old discs it is often very difficult to tell exactly what is being played. Also, the record may not have been made at concert pitch. Leadbelly, for example, usually tuned his twelve-string guitar three to five notes below concert pitch. Other players use unusual tunings on both guitar and banjo. A guitar solo conceived in, say, G tuning (DGDGBD) is impossible to play in normal tuning (EADGBE). The pitch of both the guitar and the banjo may be raised by using a capo. Thus a record may sound in the key of B♭ even though the player conceived and executed the solo in the key of G with a capo across the third fret. Nevertheless, skilled players are able to overcome all these obstacles and learn solos and accompaniments from records.

For the player of moderate ability, however, the ideal situation is one in which the aural source—teacher or record—is supplemented with a visual one. Many books and book–record combinations have been published toward this end. What follows is a brief review of the types of notation used.

Traditional notation is identical with that used for classic guitar. Its main drawback is that very few folk musicians can read it. Also, it does not accurately reflect the fretted instrument's inability to sustain notes. A note played on guitar rapidly decays into inaudibility. The decay on banjo is even quicker, so that a whole note really comes out sounding like a half note followed by a rest. When a figure is played based on a chord, the notes blend together somewhat like a piano with the sostenuto pedal held down. But since the guitar is not as rich in overtones as the piano, the effect is much cleaner. (*See* Examples 1 and 2.) Also, in

Example 3

ever, and smears, frailing, brush strokes, and similar less conventional devices are difficult to notate accurately. Probably the most basic weakness is trying to notate a two-handed technique on one staff.

Many folk song collections are published in lead sheet form. This means that the player gets only the melody, words, and chord symbols to work with. Some editions even omit the melody, since many players can't read the traditional music notes which are used to notate it. This problem is sometimes solved by writing the melody in both traditional and tablature notation, a space-wasting and awkward solution. In the hands of a skilled player, a lead sheet can be used as the basis of an elaborate arrangement. The chord symbols are used as a general guide and are varied by the use of inversions, added notes, bass runs, and the whole gamut of folk instrumental techniques. However, chord symbols are no more than the bare bones and are useless for indicating strums, hammer ons, right-hand picking, left-hand fingering, or anything even slightly unusual in the chord structure. (For a lead sheet sample, *see* Example 4.)

Example 4

On top of Old Smo - ky,

Chord frames or chord diagrams are familiar to every player of fretted instruments. They are more detailed than the chord symbol and can indicate, in addition to the name of the chord, bass notes, added notes, inversions, and special fingerings. In some editions hammer ons and pull offs are called for by circling notes, but the timing of these effects is still left to the player's discretion. A few different types of chord frames are shown in Example 5.

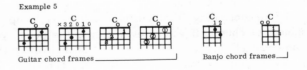

Example 5

Guitar chord frames _____   Banjo chord frames ____

Modified diagrams give all the information that is found in an ordinary chord frame plus an indication of the right-hand strum (Example 6). Although the rhythm of the strum

Example 1   Example 2

sounds like

traditional notation fairly simple accompaniments tend to look complicated. A simple Travis picking pattern on guitar comes out full of syncopation and double stemming (Example 3). Nevertheless, rhythm, bass runs, hammer ons, and pull offs can all be written with exact timing. Fingering, positions, and picking must be added separately, how-

Example 6

$5, \frac{1}{2}, \frac{2}{3}, 5, 2, 3, 1$

Means play the 5th string alone, then the 1st, 2nd and 3rd strings together, then the 5th, 2nd, 3rd and 1st strings one at a time.

is still vague, this is not necessarily a drawback, since in many cases folk strums are fairly simple, rhythmically being based on quarter and eighth notes. Sometimes counting (1 and 2 and) is placed below the strum to clarify the rhythm.

The six-line tablature for the left hand is a modification of the lute tablature in use hundreds of years ago. The six lines represent the six strings of the guitar. The numbers stand for the fret on which any note or chord is played (Example 7). This tablature is very useful in showing the

Example 7

a C scale   a C chord   D hammered   G pulled off
                                                on to E.   to E.

exact fingering of a note. Thus, unlike traditional notation, which has only one symbol for middle B on guitar, tablature has four. Each symbol represents a different place to play the same note, second string open, third string fourth fret, fourth string ninth fret, fifth string fourteenth fret. This is very valuable when transcribing single-note blues solos, breaks, and runs. Pull offs and hammer ons can also be indicated as well as chords. The tablature's main drawback is the lack of a reliable way to indicate exact rhythm. Some editions add stems to the numbers (Example 8); others add cue notes below the staff (Example 9). But these

Example 8   Example 9

G scale in quarter and eighth notes.   Same thing using cue notes.

remedies still assume that the player knows enough about traditional notation to recognize an eighth note when he sees one. Also, unlike the chord frame, six-line tablature doesn't give the player fingering, right-hand picking, or an indication of which chord form a given figure is based on.

The six-line tablature for right hand is valuable for indicating an exact right-hand strum, brush stroke, or picking pattern. Here again, the six lines represent the strings of the guitar. The letters stand for the right-hand fingers, the arrows for brush strokes, and so on (Example 10). How-

Example 10

Thumb, Index, middle and ring finger play play a simple arpeggio.   Thumb followed by up and down brush stroke.
(Left hand holds a C chord)

ever, this type of tablature must be used in conjunction with a chord diagram to show what the left hand is doing. Although hammer ons, pull offs, and other left-hand techniques can be shown, the tablature is least effective for notating these. Also, as in other six-line tablature, rhythms are not precisely indicated, although good editions attempt

to suggest the duration of notes by their spacing across the page or by adding stems or cue notes.

Five-line tablature is used for the five-string banjo. It has the same advantages and disadvantages as the six-line tablature for guitar.

Five-space tablature is used by Dick Weissman in his series of books on the five-string banjo. The spaces represent the strings; the stemless note means to strike that string; the number below means to finger a certain fret. (*See* Example 11.)

Example 11 Bluegrass picking pattern

         M   T   I   M   T   I   M   T

      0 _____   2   0 _____   2   0

It becomes clear from a review of these methods that the perfect system of notating folk music for guitar or banjo has yet to be devised. Each system now in use has advantages and disadvantages. Players with highly developed musical ears will tend to learn from teachers or records. Players who are more intellectually oriented will probably prefer traditional notation. Others in the middle ground may choose one of the tablature systems or simply playing from lead sheets.

The primary purpose of any notational system is to transmit information. Anyone who attempts to devise a new system should keep in mind that notation is only as good as its ability to evoke the best musical sound from an individual player.

67 TUNINGS FOR THE FIVE-STRING BANJO
by Dick Weissman

The first five-string banjos in the southern mountains were made without frets. To play up the neck of a banjo that has no frets, you must have a good quality instrument, or you will never be able to play exactly in tune. Also, the demands upon the player's skill are much greater; it is much easier to find the right notes on a fretted instrument. Position markings help, too. In order to play in different keys and to avoid playing in the higher positions of the instrument, many of the mountain banjo players played in different tunings.

There are other less technical reasons for trying out different banjo tunings. One is experimentation; it's nice to try playing in keys and fingerings that are new. Sometimes this brings out a creative idea that you would not ordinarily have in a standard tuning, because your fingers would be going to familiar places. On a more advanced level, you can set up different pitch intervals between the strings, and you can vary the sound of the fifth or drone string by raising or lowering it. This provides a necessary relief from that constant G note in the C or G tunings.

Most of the tunings listed come from books and records, though a few I've thought up myself (at least I can't remember where I got them). The outstanding single source of tunings is Art Rosenbaum's book *Old Time Mountain Banjo*. Whenever possible, I have listed a book or record where you can see or hear a song in the tuning. The books are indicated by authors' names only; the records by the title of the album and the musician. A list of the books and records appears at the end of the article. Unfortunately, a few of the records listed are out of print.

I have listed the tunings by letter names when they are obviously derived from a similar and more common tuning. The "C family" of tunings includes any tuning based on the GCGBD tuning, commonly known as the C tuning. The order of strings listed is fifth, fourth, third, second, and first.

Vega Tu-ba-phone Banjos

C FAMILY

GCGBD	Most common. Almost all banjo instructional books and many records provide examples. Seldom used in bluegrass playing.
GCGCD	John Burke, Muller and Koehler, and Art Rosenbaum. Many examples in these books. A number of solos in this tuning are played by Art Rosenbaum on his record *Five String Banjo*.
GCGCE♭	An open C minor chord. Wayne Erbsen, p. 48, "Honey Babe Blues," and p. 49, "Shady Grove."
GCGCE	An open C chord. John Burke, p. 63, "Casey Jones," p. 70, "Turkey in the Straw," and others. Art Rosenbaum, p. 72, "Way Down the Old Plank Road." *Old Time Banjo Project*, "John Henry," played by Winnie Winston. *Five String Banjo Jamboree*, "A Day in the Kentucky Mountains," suite played by Dick Weissman.

Note and take warning: Any tuning where you raise the pitch of the strings a whole tone or more (two frets) can result in broken strings if you are not careful. I've broken a number of strings when tuning my banjo to open C, because the first (D) string won't go much higher in pitch than an E note.

GCGCC	Peggy Seeger, p. 14. Muller and Koehler, p. 45, "Weevily Wheat."
CCGCC	(Fifth string an octave higher.) Unrecorded, Dick Weissman.
GCGAD	Pete Seeger, p. 32, "Little Birdie."
ECGBD	Muller and Koehler, p. 78, "Morpath Rant."
ACGCD	John Burke, p. 36, "Forked Deer."

D FAMILY

ADF#AD or F#DF#AD	Most common. "Old Reuben" usually played in this tuning.
F#DDAD	Lee Haring, p. 6, "I Wish I Was a Mole in the Ground."
F#DEAD	*Down to the Cider Mill*, "Little Satchel," played by Fred Cockerham.
AADF#A	Jim Connor, *Alabama Old Time Music*, "Ragtime Annie and Columbus Stockade Blues."
AADAD	Journeymen, *New Directions in Folk Music*, "Country Blues," played by Dick Weissman. I learned this tuning from an article on tunings by Stu Jamieson in a magazine called *Promenade*.
EBEBE	*Fuzzy Mountain String Band*, "Protect the Innocent."
ADAAD	"Snowbird," unrecorded song by Dick Weissman.
ADADE	John Burke, p. 25, "Pretty Little Widder." Fuzzy Mountain String Band, *Summer Oaks and Porch*, "Shortening Bread."
ADADF#	Quincy Dillon's "High D Tune." Same as open C, all strings tuned one tone (two frets) higher. Miles Krassen, p. 69.

CDF#AD — *Old Time Banjo Project*, "Banging Breakdown," played by Hank Schwartz.

ADAAD — D on the fifth string, an octave higher.

or DDFAD — Open D minor tuning. I learned this tuning from the Stu Jamieson article. Earl Scruggs, p. 96, "Nashville Blues." Dick Weissman, *The Things That Trouble My Mind*, "East Virginia."

G FAMILY

GDGBD — Most common. All banjo instructional books, many records. The most common tuning for bluegrass.

GDGB♭D — Open G minor tuning. Pete Seeger, p. 48, "All The Pretty Little Horses." Jerry Silverman, p. 93, "The Ox Driving Song," p. 94, "Buffalo Skinners," and others.

GDGCD — This is sometimes called mountain minor, sawmill, or G modal tuning. Certain songs, such as "Pretty Polly" and "Shady Grove," are usually played in this tuning. Most of the books listed include some versions of this tuning, and so do many of the records.

GDGAD — Barry Hall, *The Virtuoso 5 String Banjo*, "Willie Moore" and "Peggy-O." Pete Seeger, p. 32, "Jinny Git Around."

GDGBB — Peggy Seeger, p. 14, tuning mentioned without musical examples.

GDGDD — Peggy Seeger, p. 14, mentioned without musical examples.

GDGBE — Barry Hall, *The Virtuoso 5 String Banjo*, "Lady Gay."

EDGBD — Pete Seeger, p. 37, "Lady Gay."

DDGBD — The D can be tuned in unison to the first string, or if you have a fifth-string capo, an octave higher. I learned this tuning somewhere, but don't remember where.

GDGDD — Peggy Seeger, p. 14, mentioned without musical examples.

DDGAD — Art Rosenbaum, p. 56, "Little Sadie."

GDGAE — Art Rosenbaum, p. 79. No musical examples, but does have a few chords for the tuning. He suggests playing "Sugar Hill" and "Willie Moore" in this tuning.

The following four tunings are printed in the Pete Seeger book on page 66: GGGBD, GFGBD, GGDAE, GDGDE. They all come from the playing of Rufus Crisp. Seeger does not print any musical examples with the tunings.

GGGBD — Art Rosenbaum plays "John Henry" on his *Five String Banjo* record.

GGDAD — Art Rosenbaum plays "Got a Little Home to Go to" on his *Five String Banjo* record.

GEADE — Miles Krassen, p. 46, "Cumberland Gap." Also recorded on the sound sheet that accompanies the book.

ADGAD — Benji Aronoff, *The Two Sides of Benji Aronoff*, "Red Apple Juice."

GGGAD — *Old Time Banjo Project*, "Brighter Day," played by Hank Schwartz. The original source of this tuning was Rufus Crisp, and his version of the same tune can be heard on *Rufus Crisp*.

FDGBD — "Old Reuben," played by Larry Sandberg. Unrecorded.

A FAMILY

None of these tunings is very common.

ACACD — Muller and Koehler, p. 90, no musical examples.

ACACE — An open A minor tuning. Muller and Koehler, p. 90, no musical examples.

ADAC#E — John Burke, p. 89, "What Is Home Without Babies," and p. 94, "The Mother's Plea."

AEADE — John Burke, p. 38, "Omie Wise."

AEAEF# — *More Clawhammer Banjo Songs and Tunes*, "Sandy River," played by Oscar Wright.

AAAC#E — An open A chord tuning. *More Clawhammer Banjo Songs and Tunes*, "John Brown's Dream," played by Tommy Jarrell.

Earl Scruggs includes "Good Times Are Past and Gone" on page 168 of his book in what he calls an A tuning, but he doesn't explain what that tuning is.

OTHER TUNINGS

ECGAD — "Little Birdie." This song appears on p. 39 of Art Rosenbaum, and is recorded by Benji Aronoff on *The Two Sides of Benji Aronoff* and by Roscoe Holcomb on *The Music of Roscoe Holcomb and Wade Ward*.

EEABD — Miles Krassen, p. 32, "Sugar Babe."

EDEAD — Benji Aronoff, *The Two Sides of Benji Aronoff*, "Shady Grove."

ECGCD — Art Rosenbaum, p. 48, "Heavy Loaded Freight Train."

FDGCD — Roscoe Holcomb, *The Music of Roscoe Holcomb and Wade Ward*, "The Buffalo Skinners," played by Roscoe Holcomb.

FCDCD — Hobart Smith, *America's Greatest Folk Instrumentalist*, "Last Chance." Benji Aronoff, *The Two Sides of Benji Aronoff*, "Laughing Bort."

FCFAD — *Old Time Banjo Project*, "Ramblin' Hobo," played by Bill Vanaver.

F#CGAD — *Old Time Banjo Project*, "John Johanna," played by John Cohen.

F#DGAD — Art Rosenbaum, p. 68, "Danville Girl."

F#GEAD — Pete Seeger, p. 66. This is another one of the Rufus Crisp tunings mentioned by Pete Seeger, without musical examples.

GFGCD — Peggy Seeger, p. 14, mentioned without musical examples.

FFGCD — *More Clawhammer Banjo Songs and Tunes*, "Big Eyed Rabbit," played by Matokie Slaughter.

F#BEAD, ABEAD, F#DEAD — These three tunings are listed by Art Rosenbaum on p. 82 of his book. He suggests playing "Cumberland Gap" in any or all of them.

GEGBE — An open E minor tuning. Muller and Koehler, p. 90, mentioned without musical examples.

GCGBE — Art Rosenbaum plays "Texas Rangers" on his *Five String Banjo* record.

OTHER WAYS TO TUNE

Grandpa Jones plays his banjo in regular G and C tunings, but tunes all the strings up a whole tone. This produces a very bright sound. Miles Krassen mentions the same idea, although in his case the motivation is being able to play in D and A, which are good fiddle keys, without the use of a capo, instead of C or G with a capo on the second fret.

There is another approach to tunings which I have found very useful. Sometimes to play in A minor or D, I will simply retune the fifth string to an A and keep the rest of the banjo in the G tuning (DGBD). This gives a sound that is different from both the standard tuning and the standard tuning capoed up. A number of examples of these tunings appear in accompaniments on the *Tom Glazer* records. (*See* Records Mentioned section, below.)

Another approach is to tune the whole banjo down, a half or whole tone (one or two frets.) This gets a thunkier, more hollow sound, and could be appropriate to some mountain songs. Pete Seeger mentions a Rufus Crisp tuning that is a G tuning lowered a whole tone. The notes become FCFAC.

Finally, if you have a Pete Seeger long-neck banjo with three more frets than the normal five string, you must transpose all of our tunings down one and a half steps. The ordinary G tuning, GDGBD, will become EBEG#B. If you don't want to bother with all of these transpositions, put your capo on the third fret of the banjo, and it will be the same as the regular G tuning.

Below is a list of the records and books that have examples of the various tunings. Perhaps someone will put together a book that is devoted to banjo solos in different tunings. Many of the tunings are used on recordings not listed here, but I stuck to materials that had some documentation of the tunings. If you know a banjo tuning that is not on the list, I would appreciate hearing about it. With some encouragement from the readers of this book, I might undertake a book of solos in various tunings myself.

BOOKS MENTIONED

See Banjo section, Instructional Books, page 173, for complete reviews.

BURKE, JOHN, *John Burke's Book of Old Time Fiddle Tunes for Banjo.* AMSCO, 1968.

ERBSEN, WAYNE, *How to Play the Five String Banjo,* to be published by Carl Fischer.

HARING, LEE, *The Gypsy Laddie,* Hargail, 1961.

JONES, LOUIS "GRANDPA," *Method of Old Time Southern Style Five-String Banjo,* Self-pub., 1954.

KRASSEN, MILES, *Clawhammer Banjo,* Oak, 1974

MULLER, ERIC, and BARBARA KOEHLER, *Frailing the Five String Banjo,* Mel Bay, 1973.

ROSENBAUM, ART, *Old Time Mountain Banjo,* Oak, 1968.

SCRUGGS, EARL, *Earl Scruggs and the Five String Banjo,* Peer International, 1968.

SEEGER, PEGGY, *The Five String Banjo: American Folk Styles,* Hargail, 1960.

SEEGER, PETE, *How to Play the Five String Banjo,* self-pub., dist. by Oak, 1962.

SILVERMAN, JERRY, *Beginning the Five String Banjo,* Macmillan and Collier, 1974

RECORDS MENTIONED

ARONOFF, BENJI
The Two Sides of Benji Aronoff, Prestige 7416. Although this record is out of print, it still turns up in bargain bins.

CONNOR, JIM
Alabama Old Time Music, HAFM II-002.

CRISP, RUFUS
Rufus Crisp, Folkways FA 2342.

Down to the Cider Mill, County 713. Fred Cockerham piece. Other tunes played by Tommy Jarrell and Oscar Wright.

Five String Banjo Jamboree, Washington LP 704. OP. Originally issued on Judson Records as *Banjos, Banjos and More Banjos.* Includes Dick Weissman piece, and performances by Billy Faier and Eric Weissberg.

FUZZY MOUNTAIN STRING BAND
_____. Rounder 0010. "Protect the Innocent" is played as a banjo duet in E minor tuning.
. . . *Summer Oaks and Porch,* Rounder 0035.

GLAZER, TOM
Tom Glazer. CMS 650/4L and 670/4L. "Days of '49" and "The Sioux Indians" are played in G tuning with the fifth string tuned to A. The songs are in the key of A minor. Banjo parts by Dick Weissman, accompanying Tom Glazer's vocals. Each set contains four records.

HALL, BARRY
The Virtuoso 5-String Banjo. Folkways FG 3533.

HOLCOMB, ROSCOE
The Music of Roscoe Holcomb and Wade Ward, Folkways FA 2363.

JOURNEYMEN, THE
New Directions in Folk Music, Capitol T 1951. OP.

More Clawhammer Banjo Songs and Tunes, County 717. The tunes referred to in the article are "John Brown's Dream," played by Tommy Jarrell, "Big Eyed Rabbit" played by Matokie Slaughter, and "Sandy River," played by Oscar Wright. Several other artists also play on this recording.

Old Time Banjo Project, Elektra EKS 7276. OP. The article mentions performances of "John Johanna" by John Cohen, "Brighter Day" and "Banging Breakdown" by Hank Schwartz, "Ramblin' Hobo" by Bill Vanaver, and "John Henry" by Winnie Winston. Other banjoists also perform on this recording.

ROSENBAUM, ART
Five String Banjo, Kicking Mule KM 108.

SMITH, HOBART
America's Greatest Folk Instrumentalist. Folk-Legacy FSA-17. "Last Chance" is the tune discussed in the article.

WEISSMAN, DICK

The Things That Trouble My Mind. Capitol ST 2033. OP. "East Virginia" is mentioned in our list.

Most of these records are reviewed in greater detail in Part I.

FIGURE 1 *Chords in open G tuning.*

OPEN A: A NEW TUNING FOR ADVANCED BLUES GUITARISTS

by Larry Sandberg

FIGURE 2 *Equivalent chords in open D tuning.*

Advanced folk guitarists are familiar with several tunings other than the standard classical tuning. In most alternative tunings, the strings are tuned to an open chord—that is, playing the strings without fretting will produce a simple chord. This is not the case with standard tuning.

Folk guitarists, especially blues players, are attracted to open tunings for several reasons. Virtuoso finger-style folk guitar technique often demands that the right-hand thumb play some sort of bass accompaniment to a melody line produced by the right-hand fingers on the treble strings. In certain keys, this sound can only be produced satisfactorily with great difficulty, unless the strings are retuned. Then, the slide or bottleneck guitar style can be played most efficiently in open tunings. Finally, certain combinations of notes are impossible or inconvenient in standard tuning.

The two tunings most favored by folk guitarists are open G and open D. They are also known, respectively, as the Spanish and Sevastopol tunings, named after two traditional guitar pieces, "Spanish Fandango" and "Sevastopol." (Both tunes may be heard on Elizabeth Cotten's first record, Folkways 3526; see page 13.) Both tunings are commonly used for bottleneck style.

In open G the guitar is tuned to a G chord: DGDGBD (sixth to first strings, low to high). The four highest strings are equivalent to the commonly used banjo G tuning, and the basic chords appear in Figure 1, below. Guitarists familiar with basic chord theory will note that the intervals of the open chord are 515135. The high tonic note of the key—that is, the G note, the note that is the center and foundation of all music in this key—is easily accessible to the left-hand pinky on the first string, fifth fret. It's possible to make up a solo using the full chord shapes and open strings available on the lower frets and come to rest on that high ringing note that so well defines the sound of the key.

In open D tuning, the guitar is tuned to a D chord: DADF#AD. The four highest strings are equivalent to the less commonly used banjo D tuning, and the basic chords appear in Figure 2. The intervals in the open chord are 151351. The high tonic note is accessible on the open first string, but if you really want it to ring, you have to play it an octave higher, at the first string, twelfth fret.

Now, let's take a look at some of the similarities between

FIGURE 3 *Equivalent chords in open A tuning.*

the G and D tunings. Ignore Figure 3 for the time being. When you study these shapes carefully, or analyze them theoretically in terms of the intervals, you will notice that the relationships between strings 1–5 in G tuning are equivalent to the relationships between strings 2–6 in D tuning. The interval relationships between each of those respective sets of five strings is the same in each tuning. In open G you have one additional string on the bass side of the set, in open D on the treble side. Another way of expressing this concept is to say that if you have a lick on the first and second strings in G tuning, you can play it with the identical fingering on the second and third strings in D tuning.

I arrived at open A tuning by pushing this relationship one step further: strings 1–5 in D tuning are equivalent in their internal relationships to strings 2–6 in open A (Figure 3). The strings are tuned EAC#EAE. The lick that you play on the first and second strings in G tuning, and with the same fingering moved to the second and third strings in D tuning, now appears on the third and fourth strings in A tuning. The intervals of the strings in the three tunings compared are:

open G: 515135
open D: 151351
open A: 513515

I have found A to be a very satisfying tuning for country blues playing; it generates sounds that just don't fall under the fingers in other tunings. For bottleneck playing, the large interval between the first and second strings is unusual and somewhat cumbersome. But lines and harmonies that fall on the higher strings in G and D come out on the middle strings in this tuning, leaving room—especially when you *don't* play with a bottleneck—to expand into the newly created space on the first and second strings. And a high ringing tonic note is easily accessible on the first string, fifth fret.

It would make me very happy to see people begin to use this tuning. To encourage experimentation, I'm including here some of the many possible chord shapes, along with a transcription of a fairly straightforward blues solo. When you play the solo, try not to play all the treble notes cleanly as written. Instead, use an upward brushing stroke fairly often ("season to taste")—it will provide you with harmony notes that bring out the characteristic sounds of this tuning. Where the D chord is indicated, always finger that chord as completely as possible, in order to bring out the correct harmony notes.

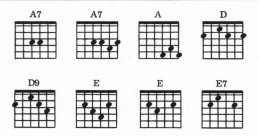

BLUES IN A

Tablature: | *or* ⊓ *or* ⊓ = 1 beat

Tuning: E A C# E A E

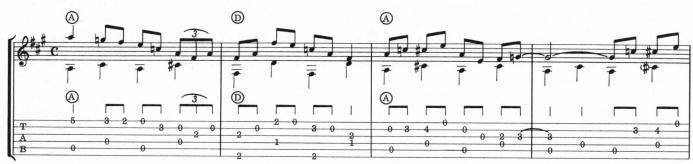

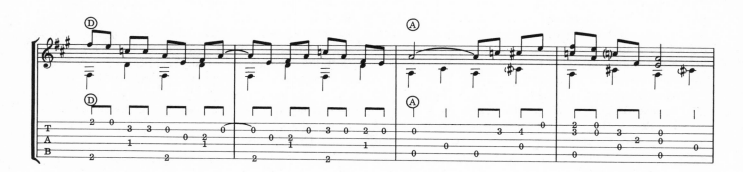

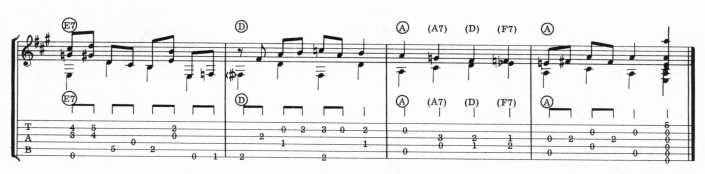

IV
HANGING OUT

Most of my hanging out was done in coffeehouses and folklore centers in New York and Philadelphia, with later, smaller doses in San Francisco and Denver. Folk music is not a very formal art, and the best music I've heard has been in people's living rooms and in informal jam sessions. Most of these sessions never happened on a stage. Talking about music doesn't necessarily help you learn about it, but it does help to clarify your own ideas about how people play or sing.

Hanging out is also a great way to meet people—musicians, fans, and just plain folks. Have fun! (—D.W.)

PROGRAMS, RESOURCES, AND ORGANIZATIONS

In addition to the national organizations listed here, there are organizations on the state level, as well as local groups that promote and share bluegrass, fiddle, and traditional music-making. An updated version of the state folklore programs list is available from the American Folklife Center, while local organizations are listed in *The Folklife Sourcebook* and *Grass Roots International Folk Resource Directory*. A *Bluegrass Directory* is published by BD Productions, Box 412, Murphys CA 95247. Experience, however, shows that addresses of local groups are extremely volatile. In New England, updated addresses are available through the annual directory of the Folk Arts Network (Box 867, Cambridge MA 02138). At this writing, the *Sing Out!* Resource Center is planning to set up an on-line directory of national scope, and issue printouts. Organizations are urged to register and update with the both the *Sing Out!* Resource Center, and the American Folklife Center. For information on ethnic organizations, consult:

American Indian Reference Book (eARTh Art, Inc., Box 2204, Kalamazoo MI 49003).

Encyclopedic Directory of Ethnic Information Sources in the U.S. (Libraries Unlimited).

Ethnic Information Sources of the U.S. (2nd ed., Gale Research Co.).

Native American Arts and Culture: A Resource Directory (Western States Arts Foundation, 141 E. Palace Ave., Santa Fe, NM 87501).

For information on archives and collections, consult:
Folklife Sourcebook (American Folklife Center).

Directory of Ethnomusicological Sound Recording Collections in the U.S. and Canada (Society for Ethnomusicology).

Directory of Oral History Collections (Oryx Press).

Directory of Popular Culture Collections (Oryx Press).

Guide to Ethnic Museums, Libraries and Archives in the United States (Program for the Study of Ethnic Publications, School of Library Science, Kent State Univ., Kent OH 44242).

Note that the former Archive of Folk Song (Library of Congress) is now called the Archive of Folk Culture.

(—L.S.)

UNITED STATES NATIONAL AND MULTI-STATE

American Folklife Center, Library of Congress, Washington DC 20540.

American Folklore Society, 1703 New Hampshire Ave. NW, Washington DC 20009.

Archive of Folk Culture: *see* American Folklife Center.

Blues Foundation, 352 Beale St., Memphis TN 38103. Trade organization for the blues music industry.

Country Dance and Song Society, 17 New South St., Northampton MA 01060.

Country Music Foundation, 4 Music Square East, Nashville TN 37203.

Folkline: Telephone hotline sponsored by the American Folklife Center and the American Folklore Society. News and professional opportunities updated Mondays. (202) 707-2000.

Hardanger Fiddle Association of America, 325 Howtz St., Duluth MN 55811.

Indian Arts and Crafts Board, Main Interior, Rm. 4004, Dept. of the Interior, Washington DC 20240.

Institute for Studies in American Music, Conservatory of Music, Brooklyn College, Brooklyn NY 11210. All facets of American music, including traditional and vernacular.

International Bluegrass Music Association, 326 St. Elizabeth St., Owensboro KY 42301. Trade organization for the professional bluegrass music industry.

International Council for Traditional Music, Music Dept., Columbia Univ., New York NY 10027.

International Society of Folk Harpers and Craftsmen, 4718 Maychelle Dr., Anaheim CA 92807.

NAIRD (National Association of Independent Record Distributors and Manufacturers), Box 568, Maple Shade NJ 08052.

National Association for the Preservation and Perpetuation of Storytelling, Box 309, Jonesborough TN 37659.

National Council for the Traditional Arts, 806 15th St. NW, Suite 400, Washington DC 20005.

National Endowment for the Arts, Folk Arts Program, 1100 Pennsylvania Ave. NW, Washington DC 20506.

National Old Time Fiddlers Association, c/o Wilson, Box 900 OSR, Kingman AZ 85018.

National Traditional Country Music Association, Box 8089, Omaha NE 68104.

North American Folk Music Association: Trade organization for the professional folk music industry. In process of formation at this writing. Contact *Sing Out!* Resource Center or California Traditional Music Society for details.

Penny Whistle Society, Box 3663, Glyndon MD 21071.

Scottish Harp Society of America, 5732 Buck Ct., Ellenwood GA 30049.

Sing Out! Resource Center, Box 5253, Bethlehem PA 18015.

Smithsonian Institution, Office of Folklife Programs, 955 L'Enfant Plaza, Suite 2600, Washington DC 20560.

Society for Ethnomusicology, Box 2984, Ann Arbor MI 48106. Consult central office for regional chapters.

World Folk Music Association, Box 4055, Washington DC 20016.

CANADA

Canadian Centre for Folk Culture Studies, National Museum of Man, Ottawa ONT K1A 0M8.

Canadian Folk Arts Council, Box 9 Station Delorimier, Montreal QUE H2N 2N6, and 1263 Adelaide St. West, Toronto ONT M5H 1Y2.

Canadian Folk Music Society, Box 4232, Calgary ALTA T2T 5N1.

Folklore Canada International, Folklore Studies Association of Canada, Dept. of Folklore, Memorial Univ. of Newfoundland, St. Johns NEWF A1C 5S7.

FOLK MUSIC CENTERS

This is a list of folk music centers in the United States and Canada, with a few more exotic addresses thrown in for spice. These centers, in one way or another, are dedicated to the propagation of folk music and the comforting of those who play.

The first folk center was founded by Israel G. Young in New York City, around 1917. It featured guitars, recorders, collections of songs, and, occasionally, concerts in the store itself. Almost every folksinger who ever made it to New York used to hang out there: but the owner tired of the constant street traffic and around 1967 moved from his original Macdougal Street location to Sixth Avenue and Third Street. In 1973 the folklore center was still in operation, but its founder, Izzy Young, had moved to Stockholm, Sweden, and opened a folklore center there.

We've compiled this list from personal experience, from ads in folk and country magazines, and with the aid of friends. Since some of the information is necessarily secondhand, we can't recommend outright every aspect of every center. We suggest you do your own checking, then let us know. If you're looking for a five-string banjo teacher or a mandolin instructional book or somebody to repair your guitar, one of these centers would be a good place to start your search.

And if you're traveling cross-country, over the endless network of interstates, centers may provide you with a pleasant drop-in spot to break the highway monotony. We have not listed folk clubs or coffeehouses because they open and close too frequently. Usually the people working in folklore centers are a good source for this information.

(—D.W.)

FOLK MUSIC CENTERS AND MUSIC STORES

Stores marked with * are known to print mail-order catalogs

UNITED STATES

ALABAMA

Golden Spring Music, 1306 Greenbrier Rd., Anniston, AL 36201

Guitar Shoppe, 113 Mitcham Ave., Auburn, AL 36830

Fretted Instruments, 2906 Linden Ave., Birmingham, AL 35209

Fret Shop, 502 Pratt Ave. NE, Huntsville, AL 35801

The Guitar Shop, 1108 7th Ave., Tuscaloosa, AL 35401

ALASKA

Down Home Guitar, 2917 Spenard Rd., Anchorage, AK 99503

Old Time Music Co., Box 4-2294, Elmendorf Air Force Base, AK 99506

M&M Music, Box 32793, Juneau, AK 99803

ARIZONA

Vallee Guitars, 2630 W. Baseline Rd., Mesa, AZ 85202

The Village Luthier, 13007, 36th Dr., Phoenix, AZ 85023

Beck Fretted Instruments, 807 S. Ash Ave., Tempe, AZ 85281

Folk Shop, 415 N. 4th Ave., Tucson, AZ 85705

ARKANSAS

Eureka String Shoppe, 10 Mountain, Eureka Spring, AR 72632

Ronnie's Steel Guitar, 881 Park Ave., Hot Springs, AR 71901

CALIFORNIA

Lundberg Fretted Instruments, 2126 Dwight Way, Berkeley, CA 94704

The Fifth String, 3051 Adeline, Berkeley, CA 94703

Marc Silber, Stefany Reich-Silber, Box 9663, Berkeley, CA 94709 (mail order only)*

Holcomb's Banjo & Guitar, 548 E. Campbell Ave., Campbell, CA 95008

Carmel Music Co., Dolores & 5th, Carmel, CA 93921

Folk Music Center, 220 Yale Ave., Claremont, CA 91711

Hobgoblin Music, 1655 Mission Rd., Colma, CA 94014

The Fret House, 309 N. Citrus, Covina, CA 91723

Blue Ridge Music, 509 First, Encinitas, CA 92024

Fiddles & Camera, Fort Bragg, CA 95437

Foggy Mountain Music, 104 W. Main St., Grass Valley, CA 95945

A B Music Studios, 19171 Magnolia St. 10, Huntington Beach, CA 92646

The Guitar Shoppe, 1027 N. Coast Highway, Laguna Beach, CA 92651

McCabe's Guitar Shop, 4209 E. Anaheim, Long Beach, CA 90804

Betnun Music, 403 N. Larchmont, Los Angeles, CA 90004

Westwood Musical Inst., 2301 Purdue Ave., Los Angeles, CA 90064

Shade Tree, 28722 Marguerite Pkwy., Mission Viejo, CA 92692

Bluegrass Music Shoppe, 514 McHenry Blvd., Modesto, CA 95354

South Seas Guitar, 247 Pearl St., Monterey, CA 93940

Acoustic Guitar, 127 Sheridan Rd., Oakland, CA 94618

Psaltery Music, 944 N. Tustin, Orange, CA 92667

Draper's Music Center, 330 California Ave., Palo Alto, CA 94306

Gryphon Stringed Inst., 211 Lambert, Palo Alto, CA 94306

Norman's Rare Guitars, 6753 Tampa, Reseda, CA 91335

Fifth String, 5522 H, Sacramento, CA 95819

Tiny Moore Music Center, 1165 48th St., Sacramento, CA 95819

Amazing Grace Music, 111 Redhill Ave., San Anselmo, CA 94960

Blue Guitar Workshop, 1020 Garnet Ave., San Diego, CA 92109

Freedom Guitar, 1053 8th Ave., San Diego, CA 92101

The Fifth String, 5957 Geary Blvd., San Francisco, CA 94121

Premier Music Co., 4102 Vachell Ln., San Luis Obispo, CA 93401

Jensen Music, 2830-F De La Vina, Santa Barbara, CA 93105

Union Grove Music, 1013 Pacific Ave., Santa Cruz, CA 95060

McCabe's Guitar Shop, 3101 Pico, Santa Monica, CA 90405

Pick 'N' Grin, Box 2186, Truckee, CA 93734

Countrywood Music, 2058 Treat Blvd., Walnut Creek, CA 94598

COLORADO

Acoustic Music Revival, 1934 S. Broadway, Denver, CO 80210

Great Divide Music, 111 S. Monarch, Aspen, CO 81611

The Music Store, 1535 Pearl St., Boulder, CO 80302

H.B. Woodsongs, 1605 Pearl St., Boulder, CO 80302

Folklore Center of Colorado Springs, 330 N. Tejon, Colorado Springs, CO 80903

Folk Source (Zither Shop), 525 E. Ohio, Denver, CO 80209
Back Porch Music, 511 Main St., Grand Junction, CO 81501
Wildwood Music, 136 W. Tomich Ave., Gunnison, CO 81230
Rockley Music, 8555 W. Colfax, Lakewood, CO 80215
Virgil Reed Music, 323 Main St., Wray, CO 80758

CONNECTICUT

Melody Music Co., 104 Asylum St., Hartford, CT 06103
Select Guitars, Inc., 43 Wall St., Norwalk, CT 06850
Country Folk Music Center, Sharon Mountain, Sharon, CT 06069
Guitar Workshop, 1074 Storrs Rd., Rte. 195, Storrs, CT 06268
The Bold Strummer Ltd., 1 Webb Rd., Westport, CT 06880*

DELAWARE

Vogel Custom Guitars, Birdhaven Rd., Millville, DE 19667

DISTRICT OF COLUMBIA

Southworth Guitars, 4816 MacArthur Blvd. NW, Washington, DC
The Guitar Shop, 1216 Connecticut Ave. NW, Washington, DC
20036

FLORIDA

F-Sharp Music, Inc., 10361 W. Sample Rd., Coral Springs, FL
33065
Metro Music, 9068 St. RD 84, Ruidge Plaza, Davie, FL 33224
Bluegrass Central, 2088 Central Ave., Fort Myers, FL 33901
Sabine Music, 305 Northwest 13th, Gainesville, FL 32601
The Banjo Shop, 5653 Johnston St., Hollywood, FL 33021
Guitar Czar, 6254 Powers Ave., Jacksonville, FL 32217
Ed's Guitars, 4047 SW 96 Ave., Miami, FL 33165
Fret Factory Discount Music, 133 Mill Spring Pl., Ormond Beach,
FL 32074
Old Dixie Pickers, Box 31234, Palm Beach Gardens, FL 33418
Blount's Music, 2025 Fernway St., Sebring, FL 33872
Bluegrass Parlor, 4810 E. Busch Blvd., Tampa, FL 33617
Don's Bluegrass Music, 6809 N. Gunlock, Tampa, FL 33614

GEORGIA

Atlanta Guitar Center, 3130 Make Dr. NE, Atlanta, GA 30305
Jay's Music Center, Inc., 927 Broad St., Augusta, GA 30901
Dulcimer Shoppe, The River, Helen, GA 30545

HAWAII

The Music Exchange, 762 Kandelehua, Hilo, HI 96720

IDAHO

Third Fret, 116 S. Main, Hailey, ID 83333
Chesbro Music Co., 327 Broadway, Idaho Falls, ID 83402
Guitars' Friend, 309 S. Main St., Moscow, ID 83843
Vintage Guitars, 316 E. 5th Ave., Post Falls, ID 83854

ILLINOIS

Golden Frets, 715 S. Illinois St., Carbondale, IL 62901
Rosewood Guitars, 313 E. Green, Champaign, IL 61820
Different Strummer, 909 W. Armitage, Chicago, IL 60614
Hogeye Music, 1920 Central St., Evanston, IL 60201
Jack Moore Guitar, 108 S. Stone, La Grange, IL 60525
Village School of Folk Music, 545 N. Milwaukee Ave., Liber-
tyville, IL 60048

Cisco's Music, 1704 Dunray, Normal, IL 61761
Hank's Country Store, 3025 Kilburn, Rockford, IL 61103
Herb Roth Guitars, 3313 Lee St., Skokie, IL 60076

INDIANA

Bluegrass Record Shop, 1250 Highway 31N, Austin, IN 47102
C&K Bluegrass, 447 E. Line, Geneva, IN 46740
Guitar Shop, 911 Broad Ripple Ave., Indianapolis, IN 46220
Mountain Made Music, Box 816, Nashville, IN 47448

IOWA

Ye Olde Guitar Shoppe, 6806 Douglas Ave., Des Moines, IA
50322
Guitar Gallery, 527 S. Gilbert St., Iowa City, IA 52240
Ed's Fretted Instrument, 206 Austin Ave., Maquoketa, IA 52060

KANSAS

Acoustic Stringed Inst., 106 E. Sherman, Hutchinson, KS 67501
Richardson Music, 18 E. 9th St., Lawrence, KS 66044
Banjo Fiddle, Etc., S. George Washington Blvd., Wichita, KS
67218
E.M. Shorts Guitars, 2525 E. Douglas, Wichita, KS 67211

KENTUCKY

Bluegrass Music Shop & Co., 302 3rd St., Carrollton, KY 41008
Flat Pickers Paradise, 323 E.K. Rd., Greenup, KY 41144
Doo Wop Ent. Inc., 1587 Bandstown Rd., Louisville, KY 40205
Pick 'N' Grin, 107 N. 4th, Paducah, KY 42002
Pro Frets Music, 815 N. Wilson, Radcliff, KY 40160

LOUISIANA

Tom's Guitar Repair, 10808 Greenwell Springs, RD2, Baton
Rouge, LA 70814
Collingsworth Guitar Service, 413 W. 77th St., Shreveport, LA
71106

MAINE

Down Home Music Shop, 43 Main, Fairfield, ME 04937
Snee Music, 175 Main, Norway, ME 04268
Buckdancer's Choice Co., 10 Longfellow Sq., Portland, ME 04101

MARYLAND

Appalachian Bluegrass, 643 Frederick Rd., Baltimore, MD 21228
Boe's Strings, Inc., 26 S. Market St., Frederick, MD 21701
Veneman Music Co., 1150 Rockville Pike, Rockville, MD 20852
House of Musical Traditions, 7040 Carroll Ave., Takoma Park, MD
20912*
Washington Music Center, 11151 Viers Mill Rd., Wheaton, MD
20902

MASSACHUSETTS

Acton Music Center, 140 Main, Acton, MA 01720
Fretted Inst. Workshop, 49 S. Pleasant St., Amherst, MA 01810
Wood & String Music Ctr., 493 Massachusetts Ave., Arlington, MA
02174
E.U. Wurlitzer Inc., 360 Newbury St., Boston, MA 02115
Jones Vintage & Custom Guitar, 295 Huntington Ave., Ste. 304,
Boston, MA 02115

Briggs & Briggs, Inc., 1270 Massachusetts Ave., Cambridge, MA 02138

Music Emporium, Inc., 2018 Massachusetts Ave., Cambridge, MA 02140

Sandy's Music, 896 A Massachusetts Ave., Cambridge, MA 02139

Strings Attached Music Center, 12 Federal St., The Tannery, Newburyport, MA 01950

Fretworks, 74 Lakewood St., Worcester, MA 01603

MICHIGAN

Herb David Guitar Shop, 302 E. Liberty, Ann Arbor, MI 48104

Fiddler's Music Co., 16209 Mack Ave., Detroit, ME 48224

Elderly Instruments, 1100 N. Washington, Lansing, MI 48906

Gitfiddler Music, 302 E. Main, Northville, MI 48167

Rochester Folk Workshop, 420 East St., Rochester, MI 48063

Pick 'N' Strum, 30081 Greenfield, Southfield, MI 48076

Northern Acoustic Instruments, 1319 Airport Rd. W., Traverse City, MI 49684

Home Grown Music, 117 S. Kalamazoo, White Pigeon, MI 49099

MINNESOTA

Don's Guitar Repair, 501 Blue Earth St., Mankato, MN 56001

Hoffman Guitars, 2219 Franklin Ave. E., Minneapolis, MN 55404

Schmitt Music Center, 12343 Wayzata Blvd., Minnetonka, MN 55343

Homestead Pickin' Parlor, 6625 Penn Ave. S., Richfield, MN 55423

Cadenza Music Center, 149 N. Snelling, St. Paul, MN 55104

MISSOURI

Mountain Music Shop, 109 N. Second, Branson, MO 65616

The Blue Guitar, 101 Orr St., Columbia, MO 65201

George's Music, 8101 N. Oak St., Trafficway, Kansas City, MO 64118

Luyben Music, 4318 Main, Kansas City, MO 64111

Fazio's Frets & Friends, 1034 Manchester Rd., Manchester, MO 63011

Brentwood Music Co., 2670 S. Glenstone, Springfield, MO 65804

St. Charles Guitar, 1026 1st Capitol Dr., St. Charles, MO 63301

MONTANA

Bitterroot Folklore Center, 4378 Last Chance Gulch, Helena, MT 59601

Bitterroot Music, 529 S. Higgins St., Missoula, MT 59801

NEBRASKA

Yanda's Music, 2200 Central Ave., Kearney, NE 66847

Dale London, 2639-1/2 N. 48th St., Lincoln, NE 68504

Browns' Music, 7351 Pacific St., Omaha, NE 68114

NEVADA

Bizarre Guitar, 2677 Oddie Blvd., Reno, NV 89512

NEW HAMPSHIRE

Vintage Fret Shop, 20 Riverside, Ashland, NJ 03217*

Fiddler's Choice Music, 41 E. Main St., Jaffrey, NM 03452

Blue Mountain Guitar Center, 2 Colonial Plaza, W. Lebanon, NH 03784

NEW JERSEY

Nolde's Music Box, Hunterdon Shopping Center, Flemington, NJ 08822

Caizzo Music, 181 South St., Freehold, NJ 07728

Guitar Emporium, 104 Brighton Ave., Long Branch, NJ 07740

Guitar Trader, 8 Broad St., Red Bank, NJ 07701

Last Chance Used Guitars, 361 Westfield Ave., Roselle Park, NJ 07208

NEW MEXICO

Candyman, 851 St. Michael, Santa Fe, NM 87501

NEW YORK

Lark St. Music, 221 Lark St., Albany, NY 12210*

Roxy's Music Store, Genesee County Mall, Batavia, NY 14020

The String Shop, 187 Norwalk Ave., Buffalo, NY 14214

Buck Dancer's Choice, 47 Main, Canton, NY 13617

Fret Shop, 1 Bartlett Ave., Cortland, NY 13045

Banjo Mart, 29 Mechanic, Hoosick Falls, NY 12090

Ithaca Guitar Works, 215 N. Cayuga St., Ithaca, NY 14850

Matt Umanov Guitars, 273 Bleecker St., New York, NY 10014

Scognetti Vintage Instruments, 138 Willowpond Way, Penfield, NY 14526

Fretted Instruments, 424 Clay Ave., Rochester, NY 14613

Guitar Workshop, 1579 Northern Blvd., Roslyn, NY, 11576

Mandolin Brothers, 629 Forest Ave., Staten Island, NY 10310*

Tom Hosmer String Instruments, 120 Julian Pl., Syracuse, NY 13210

Folkscraft Instruments, Webcetuck Craft Village, Wingdale, NY 12594

NORTH CAROLINA

Bluegrass Center, 598 Hendersonville Rd., Asheville, NC 28803

Green River Dulcimers, 31 Carolina Lane, Asheville, NC 28801

Dulcimer Shop, Main St., Blowing Rock, NC 28605

Pickin' Loft, 22-1/2 Park St., Canton, NC 28716

Harry and Jeanie West, 3815 Tremont Ave., Durham, NC 27705*

Reliable Music Co., 1001 S. Independence, Charlotte , NC 28202

David Shepherd Instrument Repairs, 1820 Spring Garden St., Greensboro, NC 27403

Ray's Music, Norwood St., Lenoir, NC 28645

Hoffman Stringed Instruments, 2660 Yonkers Rd., Raleigh, NC 27604

NORTH DAKOTA

Guitarland, 210 E. Main, Bismarck, ND 58501

OHIO

Akron Music Center, Inc., 270 S. Main St., Akron, OH 44308

Pavlov Music Center, Inc., 632 Wheeling Ave., Cambridge, OH 43725

Famous Old Time Music, 6101 Montgomery Rd., Cincinnati, OH 45213

Goose Acres Folk Music, 2175 Cornell Rd., Cleveland, OH 44106

Bluegrass Musicians Supply, 1370 S. High St., Columbus, OH 43207

Columbus Folk Music, 4760 N. High St., Columbus, OH 43214

Wildwood Stringed Instruments, 672 N. White Woman St., Coshocton, OH 43812

Drinking Gourd, 4944 Northcutt Pl., Dayton, OH 45415

Blue Grass Corner, 1058 Clark, Holland, OH 43528

Smart's Music Store, 375 Marion Ave., Mansfield, OH 44490

Durdel's Music, 2628 W. Central, Toledo, OH 43606

OKLAHOMA

Guitars & Such, 100 S. Mississippi Ave., Ada, OK 74820

Driver Music, 6600 NW. 39th Expy., Bethany, OK 73008

Peaches Music, 318 W. Main, Norman, OK 73069

Medium Rare Guitars, 1305 S. Peoria, Tulsa, OK 74120*

OREGON

Cripple Creek Music Co., 40 N. Main, Ashland, OR 97520

Balladeer Music, 296 E. 5th, Eugene, OR 97401

Mountain Music, 111 N. Central Ave., Medford, OR 97501

Artichoke Music, 3522 SE. Hawthorne, Portland, OR 97214

Pioneer Music, 505 SW. 3rd, Portland, OR 97204

PENNSYLVANIA

Medley Music Corp. 1031-43 Lancaster Ave., Bryn Mawr, PA 19010

Pickers' Delight Music Store, 412 Chestnut St., Emmaus, PA 19049

MacLaren Music, 1024 Serrill Ave., Fairless Hills, PA 19030

Troubadour Music, Valley Forge Center, King of Prussia, PA 19406

Bucks County Folk Shop, 40 Sand Rd., New Britain, PA 18901*

Barber's Bluegrass & Country Music, RD1, New Freedom, PA 17349

Flop-Eared Muse, 759 S. 4th St., Philadelphia, PA 19147

Vintage Instruments, 1529 Pine St., Philadelphia, PA 19102

Specialty Guitar Shop, 3049 W. Liberty Ave., Pittsburgh, PA 15216

RHODE ISLAND

Silva's Guitar & Banjo, 4 Goulart Ave., Bristol, RI 02809

Vintage Guitars, 2 Ella Terrace, Newport, RI 02840

Providence Guitar, 355 S. Main St., Providence, RI 02903

Music Man, 87 Tillinghast Ave., W. Warwick, RI 02893

SOUTH CAROLINA

Banjo Cason Music Co., 12 Chesterfield Highway, Cheraw, SC 29520

Fifth String Music Studio, 2320 E. North St., Greenville, SC 29607

Low Country Music, 100 N. Highway 52, Moncks Corner, SC 29461

Jerry Tillman Music, 566 Anderson Rd., Rock Hill, SC 29730

Jim Smoak Music, 890 Bacons Bridge Rd., Summerville, SC 29483

TENNESSEE

Mountain Muisc Guitar Shop, Rt. 1, Bear Creek Rd., Crossville, TN 38555

Rose Guitar Co., 1080 W. Main, Hendersonville, TN 37075

Blaylock Music Co., 7710 Hixson Pike, Hixson, TN 37343

Pick 'N' Grin, 5802 Kingston Pk., Knoxville, TN 37919

Shot Jackson's Guitar & Service Center, 105 Westchester Ct., Madison, TN 37115

Music Town, 4844 Summer Ave., Memphis, TN 38122

McPeak's Unique Instrumments, Guill Rd., Rt. 6, Mt. Juliet, TN 37122

Cotton Music Center, 1815 21st Ave. S., Nashville, TN 37212

Gruhn Guitars, 410 Broadway, Nashville, TN 37203*

Get-Tar Shop, 718 Parkway, Sevierville, TN 37862

TEXAS

Guitar Resurrection, 3004 Guadalupe St., Austin, TX 78705

Guitar Banjo Studio, 4355 Calder, Beaumont, TX 77704

Harvey's Guitar Shop, 11389 Harry Hines Blvd., Dallas, TX 75229

Frets & Strings, 4451 Lovers Lane, Dallas, TX 75225

Herb Remington's Pedal Steel Guitar Gallery, 2101 Jean, Houston, TX 77023

Rockin' Robin, 3619 S. Shepherd, Houston, TX 77098

Old Time String Shop, 216 E. Pillar, Nacogdoches, TX 75961

Guitar Stringer's Music Store, 1406 Shaver, Pasadena, TX 77502

UTAH

The Great Salt Lake Guitars, 362 W. Center St., Provo, UT 84601

Acoustic Music, 857 East 400 South, Salt Lake City, UT 84102

Intermountain Guitar & Banjo, 712 East First South, Salt Lake City, UT 84117 *

VERMONT

Maple Leaf Music Co., 49 Elliot, Brattleboro, VT 05301

VIRGINIA

Plucked String, Box 11125, Arlington, VA 22210

Pickers Supply, 902 Caroline St., Fredericksburg, VA 22401

Old Time Music Exchange, RD 2, Box 447, Halifax, VA 24558

Mountain Music, RD 1, Box 237, Lyndhurst, VA 22952

Ramblin' Conrad's Guitar, 871 N. Military Highway, Norfolk, VA 23502

Billy Cooper's Steel Guitar Shop, Rt. 2, Box 525, Orange, VA 22960

Don Warner Music, 401 S. Libbie, Richmond, VA 23226

The Fret Mill, 23 E. Salem Ave., Roanoke, VA 24011

Venemman Music, 6319 Amherst NE, Springfield, VA 22150

WASHINGTON

Ray's Fiddle Shop, 2131 Lummi Shore Rd., Bellingham, WA 98225

The Folk Store, 5238 University Way NE, Seattle, WA 98105

Lundin's Sound Hole, N. 4326 Maringo Dr., Spokane, WA 99212

Monte Vista Guitar Shop, 8328 S. Tacoma Way, Tacoma, WA 98499

WEST VIRGINIA

A Different Strummer, 150 Pleasant St., Morgantown, WV 26505

Fret 'N' Fiddle, 807 Pennsylvania Ave., St. Albans, WV 25177

WISCONSIN

Freelance Guitars, 181 E. Henry Clay Ave., Milwaukee, WI 53217

Dan's Pick-A-Way, 1011 Milwaukee Ave., S. Milwaukee, WI 53176

WYOMING

Snake River Guitar Works, 2300 Teton Village Dr., Jackson, WY 83001

CANADA

BRITISH COLUMBIA

Mainly Music, 1224 Granville St., Vancouver, BC V6Z 1M6
Rufus' Guitar Shop, 2621 Alma, Vancouver, BC V6R 3S1
West Coast Guitar Center, 1723 W. 4th, Vancouver, BC V6J 1M2
Old Town Strings (Folklore Center), 539 Pandora Ave., Victoria, BC V8W 1N5*

MANITOBA

Home-Made Music, 218 Osborne St. S., Winnipeg, Manitoba R3L 1Z3

NOVA SCOTIA

Halifax Folklore Center, 1528 Brunswick, Halifax, NS B3J 2G2

ONTARIO

Ottawa Folklore Center, 744 Brunson Ave., Ottawa, Ontario K1S 4G1
Lado Musical, 689 Wardne, Unit 6, Toronto, Ontario M1L 3Z5
Ring Music, 90 Harbrod St., Toronto, Ontario M5S 1G4
The Twelfth Fret, 920 Kingston Rd., Toronto, Ontario M4E 1S5

QUEBEC

Harmonilab, Inc., 4592 St. Andre, Montreal, Quebec H2J 2Z8

AROUND THE WORLD

There are many active folk stores in the United Kingdom. A good place to start is at Cecil Sharp House, 2 Regents Park Rd., London NW1 7AY, England. Israel G. Young, who started the first American folk shop now has Folklore Centrum, located at Wollmar Yxkullsgatan 2, 116 50, Stockholm, Sweden.

PERIODICALS

The folk music community is served by a variety of periodicals: popular and special-interest magazines as well as bulletins, newsletters, and scholarly journals issued by clubs, scholarly societies, and other organizations.

At this writing, the best complete source for folklife periodical information is the American Folklife Center's *Folklife Sourcebook.* (The standard library periodical and serial publication guides are quite inadequate in this respect.) For updates, consult the *Sing Out!* Resource Center. The short list below will get you started along the path to further knowledge. Supplement these periodicals with some of the record release newsletters mentioned in the MAIL ORDER RECORD HOUSES listings in this book's *Listening* section, and you'll stay well on top of things.

(—L.S.)

GENERAL

FOLK ROOTS Box 73, Farnham, Surrey GU9 7UN, England. Mostly about the British scene, but with plenty of interest in (and for) the U.S folk scene. Writing runs form amateurish to lively and intelligent; varied points of view abound and there is esthetic critique and social debate. Also good, of course, for events and resources in Great Britain.

SING OUT! Box 5253, Bethlehem PA 18015. The quarterly *Sing Out!* maintains its long-standing position as voice of the urban folk song movement, with columns, reviews, news, and new songs—especially topical songs—in each issue. *Sing Out!* often reflects its origin in the politics of the People's Songs movement of the fifties; whether you share them or not, you'll be best informed about the urban folk scene by reading *Sing Out!*

SPECIALIZED

ACOUSTIC GUITAR Box 376, Swarthmore, PA 19081. Quarterly; publication scheduled for 1990.

AUTOHARP QUARTERLY Lumberjack Productions, Box A, Newport PA 17074.

AUTOHARPAHOLIC Box 504, Brisbane CA 94005.

BANJO NEWSLETTER Box 364, Greensboro MD 21639. Monthly filled with information for 5-string, mostly bluegrass, banjo players.

BLUEGRASS UNLIMITED Box 111, Broad Run VA 22014. Monthly glossy, features, interviews, lots of events listings.

CADENCE Cadence Bldg., Redwood NY 13679. A jazz magazine, but some blues lovers will want it too. Good monthly features.

COME-ALL-YE Legacy Books, Box 494, Hatboro PA 19040. Reviews newly-published books in all areas of folklife. A valuable resource for folklorists, scholars, librarians.

CONCERTINA AND SQUEEZEBOX Route 1, Box 718, White Stone VA 22578.

DULCIMER PLAYERS NEWS Box 2164, Winchester VA 22601.

NA FEADANAIGH: THE WHISTLE PLAYERS Box 3663, Glyndon MD 21071.

FOLK HARP JOURNAL 31 W. Cañon Perdido, Santa Barbara CA 93101.

FOLK TRADE NEWS Box M-588, Hoboken NJ 07030. Industry newsletter; trends, chat, etc. Publication planned to resume fall, 1989.

LIVING BLUES Center for the Study of Southern Culture, University MS 38677. Current blues, reviews, etc. Bi-monthly.

MANDOCRUCIAN'S DIGEST, Box 2352, Clarksburg WV 26301. Mandolin quarterly: interviews, music, columns, etc.

OLD-TIME HERALD Box 1362, Galax VA 24333. Quarterly for fans and players of old-time music. Historical and contemporary.

REJOICE! Center for the Study of Southern Culture, University MS 38677. Non-sectarian quarterly on all aspects of gospel music.

FILMS & VIDEO TAPES

Shortly after our book was originally published, the Center for Southern Folklore published *American Folklore Films and Videotapes, An Index.* Since this is a 338-page book, I see no point in trying to publish a digest of it. It too is in need of substantial revision, but anyone looking for information on films or videotapes would do well to consult this invaluable work, put together by William Ferris and Judy Peiser. A new directory of videos is scheduled at this writing.

(— D.W.)

YOU HAVE TO PLAY WHO YOU ARE: THE BLUES IN WEST MEMPHIS

As dictated by Jerry Ricks to Dick Weissman

In the winter of 1969–70, I went on a collecting trip in Arkansas for the Smithsonian Institution. With me were Ralph Rinzler, the director of the Performing Arts Division of the Smithsonian, and Mac McCormick, a playwright and blues historian from Houston, Texas. The purpose of the trip was to find folk musicians and craftsmen who would appear at the summer folk life festival. This is an annual festival sponsored by the Smithsonian and held near Washington, D.C. The emphasis is on presenting unique and little-known performers and craftsmen who represent something indigenous to a specific geographical area. The festival includes music, crafts, and cooking; organized under the heading of what scholars call folk life.

Our trip started out in the office of the governor of Arkansas, where we met with the lieutenant governor, the director of the Arkansas Division of Performing Arts, and Jimmy Driftwood. Driftwood is a well-known folk singer and composer (he wrote "The Battle of New Orleans"), and was parks commissioner of Arkansas at that time. They suggested areas of the state in which we might concentrate our efforts, and areas where we would not be welcome, since we were an interracial group. Driftwood started us out in the Ozarks, where he introduced us to a number of interesting musicians.

In this particular article, I am going to tell about our experiences with black musicians. After we finished our work in the Ozarks, Ralph Rinzler left us and went to Fayetteville in the northwestern part of the state. Mac and I went down to the eastern part of the state, where the Arkansas portion of the Mississippi River delta is found.

In De Witt, Arkansas, southwest of Helena, we saw a man with a guitar sitting on his front porch. As we walked up, he was making up a song about Mac and me—the two guys in the red Maverick. It was the most rural music I had ever heard; there was no apparent structure. Sometimes the man would pick; other times he played rhythmic strumming patterns; he seemed to change key aimlessly. Nothing in my experience enabled me to comprehend what was happening. Was he good? Could he play? Was he keeping time? I really didn't know. He invited us to come into the house. It was a slave quarters, built on stilts, with one bed inside. The man's wife was drunk and wanted to take off her clothes. The kids asked if I was the man from "The Mod Squad" TV show (Clarence Williams III). They had probably never seen a black man with bushy hair in person.

Our host hadn't heard of Washington, D.C.; he thought the United States capital was Little Rock, and the president was Roosevelt. I guess Roosevelt was the last president with whom he'd had any feeling of personal contact; maybe he'd been on the WPA or something. When we asked for the man's address, he told us he didn't know. He never needed to use it; he got his mail at the general store.

Meeting people under those circumstances was strange. Mac is a white southerner; I'm black, from Philadelphia. We'd knock on people's doors about the time they'd get home from work—5:30 or 6:00 in the evening. It would be getting dark, and they'd look out and see first this "Mod-Squad" type of black man, and then a southern Cracker, wearing a cowboy hat, standing behind me. Most of these people had never heard of folklore, collecting, or the Smithsonian Institution. If they had any reaction at all when we explained why we were there, it was either suspicion or a fantasy about going to Washington, making records, and becoming superstars. Either way I had trouble handling the scene, because it seemed to me we were bringing something into these people's lives that was irrelevant to anything they could relate to or understand. We tape-recorded the performances, but the tapes were simply for documentation; they were to be stored in the Smithsonian vaults, not issued as records.

In Pine Bluff, Arkansas, we heard about a guitar player called Hairlong. Mac and I found him near one of the levees. His real name was James Lee, and he played and sang some beautiful songs which he had written himself. Hairlong played bottleneck guitar, and playing with him was a man named Ellis Davis, a cripple with webbed hands. Ellis played with a knife in his left hand, and somehow he managed to strum with his right hand. It was incredible music. Taping this kind of music was tricky, because we wanted to mike the singers and players correctly, but we didn't want to call their attention too closely to the tape and thus lose the spontaneity of the performances.

Our next stop was Helena, Arkansas, the hometown of the late legendary bluesman Sonny Boy Williamson. We went to a "soda fountain," where an old lady was serving up 3.2 beer, the only legal kind in Arkansas. I asked her about bluesmen, and she said, "What do you know about blues, young as you are?" She sent us on to the King Biscuit Company, right down the street. Sonny Boy used to do a radio show for them, advertising the product. There were flour sacks with pictures of Sonny Boy still on them. The people at King Biscuit were very unfriendly; they didn't dig my being with Mac. We took some pictures and left as soon as we could. Then we were able to locate Sonny Boy's old band, and the members invited us to hear them play at a club in West Memphis, Arkansas.

West Memphis is across the Mississippi River from Memphis. It's a small, rural town with a business section just about a block long. Many of the other streets aren't paved. Sonny Boy's old band played every Friday and Saturday night at the Broadway Club on Eighth Street. Mac didn't go, because things were tense at the time, and he was afraid. I couldn't blame him. I'd felt some of the same tensions in the white areas of Arkansas, when we found ourselves unknowingly integrating restaurants or hotels.

*King Biscuit Time:
Sonny Boy Williamson
No. 2*

The band started playing about 10:00. The room it played in was upstairs from another "soda fountain." Joe Willie Wilkins was the guitarist. He played electric guitar with his bare fingers in the delta blues style, using the electricity only so he could play louder. There was a young harmonica player, wearing a full-length leather coat, a suit, a big hat, and sunglasses. I can still see that leather coat. There was also an electric bass player and a drummer, who had one snare drum and one cymbal.

The band played tunes I'd never heard before, and everyone danced. Joe Wilkins said he had to go to the bathroom, and he asked if I'd play a few tunes. I knew he just wanted to hear me play, and I was really nervous. I felt like someone from another world, an urban, educated, sophisticated black man playing in a down-home rural blues joint in West Memphis, Arkansas. A band member said, "Let's play a jump." I didn't even know what that meant. It was only an up-tempo or boogie number. They liked my playing, but I felt out of place, even though I had played with Son House, John Hurt, and plenty of other rural musicians.

But I had always played the secondary parts, while Hurt or House had taken the leads. Here I was the dominant instrument, and I didn't know what to do.

Later I talked to Joe Willie about it. He said, "It was okay; it was good. You have to play who you are, and that's what you did." For the first time, I realized what it means to express yourself in playing. It doesn't matter who you are, or where you come from. Just be yourself.

Joe Willie told me something about himself. He said he'd been to Chicago, but he didn't care for it. Too much rock-and-roll. Around 11:30, after the end of the set, he told me I'd better go. Late at night there would probably be fighting, and I was a stranger, so I wouldn't be granted the musicians' traditional immunity from attack. He called me a cab, and I went back to the hotel.

I don't know which of our informants went to Washington to play at the festival. Shortly after I left Arkansas, I went to Europe, and stayed there for two years. I can still remember Joe Willie Wilkins telling me, "You have to play who you are."

AFTERWORD

Re-doing a book that is thirteen years old is an interesting and somewhat humbling experience. So many of the things we reviewed fit into more than one category. Is a Canadian children's book for guitar best classified under Canada, children, or guitar?

Doing it again re-introduced many of these problems for us, and I suppose for our readers as well. Special thanks go to Dick Burns and Lillian Krelove of Legacy Books for providing us with their catalogs and for enabling me to go through their frighteningly extensive collection of books on folklore and folksong.

The music scene today is more varied and more complex than it was in 1976. On the one hand, we have seen an incredible rise of recording technology, and the introduction of such electronic devices as drum machines, sampling devices, synthesizers of every conceivable sort, etc. At the same time we have observed artists self-producing cassettes by the hundreds, working out of basement studios. If you go to a well-stocked record store in a major city, or if you receive any of the quality mail order catalogs, the music of the entire world is literally at your fingertips. It's a long ways from the days when I used to anxiously await the introduction of a new Pete Seeger 10-inch LP. I don't know whether things are better, but I do believe that there will always be room for talented artists and audiences that take the time to seek out new and unusual music. May both groups thrive!

(— D.W.)

GLOSSARY

This glossary does not define certain terms that are defined elsewhere in the book at greater length than could be devoted to them here. If you do not find a word you want here, consult the index, which will refer you to the page where the word is defined. Some terms are defined only insofar as they apply to folk music, and not to other types of music.

(—L.S.)

ACOUSTIC Nonelectric; not using electrical amplification.

AIR SHOT A recording of a radio broadcast.

ANTIPHONY A musical form in which the melody is stated by alternating voices, so that there is a sense that they answer each other.

ARPEGGIO The notes of a chord sounded consecutively.

ARRANGEMENT The addition of anything to a piece of music beyond the original melody, or the adaptation of a piece of music from one style or medium to another.

ART SONG Songs written in the European classical tradition; a major composer is Franz Schubert. *See* song form.

BALLAD A song that tells a story.

BACKBEAT An exceptionally strong syncopated accent placed on the the second and fourth beats of each measure in 4/4 time, or on the second beat in 2/4 time.

BAR: (1) Barre, q.v.; (2) steel, q.v.

BARRE (or BAR): The placing of one finger across more than one string.

BARRELHOUSE A term used loosely to describe various blues piano styles; often synonymous with "boogie," but sometimes used even of ragtime.

BEL CANTO The vocal style particularly characteristic of Italian opera; sometimes used loosely to describe the trained vocal style of European art music in general.

BLUES SCALE AND BLUE NOTES Blues scale can refer to any of the various scales used in blues, but most often it refers to a ten-tone scale consisting of a diatonic major scale to which three extra degrees are added: a flatted third, a flatted fifth (especially in modern usage), and a flatted seventh. Any or all of these ten tones may be used, according to the preference of the individual performer or style in which he works, and according to the tonal center of the part of the harmonic structure over which the scale is being applied. For example, the flatted third and seventh may be substituted for the major third and seventh throughout; or the major seventh may be retained over the dominant seventh chord; or the major third may be used over the tonic chord but the minor third over the subdominant seventh chord. Various personal, regional, and chronological styles are characterized by the nature of these and other choices. In general, the blues feeling may superficially be described as one in which minor-quality lines are superimposed over major-quality chords. Many other scales occur in blues, including the mixolydian scale, pentatonic and other abbreviated scales, and a pentatonic scale beginning on the tone a minor third above the tonic of the piece. "Blue notes" are those notes of the blues scale that differ from those of the diatonic major scale. Various microtonal modifications also occur. All these features result from the historical interplay of African and European harmonic practises.

BODHRAN A hand drum used in Irish music. Pronounced and sometimes written "boron."

BOOGIE (boogie-woogie) A blues piano style, especially characteristic of Chicago pianists of the twenties, with repeated, usually arpeggiated, bass figures against which the right hand improvises.

BOP (or BEBOP) The dominant movement in jazz of the forties. Characteristic features include phrasing ahead of the beat and bar line, improvisation on the higher extensions of dominant seventh-type chords (ninths, augmented elevenths, thirteenths, and their chromatic alterations), use of the drums for thrust and punctuation as opposed to strict timekeeping, and a sophisticated system of chord substitutions. Typical structures were the thirty-two-measure song form and the blues (using more complex chord patterns than folk blues). Among the major stylists are Charlie Parker, Bud Powell, and Dizzy Gillespie.

BOTTLENECK GUITAR *See* slide guitar.

BOUT The upper or lower curved portion of the body of a guitar.

BROADSIDE A composed and printed ballad, usually from sixteenth- through nineteenth-century England. Many broadsides entered oral tradition.

BUTTON ACCORDION An accordion on which the right hand works a row of buttons rather than a pianolike keyboard. (All accordions have buttons for the left hand.) The instrument is used mainly in Irish, Cajun, and French-Canadian music. Sometimes the spelling "accordeon" is used to differentiate this instrument from the keyboard accordion.

CADENCE A chord progression that gives a feeling of movement coming to rest.

CAPO A clamp or other mechanical device placed across the strings of a guitar or banjo in order to raise them uniformly in pitch.

CARTER FAMILY GUITAR STYLE A guitar style in which a melody is played on the bass strings while a strummed accompaniment, between or sometimes along with the melody notes, is produced on the treble strings. Usually done with a flat pick, although the best-known older exponent, Maybelle Carter, uses finger picks.

CHANTEY *See* shantey.

CHILD BALLAD Any ballad noted in the nineteenth-century

scholarly collection of traditional British balladry compiled by Sir Francis James Child, which includes most of the older ballads.

CHORD A combination of three or more different tones played simultaneously.

CHORD EXTENSION Any note in a chord added on top of the three basic notes (triad) that constitute the simple chord. Example: C⁷ is an extended chord, since it includes a B♭ in addition to the C, E, G of the simple triad.

CHROMATIC BANJO STYLE A style of banjo playing used in contemporary bluegrass and country music; major stylists are Bobby Thompson and Bill Keith. Diatonic scales and scalar lines are used to play long series of runs; successive notes are played on different strings, requiring agile modifications of finger-picking patterns essentially derived from the Scruggs style (q.v.). In this style, the fifth string is sometimes fretted. In the precise technical meaning of the word, the designation "chromatic" is a misnomer.

CHROMATIC SCALE A scale using all of the twelve half tones within the octave.

CLAWHAMMER BANJO A melodic form of frailing (q.v.) with little or no use of brush strokes. Sometimes used to refer to the frailing style in general, or to Appalachian banjo two-finger picking styles.

CROSS PICKING A guitar and mandolin flat-picking technique used to duplicate finger-picked bluegrass banjo rhythms; major stylists are Jesse McReynolds (mandolin) and Doc Watson (guitar). The basic rhythm is eight eighth notes divided 3–3–2, the 3's produced by a down-down-up pick movement.

CYCLE-OF-FIFTHS A chord progression in which each chord is the dominant chord of the one that follows; a typical kind of chord movement in ragtime music. Example: E⁷, A⁷, D⁷, G⁷, and C.

DEGREE Any of the tones of a scale.

DELTA BLUES The country blues style characteristic of the Mississippi delta region around Clarksdale; its heyday was during the twenties and thirties. Major stylists include Charlie Patton, Son House, and Robert Johnson.

DIATONIC SCALE Scale having seven different tones within the octave; usually the normal major and minor scales.

DOZENS OR DIRTY DOZENS *See* toast.

DROP THUMBING OR DOUBLE THUMBING A modification of the basic banjo frailing (q.v.) rhythm in which the thumb executes notes on the middle strings (usually melody notes on the second string).

DYNAMICS Properly, changes in loudness within a piece of music. The term is sometimes used more loosely, as in this book, to refer to more general changes in feeling and movement.

EQUAL TEMPERAMENT *See* well-tempered scale.

ETHNOMUSICOLOGY The study of the music of "primitive" peoples. Can also refer to the study of music in any cultural context.

FAIS DO-DO Literally, "go to sleep" in Cajun French. Refers to a party that begins late at night after the children have been put to bed.

FIDDLE TUNE Any tune associated with the traditional fiddler's repertory, but most often a dance tune of Scottish or Irish descent in eighth- or sixteenth-note rhythm in 2/4 time, having two distinct sections, each repeated once, in the form AABB. In the southern highlands, fiddle tunes have traditionally been adapted to the banjo, and recently it has become fashionable to adapt them to the guitar.

FILL A statement by an accompanying instrument or singer that fills a space in the melody line produced by the lead singer or soloist.

FINGER PICKING A traditional guitar style in which the right-hand fingers pluck a melody on the treble strings, while the thumb produces rhythmically consistent bass accompaniment figures. Major stylists include John Hurt, Elizabeth Cotten, Blind Blake, and Merle Travis. The term is also used loosely of any stringed-instrument right-hand technique in which the fingers are used.

FLAT PICKING Any guitar style that involves the use of a small celluloid or nylon (formerly tortoise-shell) plectrum by the right hand. The specific virtues of the flat pick are for strumming, strong rhythmic backup work, Carter family style (q.v.), and the rapid execution of single-note figures. Some guitarists with strongly developed flat-picking styles are Doc Watson, the Delmore Brothers, and Clarence White. The mandolin is just about always flat picked, but in traditional American folk music the five-string banjo is virtually never flat picked.

FOLK PROCESS The process by which a folk song is varied or changed in the course of oral transmission from singer to singer.

FOLK SONG In the strict folklorist's definition, a song that has been transmitted orally from one generation to another. This definition is useful for Anglo-American balladry, but is unworkable when applied to blues and many other forms that can logically be considered as folk songs. The term is often used more loosely, of any song or piece of music that originates in what the observer considers to be an ethnic, naïve, or "primitive" culture. In contemporary record merchandising, the term is used to denote pop music with a soft melodic sound and guitar accompaniment.

FRAILING An Appalachian banjo style characterized by downward finger strokes by the right hand, usually but not necessarily including brush strokes. The basic rhythmic pattern is an eighth/and two sixteenth notes, consisting of a downward melody-note stroke by the first or second finger, is followed by a brush stroke with the second finger and a thumb stroke on the fifth (drone) string. This basic rhythm is subject to much further variation and modification. Some major stylists are Wade Ward, Grandpa Jones, Clarence Ashley, Rufus Crisp, Uncle Dave Macon, and Hobart Smith.

FRENCH HARP Harmonica.

FRET *n.* A metal strip set into the finger board of a guitar, etc., in order to provide precise intonation. *v.* To depress a string against a fret.

FUNKY Literally, "dirty," as in "the funk around the edge of the bathtub." Refers to the most strikingly characteristic aspects of blues rhythm and tonality. Sometimes refers in general to any performance in which emotion overrides technical precision.

GOSPEL Composed religious music, usually nontraditional, but often traditional in style. Traditional religious songs are usually called spirituals.

GUITARRÓN A large, four-stringed bass guitar used in Mexican music.

HALF TONE The interval from C to C#, or a like interval; the distance between adjacent keys on a piano or the distance of one fret on a fretted instrument.

HARP A harmonica

HB Hardback

HOLLER (1) In rural black tradition, an unaccompanied monody, (2) in Appalachian dialect, hollow, a small mountain valley.

HORNPIPE A lively dance tune in the Celtic tradition, often like a fast jig and often characterized by a sixteenth-and-dotted-eighth-note rhythm.

INTONATION The ability of a musician, singer, or instrument to keep in tune.

JIG A lively dance tune in the Celtic tradition, usually in 6/8 time.

JUG BAND A band including a musical jug, used as a resonating chamber to amplify sounds produced by vibrating the lips as though playing a brass instrument. A novelty sound often used by black and white ragtimey blues ensembles of the twenties and thirties. *See also* washboard band.

KEY The system of scales and chords that specifically relate to the tone that has the feeling of being the central and controlling sound of a given piece or section of music.

LICKS Short quasi-melodic instrumental figures, typically used as building blocks in larger statements.

LILTING The Gaelic equivalent of scat singing; singing with nonsense syllables. In the Celtic countries, lilting is done mainly with liquid consonants and with the same sorts of vowels that the Gaelic languages have. The tradition has also been carried into French Canada, where different sounds are used, corresponding more closely to the French language. In Canada the music is called mouth music *(musique à bouche),* cheek music, or *turlutage.* In both the Celtic and Canadian traditions, lilting is used as a substitute for instrumental music, even for dancing, when no instruments are present. Lilting possibly originated in the ancient system of syllable-sounds used to teach pitch and ornamentation to pipers in the days before notated music came into use.

MASTERING AND REMASTERING Mastering is the final process before a tape becomes a record; a reference disc is cut from the master tape. Remastering is the same process repeated because of some flaw in the initial process.

MELISMA A melody or ornament sung on one syllable.

MICROTONE An interval smaller than a half tone. Can be played on a fretted instrument by bending, "pulling" or "choking," the string.

MIX AND MIXDOWN Most records today are recorded on four to twenty-four tracks. A track is a discrete segment of the recording tape that receives input from one or more microphones, at the same time as the other tracks are simultaneously recording input from other microphones. In the mixdown, the producer and engineer reduce the information on the various tracks down to one track for mono, two for stereo, or four for quadraphonic sound.

MIXOLYDIAN The mode beginning on the fifth degree of the major scale. That is, the G mixolydian scale GABC-DEFG shares its key signature with the C major scale, but has intervals in relation to the tonic that are different from those of either the C major or G major scale. By transposing, it is possible to play any mode beginning on any note. A common chord progression for folk songs in the mixolydian mode is D-C-G-D.

MODE In describing folk music, mode refers to scales having other interval arrangements than those of the conventional major and minor scales.

MODULATION Changing from one key to another.

MONODY Music for solo voice.

MOUTH HARP Harmonica.

MOUTH MUSIC *See* lilting.

MONTUNO A short repeated rhythmic-harmonic structure.

MURDER-GIRL BALLAD A genre of Anglo-American balladry that deals with the murder of a young woman, often pregnant, by her lover. Some examples are: "Pretty Polly," "Omie Wise."

NEWGRASS A contemporary form of bluegrass music in which the techniques and musical conventions of traditional bluegrass are adapted to the rhythmic and harmonic requirements of the contemporary rock and pop repertory.

ORNAMENTATION Decorations or embellishments on a melody; the melody line itself remains unchanged.

OP Out of print; no longer available from publisher's stock.

OPEN STRING CHORD (open chord) Any chord formation containing one or more open strings.

OPEN STRINGS An instrument's strings as played without being fingered or fretted by the left hand.

OSTINATO A short repeated phrase or figure.

PAPER RECORD *See* sound sheet.

PB Paperback.

PENTATONIC SCALE A five-tone scale, often but not necessarily corresponding to the first, second, fourth, fifth, and sixth degrees of the diatonic major scale.

PHRASING The interpretation of a melody in regard to the

metrical placement of the notes and the rhythmic accents.

PITCH The high or low quality of a tone, as determined by the fundamental number of vibrations per second of the medium that produces it.

PLAY-PARTY An Appalachian social activity, sort of a square dance with singing and games. Play-parties are for children, but play-party songs are often sung by adults for their own amusement, and are not necessarily what we would think of as children's songs.

POLYRHYTHM A musical texture in which two or more conflicting rhythmic or accentual patterns occur simultaneously.

PRESSING The manufacture of a record from a tape master copy.

PRODUCTION Producing a record is akin to directing a movie. The producer is responsible for the final product, and relates to the record company, artist, arranger, engineer, musicians' union, etc. The producer was formerly, and still occasionally is, called the A and R (artist and repertory) man.

PROTEST SONG A song protesting or commenting upon social or economic conditions.

PUBLIC DOMAIN Not subject to legal copyright ownership or protection.

RACE RECORDS A term used in the twenties to designate records produced to be marketed for black people.

RADIO BALLAD A documentary program genre developed for the BBC by Charles Parker, Ewan MacColl, and Peggy Seeger. Tapes of traditional and composed songs, composed narrative, and narrative recorded on location are carefully edited into a continuous thematically developed whole. The BBC radio ballads, not all of which are included in the record listings in this book, have been released on the British Argo label.

RADIO TRANSCRIPTION A recording intended for radio broadcast, not for commercial release as a record.

RAGTIME A syncopated style of late nineteenth-century American music, essentially pianistic, which was derived from minstrel show and marching band traditions. It is often associated with early jazz, although it is compositional rather than improvisatory in nature.

REED PIPE An end-blown flute made of a hollow reed, often bamboo.

REEL A lively dance tune in the Celtic tradition, usually in 2/4 or 4/4 time.

RHYTHM-AND-BLUES A loosely used term, embracing the following definitions and probably others as well: (1) early black commercial music; the successor to the term "race records," (2) any blues performance which includes a rhythm section, (3) commercial blues and early black rock-and-roll music in general, up to about 1962.

RHYTHM SECTION A group of musicians whose function it is to provide a rhythmic, metrical, and to a lesser extent harmonic foundation for a band or soloist. A typical rhythm section consists of piano, perhaps guitar, bass, and drums.

ROCKABILLY Any of various styles of country music influenced by rhythm-and-blues or rock.

RUB-BOARD *See* washboard band.

RUN A linear quasi-melodic figure, usually having the function of connecting independent ideas and phrases.

SANCTIFIED Refers to the rhythmic, energetic, somewhat bluesy style of black Sanctified Church music.

SCALE An arrangement of notes within an octave, in ascending or descending order.

SCHOTTISCHE (German for "Scottish") A fashionable nineteenth-century round dance in 2/4 time, like a slow polka. It was alleged to have been of Scottish origin, but was also known during its heyday as the "German polka."

SCRUGGS-PICKING A banjo technique developed by Earl Scruggs, firmly associated with the sound of bluegrass music, in which melody notes, surrounded by other accompaniment notes, are picked in a pattern of eight eighth notes divided 3–3–2. This pattern, which is subject to some variation, is produced by a succession of finger-picking patterns called rolls, which use the thumb and first and second fingers.

SHANTEY (CHANTEY) A sailor's work song from the days of rigged ships. Songs of particular rhythms and structures were associated with particular tasks. The word "shantey" also refers to a woodsman's dwelling; a shanteyman's song is sung not by seamen but by lumbermen.

SHAPE NOTE A system of musical notation used in older church hymnals, particularly in New England and the south, in which pitch is indicated by the shape of the written note.

SHUFFLE (1) A rhythmic pattern typical of many blues and jazz styles, characterized by syncopated accents and a beat that is always actually or potentially divisible into thirds, (2) a rhythmic bowing pattern, completely different from the preceding, which is characteristic of hoedown and Cajun fiddle music. It consists of an eighth note and two sixteenth notes, the bow stroke changing direction on each note.

SIDEMAN An instrumental accompanist or band member.

SLIDE GUITAR A style of playing the guitar using a bottleneck, ring, or other glass or metal object which is slid along the strings, in effect constituting a moveable fret. Fingers not holding the slide are left free to play conventionally. The style is often used in country blues. Some major stylists are Ramblin' Thomas, Robert Johnson, Tampa Red, Muddy Waters, and Blind Willie Johnson.

SLURRED FINGERING A highly legato fingering in which one note leads into another a half tone above or below, producing the illusion of a microtone. The notes might also be produced simultaneously. Such a fingering might be notated as an appoggiatura (though sometimes beginning before the beat) or as an acciaccatura.

SONG FORM The typical structure of European art song and of much pop and jazz songwriting. The song form is thirty-two measures long, consisting of four eight-measure sections arranged AABA; the B part is known as the "bridge." Used rarely by traditionally oriented performers. Some well-known pieces in this form are "I Got Rhythm," "How High the Moon," and "Misty."

SONG SHEET *See* sound sheet.

SOUND SHEET A five- or seven-inch record pressing on flexible short-lived vinyl, designed for inclusion in a book or magazine. Also called a paper record or song sheet.

STEEL (1) The metal slide with which a Hawaiian guitar, dobro, or pedal steel guitar is played, (2) short for steel guitar or pedal steel guitar.

STEEL GUITAR (1) Any guitar played Hawaiian-style, held horizontally across the lap and fretted with a metal bar, (2) short for pedal steel guitar, (3) incorrectly, a metal-bodied guitar.

STOPPED STRING A string fingered or fretted by the left hand.

STRUM (1) Any right-hand technique applied to guitar, banjo, etc., (2) any such technique in which the strings are brushed, as opposed to being picked individually.

STUDIO MUSICIAN A musician who hires out for the specific purpose of working on recording sessions; not necessarily a usual associate or accompanist of the featured artist.

SWING (1) The ability of a musician to generate phrases and syncopated accents and rhythms free from rigid adherence to the underlying metrical structure, and characterized by a sense of relaxation and an underlying 3-against-4 polyrhythmic feeling, (2) a form of music characterized by this feeling.

SYNCOPATION A shift in accent to a beat that would normally be weak; most simply, beats 2 and 4 in 4/4 time.

TABLATURE A system of musical notation for fretted instruments, which indicates string and fret numbers rather than the formal musical notes.

TAKE A recording studio term for the actual version of a song that is being recorded. The first take would be the first recorded version or run-through of a song or any part of it.

TENOR GUITAR A small four-string guitar, tuned higher than a regular guitar, to ADGC.

THREE-FINGER PICKING An old-time banjo style using the thumb, index, and middle fingers; major stylists include Charlie Poole and Snuffy Jenkins. Scruggs picking (q.v.) is a further specialized development of this style.

TIMBRE Tone color, the particular quality a particular player or instrument gives to a tone.

TOAST The folklorist's name for a verbal game known in black folklore as the dozens or dirty dozens, in which participants insult each others' parents, personal habits, etc. The form is poetic, often rhymed and sometimes following a metrical structure, though loose enough to permit improvisation.

TONALITY *See* key.

TONE (1) A sound having definite pitch and quality. Colloquially called a note, although properly "note" refers to the written symbol for a tone, (2) loosely, timbre, q.v.

TOPICAL SONG A song concerned with social commentary.

TRACK (1) *See* mix. (2) A single selection, or "cut," from an LP album.

TRADITIONAL *See* folk song.

TRANSPORT SONG A genre of British balladry having as context or subject matter the transportation of convicted felons to serve as indentured servants in the colonies—usually Australia.

TRAVIS PICKING Properly, the guitar style of Merle Travis, but loosely used to refer to any style of finger picking, q.v.

TUNE Properly refers just to the melody of a song, but often used loosely, as in this book, to refer to the total song, including lyrics, or to any given performance or arrangement of a song.

TURNAROUND Any rhythmic or harmonic device that occurs at the end of a section of music in order to divide it more clearly from the following section.

TWO-FINGER PICKING An old-time banjo style using the thumb and index finger. A major stylist is Roscoe Holcomb.

UP-PICKING A banjo style similar to frailing, but with the melody note picked in an upward direction. The major stylist is Pete Seeger. The effect is less percussive than frailing.

VODEODO Nonsense syllables used in early white imitations of black jug band music and small-ensemble jazz. Characteristically, such imitations have lacked the rhythmic grace and swing of their models.

VOICING The arrangement of intervals within a chord (that is, the choice of inversion), with particular attention to the contextual sense of such arrangements as they proceed from chord to chord (voice leading).

WASHBOARD BAND A band including a washboard (sometimes called "rub-board") played as a percussion instrument—a prominent feature of black novelty bands of the twenties and thirties. Jug bands, q.v., sometimes included washboards, but washboard players also worked with solo bluesmen and songsters. The instrument is held across the chest; the player wears thimbles on the fingers of either or both hands and draws them across the corrugated side of the washboard to produce rhythmic sounds. Some washboard players also mount a cymbal, cowbell, etc., on their instruments. Major stylists include Washboard Sam and Bull City Red (with Blind Boy Fuller and Sonny Terry).

WELL-TEMPERED SCALE The scale used by the "equal temperament" tuning system. This system, which was first used extensively by J. S. Bach, has since the early 1800's been accepted as the standard of intonation for European concert instruments, especially the piano. Because of the mathematical characteristics that govern the qualities of intonation, a musical instrument that is tuned for perfect intonation in one key will be badly out of tune in another. The equal temperament system represents a compromise in which instruments are very slightly out of tune in all keys.

CONTRIBUTORS

DAVID FERRETTA is a banjoist, guitar player, and singer. He owns and operates the Ferretta Music Service in Denver, a folk music store and mail-order service. He is also the proprietor of the Global Village, a Denver folk music coffeehouse.

EDITH FOWKE is associate professor in the English Department at York University and teaches folklore. She is a fellow of the American Folklore Society, and has written numerous books on Canadian folk music.

DAN FOX has arranged all kinds of music for virtually every major music publisher in the United States. He has been a music editor at Warner Brothers Music and Charles Hansen Publications, and has a master's degree in composition from the Manhattan School of Music. He has recorded a number of guitar instructional records for Music Minus One Records with Dick Weissman.

DAVID P. McALLESTER is a professor of anthropology and music at Wesleyan University, and the co-founder and former president of the Society for Ethnomusicology. He has done major research among the Navajo, as well as field work with other Indian tribes. He is the author of three books on American Indian music, a book on Peyote music, and a study of Navajo ceremonial music.

JERRY RICKS has played and sung music all over the world, living in the United States, Canada, Holland, and Germany, and touring Africa for the State Department with the Buddy Guy blues band. He teaches guitar at the Denver Folklore Center and is extraordinarily knowledgeable about American folk guitar styles. His article is part of a book on the blues and its backgrounds, which he is writing with Dick Weissman.

RALPH RINZLER is the director of the Folklife Program at the Division of Performing Arts, Smithsonian Institution. He travels all over the country, rounding up musicians and craftsmen for the Smithsonian's National Folk Festival. He was a mandolinist and singer for the Greenbriar Boys, one of the first urban bluegrass groups.

PHILIP SONNICHSEN has written a number of articles and album notes dealing with the music of Mexican-Americans. His book *The Music of a Chicano Prisoner, Ramón Rivera Rodríguez* is scheduled for publication in 1976, and his doctoral dissertation, *Contemporary Chicano Music in California,* is under way at UCLA. He teaches for Chapman College on their World Campus Afloat program and was director of the Mexican and Mexican-American component of the Old Ways in the New World, one section of the Smithsonian Institution's 1975 Festival of American Folklife in Washington, D.C.

STEVE WIENCROT learned to play mandolin at the Old Town School of Folk Music in Chicago. He is the author of an excellent mandolin instruction book, and he currently teaches banjo, guitar, and mandolin at the Denver Folklore Center.

WES WESTBROOKS, who is now deceased, was originally a jazz trumpet player, playing with the Billy Eckstine band and the Leo Parker sextet. He had been a gospel music disc jockey on Denver's KDKO for over twenty years. Some of his original compositions have been recorded by the Kingston Trio, the Pentangle, the Staples Singers and others.

Left to right: Steve Weincrot, David Ferretta, Larry Sandberg, Harry Tuft, Wes Westbrooks, and Dick Weissman

ILLUSTRATION CREDITS

Mary Alfieri: 201

Arhoolie: 18; Dan Leyrer, 39; Chris Strachwitz, 24, 57, 211, 248

David Bain: 30, 31, 178

CBS Records: 38, 175

Chess Records: 189

John Cohen: 199

Denver Public Library: 140, 171, 172; C.J.
Belden, 193

Caleb Deschanel: 110, 113

Diane Deschanel: 228, 230

Flower Films: 45, 64

Roland L. Freeman, courtesy Flying Fish
records: 7

Hannibal/Carthage Records: 4, 5 (Dinner
Ladies)

Bob Kruger: 99, 207 (Collins)

Hank Lebo: 117

Library of Congress: 27, 37, 50, 78, 185,
213, 215; Delano: 177; Russell Lee: 53,
145, 182; Post-Wolcott: 123; Rossbaum:
104; V. G. Schreck: 1, 46; Ben Shahn:
91, 93; E.S. Shipp, 187; William Weiss &
Co.: 144

New York Public Library: 60

Pete Lowry: 35

Tom McKinlay, courtesy of Ome Banjo
Company; 218

Scott Newton, courtesy Keith Case Mgmnt.
and Sugar Hill Records: 3

Marc Norberg, courtesy of Bug/Capitol
records: 6 (Dixon)

Dennie Orr: 83

Sandy Paton: 67 (Proffitt), 139, 187

Playboy Records: 143

Ken Plot, courtesy Flying Fish Records: 5
(Kahn)

Stephen Ramsey, courtesy Sugar Hill
Records: 6 (O'Brien)

RCA Records: 81, 103

Larry Sandberg, copyright 1989: 8, 121,
151, 153, 154, 155, 156, 157, 204, 221,
239

Larry Shirkey, copyright 1989: 21, 25, 86,
131, 152, 164, 167, 219, 225, 228
(dobro), 234, 255

Len Siegler: 111

Courtesy of *Sing Out!*: 169, 229

Ellen Stekert: 67 (Gunning)

Lars H. Swanberg: 16

Suzanne Szasz: 115, 116, 134

Andrew Taylor: 108

Warner Bros. Records: 129, 132

Courtesy of Wesley Westbrooks: 43

INDEX

A NOTE ABOUT THE AUTHORS

LARRY SANDBERG began his music career in the Greenwich Village folk scene as a singer and guitarist during the late fifties. After some years of teaching classics and comparative literature, he returned to music and spent most the seventies in Colorado, where he performed, taught guitar at the Denver Folklore Center and at local colleges, recorded for Kicking Mule records, and wrote a number of folk instrument instruction manuals in addition to *The Folk Music Sourcebook*. During most of the eighties, he managed advertising, public relations, and promotions for a leading publisher of classical music. He is currently freelancing as a writer, photographer, and musician.

* * *

DICK WEISSMAN has been involved in music and the music business for more than thirty years. In the early sixties he was a member of a popular folk trio, The Journeymen. He has played banjo and guitar on numerous recordings and has worked as a record producer for numerous companies. After a stint as National Education Coordinator for the National Academy of Recording Arts & Sciences in Los Angeles, Dick returned to Colorado in 1988, where he is an instructor at the Colorado Institute of Art in the Music/Video/Business program. Dick has composed a number of recorded songs, two feature film scores, music for industrial films and television, and written five books about the American music scene and the music business. An album of his original, mostly instrumental, music based on American folk themes has just been released.

* * *

The Folk Music Sourcebook received an ASCAP Deems Taylor Award For Excellence In Writing About Music in 1976.

Other DACAPO titles of interest

THE ART OF RAGTIME
William Schafer and
Johannes Reidel
270 pp., 13 illus., mus. ex.
80057-8 $8.95

BIG ROAD BLUES
Tradition and Creativity
in the Folk Blues
David Evans
396 pp., many illus.
80300-3 $14.95

BLUES FROM THE DELTA
William Ferris
New introd. by Billy Taylor
226 pp., 30 photos
80327-5 $10.95

BLUES OFF THE RECORD
Thirty Years of Blues Commentary
Paul Oliver
132 pp., 17 photos
80321-6 $13.95

BLUES WHO'S WHO
Sheldon Harris
775 pp., 450 photos
80155-8 $29.50

CHICAGO BLUES
The City and the Music
Mike Rowe
226 pp., 147 photos
80145-0 $9.95

THE COUNTRY BLUES
Samuel B. Charters
With a new introduction
by the author
288 pp., 45 illus.
80014-4 $9.95

THE ENCYCLOPEDIA OF JAZZ
Leonard Feather
527 pp., over 200 photos
80214-7 $18.95

ENCYCLOPEDIA OF JAZZ
IN THE 60s
Leonard Feather
312 pp., 200 photos
80263-5 $14.95

ENCYCLOPEDIA OF JAZZ
IN THE 70s
Leonard Feather and Ira Gitler
400 pp., many photos
80290-2 $16.95

THE ESSENTIAL JAZZ
RECORDS
Volume I: From Ragtime to Swing
Max Harrison, Charles Fox
and Eric Thacker
605 pp.
80326-7 $14.95

EVERY DAY
The Story of Joe Williams
Leslie Gourse
208 pp., 26 photos
80275-9 $9.95

THE FACE OF BLACK MUSIC
Photographs by Valerie Wilmer
Introd. by Archie Shepp
120 pp., 110 photos
80039-X $9.95

IN SEARCH OF
BUDDY BOLDEN
First Man of Jazz
Donald M. Marquis
176 pp., 31 pp. of photos
80130-2 $7.95

THE LEGACY OF THE BLUES
Art and Lives of Twelve
Great Bluesmen
Samuel B. Charters
192 pp., 15 photos
80054-3 $8.95

STOMPING THE BLUES
Albert Murray
272 pp., 127 illus.
0-306-80362-3 $11.95

Available at your bookstore

OR ORDER DIRECTLY FROM

DA CAPO PRESS, INC.

233 Spring Street, New York, New York 10013